Under the editorship of
Daniel J. Levinson

JOSEPH F. RYCHLAK

A Philosophy

of Science for

Personality

Theory

HOUGHTON MIFFLIN COMPANY · BOSTON

New York · Atlanta · Geneva, Ill. · Dallas · Palo Alto

BF
38.5
.R9

To my parents

Editor's Foreword

What are the requirements, the potentialities, and the limitations of psychology as a science? What must it do to merit a legitimate place within the community of scientific disciplines? What are the essential principles of "scientific method" that should guide our theoretical and empirical endeavors? Questions such as these have been a continuing source of controversy in academic psychology. They have led to ideological struggles no less bitter than those in the realms of politics and religion. Diverse "philosophies of science" have exerted their influence at different times and places, each serving as a stimulus to certain modes of inquiry and as a block to others.

The psychologist's conception of his science involves more than a set of abstract principles, more than an operating manual for the design of research and the construction of theory. Each philosophy of science in psychology is intimately bound up with an image of man, a disciplinary identity, and a system of basic assumptions and values regarding the aims, problem areas, and investigative methods with which psychology should properly concern itself. It is, in other words, an intrinsic part of the "culture" of academic psychology and part of the "mentality" of the academic psychologist.

In the language of this book, the scientific orientation in American psychology has until recently been predominantly "demonstrative" rather than "dialectical." The prevailing approach has been tough-minded, extraspective, technically rigorous, operationalistic. The greatest value has been placed on laboratory research; naturalistic observation and field research have been largely excluded or have been regarded as mere preludes to truly scientific investigation. At the same time, theoretical attention has focused chiefly on the simpler psychological processes conceived of and studied in relative isolation. The study of learning, for example, was for several decades conducted mainly with animals in experimentally manipulable laboratory devices, such as the maze and the discrimination box. In the name of science, psychologists refrained from studying more complex forms of human learning, since these occur in, and are influenced by, complex social contexts such as the school, the family, and the work situation.

This book offers a less constraining philosophy of science — an approach suited to the development of personality and clinical and social psychology. These are the newest and the scientifically most "troublesome" fields of inquiry in academic psychology. The study of personality was established as a legitimate field only in the late 1930's, primarily through the writings of Allport, Lewin, and Murray and through the entry of psychoanalysis into the academic scene. Clinical psychology, stimulated by the growing interest in personality theory and by the demands of World War II, became a major field in the late 1940's. Although social psychology has a longer history within academic psychology, its contemporary form has been strongly influenced by developments in personality theory and in the social sciences over the past thirty years. Similarly, personality and clinical psychology are now forming a stronger social orientation (as, for example, in the field of community mental health) and are drawing more actively on the concepts and field methods of sociology.

In short, new perspectives and new aspirations are emerging in the study of human personality. It is increasingly evident that the study of man in society requires a convergence of personality-clinical-social psychology and the social sciences. It requires also a philosophy of science that will serve to free as well as to discipline the scientific imagination. In our scientific efforts we need to draw creatively on both the "demonstrative" and the "dialectical" traditions without being constrained by either. Professor Rychlak has, in my opinion, made a significant contribution toward this end. He has written an excellent textbook on substantive and methodological problems in the construction of personality theory. This is, however, more than a textbook — or perhaps it is what a textbook ideally ought to be. The author gives a clear formulation of important issues, reviews a considerable literature on each, offers his own evolving position, and issues the reader a challenging invitation to participate in the scientific enterprise. Those who read this book — undergraduate and graduate students, as well as others — will derive from it a more profound, multi-faceted conception of the human personality, of the many ways in which personality has been conceptualized and studied, and of the intriguing possibilities for further work in this field.

Daniel J. Levinson

New Haven, Connecticut

Preface

Although I was not then aware of it, I began writing this book about ten years ago, on the first day of my teaching position following the doctoral degree. It all began with the fact that I came up against people — highly competent people — with orientations so foreign to my own regarding the nature and goals of psychology that we could not really communicate without losing our tempers. The urge to solve psychology's dilemma was greatly furthered when I saw the effects of this foreign orientation upon my clinical students, some of whom actually sat mutely at case staffings and — we later learned — refused to speculate on the nature of a case because they felt psychology had not yet learned how adequately to control the behavior of rats, much less men. There was a kind of anti-intellectualism in the air, or so I thought. There was a cynicism about all that had been known by mankind, a view of history and of philosophy as somehow dead and buried in the inconsequential past. This attitude was kept from slipping into a severe morale problem — though that too was evident in some quarters — by a curious belief in the inevitability of "facts" which would some-day clear up all our problems.

This was very upsetting, and my first reactions were anger and wondering whether I had been overly sheltered in my graduate education. Somehow, I had been spared this direct confrontation in graduate school, though of course we were all dimly aware that psychology had its internal problems. But our feeling in the Psychological Clinic at Ohio State University in the late 1950's was that we were on the winning side, and that what opposition there was did not present a strong case. I was to learn with a jolt that the opposition had quite a case, one which was easier to put across to students than mine, and that I had been in my own way just as snobbish and adamant without proper background to speak as I was picturing my opponents to be. It took me a long time to discover this. The present volume is actually a record of the intellectual odyssey which began when I set out to develop my own background. I had already begun with a certain vaguely phrased framework, having drawn from my earlier interest in philosophy a "feel" for the dialectical and the demonstrative tactics in reasoning. But I did not go directly into this matter for several years. At first I merely made a systematic review of the psychological journals, tracing the history of commentary about psychology's nature. Later, the point of view began to hang together and to "write itself."

There are many individuals who, unasked and often unknowing, play a role in the research and writing of a book such as this. Frankly, much of it was lonely going, quite by design. You begin that way — almost afraid to admit even to yourself that "I am writing a book." But before long you must admit the truth and seek a certain sympathy if not support from others. You then realize that, even in the beginning, you had turned to others using the inspiration of an admired professor through your old class notes. Looking back, I can now thank Julian B. Rotter for teaching me how to think in research design terms, and George A. Kelly for showing me that data need not dictate the terms at every turn. I first drew a parallel between Freud and the dialectical tradition in a marvelous graduate seminar conducted by a true scholar, Alvin Scodel. Later, it was Jerome M. Brams, who one day as an afterthought challenged me to begin putting my ideas on paper. My first theoretical article was drafted shortly thereafter. I knew then that someday I would have to state the whole business.

There are those good friends who act as sounding boards for weird and far-fetched notions — sometimes because their area of professional specialization is not your own and therefore they are more polite about it than your academic peers. I would place in this category, with many thanks, Patrick J. Capretta, Gertrude J. Williams, Donald E. Guinouard, and Harold A. Franklin. There are the academic peers, whose dynamic and active intellects force you to sharpen your thinking and come to terms with reality in friendly but well-focused debate. I can recall many wonderful exchanges with friends like Marilyn K. Rigby, Harry A. Shoemaker, Frank A. Young, and D. Gene Davenport. There were, of course, the less friendly debates, but I will overlook them in this pleasant reverie, though they were extremely important and beneficial. The stimulation and appreciation of one's students also spurs a writer to achievement. Whether it was true or not, I told myself that I had to work out a position for my students, so that they might be spared some of the post-graduate confusion I experienced.

Getting one's ideas on paper is no easy task, and, again, without the help of many people it would never have been accomplished. In their unique ways, Douglas W. Bray and Donald H. Kausler made it possible for me to find the time to write this book. Mrs. Diane Faissler and Raymond J. Trybus helped materially in manuscript preparation.

My wonderful wife Lenore also helped prepare the manuscript and was my constant source of support in all those major and minor things that come up when one puts pencil to paper. Our children, Ronald and Stephanie, were the "silent partners" in this venture. They had to be silent, or the "philosopher in the house" would start his ranting again.

J. F. R.

Contents

> ### PART ONE • Basic Issues
> ### in Theory Construction

PART TWO • Broader Considerations in the Study of Man

EPILOGUE

A Philosophy of Science for Personality Theory

The Science of Psychology

Psychology, like any body of knowledge, has engendered many conflicts in point of view in its brief history. There are areas of agreement in psychology, to be sure, but it is clear even to beginning students that deep and significant cleavages exist. Instructors teaching beginning courses strain to present a consistent orientation across such lines as basic versus applied science, the role of animal studies in a science of man, clinical intuition and experimental rigor, and so on. Some instructors gloss over differences in orientation between the "tough-minded" experimentalists and the "tenderminded" clinicians. Others take sides, either berating the bleeding-heart thinking typical of the applied group, or challenging the adequacy of toilet training among the experimentalists. Often a more subtle innuendo goes on between camps. It is a fortunate Department of Psychology which escapes this rift in viewpoint.

When in graduate school, the student must make a decision as to where he stands; he must form an allegiance or identify with some kind of outlook. The problems he may have sensed or loosely grasped as an undergraduate now take hold in his life and become vital. "Can I be a scientist, when in reality, I have little or no control over my clients in the clinic? In fact, my clinical instructors seem to feel it is wrong even to want to control the lives of others." "Is all this stress on specific definitions and the manipulation of obscure laboratory devices really going to add up someday and say something about the behavior we know in everyday life? My lab instructors seem more interested in a significant probability level than in a significant idea which is difficult

1

to test." Such comments are not unusual among graduate students, if the instructor will only cock his ear and permit his young scholars to express their real preoccupations.

The most serious aspect of all of this is that psychologists as teachers have failed to provide satisfying answers for their students. There has been much offense and defense, much chest-beating and shaking of heads, but few real attempts to get the kind of overview, in historical perspective, which might at least clarify issues and propose answers. Many loose ends have been unraveled over the past half-century in the psychological literature; phrased in somewhat archaic terms, they continue to ensnarl the profession and threaten to stifle if not completely strangle genuine understanding. It is time for the formulation of new positions, in the hope of redefining old problems and thereby pointing the way to acceptable solutions.

Psychology has its special challenges, in that its source of data happens to be that most elusive of all things to define operationally — the *human* being. At heart it is the *image of man* which is at issue in psychology's internal conflict, let us make no mistake about that. The arguments all come down to this: How shall we theorize about the human being? Shall we say that he can think, or not? Can he grow personally and rise above his environment, or not? Can he respond to the opportunity for independent action by taking responsibility, or not? And so on. Sticks and planets, mice and monkeys may be unable to do these things, but *can man;* and if so, how, or by what theoretical maneuver, can he be so conceptualized? Customarily, that branch of science concerned with the study of human behavior has been called "personality" study, and therefore the personality theorist is most often in the center of this controversy.

Why a Philosophy of Science for Personality Theory?

In proposing to a potential reader that this volume will present "a philosophy of science for personality theory," the question naturally arises, "Does this mean that a personality theorist is not *now* in the fold of science?" Moreover, there is a hint of special treatment in the suggestion that personality theorists need "something of their own," and this naturally irritates those who believe that science — as a theory of knowledge — has been completely settled upon. It would follow that only a defeatist or "second-class" scientist could seriously argue for a change in ground rules at this late date.

We shall attempt to prove that *in point of fact* historical developments in the evolution of science have made the time propitious for the emergence of a more reasonable and honest science of man. It is the central assumption of this volume that:

Man devised his scientific methods, and he alone can adjust his thinking about how to use them most productively and usefully. Psychology's problems are at heart the fundamental problems of man's use of intellect. Before we can resolve the inner contradictions of the science of psychology, we must first revise our thinking about the nature of scientific knowledge. In doing so, we will not depart from our sister sciences, but actually come more into line with them.

We therefore do indeed feel that personality psychologists have had a difficult time of it, striving to remain within the bounds of a type of science which did not completely meet their purposes. Psychology has been especially one-sided in its talk about what constitutes scientific activity. This narrow view need no longer be held to — at least not by all psychologists who wish also to be scientists. There *is* a distinguished, completely defensible alternative to the kind of science which seems to trip us up in our attempts to catch the image of man we all carry within us. It is *this* philosophical position which we hope to present — in a sense, discover — as we move through these chapters. It is *a* position because, in truth, science *has no one* position. There is a tie binding all science — one form of evidence — but within this broad framework are all manner of potential theoretical formulations which seem to hold equally well. It is about time for those of us who take an interest in personality study to *change* things in psychology, and thereby to talk about our activity in a way that is more compatible with our interests. We must study our historical roots and sophisticate ourselves sufficiently on the nature of science, so that we no longer feel any sense of inferiority as we set out to do our particular form of scientific work.

The Plan of the Book

To bring together the myriad issues in a philosophy of science for personality theory is naturally an extremely complex task. Everything seems somehow contingent upon or in some angular fashion related to everything else, so that one finds it difficult even to choose a proper starting point. The tactic finally settled upon was to break the book into two portions. In Part One we review a number of issues which seem basic to most presentations of the philosophy of science. All the terms psychologists use in discussing their theoretical attempts and methods of study are introduced as we consider the nature of theory, the role of evidence, and the impact of science on ethics. This review of terminology is written from a considerably more liberal perspective than that of most such presentations in the past. At the close of Part One the reader should have a clearer understanding of the kinds of conflicts engendered in psychology from differences in interpretation regarding the essentials of that form of knowledge we like to consider "scientific" in nature.

Part Two undertakes to build upon this understanding, and to use the terms acquired in a search for the essential difference between those who use the more traditional "natural science" approach to knowledge, and the more "humanistically" inclined theorists who wish to capture man in other than natural science terms. This leads directly into personality study, and we begin our consideration of this topic by examining the motives to psychotherapy, where modern personality theory was first phrased. This investigation proceeds until we have proposed — more accurately, revived — a fundamental distinction in the tactics of human reasoning. The dialectical versus demonstrative bifurcation mentioned here, with its contrasting theoretical strategies and metaconstructs, then provides a framework within which to organize the terms and contradictions of Part One into a unified whole. Further, it serves as an heuristic device in the understanding of what we mean when we speak of *human* as opposed to machine-like behavior.

The two traditions of thought will prove helpful to conceptualization, but in time we must come down to the "ultimate contradiction" of their basic natures, which will force us in our inquiry to accept a stand-off at the very brink of human understanding. Perhaps it is not so much a stand-off as an interplay. But, whatever we call it, the fact remains that no one will be able to choose sides or "pick a winner" when the final thread of analysis has run its length. The intellectual traditions will continue to stand apart, as they always have and most assuredly always will.

It might be charged that the writer is presumptuous in asking a reader to undertake a dozen or so chapters of reading and study, only to arrive at a stalemate at the root of the problem. The only defense we have at this point is to observe that at least we do hold out hope of reducing the many issues into one grand issue, which might then be used as an organizing principle for future discussions. A problem well defined is only half solved, to paraphrase the saying, but then, the point of the saying is that definitions have merit. It may just be that we will sometimes have to settle for half-solutions. Rather than stake the worth of this volume on the resolution of such inscrutable problems, we would prefer to be judged as follows: *If* our problems in psychology are due in large measure to the way in which we interpret the nature of science, *then* a reassessment or possibly even a redefinition of science should help soften such conflicts. This is our fundamental theoretical proposition, and, after making his way through the chapters to follow, the reader should be in a position to evaluate the worth of his journey according to *this* standard.

Since the terminology will be in part new, and will at times be given different interpretations from those the reader may now have in mind, this will not be an easy volume to grasp on first reading. It will require rereading, study, and very likely occasional supplementary reading to bring some of the issues into sharper focus. One of the major concerns, of course, is that in trying to cover both sides of the scientific ledger we will lose readers who discard something when they find it at variance with their own biases. Those who wish to read the volume out of an interest in personality might well find Part One dreary, and possibly give up the effort before they reach Part Two. Those who are attracted more to the basic issues of Part One might not wish to venture further and consider the more speculative aspects of Part Two.

To minimize such possibilities, we have included a summary statement at the end of each chapter, and invite readers of both persuasions to read through these summaries. This will permit a rapid grasp of the logical development, and, if we have communicated successfully, can well motivate readers of diverse theoretical predilections to take a longer look at the other side of the fence. It is also possible to skip Part One for now and return to it when necessary. We have tried to index carefully and to include reasonable cross-references. We also have employed select repetition where it is necessary to the point under development. All these factors can assist the reader in a more selective reading. However, it is our hope that all students of personality will take the basic issues of Part One to heart and devote complete attention to them as background matters. We shall never evolve a common language unless such effort is expended.

In the final chapter we will attempt to summarize all the developing themes, and present them in a clear and consistent fashion within our two intellectual traditions of demonstration and dialectic. We will also return to our assessment of the major thesis of the book, and give some reactions to this point of view actually stated by students and other colleagues. We hope to leave the reader with a viable alternative to the view of science he must now so often reluctantly accept in the name of rigorous psychology.

Biases and Book Writers

One does not write about scientific theory construction without thereby taking on a bias, which is another way of saying that we all must write in certain intellectual traditions. Rather than trying to appear completely objective, the writer frankly admits he has an axe to grind. This is a book of interpretative commentary and instruction, but also decidedly one of criticism. It is written most directly for and hence phrased *to* psychologists, but it is aimed at all those social scientists in related professions — such as psychiatry, sociology, and anthropology — who find meaning in what has been said thus far. Professional identities blur at this point, and we find a common identity in a common sense of uneasiness and distaste.

It is not the reality of a writer's bias which should worry us, since higher education is a process of contrasting diverse views as a preliminary to resolving them for ourselves, but rather the consistency and reasonableness of this bias. How well does the presentation answer long-standing questions? How consistent is it, and can we sense in it a legitimate alternative to what we now have? These are the only genuine points of concern. An internally consistent alternative, even if wrong in its entirety, can enrich the meaning of our presently held positions on the questions at issue by its power of contrast.

We are long overdue in psychology for a crystallizing of our intellectual traditions; we have had "schools" and "theorists" but their connections to philosophical or sociocultural precedents have rarely been named. Biases hinge on such precedents, and one never completely avoids their silent impact. As we shall see, the issues which condition our biases are not new. They have existed — many of them — since the dawn of thought itself. We could be writing just as easily in either the first or the last quarter of this century; the chapter contents would doubtless have a contemporary significance.

We have tried to select current manifestations of the underlying bifurcation in man's thought strategies, but at times we range far back into history to make a point. One can see cycles of recurring issues even in the brief history of psychology, so it really does not matter where the examples come from. We hope the orientation of the book brings together the best from many sides. Through it all, our real purpose is to make some sense out of the human animal — the one we see in the laboratory as subject, but also the one we see in the mirror each morning.

PART ONE

Basic Issues in Theory Construction

No matter how formal or informal his comments are, when an individual decides to theorize about the nature of some item of experience, certain fundamental issues intrude themselves by definition in the act of theorizing. The theorist need not choose to become involved in these matters. He may feel they are the concoctions of woolly-minded philosophers, long since deceased, who had an imperfect grasp of modern scientific system formulations. He may feel it is unfair to label his purely empirical statements according to some arbitrary scheme, or even to enshroud them with the label "theoretical." This term has the deprecatory connotation of vagueness, phantasy, and arbitrariness for many individuals. But although they may not like it, those who theorize cannot avoid coming to grips with certain topics without paying the price of ignorance, and, possibly, decline due to a loss of vitality. To know where theory is taking us, we must know where we are, and where we have been in the history of thought.

For example, some of the questions which arise as one starts putting together ideas about his environment are as follows: When he begins the empirical description of some phenomenon, does the theorist believe that this "item of experience" need *literally exist* before his conceptualiza-

9

tion has meaning? What is the role of man's intellect in theory formulation? Is everything we say about our world of sensation in some way theoretical, or are there statements which can be called non-theoretical? When does a theoretical statement become a fact? What is the nature of evidence, and how does it determine our belief in something? Science deals with evidence. Where do theory and science come together, and what is the essence of the scientific attitude? How does theory work for the individual, and at what point in the scheme of things can we speak about knowledge? Is the universe completely determined by natural law; is man so determined also? Can one be a determinist and still believe in a freedom of choice in ethical decisions? Can we solve such ethical dilemmas through science?

These and several other questions are considered in the five interlocking chapters of Part One. They are drawn from issues of long standing in the sciences and philosophies of mankind. They would have relevance to *any* form of theory construction in the sciences, and many of the theorists cited are physical scientists who have written on these subjects. The main focus of Part One will be on psychological theory, however, and most of the classical topics in the psychological literature find their way into the presentation.

Chapter II begins with an examination of the term "theory" itself, its definition and the various ways in which theorists approach their task. A scheme for classifying theories is presented, and it provides the framework for discussion in later chapters. Chapter III outlines the functions which any theory might serve in the conceptualization of data. A distinction is made between theory and method, and the concept of knowledge is defined. Chapter IV builds on this interpretation by showing how two kinds of evidence function in method to evolve a body of knowledge. Chapter V stresses that there are many methods open to the scientist in his pursuit of knowledge. Lawfulness and its corollary, determinism, are discussed fully. Science, lawfulness, and determinism all have something in common in the "control and prediction" of events or behavior. This leads naturally into the area of ethics, the subject of Chapter VI, an important aspect of the psychological study of man. Probability theory forms the last topic of Part One.

II Fundamental Dimensions of Theoretical Orientation

What do we mean when we refer to a "theoretical" statement? There have been surprisingly few attempts in the psychological literature to deal with the preliminary job of exploring the meanings of theory, and to determine precisely how one's interpretation of theory might influence his practice of psychology as science. In Webster (1961) we find its root is the Greek word *theoria,* which means the act of viewing, contemplation, or consideration. The range of definitions then catalogued testifies to the broad signification of the term. Included are: belief, policy, or procedure proposed or followed as a basis for action; a body of generalizations derived from experience or practice in some field (as, the theory of music); a body of mathematical theorems presenting a clear, rounded, and systematic view of a subject (like the theory of numbers); a systematic analysis, elucidation, or definition of a concept; a hypothetical entity or working hypothesis, relating or explaining some observed fact pattern, with or without actual experimental evidence in its support, and so on. The notions of conjecture, speculation, and supposition are tied to the definition of theory.

Probably the definition most stressed in psychology is the one which views theory as a coherent set of hypothetical, conceptual (meaning, in psychology, operationally defined), and pragmatic (predictive) principles forming the general frame of reference for a field of inquiry. From this coherent entity, the theoretician deduces principles, formulates hypotheses, and then undertakes the actions necessary to validate these hypotheses. Clark L. Hull's (1937) well-known hypothetico-deductive technique would be an excellent example of theory in this definition.

Another definition of theory stresses the ideal or hypothetical characteristics often cited in discussions about "theoretical issues." This is

11

the "in theory" argument, and it is correct to say that psychologists, such as Hull, in promulgating a point of view concerning theory, have literally taken an "in theory" position and spelled out the nature of theory building as it "ought" to be. B. F. Skinner (1950, 1956) later rejected this tendency to talk about how we construct theories of the "in theory" or "in principle" sense. In analyzing his own scientific approach, Skinner begins by noting:

> This account of my scientific behavior up to the point at which I published my results in a book called *The Behavior of Organisms* is as exact in letter and spirit as I can now make it. The notes, data, and publications which I have examined do not show that I ever behaved in the manner of Man Thinking as described by John Stuart Mill or John Dewey or in reconstructions of scientific behavior by other philosophers of science (1956, p. 227).

Rejecting Mill and Dewey, Skinner here also rejects Hull. He forces us to ponder, and to admit — if we are completely honest — that probably very few psychologists have followed to the letter the hypothetico-deductive technique or any formalized ideal in the pursuit of knowledge. How then does this process of theorizing go on, where do hypotheses come from, and what factors are involved in the nature of theorizing? In framing answers to these questions we must first review five basic dimensions which determine one's orientation toward any given theory: abstraction, realism vs. idealism, objective vs. subjective, theoretical perspective, and formal vs. informal. These are fundamental dimensions for a classification of theories. For now, we are not seeking an answer to "What shall we call theory?" but rather to "How is it most profitable to think about what others have meant in their use of theory?"

Abstraction

Most writers on theory would agree that theorizing is a process of abstraction based upon observations of a set of phenomena. The dimension here is one from lesser to greater abstractness in the formulation of theories. The experimental psychologist observes a series of events which he has prearranged experimentally, and draws from this succession of events a set of abstractions which he then hopes to put together into a theory of learning. The clinical psychologist observes his client's behavior in psychotherapy and carefully draws from minute clues abstract inferences concerning the nature of the client's problems. What makes both these activities result in abstraction is the matter of having to leave

out details in the formulation of a theoretical notion, in describing what has taken place. We need terms, we need a way of organizing the mass of potential variables fluctuating before our eyes. Abstractions simply must be made, and they are, by definition, always selective or incomplete in nature.

Abstraction may be thought of as a universal human tendency, very much involved with the process of thought itself. Down through history, such an approach to the understanding of how man conceptualizes his world has evolved, called semanticism. This view dates back to the Greeks, and in Chapter IX we shall give it careful attention in another context. Here we might consider Wendell Johnson (1946) as a recent proponent of the semanticist position; both he and A. Korzybski (1941) have exerted a significant influence on the post-World War II development of theory in the social sciences. Johnson makes the typical semantic parallel between scientific theorizing and the theorizing of man in his everyday behavior. The fundamental thesis of his book, *People in Quandaries,* is *"that science, clearly understood, can be used from moment to moment in everyday life, and that it provides a sound basis for warmly human and efficient living"* (1946, p. 45).

Customarily, when we speak about abstracting in the context of theory, we use the term "construct." A theoretical construct, therefore, is an abstraction made from a given point of view, a refined perspective, a biased position, or the like. The elements to be included in the construct will depend upon the general nature of the theory, its purpose, the purpose of the theorists who subscribe to it, and so on. Sometimes influences of this sort are very subtle, as we shall see.

Although semanticism has had a favorable influence on theory construction in psychology, it is not without its difficulties. Before pointing to a few of the more serious misunderstandings generated by this analysis, let us briefly review the general semanticist outlook, as represented by Johnson. Essentially, this position asserts that when an individual looks out on the world about him, he perceives through his senses all the stimuli available to him at any given moment. The "meaning" of objects at this point is essentially the immediate experiencing of them through the senses, in their totality, as they impinge upon the sense organs. This sensory contact is not complete, of course, so that it i[s] correct to say that the individual abstracts at a non-verbal level, or a[t] the level of sensation. We are never literally "at one" with an object [of] observation.

As the individual now begins to name things — this is a "table," th[e]

is a "chair" — he must leave out even more details, such as the color or texture of the objects named. At this, the so-called first-order level of labeling or naming, the person can, if pressed, elaborate his verbal abstraction ("chair") through the use of additional words. If this fails, he can always simply point to a chair and assert that "that" is what he means. The word "chair" in conjunction with the pointing to a sensory object thus becomes a first-order fact.

However, other words, which do not have a first-order referent, are considered higher-order abstractions. Words like "now," "then," "future," cannot be first-order facts because there is nothing we can point to directly in defining them. They express relations between abstractions, or suggest inferences made about abstractions, which can be pointed to. Verbal levels above the first-order level of labeling are called inference levels. Essentially, we climb the ladder of abstraction by moving up these inference levels, leaving out more details, formulating higher- and higher-order abstractions. This ladder has no ceiling; one can always make an abstraction of an abstraction (termed "self-reflexivity").

Though it may seem a contradiction, our most fundamental theoretical assumptions would be considered quite abstract in character — so abstract that we might now refer to them as "metaconstructs." The prefix "meta-" carries the connotation of overriding, higher, or transcending all below, as in the philosophical study of metaphysics. Since our assumptions and presuppositions, as embodied in our metaconstructs, influence the kinds of first-order observations we make, it behooves us to sharpen our thinking about the abstracting process. There is a circularity involved, with lower-order abstractions influencing higher-order abstractions, and vice versa, as we ascend or descend the ladder of inference levels.

The first-order level in abstraction, labeling, is called the "macroscopic" level. Macroscopic description would therefore mean that we are speaking about environmental objects and actions as they appear to the naked eye, such as "chair," or "John goes to the door." If we must use an instrument to help our naked eye "see" the object in the environment, this would be an example of the "microscopic" level of description. Thus, in describing the structure of a cell, or the behavior of an amoeba, we would be functioning at the microscopic level of description. It is also possible to hypothesize certain *unobservable* entities which cannot be seen but which might exert an indirectly observable influence at microscopic or macroscopic levels. The structure of the electron is

an example of such submicroscopic description. It is precisely here that highly abstract (theoretical) inferences and assumptions must be brought to bear — in conceptualizing something that cannot be "seen" with the naked eye or with any form of instrumentation.

There is a terminology used in psychology which parallels this idea of rising from low to higher levels of abstraction: this is the distinction between "molar" and "molecular" behavioral description. Molar description is involved with formulating higher-order abstractions, taking into consideration a broad range of behavior (considering the "whole person" in formulating constructs), whereas molecular description places emphasis on breaking down behavioral manifestation into more manageable units at what is taken to be an initially lower level of abstraction (studying specific behaviors, and holding many others constant, in formulating constructs).

The semanticist position is fairly straightforward, and we readily accept its emphasis on the similarity between theorizing and everyday thinking, but two problems arise which the semanticists have difficulty resolving. The first they have pointed to in their recognition of the *multiordinality* of abstractions. Korzybski (1941) has noted that many of our most important terms are multiordinal. That is, they have different meanings at different levels of abstraction, and in relation therefore to different items of our experience. Such constructs literally have no general meaning. A term like "theory," itself, varies according to the context in which we use it, so that we can speak about higher-level and lower-level theories. It is no easy matter to try to determine which theory or which construct is more or less abstract than another. For example, it is natural to think of Freudian theory as quite abstract, that is, far removed from simple labeling, yet in point of fact the constructs "stimulus," "response," and "reinforcement" are *the* most abstract constructs in psychology. In truth, everything relating to behavior which can be pointed to or measured or even conjectured is potentially either a stimulus or a response by definition. And when the two are bound together — whether by drive reduction or an empirical law of effect — we speak of reinforcement.

The S-R theorist has gained a reputation for sticking close to the level of labeling, thanks to his emphasis on operational definitions, but this should not blind us to the fact that the S-R paradigm is multiordinal and can move quickly up and down the ladder of abstraction. Thus, we can speak about puffs of air and eye-blinks, or Russian-American relations in S-R terms. Dollard and Miller (1950) found it comparatively easy to translate Freudian theory into S-R terms, a clear indication that the latter were used more abstractly.

This brings us to the second problem with the strict semanticist position, one the semanticists seem to have lost sight of. To reverse the above process, to translate S-R theory into Freudian terms, would be essentially impossible. This demonstrates that Freudian theory can add to the meaning of S-R theory, but the latter, although more abstract, has little or no meaning to add to Freudian theory.

The point here is that, in discussing abstraction and elucidating the process by which it takes place, the semanticists have somehow lost track of the concept of *meaning* with which they began in simple sensory perception. Take, for example, the following discussion by Johnson, in which he contrasts the terms "electron" and "supernatural":

> The peculiar thing about *supernatural* is that, by definition, it refers to something beyond, or "above," or outside nature. It refers, that is, to something that is independent of anything "natural." It differs in this respect from *electron,* for example, the definition of which is rigorously dependent upon observable data and has been gradually revised in accordance with such data. Not only is it true, therefore, that such a term as *supernatural* cannot be used as an undefined term on the first-order verbal level, but also it is not clear as to just how it might be used so as to refer indirectly, like *electron,* to observable data. It represents not only a verbal abstraction, but one which bears an apparently loose and uncertain relationship to the non-verbal levels of abstraction (1946, p. 130).

If the semanticist Johnson truly wishes to speak for the individual, and if he admits that "supernatural" is an abstraction, then clearly he must explain why a term like this ever could arise. To conclude that it bears a "loose and uncertain relationship" to the non-verbal levels of abstraction fails to clarify the matter for us. To use his own terminology, we have to suspect that there are unnamed higher-order presuppositions guiding his reasoning at this point; for example, that non-verbal sensation or feelings of awe in the presence of natural phenomena cannot be abstracted as the direct experiencing of supernatural force, or that what cannot be directly pointed to cannot "exist" for the individual in an immediate and meaningful way. Reflected here is a position which suggests that man can find meaning only through the hard data of immediate experience, and this may or may not be legitimate. We suspect, therefore, that there is something wrong with Johnson's interpretation, something to do with his "theory of meaning."

Realism vs. Idealism

For a better understanding of Johnson's dilemma, we must move on to another characteristic of all theories. In addition to being more or less abstract, theories are written along a dimension known as realism vs. idealism. These are very old terms in philosophy, fraught with meanings we might hope to avoid because they will doubtless confuse our presentation. We might introduce new terms at this point, in an effort to avoid the older connotations. However, there is merit in trying to forge a continuity between the issues of yesterday and our difficulties of today, and thereby to show that a contemporary disagreement is not unique after all. The main point is to recognize that this *is* a dimension, and that it is not correct to label a theorist merely an idealist or a realist. It is more proper to think of each extreme of this dimension as a direction in which a theorist leans, with more or less conviction, according to the various tenets of his theory and the purpose he sets himself in formulating it.

The theorist who gravitates toward realism in his outlook takes the position that the world (sometimes phrased "external world") of perception and cognition has an immutable existence all its own, entirely independent of the perceiver. Man looks out onto a world that has an independent existence. Abstractions map a reality — maybe not in a one-to-one sense at all times, but such a one-to-one mapping is possible. Indeed, the scientist *must* do this in order to gain "scientific knowledge," if not in the present, then at some later time when he has refined his techniques of study and measurement.

The theorist who begins at the idealistic end of the scale would claim that there is no external world of reality apart from, or having an existence independent of the perception and cognition of the perceiver, or at least that it is not profitable to speak of such a world. Man looks out on a world of his own making. Knowledge is primarily an act of creation, of actively tying together rather than passively mapping certain of the many variables at play before our eyes. Abstractions are ordered percepts, given a name; but to assume that they map anything having a clear-cut, literal, or unchanging existence really adds nothing to our theoretical activity, and it may even hamper us.

We should note at this point a distinction often made between an "abstraction" and a "construction," for it parallels the realism-idealism dimension (see, for example, Russell, 1960). To abstract, as we have seen, is to leave out details in drawing terms for a description of our environment. This is on the "upside" of the levels of inference. But when we begin to infer, there is also an element of ascribing terms *to* the environment. This matter of "construing" experience is on the "downside" of the inference levels, and it points to a certain arbitrariness in our choice of ways of speaking about our world. The psychologist who believes that all his theoretical terms are, strictly speaking, "abstracts" would surely be on the side of realism; whereas, the psychologist who stressed the fact that he construed his data, and thus was active in creating his picture of reality, would be on the side of idealism. In modern usage these terms, "abstract" and "construct," are used interchangeably, thereby glossing over the realism-idealism issue. We will also use them interchangeably, but recognize the historical difference implied here in the nature of meaning.

"Meaning" is a relational concept; it suggests that some item to which one refers bears a certain relationship to other concepts already "grasped" — i.e., placed in interpenetrating relationship. The meaning of "love," though vague and at times difficult to point to, is carried by this term's relation with many aspects of experience, including sentimental songs, party experiences, jealousies, lust, a quiet solitude, a sharing, and so on. Now, to tie this directly into our present dimension, a complete realist would hold that the relational aspect of his constructs is provided in *nature,* entirely independent of his intellect or his behavior. We may term this the "realistic interpretation of meaning." The idealist, on the other hand, takes the view that such relations are provided more or less by a reasoning intelligence, and that reality itself need have no particular ordering of relations on which to base lasting meanings. We may term this the "idealistic interpretation of meaning."

We now can see that Johnson's difficulties with the use of "supernatural" stem from the fact that his semanticist position encompasses realism. He begins with the following assumptions: "an abstract on any level is abstracted *from something by someone*" (1946, p. 151) and "the structure of our language must correspond essentially to the structure of reality" (p. 114). It therefore follows that to speak of something above and beyond nature (reality) is to make abstractions of quite definite looseness and uncertainty, as regards that nature. Such terms imply that our map of reality is not entirely correct. Both Korzybski (1941) and Johnson (1946, pp. 131–133) have made extensive use of the map-territory analogy. The idea here is that reality is a kind of territory, which must be mapped and remapped by the individual through use of symbols (abstractions). To quote Johnson: "what we call a map is an example of a kind of language, symbols arranged in some kind of order" (p. 131). He then goes on to point out that, because they tend to confuse symbol (actually, "sign") and reality, people often do not map reality very accurately, and consequently have great difficulty in changing their maps to adjust to changing circumstances.

This is a fruitful analysis, but as we have seen it is not without pitfalls when the theorist himself comes up against a phenomenon *he* cannot map. More fundamentally we can ask, how adequate is it to conceive of the scientific enterprise as analogous to map-making? In his book, *Modern Science and Modern Man,* the renowned organic chemist, James Conant (1952), takes the map analogy to task:

> Those who still hold today with the idea that the universe has a structure which, like the geography of an island, can be discovered by successive approximations, must cling to the "in principle" argument. Confront them with the phlogiston theory, the caloric fluid, the luminiferous ether — all now obsolete (except for pedagogic purposes) — and they will say, "Yes, the first maps were imperfect, but in principle it is possible to find out what really is the structure of the universe."
>
> On this basic issue there is far from complete agreement among philosophers of science today. You can, each of you, choose your side and find highly distinguished advocates for the point of view you have selected. However, in view of the revolution in physics, anyone who now asserts that science is an exploration of the universe must be prepared to shoulder a heavy burden of proof. To my mind, the analogy between the map maker and the scientist is false. A scientific theory is not even the first approximation to a map; it is not a creed; it is a policy — an economical and fruitful guide to action by scientific investigators (pp. 96–97).

Idealism in the form stated at the outset of this section is, if not unheard of, then surely greatly avoided in American psychology. This is because psychology has been dominated by the language of realism in academic circles since the days of John B. Watson (1913). Indeed, his revolt against introspectionism was in one sense a reaction of realism (out there, in the hard reality) to the prevailing idealism (in here, the mind's eye). Over succeeding generations American psychological journal articles have been primarily occupied with the problems of how best to map the reality "out there." Usually framed in terms of lawfulness, we have shown great concern with measurement ("Let's make our maps highly precise"), operational definitions ("Let's get as close to reality as we can"), and reductionism ("Let's start with simple maps and then work our way up"). Our "toughmindedness" is tied to our realism.

This pointed rejection of idealism in psychology is very prevalent, and is pressed most strongly by those who write on the history of our discipline (see, for example, Watson, 1963, p. 35, or Kantor, 1963, p. 25). Apparently, psychologists feel particularly vulnerable to criticisms of a theoretical stance which admits of non-material influences on their data. There always lurks the suspicion that idealists harbor a desire to bring back not only mentalistic conceptions but ethereal spirits and souls of an astrological or nether land as well. In the face of such an obstinate denial of mind, it is difficult for anyone in American psychology to call himself an idealist. The term is a badge of "no honor," and he who buttons it to his lapel does so only after making perfectly clear that he has not really lost touch with reality. Take, for example, George Kelly, whom we claim advocates an idealistic position in *The Psychology of Personal Constructs* (1955). In his opening comments, Kelly is very careful to acknowledge a "middle position," lest he be accused of talking about nothing more than mental apparitions:

> We presume that the universe is really existing and that man is gradually coming to understand it. By taking this position we attempt to make clear from the outset that it is a real world we shall be talking about, not a world composed solely of the flitting shadows of people's thoughts. But we should like, furthermore, to make clear our conviction that people's thoughts also really exist, though the correspondence between what people really think exists and what really does exist is a continually changing one (p. 6).

Kelly gives thoughts an existence of their own. Ideas must be taken seriously. Man's thought processes are part and parcel of his reality, and it is just as true to say that his ideas create reality as it is to say his ideas reflect or map reality: "Man looks at his world through transparent patterns or templets [i.e., constructs] which he creates and then attempts to fit over the realities of which the world is composed" (p. 9). Thus far we find a great similarity with the semanticist position, except that, as the following quote demonstrates, Kelly's de-emphasis of realism as a theoretical presupposition permits him to view man as much less determined, much more the maker of his fate, and at all times the master rather than the slave of reality:

> . . . our formulation . . . *emphasizes the creative capacity of the living thing to represent the environment, not merely to respond to it.* Because he can represent his environment, he can place alternative constructions upon it and, indeed, do something about it if it doesn't suit him. To the living creature, then, the universe is real, but it is not inexorable unless he chooses to construe it that way (p. 8).

Though he does not like to be identified as blatantly idealistic, we do Kelly no injustice in placing his theory closer to this pole than to the pole of realism. In fact, Kelly has already named the opposite pole of the dimension on which he rests. In an unpublished paper he explicitly stated: "But I am not a realist — not anymore — and I do not believe either the client or the therapist has to lie down and let facts crawl over him" (1963, p. 5).

As an interesting contrast to Kelly, we can take the view of the realist, Skinner. Skinner has rejected the notion that he actually does any stylized or formally "active" theorizing in his approach to scientific knowledge. It is possible for him to take this extreme stand because of his extreme realism. Skinner thinks of the world as "out there," to be grabbed hold of and manipulated if man would only stop all this talking (theorizing) and start doing (experimenting): "When we have achieved a practical control over the organism, theories of behavior lose their point. In representing and managing relevant variables, a conceptual model is useless; we come to grips with behavior itself" (1956, p. 231).

In other words, from this realistic view, ideas or theories are scientifically meaningless, they are not to be taken seriously; they are kinds of epiphenomena, riding the crest of behavior. Behavior is a succession of responses made to stimuli which are themselves frequently former responses, and this succession of antecedent and consequent events is out there, flowing within the current of natural law. The current exists, and it can be counted on, it can be manipulated or changed or controlled to suit — to suit what? Man's mind, his will, his purpose, his self? Why are we tampering with the flow of natural currents? Here, of course, Skinner's formulation of man's behavior runs into difficulty because he is easily forced into an extreme position when he begins to speak about himself as man the actor, the object of study rather than the student of other actors. In one of Skinner's debates with Rogers the following exchange took place, as told by Rogers:

> A paper given by Dr. Skinner led me to direct these remarks to him: "From what I understood Dr. Skinner to say, it is his understanding

that though he might have thought *he chose* to come to this meeting, might have thought he had a purpose in giving this speech, such thoughts are really illusory. He actually made certain marks on paper and emitted certain sounds here simply because his genetic makeup and his past environment had operantly conditioned his behavior in such a way that it was rewarding to make these sounds, and that he as a person doesn't enter into this. In fact if I get his thinking correctly, from his strictly scientific point of view, he, as a person, doesn't exist." In his reply Dr. Skinner said that he would not go into the question of whether he had any choice in the matter (presumably because the whole issue was illusory) but stated, "I do accept your characterization of my own presence here" (1963, pp. 271–272).

Dr. Skinner is to be respected for his consistency, because this is truly as close to an introspective theoretical statement as this "hard-data" behaviorist could make. Our problem is, how could this state of affairs come about, and must we follow Skinner if we hope to remain within the scientific fold? Is there an alternative to this view of man? For an idealist, for a constructive alternativist, the latter question is a reasonable one, and it can be answered in the affirmative. In Part Two we shall be able to show how such an image of man could evolve in the history of thought. For now, we must take up other issues in the nature of theory construction as background preparation.

Objective vs. Subjective

The dimension objective vs. subjective has caused great difficulty in psychology, primarily because it has often been confused or identified with the dimension realism vs. idealism. Actually, of course, it is possible to define "objective" as identical to what we have been calling "realism." Immanuel Kant used the term "subjective" in the way we have been using "idealism." However, if two terms are used to express the same idea we are certainly foregoing parsimony and precision in thought. Also, if a distinction is not made, in our zeal to make psychology ever more objective we might well force ourselves into a realistic position without intending to do so.

As we shall use the term "objective," it will refer to the view that abstractions, and hence the relationship between abstractions, transcend the individual abstractor, and may be grasped or understood by all individuals in a specified class. Presumably, all the individuals in this class have had certain experiences in common so that abstractions from such experience have a common meaning — in a rough sense or in a highly refined sense. To have a common experience does not mean this experience necessarily involves a "real" object. Men have had common experiences with the concept of the supernatural, and, as the realist Johnson has already shown us, this is an "atypical" abstraction by someone from nothing. In discussing the nature of truth, the physicist Robert Oppenheimer* used the term in the way we intend to use it: "The criterion of truth must come from analysis, it must come from experience, and from that very special kind of objectivity which characterizes science, namely that we are quite sure we understand one another and that we can check up on one another" (1956, p. 130).

In checking up on one another, of course, we must all agree to certain ground rules of evidence. A discussion of evidence is better left for Chapter IV. Here we simply want to note that an objective point of view holds that we can and must presume a common frame of reference in order to begin a study or a theoretical line of reasoning. We check up on one another in order to elucidate the common meaning of an abstraction, a meaning which we believe can be generalized.

"Subjectivity," on the other hand, implies that our abstractions and the relations between them are somehow private, and difficult or impossible to circumscribe, much less to generalize beyond the behavior of the abstractor in question. The uniformity of outlook among members of a given class cannot be assumed from the subjective position, because the assumption is that experience and hence abstraction is unique. The subjective theorist would assert that it is impossible ever to know what goes on in the heads of others, or, at best, he might refuse to accept certain abstractions until he is given a rather elaborate description of their nature from the "unique point of view" of the abstractor. Henri F. Ellenberger, an advocate of existential psychoanalysis, speaks from a subjective point of view when he observes:

> Whatever the method used for a phenomenological analysis, the aim of the investigation is the reconstruction of the inner world of experience of the subject. Each individual has his own way of experiencing temporality, spatiality, causality, materiality, but each of these coordinates must be understood in relation to the others and to the total inner "world" (1958, p. 116).

Objectivity and subjectivity in psychology have often come into the picture when discussion of *nomothetic* vs. *idiographic* personality study

---

* *American Men of Science* lists this famous scientist as J. Robert Oppenheimer, but we will use the name here as given by the *American Psychologist*.

is undertaken (Allport, 1946). Nomothetic study essentially presumes that a theoretical abstraction can be made which has general applicability for several members of a given class (i.e., distribution). Idiographic study, on the other hand, emphasizes the uniqueness of personality manifestation. Once again, we must stress the fact that theorists are not either-or, one or the other, on the objective-subjective dimension. There are times when it is correct to say that a theorist takes an objective position, and times when he may be said to take a subjective position on some matter. We may be both idiographic and nomothetic in outlook, depending upon circumstances, and, as we shall see, upon the perspective requirements of our theory.

An intriguing example of a shift in position on this dimension is the highly subjective position taken by otherwise objectively inclined behavioristic psychologists when they come up against such high-order abstractions as "risk of personality." In an excellent discussion of this form of subjectivism in dealing with Rogerian terminology, David Bakan has noted:

> In the simple dictionary sense we all know what the meaning of the word "risk" is. Our behaviorist is not simply ignorant. But he may be complexly ignorant in that he consciously refuses to refer Rogers' words to his own "risk" of his personality. As a matter of fact, the avoidance of risk in just this sense in many behavioristically-inclined psychologists may be so intense that they cannot deal objectively with the experience of risk (1956, p. 657).

Though he may loudly assert that he cannot accept the "vague" notion of risk because of his need for objective, operational (first-order) definitions, the behaviorist in point of fact uses language in a highly individualized and subjective manner when he refuses to acknowledge *any* "scientific" meaning in the phrase "risk of personality." Bakan refers to this self-imposed restriction as the "postulate of epistemological loneliness" (p. 656). Behaviorists have pushed themselves into a corner; they have taken themselves out of the realm of discourse at this point; they are literally *being subjective.*

We find it difficult to think of the behaviorist as subjective in outlook because he is usually only too ready to begin his study of behavior from an objective (usually identified with "realistic") position. When "objective" is used in this sense we may find it useful to identify it as "empiricism." Empiricism in psychology rests essentially on an objective presupposition. As Conant has noted (1952, p. 41), empiricism means the observation of facts (abstracts) apart from the principles which explain them. When we are empirical we approach the study of phenomena on the basis of a common-sense attack. At first, we do not know which principles are involved in the phenomena under study. We simply formulate hunches from common-sense reasoning.

As we go along, inventing, discovering, refining a theory (however one wishes to think of this process of study), empiricism gradually gives way to a knowledge of so-called underlying principles. This knowledge of underlying principles is a matter of introducing a new set of abstractions to explain the empirical phenomena in what we might now call a different way. We become less empirical to the extent that we can explain the nature of some phenomenon in terms of general principles or laws outside the simple, macroscopic description of what is going on before our eyes in the common-sense world of experience.

This does not mean, of course, that as we lose empiricism in knowledge we lose objectivity. It does mean that as a starting point, the empirical approach, and the accrual of generalizable knowledge, must begin from an *objective presupposition:* that is, there is nothing wrong with beginning from "scratch," from the general notions we have in common sense. We follow this succession in moving from the *phenotypic* to the *genotypic* description of behavior (Brown, 1936, Ch. 2). Phenotypic description is phrased in the language of common sense, or everyday abstractions ("That child is showing off"), whereas genotypic description presumably goes beneath the overt and apparent description, as a result of previous study, and states a more "dynamic" description of behavior ("That child is attempting to gain attention because he feels rejected").

But common sense, then, with its assumption of a uniform outlook among all investigators who rummage about the laboratory poking in this and that, can be considered an appropriate starting point for scientific endeavors. This is the program Skinner offers in preference to the high-flown theory construction models of Hull: "An acceptable scientific program is to collect data . . . and to relate them to manipulable variables, selected for study through a common sense exploration of the field" (1950, p. 215). A program of this sort was also suggested to psychologists by Oppenheimer: "we may well say that all ideas that occur in common sense are fair as starting points, not guaranteed to work but perfectly valid as the material of the analogies with which we start" (1956, p. 134).

Assuming that both these men begin with common-sense approaches to the study of man, can we expect them to come to some agreement in their views on the basic nature of man? Skinner claims that he began with his common sense, and we have already seen what he has made of man — a kind of purposeless ripple in the stream of natural law. Yet Oppenheimer would not rule out purposiveness from man's nature; he would begin with this characteristic of man at the outset, as one of the common-sense truisms we all take for granted. In discussing his "nervousness" about some of the field-theory and mechanistic-physical models which psychologists seem addicted to using in drawing analogies to man's nature, Oppenheimer reflects: "I think that, especially when we compare subjects in which ideas of coding, of the transfer of information, or ideas of purpose, are inherent and natural, with subjects in which these are not inherent and natural, that formal analogies have to be taken with very great caution" (p. 134).

Our brother scientists are often disturbed by what we psychologists do with the image of man; a typical comment is this one by Conant: "The universe is not constructed along the lines of an automatic machine distributing rewards and punishments — at least not in this world of mortals" (1952, p. 150). Now, these are highly competent scientists speaking about their concern over what man the psychologist is doing with man the human, who gets up and brushes his teeth in the morning, or does not do so, because he thinks he wants to. These are not criticisms made by naive and emotional sophomores. As a sample of the kind of rebuttal one might find to such criticisms we may turn to Kenneth W. Spence, who discusses what he takes to be a deterrent to the progress of scientific psychology. This deterrent is the "tendency to criticize theoretical concepts in this field [psychology] as being too elementaristic, too mechanistic, and as failing to portray the real essence or true nature of man's behavior" (1956, p. 21). Spence then goes on:

> To the writer such criticisms reflect essentially a lack of appreciation as to the difference between *scientific knowledge* of an event and other kinds of knowledge, e.g., the kinds of knowledge the novelist and poet portray. Either by reason of their training or because of their basically nonscientific interests these critics have apparently never really understood the *abstract* character of the scientific account of any phenomenon. The only reply that can be made to such a critic is to point out that the scientist's interests just happen to be different from his. There are, of course, other perfectly legitimate interpretations of nature and man than the scientific one, and each has its right to be pursued. The science-oriented psychologist merely asks that he be given the same

opportunity to develop a scientific account of his phenomena that his colleagues in the physical and biological sciences have had. If there are aspects of human behavior for which such an account cannot ever be developed, there are not, so far as I know, any means of finding this out without a try (pp. 20–21).

Theoretical Perspective: Introspection vs. Extraspection

Although we think of theorizing as a uniform activity, standing or falling on its merit according to one perspective, this is an oversimplified and inaccurate belief. Theories, as abstractions and postulated relations between abstractions, can be formulated to meet the objectives and needs of two perspectives: introspection and extraspection. By perspective we mean here the standpoint from which the theoretical abstractions and relations are to be thought of, engaged in, or discussed. Some theories can be thought of or applied from both perspectives, but we usually find that any given theory functions most appropriately from one or the other. The perspective a theorist adopts is a function of his attitude toward the object of his study, and the purpose he sets himself in the act of formulating knowledge.

If the theorist takes an introspective attitude and perspective, his constructs will be formulated from the point of view of the *object of study*. By "object of study" we mean the contents of certain theoretical abstractions, which we might now call the "source of data" or simply "data." Sigmund Freud and the early analysts took their function to be the formulation of psychological interpretations or alternate frames of reference *for their clients,* who would then use them in achieving insight. Therefore, their data were the recorded lives of their clients, and the analysts as a group may be considered introspective in theoretical outlook. Note that we are not saying they tried to formulate explanations in the language of the client. They merely took the client seriously, as an integral aspect of the process of theory formulation. Their method of study brought man as object of study into the procedure. They then made highly esoteric genotypic comments on his nature, and gave man a new and strange language of self-description.

If the theorist takes an extraspective perspective or frame of reference, he defines his abstractions from his vantage point as observer, regardless of the point of view of the object of study. The extraspectively-inclined theorist begins from the proposition: "What do we — over here as observers — need to postulate in order to study *that* over there?" What he does not need he can leave out of his constructions. He does not pose the question a psychotherapist might well pose: "What form of underlying or dynamic terminology can I propose to my client over there, and to myself, which will somehow strike home and provide both of us with an understanding of why he does what he does?" Here, the analyst cannot leave out details which are important to the client, although he might well reconstrue them.

The history of American academic psychology since Watson is in large measure the story of an active attempt to reject all forms of introspectionism in psychological theory. It began with Watson's expression of irritation over the formal method of introspection, which had been introduced by Wundt (Boring, 1950, pp. 384–386) and was later advocated in America by Titchener. In 1913, speaking about the psychology of his time, Watson noted:

> Psychology, as it is generally thought of, has something esoteric in its methods. If you fail to reproduce my findings, it is not due to some fault in your apparatus or in the control of your stimulus, but it is due to the fact that your introspection is untrained. The attack is made upon the observer and not upon the experimental setting. In physics and in chemistry the attack is made upon the experimental conditions (1913, p. 163).

In this paper, Watson essentially argues that we — as psychological theorists — must stop analogizing from man to brute, and instead analogize from physics and chemistry to man. In short, we must adopt an extraspective attitude and take man — phrased as "consciousness" — out of the picture:

> Psychology as the behaviorist views it is a purely objective branch of natural science. Its theoretical goal is the prediction and control of behavior. Introspection forms no essential part of its methods, nor is the scientific value of its data dependent upon the readiness with which they lend themselves to interpretation in terms of consciousness. The behaviorist, in his efforts to get a unitary scheme of animal response, recognizes no dividing line between man and brute (p. 158).

In rejecting introspectionism and the importance of consciousness, Watson limited the possibility of a sophisticated form of realism developing in the history of behaviorism. To examine one's method as scientist is essentially to introspect, which in psychology has come to mean to play the metaphysician or to indulge in "armchair psychology." The theory of knowledge as it evolved stressed only those "facts" which could be discovered from without, rather than "dreamed-up" from within. Objectivity and extraspection became confused with realism, so that an honest statement of how we create our theoretical propositions rather than discover them in some inexorable reality gained little foothold in precisely that camp which was infusing the greatest creativity into the science of psychology over the first half of this century — behaviorism. Watson set the tone as early as 1913:

> The plans which I most favor for psychology lead practically to the ignoring of consciousness in the sense that that term is used by psychologists today. I have virtually denied that this realm of psychics is open to experimental investigation. I don't wish to go further into the problem at present because it leads inevitably over into metaphysics (p. 175).

So, in one bold sweep we dismiss man's unique ability to introspect and be aware, and then refuse to look into ourselves because to do so would be metaphysical and, therefore, presumably not scientific. Even so, like Skinner, Watson (1917) was prone to refer to common sense in justifying his way of going about the business of making science. Common sense was the initial vehicle for his objectivity. By 1922, a self-proclaimed "dyed-in-the-wool introspectionist," S. W. Fernberger (1922), argued for the separation of psychology into two branches: a science of behavior (study of the stimulus and response); and a science of consciousness (study of the intervening mental processes). William McDougall (1923) rather dramatically asked for a kind of rapprochement in what he termed "purposive behaviorism."

But the truth was, the extraspectionists, with their emphasis on objectivity in experimental design, were making exciting advances in the accrual of knowledge. Their success gave them the right to speak out as theoreticians and experts on knowledge, and not the least of their influences in academic circles was their early confounding of realism with objectivity. A typical example from this period is a paper written by V. F. Calverton in 1924, entitled "The Rise of Objective Psychology." Calverton began by posing a question which confounds issues at the outset: "Now what is it that distinguishes objective knowledge from subjective? *The object is there in either case;* it must be there in all cases, or there could be no knowledge" (1924, p. 419). He argued that subjective knowledge is opinion about the object, resulting in widespread disagreement, whereas objective knowledge is acceptable to all and leads to agreement. It follows, therefore, that if one is objective from

Calverton's point of view, one essentially accepts the fact that the "object out there" is really there, independent of your theoretical bias, so why be stubborn about it?

Through question-begging devices of this sort, and the early successes of their objective-realistic approach, the behaviorists created quite a fervor as well as a sense of empirical righteousness within their group. In 1928, Z. Y. Kuo asserted that all behavior — animal and human — is completely determined by the stimulus (Kuo, 1928). Man was now a completely determined responder to stimuli, which were themselves aspects of real laws, existing "out there" to be studied objectively. In 1935, while spelling out P. W. Bridgman's "Principle of Operationism" for psychologists, S. S. Stevens voiced what the writer would like to call the "Principle of Extraspection": "Psychology regards all observations, including those which a psychologist makes upon himself, as made upon the 'other one' and thereby makes explicit the distinction between the experimenter and the thing observed" (1935, p. 517).

In thus firmly implanting themselves on the side of extraspection, the behaviorists were quite prone in the 1930's to defer to their peers in the physical and biological sciences. It is certainly true that the physicist is not bothered with the necessity of formulating introspective theories; Mars does not ask to be informed on the nature of the laws which hold it in orbit round the sun. Extraspective theory is the classical perspective taken by physical science. Accurately sensing this great admiration the behaviorists held for their brother scientists, in 1936 J. E. Winter, an introspectively-inclined theoretician, used the behaviorist's model of excellence to argue back at them. He quoted the physicist Sir Arthur Eddington as saying that "Determinism has faded out of theoretical physics," and went on to point out that physicists make use of a mind concept, and essentially reject the machine as an adequate model for man (Winter, 1936, p. 143). Man, including man the scientist, does have a mind, and a purpose, at least as far as the other sciences are concerned. Winter concluded with the observation that the behaviorist "has set up a standard more drastic than physical science is able to maintain. He literally out-sciences science" (p. 144).

Hull went about answering this claim at the time he put forward his thinking on the hypothetico-deductive technique. Hull began by accepting Winter's paradox; using the behaviorist, Albert P. Weiss, and Eddington as contrasting theoreticians, he noted:

> We are presented with the paradox of Eddington, the physicist, apparently insisting that the higher forms of behavior are at bottom non-

physical, whereas Weiss, the psychologist, insists that they are fundamentally non-psychological. . . .

But what, exactly, is the issue? Is it, for example, a difference as to an ordinary matter of observed fact? Do Eddington and those who share his view claim to have made certain observations which are in conflict with a corresponding set of observations supposed to have been made by Weiss and those with a mechanistic leaning? The dispute involves nothing of this nature. It is clear that the controversy is definitely a theoretical one (1937, p. 4).

In other words, this is not a dispute of facts but of theoretical opinions. In the language of Calverton, it is a subjective and — we might as well add — unscientific argument. In a rather confident tone, Hull next goes on to lay the foundation for his hypothetico-deductive technique, and, in the process, to teach Eddington science:

The essential characteristics of a sound scientific theoretical system, as contrasted with ordinary philosophical speculation, may be briefly summarized under three heads:

1. A satisfactory scientific theory should begin with a set of explicitly stated postulates accompanied by specific or "operational" definitions of the critical terms employed.

2. From these postulates there should be deduced by the most rigorous logic possible under the circumstances, a series of interlocking theorems covering the major concrete phenomena of the field in question.

3. The statements in the theorems should agree in detail with the observationally known facts of the discipline under consideration. If the theorems agree with the observed facts, the system is probably true; if they disagree, the system is false. If it is impossible to tell whether the theorems of a system agree with the facts or not, the system is neither true nor false; scientifically considered, it is meaningless (p. 5).

These three points lay down the essential philosophy of the hypothetico-deductive method. As it has come to be known, the idea is that a psychological scientist formulates an hypothesis, makes a prediction on the basis of some experimental design devised to test that hypothesis, and then either substantiates or fails to substantiate the hypothesis in question. Presumably the hypotheses formulated are all logically deduced from the set of explicitly stated postulates which frame the theory at the outset.

To continue his examination, Hull next points out that in philosophical speculation there is no possibility of comparing a theorem with the results of direct observation. He uses as an example Spinoza's theorem which stated "Besides God no substance can be, nor can be conceived and observed," and notes that he cannot see how this could possibly be put to observational test. He then takes Eddington to task:

> Turning to Eddington, we find exactly the same paradoxical situation. Notwithstanding his positive, even emphatic, implications that moral behavior must be conscious or psychic in its ultimate nature, we find him neither presenting nor citing a theoretical system of any kind, much less one derived from psychic or conscious postulates. This paradox is particularly astonishing in the case of Eddington because he has been active in the field of physical theory and should, therefore, be sophisticated regarding the essential methodology involved in scientific theory in general. [This is an amazingly revealing comment on Hull's part; it is obvious that he did not for a moment dream that a "physical" scientist could take an idealistic position on the nature of the physical universe, which is precisely what Eddington was prepared to do if it enriched his thinking (Eddington, 1958, pp. 157–158).] Surely the same logic which demands strict deduction from explicitly stated postulates in physical theory demands it for the theory of adaptive and moral behavior. And surely if we demand it of a mechanistic theory of the more recondite forms of human behavior, as Eddington seems emphatically to do, there is no hocus-pocus whereby a psychic view of such behavior may be maintained without the same substantial foundation (p. 10).

Eddington's emphatic demands on mechanism are presumably based upon this quote which Hull offers the reader (p. 3): "Conceivably we might reach a human machine interacting by reflexes with its environment; but we cannot reach rational man morally responsible. . . . In a world of aether and electrons we might perhaps encounter *nonsense;* we could not encounter *damned nonsense*" (Eddington, 1929, pp. 343, 345).

In Chapter VI we will take up the matter of introspection and extraspection as it applies to the issue of ethics and morals. Here it should simply be pointed out that Eddington, as quoted by Hull, is merely shifting perspective. He is turning away from physical theory to a theory of man, basing his conception of man on his own personal nature and on his observations of the natures of other men. He is saying that "We, over here as observers, might go a long way in describing the behavior of that man over there mechanistically, without ascribing mind or aesthetic preference or moral responsibility to him. Yet, man *must* be thought of in these terms. I know because I am a man. Man makes judgments and evaluates, he judges not only the fact of nonsense, but the type of (damned) nonsense. He expresses *preference values* going beyond the data." Eddington, the extraspective physical scientist, here introspects, and this disturbs and even confuses the extraspective psychologist, Hull. Hull looks out at the hard data and sees behavior, of atoms, of rats, of man, but all is behavior; Eddington looks out and sees himself.

The truly startling aspect of this is that some of our most eminent psychologists could speak so confidently for and in the name of the physicists. For example, as early as 1925, Niels Bohr, one of the creators of the atomic model, warned that atomic physics could not be constructed "without resignation of the wish for sensuous presentation"; and Heisenberg later said: "an understanding of the atomic world in that primary sensuous fashion . . . is impossible" (Cassirer, 1950, pp. 116–117). Yet, here we find Bergmann and Spence, as late as 1941, speaking for the physicists, tracing the activities of what they term the "primitive physicist," who presumably derived all his scientific terms from "the hard data," "the immediately observable," or the "elementary operation of discrimination" (1941, p. 6).

So, while physics was actually becoming more idealistic in its theory (see Chapter V), and physicists were prepared to consider man from *his* perspective, many psychologists of great academic influence were placing all their hopes on the extraspective, realistic approach to the study of man. Knowledge came from "out there," the facts of life. To be sure, they did have to hypothesize a bit, basing such hypotheses on very clear-cut, precise formulations, drawn from observations of reality; but the less speculative the hypothesis the better. It is literally the case that, as a neo-behaviorist one tries, if he must hypothesize, not to get too hypothetical (see, for example, Dallenbach, 1953, p. 39).

Of course, this is the criticism many people have of the so-called laboratory or rat psychologist. Due to his realistic-extraspective position, he has limited the range of theoretical notions he permits himself to deal with. This worked well over the first half of this century, but in recent years one wonders if anything new is being added, short of a continual repetition or reliability check on the fact that conditioning can be demonstrated across a remarkably broad range of behavior. Many feel that we must go forward, that we must recognize the lower organism is not necessarily the citadel of kernel psychological knowledge some would make it. Why not be more speculative at these comparatively early stages in the development of our science? In the name of scientific discipline and rigor we are letting our probability criteria lead us down a path of triviality. Instead of bold ideas, we have safe, sane experimental designs which can show results at the .01 significance level. That is as it should be, of course, because only a well-mapped reality can give us this probability — and that is what we are after. So, why take a risk on speculation? Our battlecry in the name of objectivity becomes: "Try not to hypothesize about hypothetical facts."

This is not to say that psychologists should refrain from assuming the extraspective frame of reference in formulating their theories. Indeed, as we shall demonstrate in later chapters, this is one serious indictment of the clinical method. If the clinicians who formulated some of the outstanding aspects of introspective theory, such as Freud and Jung, had been more sensitive to the need for extraspective validation, we would not have the obfuscation of methods and constructs present today. The position the writer takes is that all psychologists should extraspect; indeed, if they are to be scientists, they *must* do so. To extraspect is to meet the objective demands of the scientific community. But at the same time, the frantic overemphasis on extraspection in psychology, which we have already reviewed, has led to certain blindspots in the theoretical sophistication of our community. We must think of theoretical perspective as a dimension, and be prepared to evaluate the worth of a theory on either end of this dimension.

Formal vs. Informal

We come now to the final dimension along which theories may be said to vary or along which they may be classified. It is a difficult dimension to deal with, even though it has long been recognized and even tacitly accepted in psychology. The fundamental reason for the difficulty is that very few psychologists want to dignify what we will call "informal theory" with the name "theory." However, more important from our point of view, difficulties arise from the fact that informal theory shares in meaning with a concept of evidence which will be presented in Chapter IV, i.e., procedural evidence. Yet, a distinction between informal theory and procedural evidence is possible, and will be made at that time (see pp. 75–76).

We have already had a statement of formal theory in the hypothetico-deductive technique outlined by Hull. This statement has had great impact on American academic psychology, where it is often held up as more than an ideal; it is held up as a standard. Mathematical systems are excellent examples of highly formalized theories. Formal theory, then, is theory stated as specifically and uniformly as possible and written to bring together all the loosely joined tenets, hypotheses, and validated facts into a consistent, interdependent unity. One need not look far to find staunch advocates of the position that theory is *nothing but* a formalized set of postulates with reduction terms, bringing the constructs of such postulates down to the level of labeling, and, based upon such operational definitions, generating discovery of lawful relations between these abstractions. This is a nice "in theory" presentation, but, as Skinner (1956) has noted, it is unfortunately not accurate as a description of what takes place. We must come to understand that the nature of the data chosen for study, and the kinds of constructs, the kinds of theoretical assertions made, are often dictated by unnamed or unrecognized tenets of informal theory. Very often these are embodied in high-level metaconstructs which have a continuing history of their own in man's thought (Chapter XI).

Informal theory, then, is theory which has not been stated explicitly, lacks a clear unifying abstraction, and, since it often goes unrecognized, does not have as its implicit goal the formulation of a logically consistent and mutually interdependent body of knowledge. If we think of theorizing as involving conjecture, speculation, hunches, and guesses, then we must certainly hold open the possibility of informal theoretical influences. There are both formal and informal tenets to every outlook, but sometimes it is difficult to identify the informal aspects of a theory which professes to be highly formal. And, on the other hand, when a theorist does not have the goal of formulating a completely integrated "postulate and deduction" system, but uses constructs which seem to *imply* an integrated view, he often misleads his reader into the belief that a comprehensive view is intended. Freud and many other analysts have been misunderstood on this score. In the case of Freud, it is probably more accurate to say that he has been misread. His style of writing is almost conversational; he makes several guesses this way and that, finally settling on one point, but often leaving the door open for another, later interpretation. This is certainly not the model of rigorous scientific writing that he followed while turning out several monographs on neurology in the laboratory of Brücke (Jones, 1953, p. 45); but it is not entirely fair to Freud as theorist to dismiss his psycho-analytic conceptions on the grounds that they do not meet the rigorous standards of his earlier writings.

To show how unnamed informal theory can operate within a highly formal theoretical position, Bakan has detected a "hidden theory" in the three basic postulates of Hull's hypothetico-deductive method. In discussing Hull's general philosophy of theorizing as presented above (p. 31), Bakan states:

> In this . . . theory the three major concepts are *theory, observation,* and *probability.* Probability is what characterizes the relation between theory and observation. Thus, on the grounds of certain observations, a theory is said to have such and such a probability. On the grounds of a given theory, a predicted observation has such and such a probability of occurring. When a predicted observation is verified, the probability of the theory goes up. When a predicted observation fails to be verified, the probability of the theory goes down. . . . This "hidden theory of learning" is more of a cognitive than an S-R theory (1953, p. 360).

Bakan points this out not to discredit the position taken by Hull, but simply to demonstrate that some of the assumptions which cognitive theorists make formally, and which are then challenged by the S-R theorists for one reason or another as not scientific, *must be made* informally by these very same S-R theorists to justify their own formal theoretical activity. Yet, since S-R theorists are not prone to introspect, these unnamed, informal theories remain anonymous. Although anonymous, they are not without influence.

Possibly the most telling demonstration of the importance of informal theory comes in Skinner's paper entitled "A Case History in Scientific Method" (1956). Skinner wrote this paper to demonstrate that he did not follow any preconceived or formal rules for scientific thinking in the research he did before writing his book, *The Behavior of Organisms* (1938). Although he was careful to note that he did "not wish to deprecate the hypothetico-deductive method" (1956, p. 226), he did say: "I never attacked a problem by constructing a Hypothesis. I never deduced Theorems or submitted them to Experimental Check. So far as I can see, I had no preconceived Model of behavior — certainly not a physiological or mentalistic one, and, I believe, not a conceptual one" (p. 227).

Yet, as a guiding principle, Skinner accepted what he called the "clue" from Pavlov, which was: "Control your conditions and you will see order" (p. 223). He did not think of this as a formal theoretical position, but we would contend that it served an informal function. If this is the real reason Skinner went into the rat laboratory — because he believed that controlled conditions would bring returns in terms of knowledge of "behavior" — then we would assert that this was his conceptual model of behavior. As he stood there in the laboratory, with all its potential for controlled observation, obviously only a limited number of observations and hence abstractions were available to him. Therefore, any discoveries reportable, any theories possible, must certainly have been affected by the Pavlovian admonition. The issue turns on how one interprets "control." Not all psychologists agree on what constitutes controls (see Chapter VI), but we do know where Skinner stands, and we can now see how he set out on the course which was to bring him to the discovery that man as we think we know him is not really in the picture. Could it be that his interpretation of "control," which placed him in the laboratory — with mute rats as subjects — and not in the bays of an industrial plant — where he might have talked over problems with workers — somehow influenced this discovery of man's behavior? We suspect this was the case.

Had not Watson hoped to achieve a study of behavior for both man and brute? And did he not suggest that this could be done in more than one context? He *did* in fact do this, by claiming that experimental pedagogy, the psychology of drugs, the psychology of advertising, legal psychology, the psychology of tests, and psychopathology were all mistakenly termed "practical" or "applied" disciplines. Watson referred to these fields of study as "truly scientific" (1913, p. 169). He believed in extending the study of behavior to these contexts as well as to the rat laboratory. Watson did not seem too certain of himself on this point, but, at least in his opening statement, he favored the study of behavior in many contexts. Psychologists should study rats to learn about rats and man to learn about man. Yet by 1930, psychology found itself studying rats to learn about man. Something had happened, and it is our contention that this "something" hinged on the interpretation of experimental controls. Skinner provides an excellent example of the way this unnamed influence has worked; there are other indications of informal theory in his "case history" paper, as when he describes how he extended the use of his experimental methods from baby rats to adult rats as sources of data: "Now, baby rats have very little future, except as adult rats. Their behavior is literally infantile and cannot be usefully extrapolated to everyday life. But if this technique would work with a baby, why not try it on a mature rat?" (1956, p. 224).

One might well take issue with this informal theoretical postulate that laws established on the behavior of young rats are not usefully extrapolated to everyday life, or even to the behavior of older rats. Why does it not follow that we can extrapolate to life directly without the intermediate step of testing an older organism? Can we not think of lawfulness as lawfulness? Did not Watson clearly assert that behaviorism "recognizes no dividing line between man and brute" (1913, p. 158)? Why then discriminate between young rat and old rat? Here is why: since Watson's battlecry of 1913, there had been much discussion of lower laws generating higher-level laws, and lower organisms teaching us something about higher organisms, so that an informal theory had taken hold of Skinner's thinking and manifested itself in his "common-sense" reasoning, the source of his supposed non-theoretical hypotheses about the behavior "out there." Historically considered, there is doubtless an additional influence here from Darwinian theory, and we can also recognize the idea of progress which has developed over the centuries with the rise of modern science (Wiener and Noland, 1957, pp. 251–275).

Summary

We have begun our consideration of theory by reviewing five fundamental dimensions along which various theoretical positions are considered in the chapters to follow. We have seen that theories involve a process of abstraction, or the leaving out of details in description, as well as the tying together of these abstractions into some kind of relationship. The question of whether one discovers such abstractions or invents them brings us to the second dimension, realism vs. idealism. To be precise, when one uses the term "theoretical construct" he acknowledges the influence of the abstractor, the theorist, on the object of study; he is moving toward the idealistic pole. On the other hand, the realist would contend that his theoretical constructs, though they are verbalized by an observer, come not from the observer's conceptualizations *about* the data, but rather from the data themselves, from the reality before his eyes. The realist would therefore "abstract," while the idealist would "construct" a theory of some sort. However, the convention in psychology has been to equate construction with abstraction, and we have followed this procedure.

There has been a long-standing confusion in psychology between our second and third dimensions. Objectivity has been confounded with realism, and subjectivity has been confounded with idealism. An objective position is based upon the assumption that abstractions can and will transcend the abstractor's understanding and comprehension. An objective theory is one which puts forth theoretical constructs understood or understandable by all individuals of a specified class. Scientific theories may be expected to meet the requirements of the scientific community, and are therefore termed objective. To the extent that a theoretical construct cannot be understood by all members of a specified class it becomes increasingly subjective. A highly subjective theory would be one which did not generalize beyond the abstractor in question. Empiricism is a special form of objectivity, beginning in the commonsense understanding of a group of individuals.

The fourth dimension, theoretical perspective, underscores the importance of the way a theory is to be formulated. Classical physical theories have been formulated and expressed or written from an extraspective perspective, and therefore meet only the needs of the observer. In the social sciences, however, it is possible to think of theory formulation from the point of view of the *source* of data.

This chapter has developed the view that a distinction between man the scientist (the observer) and man the layman (the object of study) is not only arbitrary, it is misleading and potentially dangerous. Thus, any attempt to understand the true nature of theory must take into consideration those forces which help shape the theoretician's abstracting processes, which influence his thinking. At some level, theory and thought are one. We have avoided a discussion of personal influences, those subjective forces in each man's life which we take for granted are in operation, each in their own way. Instead, we have pointed to the functioning of informal theories which can be seen transcending the individual and influencing all members of a class (i.e., objectively) in a hidden or unnamed way. This has been termed "informal theory." Formal theory is the more conventional idea of theory, with explicit postulates organized in such a way as to be interdependent and entirely circumscribed.

References

Allport, G. W. Personalistic psychology as a science; a reply. *Psychological Review,* 1946, *53,* 132–135.

Bakan, D. Learning and the principle of inverse probability. *Psychological Review,* 1953, *60,* 360–370.

Bakan, D. Clinical psychology and logic. *American Psychologist,* 1956, *11,* 655–662.

Bergmann, G., and Spence, K. Operationism and theory in psychology. *Psychological Review,* 1941, *48,* 1–14.

Boring, E. G. *A history of experimental psychology,* 2nd ed. New York: Appleton-Century-Crofts, 1950.

Brown, J. F. *Psychology and the social order.* New York: McGraw-Hill, 1936.

Calverton, V. F. The rise of objective psychology. *Psychological Review,* 1924, *31,* 418–426.

Cassirer, E. *The problem of knowledge.* New Haven: Yale University Press, 1950.

Conant, J. B. *Modern science and modern man.* Garden City, N.Y.: Doubleday Anchor, 1952. (Originally published, New York: Columbia University Press, 1949.)

Dallenbach, K. M. The place of theory in science. *Psychological Review,* 1953, *60,* 33–39.

Dollard, J., and Miller, N. E. *Personality and psychotherapy: An analysis in terms of learning, thinking, and culture.* New York: McGraw-Hill, 1950.

Eddington, A. *The nature of the physical world.* New York: Macmillan, 1929. (Also available in paperback — Ann Arbor, Mich.: University of Michigan Press, 1958.)

Eddington, A. *The philosophy of physical science.* Ann Arbor, Mich.: University of Michigan Press, 1958.

Ellenberger, H. F. A clinical introduction to psychiatric phenomenology and existential analysis. In R. May, E. Angel, and H. F. Ellenberger (Eds.), *Existence: A new dimension in psychiatry and psychology.* New York: Basic Books, 1958. Pp. 92–124.

Fernberger, S. W. Behavior versus introspective psychology. *Psychological Review,* 1922, *29,* 409–413.

Hull, C. L. Mind, mechanism, and adaptive behavior. *Psychological Review,* 1937, *44,* 1–32. Courtesy, American Psychological Association.

Johnson, W. *People in quandaries.* New York: Harper & Bros., 1946.

Jones, E. *The life and work of Sigmund Freud.* Vol. 1. *The formative years and the great discoveries.* New York: Basic Books, 1953.

Kantor, J. R. *The scientific evolution of psychology.* Vol. 1. Chicago: Principia Press, 1963.

Kelly, G. A. *The psychology of personal constructs.* Vol. 1. *A theory of personality.* New York: W. W. Norton, 1955. Copyright, 1955, by George A. Kelly.

Kelly, G. A. Personal construct theory and the psychotherapeutic interview. Unpublished manuscript, 1963.

Korzybski, A. *Science and sanity: An introduction to non-Aristotelian systems and general semantics,* 2nd ed. Lancaster, Pa.: Science Press, 1941.

Kuo, Z. Y. The fundamental error of the concept of purpose and the trial and error fallacy. *Psychological Review,* 1928, *35,* 414–433.

McDougall, W. Purposive or mechanical psychology? *Psychological Review,* 1923, *30,* 273–288.

Oppenheimer, R. Analogy in science. *American Psychologist,* 1956, *11,* 127–135.

Rogers, C. R. Learning to be free. In S. M. Farber and R. H. L. Wilson (Eds.), *Control of the Mind.* Vol. 2. *Conflict and Creativity.* New York: McGraw-Hill, 1963. Pp. 268–288.

Russell, B. *Our knowledge of the external world.* New York: New American Library, 1960.

Skinner, B. F. *The behavior of organisms: An experimental analysis.* New York: Appleton-Century, 1938.

Skinner, B. F. Are theories of learning necessary? *Psychological Review,* 1950, *57,* 193–216.

Skinner, B. F. A case history in scientific method. *American Psychologist,* 1956, *11,* 221–233.

Spence, K. W. *Behavior theory and conditioning.* New Haven: Yale University Press, 1956.

Stevens, S. S. The operational definition of psychological concepts. *Psychological Review,* 1935, *42,* 517–527.

Watson, J. B. Psychology as the behaviorist views it. *Psychological Review,* 1913, *20,* 158–177.

Watson, J. B. An attempted formulation of the scope of behavior psychology. *Psychological Review,* 1917, *24,* 329–352.

Watson, R. I. *The great psychologists.* Philadelphia: J. B. Lippincott, 1963.

Webster's *Third new international dictionary of the English language unabridged.* Springfield, Mass.: G. & C. Merriam Co., 1961.

Wiener, P. P., and Noland, A. (Eds.) *Roots of scientific thought.* New York: Basic Books, 1957.

Winter, J. E. The postulates of psychology. *Psychological Review,* 1936, *43,* 130–148.

The Multiple Functions of Theory in a Review of Classical Terminology

Introduction: Some Important Definitions

We would now do well to define some important terms which will be taken up in greater detail in Chapters III and IV. We have already used these terms but now want to see them more clearly phrased, and in closer proximity. The construct of theory will be considered first.

A *theory* may be thought of as a series of two or more constructions (abstractions), which have been hypothesized, assumed, or even factually demonstrated to bear a certain relationship, one with the other. A theoretical proposition, which defines the relationship between constructions (now termed "variables"), becomes a fact when that proposition is no longer contested by those individuals best informed on the nature of the theory, and dedicated to study in the area of knowledge for which the theory has relevance. Theories vary in their levels of abstraction, objectivity-subjectivity, realism-idealism, perspective, and formality-informality.

This is a very liberal definition, one which basically equates theorizing with thinking. It suggests that one can never escape the influence of some kind of theory, and therefore that the role of theory — its function in knowledge — is worthy of study in its own right. Theoretical propositions have various levels of meaning, so we must consider another term:

By the *meaning* of a theoretical construct or proposition we recognize the relation(s) it bears to a host of other constructs which have been clearly proposed, vaguely analogized, or factually

42

demonstrated to bear a relationship to it. The *realistic* interpretation of meaning presumes that these relationships are ultimately to be found in nature, independent of the theorist's intellect. The *idealistic* interpretation of meaning holds that such relations are provided more or less by a reasoning intelligence, and that reality need *never* have a set ordering of relations on which to base lasting and unchanging meanings.

This definition of meaning can encompass both "true" and "untrue" constructs or propositions. Nothing in our presentation thus far states how we decide whether a theory has enough supporting evidence to be considered valid, reasonable, or scientifically true. This brings us to method:

A *method* is the means or manner of determining whether a theoretical construct or proposition is true or false. Methods follow theories, though one can work back from method to a new or modified theory. Methods are vehicles for the exercise of evidence. There are two general types: the *cognitive,* which makes use of procedural evidence, and the *research* method, which uses validating evidence in addition.

A more thorough consideration of method will be left for Chapter IV, where we will take up the question of evidence in great detail. Here we simply want to recognize that theoretical propositions are put to test in more than one fashion. If, following the test of method, an enriched meaningfulness results, we then speak of knowledge:

Knowledge is the understanding of why a given theoretical construct or proposition is true *or* false *after* that proposition has been submitted to the test of method. Knowledge permits us to extend our line of theoretical reasoning even when the findings from our methods are negative, or when our theoretical reasoning has been in error. It is also possible to lack knowledge, to fall short of true understanding even though methodological tests are positive, and our reasoning seems valid as far as it goes. Knowledge is a more abstract level of meaning, encompassing both theory and method, and it is limited in scope only by the interests and intellect of a thinking, inquisitive man. The idealist would stress man's creation of meaningful knowledge, whereas the realist would stress man's discovery of knowledge.

A Miniature Theory of Personality

As a model theory around which to organize this chapter, we propose a miniature theory of personality. Suppose we hypothesize that in autumn there is a significant positive relationship between the number of leaves falling from the trees of homeowners in a given area and independent measures of the homeowners' personality dominance. To test this theory, we would count the leaves on the ground, and objectively test (using a personality scale) or rate (using a behavior sampling) the dominance tendencies of the homeowners. If one proposed this theory to one of the tougher-minded psychologists of his acquaintance, as the writer has occasionally done, he would probably meet with an immediate rejection and a disclaimer as to the scientific merit of such preposterous notions. By substituting frustration level for dominance, we might keep the discussion going a bit longer. After all, a backyard covered with leaves might well be tied to the frustration level of the man who must do the raking, or pay to have it done. But this altered formulation would probably be dismissed as unamenable to methodological test.

How could one possibly hope to make an accurate assessment of the number of leaves falling from the trees in one yard, as opposed to those in other yards? The attack would be made from method, and the disclaimer would be couched in terms of experimental design; but, and this is essential to our point, the fundamental reason for rejecting our preposterous theory hinges upon subtle, informal *theoretical* biases. That is, methods of measurement and data collection cannot define problems, nor can they assess the plausibility of a theoretical hypothesis before it is put to test. When the leaves-personality theory is rejected because it is unamenable to empirical experimentation, that is one thing; but when it is rejected because of its implausibility or because this is not the kind of basic question scientists are supposed to be attracted to, the rejection is something completely different. The latter rejections issue from theoretical biases which underlie a cognitive "test" of the proposed theory based on procedural evidence (see Chapter IV).

Theories, therefore, underlie and buttress biases. Theories nurture evidence and influence methods as much as methods influence theories. There is a reciprocal relationship here, which finds its meeting ground in knowledge — or, more properly, theories of knowledge. If one were not constrained to meet the demands of evidence, including the evidence demanded by rationality, there would obviously be no bounds to the kind of assertions he could make. Hunches, notions, and guesses are relevant or irrelevant, worthwhile or meaningless, to the extent that they meet the demands of evidence. But in that wonderful world of free theory, which in more poetic terms is called phantasy, all is fair game. One idea is as good as another, assuming that all biasing factors are absent.

Naturally, this is a big assumption, because theoretical biases are never entirely absent. Biases are not only the stuff of conservatism and timidity in cognition, they also provide the confidence and audacity to intrude a new line of reasoning into an accepted but less pliant course of thought. Without a point of view we would all be at sea. Nevertheless, it is probably true that many bold ideas emerge when the theorist is temporarily distracted by some novelty, sleepiness, or the demands of an entirely different situation. This emergence may well be a function of the relaxation of methodological requirements and the free play of phantasy, or it may be due to the heuristic benefits derived when one sequence of events is transferred by analogy to another, as an informal theory. To catalogue all the potential ways in which theoretical hypotheses emerge would be to circumscribe man's thought.

In full awareness of the arbitrariness of the endeavor, we will now outline certain major ways in which all theories may be said to function. Others have made interesting analyses of this sort (e.g., Hall and Lindzey, 1957, Ch. I; Rotter, 1954, Ch. I), and it is easy to add to the list of potential functions a theory might serve. We have endeavored to compress the list to four: descriptive, delimiting, generative, and integrative functions. We will take them up in turn, using our "leaves-personality" theory as a focal point, but we do not mean to imply that any one function is necessarily more fundamental or important than any other.

Descriptive Function of Theory

The most obvious reason for indulging in theoretical speculation is to describe the nature of some phenomenon. To describe a behavior pattern is to give a verbal (vocal or written) account of it in terms of a set of categories selected to represent the sequence in question. These categories, which may be conventional, factual or highly speculative, and even poorly articulated, we have termed "constructs." In giving his account of behavior, the theorist brings together his constructs into a formally or informally phrased proposition or series of propositions. He thereby postulates certain relations between constructs, and also between propositions, as he reasons along, both inductively and deductively (see

Chapter V, p. 101). The sum total of such speculation (and methodological verification) he terms his "theory" or "system."

Explanation

The descriptive function of theory encompasses explanation. To explain behavior is to describe fully the conditions under which it presumably varies. To do this, the theorist must usually depart from everyday language and put forth new terms to suit his line of reasoning. Thus explanation is a matter of giving increasingly sophisticated descriptions of the empirical data at play before our eyes. Genotypic description is more explanatory than phenotypic description. As the theorist introduces terms (constructs) and formulates his own point of view, he departs ever more from the layman's description of experience. The use of an esoteric language system does not imply subjectivity, however. Modern physical constructs are highly esoteric to the common man, but they are still objective in the sense that all physicists having a common history of education in the language of physics can understand one another and check one another's constructs objectively.

To return to our example of dominance and leaves in the backyard: as an initial descriptive statement we have asserted a propositional relationship between a personality trait and falling leaves. Assuming the unlikely possibility that method would substantiate this descriptive proposition, we might then ask "Why does this occur?" Answering this question would naturally call for additional hypotheses, which might have been suggested as a result of our added experience gathering leaves in the backyard (generative function). We would then be faced with the added problem of showing how our new propositions somehow relate to our initial proposition in a consistent fashion, or possibly, of tying our thinking in to some extant theory which has more data supporting it (integrative function). But as long as we continue to give birth to hypotheses which grow up through the puberty rite of scientific method and become factual propositions, we continue our work of constructing a body of knowledge. This knowledge is tentative, always subject to change, never our master, but it *is* scientific knowledge regardless of how unintelligible it at first appears.

Reductionism and Operational Definition

The procedure of analyzing propositions and constructs into simpler propositions and constructs (i.e., lower-level constructs) has been termed "reductionism." In putting forth theoretical constructs and propositions, American academic psychology has made an effort to conform to P. W. Bridgman's (1927) principle of operational definition, a tactic in the definition of meaning which has great affinity to reductionism. Bridgman's principle was popularized in psychology by Stevens, who presented it as follows: "A term or proposition has meaning (denotes something) if, and only if, the criteria of its applicability or truth consist of concrete operations which can be performed" (1935, pp. 517–518). To date, this principle has been given a realistic interpretation, although it might well be given an idealistic interpretation and be just as helpful to the researcher. The question turns on one's interpretation of "concrete operation" and "can be performed." If the psychologist has a strong realistic theoretical preference, his interpretation might be quite literal; he feels that only those constructs which can be weighed by a scale or smeared on a microscope slide can be studied. Anything beyond this, such as a mentalistic conception of behavior, is too far removed from the known "concrete data" and therefore not worthy of scientific study.

As a result of the attempt to reduce things to the lowest common denominator in explaining their nature, reductionism has come to mean something more than simply attempting to explicate any one of several points of view. Tied to parsimony (see below, "Integrative Function"), this form of reductionism has it that all phenomena must ultimately be explained in terms of a single "physicalistic" construct language. The belief in physical reductionism rests on the assumption that one set of abstractions (psychology) must ultimately be reduced to another set (such as physiology or chemistry) to be adequately explained, because the latter abstractions are more basic. The construct "Man," it is claimed, subsumes the notions gene, hormone, and blood. Reductionists of this variety therefore cannot fully accept a completely psychological psychology.

The fallacy in this thinking is reflected when we ask: "Is it really true that physiological constructs are more basic than psychological constructs?" Sometimes they are, sometimes they are not; it depends upon how the theorist is reasoning at the moment. Recall the possibility of multiordinality in the use of constructs (see Chapter II). A "basic" theory may be both more and less abstract than some other theory, depending upon the context of study. The concepts gene, hormone, and blood can all be used highly abstractly and in a way which would subsume man's blood, rat's blood, and so on. We might theorize as follows:

"Hormone X, which all animals have in common, exerts a uniform influence on all animals. Hormone X has been shown to exert Influence Y on the respiration of rabbits. It therefore follows that Influence Y will be exerted on man's respiration following the injection of Hormone X." Obviously, in this little theory the construct "Hormone X" is more and not less abstract than the construct "Man." Just because a theorist limits himself to one small part of a man — e.g., the vascular system — does not mean that his theory need be any less abstract or less complex than that of the theorist who defines his constructs at the level of the whole man, or at the level of man in a sociocultural context. Of course, it is possible to construe man complexly, as an agglutination of many sets of abstractions from the genes, the blood, the hormones, and so on. But this does not *have* to be.

It is sometimes amusing to see how seriously investigators can take their pet theoretical orientations, and how "complex" they can make the viewpoints of other theorists. *Their* theory is forced on *our* theory. The writer was once engaged in a panel discussion with a fellow psychologist who had done considerable work with rats, and a zoologist who was doing extensive research on worms of various species. We all presented views on the nature of scientific behavior study, and at one point the writer became embroiled in heated discussion with the other psychologist over the legitimacy of doing research on the "complex animal," man, before having exhausted all possibilities with a "simple animal," the rat. There was great consolation in the fact that, when he had finished with the writer, the advocate of rat behavior study had to parry with the zoologist, who felt there is entirely too little known about the flatworm nervous system for anyone to be making meaningful leaps to the considerably more complex central nervous system of the rat.

A theorist need not feel constrained to reduce his construct language to the construct language of another discipline. We each construe data from within the interlaced meanings of a theory which has been put together to meet our *purposes* as theoreticians. Our purposes and therefore our meanings will differ. Reductionism is based on the view that there is a basic, single system of interrelations for all meanings, and that only when we come to this *one* substrate can we be said to explain fully the nature of some phenomenon (see Chapter VIII). If this is incorrect, and meanings actually exist within congeries of relatively independent spheres of knowledge, then the reductionistic thesis falls. We cannot accept the reductionistic thesis as binding on all theorists, though it is an interesting theoretical presumption and might well be pursued by theorists who are so inclined.

Delimiting Function of Theory

If theories set out to define constructs and explain phenomena, then it follows that they must operate selectively because no theory uses all the data potentially available. To delimit is to select limits or fix bounds on the scope of theoretical constructs and propositions. In Chapter II we showed how the "Pavlovian clue" — to "control your conditions and you will see order" — served a delimiting function as an informal theory in Skinner's researches and subsequent theoretical views. Our little theory about leaves and personality has set rather liberal bounds within which the work of validation will proceed, assuming we ever get around to it. We must always begin to conceptualize from some vantage point. We must decide where to set down our ruler, and which variables to delimit, and begin varying systematically. A theory which does not delimit adequately will break under the weight of its own explanatory scope; some feel that psycho-analysis suffers from this descriptive overweight. Theorists delimit not just the range of convenience of their constructs and propositions, but also the form such constructs and propositions can take. The purpose of the theory usually dictates such delimitation.

The delimiting function of theory has not been greatly elaborated in the psychological literature, although it has been mentioned in passing. This is probably due to the tendency for such discussions to deteriorate into *ad hominems*. "Why does Theorist X choose Data Y, and Theorist Z choose other forms of data to conceptualize?" This question itself stimulates theoretical speculation, and psychologists with a clinical bent often seize the opportunity to put an opponent in his place with subtle innuendo. A good example of this is suggested in the report of a conference on research in psychotherapy held in Washington, D.C., during 1958, sponsored by the Division of Clinical Psychology of the American Psychological Association, and including participants from both psychology and psychiatry. Throughout the conference, and near the close of the meetings, the editors who compiled a report of its proceedings, Rubinstein and Parloff (1959), tape-recorded and took notes on the opinions expressed by the participants. In general, the participant researchers fell into two camps: so-called experimentalists and naturalists.

In summarizing the views expressed concerning supposed motives behind the two camps, the editors note:

> The experimentalist, presumably in deference to his need for structure, attempts to introduce order in a chaotic situation by selecting certain aspects of the total situation to study, and by dismissing from his attention all other data. The naturalist, however, is made less anxious by an ambiguous situation and is content to observe the naturally occurring event in its full complexity and postpone making formulations which may eventually resolve the ambiguity (p. 282).

This sounds more like a clinical report than an exchange of views among scientists. It is obviously impossible to talk to a man if he rejects your position on the basis of your need for structure and anxiety level. This has been an easy out for clinicians in the past, and they have used it many times in place of rigorous argument and clearly made points (see Chapter XII). The irritation some laboratory psychologists feel toward their clinical colleagues often stems from experiences of this sort. At the very least, reading about such views does not reassure a rigorously-inclined psychologist that he will be given an impartial hearing when he meets with his clinical brethren to exchange scientific viewpoints. But we should not let such abuses blind us to the fact that theoretical stances do, and indeed must, delimit.

Meaning

As a relational concept, which finds its significance within a particular theoretical context, meaning is tied to the delimiting function of theory, rather than to the descriptive function. When we formulate constructions from a theoretical point of view, we impose a structure, an intention, a meaning, from the very outset. Meaning does not come in secondarily, after a construct has been formulated. Of course, precisely how one views meaning depends upon his position on the realism-idealism dimension, and we might do well to review this question accordingly. Let us begin with Hull, who tended toward the realistic end of the dimension. In the first principle of the hypothetico-deductive technique Hull makes the following suggestion: "1. A satisfactory scientific theory should begin with a set of explicitly stated postulates accompanied by specific or 'operational' definitions of the critical terms employed" (1937, p. 5).

Now, assuming that we follow this reasonable proposal, as realists we could still ask: "From what hard data do I begin deriving the terms and meanings to plug into my first explicitly stated postulates and operational definitions?" Bergmann and Spence candidly admit that in formulating theoretical constructs, "there is no methodological principle, no 'operational recipe' which guarantees that no relevant factor has been overlooked" (1941, p. 3). In other words, they acknowledge that something like what we have been calling the delimiting function of theory takes place. But they would probably not agree to our designation. For them, delimitation is only a matter of overlooking certain variables which are "there" for the finding and operational defining. It is never a matter of selecting *certain* meanings (terms) for some stated purpose, from among the myriad meanings potentially applicable.

Yet, as was so ably demonstrated by Waters and Pennington (1938), operational definitions do not derive their meaning from the act of pointing to first-order abstractions which served as the root spring for the higher-level construct now being defined. Operationism must assume some form of meaning in the construct under consideration even before the mechanical task of reducing the construct to measurables is begun: "Unless we have some knowledge of a concept other than that given by a specific and concrete set of operations we cannot tell whether the operations are adequate to the task at all" (p. 421). Operationism is merely another form of deriving the implied meanings in a proposition or construct which has been creatively expressed by a theorist. The laboratory situation is an excellent environment for drawing out such implications in a carefully controlled fashion. Therefore, as Waters and Pennington note: "Operational definitions serve their best function when they point out the laboratory conditions and methods by way of which the concept may be illustrated" (p. 422).

The question raised about the derivation of first-order constructs from hard data would of course be relatively unimportant from the idealistic position. If certain data were selected for study and conceptualization, we would look to the demands put upon the theorist in his job of trying to create knowledge to understand why he used this or that construct. If someone raises a question about our theories of psychology, their meaning and intentions, the only way to treat this is to explore the context of knowledge in which the question is raised. Since we are now prepared to say that our theories can go in any one of several directions, because it is *we* rather than the "hard data" who impose the meaning, we can entertain the possibility of alternative constructions.

If we take an idealistic stand, operationism becomes a means of clarifying communication between theoreticians. Meaning comes from the communicator, who utilizes reality, but in his own unique way. If his way becomes "too unique," then he may slip into subjectivity and make statements which have different meanings for different people. This of course is an ever-present danger. To avoid this possibility, to bring the communicating theorist down to some common denominator in the conversation, the idealistically inclined psychologist demands that he provide some standard of measurement or assessment against which to judge the generality of his constructs and propositions. The "concrete example" of operationism is this standard, and the matter of performability is understood to mean that all theorists must be capable of doing what the communicating theorist is doing in order to define, or grasp the meaning of, the construct in question.

It should not be thought, because we claim meaning is asserted or expressed rather than derived, that experience bears no relationship to the accrual and expansion of meanings. The reader should not be misled and think that we have put ourselves in the position of claiming that all meaning and knowledge has its origin in the cerebral activity of the theoretician and that it is unaffected by what goes on in his environment. It is one thing to contend that meanings are rooted in the thinking human organism which is interacting with and responding to the environment, palpable and impalpable, and quite another to contend that all meaning begins within the human organism and is then projected onto the environment. We are using the former interpretation of meaning.

Logical Positivism

Hull (1943) was one of the first psychologists to draw attention to the great similarity in outlook of behaviorism, operationism, and a philosophical school of thought propounded by a group of thinkers called the "Viennese circle." This group was led by Moritz Schlick, and included other advocates, such as Alfred J. Ayer, and the man most often cited by American psychologists, Rudolph Carnap. Their philosophical viewpoint has been termed "logical positivism." Though we need not go into a complete explication of their views, we should consider their position at least briefly because of its important influence in American psychology.

The feature of logical positivism which was quickly embraced by the behaviorist was what Ayer called the "principle of verifiability." Although this carries us somewhat into Chapter IV, where we will consider methods of verification, it is important now to cite this principle as a theoretical assertion which serves to delimit the scope of philosophical inquiry. Ayer comments on the principle of verifiability as follows:

> The criterion which we use to test the genuineness of apparent statements of fact is the criterion of verifiability. We say that a sentence is factually significant to any given person, if, and only if, he knows how to verify the proposition which it purports to express — that is, if he knows what observations would lead him, under certain conditions, to accept the proposition as being true, or reject it as being false. . . . We enquire in every case what observations would lead us to answer the question, one way or the other; and, if none can be discovered, we must conclude that the sentence under consideration does not, as far as we are concerned, express a genuine question, however strongly its grammatical appearance may suggest that it does (1946, p. 35).

This criterion was set in an attempt to resolve innumerable philosophical problems about which man had ruminated for centuries. In embracing it as a vehicle for delimitation, the logical positivists were saying that many of these problems were really pseudo-problems which could not be resolved through philosophical analysis, even though they might well be studied and considered knowledge.

Take, for example, the following discussion by Ayer on the nature of ethical argument:

> We find that ethical philosophy consists simply in saying that ethical concepts are pseudo-concepts and therefore unanalysable. The further task of describing the different feelings that the different ethical terms are used to express, and the different reactions that they customarily provoke, is a task for the psychologist. There cannot be such a thing as ethical science, if by ethical science one means the elaboration of a "true" system of morals. For we have seen that, as ethical judgments are mere expressions of feeling, there can be no way of determining the validity of any ethical system, and, indeed, no sense in asking whether any such system is true. All that one may legitimately enquire in this connection is, What are the moral habits of a given person or group of people, and what causes them to have precisely those habits and feelings? And this enquiry falls wholly within the scope of the existing social sciences. . . .
>
> It appears, then, that ethics, as a branch of knowledge, is nothing more than a department of psychology and sociology (p. 112).

Needless to say, numerous psychologists today would shudder at the thought that their goal in professional life is to categorize all these ineffable emotional expressions among people, without any hope of tying such expressions down to the palpable reality from which they presumably were drawn. And, if not drawn from reality, then they lack meaning and do not merit the time required to study them. Such psychologists have taken a delimiting principle from philosophy and applied it to their own discipline. The philosopher moves the problem over to the psychologist but is checkmated. It is interesting to note how logical positivists have taken other, rather liberal positions on the question of what constitutes adequate psychological theory and study. Carnap, for example, discusses the use of quantification in psychology much more liberally than some psychologists, whom he feels are too prone to discard concepts which are difficult to quantify (1950, pp. 7–14). Philipp Frank has observed that the members of the Viennese circle rarely have branded Freudian theory as meaningless or tautological, even though such labels have been freely applied by the positivists to the doctrines of Platonism, Thomism, or Kantianism (Hook, 1959, p. 308).

Generative Function of Theory

The generative function is probably the most widely recognized function of theory, for it is what we usually mean when we speak of theoretical speculation, inventiveness, or even creativity. To come into play, either formally or informally, a theory must stimulate or suggest constructs and relations between constructs (descriptive propositions). This is the generative function of theory: to provide the essential conceptions, notions, hunches, hypotheses, and so on, which can be used in the pursuit of knowledge. At no other point in our consideration of theory is it more obvious that theorizing is identical with "man thinking"; and to attempt a complete categorization of the ways in which man might generate ideas would be to explain completely the role of thought.

It would be difficult to specify the theoretical orientation which generated our hypothesis about leaves and personality. We have only one restricted hypothesis, with no supporting propositions or constructs, and no real directions suggested. Although we might find such directions in time, as it stands now our little theory is a clear "bust" when it comes to the generative function.

Heuristic, Analogical, and Metaphorical Devices

When a theory is used to stimulate investigation, we speak of using a theory heuristically. A theorist might begin a line of "unusual" reasoning — that is, "different" or speculative — somewhat with tongue in cheek, and just see how far it might carry him in explaining or conceptualizing some phenomenon. This heuristic exercise might be carried on by design, or it might develop during a reverie or playful phantasy. Many so-called sudden insights or creative visions are probably generated when the theorist does not consciously realize he is thinking heuristically about a point of theoretical interest. Very often, the use of something like an analogy or metaphor enters at this point. That is, the conceptualization of similarities between two constructs in analogical fashion, or the use of language syntax in such a way that figures of speech are taken literally, as in metaphor, have been two of the more common heuristic devices employed. One does not need a highly formal theory to make use of analogy or metaphor. Robert Oppenheimer placed great emphasis on the role of analogy in science when he said:

> Whether or not we talk of discovery or of invention, analogy is inevitable in human thought, because we come to new things in science with what equipment we have, which is how we have learned to think, and above all how we have learned to think about the relatedness of things. We cannot, coming into something new, deal with it except on the basis of the familiar and the old-fashioned. . . . Even analysis, even the ability to plan experiments, even the ability to sort things out and pick them apart presupposes a good deal of structure, and that structure is characteristically an analogical one. . . . At each point the first scientists have tried to make a theory like the earlier theories, light like sound, as a material wave; matter waves like light waves, like a real, physical wave; and in each case it has been found one had to widen the framework a little, and find the disanalogy which enabled one to preserve what was right about the analogy (1956, pp. 129–131).

Very likely the greatest merit of Freudian theory is its generative function. Sigmund Freud was a master at using metaphors, analogies, and other rhetorical devices to explain how man reveals his nature and wishes in dreams, slang, slips of the tongue, and humor. Freud's dream interpretation methods often included the idea that we dream in concrete terms, and thereby make "a literal picture of a figure of speech" (Freud, 1953, p. 429). Thus, Freud wrote: "If a woman dreams of falling, it almost invariably has a sexual sense; she is imagining herself as a *'fallen woman'* " (p. 202). In discussing the fact that dreams sometimes contain material in direct opposition to what they intend, Freud noted that the dreamer may unconsciously provide "the replacement of a dream-thought by an allusion, by something small, a symbolism akin to analogy . . ." (1962, p. 89).

Having introduced speculation on the possible similarity between falling in dreams and sexual promiscuity, it is now fitting for us to point out that some psychologists are disturbed over the excessive use of theory generation. The so-called applied disciplines of counseling and clinical psychology frequently come under fire, no doubt with good reason, as the earlier reference to the conference on psychotherapy suggests. Spence has phrased the situation as follows:

> "Theory" has . . . come to have a very different connotation in psychology from that which it has in physics. Theories in physics are constructions which serve primarily to integrate or organize into a single deductive system sets of empirical laws which previously were unrelated. . . . In psychology, on the other hand, theories serve primarily as a device to aid in the formulation of the empirical laws. They consist in guesses as to how the uncontrolled or unknown factors in the system under study are related to the experimentally-known variables (1948, p. 72).

Much as we sympathize with distrust of the prolific and sometimes wild theorizing which goes on among psychologists, we must take issue with Spence's characterization of physical theory. He has it serving primarily what we call an integrative function. In point of fact, theorists from all branches of the physical and mathematical sciences make it quite clear that they theorize speculatively and heuristically, and thereby hope to generate a picture of the universe which will bear up under empirical test. Conant notes: "The history of science demonstrates beyond a doubt that the really revolutionary and significant advances come not from empiricism but from new theories" (1952, p. 53). Whether one begins from a realistic or an idealistic frame of reference, the desire to "theorize" very often is this desire to speculate in free phantasy. The mathematician, Jacob Bronowski, had this to say about the physical theorizing of the realistically-oriented Sir Isaac Newton:

> The world of speculation [i.e., Newton's speculation] is suddenly seen to chime with the real world, with a triumphant note like a peal of bells. It is this accord which makes us believe in Newton's picture, and underneath it in his laws. The laws are not a deduction from experiment in any obvious sense. Their success is not that they follow from the real world, but that they predict a world which is essentially like ours. And it is this success which gives us our faith in the substratum of tiny particles each obeying the laws on which Newton's picture is built (1958, p. 36).

Models

To facilitate the generation of ideas or hypotheses, theoreticians frequently use models. A model is a patterned structure or stylized means of conceptualization which the theoretician uses to order his thinking, or to bring it into agreement with an existing line of thought. When we speak of models, therefore, we might well be referring to not only the generative, but the integrative function of theory. In Chapter II we pointed out how, initially, Watson (1913) asked that psychologists study behavior at all levels. Rat behavior was to be studied as rat behavior, and human behavior as human. But in time, the rat came to serve as a model for the conceptualization of man. This is completely natural theoretical usage. In fact, man has doubtless used himself as a model to conceptualize the behavior of a rat from the very outset. E. C. Tolman was very frank about this in his own case. He not only said there were many features of rat, monkey, and chimpanzee behavior which could throw light upon the behavior of human beings (1954, p. 536), he also candidly admitted: "But, in any case, I in my future work intend to go ahead imagining how, *if I were a rat,* I would behave as a result of such and such a demand combined with such and such an appetite and such and such a degree of differentiation; and so on" (1938, p. 24).

When the theorist begins to make assumptions about non-human organisms in terms of human characteristics like this, he is open to the charge of being anthropomorphic. Anthropomorphism is the (presumably fallacious) tendency to ascribe human characteristics to objects or animals. Primitive man frequently did this with inanimate objects, such as large rocks or the moon, which he made into gods. We are prone to do this with pets, whom we like to think of as having interests and motives comparable to our own. We see knowing expressions in our dogs, and signs of personal love in our cats. It is also possible to take the opposite approach, and assign non-human characteristics to human organisms. Some psychologists feel that the behaviorist does this when he "mechanicomorphizes" man (Allport, 1940). This approach would also be subject to charges of being one-sided and therefore incorrect.

The Proper Locus of Theory Generation: "The S-R Bind"

Granting that theory generation takes place, there is still the question, when, or at what locus in the sequence of events termed "theorizing," it might be said to occur. For example, in our leaves-personality theory, is it correct to say that some unnamed theory has generated the relationship postulated, or do we merely entertain a belief in theory generation when trying to explain "why" it is that such a relationship holds, assuming that it has been demonstrated to hold empirically? When Bergmann and Spence use the term "theory," it is obvious they would like to limit it to the latter sense. It is interesting to note that, in theorizing from an S-R frame of reference, the convention usually is to begin with the S (leaves) and the R (dominance) nailed down operationally (actually, we have here an R-R situation, see Chapter V, p. 103); theory generation or speculation is then entertained only between these two ends of the presumed "lawful" connection. Rarely do we find any discussion of how "this" rather than "that" S or R came to be chosen for examination. We are bound to do our theorizing always between a stipulated S and a stipulated R, and the pairing is not given credit as a theoretical production. This is what we shall henceforth refer to as the "S-R bind," and it is a special case of the delimiting function. Psychological theory is greatly imbued with this tactic, which probably stems historically from Woodworth's adaptation of the S-R view to an S-O-R view. The "O" is the behaving organism, and psychologists have gravitated to the view that only O-type or in-between theories are necessary. Here is how the logic proceeds:

Like every other science, psychology conceives its problem as one of establishing the interrelations within a set of variables, most characteristically between response variables on the one hand and a manifold of environmental variables on the other. . . .

The problem here is two-fold: (1) the obtaining of the empirical curves and (2) the determination of their mathematical form, i.e., the specific nature of functions $f_1, f_2 \ldots f_m$. In solving this problem, physics is able to start out with assumptions as to the specific form of the f's describing elementary situations, i.e., situations of simple structure with a very limited number of variables, for it is possible to generalize or hypothesize these functions from experimental observation. More complex situations can then be adequately handled by deduction from and combination of these basic formulae. . . .

In psychology, on the other hand, the number of variables entering into even the simplest behavior situation that can be experimentally produced is so great and the structure of their interrelationship is so complex that we are unable to make even a first guess as to the mathematical form of the equations directly from the empirical data without some auxiliary theoretical device. *The terms defined by Hull's postulates provide just such a device.* They attempt to bridge the gap between the two sets of variables, those manipulated by the experimenter and those measuring the observed responses. Technically, they aim at providing the means for ascertaining a rational fit to the empirical curve (Bergmann and Spence, 1941, pp. 9–10).

Coming back to our miniature theory, if we could remove leaves from a tree one at a time, and then graft them back in good condition, we might hope to manipulate this stimulus and measure its effect on the response, the personality measure of the homeowners. Once established, any relationship between these two variables would then have to be expressed mathematically; we would hope to plot a curve and express the precise mathematical function, "so many leaves to so much increase or decrease of personality dominance." To simplify or to help in refining all the myriad variables relating the trees and the homeowners' personalities, we would use theory — as a kind of first guess. As more data were collected and more experimentation completed, our theory would help us pin down the precise relations between our S and R. This is the essential logic of theory generation, as expressed in the above quotation.

Although he accepts this account as *one* of the ways in which theory generation takes place, the writer contends that Bergmann and Spence have greatly underrated the generative functions preliminary to the so-called empirical determination of a curve. Why did we choose leaves and not blades of grass as stimuli? Why dominance and not nurturance as a response? There is a point of time in the series of theoretical ruminations when it is correct to say that theorists generate hypotheses or use models before any experimentation has been attempted, or any curves drawn. Sir Isaac Newton's discoveries were as much dependent upon the rational, mathematical approach of René Descartes as they were upon the experimental procedures of Francis Bacon. Descartes's insight — that the key to the universe is its mathematical order — came to him as a sudden revelation, in an almost mystical way. It was certainly not based upon experimentation. Newton later took from Galileo some general notions concerning the ways in which masses behave experimentally, and then, through a form of analogy, extended these findings to all masses regardless of size. Newton concomitantly applied the mathematics of Descartes and others to working out predictions which, if substantiated, would support his view, and *then* proved his "fictitious world" through experimentation after he had essentially performed an act of theory generation (Bronowski, 1958, pp. 33–35).

By stressing the "between the S and the R" form of theory generation,

American psychology has tried to keep objectivity in the forefront of all theorizing. Although this is an admirable goal, we may have paid a high price. The more we fix attention on the S and the R, and the more confidently we define particular constructs operationally — whatever their nature — the less chance we have of being vague or subjective. But also, the less chance we have of getting outside the S-R bind of limited speculation, speculation limited by an informal theory in the first instance which *dictates that we should study only those Ss and Rs which lend themselves to explicit, operational definition.* As Guthrie said about Hull: "The maxim that whatever exists in some degree is the basic guide to Hull's system. It seeks measurability at all costs, even at the cost of restricting itself to a certain class of laboratory phenomena almost unknown outside the laboratory. In this he has followed Pavlov" (1950, p. 99).

In this, Hull has also followed Newton, for Newton accepted this maxim and sought measurability — *but not at all costs.* That is, Newton did not conceptualize or attempt to study merely anything which yielded precision and objectivity. He speculated with brilliant imagination to bring an entire universe under the bold sweep of a single hypothesis. He conceived of the world as made of small particles, particles which he never literally saw, and, what is more, *never even defined* (though we came to think of them as the atoms of Democritus and the poet Lucretius) (Bronowski, 1958, p. 34). Newton had the world in mind, the world of man, the one which faced him daily in practical affairs. He would hardly have settled for a lesser phenomenon about which to speculate even if he could thereby operationally define and measure each of the small, unnamed particles of the lesser phenomenon.

In psychology, on the other hand, after almost fifty years of laboratory research on learning theory, MacCorquodale and Meehl could say: "In terms of practical application, much (if not most) of theoretical psychology is of little value. If we exclude the interesting anecdotes of Guthrie, contemporary learning theory is not of much use to school teachers" (1948, p. 105). It would not be unjust to say that this assertion is most certainly the oddity of oddities. Had something comparable been said to Newton of his theory, he would have been amused at the accuser's naïveté, even though for his own purposes Newton did not necessarily have a practical or applied goal in view when he theorized. Why can this be said of psychology? Well, it just may be that, had we paid more attention to theory generation *before the act of defining* the Ss and the Rs we took under study, we might have asked: "What significance does this particular S-R combination have in the world outside of this laboratory, the one I live in and not the one I work in?"; rather than the other question: "How can I find something suitable to precise operational measurement, even though it may be obscure and really rather irrelevant to anything but my own particular apparatus here in the laboratory?"

Keep in mind that this is not a plea for applied psychology. Applied psychology has been termed "psychology in the service of ends other than its own" (Bingham, 1923). The applied psychologist does research to suit his employer or his client's needs, rather than his own. This is not what we are advocating. We are merely raising a question about the interests of psychologists, and wondering if they have been doing researches to suit their *own* best interests. Just because we can plot a function relating two variables does not guarantee that this function has value or meaning for anyone save the one who sketched the relationship and garnered the research publication. Meanings are nurtured within contexts of other meanings, and to expect that a research apparatus far removed from daily life will *necessarily* someday add up to worthwhile meanings within daily life is of course a highly questionable theoretical assumption.

Intervening Variables and Hypothetical Constructs

MacCorquodale and Meehl (1948) have proposed a formal distinction between what they consider to be two types of theoretical variables or constructs. The issue really is one of discriminating between constructs which are supposedly defined clearly in terms of observable, operational steps and those which cannot be reduced to observables, yet are reified from theory and taken as actually existing in the organism. Since "hypothetical" implies theory generation, it seems reasonable to take a careful look at the position of these authors. They argue:

> We suggest that the phrase "intervening variable" be restricted to the original use implied by Tolman's definition. Such a variable will then simply be a quantity obtained by a specified manipulation of the values of empirical variables; it will involve no hypothesis as to the existence of nonobserved entities or the occurrence of unobserved processes; it will contain, in its complete statement for all purposes of theory and prediction, no words which are not definable either explicitly or by reduction sentences in terms of the empirical variables; and the validity of empirical laws involving only observables will constitute

both the necessary and sufficient conditions for the validity of the laws involving these intervening variables. Legitimate instances of such "pure" intervening variables are Skinner's *reserve,* Tolman's *demand,* Hull's *habit strength,* and Lewin's *valence.* . . .

As a second linguistic convention, we propose that the term "hypothetical construct" be used to designate theoretical concepts which do *not* meet the requirements for intervening variables in the strict sense. That is to say, these constructs involve terms which are not wholly reducible to empirical terms; they refer to processes or entities that are not directly observed (although they need not be in principle unobservable); the mathematical expression of them cannot be formed simply by a suitable grouping of terms in a direct empirical equation; and the truth of the empirical laws involved is a necessary but not a sufficient condition for the truth of these conceptions. Examples of such constructs are Guthrie's M.P.S.'s, Hull's r_g's, S_d's, and *afferent neural interaction,* Allport's *biophysical traits,* Murray's *regnancies,* the notion of "anxiety" as used by Mowrer, Miller and Dollard, and others of the Yale-derived group, and most theoretical constructs in psychoanalytic theory. . . .

A concept like *libido* or *censor* or *super-ego* may be introduced initially as though it is to be an intervening variable; or even less, it is treated as a merely conventional designation for a class of observable properties or occurrences. But somewhere in the course of theoretical discussion, we find that these words are being used as hypothetical constructs instead. We find that the libido has acquired certain hydraulic properties, or, as in Freud's former view, that the "energy" of libido has been converted into "anxiety." What began as a name for an intervening variable is finally a name for a "something" which has a host of causal properties. These properties are not made explicit initially, but it is clear that the concept is to be used in an explanatory way which requires that the properties exist (pp. 103–105).

Did Freud's thinking actually go this way? Did he reason the way an S-R theorist is prone to reason? If one turns to a very early formulation of this anxiety theory, he can only conclude that Freud did *not* proceed by way of S-R bind theorizing (see Freud, 1954, pp. 91–93). To bridge the gap between mind and body, Freud first had to parallel a psychical libido (S) with a physical sexual tension (S). By itself, libido did not bring on sexual intercourse; it had to combine with a physical sexual tension. Freud's insight occurred because he could next draw a parallel between physical sexual-excitement (R) and physical anxiety-excitement (R). Having first created these parallel S-R series, he could "cross" the two, so to speak.

In the case of an anxiety neurotic, he reasoned, it was not *psychical* libido which triggered proper *physical* sexual-excitement (aroused the individual for copulation), but rather a short-circuited *physical* sexual-excitement which went directly into a *physical* anxiety-excitement. This physical-physical joining of variables did not make use of even an "intervening" libidinal construct. It was just that similar pathways of discharge were used in releasing physical tension, so that anxiety had the clinical appearance of copulation (dyspnoea, palpitation, etc.). Similar arguments could be made for the constructs of censor, or super-ego. The greatness and uniqueness of Freudian thought is that it equates this S (penis) with that dissimilar S (nose), or this R (dream) with that unlikely R (hallucination), as often as it ties this S (object cathexis) to that far-removed R (slip of the tongue). If we now drop the S-R terminology, we see that Freud was creating meanings by making his theoretical speculations across a remarkable range of disparate variables (constructs). If he had limited his speculation to S-R bind theorizing, he would have ended in a far more cautious — even timid — end result. He would not be the Freud we know today, that is for certain.

Coming back to the fundamental reason for making the "hypothetical vs. intervening" distinction, it is apparent that this was an attempt on the part of two realistically-oriented theoreticians to take a slightly more liberal position on the role of theory generation or speculation. MacCorquodale and Meehl note the "almost compulsive fear [some psychologists have] of passing beyond the direct colligation of observable data" (1948, p. 95). They argue for a slight relaxation of the realistic interpretation of meaning, pointing out that even the positivists no longer contend all meaning is exhausted through operational use of reductive sentences and terms (p. 96). Meehl's later theorizing bears out this interpretation of liberalization because it reflects a willingness on his part to speculate boldly (1962). At the same time, it is clear that MacCorquodale and Meehl do not honestly believe that anyone could seriously take an idealistic theoretical stand. They contend that their position does not rest on any "metaphysical realist thesis," but in light of this it is interesting to see the faith they place in the reductive approach, which calls for psychological constructs to be reduced to physical constructs:

> Even those of us who advocate the pursuit of behavioral knowledge
> on its own level and for its own sake must recognize that some day
> the "pyramid of the sciences" will presumably catch up with us . . .
> for those theorists who do not confine themselves to intervening varia-

bles in the strict sense, neurology will some day become relevant. For this reason it is perhaps legitimate, even now, to require of a hypothetical construct that it should not be manifestly unreal in the sense that it assumes inner events that cannot conceivably occur (1948, p. 105).

Therefore, if one believes there are physical-neurological variables awaiting a discoverer in the hard real world around us which will someday engulf psychology, but that in the interim we need variables to keep ourselves busy, then this distinction between "intervening" and "hypothetical" makes sense. If one believes, as Freud did (see Chapter VII), that physical constructs will *never* convey the nature of psychic life adequately, then a distinction of this sort makes somewhat less sense. If one takes an idealistic stand, and views *all* theorizing as essentially the same process of applying to the environment meaning drawn from hypothetical speculation according to various models, levels of abstraction, and so on, then this distinction makes no sense at all. In fact, the idealistically inclined theorist would see a type of reification in MacCorquodale and Meehl's construct of the "pyramid of the sciences." The ironic point about their distinction between terms is that it does not jibe too well with the realistic interpretation of meaning, and it cannot be well received by the tougher-minded realist. Approximately a half-dozen years before MacCorquodale and Meehl's article was published, the distinction they proposed was alluded to in other terms by Bergmann and Spence:

> All scientific terms are derived terms, derived from and retraceable to what one might call "the hard data," the "immediately observable" or what Stevens calls the "elementary operation of discrimination." Any attempt then to divide this hierarchy of constructs into sheep and goats, *i.e.*, operational constructs and theoretical constructs, is of necessity arbitrary (1941, p. 6).

Integrative Function of Theory

By "integrative function" we refer to the bringing together of theoretical constructs and propositions into a more or less consistent and unified whole. When the theorist actively works to integrate, to pull together his theory explicitly and carefully into an interdependent unity, we have termed this "formal theory." He is placing greatest emphasis on the integrative function, and might disparage the generative function because it promotes multiplicity and inconsistency (Spence, 1948, p. 72). Informal theories also serve to integrate data; sometimes, thanks to the fact that they lack clear definition and interdependency, they tie together a great deal that might not otherwise be integrated. If one contrasts a carefully constructed, formalized theory of personality, such as Eysenck's, for example, with the broad sweep of Jung's personality theory, it is immediately obvious that the former loses a lot in explanatory potential, even though it is more "rigorously" defined and explicitly stated (Hall and Lindzey, 1957). Our little theory of leaves and personality is extremely inadequate when we try to integrate it with existing personality theories, or any series of internally consistent propositions. As with the generative function, we are in dire trouble even if we do happen to find an empirical relationship.

Theoretical Systematization, Parsimony, and Generalization

In the 1930's, it was quite fashionable for American academic psychologists to put together so-called systems or points of view intended as exhaustive explications of their data. In other words, theorists such as Hull were hoping to write theories of behavior which might be applied across the board, rather than attempting to write more limited hypotheses for specific kinds of problems. Psycho-analysts, and most personality theorists, are also prone to write sweeping theories, but since they do not formalize their constructs quite as much, we rarely refer to them as system builders. The implication of being systematic is that the theorist hopes to structure a formal, interdependent point of view. Since World War II, the trend in America has been away from the high-flown systematic approach, and toward miniature theories constructed around a limited series of hypotheses.

Naturally, the more theories one has to explain a phenomenon, the more likely it is that conflict and confusion will result over which view is "correct." Historically, in addition to experimental evidence, we have resorted to the "principle of parsimony" to settle such questions. Parsimony, or the effort by theorists to introduce only as many constructs and propositions as are necessary to explain their object of study, is really one type of theoretical integration. Parsimony dictates that if a simple explanation will suffice, it detracts from our knowledge to seek a more complex one. This principle has antecedents dating back to the fourteenth century, when William of Ockham introduced a rule-of-thumb to help resolve or remove such speculative arguments (see Chapter IX). Termed "Ockham's Razor," this rule stated: "it is vain to do with more what can be done with less"; or, more popularly: "entities should not be multiplied beyond necessity" (Russell, 1959, p. 162). As we have seen, physical reductionism rests on the belief that psychological constructs will someday compete with physical constructs in the explanation of behavior. When this happens we will no longer need to multiply language systems; psychology will have to give ground if not give way entirely.

Those who advocate miniature models hope that these more restricted systems "might" be integrated into higher-order, more generalizable, and simplified theoretical systems at some time in the future. Yet, what seems to be happening is that as these miniature systems are implemented they become more and more complex, and there is less hope of ever integrating the myriad approaches. We fail to realize that for any given group of facts needing explanation, there are *in principle* an *infinite* number of theoretical descriptions which might be put forth. Each of these may be phrased as explicitly and parsimoniously as possible; yet, this in itself will not guarantee a shortening of the growing list of theories proffered, nor a lessening of the difficulty of their comprehension for the man who must try to grasp them all. If the picture is to clear up, it must happen at the root source; i.e., the theorist himself will have to attempt other models and make active, integrative use of theory. Some feel that we are not ready for such integration, that we are in a so-called pre-scientific period in psychology, and that we need more data and less all-encompassing theory. It seems to the writer more accurate to say that we are in the early phases of our scientific age in psychology, but that we need more all-encompassing Newtonian-like hypotheses — extended to the world at large — and fewer of the type which are limited to some particular laboratory apparatus.

Instructiveness of Theory

To instruct is to impart knowledge, and the integrative function of theory aims at tying together such knowledge into a unified whole of greater interdependence. One of the perennial sources of argument in psychology stems from a difference in opinion about how psychological knowledge is to be integrated, and with what other bodies of knowledge this integration is to take place. In studying and commenting on their own nature over the centuries, men have projected images or models of man not only from their sciences, but also from their religions, myths, philosophies, dramas, and literature. How does one integrate *these* myriad views? Should the psychologist limit his theorizing to a scientifically acceptable machine model, or should he attempt to refine and apply some of the more humanly contrived models of man reflected in the arts? As Guthrie accurately observed (1950), it was Freud's intent to instruct in a way consistent with all human productions, including both mechanical physical science *and* the arts — through which he saw man's nature revealing itself.

From the viewpoint of the whole of cultural knowledge, the mechanical model is *not* the most parsimonious vehicle for the conceptualization of man. It is clean of design and readily adaptable to the needs of science. It has little surplus meaning. But, it violates that aspect of the principle of parsimony which states that we must have a model adequate to the characterization of our data — no more, but *no less*. Other cultural manifestations of knowledge would imply that the machine model has left out a great deal in representing man. Little wonder, then, that Freudian psychology is embraced by the dramatist and scorned by the single-minded scientist. This is what we might expect, since this is really the way in which Freud set out to instruct. We must also recognize that with the advent of science fiction and the great stress being placed on science today, *science too* is being incorporated into the arts. Who knows? In time our civilization and its culture may come to accept the machine model as "the" essential characteristic of human nature and then — at that happy time — we will finally have something like the "pyramid of the sciences and the arts" coming together in a more consistent union.

Monism vs. Dualism

Monism is the doctrine which asserts there is only one form of substance to contend with in making theoretical descriptions; for example, there is only physical matter in the universe. Dualism is the doctrine which asserts there are two substances providing referents for theoretical constructions in the universe; for example, there is the mental as well as the physical to contend with. It is tempting to equate realism with monism (there is only matter) and idealism with dualism (there is mind influencing matter), but things are not that simple. Freud was a dualist with realistic inclinations which led him to reify his constructs. The idealist might easily dismiss this distinction as he dismssed the distinction between hypothetical constructs and intervening variables, by merely pointing out that such issues are not relevant if one views all constructs as convenient labels applied to an area of study for some purpose. As long as theory construction is profitable, and evidence is presented to support the view being espoused, why should we argue over which construct is palpable and which impalpable? Let us take a stand and see where it leads us.

Monism is best viewed as an attempt to integrate and to simplify theoretical speculation. Since we have never been able to explain precisely how the mind interacts with the body, and since, therefore, the construct "mind" fails to add much to our treatment of behavioral data, why not simply drop it and speak of only one substance? This was Watson's integrative conclusion: "One can assume either the presence or the absence of consciousness [mind] anywhere in the phylogenetic scale without affecting the problems of behavior by one jot or one tittle; and without influencing in any way the mode of experimental attack upon them" (1913, p. 161). From an extraspective perspective this is a reasonable statement.

Even so, it is debatable whether psychology has ever really solved the mind-body problem. Through the assertion of monism we have repressed the term "mind"; we have skillfully avoided acting as if mind "exists." But have we solved the fundamental problem, or have we merely shifted the locus from one sphere to another? We talk about awareness, insightful learning, determinism, lawfulness, and so on, and these all have historical antecedents in the mind-body problem. Our discussions about the philosophy of science and the nature of theory also crisscross the older formulations of mind-body arguments. This volume is really on the mind and on thought, and Chapter IV in particular makes a distinction between types of evidence which is probably a contemporary rephrasing of this old mind-body theoretical issue manifesting itself in a new sphere of discourse.

Eclecticism

When an individual selects various constructs from different theoretical orientations in the hope of making sense out of some group of facts or series of phenomena, we speak of this as an eclectic theoretical orientation. Most practicing clinical psychologists find it essential to combine and patch together constructs from many personality theories in order to understand their clients. The danger here, of course, is inconsistency, and the fact that in patching together various orientations the psychologist may do violence to the construct in question. Eclecticism has gotten a bad name in psychology, primarily because of the inadequate form of integration which often results. This is comparable to the difficulty we have already considered in discussing the proliferation of miniature theories. But it is equally important to grasp the fact that all theorists are in one sense eclectic. As Rotter phrased it: "All systematic thinking involves the synthesis of pre-existing points of view. It is not a question of whether or not to be eclectic but of whether or not to be consistent and systematic" (1954, p. 14).

Growth Potential and Basic Postulate Evaluation

By "growth potential," we refer to the potential of any theoretical line of reasoning to expand, to incorporate new research findings or speculative hunches. As we have seen, theories must generate research hypotheses, but they must also be capable of integrating these findings with some fundamental picture which they imply as a meaningful assertion from the outset. The truly exciting and eventful theories of history have had considerable growth potential because they provided us with entirely new ways of looking at familiar events and things (that is, new meaning). They literally swallow up the older theories. The speculations of Newton, Darwin, and Freud had fantastic implications. One did not have to have many experimental verifications before seeing the tremendous vitality and potential scope of these conceptualizations. To grow is to integrate, to replace, to tie together, and to instruct man in a way of thinking about himself and his environment.

Finally, an adequate theory usually is said to have a self-corrective aspect. For example, Rotter suggests that theory helps us examine our basic assumptions (1954, p. 8). This is undoubtedly an important function of theory, and it is an integrative function, since to examine assumptions one must bring them in line with some extant, well-accepted, or proven point of view. This also means that for proper evaluation, a theory must be related to some general philosophical position, or theory of knowledge. The theorist must be sophisticated and capable of stating precisely where he stands in the trend of thought. He must be conscious of the biases of his position. He must know his strengths *and* his weaknesses.

Summary

Chapter III has been concerned with the functions which a theoretical position can be said to serve. We have proffered a definition of theory, distinguishing it from method, but subsuming both theory and method under the more abstract concept of a "theory of knowledge." Theory is to be thought of as a series of two or more constructions which have been hypothesized, presumed, or even factually demonstrated to bear a certain relationship, one with the other. A theoretical proposition specifies this relationship, and it becomes fact when supported by evidence and therefore is no longer contested by those individuals best informed on the nature of the theory in question. Method, on the other hand, is the means or manner of determining whether theoretical propositions are true or false. Knowledge is the understanding of why a given theoretical proposition is true or false after it has been submitted to the test of method. Meanings are created relationally, by extending theoretical constructs to ever-new ties with other constructs, now embodied in ever-changing unities of knowledge.

There are four essential functions which any theory may be said to serve. Each was examined in turn, and examples of the functions were considered in the proper context.

The first function of theory is its descriptive use. Explanation of phenomena involves a full and complete description of the conditions under which they presumably vary. In describing a phenomenon, the theorist must delimit or fix bounds on the scope of his constructs and propositions. The delimiting function of theory is tied closely to the meaning a theorist hopes to express, for in putting together a "point of view" he imposes a new structure which reorganizes experience and thereby draws new meanings from familiar data. The third function is the generative, which refers to the fact that theoretical points of view must be fruitful, stimulating, and capable of providing a steady stream of new hypotheses. Theories which run dry are like empty water holes, they have made an impression on the intellectual terrain but they are soon abandoned. Finally, theory has an integrative function, which refers to the bringing together of theoretical constructs and propositions into a more or less consistent and unified whole. We usually attempt not only to integrate within our own theoretical point of view, but also to bring together disparate points of view into a consistent picture. One goal of knowledge is to simplify the number of assumptions and assertions which must be made in order to explain phenomena. There is some question as to whether the models of physical science are appropriate for an integration with the models of, say, the arts, in conceptualizing man.

References

Allport, G. W. The psychologist's frame of reference. *Psychological Bulletin,* 1940, *37,* 1–28.

Ayer, A. J. *Language, truth and logic.* New York: Dover Publications, 1946.

Bergmann, G., and Spence, K. Operationism and theory in psychology. *Psychological Review,* 1941, *48,* 1–14.

Bingham, W. V. On the possibility of an applied psychology. *Psychological Review,* 1923, *30,* 289–305.

Bridgman, P. W. *The logic of modern physics.* New York: Macmillan, 1927.

Bronowski, J. *The common sense of science.* Cambridge, Mass.: Harvard University Press, 1958.

Carnap, R. *Logical foundations of probability.* Chicago: University of Chicago Press, 1950.

Conant, J. B. *Modern science and modern man.* Garden City, N.Y.: Doubleday Anchor, 1952. (Originally published, New York: Columbia University Press, 1949.)

Freud, S. *The interpretation of dreams* (Parts I and II). Vols. IV and V of J. Strachey (Ed.), *The standard edition of the complete psychological works of Sigmund Freud.* London: The Hogarth Press, 1953.

Freud, S. *The origins of psycho-analysis, letters to Wilhelm Fliess, drafts and notes: 1887–1902.* New York: Basic Books, 1954.

Freud, S. *Jokes and their relation to the unconscious* (1905). Vol. VIII of J. Strachey (Ed.), *The standard edition of the complete psychological works of Sigmund Freud.* London: The Hogarth Press, 1962.

Guthrie, E. R. The status of systematic psychology. *American Psychologist,* 1950, *5,* 97–101.

Hall, C. S., and Lindzey, G. *Theories of personality.* New York: Wiley, 1957.

Hook, S. (Ed.) *Psychoanalysis, scientific method, and philosophy.* New York: New York University Press, 1959.

Hull, C. L. Mind, mechanism, and adaptive behavior. *Psychological Review,* 1937, *44,* 1–32. Courtesy, American Psychological Association.

Hull, C. L. The problem of intervening variables in molar behavior theory. *Psychological Review,* 1943, *50,* 273–291.

MacCorquodale, K., and Meehl, P. E. On a distinction between hypothetical constructs and intervening variables. *Psychological Review,* 1948, *55,* 95–107.

Meehl, P. E. Schizotaxia, schizotypy, schizophrenia. *American Psychologist,* 1962, *17,* 827–838.

Oppenheimer, R. Analogy in science. *American Psychologist,* 1956, *11,* 127–135.

Rotter, J. B. *Social learning and clinical psychology.* Englewood Cliffs, N.J.: Prentice-Hall, 1954.

Rubinstein, E. A., and Parloff, M. B. (Eds.) *Research in psychotherapy.* Vol. I. Washington, D.C.: American Psychological Association, 1959.

Russell, B. *Wisdom of the west.* Garden City, N.Y.: Doubleday & Co., 1959.

Spence, K. W. The postulates and methods of "behaviorism." *Psychological Review,* 1948, *55,* 67–78.

Stevens, S. S. The operational definition of psychological concepts. *Psychological Review,* 1935, *42,* 517–527.

Tolman, E. C. The determiners of behavior at a choice point. *Psychological Review,* 1938, *45,* 1–41.

Tolman, E. C. Freedom and the cognitive need. *American Psychologist,* 1954, *9,* 536–538.

Waters, R. H., and Pennington, L. A. Operationism in psychology. *Psychological Review,* 1938, *45,* 414–423.

Watson, J. B. Psychology as the behaviorist views it. *Psychological Review,* 1913, *20,* 158–177.

IV

Methods of Evidence in Arriving at Knowledge

Introduction

Theorizing is a sequential act or process of reasoning, carried on by an individual, in which the functions of description, delimitation, generation, and integration serve as intellective counterpoints to the evolving theme or point of view. Before the resultant composition is applauded, however, like any creative work, it must be judged against some standard. Those who undertake to examine a theoretical point of view usually are — or should be — the theorist's peers who consider themselves best qualified by training and/or experience to judge its merit. They are the people best informed on the topic at hand, and the ones to whom the theorist must ultimately look for support and admiration, as well as stimulation and controversy. In this way, bodies of knowledge are developed through the collective influence of groups of people.

How do groups of people judge whether a theoretical proposition is true or false? This is, of course, a far-reaching question. Many diverse factors enter into the evolution of a body of knowledge as held by different groups of people. Sometimes the line between proven and unproven knowledge is not clearly drawn. In this chapter we will take up in greater detail two types of methods — the cognitive and the research — with particular emphasis on the form of evidence they engender. Note that we view method as an active process, a means of effecting changes in belief. One *does something* in order to show that he grasps a fact pattern; he wages an argument, he points to certain plausibilities, or he makes a prediction. Because methods do effect a change in the order of things, we sometimes use the term in a practical sense — as in referring to a method of cure, a method of engineering, or a method of debate. Indeed, this is why a distinction can be made between basic and applied science — because methods *do* have effects on the order of things. But the fundamental issue of interest at this point is, what types of evidence do our methods promote, procedural or validating? And how does this distinction help us understand the nature of knowledge?

Two Types of Evidence

Method is intimately related to evidence, and it is with evidence that we must begin our consideration of the ways in which groups of individuals decide upon the truth or falsity of any theory. When we use terms like "true" or "false," we do not ascribe any ultimate, fixed, and unchanging meaning to theoretical propositions. These terms merely signify the extent of conviction we have about verbal statements such as "If X, then Y" (i.e., theoretical propositions), based upon the evidence for or against them. Evidence refers to the *grounds for belief* or judgment which people use in settling on a position. On the basis of evidence we make decisions, state principles of general applicability, and occasionally predict the outcome of some course of events. On the basis of evidence each of us directs his own behavior. The positivistic scientist refuses to accept a "final word," preferring to deal in probabilities nurtured on past empirical evidence. The hysteric patient refuses to accept the findings of the electrocardiograph and insists that his heart is stopping. The two situations seem far removed, yet we can say that both the scientist and the hysteric are directing their behavior on the basis of the same kind of evidence. To clarify this assertion, we must first agree upon a fundamental dichotomy in the nature of evidence. The writer contends that there are two basic kinds of evidence: procedural evidence and validating evidence.

Procedural Evidence

This first type has a long history in man's thought, probably since his very beginnings. It rests upon an act of cognition, and we therefore say that this evidence emerges from the *cognitive* method. Thus, to begin a line of reasoning one must make certain assumptions, accept certain plausibilities, and accede to the weight of certain self-evidences. Philosophical argument, the weight of logic, and even the immediate personal significance of a psychological insight proffered by one's psychotherapist, all carry great impact and stimulate a sense of conviction if we take them as proofs. When we believe a theoretical proposition in this way because of its intelligibility, its consistency with common-sense knowledge, or its implicit self-evidence, we are using as grounds for this belief *procedural evidence*. The psychologist's concept of what constitutes adequate scientific methodology, and many of his other universally accepted and firmly held positions, ultimately rest not upon experimental (validated) evidence but upon procedural evidence, as incorporated in the common sense of the psychological community.

By common sense we mean the agreed-upon or accepted knowledge of a group, knowledge which is reflected in its culture and is no longer a source of contention among its members. Common sense need not refer only to the "sense of the common man." Different groups of individuals have different common knowledge, and this knowledge can change through innovation so that common sense changes over time. The theoretical propositions or "facts" accepted and used by a community of psycho-analysts might confuse and embarrass the average layman if they were reported to him in a straightforward, unvarnished fashion. This is because he has not participated in the culture of psycho-analysis and come to accept the significance of its terminology, which embodies its common sense and determines what appears self-evident to its members.

Procedural evidence and common sense are sociocultural constructs. Since there are many societies of men which hold certain patterns of behavior more or less constant (such as the scientific community or the legal community), and continually add to a body of knowledge as a result of this common experience, it stands to reason that we cannot speak about *one* form of common sense. There is, to be sure, culture contact and dissemination of knowledge. The same man can walk within several cultures or subcultures. The clinician who is also a scientist has chosen this lot in professional life, and it is at times difficult for him to integrate the mores of these two subcultures (see Chapter XII). In a larger sense, every man moves within several subcultures because he affiliates with groups such as family, church, and political organizations in addition to more restricted professional or work groups. Each of these several bodies of common knowledge doubtless influences one's grasp of the plausible, the self-evident, or the true. A man's religious or economic convictions may weaken the efficacy of logic or other uses of intellect as sources of procedural evidence for him. Some men distrust intellect in and of itself (Hofstadter, 1963).

Procedural evidence is often nurtured by unnamed theory, and for this reason we noted in Chapter II how informal theory (one kind of unnamed theory) is likely to be confused with procedural evidence. In order to distinguish between informal or unnamed theory and procedural evidence, we re-emphasize the distinction between theory and method. Theory embodies propositions which assert relationships between constructs. Method is a vehicle for the exercise of evidence. Informal theory might therefore be operating in an unnamed fashion, and if accepted among, let us say, a community of scientists, it would be encompassed as knowledge within this subculture. The use of procedural evidence as a *method* for testing the plausibility of *newly generated* hypotheses, on the other hand, would occur when this community of scientists, or, more properly, one of its members, assessed the new hypothesis in terms of the already accepted body of knowledge. In this case, the body of accepted theory serves as a standard of comparison, but the *method* of assessing *this* newly generated proposition against *those* well-accepted propositions (that is, the cognitive method) is something else again. If the already accepted propositions were used merely to further a theoretical line of reasoning, and not as a standard for establishing *proof,* we might refer to this as an act of theoretical integration in the process of carrying out a speculative cognition. But when a decision must be made concerning the truth or falsity, plausibility or implausibility of a theoretical proposition, we are no longer dealing with theory, we are dealing with method. This method bases its decision — true or false, plausible or implausible — on the consistency with which the entire body of knowledge — the "common sense" — hangs together.

Probably the most widely known example in psychology of the interlacing of procedural evidence with informal theory occurs in Boring's use of *Zeitgeist,* a term introduced by Johann Gottfried von Herder and other eighteenth-century sociopolitical thinkers (Becker and Barnes, 1952, p. 487). On the opening page of *A History of Experimental Psychology* (1950), Boring says:

> The progress of science is the work of creative minds. Every creative mind that contributes to scientific advance works, however, within two limitations. It is limited, first, by ignorance, for one discovery waits upon that other which opens the way to it. Discovery and its acceptance are, however, limited also by the habits of thought that pertain to the culture of any region and period, that is to say, by the *Zeitgeist:* an idea too strange or preposterous to be thought in one period of western civilization may be readily accepted as true only a century or two later. Slow change is the rule — at least for the basic ideas. On

the other hand, the more superficial fashions as to what is important, what is worth doing and talking about, change much more rapidly, depending partly on discovery and partly on the social interaction of the wise men most concerned with the particular matter in hand — the cross-stimulation of leaders and their followers, of protagonists and their antagonists (p. 3).

In emphasizing that habits of thought and the discovery of new facts interact to make up the slowly changing common sense of a scientific community, Boring has provided us with a natural transition to the second major type of evidence now at work in the process of expanding knowledge.

Validating Evidence

When we believe a theoretical proposition on the basis of observable consequences that follow a prescribed succession of events designed to test that proposition, we do so on the basis of validating evidence. This form of evidence is a comparatively late arrival in the history of thought, dating from approximately 1600, when Galileo triggered the Scientific Revolution. As Bronowski has observed: "The outlook before the Scientific Revolution was content with scholastic logic applied to a nature of hierarchies. The Scientific Revolution ended that: it linked the rational and the empirical, thought and fact, theory and practical experiment. And this has remained the content of science ever since" (1958, p. 31). The method of creating an effect, a change in the order of our knowledge through validation, we have called *research*. Validating evidence relies upon research methods, and obtaining it is the goal of all those disciplines which today employ the scientific method (Chapter V). It serves as a check on the more fundamental procedural evidence, which theorists have come to mistrust and to challenge in the Age of Science.

Note that we stress a *prescribed* succession of events. We must design an experiment to test the theoretical proposition *before* we actually submit it to test. In this way we make quite clear what outcome will affirm, and what outcome will negate the proposition under test. We agree on a set of ground rules and then play the game, to win or to lose. Further, by demanding the construction of a procedure permitting *observable* consequences we tend to shift the theoretical emphasis to the extraspective end of the continuum. Our constructs need not be *only* extraspective, but it is certainly true to say that validating evidence is conducive to extraspection and vice versa. One could easily settle for extraspective constructs and let it go at that. When we study to validate, we study an object which has been nicely packaged within our experimental design "over there." What this object may think about the validity or accuracy of our design — assuming that the object of our study can think — is not considered. Even if the object of study can think, we certainly do not permit its ideas or attitudes to influence the prescribed sequence of events in any way other than that which is called for in the research at hand. We study an object in a certain way, and its influence on the method of study is, or should be, non-existent. (Such influences would, of course, result in unreliable data.) We then act in relation to the theoretical proposition according to the observed consequences of the succession of prescribed events, that is, according to the experimental findings. We may accept the import of the proposition as being true (as having validity), reject it as being false, or modify it in some way.

Theoretical propositions which have been thus validated are incorporated into the common sense of the scientific community at some point in time. This slightly revises the corpus of knowledge on which *procedural* evidence is based. That is to say, yesterday's validated propositions become today's bias in the use of procedural evidence. To discredit the older proposition in the scientific community, newly validated evidence must be presented, which then — in time — has an effect on the corpus of knowledge. Knowledge is constantly changing and extending its scope; we like to think of it as growing or advancing. Precisely when a validated proposition is incorporated into a body of knowledge, into a group's common sense, depends upon many things, such as the amount of attention research findings receive (the vogue among the scientific community), or the status of the individual scientist who reports the research findings. Probably the most important prerequisite for the incorporation of a validated proposition is its credibility, i.e., the strain it places upon the already accepted tenets of the scientific community. The less strain, the more credible a proposition is and the more readily is it incorporated.

The same applies, of course, for new items of knowledge accepted on the basis of procedural evidence. Let us take as an example the principle of operationism. To propose that we define things operationally is very reasonable on the face of it; this prescription for an appropriate relationship between the theorist and his construct places very little strain on other practical rules of thumb which we incorporate in our professional common sense, such as: "Put up or shut up"; or "Make sure you know what you are talking about." Freud's theoretical propositions placed considerably more strain on the common-sense notions of both the general public and the scientific community. As a result, whether he was *in fact* right or wrong — even as judged by validating evidence — he found it extremely difficult to get general acceptance for his terminology and point of view by procedural evidence. The process of cultural assimilation was considerably slower in this case. Although accepted in part now by almost everyone, there are still fundamental aspects of his view (e.g., the unconscious mind) which certain groups fail to incorporate in their common-sense knowledge.

The Interdependence of Evidence

Having made a bifurcation in evidence, it is tempting to rank order the two kinds of evidence as to importance or merit. Is not procedural evidence basic to validating evidence, and therefore the "real" source of all knowledge? Validating evidence was ushered in with the advent of science. Considering the great achievements of science, does this not clearly establish the superiority of validated proofs? There seems little to gain from such arguments, and it was not our intention to foster a status hierarchy in making the distinction. It was made arbitrarily, as a heuristic device to facilitate conceptualization and discussion. We must come to recognize the reasons for employing each kind of evidence, their merits and weaknesses, and thus fully appreciate the contribution of each in the evolution of knowledge. It is also possible to misidentify idealism with procedural evidence, since both call for the use of creative intellect, and realism with validating evidence, since both stress the importance of empirical observation. This would be an error, of course. George Kelly's observer (Chapter II) may see consistency through his templets as he looks out onto the world; he may report the same observations we report seeing through our templets, and he may validate propositions like any of us. But this does not mean he must therefore assume that "the other side" of his templet exists any more fundamentally or tangibly than "this side."

One of the first points to appreciate in the use of evidence is that objectivity is based upon procedural evidence, or presumes that it is in operation. If we follow Skinner's suggestion to begin our study with a "common sense exploration of the field" (1950, p. 215), we would begin with procedural evidence and return to it as often as dictated by our identification as psychologists or toughminded psychologists or "students of the mind." Professional conflicts — as between the applied and the basic scientists — result because we begin from different identification groups, and evolve different bodies of knowledge. There is much overlap between groups, but also much disparity. No matter what group of men we choose to examine, including the so-called common men, the process of theoretical reasoning or discourse is the same. It always begins with, and then returns to, a reliance upon procedural evidence. Clark Hull recognized this when he wrote: "At first sight the formal characteristics of scientific theory look very much like those of philosophical speculation and even of ordinary argumentation, from which philosophical speculation can scarcely be distinguished" (1937, p. 5). But Hull goes on to say that there *is* a difference between the philosopher and the scientist in their use of theory: "The difference is that *in philosophical speculation there is no possibility of comparing a theorem with the results of direct observation*" (p. 6).

By asking for direct observation, Hull does not mean the kind of observation any of us might achieve in our everyday routines. Philosophers frequently begin their arguments with descriptions of everyday, easily observed activities. For example, the philosopher might begin an argument for or against determinism in human behavior with the description of a man reaching for a glass of beer (Black, 1958, p. 15). As he goes along, making his case, there may be several opportunities to compare his argument with direct observations of an informal variety. This is the way a philosopher makes his case, by bringing his knowledge to bear on the self-evident aspects of our everyday life. This gives us a sense of conviction for which there is no substitute. What Hull really wants the philosopher to do is to move from the cognitive to the research method, to design an experimental test drawing on the implications of the theory in question, and in this way test it empirically. Hull's extraspective attitude goes something like this: "You can sit around and argue about things all you want to, but unless this speculative argument leads over into some kind of observable test, all the skillful rhetoric in the world isn't going to settle the issue for me."

Why does the philosopher not take Hull's admonition to heart? Why does he not settle his questions through experimentation? There are several good reasons why he does not. One of them was presented to Hull in 1937 by Donald K. Adams:

> Consider the logic of this. Major premise: If this theory is correct, under conditions *A* event *a* must occur. Now if the deduction is what Hull calls "verified" [in our terms, validated], we have for the minor premise: Under conditions *A* event *a* occurs. We have "affirmed the

consequent" of an hypothesis, which proves nothing whatever, though many others beside Hull write as if it confirmed the theory (1937, p. 215).

Affirming the consequent is a form of logical error that occurs when we uncritically accept the affirmed or confirmed results of an "If, then" sequence in reasoning. It is a clear demonstration that validating evidence is never as convincing as procedural evidence. For example, we might want to test a little theory such as this: "Disobedience to law and order is at the root of mental illness." We deduce from this that areas of a city which have the highest crime rates, indicating the greatest disobedience to law and order, will also have the highest incidence of mental illness. Or: *If* high crime (the antecedent), *then* high mental illness (the consequent), in a given city area. Our research data may serve to affirm the consequent, which has indeed been generated by our theory. But what will we have proven with certainty? Not our little theory, for there could be any one of a number of reasons explaining the high incidence of mental illness in this particular city area. This is why philosophers are wont to point out that for any given fact pattern which can be demonstrated or "discovered" empirically, an infinite number of theoretical explanations are possible. This is also why we say theories remain theories, even after they have been validated. All validating evidence can establish convincingly is the *negation* of a theoretical proposition. Having postulated an *If A, then B* sequence, when our researches *fail* to confirm this sequence, we can logically reject the theoretical relation originally postulated.

Now this situation bothers philosophers. They would like to fill a role in the area of knowledge which would give them a chance to reduce statements to the more convincing procedural evidence. That is, they would like to make statements of a more lasting, more absolute nature than scientific statements, which must rest upon the most flexible and changing of grounds for belief imaginable, i.e., the latest data collected. At any point in time, science is prepared to shift positions as new data are forthcoming.

There are other reasons why the philosopher cannot settle questions he deems important through the use of validating evidence. One of his self-proclaimed functions is to attempt to bring scientifically validated data *themselves* back into the corpus of knowledge we call philosophy. In the terms of Chapter III, he hopes to integrate theories and round out knowledge. Empirical data are sometimes accumulated so rapidly that they literally outrun the common sense of any group, including the scientists who amass them. As Philipp Frank has expressed it: "Science starts from common sense, and from generalization by induction or imagination one derives science; but the derived principles themselves may be very far from common sense. To connect these principles directly with common sense — this is the work done by philosophers" (1957, pp. 46–47). A datum accrued is not always knowledge gained, because sometimes genuine understanding is lacking. One can have a great deal of information and still suffer for lack of knowledge. Findings occur which defy explanation in terms of older philosophical preconceptions in the history of thought. Philosophers see it as their role to help tie these rapidly accruing data back into the "self-evident" beliefs growing out of everyday, observable acts, such as reaching for a glass of beer. Only in this way can the knowledge man possesses carry a sense of real conviction. We badly need people who can do this and we must recognize that philosophy, which attempts to do this, is an integral aspect of all science.

We have already noted that validating evidence encourages the theorist to take an extraspective perspective. It is equally true that procedural evidence has a greater affinity to the introspective than the extraspective theoretical perspective, and it is from this affinity that the historical conflict between introspective and extraspective psychologists stems. The drawback to procedural evidence, and the reason validation is needed, is that sometimes a very plausible theory which rests on self-evident assumptions leads us astray. Speculative philosophy received a bad name in psychology because some of the analyses done were based upon rather plausible, self-evident conceptions. Boring summed it up for psychology when he observed: "The trouble seems to be that what is introspectively obvious is not necessarily true" (1936, p. 522).

Self-evidence and common sense are concepts many extraspective psychologists have felt they successfully dispensed with years ago. The complete rejection of introspectionism carried with it a dismissal of all such "armchair" criteria. In their desire to be scientific, they patterned themselves after what they took to be the extraspective sciences, physics and biology, emphasizing the role of validating evidence in the context of laboratory experimentation. Scientific activity in psychology has come to mean *nothing but* the use of validating evidence. And the fact that procedural evidence also influences behavior has been set aside as an area of study and consideration in psychology, as if it were an unrealistic, or at least an unscientific problem.

Physicists, on the other hand, have learned over time that their biases must be considered in evaluating their theories, their experimental methods, their objects of study, and their empirical findings. And biases hinge upon procedural evidence. One of the most significant and dramatic events in the post-World War II years was Oppenheimer's (1956) sophisticated exhortation to psychologists to consider their biases, to ask themselves how fruitful it is to use a machine as a model for man, to question their too-eager identification with physics, and essentially to strike off on their own and trust their common-sense knowledge of people. The physical scientists have come to appreciate the importance of procedural evidence — very likely the result, in part, of significant advances made when a bold thinker such as Einstein took a different tack, viewed the universe from a theoretical position outside and ahead of the common sense of the traditional scientific community, and made significant predictions which are even today being validated for the first time.

At the very least Oppenheimer wanted psychologists to familiarize themselves with some of the more recent tenets or beliefs embodied in the common-sense knowledge of the physical science community. He wanted thus to protect psychology from identifying with the physics of yesterday. If psychologists cannot evolve their own science without analogizing to physics at every turn, then "the worst of all possible misunderstandings would be that psychology be influenced to model itself after a physics which is not there any more, which has been quite outdated" (p. 134). For those clinically-oriented psychologists who doubt they can be completely scientific and at the same time conceptualize man in a meaningful way, Oppenheimer had some comforting words. He was willing to accept psychologists as scientists if they think of people as people rather than as electrical machines, refuse to accept the world as completely determined, are unable to define every construct operationally, recognize the importance of individual bias in observation, admit being unable to predict every event (even in theory), and speak about organic wholes (p. 134). In fact, he points out that these are some of the most generally accepted tenets of modern physical science. If a physical scientist of this sort were teaching the science and laboratory courses psychology students attend, there might be less conflict for the student when he leaves the academic circle and enters the clinic, because such procedural evidences certainly fit the common sense of the clinician's culture.

Unfortunately, the procedural evidences of psychology often work against an easy transfer from course to clinic. The student is given a mechanistic orientation well suited to the experimental paradigms of the laboratory, and all the accompanying hortatory cliches about precision, operational definition, and the lawfulness of behavior which accompany such courses serve merely to give him an unnecessary sense of inferiority. Lest the clinical student feel he is a special case in this cross-cultural conflict, let us hastily note that other areas of study, of which the best examples are hypnotism and extrasensory perception, face the same kinds of problems. Gardner Murphy, speaking about those toughminded psychologists who refuse to accept the validating evidence of extrasensory perception, quotes from Donald Hebb, as he observes "that it is not a question of evidence, for the evidence would, in its own right, be adequate. The trouble is that 'ESP does not make sense' " (Murphy, 1958, p. 69).

Here we have a perfect example of what philosophers have been telling us for centuries: procedural evidence carries enough conviction to take precedence over validating evidence whenever the validated material fails to be consistent with the common sense of the individual or group doing the validating. Those psychologists who have attempted to publish unique papers in our research journals have found such resistance to innovation from time to time. Getting a "new idea" into the literature is no easy matter, since it has to buck the procedural evidence biases of those in editorial control. Having empirical validating evidence at the .01 level of probability is no assurance that innovation will take place or that your paper will reach print. When one adds to this the awarding of research grants, and recognizes how much these fundings rely upon vogues and ideas with a comfortable, familiar ring about them, only a truly unthinking individual could assert that scientific psychology relies *only* on validating evidence to evolve its body of empirical knowledge. The other side of the coin is that clinicians have frequently confused procedural evidence in psychotherapy with validation. If many research psychologists have naively identified scientific activity as exclusively validational in nature, equally as many clinicians have mistaken procedural evidence as *necessarily* validating a clinical hypothesis.

Evidence in Psychotherapy

Although the clinician's method of study in psychotherapy may parallel that of the laboratory scientist's in the sense of formulating abstractions, propounding descriptive explanations, and so on, we cannot overlook the important difference between the two situations in the *focus* of evidence. When it comes to psychotherapy, procedural evidence holds sway over validating evidence. But this is the procedural evidence of the client and not of the psychologist.

It is well known that all schools of psychotherapy have certain basic principles in common, such as accepting the client on his own terms, or placing the responsibility for most decisions on the client. The ethical canons of the psychotherapeutic profession make it clear that an individual must not be coerced into therapy of an interpersonal "relationship" variety. What is often not made clear is that all such practices emphasize and cultivate the client's reliance on procedural evidence. The laboratory experimenter does not deliberately encourage his subjects to make shifts in behavior on the basis of their personal procedural evidence. He is not much interested in this question and does not allow their decisions to influence his experimental design in any case. He is studying the subject and never the procedure, which he has designed at the outset. The subject has little to say about the procedure, except possibly in the pretesting manipulations. In this fashion the experimenter learns a great deal about a circumscribed hypothesis. From his extraspective vantage point, he can in fact learn very little beyond or unrelated to the predesigned sequence of events he calls his experimental paradigm.

In the clinic the situation is different. The clinician must continually take into consideration the client's procedural evidence whenever a theoretical proposition is phrased as an interpretation. Since it is the client who must come to accept an interpretation, and since he may — like the scientist regarding ESP — exercise his prerogative as a thinking, feeling individual (who can separate the two?), there is every chance that the client will reject perfectly *valid* evidence. Or, the client may accept 80 per cent of a valid interpretation, but alter it by 20 per cent to jibe with his personal common sense. Frequently this is not verbalized, so the clinician is unaware that his interpretation has been modified in the client's assimilation of it. To put this another way, the clinician does not have to be *right,* that is, valid, in order to get a client to find meaning in an interpretation, to accept this interpretation, or to act on the basis of it. The client is always manipulating the "method" of psychotherapy as he could never do if he were behaving within an experimental method or paradigm; and the instrument for his manipulation is procedural evidence. As Jung sagely expressed it: "I do not need to prove that my interpretation of the dream is right (a pretty hopeless undertaking anyway), but must simply try to discover, with the patient, what acts for him — I am almost tempted to say, what is actual." *

We should point out that Jung had a theoretical justification for the acceptance of procedural evidence. He thought of people and their psychic systems as infinitely variable, and his psychology was a kind of limited relativism of the psychic sphere. Freud was correct, and so was Adler, and so are the other personality theorists; each man gives what is true for himself in projecting his psychology. Freud gave us a picture of the neurotic side of man's nature (Jung, 1961, p. 334). From Jung's point of view, if a client accepts an interpretation, finds meaning in it, and acts on the basis of it, this interpretation *is true* for that client's particular psychology. Thus we find Jung making statements such as this: "The [dream] interpretation just outlined was apparently the correct one, for it struck home. It won the spontaneous assent of the dreamer. . . . " † If we extended Jung's thinking, we would of course end in a completely subjective position on the nature of psychological knowledge. It would follow that every man's plausible understanding of how he behaves as he does is a correct belief — correct for him, for his psychology. Jung avoids this pitfall by reasoning thus:

> Since the individuality of the psychic system is infinitely variable, there must be an infinite variety of relatively valid statements. But if individuality were absolute in its particularity, if one individual were totally different from every other individual, then psychology would be impossible as a science, for it would consist in an insoluble chaos of subjective opinions. Individuality, however, is only relative, the compliment of human conformity or likeness; and therefore it is possible to make statements of general validity, i.e., scientific statements.**

For Jung, validity is tantamount to generalizability, and the matter of having to lay down a prescribed succession of events before validly testing a proposition is not part of this process of generalizing theoretical statements. Since people are not unique in all their particular individualities, even though several theories of personality can apply, the variations will begin re-echoing or rephrasing common themes in making therapeutic interpretations. It is at this point that subjective variation becomes objective generalization and the science of psychology can

* From *The Collected Works of C. G. Jung*, Vol. 16, p. 45, *The Practice of Psychotherapy*, Bollingen Series XX.16. New York: Pantheon Books, and London: Routledge & Kegan Paul Ltd, 1954.
† *Ibid.*, p. 155.
** *Ibid.*, pp. 4–5.

begin. Although it is highly ingenious, Jung's position leaves open the possibility of having an invalid (in our terms) but generally held belief masquerade as objectively true. There is always the chance that all the people can be wrong and communally hold to a conventional belief which would be easily disproved if put to the test by research methods.

Jung seems to have minimized this possibility. In his view, the use of what we have termed "procedural evidence" *can* serve to validate theoretical propositions (therapeutic interpretations). Whether we accept his justification or not, the important point is that Jung candidly admitted that he cultivated the operation of, and rested with, a form of evidence which fails to satisfy most of the scientific orientations in operation today. It is for this reason that the more rigorously-inclined psychologists view "clinical insight" with a great deal of suspicion. This has always been true in the area of psychotherapy, since the very beginnings — the self-analysis of Sigmund Freud. In 1897, Freud commented, in a letter to Fliess: "Outwardly very little is happening to me, but inside me something very interesting is happening. For the last four days my self-analysis, which I regard as indispensable for clearing up the whole problem, has been making progress in dreams and yielding the most valuable conclusions and evidence." *

The evidence to which Freud refers was procedural. It is a curious fact that, though Freud had an early example of how procedural evidence might "work" for any given client — i.e., convince the client of the truth of a presumably generalizable interpretation which later proved to be wrong — Freud did not give the potential influence of procedural evidence much weight in his later theorizing. Thus, his early view of hysteria was that *all* such neurotics had been seduced as children (a generalizable principle of etiology). He came to this view as a result of the recollections given by his clients while under hypnosis or in the process of freely associating to their memories.

However, Freud eventually reasoned that *every* case of hysteria could not have a sexual attack in the background because "it was hardly credible that perverted acts against children were so general" (written in 1897).† His self-analysis helped him to decide that most of these recalled sexual assaults were really nothing but phantasies, and that they had never taken place: "I have accomplished a piece of self-analysis

---

* From *The Origins of Psycho-analysis, Letters to Wilhelm Fliess, Drafts and Notes: 1887–1902,* by Sigmund Freud, Basic Books, Inc., Publishers, New York, 1954, p. 218.
† *Ibid.,* pp. 215–216.

which has confirmed that phantasies are products of later periods which project themselves back from the present into earliest childhood; and I have also found out how it happens, again by verbal association" (written in 1899).* Despite this chain of events, Freud did not come to any Jungian-like position on the nature of evidence. He continued to rely on procedural evidence, and even took signs of improvement in his client as essentially validating the truth of his now revised theory of neurosis.

Freud's view on the matter of interpretation was that if the therapist was wrong when he had made an interpretation, the client's unconscious processes would eventually rectify the situation. For example, the client would soon dream in such a way as to contradict the interpretations which had earlier been made in error (see Breuer and Freud, 1955, p. 295). To buttress this argument, Freud asserted that mental contents were determined and were in no way arbitrary or subject to alternative interpretations (see Freud, 1952, p. 462). Yet, the fact remains that it is the therapist who proffers the interpretations, or at least sets the style for such interpretations. Once a given life history has begun to unfold, and the therapist provides a series of constructs in which to array the sequence, along with a line of thought fully describing the life in question, it is easy to see how *any* dream might be twisted and turned to meet the demands of the theoretical reasoning already under way.

The clinical office or the analyst's consulting room is *not* the appropriate location for validating certain hypotheses. If one is studying the nature of psychotherapy, then naturally one must validate hunches relating to therapeutic behavior change in this context. However, though it may be a fruitful and unparalleled source of hypotheses, the clinical relationship should not be considered the sufficient criterion for validation of personality theories. Research findings to date suggest that, no matter what theory the clinician subscribes to and uses to phrase his interpretations, changes in client behavior and claims of newly discovered "insights" always serve to validate the personality theory held by the clinician. This is in part due to the nature of theorizing, and in part due to factors in the relationship other than the clinician's theory of personality (e.g., suggestion).

Problems result when the clinician takes the client's behavior, based on the client's personal (including subjective) procedural evidence — an unreliable criterion at best — as *necessarily* validating a clinical interpretation. Several personality theories have been developed this

* *Ibid.*, p. 270.

way. Many of the constructs so postulated and "clinically validated" have stood up in subsequent experimentation, but many have not. The behavior change, the cure, the expressions of insight, the personal growth of the client *may* be the result of some generally true principle now in operation within his life, but this is not necessarily true. Clinical practice is a fruitful source of hypotheses and may even be viewed as a kind of pretesting; but we should always submit our theories to "extra-clinical" test, particularly since they make reference to life beyond the therapy room.

Now, to the clinician who desires to be completely scientific in his practice, underscoring the play of procedural evidence in his work seems to strike at the heart of the matter and to remove him from the charmed circle of "scientific disciplines." He knows that people can believe many things in the name of common sense. They may believe things which are not validated, or which cannot be validated — such as the belief in supernatural forces (see Chapter II) — and as a result of these beliefs show improvement in their conditions. Does this not establish clearly that clinical practice will always remain unscientific? We contend that it most certainly does not. To conclude this would mean that we had overlooked the comparable play of procedural evidence in science, already discussed, and also that we had chosen to ignore the influence of all other theories of knowledge (such as the philosophical or the theological). Though a psychological scientist might dismiss a theory of knowledge which permits of supernatural forces, he cannot in good conscience dismiss the *fact* of influence which supernatural forces as conceived by his clients have upon their behavior. He can even follow Ayer's suggestion (see Chapter III), and do research in this area, and prove through validating techniques that a belief in such forces does exert influence among a given community of people. If he goes beyond this, and pronounces judgment on the content of the belief, he is impelled immediately into the area of morals and ethics. To safeguard themselves, and to try as best they can to remain socioethically neutral, clinicians have consistently tried to enforce their own ethic of client responsibility, thereby identifying with the client and taking his viewpoint in introspective fashion.

When the time is propitious in the sequence of therapeutic contacts for the clinician to proffer some *new* term, some new construct into the conversation as a form of interpretation, he should strive to use genotypic description which has been validated. If it has not been validated, if his terms and line of reasoning have never even been attempted in a research project to date, this should not disturb him for the present. He should go ahead with his interpretation, noting its assimilation by the client and the effect it has upon the client's behavior. This may be an item of subjective knowledge, one which does not generalize to other clients. But, if the clinician wants to make an objective generalization of this interpretation, and apply the theoretical proposition to all or most members of a given group, then he must think in terms of validating the proposition. To simply write up this "finding" as a case history and sagely express it as a fact of human behavior is not sufficient. The interdependence of evidence in psychotherapy means that the clinician accepts his client's belief system as meaningful and relevant to this client's behavior, even though he as a scientist might not personally accept the body of knowledge on which this belief system rests. This is the *client's* theory of behavior, so to speak, as learned within his subculture.

It is at times very difficult to base a line of reasoning or a decision as to what is true or false upon the findings of psychological research. This leads some clinicians to give up hope of ever making sense out of the morass of researches engulfing our journals. Does not this re-affirm the view that clinical activity can never be scientific, and that it will always need an educated guess or have its artistic side? Suppose an atomic scientist tells us that fallout is going to destroy our children's minds and ultimately the entire race if atomic tests are continued. Does this suggestion make him any less a scientist? He may be right, or he may be wrong. Certainly not all scientists agree on this point, which presumably can be determined from empirical research findings. But as long as he bases his decision on the validated knowledge of his specialty, whether he has the minority or the majority view, who will deny him the right to speak? Further, what we as a nation decide to do about it is up to us. He has fulfilled his professional responsibility.

It is the same with the clinician. He has an *ethical* responsibility to keep in close contact with, and contribute to when possible, the validated and validatable evidence of his profession (i.e., the scientific literature), and to make his therapeutic interpretations in light of these findings. By continually accepting therapeutic change as validating theoretical hypotheses we have both learned much and consistently confused issues. This is the reason clinicians are and must remain scientists, must subject their hypotheses to public trial, and must keep in touch with other points of view (the larger body of scientific knowledge). The clinician need not be caught up in role conflict, for he can be a scientist to the extent that he follows such a program. This is nothing more than anyone with an interest in people and a desire to be correct could be expected to do. If he prefers to abstract himself from the larger scientific community, to neglect the research literature, to deride the attempts of his peers to validate some of the notions "he knows" can never be validated, he certainly cannot be considered a scientist. Again, the decision is with him.

Meaning and the Nature of Knowledge

Now that we have completed a review of theory, its functions, and the methods by which it is tested, we can further crystallize our interpretation of knowledge. To do so, we build on our interpretation of meaning, for knowledge too is a relational concept. We have said that the meanings of theoretical constructs and propositions depend upon the relationships they bear to other constructs and propositions within our total grasp of experience. When the ties between terms are clear, we can speak of the denotative meaning of theory as expressed in language; when they are less certain, we can speak of connotative meanings. Denotations and connotations refer to meaning in the verbal expressions a theorist uses. A highly mystical theorist may well limit himself to the more vague, analogical, connotative meanings of terms. We are never sure how much truth he is expressing, until such time as we can place his commentary within a framework of methodological test — either cognitively or through a research experiment.

So long as we limit consideration to the *theoretical* (denotative and connotative) meaning of constructs or propositions, we are not speaking of knowledge. There is meaning, but as yet the question of "knowledge" remains open. Knowledge is a more abstract concept, subsuming *both* meaningful relations *and* the play of methodological evidence. Knowledge is the understanding of why a given theoretical proposition is true or false after that proposition has been submitted to the test of method. Meaning as a concept is on the side of theory, as it is used to explain data sequences, but knowledge embraces both theory and method. Methods have meaning, of course, but when we speak of them in this sense we usually refer to them as based upon a *theory* of knowledge. Methods are acts of evaluation or assessment, whereas theories merely "bring together" any of a number of constructs, thereby generating meaning but not necessarily knowledge.

Meaning, we have argued, *begins* in theory delimitation, as an expressive act of conceptualization from the very outset of a line of theorizing. Knowledge demands that such meanings be evaluated, and widened. Knowledge reaches out beyond the individual case, beyond the subjective meaning of some limited fact pattern, and interlaces with the meanings of an ever-broadening community. It is for this reason that when we speak of "knowledge" we seem to suggest a superordinate grasp, a scope and depth of insight far transcending the usual realm of man's understanding. Theoretical explanations which have been proposed on a limited basis begin melting one into another, and a uniformity of outlook catches us up in the aesthetic delight of seeing parallels and explanations where none were to be had before. But there are many levels of knowledge, just as there are many levels of theoretical explanation. Man seeks to enlarge his meanings, to extend and to combine his theoretical explanations, and thus to understand in a "new way" the older facts of experience. He seeks knowledge.

This is not to say that subjective items of knowledge are impossible. For example, if we study an individual and come to know him as a person within the framework of his own subjective beliefs, we do have knowledge of that single person. However, the truly wise psychologist doubtless can see — as Freud and Jung did — that within each individual there are common themes, tying this "one" man to others, this idiosyncratic belief to a certain tradition of belief, this highly bizarre delusion to a commonly expressed prejudice, and so on. To the extent that the theorist can see beyond his single object of observation — his subject in an experiment or client in psychotherapy — he is more likely to extend the horizons of knowledge for mankind. When his subjectively derived insights strain at yesterday's meanings for *all* men, and especially if these meanings are changed in the process, then we are more likely to consider that theorist a wise man. The more he can extend the scope of his explanatory theory, as long as it meshes well with other aspects of knowledge, the wiser we take him to be.

Another point which this interpretation of knowledge recognizes is that convention and arbitrariness are never entirely absent from bodies of knowledge. Truth or falsity is merely another way of expressing our conviction, nurtured by the two types of evidence, that some verbally expressed proposition can be counted on to bear up under experience. Meanings which can be counted on in experience make the greatest sense, and hence for all practical purposes may be considered "true." Nevertheless, the meanings of constructs are never settled, and theoretical propositions never quite circumscribe all that there is to experience, even at the most rudimentary levels. Especially when it comes to the description of human personality, there is always room for alternative explanations.

A final question is suggested by all this: "How does one evaluate knowledge?" We must first recognize that a question phrased so broadly encourages confusion due to the multiordinality of the term "knowledge." Obviously, some items of knowledge are susceptible to validation; others require primarily procedural test; in one sense, all such assessments draw from both kinds of evidence. But to say that we wish to evaluate a "body" of knowledge *en masse* — such as psycho-analysis, or science — is to phrase a distinctly philosophical question which would demand considerable discussion of ground rules for what we, the propounders of this knowledge, hope to gain, what we expect of our bodies of knowledge, what factors are to be integrated and brought under the rubrics of a point of view so that it might instruct us, and so on. In short, we would have to talk about the purpose any given body of knowledge is to serve, how it historically evolved, and what it is now expected to do for those who nurture it. This brings us back to Chapter I, where it was avowed that we would attempt such an assessment of psychology. We are continuously involved in precisely this task of evaluating the body of knowledge called psychology, as we make our way through the many issues of succeeding chapters.

Summary

In Chapter IV we have distinguished between two forms of methodological evidence which enter into the evolution of knowledge, and we have shown how one form serves to influence the other and vice versa. Procedural evidence involves the belief in a theoretical proposition because of its intelligibility, its consistency with the common-sense knowledge of one's group then in ascendance, or its implicit self-evidence. On the other hand, when we believe a theoretical proposition on the basis of the observable consequences following a prescribed succession of events designed to test that proposition, we do so on the basis of validating evidence. Procedural evidence carries a greater sense of conviction than validating evidence, but this does not make it an infallible guide to the truth of a proposition, if by "truth" we mean something which is demonstrable, observable, and predictable. It is a truism to say that both forms of evidence are equally essential to the development of a scientific psychology. Unfortunately, certain psychologists have mistakenly identified the method of science as *nothing but* the use of validating evidence, while other psychologists have mistakenly accepted procedural evidence as *necessarily* validating theoretical propositions. Chapter IV closed with a discussion of knowledge, stressing the fact that it is a higher-order meaning construct which considers both theory and method in propounding a point of view.

References

Adams, D. K. Note on method. *Psychological Review,* 1937, *44,* 212–218.

Becker, H., and Barnes, H. E. (Eds.) *Social thought from lore to science.* Washington, D.C.: Harren Press, 1952. 2 vols.

Black, M. Making something happen. In S. Hook (Ed.), *Determinism and freedom in the age of modern science.* New York: New York University Press, 1958. Pp. 15–30.

Boring, E. G. Temporal perception and operationism. *American Journal of Psychology,* 1936, *48,* 519–522.

Boring, E. G. *A history of experimental psychology,* 2nd ed. New York: Appleton-Century-Crofts, 1950.

Breuer, J., and Freud, S. *Studies on hysteria.* New York: Basic Books, 1957. Also Vol. II of J. Strachey (Ed.), *The standard edition of the complete psychological works of Sigmund Freud.* London: The Hogarth Press, 1955.

Bronowski, J. *The common sense of science.* Cambridge, Mass.: Harvard University Press, 1958.

Frank, P. *Philosophy of science.* Englewood Cliffs, N.J.: Prentice-Hall, 1957.

Freud, S. *A general introduction to psycho-analysis.* In Vol. 54 of R. M. Hutchins (Ed.), *Great books of the western world.* Chicago: Encyclopedia Britannica, 1952. Pp. 449–638. (Also published —New York: Liveright, and London: George Allen & Unwin, 1963.)

Freud, S. *The origins of psycho-analysis, letters to Wilhelm Fliess, drafts and notes: 1887–1902.* New York: Basic Books, 1954.

Hofstadter, R. *Anti-intellectualism in American life.* New York: Knopf, 1963.

Hull, C. L. Mind, mechanism, and adaptive behavior. *Psychological Review,* 1937, *44,* 1–32. Courtesy, American Psychological Association.

Jung, C. G. *The practice of psychotherapy.* Vol. 16 of H. Read, M. Fordham, and G. Adler (Eds.), *The collected works of C. G. Jung.* Bollingen Series XX.16. New York: Pantheon Books, and London: Routledge & Kegan Paul, 1954.

Jung, C. G. *Freud and psychoanalysis.* Vol. 4 of H. Read, M. Fordham, and G. Adler (Eds.), *The collected works of C. G. Jung.* Bollingen Series XX.4. New York: Pantheon Books, 1961.

Murphy, G. Trends in the study of extrasensory perception. *American Psychologist,* 1958, *13,* 69–76.

Oppenheimer, R. Analogy in science. *American Psychologist,* 1956, *11,* 127–135.

Skinner, B. F. Are theories of learning necessary? *Psychological Review,* 1950, *57,* 193–216.

The Meanings of Lawfulness and Determinism in Modern Science

Introduction: The Lawfulness Construct

One of the essential characteristics of scientific knowledge is that it consists of lawful regularities garnered from observation. Psychologists accept with varying degrees of conviction the belief that all behavior is lawful. But what is meant by this assertion? A psychologist who claims that "all behavior is lawful" may be using "lawful" here in a methodological or theoretical sense. He may mean that all behaviors which have thus far been studied, such as eye-blinking, walking, or talking, have shown "lawful" regularities going beyond chance occurrence. This would be a methodological usage of "law." Or, he may mean that all eye-blinking, all walking, and all talking are lawful behaviors. Now, he is using the word "law" as a theoretical speculation. He is implying that, in time, we will be able to show that all behaviors are completely regular and extraspectively predictable. We shall take up this latter usage of lawfulness first, and then consider the methodological usage.

Lawfulness as a Theoretical Construct

Probably the most pervasive use of lawfulness as a theoretical construct emanates from the so-called "S-R lawfulness" usage. This view essentially states that there are myriads of antecedent and consequent events tied together in (efficiently) causal connections, permitting an eventually complete explication of the nature of the universe by carefully studying the lawful interrelations of these events, now termed stimuli and responses. This antecedent-consequent view dates far back in history, and is probably based upon Aristotelian terminology used in

96

the explication of "If, then" logical propositions (see Chapter IX). What is more, it is clearly a *theoretical* position, because at this point in time our validated evidence does not support the catholicity of this view. A completely objective conclusion in the present, one which could be drawn by any theorist and which would have broad applicability would seem to be: "All behavior is not lawful, but much — maybe most of it — is." Some psychologists dislike this form of "word-bantering," because they feel that unless the assumption of complete lawfulness is made we could not have an experimental psychology. Levy takes this stand when he claims: "For if we did not make this assumption [i.e., the lawfulness of all behavior] there would be no point in performing any research; the results of any given study would have to be considered fortuitous and no generalizations would be possible" (1963, p. 58).

Although it is very likely true that belief in lawfulness of all behavior acted as a spur to the early experimental psychologists of this century, one might well ponder whether things would be as bad today as Levy paints them if psychologists had concluded: "All behavior is not lawful, but much of it is." This is, after all, a *generalization*. It is a verbal statement purporting to refer to a broad range of data. One suspects that the extreme position taken by some psychologists, who believe that only if lawfulness is accepted as some form of ultimate certainty is a psychology possible, draws its strength from a realistic thesis of so-called natural laws which *themselves* generalize across a real world of implacable events. It would then seem to follow that experiments done in one context could never generalize to another if the existing laws somehow "broke down." But if one views theoretical statements as *verbal* propositions, being applied idealistically to a world of phenomena, then the generalization referred to has nothing to do with any fixed reality, but rather with the way we prefer to speak about our phenomena.

There would still be a spur to research for the latter psychologist. The aim then might be to show under what conditions behavior could be considered lawful or unlawful. Even if a psychologist took the extreme position of direct opposition — i.e., "all behavior is unlawful" — there would be some point in doing research to establish *this* verbal generalization. Of course, the latter position is not likely to be taken, but at the level of theory *qua* theory it has no less need for method than does the opposite and more popular assertion. Generalizations are made by intelligent men, not by implacable realities. A theory is a theory, and without method, without a generalized acceptance among some group of people who know the theory, it would die its own death because it was ignored.

Another manifestation of the theoretical use of "lawfulness" stems from the belief often voiced by psychologists that laws which are discovered at a so-called lower level will somehow generate laws at a more general or higher level (level of abstraction, presumably). The psychologist hopes to begin with simple relations, simple laws, and then work his way up to more general laws, which are sometimes phrased as more complex laws. Clark Hull was doubtless very influential in promulgating the view that lower-level psychological laws are somehow tied to higher-level laws, and if discovered through experimentation, they will eventually generate higher-level or more abstract laws in a quasi-mathematical way. To show how he came to this position, we will first follow his thinking on the matter of theory vs. method in science, or, to use his terms, theoretical vs. empirical (method) science. Hull viewed theory and empirical test as two sides of the same coin, each checking on the other, each potentially congruent with the other:

> The fact that, in certain fields at least, practically the same statements or propositions can be attained quite independently by empirical methods as by theoretical procedures is of enormous importance for the development of a science. For one thing, it makes possible the checking of results obtained by one method against those obtained by the other. It is a general assumption in scientific methodology that if everything entering into both procedures is correct, the statements yielded by them will never be in genuine conflict. . . .
>
> We note, next, that in scientific systems there are not only many theorems derived by a process of reasoning from the same assemblage of general principles, but these theorems take the form of a logical hierarchy; first-order theorems are derived directly from the original general principles; second-order theorems are derived with the aid of the first order theorems; and so on in *ascending* [italics added] hierarchical orders (1943, pp. 5–6).

Hull was elaborating here on the logical interrelationship of theorems within his system, but it was an easy matter to extend this hierarchy notion to the empirical side of science. If we were to change his term "derived" to "inferred," Hull's discussion of hierarchical orders would pass nicely as a definition of induction, the generation of new theoretical hypotheses or propositions based upon lower-level, less abstract propositions. As it now reads, we fear that Hull has confounded induction with deduction (see below, pp. 101–102). But if logical theoretical hierarchies (theoretical science) paralleled quantitative empirical hierarchies (empirical science), then it would follow that a logically consistent theoretical system would have its counterpart in a quantified reality.* Many psychologists since Hull have stressed the latter "order in natural reality" which supposedly can be measured accurately via the method of research experimentation, and have soft-pedalled the theoretical order of free discovery. The view has evolved that nature is quantified and will generate her own hierarchy of quantified knowledge if we will only follow diligently the rules of scientific experimentation.

Lawfulness as a Methodological Construct

The second usage of lawfulness has nothing to do with a theoretical position on the nature of the universe, although it might well accompany such a theory. In conducting an experiment, the psychologist defines, let us say, two variables as independent and dependent, then proceeds in as well-controlled fashion as he possibly can to demonstrate the relationship between them. Data are then recorded as the findings of his investigation, and the relationship which he can graph as a quantitative function is said to be the description of a law, or the manifestation of a general law in a specific instance. In this case, "law" is used as a kind of methodological artifact. Stafford uses the term this way when he states: "A law in any science today is simply a stable, generalized relationship between facts operationally observed and quantitatively expressed" (1954, p. 63). Note that anyone could agree to this, even those psychologists who would not agree to the theory that the universe consists of myriads of antecedent and consequent variables which are potentially interrelated and generative of one another in some quantitative sense.

When it is said that psychologists seek lawfulness in behavior, it is this methodological usage of "law" which usually is meant. That is, in a superficial sense, experimentation seems more oriented to the *fact* of relatedness than to the matter of what variables happen to be related to what other variables. It is possible to think of method without theory

* This is clearly a neo-Platonic line of reasoning, and it suggests to the writer that Hull was not as close to the realistic end of the dimension as he would have liked temperamentally to have been. It is possible to think of Platonism as realism, and, indeed, the term "scholastic realism" has been used to classify Plato. But as Russell has indicated, "Because scholastic realism is connected with the theory of ideas, it has in modern times also been called idealism" (1959, p. 147). It is in the latter sense that we have been using "idealism" and we see in Hull's quotation a direct affinity. In Chapter IX we shall take up this question in great detail.

if one ignores the influence of informal theory. In the present volume, we would prefer to think of the process of experimentation as follows: Theory defines the variables as constructs and speculates on the relationship between these variables. Method establishes the fact of an interrelationship, which is then referred to as law. Rather than looking for lawfulness, it is more correct to say that the experimenter looks for an hypothesized relationship (formal or informal) between variables. If he does not find this relationship, he might do one of three things: (1) refine or change his theory; (2) refine or change his experimental design; (3) decide that the problem cannot be investigated at the present time, but retain his theory intact.

There is a fourth alternative, which psychologists sometimes follow too easily in the name of basic science, and that is to seek lawfulness come what may. This involves forsaking an interest in a *given* formal or informal theory in favor of literally finding a "significant" relationship between *any* two (theoretically defined) variables, no matter how irrelevant or esoteric the relationship proves to be. There is a common belief that "we have to start with statistically significant, concrete relationships before we can even think of formulating any theories." The mad chase after a significant probability level is often a dash to mediocrity. Any psychologist who does literally search for lawfulness and not for the relationship between certain variables can justify his activity only on the basis of a theory of natural law. He is no longer primarily interested in law as a methodological construct, he must hold to the theory of lawfulness already discussed.

What about the investigator who really has no view on the nature of lawfulness but simply enters the laboratory one day and begins poking around in this and that, seeking a loosely phrased "common sense exploration of the field" (Skinner, 1950, p. 215). Do we mean to assert that he could not stumble across an exciting advance in knowledge without having first defined his variables from a theoretical point of view? The answer here, of course, hinges upon one's definition of theory. In order to "stumble onto" a discovery, a man must first have a frame of reference in which to cast and subsequently evaluate his observations, or he would fail to take note of a discovery. Such common-sense frames of reference we have termed informal theories, and in Chapter IV we have added the concept of procedural evidence to help us understand how sudden insights might develop. It is therefore possible accidentally to note (generative function) a relationship between two informally defined constructional variables, and then work back to a clear definition and the gradual evolution of a formal theory. In doing this, the psychologist naturally makes use of new experimental controls to clarify his thinking about the validity of his insight.

The Use of Lawfulness Constructs: Induction vs. Deduction

We have said that theories suggest both the relevant variables in an experimental test and the nature of the relationship between these variables. It might appear that in using the term "relationship" here, we have presumed a form of theoretical lawfulness at the outset. If variables are related, is this not tantamount to claiming that they are tied together by some kind of natural law? How else could one hope to study them in a uniform, generalizable way? Actually, the way we have used the term "relationship" has nothing to do with lawfulness in nature (though once such a relationship stands up under validation one might begin referring to it as a law in the methodological sense).

The term "relationship" is an important aspect of the *verbal meaning* of a theoretical proposition. Meaning, we have argued, is a relational concept, and therefore to begin to know an item of experience is to relate it to other items of experience. It is for this reason that we must evolve theoretical statements or propositions. But this does not mean that one must believe all items of experience are necessarily lawfully related independent of one's intellect. There are many methodological ways to slice the pie of experience. A *less lawful* relationship may have more significance, may be more instructive, than a *more lawful* relationship in experience. The extent of relationship found methodologically cannot be the only grounds or even the main grounds for assessing the worth of our theoretical constructs. One does not have to assume that all items of experience are lawfully related before he begins to bring new items of experience into a theoretical relationship, one with another.

To understand better the generalization of theoretical propositions, we must introduce the topic of inductive vs. deductive reasoning. To reason inductively is to reason from the particular case to the universal, as in Hull's discussion above (p. 98). Induction proceeds from lower levels to higher levels of abstraction, in that more and more details are left out, and gradually a so-called highly generalized proposition can be stated. Since one can never derive — in a logically necessary way — a proposition of higher generality or abstractness from a proposition of lower generality, inductive reasoning always involves a guess or a hunch, or more properly, an *inference*. It is in this sense that we feel Hull misused terms in speaking about "deriving" a hierarchy of theoretical propositions in *ascending* order (p. 98); one does not derive but infers *up* the ladder of abstraction. These inferences are not completely free agents; they are made from within some kind of framework, one we would call informal or formal theory, and their plausibility is tested in the ways discussed in Chapter IV.

Deduction, on the other hand, is reasoning from a universal to a particular case. Deductive reasoning begins with a more abstract or general proposition, and from this derives a less abstract or more specific proposition. Induction and deduction are two sides of the same coin in the process of reasoning. To perform an experiment the psychologist uses deduction from an informal or formal theory, states a hunch of any degree of formality, and then carries out the method of testing that hunch. On the basis of his findings, he returns to induction, and once again infers a new proposition or modifies an old one within his theory. He never foregoes the influence of theory, even when making inferences from empirical findings.

The important point to keep in mind is that, when lawfulness is used in the methodological sense, it is tied to induction and *not* to deduction. What we call a law in this sense is what we have found empirically "thus far." This methodological usage does not provide us with the logical rationale for making a generalization of the sort, "All behavior is lawful." This is an inferential leap and it is *never* proven deductively. Rather than assuming that a world of intertwining laws must exist before we can generalize our experimental findings, all we need do is keep in mind that experimental findings are the tested derivations of theories initially phrased as presumed generalizations and then either taken seriously as facts or rejected as unproven statements of relationship between variables.

There is a way in which law as a methodological construct might be said to be general or stable; in our terms, this would mean that the theoretical proposition it supports can be cross-validated. Of course, it is usually the rule that the statistical value of the law expressing the relationship between variables in the theoretical proposition does not in itself cross-validate. This value changes, and the belief in psychology has traditionally been that these differences in the manifestations of the law are due to the uncontrolled conditions which plague all experiments. We presume that an absolute law shines either brightly or dimly through any given experimental test of a theoretical proposition, and that it could be measured perfectly if only the uncontrolled conditions in our imperfect methods could be rectified. In light of present-day findings of other sciences, this belief may certainly be challenged. Rather than viewing statistics as a kind of rough or crude means of estimating the absolute law hiding behind our lack of experimental controls, one might well think of natural laws as themselves constituted of statistical probabilities, which summate in any given experiment to support or fail to support a theoretical proposition, or to support it in varying degrees at different times. Even assuming that our methods were completely refined and that there was *no* uncontrolled variance due to instrumentation in an experiment, this view would contend that the *perfect* functions (relationships) between variables called for by some psychologists would be impossible. The atomic theorist and Nobel laureate, Erwin C. Schrödinger, took such a position on natural law when he wrote:

> It is quite possible that Nature's laws are of thoroughly statistical character. The demand for an absolute law in the background of the statistical law — a demand which at the present day almost everybody considers imperative — *goes beyond the reach of experience*. Such a dual foundation for the orderly course of events in Nature is in itself improbable. *The burden of proof falls on those who champion absolute causality, and not on those who question it.* For a doubtful attitude in this respect is to-day by far the *more natural* (1957, p. 147).

S-R Laws vs. R-R Laws and Methods of Study in Psychology

Kenneth W. Spence has introduced a distinction into the psychological literature which is sufficiently important to be considered as a special subtopic of lawfulness. Framed in terms of *methods* of scientific investigation, this distinction actually hinges upon a *theory* of lawfulness of the sort we have already discussed. Spence distinguishes four types of laws, but we will take up only the two really important types. He cites differences between R-R and S-R laws as follows:

> R = f(R) laws describe relations between different attributes or properties of behavior; they tell us which behavior traits are associated. This type of law is investigated extensively in the fields of intelligence and personality testing, and the laws that have been discovered have formed the basis of much of our technology in the areas of guidance, counseling, and clinical diagnosis. These empirical R-R relations also

form the starting point for the theoretical constructs of the factor analysts. . . .

The second class of laws, $R = f(S)$, relates response measures as the dependent variable to the determining environmental conditions. There are really two subclasses of laws here, one relating to the environmental events of the present and the second to events of the past. The first subclass includes the traditional laws of psychophysics, perception, reaction time, and emotions. . . . Insofar as the behavior at any moment is a function of environmental events that occurred prior to the time of observation one is dealing with laws of the second subclass. The most familiar instance of this kind of relation is represented by the so-called learning curve which relates the response variable to previous environmental events of a specified character (1956, pp. 16–17).

Spence goes on to note that these two kinds of laws form the bulk of current psychological investigation. Why do we need a distinction of this sort, and what are some of the probable reasons for making it? As they stand, one cannot quarrel with such attempts to refine thought concerning our styles or methods of investigation. Regrettably, however, this breakdown into R-R and S-R laws has been viewed by many psychologists as a kind of status distinction. Spence has done little to counteract this view, and indeed, seems to subscribe to it himself when he observes: "These R-R laws represent only one small segment of the total framework of a science of behavior, and unfortunately not a very basic one at that" (p. 9). As it has evolved in psychology, this attitude suggests that an "applied" scientist makes use of R-R laws, while a "basic" scientist capitalizes on the heart of the matter, i.e., S-R laws. This is no minor point, as witnessed by the fact that Lee J. Cronbach eventually felt it necessary to devote a Presidential Address to the American Psychological Association to the distinction between what he called "two disciplines of scientific psychology," the experimental and the correlational:

The experimental method — where the scientist changes conditions in order to observe their consequences — is much the more coherent of our two disciplines. . . . While the experimenter is interested only in the variation he himself creates, the correlator finds his interest in the already existing variation between individuals, social groups, and species. . . . The correlational method, for its part, can study what man has not learned to control or can never hope to control. Nature has been experimenting since the beginning of time, with a boldness and complexity far beyond the resources of science (1957, pp. 671–672).

Cronbach then argues for a "true federation of the disciplines," pointing out that only incorrect answers can result from a one-sided approach (p. 673). By accepting the distinction between experimentation and "something else," his paper has served to perpetuate what the writer believes to be a detrimental feature of current thinking on the nature of evidence in psychology. Graduate psychology students are occasionally instructed that psychologists do at least two types of studies: experiments (S-R laws resulting) and correlational researches (R-R laws resulting). There is often the additional connotation that the latter falls short of the former because only the experimenter has "control of the stimulus." Since we feel that this status discrimination rests on an unnamed theory of lawfulness, and also on an incorrect interpretation of evidence, we will now consider it in some detail.

First of all, we might ask, how legitimate is it to distinguish between R-R relations and S-R relations? What makes a variable or a measurement an S and what makes it an R? Is this some kind of spontaneous dichotomy provided by nature, or do we as experimenters assign such labels to our data? Spence has taken the theoretical position that this world consists of antecedent events which lawfully tie into consequent events. This takes place over time, so we might diagram the S-R relation as follows:

Time dimension ————————————————→
S (antecedent) . . . . R (consequent)

If the bond between the S and R can be shown to bear a consistent relationship, then Spence would speak of an S-R law. Now, it is also possible on this theory for S-R regularities, occurring over time, to parallel one another. We might represent this situation as follows:

Time dimension ————————————————→
S (antecedent) . . . . R (consequent)
S (antecedent) . . . . R (consequent)

In this situation, one might actually find a relationship between the two consequents, which move systematically in parallel, and it is in this sense that Spence speaks about the emergence of an R-R law (symbolized by the dotted arc). A law of this sort would of course be "less basic" because it would not give us a true picture of what is causing what. In place of the true controller of the R, we have a parallel variation in two Rs. Indeed, it could well be that *one* antecedent S is in control of both consequent Rs. An individual who always gets a headache (R) when he gets a stomach-ache (R) may come to think that his headache causes the stomach-ache, when in fact it is some virus (S) in the bloodstream which is the real cause of both disorders. The headache might actually be the cause of the stomach-ache, of course, but we can never know, until such time as we have ruled out alternative explanations, which means, in S-R terms, until we have identified the correct S by having manipulated it in relation to the R of our interest.

This is a plausible theory, but an unfinished one. That is, it should be possible to have S-S laws, but Spence does not develop this possibility in quite the way he develops the R-R variety of laws. That is, Rs are said to tie into other Rs and they might be studied through correlational techniques. We might learn that passivity (R) is tied to schizophrenia (R), but we would not have elaborated the Ss of either condition by having thus named an R-R law. But why could not passivity and schizophrenia be intercorrelated Ss, each of which has some as yet undiscovered R attached to it? Why do we not take an interest in them as an S-S tie-up, rather than as an R-R tie-up? Because this form of S-S tie-up does not seem so reasonable on the basis of procedural evidence. The S concept is always taken to be an *antecedent* on the time dimension, and how could we have two antecedents being connected over the passage of time? One might well have two consequents, two Rs, both tied to the same antecedent S, or two Rs correlated with one another though actually controlled by two different antecedent Ss. But to think of intercorrelated antecedents is a bit too complex for our common sense, though of course it is theoretically possible on the S-R world view. What differentiates R-R from S-S is the construct usage of the experimenter.

When Spence (1951) actually turns to an S-S usage, as in discussing Tolman's cognitive approach to learning, he does an interesting thing. He makes the cognition S an *intervening variable* between the more basic environmental S (reality) and the eventual R (behavior) of the organism. He applies the same S-R bind which we discussed in Chapter III (p. 57). In commenting on Tolman's "cognitive structures," or the cognitive map which an organism presumably acquires when he interacts with his environment, Spence notes: "These cognitions are introduced as intervening variables that refer to organizations or connections that become established among the perceptual systems of the subject" (p. 256). In short, we slip Tolman's cognitive map between the S and the R, so that now we have a so-called S-S complex which eventually brings on the R. However, it would be just as correct to call this an S-R complex in disguise, which then eventually brings on a further R. The essential idea is that S (environment) *leads to* R (cognitive structure) which eventually *leads to* a further R (behavior). It is not truly S-S, as for example, in the sense of "S (passive father) *when correlated with* S (dominant mother) *leads to* R (effeminate male offspring)." In the latter case, if it could be shown that passive men *invariably* sought dominant women, and if we accepted Spence's terminology and world view, we might have a true S-S law.

But one cannot accept the Spencian terminology, because strictly speaking it is incorrect to think of Rs apart from the Ss which presumably control them. The S and R conceptualizations are inextricably bound up with one another as theoretical products. As Bakan observed, "The stimulus does not exist as a stimulus except by virtue of the responses of the organism. The delineation, abstraction, and identification of the stimulus *is the response*" (1953, p. 48). In our terms, the delineation, abstraction, and identification of the stimulus and the response *creates meaning* by relating one phenomenon to another. If we could free ourselves of the S-R terminology and think of these ends of a time chain as simply two variables, functionally linked to one another and thereby framing a valid (or invalid) meaning, we would be far better off (see Chapter VIII).

The meanings are never in reality, but always in the theory under elaboration and study. Whether we point to R-R or S-R relations, the worth of a theory is to be judged on the kinds of meanings thus generated. Now, it is true that in explaining the nature of some phenomenon, the theorist might err and ascribe a fallacious causal connection between two variables which co-vary. This is a point in logic, much like the point about affirming the consequent (pp. 80–81). David Hume wrote an historically important analysis in which he clearly demonstrated that the correlational influence of antecedent to consequent in itself *never* establishes causation with certainty (see Chapter IX). Correlations are not causes, even when the correlation occurs before our very eyes in the striking of one billiard ball against another. How do we know for *certain* that we ever have "the" S for a given R? We never do, actually. But, by ruling out alternative Ss through experimental controls and the manipulation of one antecedent (independent variable) in relation to one or more consequents (dependent variable), we can at least feel a little more self-assured. If there are no loopholes in our experimental design, and it bears up under retest, we can begin to speak of more or less meaningful "facts." Just how instructive these meanings prove to be, how interesting and insightful they are, is another matter.

If we think of the S-R vs. R-R distinction as one which involves the creation of meanings by tying certain constructs into other constructs, then we can see how it can have some merit. *One gets two different levels of meaning here.* It might well be that an S-R law is denotatively clearer than an R-R law, but the items of experience which are theoretically integrated in the former may be trite and obvious alongside the so-called less basic (less explicit, connotative) contents of the latter. On the other hand, a too-ready acceptance of so-called R-R laws probably signifies that the theorist lacked the tenacity to carry through on the meanings he was evolving. In time, he will surely be embarrassed if he builds his case uncertainly, on an unfinished examination. But he should never be intimidated into foregoing a study which relates one broadly conceived variable to another, where he cannot say with great certainty that *this* variable and *this one alone* relates to *that* variable. He should not shrink from correlational studies, because in doing his work he evolves meaning which must ultimately alter our course of thinking as regards his data — so long as he finds something of interest, a relationship (which is meaning) worth mentioning.

If we recast this lawfulness issue in terms of evidence, can we remove the invidious comparison of the "experimenter" and the "correlator," the precision expert and the guesser? We think so. The fundamental issue here is the matter of validating evidence. Does the experimenter lay down a prescribed or *predictable* course of events before submitting his theoretical proposition to the test? Experimentation as a form of method is done to *demonstrate* (see Chapter IX) or, as Bakan (1953) has said, it is done to teach equally as often as it is done by a given psychologist to learn. The experimenter has already accumulated some information and formulated his formal or informal theoretical hypothesis. We call this preliminary systematic inquiry "research." He now designs a *further* test of that hypothesis, and *predicts* that such and such will occur. We call this an "experiment." When this trial run is carried out, his hypothesis is strengthened or weakened as the case may be (though it is never logically proven, because the evidence affirms the consequent). One cannot reduce every hypothesis about behavior to the highly instructive, didactic demonstrations of the physics class variety, but this need not detract from the predicted demonstrations made in life situations. Why should one type of prediction be called an experiment, and the other some kind of research falling short of experimentation? The confining and restrictive view of life which one's laboratory apparatus provides is no sure ticket to the accumulation of worthwhile knowledge.

There is no essential difference in cognition between what the psychologist does in the laboratory preliminary to his application of validating evidence, and what he might do in the field. In the laboratory, he might well fiddle around in this, and dabble in that. Suddenly, or possibly slowly, after much painful pretesting, a regularity in the behavior of his object of study — let us say, a rat in a maze — is observed by the psychologist, but he cannot be certain precisely what variables are at play. He is not certain whether the observed order is merely a chance R-R, or whether he can more carefully elucidate the conditions under which this order is taking place and thereby shift terminology and confidently assert an S-R regularity. He goes on to design an apparatus to test the specific hunch about what the presumed S really is, calling his shots *beforehand* in an attempt to validate his hypothesis positively. In the same way, a psychologist in the field might begin with a fiddle here and a dabble there, correlating this test variable against that behavior variable in quite random fashion at the outset. If he then notes some kind of order emerging from his personality test data, he must carry this further to cross-validate, expand, and refine his results. Finding relationships in *post hoc* fashion is a form of research, in the sense of inquiry, but this is not completely validating evidence. Since there is a community of science, it is not wrong to publish such findings as a first step in a series of researches, or in an effort to attract other investigators to one's area of interest. But at some point, the "experimenter" is called upon to validate fully his data.

What rigorous psychologists decry is the loosely organized, "shotgun" study which uses several objective tests correlated against one another and often thereby capitalizes on chance relations. An investigator might find a few significant correlations between variables, which he had not even predicted and probably was surprised himself to find. These results are then written up for publication, with a strained rationale, and nothing further is done until at some later date a second investigator shows that these earlier correlations were due to chance, or to unique sample differences which cannot be cross-validated (see Cureton, 1950). The psychological research journals have doubtless been cluttered by work of this sort, which in our terms has fallen short of *validating* an hypothesis, and the criticism implicit in the R-R conceptualization is certainly warranted. But things can go too far, as they have in some universities, where graduate students feel they are not being scientific unless they do a doctoral study in which they can somehow lay claim to "manipulating an independent variable" (the stimulus, the antecedent event) and recording its effect on some dependent variable (the response, the consequent event). We would do well to drop such experimental snobbishness and conceptualize lawfulness in terms of one form of evidence — what we shall come to call "control and prediction" in validation — rather than in terms of two or more kinds of psychologies.* To illuminate this point, we turn now to the history of science, and ask ourselves what experimentation has meant in the scientific method. What is the essence of the scientific method?

Scientific Method

What Is Science?

The term "science" is derived from a Latin root meaning "knowledge," or "to know" (*scire,* to know) and the "scientific" usage adds "to make, or to demonstrate in the sense of doing something to show one's knowledge" (*facere,* to make, do). When we refer to science we therefore refer to knowledge, or to a certain theory of knowledge which has been propounded over roughly the past four hundred years. Though we are accustomed to speaking of science as a unified whole, particularly when referring to the scientific method, in point of fact science does not find its common ground on the matter of a single method or type of experimentation. Kantor has accurately typified science as "an enormous accumulation of specific jobs" (1953, p. 4). An experiment is a trial run which the scientist undertakes to prove some point, to substantiate his hypothesis; or, the converse, to disprove some point held by his peers. Since he is seeking knowledge, his use of method is aimed at proving his theoretical point of view to his own satisfaction, and to the satisfaction of his fellows in the scientific community. Validating evidence is therefore the tie that binds.

If we now turn to two of the recognized founders of the theory of

---

* Although he has accepted a different experimental terminology, Cronbach (1957; also Cronbach and Meehl, 1955) has been instrumental in laying the groundwork for a union *through prediction* in the notion of Construct Validity. (See especially his comments, 1957, p. 676.) In seeking construct validity, a psychologist would most certainly be doing experimentation in the true sense of that word.

knowledge embodied in science, it will be clear that they never intended to restrict their scope to experimentation of the laboratory variety. This was not even their ideal. The first, a man who is sometimes called the "father of the scientific method," William Gilbert (1540–1603), devoted only about 40 per cent of his important work *De Magnete* (appearing in 1600) to what we would now call basic science pursuits (physical or laboratory experiments). The remainder of this first physics book had to do with navigation, nautical instruments, mining, the fashioning of iron, speculations on the terrestrial globe as a magnet, and the medical effects of iron. During Gilbert's time a distinction had been drawn between the liberal arts (i.e., intellectual, gentlemanly skills) and the mechanical arts (i.e., use of manual labor, working-class skills). Science, as the method of constructing experimental apparatus to attempt validation of what seemed plausible to the mind's eye, was considered a mechanical art.

Gilbert sought the association of men who were doing things in the workaday world. Though he was a man of means and a "physician in ordinary" to Queen Elizabeth, he nevertheless visited miners at work and was proud of his friendship with members of the sailing trade. He was not greatly taken with the mechanistic view of the universe, and his quantitative studies were fairly mediocre. But he did adopt and adapt the practical methods of problem verification used by men in the foundries. Gilbert felt that the gentleman-philosopher might observe, and draw conclusions in the serenity of his library, but he was not called upon to test such conclusions empirically in the practical world of affairs. Thus, as Zilsel has noted, Gilbert's "spirit of observing and experimenting was taken over not from scholars but from manual workers" (1957, p. 233).

Sir Francis Bacon (1561–1626), whose *Advancement of Learning* was published five years after Gilbert's *De Magnete,* is our second major figure in the founding of science. Bacon succeeded in fixing the attitude of skepticism which has come to typify the modern scientist. He strongly argued that one man's intellect could not be relied upon to bring all of nature's truths into an ordered body of knowledge. It would take many men, working over time with a common purpose, to promulgate a body of knowledge which might then progress to certainty by degrees or stages (Prior, 1957). Since man's senses are imperfect, Bacon called for instrumentation and experimentation to correct these natural deficiencies. Man must correct for the defect of overestimating the power of his personal intellect, for "If a man will begin with certainties, he shall end in doubts; but if he will be content to begin with doubts, he shall end in certainties" (p. 384). He thus severely criticized those who would rest with the plausibilities of procedural evidence.

Even so, the ideal for Bacon was *not* the pleasure of study or the excitement of discovery which we today associate with the so-called basic sciences. His goal was rather to improve man's lot in life. As he phrased it: "Now the true and lawful goal of the sciences is none other than this: that human life be endowed with new discoveries and powers" (p. 386). Although he had helped shape the scientific attitude we now take for granted, Bacon did not introject the notion of two disciplines in science. How then did this distinction arise? As the vogue of experimenting with apparatus caught on, it was no longer socially frowned upon for a gentleman of the seventeenth and eighteenth centuries to work with his hands, because he was still in pursuit of knowledge. The leisured scholar who used to pour over philosophy texts was now checking his theoretical propositions in a new way (validation). The spirit of empiricism was taking hold, in combination with Bacon's concept of scientific progress, and it was exciting to be part of a "classless" movement in knowledge. But, as John Dewey (1916) has pointed out, class distinctions are not so easily blurred. A scholar of the eighteenth or nineteenth century who actually had to earn a living from knowledge was simply not leisured. He was not pursuing knowledge only for the pleasure it afforded, but was working for a practical reason. There were other men who could afford the luxury of a completely disinterested attack on knowledge with no material purpose. Gradually, a special class distinction evolved within the scientific community between the leisured or "pure" scientist and the practical or "applied" scientist. Physicians thereby became applied scientists when they took money for their demonstrations of knowledge, gained through their practice, by effecting further cures. This is the historical root of the basic vs. applied science distinction, and one can be excused if he sees in the S-R vs. R-R, or experimentation vs. correlational study dichotomies of psychology, a possible rephrasing of this old class snobbishness.

Science, therefore, seems to be above all an attitude or desire for a certain type of truth. If one claims to be scientific in his approach, he must do something from this point forward to show us that he really has a grasp, an understanding, a fund of knowledge. He must predict the outcome of a course of events, and control to our satisfaction all extraneous factors which might influence this course besides his purely logical claim on knowledge. Thus, part of this control is his line of argument and the amount of systematized knowledge he can muster for his case. Not everyone would insist that it is necessary to experiment to be scientific. Some would contend that any systematization of information into a body of knowledge is a scientific endeavor, so that logic and philosophical inquiry are in one sense scientific. But the more generally accepted view of science centers in that *special type of inquiry* we know as research, with its carefully preconstructed trial run known as experimentation. This produces validating evidence, and the phrase "control and prediction" further describes such evidence. This phrase essentially defines what we mean by validation in the practical terms of experimentation. The desire to be scientific is a desire to move whenever possible from complete reliance on procedural to *at least partial reliance on validating evidence*. This is the essence of scientific activity as the writer views it. To appreciate the strengths and weaknesses of validating evidence in physical science, we will now follow the course of "control and prediction" in the history of science.

Control and Prediction in Physical Science

Although the age of modern science is usually dated from about the year 1600, with the writings of Gilbert, Bacon, and especially Galileo (1564–1642), the prediction of events dates back to the time of the Greeks, as embodied in their mathematical and practically motivated astronomical studies for navigational aids (Koyré, 1956). In Galileo's thought several important lines of historical influence converge. First of all, from the writings of Copernicus, who had been influenced by the revival of neo-Platonism in medieval Italy, Galileo obtained the following Pythagorean view of the universe:

> Philosophy is written in that great book which ever lies before our eyes
> — I mean the universe — but we cannot understand it if we do not first
> learn the language and grasp the symbols, in which it is written. This
> book is written in the mathematical language, and the symbols are tri-
> angles, circles, and other geometrical figures, without whose help it is
> impossible to comprehend a single word of it; without which one
> wanders in vain through a dark labyrinth (Burtt, 1955, p. 75).

In order to decipher the knowledge which nature possesses, according to Galileo, man needs a grasp of mathematics. He does not need to experiment at every turn. Galileo was not as skeptical as Bacon, for he placed great faith in the power of mathematical intellect. He believed that from a few experiments one could generalize or make inferences extending far beyond the reaches of immediate experience, because as he said: "the knowledge of a single fact acquired through a discovery of its causes prepares the mind to understand and ascertain other facts without need of recourse to experiment" (p. 76). Galileo was, in our terms, closer to the idealistic than the realistic pole in theoretical outlook.

With this mathematical view of the universe Galileo combined the pragmatic and machine-like models of empirical investigation used by Gilbert and, in the century before, Leonardo da Vinci. The natural result was a theoretical world view which we have come to call mechanistic. As Burtt has noted, Galileo helped introduce into the common sense of the scientific community the view that nature was "a perfect machine whose future happenings can be fully predicted and controlled by one who has full knowledge and control of the present motions" (p. 96). The advent of experimentation generated a dual interpretation of the terms control and prediction. They no longer referred only to man's application of his knowledge, as when the Greek sailor guided (controlled) his course on the basis of predictions from the stars, they also served as guiding principles for observation and validation. The scientist formulates an hypothesis, makes a prediction, and through the application of controls either supports or fails to support his hypothesis. This is another way we distinguish between applied and basic science. Although he controls and predicts, the modern scientist does not always apply knowledge, but "basically" seeks it through a machine-like experimental apparatus.

The next important figure in physical science, and the one who has been most influential in modern psychology, is Sir Isaac Newton (1642–1727). Unlike Galileo, whom we have already described as leaning to idealism, Newton was a confirmed and uncompromising realist. He made a distinction between mathematical truths (in the mind) and physical truths (in the physical reality of the universe) and contended that there was no such thing as *a priori* certainty. In our terms, Newton distrusted procedural evidence — the evidence of creative mathematics — so much that he insisted only validating evidence was involved in his method. He demanded experiments at every turn, in order to stay very close to physical reality, and he denied that he had to make any speculative assumptions or hypotheses in the pursuit of science. He brought together mathematics and experiment in a new way. Whereas Galileo viewed experiment as something he did when, for example, mathematical reasoning (intellect) led to two alternative outcomes and one had to be eliminated by experimental evidence, for Newton experimentation was the means by which a man clocked or mapped the fluctuating and mathematically precise lawfulness of the mechanical universe (reality). Newton believed that even geometry was part of the physical universe's mechanics, and that it accurately demonstrated the art of measuring in nature (p. 215).

Newton's world was most certainly a huge, precise, and perfectly running machine. Laws of precision and exactitude existed "out there," and for any event taking place before his eyes there was a discoverable antecedent event (efficiently) *causing* it or bringing it about. The machine model, initially used as a paradigm for experiment, became the paradigm for a world view. Newton and his followers succeeded in making a metaphysic out of a method (p. 243). Man discovers, he does not create in the world of reality. Bronowski underscores the change in use of the machine paradigm from da Vinci's time to Newton's: "when da Vinci wanted an effect, he willed, he planned the means to make it happen: that was the purpose of his machines. But the machines of Newton (and he was a gifted experimenter) are means not for doing but for observing. He saw an effect, and he looked for a cause" (1958, p. 25). Man was not an initiator but an extraspective, passive observer, who watched while nature played out her symphony of lawful processes. There was as yet no hint of the significant role man as theorist would find himself playing in the *act* of observing or discovering. Man had his future in hand, but it was a comparatively conservative future of discovery rather than of conceptualization in the pursuit of knowledge.

Following Newton, eighteenth-century scientists elaborated the machine model, and looked for mathematical finality in all things. The pushes and pulls of basic, immutable laws, probably few in number and mathematically related to one another, were to be found in the world of reality, not postulated in the world of intellect. It was the great age of 100 per cent determinism in science. This metaphysical assumption held that if only man knew the basic laws of nature, he could predict the future with as much assurance as he had in the knowledge that two times five equals ten. Determinism reached its most elevated and eloquent expression in the famous remark of Laplace (1749–1827), "that a superhuman intelligence acquainted with the position and motions of the atoms at any moment could predict the whole course of future events" (Burtt, 1955, p. 96). The natural clock of time was wound: it would run its eternal and inflexible course.

This mechanistic and completely deterministic attitude was modified in the late nineteenth and early twentieth centuries, as reflected in the writings of Hertz, Poincaré, and Duhem (Cassirer, 1950, Ch. V). Man was now seen to play a more central role in the accrual of scientific knowledge, as the influence of theory and conceptualization was given its proper due. Man did not discover the facts of nature so much as he applied theoretical systems or paradigms to it. The paradigm did not *have* to be a mechanical one. Einstein's theory of relativity demonstrated that even the axioms upon which geometry is founded are not fixed once and for all by some naturalistic providence. Einstein returned to a Galilean outlook on the nature of creativity, as this quote clearly shows: "Experience remains, of course, the sole criterion of the physical utility of a mathematical construction. But the creative principle resides in mathematics. In a certain sense, therefore, I hold it true that pure thought can grasp reality, as the ancients dreamed" (Einstein, 1934, p. 18). Einstein was basically realistic in theoretical outlook, but more moderate on this dimension than Newton.

Though some physicists may find it difficult to accept this "appellation," in the terminology of the writer modern physical science has reflected a clear trend to idealism. Control and prediction has been retained as the standard for all knowledge reputed to be scientific, but the old certainty and trust in explanations based on the empirical behavior of nature is no longer present. Intellect has won, for the present at least, if only in the negative sense of showing that even intellectual proofs are not what they were once thought to be. For example, in 1931 Kurt Gödel proved mathematically that it is impossible to establish the logical consistency of a very large class of deductive systems, including elementary arithmetic. In other words, mathematics is not the neatly closed package we once took it to be, with 100 per cent internally consistent axioms and propositions; inconsistency and unpredictable outcomes are possible and indeed probable in the simplest mathematical systems (Nagel and Newman, 1958). If mathematical systems lack closure and internal consistency, how can we go on accepting the view of nature handed to us by Newton — that the world of reality forms an interlocking network of related laws?

The physical universe as a comprehensible, demonstrable means of validation is no longer the reality it once was. Theoretical physicists no longer demand that their conceptual models be even remotely connected to our conventional picture of empirical reality. Due to Heisenberg's "Principle of Indeterminacy," and related conceptualizations, physicists no longer feel constrained to search for the "ultimate" in causal reality.

Heisenberg's principle strikes at the heart of determinism in the sub-atomic world, for it essentially states that a scientist cannot measure both the position and the velocity of an electron without thereby influencing the electron's speed or direction of movement. Predicting the future in the subatomic world is a matter of probability, and so it shall always remain. There is no hope at present of ever finding the immutable law shining through the apparatus; as Schrödinger said, absolute causality in modern physics simply does not meet the facts (see above, p. 103). This has strained the common sense of not a few physicists, who find it hard to accept an altered view of reality because they are so accustomed to explaining phenomena in causal terms drawn from a real universe. As the physicist Bridgman has observed:

> Involved in all this, in a way that is perhaps not always very explicitly evident, is the insight that, since an object never occurs naked but always in conjunction with an instrument of measurement or the means by which we acquire knowledge of it, the concept of "object," as something in and of itself, is an illegitimate one. Acceptance of this insight with all its implications is obviously going to react strongly on our idea of "reality," and many of the objections to the orthodox view arise precisely from unwillingness to accept the altered view of "reality" (1958, p. 48).

The altered view to which Bridgman refers here we would call: idealism. This is a Kantian insight (see Chapter IX). As the physicist sharpened his thinking concerning the role of theoretical paradigms, heuristic devices, and so on, it became evident that predictions and controls cannot always be counted upon to decide finally between opposing points of view on the nature of reality. Although a theory is rarely if ever rejected simply and only because of its empirical performance (that is, because it has generated some predictions which have failed to be substantiated), the theoretical formulation which meets with observational experience most consistently certainly has a strong position. If we had to make a best guess at any given time, the prudent choice would be to rely upon the better performer. Granting this point for the moment, it is in fact possible to predict the same phenomena in reality from diverse theoretical positions. For example, both Einstein's and Whitehead's laws (in our terms, "theoretical laws") of gravitation predict certain natural phenomena equally well, even though the respective laws are based upon diverse philosophical positions, theoretical formulations, and mathematical devices. The laws also generate incompatible predictions, but since these hypotheses cannot as yet be tested, there are no grounds on which to choose one law over the other — except possibly of an aesthetic nature (Palter, 1956).

This now leaves us with two rather interesting developments: First, other considerations besides predictive efficiency may determine the choice of one theoretical view over another at any given time. Second, it is within the realm of possibility that *more* than one view of the cosmos may function jointly and efficiently at any point in time, or *even for all time*. Empirical data may be amenable to diverse points of view. There is no logical reason why a given series of theoretical abstractions drawn from some time series in the past and projected into the future — to be evaluated at that point by abstractions consistent with the theoretical view — must lead to greater predictability than another series of theoretical abstractions so construed and evaluated. Some middle ground between an attitude of this sort and the eighteenth-century attitude of "discovery" of concrete, immutable laws seems warranted, if the history of physical science to date is correctly interpreted.

Despite the reasonableness of this conclusion, based upon the experiences of our brother scientists, whom we were once only too pleased to emulate, psychologists have disregarded the lessons of history and persisted in patterning themselves after a nineteenth-century brand of physics. The science of modern psychology is essentially Newtonian. Physics has changed since Newton's time, but psychology has retained his world view. Oppenheimer's admonitions about patterning ourselves on a "physics which is not there anymore" (1956, p. 134) fall on deaf ears. We have our older heroes, with their more confident assertions about the nature of scientific investigation to cling to. The lessons of history are, after all, subject to varying interpretations as conditioned by one's procedural biases. It is no doubt for this reason that one realistically-oriented historian of scientific psychology can dismiss the views of several eminent physical scientists with the charge of naïveté:

> Schrödinger adopts the popular modern view that in the process of scientific study the scientist creates his data. This view implies that the scientist is not merely a spectator but a part of the events studied. I submit that this opinion reflects the exact opposite of the correct relations that exist between scientists and the events they study. Schrödinger, Bohr, Eddington, and the other scientists who adopt this postulate are surely confusing events and the constructs created with respect to them (Kantor, 1963, p. 25).

Control and Prediction in the Choice of Theory

The discovery that control and prediction was not an infallible guide to the accrual of scientific knowledge, nor to the fundamental decision of which point of view to accept and "believe in," was not easy to come by in the sciences. It took a few centuries of experimentation and a number of surprises to alter the Newtonian world view. For example, it was once believed that if two theorists disagreed in outlook, the construction of a crucial experiment testing some vital point at issue would make clear which theory was true; however, as Frank has noted:

> A single experiment can only refute a "theory" if we mean by "theory" a system of specific statements with no allowance for modification. But what is actually called a "theory" in science is never such a system. If we speak of the "ether theory" or the "corpuscular theory" of light, or of the "theory of evolution" in biology, each of these names covers a great variety of possible systems. Therefore, no crucial experiment can refute any such theories. A famous example was the "crucial experiment" which Arago proposed in 1850 to test the corpuscular theory of light. This theory was refuted in 1855, but in 1905 Einstein again made use of this theory in a greatly modified form known as the hypothesis of "light quanta" or "photons" (1957, p. 31).

In 1905, the physicist Duhem made the following observation: "In physics the crucial experiment is impossible" (p. 31). The same point applies in psychology. We will occasionally have to look elsewhere than the experimental method to make choices between theoretical points of view. The writer once heard a commentary on the supposed motives of Gordon Allport, who takes a somewhat more "above the belt" view of man than does Freud. It was said that: "Gordon Allport wants to take man out of the lavatory and place him in the living room, where he feels man belongs." Although this was said in a tauntingly humorous vein, assuming this really was Allport's motive, as long as he could account theoretically for all of the validated behavior that Freudian theory accounts for, there would be nothing unscientific about this motive. Preferences or values, as conditioned by one's aesthetic or ethical inclinations, are occasionally legitimate reasons for making a choice between psychological theories. Similarly, at this time, and possibly at any time, one's acceptance of either Whitehead's or Einstein's theory of gravitation is a purely aesthetic matter (Palter, 1956).

Determinism

Growing out of earlier philosophical problems, and paralleling the rise of modern science, the issue of determinism in nature has plagued man as he strove to outline patterned change in lawful terms. Lawfulness implies determination of one sort or another. Since it also relates to probability, a topic taken up in Chapter VI, this seems a good point at which to consider briefly the matter of determinism. This term is ambiguous due to a variety of usages, but we shall try to summarize the most important points in the deterministic view. Some define determinism very broadly as the belief that "all phenomena, including those of human behavior, fall into causal patterns" (Grunbaum, 1952, p. 669). Others, though not necessarily rejecting this definition, take issue with the way certain determinists use the term because they feel it takes on the added connotation of a *necessary* influence. Cassirer refers to the historian Buckle in this sense: "He [Buckle] sometimes speaks of statistical laws in a rather queer way. He seems to regard them not as formulae which describe certain phenomena but as forces which produce these phenomena. This is, of course, not science but mythology" (1944, p. 250). One of the problems with accepting determinism as the view that all events are caused is that there are at least four kinds of causes which can be used to describe an object in experience. We must ask the determinist to which cause he is referring.

The Four Types of Causes: Aristotle vs. Bacon

Aristotle was the first to note that man invokes the idea of cause because he hopes thereby to demonstrate his knowledge of some phenomenon: "We think we have scientific knowledge when we know the cause . . ." (Aristotle, 1952, p. 128). If a man cannot point to the causes of something, he is probably merely stating opinion and thus cannot make a claim on knowledge. He must demonstrate his knowledge by making his case in terms of four causes, said Aristotle: (1) material, (2) formal, (3) efficient, and (4) final (p. 271). The material cause of an object is the substance from which it is made. In building a stereophonic system, the metals and plastics going into the components define a material "cause" of the finished product. The formal cause is the blueprint from which we organize the components into a whole to match the intended form of this class of electrical equipment. The ways we manipulate our eyes and hands in reading the blueprint and building the set act as the efficient cause of the finished product. Last, "that for the sake of which" (p. 270) we built the set — e.g., our desire to hear good music — would be the final cause of the completed stereo system. Putting these four types of causes together, we can now fully explain the "why," the "nature" of our newly acquired personal possession. This, in brief, is Aristotle's basic theory of scientific knowledge and we shall be making ever greater use of its tenets in the chapters to follow.

The first point we wish to make concerning this theory of causation is that, with the advent of what we now call "natural science," or modern physical science, the legitimacy of using formal and final causes to explain natural phenomena was first questioned, then denied. Bacon was very influential in pointing out that "to inquire the form of a lion, of an oak, of gold; nay, of water, of air, is a vain pursuit. . . . If the cause of whiteness in snow or froth be inquired, and it be rendered thus, that the subtile intermixture of air and water is the cause, it is well rendered; but nevertheless is this the form of whiteness? No; but it is the efficient [cause], which is ever the *vehiculum formae*" (Bacon, 1952, p. 44). Thus, formal causes are not the proper means of explaining the "why" of natural events because they fail to instruct us properly. This is because all we can do by citing a formal cause is classify things another way, without adding any new empirical meaning to the conception, or so Bacon contended.

In psychology, Kurt Lewin (1935, pp. 1–42) has referred to the rather stylized attempt to explain behavior by classifying it into types, such as the "oral personality" or even "dominant vs. submissive personality," as representative of Aristotelian thought. He contrasts this mechanical approach with what he terms "Galilean thought," which is presumably a more dynamic approach taking into consideration not only the form (the "labeled" nature) of individuals, but their life circumstances (their behavioral environments) as well. Of course, it is really not appropriate to claim that Aristotle's thought is characterized primarily in terms of class or formal causes. Lewin's analysis and criticism is well taken as applied to many theorists, but the choice of "Aristotelian thought" is an unfortunate one because formal causation by no means exhausted Aristotle's theoretical analysis. He felt that the more causes we could bring to bear in making our descriptive analysis, the more knowledge we possessed concerning any item of our attention.

It is even more important to observe that final causes were considered far less acceptable to natural science explanation than formal causes. Since final causes deal with "that for the sake of which" something exists (a stereo system, or an "act" of behavior), there is an implication here of intentions, purposes, or goals toward which the item being described is moving or striving. In his *Physics,* for example, Aristotle theorized that leaves exist for the purpose of providing shade for the fruit on trees, and he concluded thereby: "that nature is a cause, a cause that operates for a purpose" (1952, pp. 276–277). Bacon noted that one settles for nonscientific explanations when he tries to find the "goal" (final cause) of natural structures; for example, if one were to claim that: "the bones are for [have the goal of] the columns or beams, whereupon the frames of the bodies of living creatures are built . . ." (p. 45). Bones do not have it as their "aim" to hold up the muscles and flesh of our bodies, and it adds nothing to our knowledge of bones to claim that they do. This form of "intentional" analysis of nature had become customary in the Middle Ages, due to the tendency for theologians (scholastics) to ascribe intentions to physical matter by way of showing God's hand at play in nature. Thus, it was *God's* intention that the bones provide a structure for the frame of the body. Bacon was in revolt against this tendency, as was Voltaire, in a more satirical vein, when he had the "metaphysico-theologo-cosmolo-nigologist" *Pangloss* teach his young charge, *Candide,* that: "everything is made for an end . . . noses were made to wear spectacles; and so we have spectacles" (Voltaire, 1930, p. 14).

As with formal causes (designs in nature), final causes imply a rationality in the data being described which may well transcend the empirical facts. The approach which explains either natural phenomena or human behavior on the basis of its purposive or intelligent striving toward some goal is called *teleology.* A teleological explanation places as much or more emphasis on the future as on the past. Teleological theorists are sometimes called "vitalists," in contrast to the more "mechanistic" theorists, who stress the past with its fund of efficient causes. When vitalism is extended to a discussion of the nature of man, we often see the term "humanism" used. Humanism implies that man is a datum different in kind from the data of inanimate nature (natural science view), and the humanist ordinarily argues against relying exclusively on efficient causes to capture the essence of man as actor (see Chapter VIII).

Bacon feared that if men of science accepted formal and final causes as explanatory they would not go forth and actively seek empirical knowledge through experimentation. To experiment is to ask a question different from "What is the form or the purpose of this object?" To experiment is to ask, "What brings about this state of affairs?" This is the attitude which Bacon helped fix as the proper one for a *natural* science. He limited theoretical explanation to material and efficient causes, and natural science has continued in this vein down to modern times. Formal and final causal explanations were to be used only in ethical and/or metaphysical argument, in itself a legitimate and worthwhile activity though not suited to science. This is at least one of the reasons scientists have always contended that their form of study was not involved with ethical matters. Ethics went to final causes in getting at the purpose of things. Science must content itself with efficient causes.

Chance, Hard vs. Soft Determinism, and Indeterminism

We have already seen how the eighteenth- and early nineteenth-century scientists believed in a completely determined, Newtonian and Laplacian universe of immutable lawfulness. On this view, spontaneous or "chance" occurrences would not be possible, except as a term used to cover those cases of ignorance where the scientist does not know enough to predict events with complete accuracy. The belief here is that the scientist has not yet learned enough to refine his experiments and thereby capture the 100 per cent predictive efficiency which nature permits. Some people would call this 100 per cent determinism "fatalism." Opposed to this, what we might call "hard" determinism, is the view that chance is not inimical to causal nature, and that a limited or "soft" determinism is possible. On this view, "chance causes" would result when two lines of action — each in itself determined completely — coincide to bring about a single, unpredictable and entirely novel result. The world need not be fatalistically certain. Aristotle referred to this form of chance possibility as an *incidental cause,* thereby extending his use of the causal term even further (1952, p. 273). Finally, there is the view that all actions or behaviors are completely undetermined, fortuitous, or even somewhat chaotic. Virtually no one in the sciences holds to this view of 100 per cent indeterminism, although some people use the word "indeterminism" to cover both 100 per cent lack of determinism and what we have been calling soft determinism. Thus, though the terminology varies, debate actually focuses on the tenability of a soft vs. a hard determinism.

Soft determinism is also referred to as *statistical determinism* (Grunbaum, 1952), and to explore the differences between hard and soft determinism we would have to take up at this point the matter of probability in prediction. However, since the latter topic has been reserved for Chapter VI, we will do no more here than merely point out this identity between soft and statistical determinism. We might now more properly take up the question: "Is one justified in holding to both a soft and a hard determinism at the same time?" For example, can a physicist accept the Heisenberg principle of indeterminacy at the subatomic level, yet stick to hard determinism in the macroscopic world? Basing his argument on the increased information which instrumentation can give us in the macroscopic world, the physicist Bridgman answers this question affirmatively:

> Take in the first place the consideration that the object of knowledge is not to be separated from the instrument of knowledge. Two extreme limiting cases are to be recognized: the instrument is very small compared with the object, and the object is very small compared with the instrument. Since *we* are in the last resort the instrument for acquiring knowledge, the two limiting cases are: objects large compared with us and objects small compared with us, or, in other words, simply large and small objects. Now, it seems to me to make sense to suppose that a small instrument can find out more about a large object than a large instrument can find out about a small object. The small instrument can explore the large object bit by bit in a way impossible for a large instrument with a small object. It also seems to me to make sense to suppose that more perfect knowledge of the large object would make possible more effective ways of dealing with it. In particular, I think it makes sense to find that we can predict the future behavior of a large object but not that of a small object. This is merely another way of saying that it makes sense that causality should fail for small objects (1958, p. 59).

Though he has resolved the problem to his own satisfaction, as M. K. Munitz later suggested (1958, p. 64), Bridgman's resolution sounds like the old hard determinism view, attributing our inability to predict at subatomic levels to a lack of adequate knowledge (in this case, instrumentation), and *not* to the possible lack of 100 per cent predictability in nature per se. Be that as it may, we have here the position of a leading physicist who is a soft determinist in outlook. Others would not agree that a soft determinism is admissible. For example, Grunbaum (1952) contends that moral arguments used against hard determinism (e.g., responsibility for personal actions) are equally valid against soft determinism, which he rejects. For him, one is either a determinist or an indeterminist. William Barrett arrives at the same conclusion, but does so while attacking determinism's insufficiencies: "For determinism predictability in general is not enough: it has to assert (and prove, if it can) predictability down to the last detail — lock, stock, and barrel, and even down to the last scratch on the barrel. Anything less than this, and the thesis of determinism must crumble" (1958, p. 32).

Physical vs. Psychic Determinism

There is another distinction to be made in the kind of determinism a theorist adopts — that between physical and psychic determinism. This distinction, which hinges on the theorist's interpretation of final causes or teleological explanations, is often glossed over, and then muddled thinking on ethical issues results. Although both physical and psychic determinism provide rationales for theoretical explanations in the present as conditioned by the past, psychic determinism does not have the "blind" regulative connotations or the inexorable demand character of physical determinism. Teleological or final cause explanations may be quite inappropriate for the physical universe, since they fail to capture the flavor of these data; but what about for man?

We have already seen an example of a physical determinist's image of man in Skinner's conceptualization (see Chapter II, pp. 21–22), but a more poetic phrasing of this view can be seen in what Clark Hull (1937) called the "beautiful presentation of the raindrop analogy" written by the psychologist Albert P. Weiss. Weiss was a behaviorist who took the following view of teleological or purposive behavior:

> We may start with the assumption that every drop of rain in some way or other gets to the ocean. . . . Anthropomorphizing this condition we may say that it is the *purpose* of every drop of rain to get to the ocean. Of course, this only means that virtually every drop *does* get there eventually. . . . Falling from the cloud it may strike the leaf of a tree, and drop from one leaf to another until it reaches the ground. From here it may pass under or on the surface of the soil to a rill, then to a brook, river, and finally to the sea. Each stage, each fall from one leaf to the next, may be designated as a *means* toward the final end, the sea. . . . Human behavior is merely a complication of the same factors (p. 2).

Hull goes on to point out that Weiss was referring, of course, not to increasingly complicated processes of evaporation, condensation, and other vicissitudes of water, but rather to the electrons and protons of the physical universe. Man is a more complex composite of the same laws which make up the motions of submicroscopic particles in the humble raindrop. At no point does self-awareness, level of aspiration, or purposive decision-making come into the picture to define man. So-called purpose is the measurable end-state of a sequence of behavior which we, as extraspective observers, can measure from our vantage point. The raindrop gets to the ocean, and the man gets to the office in the morning. The man has no more "purpose" in his behavior than the raindrop, says Weiss.

As can now be seen, it is the exclusive wedding of determinism to physical efficient causation that has generated the real problem in theorizing about lawfulness. If laws are nothing more than efficient and physical (material) causes of phenomena, operating under their own weight out of the past, then we have a blind regulator of present behavior. And if this regulator is postulated to operate with 100 per cent consistency, then there is no room for self-directed, alternate actions, either for the raindrop or for the man. We have the Skinnerian and Hullian views of purpose in behavior. If, on the other hand, determinism admits of other than efficient (and material) causes, soft determinism seems to pose a way out of the dilemma. The resolution seems to hinge upon whether or not science is prepared to readmit final and formal causes into its body of explanatory principles. We shall return to this issue in Chapter VIII, when we consider in more detail some of the problems in describing human behavior.

Let us turn now to Sigmund Freud, a theorist who believed in psychic determinism. First, it should be entirely clear that Freud *did* distinguish between "psychical reality and material reality" (1952, p. 472). Freud was a dualist who, at least early in his career, took a realistic position on *both* mind and matter. One is not necessarily an idealist because he holds to a dualistic conception. But why did Freud find it necessary to distinguish between a psychical and a material reality? Did he feel that man was determined by the inexorable and efficient-cause hand of nature in some way transcending man's intellect or act of choice? We do not think so (see Chapter VIII). Psychic determinism was his tool for answering those who doubted his method of study. Using our terminology, Freud *needed* something like psychic determinism to counter the charge that he made interpretations on the strength of procedural evidence. It was not that he "made up" interesting or amusing explanations of dreams or slips of the tongue, but merely that he interpreted correctly what the *individual himself* had rationally, albeit unconsciously, selected to *tell himself* for some purpose. Take, for example, the following argument, which Freud gives in *A General Introduction to Psychoanalysis*;

he has been discussing slips of the tongue that a client might make, and now addresses himself to those who challenge his approach as a fanciful illusion due to the client's cooperation:

> Are you [i.e., his doubters] not eager to object that information supplied by the person enquired of, who committed the slip, is not completely reliable evidence. He naturally wishes, you think, to meet your request to explain his slip, and so he says the first thing that he can think of, if it will do at all. There is no proof that that is actually how the slip arose. It may have been so, but it may just as well have been otherwise. Something else also might have occurred to him that would have met the case as well or even better. It is remarkable how little respect you have, in your hearts, for a mental fact. . . . The truth is that you have an illusion of a psychic freedom within you which you do not want to give up. I regret to say that on this point I find myself in sharpest opposition to your views (1952, p. 462).*

This is the most plausible explanation of why Freud chose to employ a psychic determinism. He approached man from the latter's perspective — i.e., introspectively — and wrote a psychology for man as a purposive organism. Of course, a good deal of man's purposiveness emanates from his *unconscious* mind, but this does not obviate the fact that *in principle* Freud was not opposed — as Weiss was — to the explanation of human behavior in teleological or purposive terms. Man may be impelled in the psychic sphere, but he need not be completely determined thereby in the physical sphere, because the former *takes precedence* over the latter. As he said when talking about neurotic phantasy behavior (though of course such explanations have been extended to all behavior, including normal behavior): "In contrast to *material* reality these phantasies possess *psychical* reality, and we gradually come to understand that *in the world of neurosis* PSYCHICAL REALITY *is the determining factor*" (p. 598).† What is the benefit, therefore, of understanding one's dreams or slips of the tongue? As unconsciously motivated and rational processes, slips of the tongue can help one to make rational conscious decisions and actually to *gain freedom* in the world of physical reality:

> Every one of us who can look back over a fairly long experience of life would probably say that he might have spared himself many disappointments and painful surprises, if he had had the courage and reso-

---

* From: *A General Introduction to Psychoanalysis* by Sigmund Freud. By permission of Liveright, Publishers, New York, and George Allen & Unwin Ltd, Publishers, London. Copyright © renewed 1963 by Joan Riviere.
† *Ibid.*

lution to interpret as omens the little mistakes which he noticed in his intercourse with others, and to regard them as signs of tendencies still in the background (p. 467).*

If Freud was a hard determinist in the psychical sphere, he was most certainly a soft determinist in the physical sphere. Thus he could say: "I believe in external (real) chance, it is true, but not in internal (psychical) accidental events" (1960, p. 257). Moreover, his psychic determinism was not of the blind, but the rational variety. It is correct to say that the individual as conceptualized by Freud determines his own fate, either through unconscious motives and goals, or through conscious insight and understanding. As Phillip Rieff has noted, the latter situation is essentially the Freudian view of normalcy (1959, p. 49). The neurotic is tied to his past, but the normal man is at least partially emancipated from earlier conflicts and fixations. This is truly the hope of Freudian psycho-analysis — to set tormented minds free, to define for man his self-determined and unique nature (see Chapters VIII and XII).

Summary

Chapter V traced the development of modern science and tried to capture some of the major characteristics of the scientific turn of mind. The concept of lawfulness was taken up first, and it was pointed out that the term "law" can be used in both a methodological and a theoretical sense. The usage which has the greatest applicability in psychology is the one viewing law as an abstract and therefore generalizable verbal statement of a relationship between variables which have been experimentally defined and statistically proven. A law is the verbal statement of an objective fact, in which the statistical evidence supporting this statement may vary across validation samples but the finding of a relationship must stand up as predicted. One does not have to assume that the world is constituted of an interlocking network of potentially quantifiable laws in order to use the term "law" in a methodological sense. When one does see the universe as a myriad of causally linked antecedent events and consequent events, which is then translated into "natural lawfulness" with the accompanying phrase "All matter, including behaving matter, is 100 per cent lawful," this is a *theoretical* assertion. The experimental evidence from all sciences now reporting data fails to support completely this all-inclusive theoretical generalization.

A distinction sometimes made between experimentation and correlational research was next taken up, along with its corollary assertion of

* *Ibid.*

S-R vs. R-R laws. The position settled on views research as enlightened inquiry and the experiment as a trial run done to validate an hypothesis emerging from preliminary research investigation. Many types of experimental methods are possible in science, but all of them aim at proceeding from exclusive reliance upon procedural evidence to at least partial reliance on validating evidence. To move from the former to the latter is the essential nature of the scientific intellect. The "unity of the sciences" is the result of an emphasis on one kind of evidence, *not* on one theory of the nature of the universe. This involves "control and prediction" as a further elucidation of what one does to validate a theoretical hypothesis. The course of control and prediction in the physical sciences was traced historically. Basic vs. applied science was discussed, and the conclusion drawn that control and prediction in the "crucial experiment" cannot always help us to select one view of the universe, or of behavior, over another.

The eighteenth-century Newtonian world view of a mechanistic universe, with complete predictability *in principle,* has had to undergo some revision. In the twentieth century physical science has turned more toward the idealistic emphasis which gave it an initial impetus in the neo-Platonic influence on Copernicus, and through him, Galileo. Unfortunately, scientific psychology has been reluctant to follow suit.

The final topic in Chapter V was determinism. Various grades of determinism are accepted in the natural sciences today, and, for the present at least, a soft determinism seems to have taken precedence over hard determinism. The important differences between physical and psychic determinism were explored, and it was shown how Freud could be considered a hard determinist only in the psychic sphere. Freud's intent was to capitalize on the determinism of the mind in order to gain more personal *freedom* for the individual in the material world of reality.

References

Aristotle. In Vol. 8 of R. M. Hutchins (Ed.), *Great books of the western world.* Chicago: Encyclopedia Britannica, 1952.
   Physics. Pp. 257–355.
   Posterior analytics. Pp. 95–137.
Bacon, F. *Advancement of learning.* In Vol. 30 of R. M. Hutchins (Ed.), *Great books of the western world.* Chicago: Encyclopedia Britannica, 1952. Pp. 1–101.
Bakan, D. Learning and the scientific enterprise. *Psychological Review,* 1953, *60,* 45–49.

Barrett, W. Determinism and novelty. In S. Hook (Ed.), *Determinism and freedom in the age of modern science.* New York: New York University Press, 1958. Pp. 30–39.

Bridgman, P. W. Determinism in modern science. In S. Hook (Ed.), *Determinism and freedom in the age of modern science.* New York: New York University Press, 1958. Pp. 43–63.

Bronowski, J. *The common sense of science.* Cambridge, Mass.: Harvard University Press, 1958.

Burtt, E. A. *The metaphysical foundations of modern physical science,* rev. ed. Garden City, N.Y.: Doubleday & Co., 1955. Quotations used by permission of Humanities Press, New York.

Cassirer, E. *An essay on man.* Garden City, N.Y.: Doubleday, 1944.

Cassirer, E. *The problem of knowledge.* New Haven: Yale University Press, 1950.

Cronbach, L. J., and Meehl, P. E. Construct validity in psychological tests. *Psychological Bulletin,* 1955, *52,* 281–302.

Cronbach, L. J. The two disciplines of scientific psychology. *American Psychologist,* 1957, *12,* 671–684.

Cureton, E. E. Validity, reliability, and baloney. *Educational and Psychological Measurement,* 1950, *10,* 94–96.

Dewey, J. *Democracy and education.* New York: Macmillan, 1916.

Einstein, A. *Essays in science.* New York: Philosophical Library, 1934.

Frank, P. *Philosophy of science.* Englewood Cliffs, N.J.: Prentice-Hall, 1957.

Freud, S. *A general introduction to psychoanalysis.* In Vol. 54 of R. M. Hutchins (Ed.), *Great books of the western world.* Chicago: Encyclopaedia Britannica, 1952. Pp. 449–638. (Also published—New York: Liveright, and London: George Allen & Unwin, 1963.)

Freud, S. *The psychopathology of everyday life* (1901). Vol. VI of J. Strachey (Ed.), *The standard edition of the complete psychological works of Sigmund Freud.* London: The Hogarth Press, 1960.

Grunbaum, A. Causality and the science of human behavior. *American Scientist,* 1952, *40,* 665–676.

Hull, C. L. Mind, mechanism, and adaptive behavior. *Psychological Review,* 1937, *44,* 1–32.

Hull, C. L. *Principles of behavior.* New York: Appleton-Century-Crofts, 1943.

Kantor, J. R. *The logic of modern science.* Chicago: Principia Press, 1953.

Kantor, J. R. *The scientific evolution of psychology.* Vol. 1. Chicago: Principia Press, 1963.

Koyré, A. Influences of philosophic trends on the formulation of scientific theories. In P. G. Frank (Ed.), *The validation of scientific theories.* Boston: Beacon Press, 1956. Pp. 192–206.

Levy, L. H. *Psychological interpretation.* New York: Holt, Rinehart & Winston, 1963.

Lewin, K. *A dynamic theory of personality.* New York: McGraw-Hill, 1935.

Munitz, M. K. The relativity of determinism. In S. Hook (Ed.), *Determinism and freedom in the age of modern science.* New York: New York University Press, 1958. Pp. 63–69.

Nagel, E., and Newman, J. R. *Gödel's proof.* New York: New York University Press, 1958.

Oppenheimer, R. Analogy in science. *American Psychologist,* 1956, *11,* 127–135.

Palter, R. Philosophic principles and scientific theory. *Philosophy of Science,* 1956, *23,* 111–135.

Prior, M. E. Bacon's man of science. In P. P. Wiener and A. Noland (Eds.), *Roots of scientific thought.* New York: Basic Books, 1957. Pp. 382–389.

Rieff, P. *Freud: The mind of the moralist.* New York: Viking Press, 1959.

Russell, B. *Wisdom of the west.* Garden City, N.Y.: Doubleday & Co., 1959.

Schrödinger, E. *Science theory and man.* New York: Dover Publications, 1957.

Skinner, B. F. Are theories of learning necessary? *Psychological Review,* 1950, *57,* 193–216.

Spence, K. W. Theoretical interpretations of learning. In C. P. Stone (Ed.), *Comparative psychology,* 3rd ed. Englewood Cliffs, N.J.: Prentice-Hall, 1951. Pp. 239–291.

Spence, K. W. *Behavior theory and conditioning.* New Haven: Yale University Press, 1956.

Stafford, J. W. Fact, law, and theory in psychology. *Journal of General Psychology,* 1954, *51,* 61–67.

Voltaire, F. M. A. *Candide.* New York: J. J. Little & Ives, 1930.

Zilsel, E. The origins of Gilbert's scientific method. In P. P. Wiener and A. Noland (Eds.), *Roots of scientific thought.* New York: Basic Books, 1957. Pp. 219–250.

The Enigmas of Control and Prediction for a Science of Man

Introduction

The phrase "to control and predict" has exerted great influence on the development of the discipline of psychology, not only as a key phrase in the definition of what constitutes scientific psychology, but also as a kind of verbal adhesive which binds the various psychological specialties. There is just enough latitude in use and definition of these words that psychologists of any bent can say with relief that they too "control and predict behavior." This very likely represents the constructive utility of language, and the fact that this shopworn phrase has attained such eminence is not disturbing in itself. But if an easy acceptance of this professional self-definition serves to mask ethical issues, then it behooves the psychologist, as one who often deals directly with the lives of people, to ask himself, "What precisely do these terms signify?" Is the clinician's goal to control the behavior of his client, to predict the outcome of his client's contacts with him, to plan in advance a therapeutic schedule of reinforcements? The denotations and significations of "control and prediction" are not clear-cut. To dismiss their importance, however, would be naive in the extreme, if only because of the dramatic and exciting advances of science. Since these terms define scientific psychology, and since achievement breeds idealization, positive halo effects may spread to the terms per se, leading to easy generalizations and consequent confusion when we turn to ethical and/or aesthetic issues — issues which also have something to say about behavior.

We have already seen in Chapter V that the phrase "control and prediction" is an important elucidation of the concept of validating evi-

132

dence. It originated in the mechanistic world view promulgated by Newton, who constructed experimental machines to observe the flux of cause and effect in natural law. The phrase, if not actually brought into psychology by John B. Watson, was at least given its greatest impetus by him. Watson was a student in the laboratory of James Rowland Angell at the University of Chicago early in this century, and his behavioristic point of view drew strength from the intellectual tradition of functionalism then being furthered by Angell and John Dewey. Let us return to the opening statement of behaviorism made by Watson:

> Psychology as the behaviorist views it is a purely objective experimental branch of natural science. Its theoretical goal is the prediction and control of behavior. Introspection forms no essential part of its methods, nor is the scientific value of its data dependent upon the readiness with which they lend themselves to interpretation in terms of consciousness. The behaviorist, in his efforts to get a unitary scheme of animal response, recognizes no dividing line between man and brute (1913, p. 158).

The implications of this credo of behaviorism blur more distinctions than merely those dividing man and brute. Behavior is behavior, whether it is manifested in the laboratory or at a cocktail party. Thus, Watson claimed that advertising and psychopathology are "truly scientific" (p. 169), for they deal with control and prediction of behavior. But in what sense? Are they scientific because they make use of validating evidence, or because they attempt to manipulate — to control and predict — the lives of people? A distinction of this sort is not relevant to the behavioristic viewpoint, for it is a neo-Newtonian world view of interlocking laws obeying a mechanistic principle of antecedent-consequent event. To validate is to capitalize on the regular flux of such natural laws. To apply this knowledge — to manipulate and thereby make advances for mankind — is part and parcel of the validating process. Since the laws are there, in any case, it is better to have a conscious than an accidental progress (to use Dewey's phrasing; 1916, p. 266). Therefore, when Watson slips into the following usage of control he is not changing the meaning according to his fundamental outlook: "It is . . . part of the function of psychology to establish laws or *principles for the control of human action* so that it can aid organized society in its endeavors to prevent failures in such adjustments" (1917, p. 329).

But for those who do not hold to the behavioristic viewpoint, this is decidedly a shift in meaning. For those clinical psychologists who think of themselves as consciously striving *not* to control the lives of their psychotherapeutic clients, the program outlined by Watson to find laws for the control of human action is most certainly unpalatable, at least as it applies to the therapeutic relationship. In fact, such a program represents an ethic going distinctly against the fundamental ethical principles they follow as psychotherapists. The difficult and emotion-laden problem of ethics is receiving more and more consideration in psychology, and much of the discourse concerns the use of the term "control," though very often "and predict" is tacked on automatically. The writer has observed that often in such discussions the meaning of the phrase shifts between the way it is used by the behaviorist and the way it is used by the non-behaviorist. Before turning to the problem of ethics and science generally, we shall first identify three ways in which the phrase is used.

Usages of "Control and Prediction"

The writer contends that there are three major usages of the phrase "control and prediction" in psychology, and that misunderstandings sometimes arise because we do not make the distinctions between them clear in our verbal exchanges. The toughminded experimentalist occasionally feels his clinical peer is bringing ethical considerations into the discussion unnecessarily. The clinician, in turn, feels he is being led to say that he controls the behavior of his client, when in fact he is striving *not* to control client behavior. To help clear up such points of confusion, it seems profitable to take up in turn the three ways in which the phrase "control and prediction" may be used. We argue that psychologists use this phrase (1) methodologically, as part of a "theory of knowledge"; (2) theoretically, as a "language of theoretical description"; and (3) as a "means of social control," which takes us into the realm of ethics.

Theory of Knowledge

We noted in Chapters IV and V that knowledge is contingent upon both theoretical *and* methodological factors, and outlined there the nature of validating evidence, which hinges upon the phrase "to control and predict." This seems the most legitimate use of the phrase, as a summary term for what the scientist "does" to prove his theoretical case. In this sense, it is certainly true that all psychologists as scientists aim to control and predict behavior. For this usage refers to the predetermined construction of experimental designs, selection of probability levels, construction of actuarial tables, and so on, all of which go into the production of validating evidence. We control as best we can the empirically defined variables which we feel are relevant to our hypothesis and predict the outcome in such a way that our peers will take our facts (verified hypotheses) seriously. Empirical validation demands that our peers give our verified hypotheses at least minimal attention. In this sense, experimentation is the great equalizer. It makes any man potentially as important as any other man when he sits down to "talk science."

Anyone who would not agree to this procedure for accruing knowledge — no matter how limited that knowledge is at any particular time — cannot be permitted to sit at the conference table of scientific knowledge. This standard is the tie that binds all scientific disciplines. It is properly referred to as a theory of knowledge, and we owe the early extraspective psychologists a great debt for their forceful promulgation of this ground rule. Today, no one denies its importance, although many are impatient with the need to construct an experimental design to demonstrate what is for them a "truism."

Before leaving this topic, it should be recalled that there are two methods — the research *and* the cognitive — and that some psychologists would like to consider a certain contribution which the *latter* method makes to the scientific process. The neo-behaviorist position often demands that, ideally, the research experimenter must *literally control* observed behavior, much as one might control a marionette on strings. In this case the strings would be natural laws, or lawfulness, and the fact that the experimenter predicts "Look, I'll reinforce that pigeon so that he'll walk a figure eight" clearly demonstrates that the experimenter has knowledge — rock-bottom, non-speculative, non-theoretical knowledge. As Skinner put it: "When we have achieved a practical control over the organism, theories of behavior lose their point" (1956, p. 231). Like mental or verbal contents, theoretical contents are epiphenomena in the face of practical control. Here is the right wing speaking out on the matter of science through experimentation, the *only* method it takes to be scientific.

The left wing is more sympathetic to procedural test in theoretical speculation as one aspect of science. It stresses control as a *logical,* and not only a literal activity of the experimenter. Since the experimenter is seen as initiating the process, he is given more leeway to reason through on the important variables, dismissing some on the basis of procedural evidence, in the belief that if he is wrong the oversight will work against his finding subsequent experimental verification (see

"The Line of Development," Chapter VIII). Constructs are more likely to be applied in bold sweep, presumably with more meaning but with less overt precision. Indeed, one-to-one precision is not seen as essential, and probabilities are accepted as the natural course of events. It would take a fantastic apparatus to insist upon literal experimental control before studying the machinations of, say, the stock market, today or at any time. Proponents of the left argue that their method never enslaves them, never limits their range of interest.

Language of Description

There is a way of using these terms as constructs — to classify the typical personality patterns of people — which is best thought of as a means of behavioral and/or theoretical description (see Chapter III). So-called prediction is continually used as an informal method of behavioral description in routine assessment statements. In fact, all one need do to predict is to make a personality statement — any statement — about another person. If we say, "Jim is hostile," since we are in a time-bound universe, what we are doing in this sense is predicting that the next time Jim gets a chance to behave, his behavior will be patently hostile. But this is hardly the same usage implied in predicting to validate an experimental hypothesis. For one thing, this makes all such statements predictions, when often they are not, as in the case of descriptive definitions. Second, as Stone (1952) has already noted, such informal clinical hypotheses do not always allow for a clear-cut confirmation or negation, since evaluation at the criterion end (what is hostile behavior?) is rarely as well defined as it would be in an experiment.

The experimental subject is never in the position of some psychotherapy clients, who are "damned" no matter how they behave. Criteria for his behavior have been carefully worked out in advance to meet the demands of validation. If we define as hostile behavior flushing in the face, pushing and shoving, heated discussion, and so on, and then find that our experimental subject behaves docilely, mutely, and without open displays of emotion following administration of an experimental frustration, we cannot resort to "reaction formation" or "repressed hostility" as a theoretical justification after the experimental treatment has been carried out. However, in the clinic, such *post hoc* or other justifications for client hostility are always possible (and sometimes accurate, but sometimes not).

Perhaps "control," as a descriptive term, is even more likely to obscure issues than "prediction." If one person is speaking and a second listening, we sometimes hear it said that the former is controlling the latter's behavior, or that a reciprocal control is in effect. Skinner includes as techniques of control education, seduction, moral suasion, and threats of force, and he even hints that the "tyranny of the beautiful woman" (Skinner, 1955, p. 549) may be so conceived. "Control" in this sense is a descriptive attempt to subsume all forms of influence for consideration and the elucidation of a point, but it must not be equated with or even compared to the notion of experimental control.

Since an S by definition *controls* some R, as long as it is possible for us to conceptualize data in S-R terms, we can — again by definition — speak of the control of this R by that S. When we do this, we can group together several otherwise unrelated S-R sequences, as Skinner does, and speak of "control in general." However, this should not mislead us into thinking we have added anything to the S-R conceptualization with which we began. We have actually added nothing by changing terms; we have, in fact, expressed a tautology. To add meaning there would have to have been some way to speak about an R going begging for an S. We would have to say that "there" is an R which now fails to follow or to be controlled by its rightful S. But since Rs are always controlled by Ss, we could not say this and be correct; indeed, we would not know that Ss existed if it were not for the Rs they control.

It is true that the investigator might, for example, err, and assume that a given variable which he takes to be an S is connected to or controls a given variable which he takes to be an R; in this case he is merely misusing the terms S, R, and control. Control has meaning here only if an S-R sequence has been established. When the S and R are proved related, when a woman's beauty moves a man to respond, then we can speak of "control" if we wish to do so as a variant language. In this sense, *all* behavior characterizable in S-R terms becomes controlled behavior, and the idea of control is merely the further definition, elaboration, or, more precisely, description of an S-R relationship between two arbitrarily designated variables. Of course, if we are wont to call everything expressible in S-R terms "controlled behavior," then, like adding a constant to a series of numbers, we lose discriminatory power in the application of our term "control." This is especially important when we get to ethical distinctions, as we shall see in the next section.

Means of Social Influence

We come now to the usage which has ethical implications for many clinical psychologists, and, even more basic, which threatens the very assumptions of freedom, acceptance, permissiveness, candidness, openness, and non-directiveness that permeate their theories of psychotherapy (Rogers, 1955; Jourard, 1959). For this usage implies that psychotherapists literally set out to control and presumably predict the course of their clients' lives. Advocates of this approach (Krasner, 1962a) argue that clinicians already do control clients' behavior, so they find it difficult to understand why there should be all this furor about the matter of social control. Apparently one of the preferred explanations for the furor is that psychologists have permitted the American democratic political philosophy to permeate their outlook as scientists (Skinner, 1955, p. 551).

Now, it seems obvious to the writer that the basic reason for the lack of understanding on this matter of behavior control is that the two sides speak in different intellectual traditions. We have here the extraspectionists and the introspectionists locked in debate. If the arguments are read carefully, one can see clearly that the extraspectionists are still speaking primarily about "that" and the introspectionists about "me." One man's ethic is another man's "empirical problem." For example, after first dismissing Carl Rogers' points about the therapist's personal investment in the therapeutic process, the behavioristically-oriented clinician Krasner (1962a) goes on to ask for research on ethical problems ("Let's have the apparatus define our ethics"), and proffers as a defense against unethical manipulation of people the factor of "awareness." Presumably, if people knew what psychologists were doing in studies aimed at controlling human action, they could defend themselves against being unethically controlled. Krasner seems to overlook the fact that awareness is precisely what Rogers is seeking for his client. Rogers is trying to provide a therapeutic situation in which complete openness, acceptance, and awareness are the goals sought for in the "here and now." These are his tools in the job of working *against* control.

For Krasner, the extraspectionist, awareness seems to mean communication between researchers, and the edification of the public concerning such things as sensory deprivation studies (1962a, p. 203). He does not apply his principle to the "me-you" therapeutic relationship. Rogers (1955), the introspectionist, has always placed himself on the line, he has always exposed himself as a "person" with his clients. Everything is geared for awareness and if it does not exist, then a change of therapeutic affairs is called for. To the extraspectionist, who tends to see himself adjusting the mechanical laws of nature, this talk of personal exposure is difficult to grasp. Krasner phrases the Watsonian tradition well:

> A science of psychology seeks to determine the lawful relationships in behavior. The orientation of a "psychology of behavior control" is that these lawful relationships are to be used to deliberately influence, control, or change behavior. This implies a manipulator or controller, and with it an ethical and value system of the controller (1962a, p. 201).

The interesting thing about this passage is that it takes the matter of ethics out of the decision to move from the first sentence to the second. We have science, and we have behavior control, and if you do not stop to contemplate the sequence it seems like the most natural thing in the world to move from the first sentence to the second. Problems of ethics are empirical and come in after the decision to influence has been made; and this decision to influence is not itself stressed as an ethical one. Over against this we have the position of many clinicians that they consciously strive *not* to control the lives of others, not to manipulate but to elaborate and elucidate, to clarify the situation and make the client aware. If effective control could be achieved without the client's awareness, which direction would the clinician take? Many would settle for less control (means of social influence) and greater awareness on the part of the client, even though he may be made less happy in the process. In a very real sense, then, ethical positions are being propounded in these views on whether to control or not control. This depends somewhat on how one defines ethics, but if we take ethics to mean a man's character, his ideals (even those he may feel are unrealizable), then we — as potential clients for psychotherapy — have a choice between one psychotherapist who tells us he will strive as best he can ethically to keep from controlling us and another who tells us he will strive to control us, but ethically so, as defined by science.

And with this prospect, what must pass through our minds? How much faith can we put in this science? If the one man isn't trying to control us, how successful will he be? Science, as knowledge, owes allegiance to no one; it can be fickle — incorrect today and correct tomorrow — and then incorrect again as new validating evidence emerges. Can ethics as a guide for behavior rely on such knowledge to fix its norms of behavior? If a man is trying not to control us, will he let us know when things are going wrong and he really is controlling us, and how will he know that? Will the man who strives to control us tell us how he will do this, or will it just happen mysteriously and wonderfully? And suppose we want to be different and moody and slightly blue — will this be all right or will we have to smile and like to be with other "happy" people?

These are only a few of the questions which must pass through the mind of the man in the apparatus. But such questions are not reality-oriented, from the extraspectionist's point of view. For, have we not proved that clinicians *do* in fact control behavior, whether they admit it or not? The writer asserts that we most certainly have *not* proved that all clinicians or even most clinicians "deliberately influence, control, or change behavior" (Krasner, 1962a, p. 201). Clinicians certainly influence in the S-R "language of description" sense described above. But then, so does everyone who "behaves" within an S-R perspective. This is the practical result of the abstract character of S-R terminology (see Chapter II). Surely such a usage obscures the significance of the word "control," and the clinician cannot be singled out as this form of "controller" any more than another individual with whom the client comes in the most casual contact. The clinician influences through his interpretations or his uh-huhs and the cigarette girl influences through her smile; who is to say which individual exerted the greater control or the greater influence on the client's self-confidence this day, the therapist or the cigarette girl?

But to assert that clinicians set out *deliberately* (means of social influence) to influence a client *this* way over *that* way is certainly fallacious for many therapeutic orientations. This is not to say that what a clinician believes in will not influence his client in some fashion (theory of knowledge evidence may establish this); rather, it is to say that the clinician does not consciously plan beforehand to control his client, and indeed his ethical stand often dictates against this. Extraspectionists make no distinction between deliberate fore-planning and what can be demonstrated through observing lawful regularities in "that, over there." There is a kind of observer's error that they make: "What we don't need to distinguish in order to predict doesn't exist; and what we do distinguish so that we can predict does exist." So control becomes control. If Rogers influences (i.e., reinforces) his client through fore-planned, directive counseling, this is control; and if he influences his client through non-foreplanned, non-directive counseling, this is also control. What constitutes non-control? Why, non-influence, of course. So, through this kind of logic, non-directive and directive are equated on the matter of controlling behavior.

If we teach a pigeon to walk a figure eight through reinforcement by successive approximations, we have certainly demonstrated knowledge of how behavior is shaped (theory of knowledge). But the subtle question remains — and it is either an aesthetic or an ethical (means of social influence) one — "why a figure eight and not a circle?" To answer this question, the extraspectionist would have to talk about himself and not about the hard data. This kind of ethical talk (really, "final cause") is likely to be passed over. He could hardly ask that we do a study to determine which is better: to deliberately control a pigeon to make an eight-walk or a circle-walk. If we had chosen a circle in preference to a figure eight to begin with, and this is certainly a deliberate choice, at the completion of training this would have still been an example of control. But who would argue that there is no difference between the figure eight and the circle, at least from the pigeon's perspective? Perhaps if pigeons could know — that is, had the awareness — that this experimenter preferred eights to circles whereas that experimenter held the opposite preference, and if they had a choice, no matter what the current walking vogue was among their feathered peers, certain pigeons might pick one experimenter over another to collaborate with. Or, they might prefer other alternatives not now in the experimenter's repertoire. Carrying the analogy to psychotherapy, this is the way many clinicians would like to see the matter of ethics discussed.

In the writer's opinion, the only real distinction the extraspectionist, Skinner, makes in his thinking about controls is that between positive and negative reinforcement (Rogers and Skinner, 1956). His personal ethics dictate that so long as positive reinforcements are used to control behavior, and the controller is unselfish (Skinner, 1956), then the palatability of social control (means of social influence) is greatly enhanced. He was understandably hurt, then, when his novel *Walden Two* (1948) was badly received by certain critics (Rogers and Skinner, 1956, p. 1059). It is the story of a brilliant, unselfish behavioral scientist by the name of Frazier, who establishes a utopian community through the Promethean task of setting natural behavioral laws right so that a small body of people find communal happiness and an enriched personal life. Skinner once again puts the blame on the democratic traditions of this country and concludes that the only thing wrong with his Utopia so far as he can see is that someone (Frazier) "planned it that way" (p. 1059). Though we might question the legitimacy of the claims made against over-generalized democratic ideals, we suggest that Skinner has put his finger on the real source of irritation in the latter comment. The book is a monument to the achievement of one man — the successful extra-spectionist who put things in order, *à la* Laplace. For the reader who finds it difficult or impossible to identify with Frazier, as he stretches out on the hill overlooking Walden Two, all that is left is the apparatus, the controlled existence in the valley below. Therefore, the author must absorb the hostility this generates in his reader.

This is the real lesson of awareness. Skinner's readers, like Rogerian clients in psychotherapy, assuming they are not so disturbed that they have lost all sense of reality, would prefer to be "in" on the developing process of change which we have been calling control. A client — or a book reader — who feels used is one who feels hostile, no matter how well-intentioned and unselfish the control exerted was meant to be. In the book, the Walden Two residents were *not* aware of what had taken place; they only realized that they were happy or content. Such happiness the reader does not want, such contentment he cannot find. For he realizes that only through a covert control could he feel that good. Someone once said that a man is free who is conscious of being the author of the law he obeys. Although Frazier is presented not as the author but the "discoverer" of the laws guiding Walden Two, he is certainly presented as the person most conscious, most aware of them. Of course, we are taking the book's content at face value here. There is obviously the real question of whether or not such setting straight of natural laws could ever be possible. Considering the developments of physical science to date, the recognition of man's personal bias in his view of reality, the fact that more than one law of gravitation is capable of functioning adequately at the same moment, and so on, one wonders where and when a Frazier would find these immutable laws with the correct buttons attached for him to push. Even Bridgman, on whom the extraspectionists leaned heavily in the 1930's, has concluded: "I suspect that behavior control will always have to be on a probability basis — even if one accepts the thesis of the sufficiency of atomic analysis, the instrumentation necessary to completely control any single individual would be so complex as to entirely swamp the individual" (1959, p. 232).

Control and Prediction as an Ethical Position

We have now looked at three ways in which psychologists can be said to participate in the control and prediction of behavior. One of these ways, means of social influence, is seen as the statement (or presumption) of an ethical principle, namely: "It is right and good that I, as a psychologist, with certain knowledge and training, make decisions for others, and consciously, deliberately influence others' behavior in ways which my researches tell me are good ways, correct ways, or at the very least conventional ways of behaving." This is the proposition "for the sake of which" certain psychologists *intend* to behave. As such, it is the framing of a final cause. It presumes a value system which transcends the dictates of empirical findings, and it was for this reason that Bacon wanted to remove such propositions from the rigors of science. Of course, not all extraspectively-inclined psychologists are attracted to this ethical principle; some feel they are empiricists and not social reformers, but in general more extraspectively- than introspectively-inclined psychologists may be expected to advocate it.

Needless to say, there is absolutely nothing improper in holding to this ethical principle, although we might discuss the merits of the position as a professional goal for psychologists as compared to physicians, priests, ministers, politicians, or court authorities. It is important, however, that this position be recognized as an ethical principle, and *not* as something which has emerged from empirical data. This is "*me* talk" and not "*that* talk." Even more important, the other two usages of control and prediction should never be confused with the usage underlying this ethical stand. A clinical psychologist is not committed to accept this principle simply because research demonstrates that he influences his client to change behavior (Rosenthal, 1955). Krasner feels that clinicians place themselves in "the paradoxical position of saying to the patient, 'we will change your behavior, but we do not really want to change your behavior'" (1962a, p. 200). We can remove the so-called paradox by realizing that he has shifted here from one usage (theory of knowledge, or language of description) to another (means of social influence) in the same sentence.

For example, in some of his own work, Krasner (1962b, p. 84) has shown how it is possible for schizophrenic patients to take the role of an experimenter or pseudo-therapist, and, using college students as subjects or pseudo-clients, to verbally condition the college students. Although Krasner views this as a form of training for the psychotic (so that he becomes sensitive to certain interpersonal cues), what he has done here is to show, through actual experimentation, that a patient need not be only at the *receiving end* of social influence. He, too, given the opportunity and the respect as a human being in an interpersonal situation, can exert influence on another person. Rogers is asking therapists to do this as a matter of course. If the patient can influence the doctor while the doctor is influencing the patient, then it is just possible that doctors can permit more patient influence to develop in a therapeutic contact by taking an open and "equal" role with their clients. Patients can be given the "lead" in determining the ground rules on which they will operate as human beings. It is up to them to decide how to run their own lives, with the help of a person interested in bringing them to this responsibility.

A clinician who takes the position, "It is right and good that I should try, as best I can, to refrain from making decisions for my client, even though I realize that social conventions, the force of my personality, and my personal values may very well exert a selective influence on him as we move along; in fact, when appropriate, I intend to bring up all of this and talk it over with him," is stating an equally legitimate ethical position, though it too can be examined in light of acceptable professional goals. But to say that he cannot live up to this, or that he is deluding himself into ignoring the fact that he is really controlling behavior (means of social influence) is not only incorrect, it is naive. There are controls, and there are controls. In the case of ethics, the man in the apparatus *does* have a voice, no matter how the presumably unbiased extraspective observer may wish to formulate things for him. A clinician with this ethic has climbed into the apparatus along with his client. He peers out at his fellow psychologist, who is deliberately planning things for clients from the outside, and wonders what he is up to. Such wondering is at times frightening. But that is how it is when you are on the inside looking out, as any of our human experimental subjects in their controlled circumstances can testify.

Ethics and Science

The term "ethics" in Greek philosophy referred to the elements and components of man's character as opposed to his intellect (Sidgwick, 1960, Ch. I). Ethical study therefore deals with all those aspects of life and behavior which are *good* for, or valued by man. It asks: What are the valued principles "for the sake of which" men behave? Theology deals with the Absolute Good as embodied in the belief in a Supreme Being, and thereby goes beyond considerations of "man" as such. Though "moral" has been used as the theological equivalent of "ethical," in common practice these two terms are considered to be synonymous, and we shall follow that practice. When we speak of ethical decisions, we are speaking of reasoned and deliberate choices between alternatives for some implicit or explicit reason, of preferences (values) for one form of behavior over another or one way of living over another. These are all forms of what Aristotle called a "final cause." Ethical decisions are at times difficult to distinguish from aesthetical decisions, which also deal with preferences (values). Recall that Bacon relegated final causes to both ethics and aesthetics. Aesthetics is that branch of philosophy which deals with the grounds for a judgment of beauty in life. Of what does beauty consist? Since considerations of good taste are based on such factors, it is easy for an ethical question to shade into an aesthetical question; for example, if blackface comedy detracts from the image of the Negro, is it ethically wrong to stage a minstrel show, or is this merely a matter of poor taste in an art form? How do we settle such questions, and what kinds of disagreements are likely to arise in their settling? As we shall see, the ethical thinker cannot find the personal faith and sense of conviction in empirical study and validating evidence that many of his scientifically-inclined friends seem to find. There are certain basic differences in the grounds for an ethical decision and the grounds for a scientific decision as to which way to behave.

Ethical vs. Statistical Norms

The first point at which an ethical thinker is likely to depart from one who is reasoning according to empirical — hence "scientific" — data is on the matter of how to interpret a normative finding. Considered statistically, a norm is the report of a measurement, a count, an assessment, drawn from some sample, which approximates the parameter — i.e., the value ascribable to the entire population under study. Assuming that our sampling procedure has been carried out correctly, our statistical norm estimates clearly and precisely "what is." We can then use this finding as a standard against which to judge any single individual. If we know that 90 per cent of our school children cheat on examinations when given a chance, it does not surprise us, nor do we necessarily become concerned about the psychotherapy client who admits to this practice. If only 1 per cent of school children enjoy maiming wild birds, given a chance, and our psychotherapy client admits to a pleasure in such activity, we judge his behavior to be more atypical and thus become more concerned. This is the way many psychologists conceive the process of evaluation based upon empirically derived norms of behavior.

The ethical thinker, on the other hand, is moved to express concern about this logic based upon empirical findings. For him, an *ethical* norm is not a measure of "what is" but rather "what ought to be." Historically, ethical investigation has been devoted to the finding of a universal rule, principle, or standard by which to judge the act itself, regardless of what the practice is. The Golden Rule or Kant's Categorical Imperative are examples of such universal rules. This is somewhat of a chicken-egg question, but it is a moot point whether ethical principles emerge from the common practice or whether ethical practices emerge from the stated principle. Doubtless there is a certain amount of reciprocity here.

But, from the viewpoint of an ethical philosopher, when the psychologist reasons that if 90 per cent of a population does something defined by the broader culture as being "bad" it cannot really be so bad after all, he has made *at this point* an ethical judgment. His judgment is not *forced* on him by the data. He could just as well have concluded — as many do — "where have we fallen down in developing the character of our young people?" He could still judge the *act* of cheating on examinations as bad, and then also judge himself as somehow at fault for not having checked such a tendency in the children. Presumably, religious leaders would reason in the latter sense if this finding on cheating were actually reported. When empirical scientists discuss ethics with religious, political, legal, and other leaders in the society, suffice it to say, there is considerable room for disagreement as to what is the correct or the *good* in life. There is also room for agreement. The point is, agreements would not be reached on the weight of empirical or validating evidence in any more fundamental sense than they would be reached on the basis of procedural evidence. A question such as "what is the good?" lends itself to procedural biases.

The Criterion Problem

At no other time is the prescribed, predicted, decided-beforehand methodological demand of validating evidence more clearly in the picture than when we turn to the possible use of scientific methods to settle ethical questions. This has to do with what is sometimes called the "criterion problem" in deciding on an experimental test of some ethical conclusion. The scale of measurement of an experimental test must be settled on beforehand in order to validate. This means that when we turn to the test of an ethical hypothesis, we must agree upon what will constitute a positive or negative outcome at the criterion end. We can then decide upon an experimental design and test the hypothesis, as, for example: "Treating others with respect leads to a happier and more fruitful life for all concerned." But here is the rub. In defining respect, happiness, and fruitful life we must inevitably rely upon ethical considerations at the outset, even before we have nailed down our criterion measurements operationally. In this very fundamental sense, all attempts to validate ethical hypotheses must ultimately beg the question.

Many social scientists and modern philosophers are aware of these difficulties with the empirical approach to ethical issues, yet they feel that ethical pronouncements can be put to the test nevertheless. For example, although he notes that science cannot dictate value standards, Herbert Feigl feels that "a mature mankind should be able to determine its own value standards on the basis of its needs, wants, and the facts of the social condition of man" (1953, p. 18). He then goes on to note: "There is an important common element in mature thinking (as we find it in science) and mature social action (as we find it in democracy): progress arises out of the peaceful competition of ideas as they are put to intersubjective test" (p. 18). This is a friendly evaluation of man's maturity, and from our ethical perspective, talk of this sort is certainly correct. We firmly believe in science and in the strengths of democracy. But what makes democracy more "mature" than communism is an evaluation of the strengths of democracy along *certain* preselected dimensions, which frame our major premises. We advocate individual freedom and the expression of alternative points of view over the ethics of the state. We advocate competition and the accumulation of wealth — both intellectual and economic. The "best" (the good) thinker, with the most convincing argument blocks the ideas of his opponent; the "best" (the good) and most hard-working businessman sells his products and thereby adds to his personal wealth. From the Marxian ethic of a classless society, such clashes of ideas and accumulations of wealth must inevitably foster various class distinctions and an unequal distribution of material wealth within the state.

The free play of alternative ideas and the operation of a profit motive are considered ethically *bad* in the communist world, where it is held that they negate the quick and easy redistribution of material wealth throughout the state. If it happens that a communist country succeeds in getting more of its wealth to more of its people than a democratic society, since this is the basic value dimension along which it has decided to evaluate *its* maturity, it could rightfully conceive of itself as far more mature than the "dog eat dog" pattern of behavior in the democratic and open societies. When one places the state over the individual it is possible to think of the *good* in these terms. Let us assume for a moment that this were found: in the communist countries, although there was no freedom of personal decision and expression as we know it, there was in fact a greater sharing in the fruits of the gross national product by each individual citizen. Would this *scientifically* established fact prompt us here in America to change our political philosophy? Hardly. We would cling to our ethic of personal freedom and seek to aid the economically depressed groups which open competition might have engendered in our country. Of course, because of the potpourri of political outlook which our open society permits, we would see many alternative views expressed concerning the extent of government control to be permitted in redistributing such material wealth through taxes, and so on, with all sorts of pressure politics and attempts to block legislation in congressional committees. The communist sees this as *bad,* as a hindrance; we see it as *good,* as an expression of freedom in an open society.

The Goals of Psychotherapy: Intrinsic vs. Instrumental Values

If a clinician maintains that he really does not want to make decisions for his client, the frequent rejoinder is: "But you do have certain goals for him. At the very least, you have some notion of what psychological health is. And you are trying to get him to this point, are you not?" Standing off, the clinician can see the reasonableness of this claim that he does have at least some vaguely or generally defined goals. Yet, to admit in any way that he is trying to "get" his client anyplace seems to strike at the heart of his ethical position. This is extremely upsetting to some clinicians and in their zeal to deny any desire to direct a client's life, they sometimes put themselves in untenable positions. There is a sound reason for not wanting to accede to the point made about having goals in psychotherapy. There is a comparable point of disagreement in the history of ethical philosophy, and it has to do with the distinction between *intrinsic* and *instrumental* value.

On the one side, we have had over the centuries ethical philosophers who believed that each man holds within him the rational — sometimes called the intuitive — power to know the *good* implicitly, and to carry out ethical obligations for their own sake as a matter of duty. There is no calculation from means to ends on this view; the *good* is not the pursuit of happiness so much as it is the fulfilling of duty which thereby makes one worthy of happiness. Immanuel Kant reasoned in this tradition, and the following admonition of his captures the flavor of the view: "act so as to treat humanity, in thyself or any other, as an end always, and never as a means only" (Sidgwick, 1960, p. 274). On the other side, we have ethical philosophers who believe that all men seek happiness — sometimes phrased as "pleasure rather than pain" — and that they decide on what is good in the particular case by referring to this end. The goal of "general happiness" for oneself and one's fellow man is what defines the good of any present act of behavior. The British utilitarians Jeremy Bentham and John Stuart Mill reasoned in this tradition when they argued that pleasure is what people pursue in life, and that the greatest pleasure over pain for the greatest number of people is the foundation of ethical obligation. Man does not have a sense of moral intuition, nor can he be counted on to do the *good* things through rational cogitation; it is the ultimate pleasure or pain associated with the observance or violation of moral rules which directs man's behavior. His present behavior, therefore, is the *instrument* for achieving the ultimate value. Another term more widely used to describe this viewpoint in psychology is *hedonism*.

Bentham was one of the early British associationists, and, combined with the empiricism of Newton, it is this British tradition of extraspection and utilitarianism which is most influential in present-day American associationistic psychology (Russell, 1959, p. 264). The experimental tradition of Watson is practical, instrumental, and utilitarian. Validating evidence demands that we think in terms of a predetermined end, a goal, or an experimental criterion. This is a natural way in which to conceptualize problems experimentally, and we become so habituated in this extraspective manner of thought that it is understandable how we might want to extend it to the therapy situation. But how adequate is this analogy for therapeutic approaches like that of Rogers? He has expressed the introspective, intuitive tradition of ethics, which sees ethical behavior not as some means to an end, but as an intrinsic end in itself. Rogers has a goal, but it is a goal to be realized in the present relationship *as well as* in all relationships that a man is to have with his fellow men (see Chapter VII).

When a psychotherapist states that his aim or "goal" is to avoid controlling his client's behavior, he is speaking about the implicit and intrinsic value of behaving this way *for its own sake*. He wants to treat his client as an *end,* as an entity worthy of acceptance in the present, not as a *means* for alteration to fit some preconceived pattern of what he takes to be normal or healthy, or "better." His belief — like Kant's view on man's morals — is that each man implicitly has it within himself to find the solution to his behavioral problems, given the opportunity. If we then say to this therapist that he is really saying these things about accepting people as they are only because in the long run this talk of not controlling client behavior is a successful technique for *in fact* controlling client behavior, we strike at the very heart of his ethic. We say to him that he holds to his ethic *not* for intrinsic, but for instrumental values or *goods*. There is no reason Carl Rogers cannot hold to his ethic, his "one goal" in the here and now, based upon what he takes to be an intrinsic value in interpersonal behavior. By foisting a utilitarian ethic on him, we are calling him unethical — or at least phony and ingenuine — by the standards of his own ethical self-definition. He therefore has every right to be upset and irritated with us.

Experimental Ethics

In most cases, when psychologists express the view that ethics or the "good life" can be founded upon an experimental science, they are referring to some form of utilitarian ethic (see, for example, Rogers and Skinner, 1956). The view is usually expressed as follows: "If we want to test what is the best or most appropriate way to behave, we must find out what promotes the common good, what makes most people happy and productive." The greatest pleasure over pain for the greatest number is taken as the criterion — the goal (really, final cause) — against which to judge present behavior. We should all behave in a way that furthers this goal. We have already discussed the criterion problem; but suppose that a free and open society could agree upon what constitutes the *good* in life. Would this not make an experimental ethics possible? Yes, it probably would. But let us examine another flaw in this utilitarian approach to ethics by posing an experimental study.

Imagine that we were actually to do a large-scale study covering so-called unethical business practices over one decade in America. Assume that we could systematically vary such practices across the United States, encouraging them in one region and discouraging them in another. Behaviors such as selling inferior products, or using high-pressure sales techniques or misleading advertising would all be investigated. Since inferior products break down and call for replacements, and false advertising might well encourage spending, the producer stands to gain by unethical means. Suppose we found that the economy thrived in the regions where unethical business practices were the rule, so that in these regions there were many jobs, a high standard of living, and much general happiness, while in the other regions there were frequent recessions and considerable unrest among the populace. Are we to conclude from this that the old-fashioned unethical business practices are now good, and that they should be actively encouraged throughout the country?

It does not seem likely that validating evidence will ever provide answers to ethical questions, though admittedly such proofs can be one of the arguments to consider in making an ethical decision. Ethical thinkers can make use of scientific methods to check on their assumptions and beliefs about what is actually happening in a given population. But, as David Hume long ago noted, we shall never deduce the "ought" from the "is." Nor shall we "find" the former in the latter. It seems that the visionary, the social critic, the religious reformer, the "heretic" will always have his place in this world of man. In Part Two we shall propose a means for understanding how men come to project their "oughts."

Probability and Prediction

We have thus far placed greatest emphasis on the "control" aspect of our phrase. Prediction, as such, has been an equally important topic for consideration in psychology. We will therefore take a closer look at what is involved in making predictions. To predict is to prophesy or to foretell the outcome of an event before it happens. This foretelling of the future is what gives validating evidence its impact, and it is the reason for our sense of conviction when such evidence is presented. Since predictions are never certain as to their ultimate accuracy, we usually think of prediction as one aspect of probability. How do we determine the likelihood of a potential occurrence? This is a question for probability theory to answer, and, in answering it, the issue of predictability falls into line.

The Meaning of Probability

Ernest Nagel believed it was impossible to give a single definition of the term "probable" (1947, Ch. I). He cited three ways in which the term may be used: (1) the extent of conviction or strength of belief that we have in our completely subjective expectations ("I really and truly expect that such and such will take place"); (2) a unique logical relationship between propositions, analogous to the relation of deducibility ("If this, and if this, then what is the probability of that?"); and (3) the relative frequency with which a property occurs in a specified class of elements ("What is the probability of drawing a black marble from an urn having 10 black and 40 white marbles all mixed together?"). The first of these types of probability rarely becomes a problem, since it is usually taken to be a kind of emotional accompaniment of the other two. Most probability theorists find their points of departure around the latter two kinds of probability, termed (2) nonfrequency and (3) frequency approaches, respectively.

Though it is true that logic and mathematics have common characteristics at one level of philosophical analysis (Russell, 1959, p. 283), it is also true that mathematics deals with more exact relations between magnitudes than does logic. Logic deals with the process of reasoning, a process which is open-ended and generative. The essential difference between frequency and nonfrequency theorists is that the former approach probability from mathematics, whereas the latter view probability as one form of logic, particularly the logic of decision-making in the face of the unknown or the imperfectly known. The view that probability is a branch of mathematics, making the probable a stipulated ratio within a closed system (either actually known, as with the marbles above, or guessed at through empirical samplings) had its origins in the philosophy of Aristotle. Nonfrequency theory, with its emphasis on the logical weighing of one proposition against another, received its initial impetus in the writings of Leibnitz, and its greatest modern popularization in the work of the economist, John Maynard Keynes.

The frequency view of probability is the one most often held to in psychology, which has been more closely identified with statistics than with logic. Frequency theory presumes a distribution of events, a class or a parameter within which the actuarial possibilities for a given event may be calculated with mathematical precision. We construct objective tests, and capitalize on our knowledge of the actuarial possibilities. But what happens when we must predict the possibilities of an event which has no known frequency, which has never even occurred before? For example, what if one of our clients in psychotherapy threatens to commit suicide. To which class do we refer this threat in order to determine the probability that he actually means to do himself in? Frequency probability is clear-cut in a case such as the toss of a six-sided die. If we were tossing a die, and the number one signified "real suicide," then the probability would be a neat ratio of one in six (1/6). But what about our client's probability for self-destruction? Paul Meehl has published (1954) a well-reasoned analysis of such cases, and he has concluded that the classes to which we would refer this probability of client suicide might have nothing to do with our client, nor merely with suicide for that matter; there are hierarchies of probabilities, claims Meehl, each of which has something to say about the probability of successful prediction as embodied in a verbal statement made by any given clinician:

> The crudest example is to order the prediction (treated as a sentence occurring in the clinician's verbal behavior) to the entire class of sentences the clinician emits qua clinician. This is the largest class and although its relative frequency is very stable, it is too broad to be very informative. . . . We may define narrower classes, e.g., what is the relative success frequency of clinician A when he is concerned with the prediction of suicide? Or, what is the relative success frequency of clinician A when he is making predictions about patients of a given sort? Or, what is the relative success frequency of clinician A when he attaches to his individual prediction the statement "I am very certain about this one"? . . . The best bets will be based upon the relative frequency of success of predictions for joint (multiple predicate) classes, including the clinician, the situation, the nature of the predicted events, and all the information about the individual (Meehl, 1954, pp. 33–34).*

Although he is a frequency theorist, Meehl's soul-searching presentation is far from dogmatic and certain. He impresses the reader with his honest attempt to discover the essentials of clinical activity. The most

* This (and several quotations on succeeding pages) from *Clinical versus Statistical Prediction*, by Paul E. Meehl. University of Minnesota Press, Minneapolis. Copyright 1954 by the University of Minnesota.

sophisticated spokesman for the nonfrequency position in psychology is David Bakan (1953, 1956). Bakan begins by noting that frequency theorists insist on an "objective" definition of probability in terms of relative frequency. He then takes a quote from A. De Morgan (1838) which captures the nonfrequency definition of probability, as: "The state of mind with respect to an assertion, a coming event, or any other matter on which absolute knowledge does not exist" (Bakan, 1953, p. 361). We imagine that Bakan, if he were to take up the question of a client's threat to commit suicide, would be more likely to treat its probability as follows: "The probability that this client will commit suicide depends upon the probability that he would make this threat in his given life situation (let us say he is destitute and depressed), and *inversely* dependent upon the probability that he would make this threat whether or not his current life situation were the case (that he would threaten this even when he is not destitute or depressed)."

This is the essential logic of inverse probability, or The Rule of Bayes. In this case, the ratio of probability is called a "likelihood ratio" (R), and it consists of weighing one probability (P) against another (P) as follows:

$$R = \frac{P(B_o/E_oh)}{P(B_o/\bar{E}_oh)}$$

to be read as "The probability of behavior B_o on experience E_o, over the probability of B_o on not-E_o, under all conditions h' . . . the probability of the experience E_o on the basis of observing B_o depends directly on $P(B_o/E_o)$ and inversely on $P(B_o/\bar{E}_o)$" (Bakan, 1956, p. 661).

If the client is experiencing genuine impulses for self-destruction (E_o) under his life circumstances (h), and if his threats and generally depressed demeanor (B_o) present enough of a contrast to the opposite situation — making such threats and appearing so depressed (B_o) *without* genuine feelings of self-destruction $(\bar{E}_o)$ under his life circumstances (h) — then the ratio (R) is large and the likelihood of a real suicide is entertained. If the ratio is small, the probability of suicide is considered low. Of course, this is a simplified example, because it usually takes several such assessments by inverse probability to make a clinical prediction as to the threat of self-destruction. The client may be questioned, and a continuing series of such inverse probability judgments might be necessary before a confident prediction could be rendered. Knowing something about his financial, marital, and physical health status would naturally help the clinician to weigh probabilities (possibilities).

How does the clinician get to know the probabilities which enter into the likelihood ratio? In this regard, Meehl contends that the frequency thesis is merely pushed back a notch because the probabilities being contrasted must themselves be determined by some known class of conditions: "You cannot apply Bayes' Theorem to a problem until you have specified the initial conditions; and this means to state what are the various urns, and what are their contents" (1954, p. 63). Bakan, on the other hand, begins from the assumption that: "after all, we are all pretty much alike" (1956, p. 661), which means that the clinician and his client have much in common as human beings participating in the same culture. This similarity in human nature and experience is what forms the basis for probabilities. Bakan is recognizing that the clinician must assume the role of his client. The clinician says to himself, at some level of awareness: "If I were in that man's predicament, and if I were that kind of personality, and if I were saying that, what is the probability that I would mean it?" Indeed, the clinician's training should have prepared him to know himself, and to know other people as a consequence of such self-knowledge. If he does not have a broad background of knowledge, he might well misperceive the "likelihood ratio" of certain claims made by his client.

It is fairly obvious that Meehl's treatment is analogous to mathematics. When he speaks of probability he means the given boundaries within which certain events distribute themselves in relation to other events. Bakan, on the other hand, is speaking of the logical weighing of one imperfectly known and unquantified possibility against another. He is trying to capture the essence, the nature of how we cognize in an ordinary life situation. The simple truth is that we often must formulate probabilities on the basis of unquantified, and unquantifiable, material, which will never enter into a determinable frequency distribution or class of events. If we must defend the frequency thesis in part by going to our own verbalizations rather than those of the client, as Meehl found it necessary to do, how adequate can it be as an honest representation of what goes on in actual life? On the other side, is not Bakan's call for self-study actually one kind of frequency distribution, in that the clinician will have many "learning events" spread over his personal life history? How can we overlook this obvious frequency influence on any given clinical prediction? As we turn these matters over in our minds, it is apparent that both the frequency and nonfrequency positions have merit; how then do we resolve things satisfactorily? Before looking at a possible resolution, we should review a few topics related to prediction.

Clinical vs. Experimental Prediction

There is a tendency for some psychologists to equate clinical and experimental activity on the strength of their presumed similarity in the prediction of future events. Sigmund Freud was the first in a long line of modern clinicians who take it as their role in professional life to foretell the outcome of certain behavioral events. "Clinical intuition" has always been a highly prized quantity in field practice, and such intuition must ultimately hinge upon the clinician's ability to foretell the future. Following World War II, there was great interest in cementing the so-called applied disciplines of clinical–counseling psychology with the basic discipline of experimental psychology. F. J. Shaw wrote one of the earliest papers drawing a parallel between the experimenter and the clinician on the basis of prediction:

> The experimental psychologist sets up hypotheses which are in the nature of predictions and tests them. The clinical psychologist does the same thing in reality when he selects, let us say, one therapeutic procedure rather than another. . . . A man's adjustment to his culture is considerably more "molar" and less "molecular" than a rat's adjustment to a maze. The methodology, broadly conceived, that is involved in the search for the kind of knowledge that makes possible prediction does not differ, however. If this can be demonstrated, the distinction between experimental and clinical psychology can perhaps be erased (1950, p. 388).

Shaw is attempting here to weld a bond through a presumed methodological similarity. He is saying that prediction in the clinic may be viewed as a theory of knowledge just as it is in the experimental laboratory. Validating evidence may be accrued in the consulting room. As with the matter of goals in therapy, there is a certain plausibility in speaking about the clinician making predictions and subsequently confirming or disconfirming them as he goes along in the psychotherapeutic contact. Many clinicians and experimentalists have been quick to accept this analogy in method, as we have already seen; but the fact remains, there are fundamental differences between the clinic and the laboratory. G. R. Stone responded to Shaw's paper, and stipulated the crucial requirement of validating evidence: *"Postulates must be stated in such a way that predictions (deductions) from them allow for the operations of both confirmation and failure of confirmation"* (1952, p. 95).

This is the one methodological requirement that at least some clinicians cannot impose on their therapeutic approaches without violating their ethical stands. One might study people and learn a great deal about them in therapy; but to impose a sequence of rigid controls in order to predict as one *must* in validating an hypothesis goes beyond the demands of the clinician's ethic.

Clinical vs. Statistical Prediction

In his scholarly book, *Clinical versus Statistical Prediction* (1954), Paul Meehl proposed a distinction which created considerable stir within the clinical profession. He based his analysis on two types of prediction: the clinical, and the actuarial or statistical, as follows:

> The mechanical combining of information for classification purposes, and the resultant probability figure which is an empirically determined relative frequency, are the characteristics that define the actuarial or statistical type of prediction.
> Alternatively. . . . On the basis of interview impressions, other data from the history, and possibly also psychometric information of the same type as in the first sort of prediction, we formulate, as in a psychiatric staff conference, some psychological hypothesis regarding the structure and the dynamics of this particular individual. On the basis of this hypothesis and certain reasonable expectations as to the course of outer events, we arrive at a prediction of what is going to happen. This type of procedure has been loosely called the clinical or case-study method of prediction (pp. 3–4).

Meehl made this distinction while ferreting out the factors at play in the process of clinical activity. He has been accused wrongfully of desiring to downgrade clinical intuition by some clinicians who have not read him carefully. This charge stems from the fact that he has bravely faced up to the question: "How well do we actually do in making clinical predictions when compared to the simple and straightforward actuarial procedure of a mechanical formula?" In answering this query, Meehl has taken the wind out of the sails of many high-flown clinical intuitionists. Thus, in discussing the findings of twenty-seven empirical studies comparing clinical with statistical prediction he once noted: "Of these 27 studies, 17 show a definite superiority for the statistical method; 10 show the methods to be of about equal efficiency; none of them show the clinician predicting better" (1957, p. 272). Now, as we read these findings and listen to his argument, an interesting thing is happening if we will only take note. We, as readers, are actually forming a type of "likelihood ratio" (R) on the order of Bakan's inverse probability.

When at some point in the future we face the practical problem of either staying completely with an actuarial formula or adding to it our own clinical intuition (which will foul up the formula and probably detract from its precision, if we can believe Meehl), we will doubtless behave more like what Bakan has us doing than what Meehl has us doing. We will not really base this decision on the frequency of Meehl's twenty-seven sample cases; we will make it on the strength of his argument ("You can't better empirical findings") and the evidence he presents ("Look at the men who tried and couldn't"). How *probable* is it that we will depart from the actuarial formula? Since he has not done twenty-seven studies *on us,* this is not the frequency of importance. It is the inverse probability of one P (actuarial data alone) over another P (actuarial data *plus* clinical intuition) which will convince us one way or the other. Meehl is saying to each of us who has not actually participated in one of the twenty-seven studies, "Clinicians are all pretty much alike, so don't dismiss my logic; take heed, and weigh the evidence thus far accumulated." Those of us who feel these were not "real clinicians" but poorly trained individuals, or students, or men with little ability, will not take heed. In this case, the belief will be that clinical intuition can add something to the formula. If we then do a study of our accuracy and find we cannot in fact add anything ourselves, an N of *one* such attempt will probably make us quick converts to Meehl's position. But is this a shift in our probable behavior on the basis of some frequency, or on the basis of a logical weighing of two propositions now taken seriously?

When Meehl (1954, p. 73) turns his attention to clinical intuition or hypothesis formulation, he discusses it in terms of Reichenbach's (1938) "context of discovery." The context of discovery is essentially the same idea embodied in what we have called "theory generation" (see Chapter III); it is the creative act of "coming up with" an idea. Of course, all our theoretical functions would come into play before a given hypothesis was put to empirical test. Reichenbach's "context of justification" is what we have been calling the methodological validation of hypotheses. These two contexts parallel our distinction between theory and method. Meehl, therefore, sees clinical intuition as a *theoretical* act and probability as primarily a *methodological* act. He does not argue for me-

chanical actuarial formulas in the generation of hypotheses; he argues
for this mechanical procedure only in the testing of hypotheses:

> So it seems to me it is dangerous to require that in the process of
> hypothesis creation, i.e., *in the context of discovery*, a set of rules or
> principles (recipes, for example) is a necessary condition for rationality.
> What should be required is that a hypothesis, once formulated, should
> be related to the facts in an explicit although perhaps very probabilistic
> way. But to *come* to the hypothesis may require special psychological
> dispositions on the part of the clinician which are only acquired by
> experience superimposed upon what may or may not be a fundamental
> personal talent (1954, p. 73).

Having read the literature and considered the issue (to paraphrase one
of Meehl's papers, 1957): "When shall we use our heads instead of a
formula in making clinical predictions?" Says Meehl, "Obviously we
must use our heads when no formula for selection in prediction exists."
This is the most usual circumstance, since very few formulas for clinical
predictions exist. Yet, when an actuarial table does exist, it would be
foolhardy to ignore it. Is there any time when the clinician might choose
to ignore an already established formula? Yes, but only when he knows
something dramatic about the client regarding whom he is making the
prediction, such as the fact the client has a sudden illness or a broken
leg. Only in this case, which the actuarial formula has not taken into
account, should he depart from a mechanical prediction; "otherwise,
very, very seldom" (p. 273).

Theoretical Perspective and Evidence in Prediction

Meehl's analysis of prediction in terms of Reichenbach's *contexts*
(1938) provides us with an initial clue to the proper conceptualization
of probability. As one contemplates the treatments of probability by
frequency and nonfrequency theorists, it seems clear that they are trying to answer somewhat different questions. Nonfrequency theorists are
trying to explain how a man *in* a time series is actually reasoning, or as
he might reason if he were to reason sensibly, logically, or correctly.
They are writing an *introspective* theory of probability. Frequency
theorists, on the other hand, are writing from the *extraspective* theoretical perspective. They are consequently able to think of the time
series within which the man behaves as a unit. It can be so conceived,
if one rises above the given situation and thinks of "this event" as part
of a distribution over time. Life situations usually force themselves on

us with such immediacy that we do not think of a present crisis, for example, as one of many which have occurred and which will occur again in the course of our lives.

We are presently in a jam, and "this is it." What shall we do? Let us decide. Interestingly, the decision we eventually make is not unlike the decision we made last time, and it also bears a resemblance to the one we will make the next time we are in a jam. Standing off a bit, a man who has measured our decisions can predict this regularity with surprising accuracy. Is this because we are so consistent in making a series of decisions, or are we maybe *not* deciding at all? Maybe we are just going along in a fixed rut, thinking we are in a decision crisis when we really are not.

People are remarkably unindividualistic to the actuary, at least in his professional role. He does not have to know how any given man came to be an alcoholic in order to predict with some success that he is probably basically dependent and a poor risk for automobile insurance. In the same way, if all we ask ourselves is "what verbal products are emitted by a man?" the question "how does man think?" need not arise. We can go on predicting with satisfying accuracy the emitted products of such mental cogitations. But since Meehl is a clinician and concerned about how clinicians think, the question has arisen for him. Much of his writing has attempted to resolve an introspective problem in probability theory extraspectively. When an introspective probability comes along, Meehl does not know quite where to place it in the scheme of things. For example, in discussing Carnap's "inductive probability," which is the nonfrequency logical support given to an hypothesis, he is somewhat nonplussed: "If Carnap and some of his fellow-logicians are right, the idea that *relative frequency* and *probability* are synonymous is a philosophical mistake" (1957, p. 271). Not having a way of using this introspective form of probability, Meehl goes on to ask for an evaluation of the predictive efficiency of the two types of probability as follows:

> The philosophical recognition of a non-frequency inductive probability does not help much to solve our practical problem. No one has quantified this kind of probability (which is one reason why Fisher rejected it as useless for scientific purposes). Many logicians doubt that it can be quantified, even in principle. What then are we to say? The clinician thinks he has "high" (How high? Who knows?) inductive support for his particular theory about Jones. He thinks it is so high that we are rationally justified in assigning Jones to the 25 per cent class permitted by the formula. The actuary doubts this, and the data

do not allow a sufficiently sensitive statistical test. Whom do we follow? (p. 272).

Meehl then goes on to show how, in a contest with the formula predicting "Jones'" behavior, the clinician would lose; hence, what is the conclusion? Nonfrequency theory is inferior, of course. Now what has happened here? Meehl has not addressed himself to the question "how did the clinician arrive at his theory about Jones which departs from the actuary's formula?" Rather, he wants us to compare the accuracy of the emitted clinical hypothesis with the accuracy of the statistical formula. He has framed the question in extraspective terms, whereas the logicians Carnap and Bakan are *not* formulating an extraspective, but rather an introspective issue. They do not deny the existence of frequency probability, nor do they feel that it has no utility. They are merely presenting the case for another kind of probability, because unfortunately, frequency probability simply does not cover all the issues there are to be explained.

If we pose the question "how did the clinician arrive at his hypothesis?" then frequency theory sags under the burden of explanation, just as in this case nonfrequency probability sags under the burden of performance when compared to an already worked out, validated, and cross-validated formula. Keep in mind that the formula did not spring full-blown from the calculator; it too began as a theoretical hypothesis (with a nonfrequency estimate of probability), which was then put to empirical test. And, as Robert Holt noted (1958), Meehl's twenty-seven studies had formulas which were being cross-validated, whereas their clinical predictions were initially being validated. It is therefore not surprising to find that the formulas performed better than the clinical hypotheses. Hard determinism is based upon the extraspective totality of frequency probability. Since we can actuarially predict a course of events from our vantage point as observers, the compulsion is strong to reify natural laws and simply claim that complete measurement would make for complete predictability.

In his philosophy of constructive alternativism, George Kelly (1955, Ch. I) has proposed a highly original resolution of the problem of prediction. He has taken the opposite approach to that of Meehl. Rather than trying to use extraspective theoretical formulations to explain client and clinician behavior alike, Kelly has tried to draw a similarity between these two, and indeed between all humans on the basis of an introspective account. He begins from the outset to break down the distinction between observer and subject, as follows:

It is customary to say that *the scientist's ultimate aim is to predict and control*. This is a summary statement that psychologists frequently like to quote in characterizing their own aspirations. Yet, curiously enough, psychologists rarely credit the human subjects in their experiments with having similar aspirations. It is as though the psychologist were saying to himself, "I, being a *psychologist*, and therefore a *scientist*, am performing this experiment in order to improve the prediction and control of certain human phenomena; but my subject, being merely a human organism, is obviously propelled by inexorable drives welling up within him, or else he is in gluttonous pursuit of sustenance and shelter" (p. 5).

It is clear that the intent here is to break down the inconsistency of the psychologist who thinks about himself one way (introspectively) and his client another (extraspectively). Kelly casts his lot with an introspective approach by essentially making each man a scientist who sets out to control and predict behavior — in others, and in himself. To do so, each individual "construes" or formulates abstracts and hypotheses about his world which help him to order it and to predict within it. Where do these new hypotheses come from? In explaining how they arise, Kelly eschews the frequency explanation, or at least downgrades it: "The statistical-dragnet method provides a quick and sure exploitation of ideas that have already been expressed or applied. It tends to be sterile from the standpoint of developing new ideas, and it commonly falls into the error of assuming that the greatest volume defines the greatest truth" (p. 34).

Kelly gives the individual in the time series much more to say; he takes a position in opposition to hard determinism. People can shift their stances, or realign the coordinates of their construct systems, on his view, precisely because Kelly has personally construed events from the introspective perspective as a theoretician. If people have regular habits, and fall into line from the construct vantage point of an extraspective observer, that is to the benefit of the observer. That is *his* control and prediction in operation. But he, as a person, is not any more necessarily and blindly driven in making his predictions than is the object of his observation, the man behaving over at the other end. Kelly's view is therefore strong where Meehl is weak, and weak where Meehl is strong. Kelly provides us with great insights into how man might approach his world, but he is prone to draw easy parallels between the clinic and the laboratory, and thereby falls prey to the criticism made by Stone (1952; see above, pp. 156–157). On the other hand, Meehl gives us the methodological procedure for assessing clinical predictions in an empirical manner after they have been made, but he is not very helpful in describing theoretically the cogitation of the clinician.

We therefore conclude that the only resolution possible to the problem of frequency vs. nonfrequency probability (and prediction) is to appreciate that both conceptions have their place. If Meehl is unhappy about the fact that nonfrequency theories of probability remain unquantified, hence presumably unscientific, this discomfort is due to his particular conception of science. Science, as we have seen, rests *not only* on well-quantified evidence, but also on the less precisely measured procedural evidences of self-evidence, the logical weight of argument, and so on. Empirical studies, alas, are rarely clear-cut and consistent in their findings. We are often disappointed in our cross-validations, since they may not completely support our earlier study. *Someone* must put in order the inconsistencies we find in empirical reports, and thereby fashion an unquantified probability of the "true." That someone is the man in the time series, and the way he does this is very likely what we can learn from Bakan, Carnap, and Kelly.

Summary

Chapter VI completes a review of the basic terminology and issues which confront the psychological theorist. It dealt with the phrase "control and prediction," and took up the explicit and implicit ethical issues which tie into one's interpretation of this prerequisite for the exercise of validating evidence. We noted that "control and prediction" as a professional goal was brought into psychology by Watson, who was greatly influenced by James R. Angell and John Dewey. The phrase has three major usages, and misunderstandings sometimes arise because we do not make clear the distinctions between them. The first usage is as a theory of knowledge, for it refers to the predetermined construction of experimental designs, selection of probability levels, construction of actuarial tables, and so on, all of which go into the production of validating evidence. The second usage is as a language of description, in which we try to classify the typical personality patterns of individuals, their impact on one another, and so on. Finally, the phrase is used as a means of social influence, in which the psychologist's aim is literally to control and predict the course of his clients' lives by making decisions for them and then (sometimes covertly) influencing their behavior one way rather than another.

Ethics has traditionally referred to the elements and components of a man's character as opposed to his intellect. It is common practice to use *"moral"* and *"ethical"* synonymously. Ethics has to do with reasoned and deliberate choices between alternatives for some "good," as defined by the ethical thinker. Aesthetics deals with the grounds for the selection of beauty in life, and since it therefore relates to preferences (values), aesthetical questions sometimes shade into ethical questions. The ethical norm is the "ought," whereas the statistical norm refers to the "is." After some discussion, it was concluded that we shall never be able to obtain the former from the latter, as some psychologists feel we might through the use of validating evidence. Since experimental designs call for an explicit, beforehand decision as to the nature of a positive or negative outcome (the good or the bad), empirical investigations always must beg the question on the matter of preferences (values). This "criterion problem" is what makes it impossible for us to hope that empirical studies can in themselves solve our ethical questions. Empirical data may help in the evaluation of an ethical question, but they will never suffice as grounds for an ethical decision any more fundamentally than will self-evidence, for example. Ethical positions are introspective, procedural decisions as to the *good* in life. Psychologists who take the position that they do not control their clients' behavior hold to a non-utilitarian ethic. By insisting that such protestations are merely gimmicks or methods for successful client control, we essentially accuse them of being phony if not unethical.

The issue of prediction in psychology was tied to the more general problem of probability theory. It was pointed out that there are two major types of probability theory — frequency and nonfrequency theory. Psychology has been most directly influenced by the frequency theory of probability, which is a mathematical formulation well suited to the statistical and nomothetic use of test data. Nonfrequency theory, which has a more recent origin in the history of philosophical thought, is closely related to logic. Various implications of these two approaches to prediction were discussed, and the major point was made that frequency probability is an extraspective formulation, whereas nonfrequency probability is an introspective formulation. Frequency theorists look for the class or distribution of events within which to judge the likelihood of a given event's occurrence; they take the extraspective perspective and view their task as one of accounting for questions of probability through the use of validating evidence. Nonfrequency theorists try to capture the essentials of how we reason when confronted with a mass of unquantified material; they deal with the weighing of procedural evidences, some of which may well have been validated earlier. But at "this point in time" each man must decide as to what is probably true, and he cannot rely on validating evidence alone; procedural evidence is not to be denied. There is a need for *both* forms of probability theory, to explain fully the types of data which face us as theoreticians.

References

Bakan, D. Learning and the principle of inverse probability. *Psychological Review,* 1953, *60,* 360–370.

Bakan, D. Clinical psychology and logic. *American Psychologist,* 1956, *11,* 655–662.

Bridgman, P. W. *The way things are.* Cambridge, Mass.: Harvard University Press, 1959.

De Morgan, A. *An essay on probabilities.* London: Longmans, 1838.

Dewey, J. *Democracy and education.* New York: Macmillan, 1916.

Feigl, H. The scientific outlook: Naturalism and humanism. In H. Feigl and May Brodbeck (Eds.), *Readings in the philosophy of science.* New York: Appleton-Century-Crofts, 1953. Pp. 8–18.

Holt, R. R. Clinical and statistical prediction: A reformulation and some new data. *Journal of Abnormal and Social Psychology,* 1958, *56,* 1–12.

Jourard, S. I-thou relationship versus manipulation in counseling and psychotherapy. *Journal of Individual Psychology,* 1959, *15,* 174–179.

Kelly, G. A. *The psychology of personal constructs.* Vol. 1. *A theory of personality.* New York: W. W. Norton, 1955. Copyright, 1955, by George A. Kelly.

Krasner, L. Behavior control and social responsibility. *American Psychologist,* 1962, *17,* 199–204. (1962a)

Krasner, L. The therapist as a social reinforcement machine. In H. H. Strupp and L. Luborsky (Eds.), *Research in psychotherapy.* Vol. II. Washington, D.C.: American Psychological Association, 1962. Pp. 61–94. (1962b)

Meehl, P. E. *Clinical versus statistical prediction.* University of Minnesota Press, Minneapolis. Copyright 1954 by the University of Minnesota. Quotations used by permission.

Meehl, P. E. When shall we use our heads instead of the formula? *Journal of Counseling Psychology,* 1957, *4,* 268–273.

Nagel, E. Principles of the theory of probability. *International Encyclopedia of the Unified Sciences.* Vol. 1, No. 6. Chicago: University of Chicago Press, 1947.

Reichenbach, H. *Experience and prediction.* Chicago: University of Chicago Press, 1938.

Rogers, C. R. Persons or science? A philosophical question. *American Psychologist,* 1955, *10,* 267–278.

Rogers, C. R., and Skinner, B. F. Some issues concerning the control of human behavior: A symposium. *Science,* 1956, *124,* 1057–1066.

Rosenthal, D. Changes in some moral values following psychotherapy. *Journal of Consulting Psychology,* 1955, *19,* 431–436.

Russell, B. *Wisdom of the west.* Garden City, N.Y.: Doubleday & Co., 1959.

Shaw, F. J. Clinical psychology and behavior theory. *Journal of Abnormal and Social Psychology,* 1950, *45,* 388–391.

Sidgwick, H. *Outlines of the history of ethics.* Boston: Beacon Press, 1960.

Skinner, B. F. *Walden two.* New York: Macmillan, 1948.

Skinner, B. F. The control of human behavior. *Annals of the New York Academy of Science,* 1955, *17,* 547–551.

Skinner, B. F. A case history in scientific method. *American Psychologist,* 1956, *11,* 221–233.

Stone, G. R. Prediction in clinical psychology and behavior theory. *Psychological Review,* 1952, *59,* 95–97.

Watson, J. B. Psychology as the behaviorist views it. *Psychological Review,* 1913, *20,* 158–177.

Watson, J. B. An attempted formulation of the scope of behavior psychology. *Psychological Review,* 1917, *24,* 329–352.

PART TWO

Broader Considerations in the Study of Man

Part One has taught us that all theories have a structure and a style which can be analyzed independent of the specific theory under consideration. Building upon this knowledge, a major thesis of Part Two will be that personality theories are best understood as functions of the heuristic, analogical, and technical means by which those who concoct them set out to describe the data in which they have an interest. Differences between personality theories are best understood in terms of such technical variations in the description of data. How does one conceptualize the "human" being? What does it mean to be human, and how does a human being behave in contrast to a non-human organism or mechanism? Can one identify such differences in behavior, or is all behavior the same, regardless who or what is doing the acting? We know from Part One that for any sequential fact pattern in human behavior there are N personality theories which can potentially describe the sequence of events. Many of these personality theories can be supported by the same validating evidence, even though their assumptions about the nature of the data are disparate. How then are we finally to decide which is true? Who is to choose the standard against which

167

we judge the worth of psychological theories — the theorist who concocts them or the man being described?

If it were possible to ferret out the various technical devices used by different theorists as the assumptions upon which their descriptions of personality are built, then it should also be possible to answer some of the more subtle questions as to the nature of man, the image of man, the differences intended when we speak about man vs. animal, or man vs. machine. This is so because theoretical gulfs in description develop when theorists limit themselves to certain constructs and metaconstructs which they take to be more appropriate to their efforts, or more accurate for capturing their data than other constructs.

It will be our purpose in Part Two to draw out all the issues which are involved in the conceptualization and study of man. We shall try to show how and why the non-manlike image which has held sway during the first two-thirds of the twentieth century in psychology arose in the first place. We shall argue that the human side of man was dropped in natural science for a good reason, but that it is now being avoided in the social sciences for a bad reason. To alter our image of man it will be necessary to readmit theoretical devices formerly outlawed, and to liberalize our interpretation of the scientific enterprise. As a fundamental principle and an underlying metaconstruct in the proper conceptualization of man, the dialectic will be presented and discussed at great length. This will be contrasted with the demonstrative conceptualizations which have been in ascendance in the twentieth-century images of man.

Chapter VII begins with a discussion of the origins of personality theory in the psychotherapeutic contact and what this has meant to the study of man, particularly since psychologists have moved ever more from the consulting room to the laboratory in their efforts to be scientific. Chapter VIII then broadens this theme by taking up the role of introspection for a science of man, and an analysis of the causes of human behavior. This leads into an historical overview in Chapter IX of the dialectical vs. demonstrative reasoning distinction in the history of Western thought. Chapter X takes up a thesis which the writer proposes regarding the unique contribution psycho-analysis has made to the image of man in our century. Developing from the dialectical vs. demonstrative bifurcation, Chapter XI then takes up various related metaconstructs which have been employed in describing human behavior, and thus in framing the human image. Finally, Chapter XII shows how this same bifurcation lies at the heart of the clinicians' revolt against what they take to be a stifling "basic science" academic atmosphere.

VII

Psychotherapy, Personality Theory, and the Proper Study of Human Beings

Introduction

It is significant that modern personality theory, which presumably has something to say about man's behavior, has issued more from the field of psychotherapy than from the laboratories of academic psychology. It is in academically poor taste to say that psychology is dedicated to the study of mankind, or even to the study of human behavior as such. Psychology is supposedly dedicated to the study of *all* forms of behavior; consequently, the respective roles of the personality theorist versus the general psychologist are not at all clear. Robert M. Yerkes once proposed that a distinction be made between psychology and psychobiology (1933). Candidly admitting that he had never been a psychologist by interest, "save by reason of the unprofitable identification or confusion of psychobiology with it," Yerkes argued for the study of "introspective and otherwise profitable investigation[s] of mind" (p. 211). This division of ways would have provided a clearer role for the student of personality, but psychology never made such a bifurcation. Watson's edict of not recognizing a "dividing line between man and brute" has been maintained (Watson, 1913, p. 158).

Though straining in the process (see Chapter XII), psychology has been reasonably successful in the attempt to keep all behavioral data under one construct. All manner of behaviors have become "behavior." Such singlemindedness has been instrumental in forging an image of psychology as a laboratory science. This reputation has often been gained at the expense of psychological knowledge having direct relevance for the culture at large, but even this outcome has been justified in the name of "basic" science. But what of man, what of the individual they write

169

novels about, or send off to college to educate, cultivate, and promote his self-growth? An honest assessment would be that formal academic psychology has not seen as its responsibility studying this side of the line which used to be drawn between man and brute. Sigmund Koch has remarked that psychology (as all social science) in the twentieth century, "has perhaps done more to solidify, sharpen, perpetuate, thus obfuscate, the division between science and the humanities than any other 'force' in the culture" (1961, p. 629).

This leaves us with a void in knowledge, a void which has been filled by those who take a serious interest in man — *as man knows himself to be*. Modern personality theory begins with Freud precisely because he had this interest — to reconstruct an account of man from his own lips, to capture man's behavior as historically lived, in one life or in a collective society. It is this heritage to which the psychotherapist has laid claim over the years. He speaks as a personality expert because he has taken the time to listen and to reconstruct a more valid, insightful account of the human condition. He has often turned his gaze to the humanities to see there additional confirmations of these insights. He welcomes rather than rejects parallels with the humanities, for that is his interest — the *human* being in all his manifestations.

By what right can a "therapist" come to speak for man in this way? Is he not, as an applied scientist, merely putting to good use what the basic scientist already knows, or easily comes to know through his more fundamental investigations? Why should a therapist want to make such statements in the first place, since his role is that of healer and not social scientist? Or is it? People go to therapists to be helped through an illness, to be cured of a nagging condition. Some of them might go to find a substitute for other satisfactions in life, to give meaning to an empty existence, or to rekindle values long since exhausted. But no one goes to a therapist to act as a guinea pig in some quasi-laboratory, seeking the distinction of becoming a "case history" for the medical journals. Or do they? This is surely a very special laboratory, for the guinea pig is just as likely to become co-investigator and, as a result, co-author of the study eventually accomplished.

To set the scene for a broader understanding of personality study, we will first consider this topic, the motives to psychotherapy. We must come to see this as a preliminary step, a necessary adjunct to the proper conceptualization of man as a social animal. It is becoming ever clearer that, if psychotherapists need the methods of science against which to test their theories of personality, then the scientific method needs the psychotherapist, or someone like him, to generate proper theories of man. Methods test theoretical hypotheses framed from a certain bias. Psychotherapists have given us man's bias, and we as scientists must not overlook this need to *instruct man* in framing our testable hypotheses about his "behavior."

The Motives to Psychotherapy

It may seem strange and even perplexing to inquire into the motives for doing psychotherapy. Aside from the economic benefits which accrue to one of the participants, is not psychotherapy clearly a therapeutic endeavor? Why else would a client engage in such activities, and how else could a therapist sell his services, unless there was some understanding that this activity would provide a cure, or maybe insight, or self-growth? Are these really three ways of saying the same thing? As we contemplate such factors, it becomes clearer that the motives to psychotherapy — both for the client and for the therapist — are complex. Unfortunately, we have failed to distinguish between them, even though doing so might help us to understand our roles much better. It is the writer's contention that three major motives lie behind the activity known variously as counseling, psychotherapy, or psycho-analysis.

In order to clarify these points, we will use three well-known psychotherapists, each of whom, we contend, places greatest stress on *one* of the motives and less stress on the others. This implies that any one therapist might have an interest in all three motives, but that his particular interpretation of the therapeutic contact — the reasons for being involved in it — stresses only one. Our therapists are Sigmund Freud, Carl Rogers, and Joseph Wolpe. Our three motives to therapy are the scholarly, the ethical, and the curative.

The Scholarly Motive

Students applying for graduate study in clinical psychology often give as their reason an untiring "interest in people." Taken at face value, this interest reflects our first motive to psychotherapy. We do psychotherapy to learn about people. Many clients who enter therapy do not think of themselves as necessarily maladjusted, and many more would so enter if they could financially afford it. They come to learn, to be educated, to be — as we say — provided with insight. The point is, even if some "magic pill" were to suddenly remove emotional maladjustments, unless it immobilized and sent the entire population into a stupor, there would still be a call for what we now term "psychotherapy." Indeed, there would be a call even if there were no scholarly motive, but we shall save this for the next section. Here, we want to emphasize the scholarly motive, for it was uppermost in the hierarchy of motives of the man who first practiced psycho-analysis, Sigmund Freud.

The fact that Freud was not greatly interested in becoming a physician has been well documented (Jones, 1953). We know this from his performance in medical school, where he lagged behind his class for a full three years while doing neuro-anatomical research in the laboratory of his beloved teacher, Ernst Brücke. In 1878 he wrote to a friend, Wilhelm Knoupfmacher, saying: "I have moved to another laboratory and am preparing myself for my proper profession — mutilating animals [i.e., anatomical research] or tormenting human beings — and I decide more and more in favor of the former alternative." * Even after taking the M.D. degree in 1881, Freud continued to be an economic burden to his father by working an additional fifteen months as an unrecompensed, aspiring academician in Brücke's laboratory. It was only after the venerated professor took it upon himself to spell out the facts of life to his young scholar that Freud actually gave up his dream of a career in the academic setting. As Freud tells us, "The turning point came in 1882 when my teacher, for whom I had the highest possible esteem, corrected my father's generous improvidence by strongly advising me, in view of my bad financial position, to abandon my theoretical career. I followed his advice, left the physiology laboratory and entered the General Hospital." †

Brücke was later instrumental in obtaining a travel grant for his former student, and with this modest sum Freud traveled to Paris, where he studied with Charcot and also heard of Bernheim, whom he was later to visit. But it was rather evident from the outset that Freud's interests were never primarily in curing, or in changing behavior, as it is often phrased today. He was of course not *opposed* to helping people, and in time, he became a social critic of major importance. But he seems never to have accepted his role as *merely* the practitioner. Ernest Jones notes: "I can recall as far back as in 1910 his [Freud's] expressing the wish with a sigh that he could retire from medical practice and devote himself to the unraveling of cultural and historical problems — ulti-

---

* From *The Life and Work of Sigmund Freud,* Volume I, Copyright 1953 by Ernest Jones, Basic Books, Inc., Publishers, New York, p. 53.
† *Ibid.,* p. 59.

mately the great problem of how man came to be what he is." * In his later years Freud observed: "After forty-one years of medical activity, my self-knowledge tells me that I have never really been a doctor in the proper sense." †

If he was not a medical doctor, a healer, then what was he? It is clear that Freud thought of himself first and foremost as a *scientific scholar*. He made of his method of therapy a device by which he could look into the depths of man's nature. The method of analysis, beginning with hypnosis, then a form of waking suggestion, and finally free association, was to Freud a scientific *method* to complement the scientific method he had used for six years in Brücke's laboratory. Freud was an intrepid and highly ambitious intellectual, who found it extremely difficult to settle for a practitioner's role in life. It was inevitable that he make a miniature laboratory of his consulting room and seek to find the secrets of *all* men through his "investigative" research — and incidentally, therapeutic — technique.

The technique is properly referred to as investigative, for Freud's approach was very much that of the detective, the exposer of mysteries, *à la* Sherlock Holmes. In discussing Freud's literary style in case presentations, Hyman notes:

> We can see Conan Doyle's hand in the titles Freud gives the dreams, so like Holmes cases: The Dream of Irma's Injection, The Dream of the Botanical Monograph; and Doyle as well as Sophocles has had a clear influence on Freud's form of delayed revelation and suspense. . . . When Theodor Reik suggested this comparison with Holmes (for Freud's technique, not his tone) in 1913, Freud said he would prefer a comparison with Giovanni Morelli, a nineteenth-century art scholar who specialized in detecting fakes (1962, p. 313).

But what sort of scientific method is this? How could Freud think of the analytical situation and the method of free association as somehow analogous to what he had done as a medical student? It is significant here that Freud's medical research activity was almost exclusively tied to dissection and the use of the microscope in histological investigations. He sought the proper locus of the testes in eels, studied the structure of the nerve cell, and so on. On the three occasions when Freud used the experimental method in attempts to validate hypotheses he was unsuccessful, and he never published an article of an "experimental" nature,

* *Ibid.*, p. 27.
† *Ibid.*, p. 28.

though he published several of the structural variety. Jones ascribes Freud's modest use of "control and prediction" as a vehicle for evidence to his passive personality (1953, p. 54). Freud was more the passive observer and dissector than the active experimenter and "doer." To press our detective analogy, he was more the Sherlock Holmes than the Mickey Spillane. Whether this is the correct interpretation or not, the important thing seems to be that Freud very likely analogized from the microscope to the method of free association, rather than from the model of experimental design to the method of free association.

His analytical method, in use, was like discovering the facts under one's lenses in the histological laboratory. Unfortunately, whereas nature provides certain built-in constancies (controls) within the bodies and cell structures of animals, so that laboratory research can in our terms actually come up to the demands of "control and prediction," the analytic situation falls short of this constancy and relies in greatest measure upon procedural evidence (see Chapter IV). It was because of this essentially false analogy that Freud failed to develop the concern for validating evidence which preoccupied his scientific colleagues.

To understand fully the importance Freud attached to his method as a source of scientific knowledge rather than as merely a technique of therapy, we must review a few of the early years in his developing thought as reflected in Freud's correspondence with Fliess, whom he had met through Breuer (Freud, 1954). The letters began in 1887, roughly five years after Freud had left Brücke. He had, in the meantime, formed an association with Breuer, studied with Charcot, married, and set up a practice as a specialist in nervous and mental diseases. The first letter published is dated November 1887, and it has to do with a case which Fliess had referred. In discussing this patient, Freud ascribes the malady to a "weak spot in the central nervous system." *

Up until the year 1895 one notes a decided physical emphasis in the theoretical formulations proffered by Freud. But in January of 1895, as he discusses his abortive treatment of a female patient with paranoid tendencies, one senses a different emphasis. Freud begins now to introduce the role of societal values as introjected by clients and influencing their attitudes, so that "The purpose of the paranoia . . . was to fend off an idea that was intolerable to her ego by projecting its subject-matter into the external world." † Here is a decidedly psychological ex-

---

* From *The Origins of Psycho-analysis, Letters to Wilhelm Fliess, Drafts and Notes: 1887–1902,* by Sigmund Freud, Basic Books, Inc., Publishers, New York, 1954, p. 51.
† *Ibid.,* p. 111.

planation, a commentary on how the *content* of the mind works without regard for the *organic mechanism* by which the mind works. Freud apparently recognized this transition in theoretical approach, for in May of 1895 he writes to Fliess:

> I have found my tyrant, and in his service I know no limits. My tyrant is psychology; it has always been my distant, beckoning goal and now, since I have hit on the neuroses, it has come so much the nearer. I am plagued with two ambitions: to see how the theory of mental functioning takes shape if quantitative considerations, a sort of economics of nerve-force, are introduced into it; and secondly, to extract from psychopathology what may be of benefit to normal psychology.*

These are decidedly scholarly interests. The year 1895 is the year of crystallization in Freud's theoretical development, and he later pinpoints the precise date when his "once in a lifetime" psychological insight burst upon him. He wonders aloud to Fliess whether they will ever place a tablet on his house, inscribed with the words: "In this house on July 24, 1895, the Secret of Dreams was revealed to Dr. Sigmund Freud." †

Thus, by the summer of 1895 we note the following developments in Freud's theoretical approach to behavior description: first, he is gradually shifting away from the purely extraspective, medical orientation which he had followed in his student days and association with Breuer. Second, he has decided that a knowledge of *all* men can be gleaned through the medium of studying neurotic men. Finally, by bringing in the dynamic factor of ideas which are so intolerable that they must be projected onto the environment, Freud is being impelled into our *second* motive to psychotherapy — ethical or moral considerations. Each of these trends continues over the next decade of Freud's life.

Fliess, in addition to being valued as a friend, seems to have acted as a kind of professional sounding board for Freud. Fliess was a nose and throat specialist with a successful practice in Berlin and he, like Freud, had scientific interests transcending his specialty. He seems to have been well versed in biology and physiology, and was better informed on the general science of his day than Freud. We can surmise from the succession of events in the pivotal year, 1895, that Fliess was also probably more imbued with the values of science than his friend, particularly as regards the need to reduce behavior to physiological under-

* *Ibid.*, pp. 119–120.
† *Ibid.*, p. 322.

pinnings when at all possible. For his part, Fliess was propounding an explanation of behavior based upon genetically determined "periodic cycles" of 28 and 23 days. Not only menstruation and biological development, but all physical diseases (including neurological) were to be viewed in the light of such cyclical variations. Because of this atypical explanation of behavior, some of Freud's interpreters claim that Fliess was no more science-oriented than Freud, and that the association was probably formed in part on the basis of two highly idiosyncratic theorizers each needing a friendly ear (Bakan, 1958, p. 61). Whether this was the case or not, the correspondence clearly suggests that Fliess was more the advocate of physical reductionism, and he seems to have had a greater appreciation for validating evidence than Freud. The two gentlemen of science and medicine used to meet in some resort city of the area from time to time, and exchange their ideas in what were called "congresses." In September of 1895 such a congress was held, and we can piece together from the course of subsequent events that Fliess had in fact brought home to Freud the need for firming up his theory of behavior, into a more extraspective, formal, physically based unity.

On the train, returning home to Vienna, Freud begins to write what is now called his *Project for a Scientific Psychology,* and he continues to work on it so that by October of 1895 he has completed and sent off to Fliess three parts of a projected book. In this work he strives to write an extraspective account of behavior, based primarily on non-psychological constructs. He must have worked under tremendous inspiration, but this soon dissipated, for by November 1895 he could write and say: "I no longer understand the state of mind in which I concocted the psychology [the *Project*]." * He never completed the *Project.* At the opening of 1896, Freud surely must have been aware that he had moved into a new sphere of theoretical activity, one which had little to do with his earlier studies as a medical student. From this point onward, we note his rather awkward attempts to explain how he is doing what he is doing. He seems uncertain whether apologies are necessary; he is, after all, scooping up from the depths of the unconscious some of the most profound and important comments on man. He tries to get Fliess to understand this — that at bottom they are both medical scientists, working toward the same goal: a fuller understanding of man. In January 1896 he writes:

* *Ibid.,* p. 134.

The thought that we should both be busy with the same work is the happiest that I could have just now. I see that you are using the circuitous route of medicine to attain your first ideal, the physiological understanding of man, while I secretly nurse the hope of arriving by the same route at my own original objective, philosophy. For that was my original ambition, before I knew what I was intended to do in the world.*

Freud is striving to make clear to Fliess, first of all, that he is not merely a practitioner, and second, that a psychological view of man — and an introspective view — is necessary. But Fliess seems to have been a difficult man to convince. One must guess at much of this; unfortunately, Freud did not save his letters from Fliess, so we cannot document each point. In April 1896, Freud writes: "When I was young, the only thing I longed for was philosophical knowledge, and now that I am going over from medicine to psychology, I am in the process of attaining it. I have become a therapist against my will." † Following this, he made a few sporadic attempts to patch up the physicalistic theory introduced in the *Project,* but by the close of 1896, Freud no longer made the effort to explain behavior extraspectively. His father died in October of 1896, and this precipitated his self-analysis in 1897. In May of 1897 the theme of morality emerges clearly and explicitly when Freud notes: "Another presentiment tells me, as if I knew already — though I do not know anything at all — that I am about to discover the source of morality." ** We can only imagine what effect such talk may have had on Fliess.

In late 1897, Freud begins to use his argument from psychic determinism to support some of his assertions (see Chapter V). During 1898 Fliess seems to have continued to hound him for explanations of behavior in organic terms. Freud tells him that he does not disagree with this in principle: "But, beyond a feeling of conviction [that there must be such a basis], I have nothing, either theoretical or therapeutic, to work on, and so I must behave as if I were confronted by psychological factors only." †† In March 1899, Freud discussed his method — one of the few times he does this in the correspondence — and mentioned a new theme, which came to be known as the transference aspect of treatment: "From time to time I visualize a second part of the method of

* *Ibid.*, p. 141.
† *Ibid.*, p. 162.
** *Ibid.*, p. 206.
†† *Ibid.*, p. 264.

treatment — provoking patients' feelings as well as their ideas, as if that were quite indispensable." * In April 1900 he uses the term "transference." †

Possibly their relationship might have been saved had Fliess been occupied in the same type of therapy as Freud. He might then have come to participate in the procedural evidence being nurtured by Freud, who was single-handedly laying down the guidelines for a strange new subculture. But as things stood at the turn of the century, it was a foregone conclusion that the tension being generated between them would end in a definite confrontation. This took place at their final congress in Achensee in 1900. Apparently, Fliess pressed for an explanation of the neuroses based at least in part on his theory of periodic variations. Freud presumably continued his defense of a completely psychological explanation of the neuroses and noted that he could find no evidence of the periodic cycle. Here is Fliess's account of the argument:

> I claimed that periodic processes were unquestionably at work in the psyche, as elsewhere; and maintained in particular that they had an effect on those psychopathic phenomena on the analysis of which Freud was engaged for therapeutic purposes. Hence neither sudden deteriorations nor sudden improvements were to be attributed to the analysis and its influence alone.**

This is an especially interesting statement. Note the role Fliess assigns to Freud — that of a *therapist* who naively presumes his therapeutic method is the sole mediator of the cure. Freud's method is not a tool for the discovery of intricate truths about all men: it is first and foremost a therapeutic method. Fliess obviously never appreciated the scope and significance Freud ascribed to his method of psycho-analysis. In the argument which followed, Fliess apparently criticized Freud along the lines we developed in Chapter IV, implying that Freud's uncontrolled method of investigation fell short of scientific validation, and he must have added the appellation that Freud was a "thought-reader" who projected his own ideas onto his clients. An attack against his scientific rigor Freud could have sustained, as he did in later years; but to have his role in life misconstrued as that of a therapist was the cruelest blow of all. His dear friend and correspondent of all these years *really* did not understand his true purpose, even after he had tried to make it per-

---

* *Ibid.,* p. 280.
† *Ibid.,* p. 317.
** *Ibid.,* p. 324.

fectly clear to him. Freud reveals this disappointment when he makes to Fliess a touching comment following their quarrel: "The only thing that hurt me was another misunderstanding in your letter, when you connected my exclamation [presumably at the meeting in Achensee] 'But you're undermining the whole value of my work' with my *therapy* [italics added]." * An editorial omission follows this comment, but it is quite obvious Freud is very hurt indeed that his comrade does not recognize that to strike at his method does more than detract from his proficiency as a therapist; it strikes at his *scientific* or scholarly pursuits and the theory of human behavior which resulted from such activities. Freud was not cooking up subjective flights of fancy merely to cure people; he was rather doing the "work" of a science of man.

Freud continues:

> I was sorry to lose my "only audience," as our Nestroy called it. For whom shall I write now? If as soon as an interpretation of mine makes you feel uncomfortable you are ready to conclude that the "thought-reader" perceives nothing in others but merely projects his own thoughts into them, you really are no longer my audience, and you must regard the whole technique as just as worthless as the others do.†

By "worthless," Freud is not referring to the method's therapeutic efficacy. He is saying that Fliess refuses to accept this form of scientific method as a legitimate key to man's nature. This is the bone which sticks in his throat. Little wonder, then, that Freud verbally attacked Fliess with what the latter termed a personal animosity and violence. Freud's reference to the uncomfortableness of interpretations suggests that he may well have tried some "brief analysis" of Fliess on their holiday in Achensee, but we shall never know.

In a few years, Freud had attracted a group of students and thereby acquired a lasting audience. Prompted by his students, many of whom stressed the curative motive, he also began to devote more energy to the discussion of psycho-analysis as a technique or vehicle for cure as such. But his *main* emphasis on the technique of psycho-analysis was always as a tool for the discovery of truths about man, rather than as a tool for the therapeutic cure of man. Not all analysts share his attitude today — some of them feel the reason one analyzes is to cure patients — but this theme of scholarly assessment, of the hushed excitement of unraveling aspects of man's nature never before unraveled

* *Ibid.*, pp. 336–337.
† *Ibid.*, p. 337.

continues to be a major one in the psycho-analytical literature. Psycho-analytical case histories are not to be taken merely as subjective accounts of some unique and interesting personality. They are commentaries on man, generalized from one specimen who has been microscopically investigated. The personality descriptions given have been "tested" and are now put forth as proven — tentatively phrased, nurtured by words of caution, but proven, nevertheless.

How different it is when we turn to our other therapists, Rogers or Wolpe; for both these men have accepted the tenet that objective truths, generalizable commentaries on man, must come from the more universally recognized scientific method. This is, of course, the great failure of psycho-analysis — not being able to sell its method to academic psychologists or to many other medical and physical scientists. The image of the thought-reader plagues them in professional circles. Rogers and Wolpe look to the scientific method of control and prediction in the use of validating evidence as the only genuine source of objective knowledge. In contrasting research and therapy, Rogers expresses it as follows:

> Therapy is the experience in which I can let myself go subjectively. Research is the experience in which I can stand off and try to view this rich subjective experience with objectivity, applying all the elegant methods of science to determine whether I have been deceiving myself. The conviction grows in me that we shall discover laws of personality and behavior which are as significant for human progress or human understanding as the law of gravity or the laws of thermodynamics (1961, p. 14).

For Rogers science is an extraspective activity, aimed at the discovery of laws which can be gleaned objectively from observing individuals who are behaving subjectively over at the other end. Therapy is one such subjective activity, and to do it properly one must enter into it completely, spontaneously, subjectively, as a "person." In his view, therapy is clearly not a method, but rather a form of "subjective encounter," which is the term we shall use for purposes of discussion. In a real sense, the manner in which this subjective encounter is carried out represents Rogers' personality theory. He has recognized this by noting: "client-centered therapy . . . has grown to a ramifying theory of personality and interpersonal relations as well as of therapy . . ." (p. 247). Whereas Freud found support for his personality theory *within* the method of psycho-analysis, Rogers seems to feel that if empirical (validating) evidence can be presented to show that the *outcome* of his subjective encounter (practiced as he says it ought to be practiced) is beneficial, then this validates the essentials of his image of man as embodied in his view of how the subjective encounter should be carried out. Thus, Rogers is very much interested in doing empirical studies of his therapy, and it is the "client-centered" philosophy (really, ethic) which is under test. The neo-Freudians are not nearly so impressed with the empirical methods of science, because they have their own method which tests their own image of man every day, in every session, with each client. Why should they then do follow-up or outcome studies?

Although he comes to the practice of psychotherapy for reasons fundamentally different from those of Rogers, Wolpe shares Rogers' belief in the primacy of validating over procedural evidence in the pursuit of knowledge. Wolpe bases his therapy on the principle of reciprocal inhibition, which is defined as follows: *"If a response antagonistic to anxiety can be made to occur in the presence of anxiety-evoking stimuli so that it is accompanied by a complete or partial suppression of the anxiety responses, the bond between these stimuli and the anxiety responses will be weakened"* (1958, p. 71). If we wish to remove the anxiety-response of a client who is gripped with such an emotion every time he enters an elevator-stimulus (claustrophobia), we might begin by sitting him down to an electric machine and getting him to take increasingly large doses of electric shocks. At the point where he can no longer stand the level of electric shock, we have him say aloud the word "relax," and then cut off the current, which brings blessed relief. The verbal term "relax" therefore acts as a stimulus for the response of good feeling, thanks to the disconnected electric current. The procedure is repeated many times, of course. The next time our client gets into a crowded elevator-stimulus and begins to feel the mounting anxiety-response, he can use the device of saying to himself "relax," and the good feeling which has been conditioned to this verbal term (i.e., the response antagonistic to anxiety) serves to weaken the bond between the elevator-stimulus and the anxiety-response. We "pair" two S-R sequences, so to speak, and one serves to inhibit the other.

Wolpe's view of the role of therapy is *not* as a method. Indeed, he tells us at the outset of his book, *Psychotherapy by Reciprocal Inhibition* (1958), that his principle is itself a scientifically valid one, established initially through laboratory methods of experimentation. Thus, he notes: "Both experimental and clinical observations supported the conclusion that *fundamental psychotherapeutic effects follow reciprocal inhibition of neurotic responses.* The experimental observations came first. They were made on cats in which lasting neurotic states had been induced by the administration of several punishing but nondamaging shocks in a small cage" (p. ix). Wolpe has his technique of therapy in hand as he enters the consulting room. His is not a subjective but an objective encounter, a direct analogue of the methods of experimentation practiced in the laboratory, where the theoretical hypothesis first suggesting the possibility of something called "reciprocal inhibition" was completely validated. He is the applied scientist in the tradition of Newton and Laplace. He studies man — or more properly, behavior — in one context, and adjusts or cures that same behavior in another.

Wolpe does not view the objective encounter as a source of methodologically valid new insights into the nature of man; at best, it is a kind of cross-validation of knowledge already established. In fact, he is perfectly willing to say to the client: "I have no intention of devoting a great deal of time to raking up past history, because although it would be interesting and perhaps helpful it is not necessary: *for to overcome his neurotic reactions it is of greater relevance to determine what stimuli do or can evoke them at the present time*" (p. 105). How unlike Freud! This is clearly the twentieth century, and active "doers" have replaced the nineteenth-century intellectual "seers." Mickey Spillane now sits restlessly in the consultant's chair, wanting to finish in a hurry all this Holmesian theorizing and get moving on the *real* facts of the case.

The Ethical Motive

There are undoubtedly many therapists who practice psychotherapy out of what can only be considered an ethical interest. Either they see in the nature of mental illness a reflection of the ethical injustices which have been wrought upon their clients (see Chapter VI) — a situation they hope to rectify — or they feel that the therapeutic benefits of the contact itself emanate from the "relationship," the coming together of two people in a certain way. Our prime example of the latter type of therapist is Carl Rogers, though keep in mind, we do not claim this is his only motive to the therapeutic contact.

The question naturally arises, "Is this the reason clients seek therapy, and pay their fees — to relate to someone in a certain way, or to solve ethical problems?" Obviously, not all clients have this motive, but there is growing evidence garnered by Rogers and his followers that many do, and that a desire to change or to grow toward self-realization represents at least one of the motives to therapy for paying clients. People will come to psychotherapy to improve, to reform, and to grow. They seek a non-threatening environment in which to examine themselves, in the company of a sensitive and genuine listener who takes a certain ethical stance in relating to them which is aimed at furthering this goal of individual growth and freedom. The client may begin by seeking definite help for definite problems, but in time this need evolves into something quite different. Along with insight, or possibly instead of insight proffered by a therapist, many clients need — are actively seeking — an examination of themselves *in their own terms*. They do not want to be "interpreted" so much as they want to be appreciated and accepted for themselves. Once such an atmosphere is made available to them, Rogers believes — and continually seeks to demonstrate, with some success — they tend to change and to advance under the weight of their own potentiality. Still other clients come to therapy to find a substitute for religion, a new faith, a different orientation to which they can cling to make meaning out of life. Critics of psycho-analysis often claim that this is the primary attraction for its clients.

Rogers published a theory of the technique of therapy even before he had published a theory of personality which could encompass the changes wrought by therapeutic contact. In this sense, "early Rogers" may be diametrically opposed to "early Freud." Whereas Freud filled his letters to Fliess with theoretical accounts of illness and personality, to the relative exclusion of a discussion of therapeutic technique (transference and the technique papers came in much later), Rogers is little motivated to attempt a scholarly accounting of the nature of man as gleaned from his early therapeutic contacts (1942). Later, in response to demand more than anything, Rogers borrowed from the neo-phenomenological point of view to explain how personality change comes about (1951, Ch. 11). But his real preoccupation and his fundamental attraction to the therapeutic situation has always been to further what we might now term "the ethics of self-determination through congruent interpersonal relations."

If we follow his development, we note that Rogers has staunchly defended two points regarding his client-centered approach: (1) He does not attempt to "do" anything to his clients, on the order of Wolpe's use of reciprocal inhibition. Indeed, this would run counter to his ethical stand, on which he bases his therapeutic outcome. (2) He does not attempt to "study" his clients, or to label their behaviors according to some theoretical scheme of his own, as Freud did. He feels that diagnostic and theoretical labels tend to remove the individual one is relating to as a "subjective" person and to put him off in the relationship extraspectively as an "object" (1961, p. 52).

Rogers' early phrasing of his ethic was reflected in his well-known *"Basic Hypothesis"* which the client-centered therapist makes before engaging in a relationship with the client: *"Effective counseling consists of a definitely structured, permissive relationship which allows the client to gain an understanding of himself to a degree which enables him to take positive steps in the light of his new orientation"* (1942, p. 18). By 1951, he had reworded this slightly as the "Therapist's Hypothesis" to the effect: "the [client-centered] counselor chooses to act consistently upon the hypothesis that the individual has a sufficient capacity to deal constructively with all those aspects of his life which can potentially come into conscious awareness" (1951, p. 24). Thus far, we clearly have an ethic of self-determination, and it is sometimes referred to as the "Rogerian growth principle." Rogers believes that people can solve their own problems, because change is implicit in the process of life; but such change is possible only if we provide the individual with the proper environment or milieu in which to function. In more recent years, after many attempts to work out the essentials of this relationship milieu — acceptance, permissiveness, respect for the individual, lack of defensiveness, and so on — Rogers has finally hit upon a meaningful descriptive term for his ethic in "congruence." As he phrases it,

> personal change [of the client] is facilitated when the psychotherapist is what he *is*, when in the relationship with his client he is genuine and without "front" or facade, openly being the feelings and attitudes which at that moment are flowing *in* him. We have coined the term "congruence" to try to describe this condition. By this we mean that the feelings the therapist is experiencing are available to him, available to his awareness, and he is able to live these feelings, be them, and able to communicate them if appropriate. No one fully achieves this condition, yet the more the therapist is able to listen acceptantly to what is going on within himself, and the more he is able to be the complexity of his feelings, without fear, the higher the degree of his congruence (1961, p. 61).

Unlike Freud, who began with an interest in the dynamic features of his *client*, as evidenced in the latter's mental cognitions, Rogers begins with an interest in the attitudinal features of the *therapist*, as evidenced in the latter's emotional responses. The Rogerian therapist is wont to speak of feelings rather than ideas; one rarely "thinks" from this orientation, one usually "feels" that such and such is the case. The therapist need not have intellectual or scholarly interests, so long as he is congruent. Rogers stated as much early in his career: "The essential qualifications of the psychotherapist lie primarily . . . in the realm of attitudes, emotions, and insight, rather than in the realm of intellectual equipment" (1939, p. 284). By "insight" Rogers was of course referring to the therapist's awareness of his genuine feelings, rather than to some theoretical understanding based upon a given personality theory. One does not have to be eased into the "Zeitgeist" by a personal series in (client-centered) therapy before he assumes the role of therapist, as one must to be a full-fledged member of the psycho-analytical profession. In one sense it is more true of the Rogerian than the analytical therapist that he is (spontaneously) "born and not made."

If Rogers is not the scholar that Freud was, how has he acquired the well-earned reputation as a researcher in addition to the one as a healer? It is because, as we mentioned above, Rogers turns to science as a proving ground for the validity or invalidity of his Basic Hypothesis, as well as his belief in the necessity of being congruent if one is to be a therapist. These are the hypotheses he desires to put to test: "It would seem justifiable to say that the faith or belief in the capacity of the individual to deal with his psychological situation and with himself is of the same order as any scientific hypothesis. It is a positive basis for action, but it is open to proof or disproof" (1951, p. 23). *If* his ethic is not to deceive him, *then* a follow-up on clients to whom the client-centered counselor has related should show that they are better adjusted, or as well-adjusted as clients from other therapeutic approaches. He first puts down his "Golden Rule" and then submits its effects to empirical test. Thus, in a forthright and courageous way he has consistently experimented and, as he says, for his researches, *"the facts are friendly"* (1961, p. 25).

Rogers has not found it convenient to limit his ethic to the therapy situation. As with most ethical thinkers, in his book, *On Becoming a Person* (1961), he assembles several papers which extend his view to education and social interactions of all types. As is well known, Freud was also prone to generalize ethical evaluations based on his cases to the culture at large, and he is interpreted today, rightfully, as a moralist of major importance (e.g., see Rieff, 1959). He was the type of ethical thinker who felt he had seen in his clients the unnecessary transgressions of an unreasonable and unbending environment, particularly as reflected in the contents of the super-ego. In psycho-analysis, one can always find an alternative interpretation for the most hallowed and accepted tenets of everyday morality. It should also be noted that Freud originated the current ethical vogue among all therapies, even as epitomized in the outlook of Rogers, that the *client* — later, the therapist — must be as honest and open and self-knowing as possible, if therapy is to proceed successfully. The reason for being psycho-analyzed before practicing psycho-analysis is so that, as therapists, we have already come to know ourselves as we "truly are." Only the priestly anointed are competent to carry the message. As David Bakan has noted, "Freud's whole psychoanalytic contribution shares many of the characteristics which we generally subsume under the rubric of religion" (1958, p. 136).

Bakan also makes the interesting case that Freud, having first traced the source of neurosis to the demands of a repressively harsh super-ego which had been inflicted on man by a Jewish religious tradition, sought to rectify this situation in his closing years. Thus, in his last book, *Moses and Monotheism* (1964), Freud is said to have tried to lift the onerous weight of responsibility for the super-ego from the shoulders of the Jews by claiming that Moses (the father of religion) was *not* a Jew, but an Egyptian. It was not a religious Jew, but a religious Gentile who brought about the unreasonable and unbending type of super-ego which now has Western Man in its clutches. In making this claim, says Bakan, Freud was "trying to remake and rework our conceptions of morality in a way which would make it possible for the individual to live a richer and less hampered existence, freed from the taboos which Judaism had imposed upon itself for its survival and which had been accepted by the Christian world as a way of life" (1958, p. 167).

Although this is an interesting thesis, the writer feels it would be wrong to conclude that Freud *set out* to make the Judaeo-Christian moral tradition the harbinger of the rigid super-ego. Bakan suggests that something akin to this might have taken place, due to Freud's conscious or unconscious secularization of Jewish mysticism, which has traditionally aimed at lessening the rigidities of religious practice and dogma. However, a careful reading of Freud's early theorizing and letters clearly suggests to the writer that his ethical pronouncements were the result of his early scholarly and "scientific" interests. After all, it is surely inevitable that he who can lay claim to being the "first mortal to set foot" in the "unexplored regions of the mind" (Freud, 1954, p.

318) *must* eventually come up against highly dramatic ethical aspects of that complex terrain. Though doubtless Freud's Jewishness played a role in his style of theoretical reasoning — an important point which we will explore in detail in Chapter X — we do not want to ascribe to him, at least at the beginning of his career, a *primary* interest in ethical matters.

It goes without saying that Wolpe's S-R approach to psychotherapy denies any direct ethical involvement or motive. Based as it is on a laboratory analogue, the usual claim made is that the scientifically-oriented therapist refuses to be drawn into any given ethical posture, but rather attempts to speak directly to the variables in client behavior and to control those which need controlling to remove a symptom. Yet, Wolpe is not above making the following comment:

> All that the patient says is accepted without question or criticism. He is given the feeling that the therapist is unreservedly on his side. This happens not because the therapist is expressly trying to appear sympathetic, but as the natural outcome of a completely nonmoralizing objective approach to the behavior of human organisms. For example, when the patient shamefully recounts an extramarital love affair, it is sincerely pointed out that this is no reason for shame, because factors in the circumstances made it a natural thing to happen — as indeed they must have (1958, p. 106).

By the factors which made it natural, we presume that Wolpe has in mind some form of reinforcement history, ultimately relying on natural lawfulness, and that he, as a hard determinist, is entirely consistent in his approach by reassuring the client in this fashion. We do not take issue at this juncture with the ethic embodied in this reassurance to the client, where there seems little desire on the part of the therapist to permit the client a congruent expression of shame, but we do wonder why therapists sometimes find it necessary to deny the fact that they are taking what has classically been called an ethical position in their treatment procedures. After all, if it was natural for the client to have carried on an extramarital affair, it is no less natural now for him to experience the shame associated with this event. On what *but ethical* grounds can the therapist dismiss nature in one context and accept it in another? This must surely be one of those instances Rogers speaks about, in which the rigorous and objective scientist first defines himself out of a situation and then defines his client out of responsibility just as easily.

The Curative Motive

Our final motive to psychotherapy is the most apparent and possibly the most popular one moving individuals into the relationship. People come to doctors to be cured of illness. When the illness has to do with their "minds" (translated by the psychologist into behavior), then it is only natural that they analogize to physical illness and expect some kind of concrete assistance, manipulation, or prescription which might set matters straight. They come into therapy as "patients" in the true sense of that word, as passive recipients seeking help. Many people would no doubt love to submit to thought control from a nice "smart" doctor. If such a patient entered into psycho-analysis or client-centered therapy, he would have a tough time of it, at least at the outset. In time, however, if he also has or acquires some of the other needs — for self-insight, self-integrity, self-growth — he stays on and is lofted into another sphere of motivation. Suddenly, things seem different; he is going to the therapist for quite other reasons. Whether these other reasons will also lead to an eventual "cure" is an issue still in doubt. Surely, if he is in analysis, the period of time considered necessary to effect a cure is dramatically lengthened. Is this not a mark against the technique of analysis? Rogers seems to do well over shorter periods of time, as supported by empirical investigation. But does he really get "at" the core of the individual or does he merely "adjust" the client superficially? If the patient comes in for a change in behavior, why should we not pitch our therapy to this end, and this end alone? Do not many people just walk out of the "insight" therapies in disgust? These are the questions raised, and we are impelled into the round-robin of conflicting attitudes nurtured by different motives to the therapeutic contact.

It is evident to anyone who has instructed graduate students in clinical psychology that many of them come into the profession out of a need to help others, to cure, to fight mental illness. The problems of mental illness are staggering to the comprehension of all. One may analyze the personality of a select number of clients, usually drawn from the better educated, more verbal, better motivated upper levels of the social hierarchy (Strupp, 1963), but what about all those miserable souls who lack the sociocultural motivation or the abstracting ability for psychoanalysis? We have to help them as well. These are not infrequent comments made by the therapist who is moved to cure, to help, or to change behavior. For the extraspectionist, who has gleaned his "insights" into man's behavior from the laboratory, this change of behavior motive is particularly appealing (see, for example, Spence, 1944, p. 57).

On Wolpe's view, we move from the R-R to the S-R law via experimentation, and then take hold of the latter S and manipulate the client's behavior. In Chapter VI we discussed the tenets of this view and pointed out that, in a sense, it too can be viewed as an *ethical* motive to psychotherapy, albeit an unnamed one. We have chosen to refrain from lumping this particular phrasing of an ethic under the ethical motive above, however, in deference to the frequently stated belief by the S-R or "behavior" therapists that they do not make an ethical choice when they decide to take hold of the S and begin their manipulation; they are merely curing or changing behavior.

It would follow that in an approach which draws its strength from the cure or change of behavior motive, follow-up research giving clear-cut figures on "proportion cured" would be very important. It is therefore not surprising to find a comment of the following sort being made by Wolpe, who clearly equates the value of therapy with its therapeutic effects alone: "The only valid measure of the value of any system of psychotherapy is its success in bringing about lasting remission of the undesirable reactions that distress and disable neurotic patients. Success is the yardstick by which alone comparison can be made with other modes of psychotherapy" (1958, p. 204). This is a rather confident assessment of the scope of therapy, but it follows from Wolpe's general motives to the therapeutic contact. Rogers would not go quite this far. As we have seen, he is attracted to scientific evidence as a source of support for his ethical outlook, but this does not mean that he would see great merit in the analogy between laboratory and consulting room. Indeed, his well-known exchanges with Skinner are on precisely this point, and in the following quote we get an accurate reflection of his basic view on science as a tool for the manipulation of others:

> I am not blind to the value of science as a tool, and am aware that it can be a very valuable tool. But unless it is the tool of ethical *persons*, with all that the term persons implies, may it not become a Juggernaut? We have been a long time recognizing this issue, because in physical science it took centuries for the ethical issue to become crucial, but it has at last become so. In the social sciences the ethical issues arise much more quickly, because persons are involved. But in psychotherapy the issue arises most quickly and most deeply (1961, p. 214).

Rogers does not want to "do," to "change," or to "cure" so much as he wants to "relate," to "provide," and to "experience" the self-growth of the client. He is betting that empirical research will prove him right, but if necessary he would forego client improvement rather than violate his ethic. When someone begins getting the urge to cure others, this goes in opposition to his ethic, and therefore we find Rogers getting very uneasy with such therapeutic goals. As he puts it, the proper "helping relationship might be defined as one in which one of the participants intends that there should come about, in one or both parties, more appreciation of, more expression of, more functional use of the latent inner resources of the individual" (p. 40). Live, accept, be a human person, and the potentials are there for self-correction; for that is the nature of life.

We have already documented the fact that Freud was reluctant to take on the therapeutic urge. Although Fliess may have seen him as primarily a therapist at the turn of the century, in 1919 Freud could say: "at the present time theoretical knowledge is still far more important to all of us than therapeutic success . . ." (1955, p. 183). The analyst's commentary is on mankind as a unit, and what may appear to represent a "cure" on the face of things may for him merely conceal an underlying character disorder of conformity to the public norm, or some such. For those of us who have a greater appreciation of validating evidence, this is surely a most unsatisfactory view. But we should make the attempt to understand that analysts shy away from follow-up research not *only* because they fear being exposed as ineffectual, though that may also be involved. They merely question the right of one *method* to check on another, when the two methods are based upon diverse presuppositions.

This attitude of commenting on mankind as a whole is very important to the proper understanding of Freud's views on the curing of patients. That is, a good case could be made that Freud was more the social revisionist than the individual therapist. His ethical message was aimed for all of society, and he recognized a kind of interdependence between behavior change in psycho-analysis and "good" vs. "bad" or "healthy" vs. "unhealthy" behavior in the society at large. In a lecture on "The Future Prospects of Psycho-Analytic Therapy," delivered to the Second International Psycho-Analytical Congress in 1910, Freud noted how it is impossible for a client *always* to be helped by the technique of psycho-analysis; sometimes he is made worse. Neurosis provides a certain *advantage through illness,* and sometimes by relieving him from the burden of neurotic illness the therapist might well unleash energies which will drive the individual to commit those outrages he was trying to avoid when he took flight into the neurotic illness. Freud remarks, therefore, "that our attitude to life ought not to be that of a fanatic for hygiene or therapy" (1957, p. 150). He then goes on to advocate treating all neurotics, even those who might get worse from the treatment (surely an enigmatic statement from Wolpe's view) because in this case some form of *social change* might be achieved:

> The unhappiness that our work of enlightenment may cause will after all only affect some individuals. The change-over to a more realistic and creditable attitude on the part of society will not be bought too dearly by these sacrifices. But above all, all the energies which are to-day consumed in the production of neurotic symptoms serving the purposes of a world of phantasy isolated from reality, will, even if they cannot at once be put to uses in life, help to strengthen the clamour for the changes in our civilization through which alone we can look for the well-being of future generations (pp. 150–151).*

A Confusion of Motives

Why do we do psychotherapy? Quite obviously, the therapy, like the illness, covers a multitude of sins. What is therapy to one man may literally be an act of unethical behavior to another. What is a method of discovery for one may be an invalid source of unessential verbalisms for yet another. Who is to say which factors are uppermost in any given case? Who is to say that one is not as important as the other? This issue gets particularly sensitive when we consider the professional relations of the "psychiatric team" (see Chapter XII) which sets out to treat the mentally ill — whatever that means, and it usually means different things to different professions, and to different "schools" within these professions. Today, mental illness is conceived as a lack of insight, a personality dimension, an ethical conflict, and it also is seen as having possible genetic and physiological causes. Do we treat it with medicine, change it by reinforcement, provide it with insight, or expiate it through a recognition of its moral-ethical features?

* By permission of Sigmund Freud Copyrights Ltd, Mr. James Strachey, and The Hogarth Press Ltd. From "The Future Prospects of Psycho-analytic Therapy" (1910), in Volume XI of *The Standard Edition of the Complete Psychological Works of Sigmund Freud.* Also in Volume II of *The Collected Papers of Sigmund Freud,* Basic Books, Inc., Publishers, New York, 1959.

The Parting of Ways in Psychotherapy and Personality Study

Personality Theory in Classical Psycho-analysis and Psychotherapy

It may be taken as a maxim that beliefs founded upon or supported by the psychotherapeutic contact are certain to be generalized beyond the walls of the consulting room. Freud did this quite by design, and thereby initiated the modern practice of commenting on the personalities of all men through a discussion of his clients in "case histories." These were really personality sketches, reflecting a unique approach to the conceptualization of man. Rogers finds it easy to move from ethical talk as a therapeutic endeavor to ethical talk about man's relation to man in education, business, or international affairs. And behavior therapists like Wolpe find their laboratory analogues coloring their view of all men (see Chapter VIII). The history of modern psychotherapy is at the same time the history of modern personality theory. It is in some ways unfortunate that so much stress has been placed on the "abnormal" features of this theory, with extensions made to the normal as an afterthought. Yet, Freud's self-analysis was, after all, an analysis prompted by certain neurotic aspects of his personality. The period 1895 to 1897 seems to have been the time of neurotic stirrings in his personality. The habit he began of tying the abnormal to the normal dates from this period and saw its original expression in the 1901 work, *The Psychopathology of Everyday Life* (1960). It is possible to accept the Freudian viewpoint, yet reject aspects of the personality theory as evolved by the master himself, such as the literal belief in infantile sexuality. But for Freud, the great theoretician, whose *method* was not founded upon validating evidence, the personality theory he advocated, the insights he provided for his clients to help them along the way to cure, were never to be modified — at least not in any basic way and surely not by anyone but Freud himself. As long as he clung to "therapeutic verification" — i.e., the evidence that a client had been cured of neurosis by analytical insights (see Chapter IV) — Freud's personality theory was certain to run into difficulty. As he acquired talented students it was just a matter of time before splits within psycho-analysis would occur.

Jung and Rank were especially sensitive to the fact that more than one explanation of (neurotic) personality could result in the removal of symptoms from the same client. Freud made these splits appear to be due to the ambitions of his younger colleagues, or to father-son reactions, but a more objective truth seems to be that a growing disenchantment with the *method* of psycho-analysis as a proof for personality theory was developing. Jung was to talk more about the normalcy of man, and Rank was to speak of man's creative nature, but what they really were saying to Freud was: "You have not said all there is to say about man, and furthermore, your interpretations of how man lives, gets sick, and gets well are not the *only* interpretations which can be true."

Since there was no objective means for settling such differences in the psycho-analytic method, short of appeals to authority, and since Freud's students consistently got their own "therapeutic verifications" for their own personality theories, the only path open was to leave the master and make their own ways — and this is what they did. These men were, like their teacher, great intellectuals and much attracted to the profound questions of existence. Their comments — ostensibly based upon a "therapeutic" rationale — were always sweeping and inclusive commentaries on the human condition. Thus it was that, at least up to World War II, the tradition of psycho-analysis and of all psychotherapy was to "lead the way" in personality theory. The "doctor of the mind" was not only an effective technician but a wise person in general. This image was to change following the world conflict, with the rise of social science and the rapidly growing emphasis on the healing professions.

The Transition to Non-Depth Psychotherapy and the Loss of Personality Studies

In the 1915 *Introductory Lectures on Psycho-analysis* (1963), Freud made a very significant comment in defense of his therapeutic approach. After observing that psycho-analysis cannot remove psychotic delusional beliefs, he said:

> Even if psycho-analysis showed itself as unsuccessful in every other form of nervous and psychical disease as it does in delusions, it would still remain completely justified as an irreplaceable instrument of scientific research. It is true that in that case we should not be in a position to practise it. The human material on which we seek to learn, which lives, has its own will and needs its motives for co-operating in our work, would hold back from us (p. 255).

Thus, Freud did not believe that people would come to be analyzed out of a desire to learn about themselves even if they were healthy. His attitude that cure was the only motive to a client was probably correct for his early days, but it is surely incorrect for today, as any psycho-analyst can soon discover if he begins offering his services to people he considers relatively healthy without charge. If Freud had only been able to sell his service as "self-study not *necessarily* aimed at cure," much of the confusion in motives we have already outlined might have been forestalled. One could study individuals, learn from them, instruct others on the basis of what was learned, and build a science of the human person, based upon a *general theory of personality.*

But it did not work that way and, realistically speaking, it doubtless could not have worked that way, for personality study was surely a luxury, and only when Freud could show its relevance for a practical problem like mental health did it become an area of concern. Mental health provided the psycho-analyst his initial impetus as personality theorist for mankind, and then, ironically enough, it threatened to extinguish him completely in this role.

In order to show how this occurred it is necessary to discuss the emergence of "non-depth" approaches to psychotherapy. This term was doubtless introduced by the psycho-analytically or "dynamically" inclined psychotherapists, who were trying to capture approaches such as those of Rogers and Wolpe by naming the one feature they have in common: i.e., they do not purport to unfold a complex inner life of personality. They are not "depth" approaches, and have no commitment to a doctrinaire view on the nature of man. They have certain personality theories at their base, to be sure, but there is not the direct personality-cure tie that we find in the classical analytical approaches. As a result, the "case histories" of the non-depth approaches lack all the color and complexity that we find in the more Freudian tradition.

The rise of the non-depth approaches, and the consequent decline of the depth therapies with their more involved personality theories, can be traced to three major influences. First, there was the effect of a popularization or "vulgarization" of the therapeutic role, extending it to the less scholarly or uninitiated (unanalyzed) individuals who were out to help cure their clients in the most effective way possible. Otto Rank was instrumental in extending therapy to the minimally trained (by Freudian standards) social workers, who were moved by the curative or ethical motive. Carl Rogers was to take strength from this tradition, and to disparage the need for intellectual prowess to help others. Science became something apart from the therapeutic contact, and personality theories were suspect, in that they often got in the way of the cure. The proper attitude for a therapist was something removed from this needlessly intellectualized game of finding "the man within."

This splitting-up of psychotherapy into "curing" or "relating" vs. "studying" was reinforced by the need in American psychology for a proper science of man. It was out of this more academic need that a watering down of Freudian constructs resulted. Shortly after World War II, Dollard and Miller (1950) tried to translate Freudian analytical therapy into this more precise, "scientific" language. They were highly ingenious in this task, and for all practical purposes their work must be considered a success. However, rather then welding the consulting room to the basic-science laboratory, their book merely proved to the behavioristically-inclined psychologists that Freudian constructs could be better phrased in this supposedly more appropriate language. If one defines repression — the foundation concept of Freudian psychology — as "stopping thought as a response," and this leads to someone's inability to "label" items in his experience and to make proper discriminations (Dollard and Miller, 1950), then it soon appears that Freudian terms may be superfluous. Why build up a personality theory of the unconscious mind with all its coordinate notions, such as censors and psychic energies, when the basically scientific terminology of S-R theory can account for the same data? And, before long, as Wolpe and others have extended this tradition, the whole of psychotherapy can be subsumed under the abstract, yet simple and clear construct of "reciprocal inhibition."

We move, therefore, from an initial reliance on Freud to a completely independent S-R conceptualization, which draws its legitimacy *not* from the consulting room but from the laboratory. It is basic science now being applied in a new context. This did not seem to be Dollard and Miller's goal, but they must be considered as transitional in this process of eclipsing the terminology of Freud. A host of behavioristically-inclined psychologists were to follow, only too ready to prove empirically that all the Freudian speculation about personality was something less than mythology, and totally unnecessary to therapeutic success in any case.

The final comedown for psycho-analysis as personality study occurred when it was forced to stand up in competition with other forms of *therapy*. Though the complete picture will probably always remain muddled, due to the criterion difficulties in defining what we mean by mental health, one thing seems certain: psycho-analysis is not any better as therapy than many other approaches, including the non-depth varieties. Every type of psychotherapy seems to garner its quota of cures. If psycho-analysis is to survive only on its merits as a healing agent, then its future is dark, for it is a long, expensive, and often quizzically ineffective method of change which occasionally turns failures into successes by a turn of phrase or criticism of the criteria under which it is judged. It also disparages as "superficial" the obvious successes of its non-depth competitors. Were it to be evaluated on scholarly grounds, however, there would be little contest; for here, Rogers' simple personality theory and Wolpe's refusal to speculate on personality matters would assure its ascendance by default. Psycho-analysis, whether right or wrong, at least aims to instruct men about their natures, though it may not be any better at curing them than other approaches. Freud would have preferred to be evaluated on such a scholarly dimension, but, due to his own inability to meet the needs of the conventional scientific community, today he would face a threat even on this score.

For, since World War II there has been an increasing trend away from the consulting room as a locus of theory generation in the conceptualization of man and toward the psychological laboratory. The "all behavior is behavior" approach mentioned at the outset of this chapter has meant that the behavioral scientist no longer draws his constructs from an intimate personal contact with his data. This "naturalistic" version of science may be so "basic" that it is far removed from the anthropomorphic problems of the man it is committed to instruct someday. As we have seen in Part One, there is a great gulf between the theory of the laboratory and the theory of the clinical office. Even so, though he may not take an interest in the personality of his client for curative purposes, the modern behavior therapist can take some of his laboratory knowledge and apply it in a "healing" way to his client. It is not inaccurate to state that, in this case, ignorance of personality is no handicap as long as the symptom picture is clear. And the ethical theorist, with his disinterested "giving" of himself to a relationship can find justification in what was once taken as verification for theories of personality — therapeutic success! Here again, ignorance of personality is no handicap, because it is an attitude that provides the cure and not some complex personality study. Who then remains to speak for personality theory, and how do we set about doing this work?

Theoretical Gulfs and Proper Personality Constructs

When the locus of personality study began to shift from the consulting room to the laboratory, it meant more than simply the fact that now all observations made on man, and descriptions arising from them, were subject to better control. It meant that man was being framed in different (meaningful) terms *at the outset* of such observations. Whether or not he was correct in his theorizing about man, Freud was at least attempting to write a theory which could instruct men in a way consistent with their aesthetic, moral, and political history. The move to natural science in the laboratory is accompanied by a pulling away from the man we have known in psychotherapy, introspective and "alive," with a history, in favor of the man we know in the laboratory, extraspective and mechanistically uniform, with no need of a history to be subsumed by a properly "scientific" theory. Mars was much the same planet centuries ago, as to behavior, but how about the behavior we call personality in man, even a few decades ago? Is there some "basic nature" or essence of man that we can someday discover or generate through laboratory experimentation, which will stand for all time as a human law of gravity or some such? Or is the essence of man a more subtle point, relying on knowledge unattainable in the laboratory and calling for something akin to the Freudian study of clients in the consulting room? Surely the answer is obvious.

As we have seen in Part One, there are those who would argue that questions dealing with the nature of man are *not* scientific questions at all. They may be philosophical or artistic questions, but they have no place in a science of man. Yet, how naive such claims are, for it is precisely this interweaving and overlapping of artistic with scientific conceptualizations of man that continually result in dissatisfactions being expressed over the personality theory propounded by modern laboratory psychology. We have defined theory in Part One. Now what do we mean by *personality* theory? To answer this we must first understand what we mean by a person, as opposed to any living animal. We must phrase a proper retort to the Watsonian claim that there is no line dividing man and brute. How can one say that questions raised to elucidate the construct *person* are not scientific matters? Is there not the possibility of distorting the data by choosing inappropriate theoretical devices to explain them, simply because we have not taken the time to conscientiously examine our "image" of the data we seek to conceptualize more clearly in testable constructs and propositions?

Wolpe may someday "discover" his *person* in the natural science laboratory, and Rogers may truly experience his *person* in the spontaneous and subjective relationship, but when we come to theoretically describing what in fact we mean by the person or the human being, we will have to frame our observations in *person* terms. We will have to use constructs and theoretical devices of one sort or another. And these devices are not necessarily unique; they have a history. We want now to review that history, and to find out which devices most accurately capture the man we intend to study. The very existence of our science depends upon such a review and careful selection. Interestingly enough, though we may continue to study him in the laboratory, if we use the full range of historical metaconstructs and devices open to us, and the proper theoretical perspective, man will come out looking pretty much like the kind of man psychotherapists have been seeing in their practices for years past. There will still be the range, and the diversity in lower-order abstractions; but the basic continuity of intelligent, striving, growing, self-directed, and even arbitrary human beings as most personality theorists think themselves to be in greater or lesser degree, can be preserved. Neither science nor personality theory need suffer in the process of putting psychology more in tune with the human beings who turn to it for self-knowledge.

Summary

Chapter VII began our consideration of personality theory in Part Two by underscoring three broad motives to psychotherapy. Both the therapist and the client, it was maintained, can be attracted to the therapeutic relationship by these motives, which probably all operate to some extent in the same series of contacts: scholarly, ethical, and curative. Freud, Rogers, and Wolpe were discussed in the light of these three motives. The point was made that personality theory classically has issued from the scholarly motive, and that it is this tradition which has given psycho-analysis a reputation as the "science of man." Unfortunately, due to the identification of psycho-analysis as a curative agent, and the rise of other, equally effective non-depth therapies, psycho-analysis and other insight therapies have been giving ground on the scholarly dimension. Personality theory has been shifting its locus of generation from the consulting room to the laboratory.

Now, in the shift to the laboratory there is a certain danger, for theory is then constructed to meet the needs of an extraspective observer, rather than an introspective client. Further, by attempting to extend the natural science approach to a study of man there are pitfalls in conceptualization which may so distort the image of man we seek to capture that a complete violation of our data may result. It is maintained that the proper conceptualization of man (even in laboratory study) must surely be something approximating the style of theorizing which Freud and other personality theorists — who also happened to be psychotherapists — advocated and furthered. This is not to say that Freudian theory *per se* is correct. The important point is to recognize the specific theoretical devices and metaconstructs which various personality and/or behavior theorists have utilized in conceptualizing man.

References

Bakan, D. *Sigmund Freud and the Jewish mystical tradition.* New York: D. Van Nostrand, 1958.

Dollard, J., and Miller, N. E. *Personality and psychotherapy: An analysis in terms of learning, thinking, and culture.* New York: McGraw-Hill, 1950.

Freud, S. *The origins of psycho-analysis, letters to Wilhelm Fliess, drafts and notes: 1887–1902.* New York: Basic Books, 1954.

Freud, S. "A child is being beaten"; A contribution to the study of the origin of sexual perversions (1919). In Vol. XVII of J. Strachey (Ed.), *The standard edition of the complete psychological works of Sigmund Freud.* London: The Hogarth Press, 1955. Pp. 175–204.

Freud, S. The future prospects of psycho-analytic therapy (1910). In Vol. XI of J. Strachey (Ed.), *The standard edition of the complete psychological works of Sigmund Freud.* London: The Hogarth Press, 1957. Pp. 139–151. Also in Vol. II of *The collected papers of Sigmund Freud.* New York: Basic Books, 1959.

Freud, S. *The psychopathology of everyday life.* Vol. VI of J. Strachey (Ed.), *The standard edition of the complete psychological works of Sigmund Freud.* London: The Hogarth Press, 1960.

Freud, S. *Introductory lectures on psycho-analysis.* Part III: *General theory of the neuroses* (1915–1917). Vol. XVI of J. Strachey (Ed.), *The standard edition of the complete psychological works of Sigmund Freud.* London: The Hogarth Press, 1963.

Freud, S. *Moses and monotheism.* In Vol. XXIII of J. Strachey (Ed.), *The standard edition of the complete psychological works of Sigmund Freud.* London: The Hogarth Press, 1964. Pp. 1–137.

Hyman, S. E. *The tangled bank.* New York: Atheneum, 1962.

Jones, E. *The life and work of Sigmund Freud.* Vol. 1. *The formative years and the great discoveries.* New York: Basic Books, 1953.

Koch, S. Psychological science versus the science-humanism antinomy; intimations of a significant science of man. *American Psychologist,* 1961, *16,* 629–639.

Rieff, P. *Freud: The mind of the moralist.* New York: Viking Press, 1959.

Rogers, C. R. *The clinical treatment of the problem child.* Boston: Houghton Mifflin Co., 1939.

Rogers, C. R. *Counseling and psychotherapy.* Boston: Houghton Mifflin Co., 1942.

Rogers, C. R. *Client-centered therapy.* Boston: Houghton Mifflin Co., 1951.

Rogers, C. R. *On becoming a person.* Boston: Houghton Mifflin Co., 1961.

Spence, K. W. The nature of theory construction in contemporary psychology. *Psychological Review,* 1944, *51,* 47–68.

Strupp, H. H. The outcome problem in psychotherapy revisited. *Psychotherapy,* 1963, *1,* 1–13.

Watson, J. B. Psychology as the behaviorist views it. *Psychological Review,* 1913, *20,* 158–177.

Wolpe, J. *Psychotherapy by reciprocal inhibition.* Stanford, Calif.: Stanford University Press, 1958.

Yerkes, R. M. Concerning the anthropocentrism of psychology. *Psychological Review,* 1933, *40,* 209–212.

# VIII

| Introspective and Causal
| Analysis in the Study
| of Man

Introduction

At the beginning of the present century, psychology was already caught up in serious debate over its nature as a science. Two major issues were being discussed at that time: mind, or consciousness, and the proper method of studying man's mind, assuming he had one in the conventional sense. The introspectionists of that period defined psychology something like this: "psychology is the science of mind — of the mental life and mental development of the individual man" (Ladd, 1899, p. 121). The introspective method was taken as the proper vehicle for the study of mind, and it was even viewed somewhat like Freud's analogy, as the "internal microscope of attention" (Munsterberg, 1900, p. 1). The first threat to this view of psychology as science came from physics. The question arose, could psychology be reduced to physics, to material explanations, or was it an area of study having its own mentalistic needs and consequently unique methodology? (See, for example, Sanford, 1903; Boodin, 1909.) After all, is it not true that man's conscious state makes a difference in his physical behavior? (See R. McDougall, 1912.)

Watson then stated flatly that psychology was a purely objective branch of *natural science,* and that it therefore had as its scope the same methods and procedures as physics and the other extraspective sciences (Watson, 1913). The view the behaviorist took was that psychologists had been reifying neural behavior and making it something independent of the measurable neural events, when there was no justification in this practice. The behaviorist, Weiss, noted that psychology had: "passed through successive stages, from the frankly confessed personal soul or

201

spirit, to the more restricted use of the term ego or self and finally to the guarded use of the conceptions mind or consciousness" (1919, p. 334).

We now have to ask, what precisely was involved in this debate over the nature of psychological investigation? Was it the reflection of a growing scientific sophistication in psychology? Were the introspectionists defending an outmoded, unscientific, and possibly even mystical method of investigation? Although it is sometimes phrased this way by the more empirical, toughminded psychologists, no one who reads the actual discussions of science proffered by the introspectionists can accept this evaluation of their position. These men were extremely knowledgeable about the nature of theory and method (Ladd, 1899), were prepared to discuss and even to accept a mechanistic view of the universe as a working hypothesis (Fullerton, 1902), and in no way seem to have been blinded to the subtle influence of one's method on his conceptualization of data (Sanford, 1903). Titchener's (1914) discussion of the scientific method as taken from physics, with its contingent and necessary assumptions about the order in nature, is very sophisticated and of lasting interest to any student of science. These men do not strike one as dogmatic or extreme in their outlook; they do not seem prone to making naive reifications of certain aspects of their data. They are, in fact, very impressive in their grasp of and willingness to discuss the nature of science.

What then is reflected in this debate between the introspectionist and the extraspectionist? It is no less than a disagreement over the proper *image of man* to be incorporated by the science of psychology. How to conceptualize man, that is the point at issue. In the present chapter we shall take up this matter from several directions. First, we shall look into the strengths and weaknesses of introspection, its role in the conceptualization of man, and attempt to place it in proper alignment with the demands of validation. Then we shall move on to consider in greater detail how it is that causal explanation is directly involved with the images of man now being propounded by various students of behavior in psychology.

The Nature of Introspection

Introspection as Method

Even though the arguments which raged over introspection are long since exhausted, Boring has observed, "introspection is still with us, doing its business under various aliases, of which *verbal report* is one" (1953, p. 169). The clinical methods of interview, projective testing, and psychotherapy are often cited as contemporary examples of introspection. How can we best assess the nature of introspection, both historically and in terms of proponents of this method in recent years? One approach which may prove fruitful is to consider introspection as first a methodological and then a theoretical problem. The great advocate of American introspection, Titchener, proposed that we accept his tool as a methodological standard, a vehicle for evidence which he took to be validational. For him, science was an act of trained observation, followed by analysis of data. The more direct the observation, the better the science. Measurement and experimentation were viewed as "roundabout" ways of practicing scientific observation (1914, p. 43). The most direct means of gaining scientific knowledge was through the exercise of trained, disinterested, self-observation and analysis. It took training to become an introspectionist, and, in theory, there was to be no conflict over findings because trained observers were expected to be reliable observers.

Unfortunately, this was not always the case, and one of the most widely publicized disagreements in the history of psychology was Titchener's opposition to the belief in imageless thought. The introspectionist Wurzburg school, of Külpe, Buhler, Ach, and Marbe, contended that certain thoughts were not sensory-imaginal patterns. Titchener claimed these so-called imageless thoughts were merely difficult thoughts to analyze, and he proposed various weak explanations to account for the phenomena (Boring, 1950, p. 415). No successful and mutually satisfying way out of this impasse was ever effected, and when that happens to a scientific method it means that proof is suspect, even for the more generally accepted findings of the method in question. Thus it is probably not surprising that psychology found itself gravitating toward the more roundabout but also more trustworthy research method of experimentation.

David Bakan (1954) has made an interesting case for what had probably taken place among the Wurzburg group. He notes that, at the time of the controversy over imageless thought, the Wurzburg psychologists were doing investigative "experiments" which clearly paralleled the free-association method used by Freud. For example, a subject might be asked to free-associate to a verbal stimulus, giving all the inner reasonings which transpired as he went along associating to the particular stimulus. At various points in their study, unconscious processes were posited, "will" was introduced as an explanatory term, and even the importance of rapport (or transference?) for proper experimentation was brought into the discussion by the Wurzburg group.

Then, quite suddenly, the entire area of study was dropped. In the end, Külpe's system of psychology, although thorough in other ways, lacked an adequate treatment of *thought*. Why should there be such an important omission? Was it due to the inability of the introspectionists to solve their imageless thought question? Rather than accepting this easy explanation, Bakan proposes a more intriguing alternative. It is his belief that the Wurzburg investigators, using one another as subjects so that they were intimately involved in the research, had come upon the workings of the unconscious in the same way that Freud had. However, unlike Freud, the Wurzburgers were not prepared to undergo the personal scrutiny and struggle to overcome their resistances in a thorough investigation of the unconscious (p. 106).

Here is the core argument for free association as *method* in personality study. The belief is that only through the use of something like free association can we overcome our *natural* tendency to resist revealing certain *truths of our natures* to ourselves. And free association is clearly an introspective exercise, born of Freud's personal experience during his self-analysis. In an early letter to Wilhelm Fliess (October 27, 1897), Freud observes that since business is bad he is living only for "inner work" (i.e., self-analysis); he then writes that his self-analysis "gets hold of me and hauls me through the past in rapid association of ideas; and my mood changes like the landscape seen by a traveller from a train. . . ." * This is a personal account of Freud's act of introspection, and when he later formulates his instructions for free association he makes use of the same metaphor. Thus, in 1924 he explains that during the structuring of free association for the patient the analyst should say something like: "Act as though, for instance, you were a traveller sitting next to the window of a railway carriage and describing to someone inside the carriage the changing views which you see outside" (Freud, 1958, p. 135).

But the difference between Freud's introspective method and the method of introspection advocated by Titchener is that the former is devoted to the overcoming of *resistances,* whereas the latter presumably gets directly at observations of a valid nature. Both theorists believed, how-

---

* From *The Origins of Psycho-analysis, Letters to Wilhelm Fliess, Drafts and Notes: 1887–1902,* by Sigmund Freud, Basic Books, Inc., Publishers, New York, 1954, p. 225.

ever, that their methods were scientifically acceptable and resulted in generalizable truths. In the case of Freud, such truths had to do with man's fundamental, albeit hidden, rejected, and repressed nature; in the case of Titchener, such truths were presumably facts about man's sensory apparatus, his mechanisms of thinking, and so on. The issue of man's nature was for Titchener a hidden one, submerged in the fight over the proper method of psychological investigation which he carried on with his peers.

To grasp better the nature of data generated by an introspective method, we would do well to consider two examples of such a practice drawn from the literature. One is Bakan's (1954) use of the "Method of Retrospective Analysis," the other is Jung's highly graphic account of his self-analysis, dating from roughly 1913 through 1917 (1963, p. 208). Bakan describes his brief encounter with introspection as a "miniature" investigation, conducted for roughly an hour and a half on each of five successive days. He first chose a topic to associate to — in this case "secrets" — and then sat down to the typewriter to begin. Hence, "The procedure simply involved sitting down to the typewriter and typing whatever came, after the decision concerning the topic was made" (Bakan, 1954, p. 111). The choice of a typewriter was purely arbitrary, based on the fact that Bakan found himself most fluent when using this writing aid.

Jung's introspective odyssey began far more dramatically, following his split with Freud in 1912, during a period when he felt unsure of himself and somewhat at sea. As his inner turmoil increased, reflecting itself in dreams, phantasies, and even visions, he felt as though — and surely writes as though — a transitory psychosis had overtaken him (Jung, 1963, p. 176). In 1913 Jung began to sense a heavy air of oppression, and an inner pressure which seemed to have implications for mankind in general. He was seized by an overpowering vision in which he saw a large portion of Europe covered by a flood, and he had dreams that an Arctic cold wave had frozen the whole of Lorraine (pp. 175–176). These he later took to be fateful visions and dreams, for in August of 1914 World War I broke out, and he launched into his own analysis, or as he termed it "experiment," eventually resigning a teaching position to devote full time to his practice and introspective efforts: "I had to try to understand what had happened and to what extent my own experience coincided with that of mankind in general" (p. 176).

Bakan, on the other hand, seated at his typewriter, begins with the rule of thumb that he is to write "as though" the written content would never be released for publication. He must have been effective in removing some resistance by this maneuver, for he found it circumspect to publish only a limited example of his total production concerning secrecy. Jung also observes how surprised he was at the similarity of his unconscious mental productions to those of the psychotic, and how, although such imaginative productions are to be found everywhere, their free expression and recognition is tabooed and dreaded (1963, p. 188). Although Freud published analyses of his personal dreams, and we do have some gleanings from his self-analysis, it is also true that Freud was rather guarded concerning the explicit details of his introspections. This is, therefore, a common finding when one uses free association — he is amazed and often threatened by the kinds of material generated. Little wonder we are resistive at first.

What kinds of data issued from the introspections as reported by our two model investigators? Bakan gives us a sample of his work as follows:

> What is one of the secrets such as *thee and me* have? I once talked to a professor of zoology at lunch about the academic life. He commented that over the head of every academician hangs a sword on a thin string. No matter how much you do, you never feel that you are doing enough. I am reminded of Freud's dream of Irma's injection. He says, "I am always careful, of course, to see that the syringe is perfectly clean. *For I am conscientious.*" The italics are mine. If he felt that he were really conscientious, if he had no feelings of short-comings in this connection, why did he have to protest that he *was* conscientious? The guilt of lack of conscientiousness haunts most of my friends. My lack of conscientiousness is my "secret." But here I find myself confessing to lack of conscientiousness. But I was not able to do so until I was able to remember something which would make it possible for me not to have my guilt alone. I brought up the zoology professor. When I wrote the above line about him I hesitated for a moment on the question of whether or not to use quotation marks, or to write it in the way that I did. The quotation marks would have had to come, in all honesty, after the word "string." I wrote on, however, "No matter how much you do, you never feel that you are doing enough." This is what I would have liked him to have said. I added it to give the impression that he had said it, but not quite lying about it.
> I think that what has been said above can be generalized. *We are more prone to confess a secret guilt when we can believe that others have the same secret guilt* . . . (1954, p. 111).

Bakan here seems to have played the game correctly, observing the two cardinal rules of free association, to be completely honest and to record everything (even the unpublishable) which comes to mind. The italicized sentence at the close of the quote is then taken as an item or datum, and through a similar procedure he concocted several other propositions which he presents to the reader; for example, that secrets help maintain a given perception of one's self in the eyes of others, or that when an individual has a secret he will protest that the opposite is true. Bakan describes his method of writing as "an oscillation between a free expressive mood and an analytic mood, with the free expression being the subject of the analysis" (p. 111). In the classical analytic situation the patient would provide the free expression and the therapist the analysis.

Jung's stream of phantasies and visions continued to press on him, so that he felt as if another will, greater than his own, were making itself felt in his consciousness. He recorded the phantasies as they arose, and when they occasionally ceased, encouraged their reappearance through some form of artistic activity, such as painting a picture or hewing a stone (1963, p. 175). And so the phantasies continued, until a fateful day: "When I was writing down these fantasies, I once asked myself, 'What am I really doing? Certainly this has nothing to do with science. But then what is it?' Whereupon a voice within me said, 'It is art.' I was astonished. It had never entered my head that what I was writing had any connection with art" (p. 185). Jung did not dismiss this voice from within as unimportant. Rather, he decided to challenge it in dialogue fashion: "I said very emphatically to this voice that my fantasies had nothing to do with art, and I felt a great inner resistance. No voice came through, however, and I kept on writing. Then came the next assault, and again the same assertion: 'That is art.' This time I caught her and said, 'No, it is not art! On the contrary, it is nature,' and prepared myself for an argument" (pp. 185–186).

He was to carry on his verbal exchange with this internal opponent. The "voice" speaking to Jung here was that of a woman patient, whom he later theorized had become a living figure in his mind speaking for the "anima," the contra-sexual portion of the psyche in the male. But for our purposes the interesting thing to note is that Jung is here denying an artistic motive to his phantasy productions. If they were merely artistic phantasies, then he would not take them seriously, and his method of experimentation would lack scientific merit (p. 187). Here again, accepting the artistic interpretation would aid the cause of resistance. But Jung would not be dissuaded. He continued in his search for the contents of unconsciousness as a scientific quest, and by 1917 the stream of phantasies subsided. But in this span of time he had laid down a new psychology, one which stamped him clearly as independent of his teacher, Sigmund Freud. He could sum it up in later years by observing: "My life is what I have done, my scientific work; the one is inseparable from the other. The work is the expression of my inner development; for commitment to the contents of the unconscious forms the man and produces his transformations. My works can be regarded as stations along my life's way" (p. 222).

At this point, we would do well to step back from our introspective demonstrations and ask ourselves precisely what has transpired. Have Bakan and Jung shown us the operations of a *method* as we have construed the term; i.e., as a means or manner of determining whether theoretical propositions are true or false? Are they viewing method as the vehicle for the exercise of evidence, and if so, what kind of evidence are they advocating? Could we sit down to the typewriter or plunge into our own reveries and come up with data similar to the ones they report, the insights into "secrecy," or man's unconscious psyche, as the case may be? If indeed we attempted to replicate their efforts, we might be surprised by the similarity of our results — at least, with the productions of Bakan, for even he notes that his propositions have a ring of self-evidence about them (1954, p. 115). Jung's propositions concerning the collective unconscious, which surged forth from his inner being, the meanings of archetypes in his reveries and dreams, would doubtless be considerably more difficult to come by; but even here, with the proper orientation, at least some of us might duplicate Jung's findings if we gave his method an honest try.

Yet, in terms of our discussions in Chapters III and IV, it seems clear that Bakan's and Jung's use of introspection as method combines and at times confounds theory generation with procedural evidence (cognitive method). The findings of introspection, although often highly convincing as they apply to the individual personality undergoing the "method," never carry the *objective* weight of experimental evidence, because there is always the good possibility that one has generated a subjective theoretical proposition of no generality, or at best highly limited generality. The proposition's claim to validity must ultimately depend upon something other than the method used, which rests only upon procedural evidence. This may mean, of course, that the proposition is generally applicable to all members of a class, to all people of a given socio-historical period; but on the other hand, it could also mean that the proposition is not generally applicable, that it lacks objective truth, that it is not a scientific law or finding at all.

Since they are both highly sophisticated theoreticians, Bakan and Jung clearly recognize this incompleteness in their introspective methods. Bakan notes that the propositions which emerged from his investigation are at the very least hypotheses, which could be investigated by other methods, such as the experimental; or, he comments, "the method could be used as a device whereby an investigator, having got some experimental results which he cannot understand, provokes his imagination to arrive at some kind of an explanation of his results" (1954, p. 114). However, Bakan is of the opinion that his method has merit beyond what we would call its usefulness as an act of theory generation or theoretical integration. He feels it has a *directness* which cannot be found in any other attempt to study psychological phenomena (p. 115). This is reminiscent of Titchener's claim for introspection as the most direct form of observation open to man. Bakan also goes on to make the point that an introspective analysis can give the investigator not only literal truths, in the sense of objective validity, but also various *possibilities* for behavior, which can sensitize the investigator to alternatives he may not have thought of because he has not found them in reality:

> In the matter of prediction and control of human behavior, a knowledge of what an individual might *possibly* do, or *possibly* feel, or *possibly* think places us well on the way toward the achievement of our objective. Given a detailed knowledge concerning the possibles we can act in such a fashion as to discourage some from becoming actualities, and to encourage others into becoming actualities. The pragmatic usefulness of knowledge of possibles extends from the clinical situation to world affairs (p. 117).

The idea of possibilities or alternatives not now under consideration by a theorist is an important derivative of the classical introspective method, due to what we shall come to call in Chapter IX the dialectical reasoning process. But for now we merely stress that Bakan has acknowledged the fact that the introspective method fails to generate an unequivocal statement of what "is." The method tells us what "might be," what "is plausible," or what could possibly someday "come to be," but since it rests upon the interplay of theory generation and the procedural testing of propositions so generated, it cannot give us the sense of scientific conviction that the research method and its validating evidence provides. Jung solves this problem of how to generalize to all members of a class (objectivity) by going to the myths, religions, and histories of mankind. He postulates a collective community within his own psyche — the so-called collective unconscious — which he then views as making itself known in his unique life. If this collectivity exists, if it moves the minds of men in some commonly recognizable way, then an examination of the products of other men's minds should reflect its influence. Why not, therefore, turn to the study of mankind and in this way substantiate the theoretical constructs and propositions generated initially through the supposedly "subjective" act of introspection? This is how his logic runs, as we can see in the following excerpt:

> First I had to find evidence for the historical prefiguration of my inner experiences. That is to say, I had to ask myself, "Where have my particular premises already occurred in history?" If I had not succeeded in finding such evidence, I would never have been able to substantiate my ideas. Therefore, my encounter with alchemy was decisive for me, as it provided me with the historical basis which I had hitherto lacked. Analytical psychology is fundamentally a natural science, but it is subject far more than any other science to the personal bias of the observer. The psychologist must depend therefore in the highest degree upon historical and literary parallels if he wishes to exclude at least the crudest errors in judgment (1963, p. 200).

This is a rather sophisticated defense of his introspective efforts. "Man is men," so to speak, and through the examination of man's history, his literary products, both of which reflect his struggle for identity, man has expressed meanings from that alien world of the unconscious which must be taken into account if his true nature is to be known. With the proper intelligence and a lack of defensiveness, the individual man can turn into himself and discover the legitimacy of Jung's claims. He can record dreams, cultivate phantasies, hew a rock or paint a picture; archetypal prefigurations will be discernible in any of these productions. And this effort is not art, it is (man in) nature.

The problem with this justification of introspection is that it must ultimately rest on one's point of view, for history, like science itself, is subject to varying points of view. As we saw in Chapter IV (p. 86), Jung, like Bakan, was aware of the fact that many alternative views of man were "possible" through introspection. However, Jung believed there were only a limited number of possibilities open to anyone who hoped somehow to capture the behavioral nature of man. Therefore, at some point, objective commentaries on man could be made. Freud was right in that he gave us a legitimate view of neurotic man. Adler was right in that he gave us a legitimate view of conscious man, and so on. Like the skilled craftsman who fashions a valuable jewel by cutting many facets from the rough face of the natural diamond, each personality theorist enriches our knowledge of man by giving us his own personal psychology, as issued from his unconscious psyche and somehow put into words.

Introspection as Theoretical Perspective

Despite their defenses of introspection as something more useful than what one might expect to derive from the free play of intellect (theoretical functioning) and the procedural testing of propositions resulting from this activity, it seems clear enough that introspection can never be a substitute for the more public and therefore more objective methods of validation. To attempt a defense of introspection as the sole vehicle for evidence is doomed to failure, and to carry it further, as Jung did, merely acknowledges that introspection as proof is not sufficient. We cannot accept introspection as an adequate scientific method. This does not mean, however, that we must dismiss the related issue of why introspection was seen as so important to the development of psychology in the first place. Jung's emphasis on the history and arts of mankind alerts us to the fact that, after all, the study of human behavior is the oldest of all scholarly attempts. Who has a better right to speak for man than man himself? Considering the force of history and the weight of culture on procedural evidence, it is surely correct to think of a man as men-like in nature, and Jung's thesis makes great sense.

Although he formalized the approach in his method, Jung is not the only eminent personality theorist to advocate a study of the arts in order to gain a fuller and more meaningful picture of man. In his analysis of Jensen's novel, *Gradiva,* Freud said that: "creative writers are valuable allies and their evidence is to be prized highly, for they are apt to know a whole host of things between heaven and earth of which our philosophy has not yet let us dream. In their knowledge of the mind they are far in advance of us everyday people, for they draw upon sources which we have not yet opened up for science" (Freud, 1959, p. 8). Otto Rank (1945) was also greatly taken by the presumed wisdom of the creative artist. In more recent years, Carl Rogers has observed: "what is most personal and unique in each one of us is probably the very element which would, if it were shared or expressed, speak most deeply to others. This has helped me to understand artists and poets as people who have dared to express the unique in themselves" (1961, p. 26). The great champion of individual uniqueness, Gordon Allport, has also suggested that: "Personality is not a problem for science or a problem for art exclusively, but for both together. Each approach has its merits, but both are needed for even an approximately complete study of the infinite richness of personality" (1960, p. 15).

The study of man has always been phrased as if it involved an antinomy between the opposing propositions of science and art, or science and theology, or science and mysticism. Those who take a more toughminded view of the nature of psychology have seen in this bifurcation a serious hindrance to the advance of objective psychology. For example, Kantor has traced the rise of introspection to Plotinus (Egyptian philosopher, A.D. 205?–270), who presumably invented "the introspective tradition of spiritistic psychology" (Kantor, 1963, p. 264). St. Augustine (A.D. 354–430) supposedly helped crystallize this method as a means of studying the soul, for: "soul is spaceless and known only by inner awareness or introspection" (p. 285). Hence, the introspective method is the heritage of the Middle Ages, when the completely empirical and objective science of Aristotle was diverted and in its place, due to the desire of various medieval thinkers to establish their vested subjective interests (belief in deities, souls), a shift from extraspection to introspection supposedly took place (p. 345). Psychology was "adversely affected" in the process (p. 310), and any attempt today to formulate psychological data introspectively is presumed to be a return to these highly suspect pseudo-scientific periods of subjectivity and vested interests. If not a return to spirits or theology, then at the very least, all attempts to conceptualize man in introspective terms are taken to be nonscientific or prescientific, and the proponents of rigor speak derisively of those psychologists who take an interest in "the kinds of knowledge the novelist and poet portray" (Spence, 1956, p. 20).

What an impasse for the scientific-minded student of personality! Even if it is true that introspection was the vehicle for the study of soul or spirit or mind or essence, the important point would be that one's data — men — are making interesting attempts to study themselves for strange and interesting reasons. Where do these attempts spring from, why are they continually expressed, and what are the contents of the statements they are seeking to make? Further, since so many of the artistic propositions are vested and subjective, is it possible for a psychologist who takes an interest in man to capture these views of men in a more disinterested, objective fashion? When we have phrased the problem in this way, it is clear that the *essential* feature of introspection is *not* its utility as a vehicle for scientific evidence of another sort, but rather its contribution to a certain theoretical perspective. *It is the introspective theoretical perspective which we really seek to capture through introspection,* and this theoretical perspective must be retained even though we might easily drop the use of introspection as a form of methodological test due to its contaminations and unreliabilities. We need and want the truths which it generates as an exercise of theoretical functioning, but we do not want to rest with a procedural testing of its propositions because not all of these are sufficiently generalizable to attain the status of what we call scientific truths.

Although the personality theories of our well-known psychotherapists often lack the weight of validation, they do not lack meaning for us, they are not without a certain modicum of objectivity and relevance to the population at large, or at least to certain elements within the broader population. Freud's view may be somewhat more relevant for an upper socioeconomic group, and Adler's might adapt itself somewhat better to the lower economic classes (Ansbacher, 1959), but to some extent all personality theorists have said meaningful things about various aspects of man's behavior. We have been personally instructed by the writings of Jung, Rogers, Rank, and others, even though everything they have said has not been subjected to empirical test. But it is the point of view (meaning), the style of thought issuing from the clinical relationship which has been a genuine and lasting product of psychotherapy.

It is possible to conceptualize psychotherapy (of the insight variety) as approximating a kind of "theory generation in discourse." Two people talk and together generate theories of personality. What sorts of ways do we have of speaking about man? Jung suggests that we have as many ways as we have theorists (usually therapists) who have deflected their (presumably hereditarily and unconsciously directed) natural characters into the mainstream of thought about man. Whether one accepts this biogenetic view of the nature of mind, or prefers to translate Jung's thesis into a sociocultural (Zeitgeist) explanation of how men deflect their traditionally learned self-images into their artistic products, the point is, this view implies a certain arbitrariness in the ways we might describe any one man at any one time — at least, up to a point.

If one begins with a realistic thesis about the nature of his data, then to speak of arbitrariness in the conceptualization of man strikes a chord of discontent. How can man have one and then another pattern of behavior, depending on who is doing the describing? This most surely sounds like unreliability, occasioned and defended by those who cannot accept the "truths" of science. On the other hand, the idealist, who accepts from the outset *potentials* in behavior not now realized but always *possible* (to recall Bakan's point above), an infinite variety in human behavior is to be expected. The idealist does not concern himself with the question "how does man really behave, once we have stripped off all the verbiage he uses to describe his own behavior?" Rather, he follows up on the question "which form of verbal self-description used by man seems to capture best all the behaviors man exhibits?" He responds to the latter question for he hopes to educate man in an area of self-exploration. To answer this, he must dislodge himself from the extraspective perspective and at least attempt to validate theoretical propositions generated from the point of view of his data. He must give man a chance to speak. Historically, it has been the clinician who has afforded man this opportunity.

The issue of meaning is germane to our discussion at this point. Although one may limit his consideration of human behavior to glandular responses, or to some highly stylized responses to technical laboratory equipment, what after all can such things say about man in historical perspective? In doing experimental research we define constructs operationally so as to make our thinking clear to professional peers. Operationism is tied to the meaning of our constructs, both formal and informal. As we do research, we educate one another, we manipulate meanings and bring them into line with the common sense of the psychological community. We call this spread of scientific knowledge "communication," or the dissemination of meanings. But in a comparable fashion, for centuries the storyteller, the poet, the novelist, have defined meanings operationally for those who listened to them or read their works. The "operations" here are accomplished by taking the individual reader through an introspective excursion for which his sociocultural learnings to date have prepared him. We can identify with the expressions of a poet (at times) or with the hero of a novel because we too are human, we too have faced analogous situations. It is instructive and insightful to read literature in order to learn about personality, simply because literary works of art educate one concerning the human condition. They explore avenues of meaning consciously closed by the extraspective theorist.

Great authors define for us the nature of men as they have experienced it, in their own identities, or in their living contacts with others. Measurement of such dimensions as they may use to describe man is not an issue, for they do not seek to validate their theoretical propositions on the possible (the "fictional"). This is why we can learn so much through a study of literature. Man is truly men. Man is a sociocultural heritage of patterned behavior determined not by any *necessary* system of laws, but in a way arbitrarily, by the adjustments other men have made to the ravages of nature, the competing needs of groups of men, with the resultant philosophies, prejudices, and theologies generated. The truly amazing side of this is the amount of objective understanding — "empathy" maybe — that man has for his fellow human beings. His grasp of the nature of other men seems immediate, once he can identify himself with the sociocultural context in which these other men operate. He may not agree with their behaviors or their philosophies, but he understands them. The experiences of our fellow human beings have meaning, once we put ourselves in their shoes, in their sociocultural situation. This introspective act is not easy, but once it is attained, meanings flood our awareness in an immediate and clear fashion. Such meanings (points of view) may or may not be highly objective, or highly generalizable to all men, but there is no way to determine this, short of scientific investigation. The problem then, is to move from the introspective theoretical perspective to the research method, which, as we know, has a greater affinity for extraspection.

Compatibility of Theory and Method: The Line of Development

What makes a psychologist an "S-R theorist" rather than any other kind of theorist? For some, the connotations of S-R theory include: experimentation, rigor, candor, accuracy, and dependability. For others, the connotations include: narrowness, rigidity, triteness, distortion, and stagnation. Are the terms S-R theorist and S-R experimenter interchangeable as to meanings? Can one experiment to validate in the usual scientific sense and yet avoid the label of "S-Rist"? The writer is of the opinion that many personality-oriented psychologists avoid experimentation, at least in part, through an emotional rejection of what is for them the deprecatory connotation of "S-Rism." This unfortunate state of affairs results from an inability on the part of most psychologists to distinguish between what is theory and what is the methodological validation of a theoretical proposition.

The writer was once speaking before a group on the difficulties facing the clinical personality theorist, who hopes to take the verbal productions of his client — his "data" — and translate these (essentially) theoretical propositions into experimental designs, without having to embrace the S-R image of man. After the talk was finished, as he was leaving the auditorium, one of the writer's peers engaged him in conversation the point of which was: "why are you fighting the acceptance of S-R theory so when it is all based upon empirical validation, and to that extent is scientifically proven and really unquestionable?" What this friend had done was to gloss over a distinction between "before and after" as it applied to a theoretical view (S-R theory), and as it applied to a research methodological act (experimentation). The writer's response to his friend was therefore: "What makes you say that the IV-DV sequence we use to validate theoretical hypotheses must necessarily support *only* the S-R theory of human behavior?"

And here we have the crux of the issue. Some theories of personality (and for now we will assume that S-R theory is a "kind" of personality theory; see below, p. 248) are more compatible with the method of validation commonly accepted in psychology than others. Classical learning or S-R theory has been tied *extremely* closely to this method, and in one sense it is *identical* to it as a metaconstruction. That is, the antecedent-consequent metaconstruct introduced by Aristotle (see Chapters IX and XI) is at the heart of experimental method both in psychology and in S-R theory as usually phrased. What real difference in meaning is there between the following constructs: antecedent condition and consequent condition; stimulus (S) and response (R); independent variable (IV) and dependent variable (DV)? There is no difference, really; all three constructs rely on the fact that we move in a time-bound universe, and that one event succeeds another and may well be related to it in some lawful way. Therefore, although the personality theorist might generate interesting hypotheses on the nature of man from an introspective investigation, possibly in cooperation with a therapeutic client, the moment he attempts to test this proposition empirically two things are likely to happen: (1) he finds that at the present time it is impossible to put this proposition into a workable or acceptable design; or, having done so, he may find that the meaning has shifted in the translation to experimental design; (2) even if he has put his introspectively generated proposition into the IV-DV validational paradigm, his S-R brethren immediately shift their thinking along the lines already suggested, and take his insight as just another validation of the S-R theory and image of man. Both of these alternatives are very demoralizing, to say the least. There is really no way out of the former; public scientific knowledge is probably always going to lack some of that immediate significance (meaning) which highly personal knowledge seems to have. But there is a way out of the latter alternative, and that is by recognizing that IV-DV sequences follow from the generation of a theoretical hypothesis, and that they do *not necessarily* establish the view which generates them (they affirm the consequent; see Chapter IV, pp. 80–81), much less the view which seems most applicable to them.

What has actually taken place in academic psychology, where the extraspective perspective has been most stressed, is that the methodological procedure has subtly and informally been extended to the side of theory, so that man is now seen to behave the way we want our methodological apparatus to behave. Modern psychology is in danger of making a metaphysic out of a methodology, as Newton once did. The S-R bind (see Chapter III, p. 57) is greatly ensnaring, so that any time the scientifically conscientious personality theorist wishes to speak he must use "the language of experimentation" and begin laying down the stimuli to which various responses are to be postulated in his research design. He is unknowingly asked to equate S-R and IV-DV, so that, having proven his proposition through the latter, he protects the integrity of the image of man implicit in the former. Thus, the "discovery" that man is after all a responder to stimuli, a kind of mechanical robot lacking in intellect or mind is carefully foreordained by the very psychologists who often decry the images of man subjectively handed to us by the poets and the novelists.

It is natural for a given theoretical view to seek a compatible method. Freud recognized this, and rather stubbornly clung to his introspectively "verified" theoretical constructs and propositions even though they flew in the face of the more traditionally conceived scientific methods. It is also natural for a method to come to exert considerable influence on the free play of theory generation. We recognize this influence in the old adage "A good theory must generate testable hypotheses." This is not, of course, completely true, because it merely emphasizes one of the four functions which "good" theories must fulfill. Actually, some of the so-called good theories which generate testable hypotheses get increasingly complex, and hold out less and less hope of ever coming to fruition. The notion of generating testable hypotheses, for Freud, would mean putting forth interpretations which can integrate the introspectively delivered free associations of the client, which in turn would provide the insight through which a cure could eventually be achieved. To ask Freud for a theoretical hypothesis amenable to the demands of laboratory validation is like asking the S-Rist to educate a client who is at the introspective end of the perspective continuum. Both views (images of man) have their difficulties when they swim in strange waters. Yet we must expect Freud and others like him to make the accommodation if an objective science of personality is ever to be achieved. We must look beyond the walls of the consulting room for a more objective support for our theoretical speculations subjectively arrived at. How can we increase the compatibility of introspectively phrased theory and extraspectively organized methodology?

The writer feels this is possible, by extending the reasoning already begun in this section. Methods never validate the theoretical propositions which they seek to test in a *logically necessary* way, due to the fact that methods always affirm the consequent. A corollary to this insight is the recognition that there is always a *line of development* stemming from the theory-to-test sequence, even in the act of validation. Any fact pattern observed can be explained by *more* than one theory. Precisely how long the line of development is, from the theorist's hunch to the variables he ultimately defines to test this hunch, varies according to the nature of the theory under consideration. The S-R theorist is in the fortunate position of having a highly multiordinal construct, which he can use very close to the level of labeling (see Chapter II), or at a considerably more abstract level. For example, the writer contends that Osgood's analysis of United States–Russian relations is a highly sophisticated, very abstract attempt to apply S-R principles to international relations (Osgood, 1962). However, the S-R theorist is not likely to establish the validity of his thought on such highly speculative (even if creative) forms of analysis.

When he decides to prove the validity of his thought, the S-R theorist usually permits himself very little line of development, at least in a formal sense. He is more prone to construct an apparatus, or to settle on a series of studies, all varying slightly on some common theme, and then seek changes in the DV as a function of various manipulations he can make in the IV. Since his S-R theory so closely approximates his IV-DV methodological apparatus at this lower level of abstraction, he does not see the need for a line of development from some more abstract height. Thanks to the multiordinality of the S-R construct, at the time he is gathering data his theoretical and methodological constructions (S-R and IV-DV) are for all practical purposes "one." His line of development in these laboratory instances is most often accomplished by way of his preparations to doing the research (designing the apparatus), and it is very often hidden in the confines of informal theory (see Chapter II).

The personality theorist, on the other hand, deals with less multiordinal, less "flexible" constructions. In having to define operationally some concept which any normal human being would find little trouble in accepting or understanding — such as "love" or "ambition" — he must in most instances show a long line of development from the construct as grasped to the construct as realized in methodological terms. Often, he cannot hope to capture the full meaning of the construct to which he alludes, for at the level of abstraction at which he is theorizing the construct defies reduction to a lower level, operational definition. Is it right, therefore, to tell him he should stop thinking in these terms, which he finds so instructive and informative? Would it not be more profitable to permit him to continue, with only the proviso that he must show us the implications of his thought at some point along the line of development through an extraspective act of validation? In permitting him a longer line of development from theory to test, we must accept his inevitable reliance upon procedural evidence, and he must accept the inevitable fact that his construct may never be truly circumscribed in the methodological framework (see Chapter XI, "purity" criticism). He may only have the remnants of the construct as he views its nature rather than the construct as such. Rather than "love" he has some scores on a paper-and-pencil test; we have to accept his argument that his scale taps love, unless we apply our own counter-arguments (procedural evidence) and undermine the psychometric scale he has devised by showing that there are certain variables which he has neglected (loss of control).

By stretching the acceptable line of development in psychology we liberalize our interpretation of the scientific enterprise. We recognize that logical controls are at times as important as experimental controls. Better a "loose" design and an exciting idea than a "tight" design and a pedestrian idea. It is the theoretical side of the scientific process which we elevate in liberalizing research in psychology. Man can then be talked about as man-like, and the personality theorist will be held back only by the limits of his own ingenuity from demonstrating his line of development by an innovative research design, even if this is somewhat removed from the more abstract level at which he would like to test his hypotheses. As a counter to the charge of looseness, the line of development can be further elaborated through cross-validations. Rather than trying to "control all variables in your experiment" — which as it is often taken means "don't risk chances on being wrong in any *single study*" — this more liberal view would ask that we "sharpen our reasoning, flirt with error, but continually seek to demonstrate the effectiveness of our reasoning through repeated data collections along the way."

There are, of course, dangers in this approach, suggesting as it does the possibility of "wild theorizing" and settling for merely tepid attempts to validate a few propositions now and then along the way to a phantasy world. Yet, there is no need for such alarm, since this is merely a statement of policy alternative to the one we have been following in academic psychology, one which is not free of pitfalls itself. The writer is reminded of a research colloquium he once attended, where the speaker described spending several months worrying and struggling to design an apparatus which would in due time produce marvelously clear measurements of a certain phenomenon. After taking his audience through the growing pains of an apparatus, he then frankly admitted that he had not had any clear-cut goals in mind for how this apparatus might be used (though one could see the operation of an informal analogy which got him underway initially). A member of the audience, a fellow research-design enthusiast, then spoke up and put the dilemma rather succinctly to the speaker: "You seem to have here a marvelous dependent variable, but what you need now are some independent variables." This is the problem with a policy of "tight design." It encourages weakness on the side of theory, where either independent variables are selected in the context of some worthwhile, meaningful theory, or they are not. Rather than err on the side of method, on the side of the measurement of something — anything, just so it is clearly possible to get a fix on it — we would rather err on the side of theory, error, and vagueness in speculative attempts. It is *easier* to "feel scientific" the former way, but it is more exciting and meaningful the latter way.

Causes of Behavior and the Behavior of Man

It is the hope of many psychologists to make psychology a "natural science," paralleling physics, biology, and chemistry. Aside from the respectful identity it affords one to know that he is a member of the community of natural sciences, just what does it mean to be so identified? Apparently, it means or at least suggests that psychology hopes to explain the behavior of men in precisely the same fashion as the physical sciences have explained the behavior of inanimate, "natural" events, such as the motions of stars, the forming of earthquakes, or the falling of rain. It is a policy designed to end completely the conceiving of human behavior as in any way mental, self-directed, or organized from within the individual. Man walks and talks but is not the locus of innovation, behavior change, or uniqueness that he thinks he is.

One is tempted to see in this rejection of mind the anti-intellectualism and anti-rationalism attributed to the twentieth century by historical and literary analysts (e.g., Hofstadter, 1963; Hyman, 1962). We cannot downgrade the role of man's ideas in one breath and take his rational intellect as a serious force in the next. There is a certain theoretical beauty and simplicity gained in the denial of mind, if one takes his stance from an extraspective perspective. This not only makes it easy to theoretically conceptualize man as actor (albeit an extremely complex actor), it permits one to turn a deaf ear to the highly florid, or at times cacophonic, strains of thought being orchestrated by other theoreticians. The tune setting a man's mouth to dancing is not the one he thinks he has composed, but rather a far more subtle one, out of his range of hearing, though perfectly identifiable by an observer with the proper equipment. Forego the dance, and get to looking for the real tune. Stop the talk and start the action. And so, the great rational intellects of the nineteenth century, men like Freud and William James, Hegel and Marx, become the "armchair theoreticians" of today — the non-doers. Walden was founded by a contemplative thinker who rejected technology and utility; Walden Two was founded by a "doer" of the first rank, who made of this monumental reaction to technology a kind of nightmarish anti-Thoreauian world of gadgets and gimmicks all calculated to make, to do, to move, to behave (Skinner, 1948).

Of course, there are some very good reasons why mental conceptions cannot be used, according to the rules of science as evolved in the physical or natural sciences. To understand fully these reasons and the consequences of them we must look into the question of causation and the types of causal explanation used by scientists up to the present time. We will then have to judge whether it is really correct or truly representative of man to continue in this vein of causal explanation, or whether it will be necessary to broaden our base of scientific explanation.

Efficient Causation: The Extraspectionist's Hope

We have already seen, in Chapter V, that Sir Francis Bacon was one of the first men to discredit the use of formal and final causes in the explanation of natural phenomena. He had good reason for doing so, and it was a reasonable step in the evolution of science for Sir Isaac Newton to try to establish a physics entirely on the basis of an efficient-cause explanation. It is an interesting fact that two historically eminent psychologists of the latter half of the nineteenth century, Helmholtz and Wundt, were strong advocates of the Newtonian position at the same time physicists themselves were beginning to alter their views on the nature of theoretical explanation.

Helmholtz argued that a complete explanation of any event in physics cannot be obtained until we have penetrated to the ultimate (efficient) cause(s) of that event (e.g., behavior), and have fully described the immutable law which will always reflect this same event sequence as long as conditions remain constant. As Helmholtz said, "The work of science will have been completed only when phenomena have been traced back to the simple forces, and when it can be shown also that the given account is the only possible one admitted by the phenomena" (Cassirer, 1950, p. 86). Note the reference to *simple forces,* which implies that there is some basic, underlying substratum to the universe, to which everything must be reduced before it can be meaningfully understood. Efficient causality as such refers to the sequence before-after or anteced-ent-consequent, but this concept of a hierarchy in nature (simple to complex) goes beyond the principle of efficient causality. It implies a mechanistic substrate of act-react, or some such, and has traditionally been called "mechanism" in the physical sciences.

It was Wundt who tied the causality construct to an even more basic idea: "We must trace every change back to the only conceivable one in which an object remains identical: motion" (p. 88). The position taken by Wundt, as the father of experimental psychology, clearly implied that the psychologist must perform reductive experiments, bringing his concepts down to the motoric demands of laboratory procedures. However, neither Helmholtz nor Wundt thought to distinguish clearly between their *methods* of demonstrating a causal tie of IV to DV and their underlying and somewhat removed mechanistic *theory* of the world as a mechanism. Before this distinction could be made in physics, it was necessary to weaken realism with its corollary assumption of a "hierarchy of existence" (p. 90). As the twentieth century approached, grave doubts were cast on the older view that a more basic knowledge could be gained by reducing a higher-order concept, such as behavior, to a lower-order concept, such as motion. The concept of "function" came to supplement and weaken the earlier concept of "cause-effect" in physics due to the entirely intellectual mathematical manipulation of data. Pure correlation between constructs to enrich their meaning came to rule (the so-called R-R laws of Chapter V were now the order of the day): "Once the physicist's idea of force has been recognized as merely a special case of the function concept, all necessity disappears of conceding to mechanical forces any sort of exceptional position and there is no need to treat the phenomena of motion as 'better understood,' or 'simpler,' than any other phenomena" (p. 90).

It was Ernst Mach who argued most cogently against the theory of knowledge being advanced by Helmholtz and Wundt. He pointed out that: "The law of causality demands nothing more than certainty and determinateness in what happens; it says nothing, however, about one realm of events being in principle of a higher order than all others. Hence it is absolutely impossible to prove that all strict and actual causality must be of mechanical nature" (p. 91). Mach defended what he called in the 1890's a "phenomenological physics," in contrast to the mechanistic physics of Helmholtz and Wundt (p. 93), and in it he idealistically challenged the metaphysical idea of matter. Psychology has yet to weaken its strong ties to Newtonian realism, thanks to the impetus of our great founding fathers, Helmholtz, Wundt, and others who followed their lead.

The hope of the psychologist who claims to seek a natural science explanation of man is that he can, somehow, account for all of man's behavior in terms of efficient causes, among which the S-R conceptualization is the most eminent example. This places him firmly in the extraspective stance, for to take the opposite, introspective perspective, would be to admit eventually of other causal possibilities (such as goals "for the sake of which" a man might behave). He may still cling to the view that ultimately all of behavior will reduce to the fundamental forces or motions of Helmholtz and Wundt, or he may simply try to show how various forces of act-react and antecedent-consequent are at play in man's patterned behavior as efficient causes, in the belief that this will somehow prove that man is a mechanism. He consciously sets out to create an *empty organism* in his theoretical view of man, as Boring notes:

> I conceive of myself as supporting the main thesis of B. F. Skinner. Skinner deals with the properties of the empty organism. He ignores, by intelligent intention, the nervous system and all the hypotheses, speculations and intervening variables with which the skins of most organisms are supposed by psychologists to be stuffed. The properties

of an organism are for him and for me simply the ways in which stimulus and response are related, just as the properties of an electronic instrument are the ways in which the electric output is dependent upon the electric input (1946, p. 177).

If we stuff our image of man with unnecessary concepts, such as hopes, dreams, or possibilities, we have transcended the bounds of efficient-cause explanation. We will at this point have moved into what traditionally has been called a final-cause explanation of behavior. As William James made very clear:

> *The pursuance of future ends and the choice of means for their attainment are thus the mark and criterion of the presence of mentality* in a phenomenon. We all use this test to discriminate between an intelligent and a mechanical performance. We impute no mentality to sticks and stones, because they never seem to move for *the sake of* anything, but always when pushed, and then indifferently and with no sign of choice. So we unhesitatingly call them senseless (1952, p. 5).

This insight is of the utmost importance to a proper understanding of how best to theorize about man: In formulating theories of behavior, phenomena which may be said to move "for the sake of something" (Aristotle's definition of final cause) — a principle, an aspiration, a goal — carry a self-direction which we have traditionally taken as the mark of intelligence. *Concepts of mentality demand the use of a final-cause construct.* In Chapter V we learned that this was the essential reason men like Bacon rejected final cause as an adequate descriptive concept for "nature." As natural scientists, we no longer ascribe motives to inanimate objects, nor do we make the parallel assumption of the hand of some beneficent deity operating within nature to further man's ends. Nature is impersonal and operates by its own rules, quite independent of man. As it has evolved, therefore, natural science has "put man down"; and modern psychological "natural" science now threatens to put him as a "person" down even further, for now presumably even *he* lacks a final-cause direction (mentality) from within his own identity. Skinner voices this natural science tradition well, even as he applauds its advance:

> As science advances, it strips men of fancied achievements. . . . The crowning blow to the apparent sovereignty of man came with the shift of attention to external determiners of action. The social sciences and psychology reached this stage at about the same time. Whenever some feature of the environment — past or present — is shown to have an

effect upon human conduct, the fancied contribution of the individual himself is reduced. The program of a radical behaviorism left no originating control inside the skin (1957, pp. 458–459).

What has happened here is that Skinner has substituted in his theory of knowledge the concept of extra-individual sources of control for the earlier Helmholtzian view of simple forces. If we can demonstrate experimentally how man is influenced by his environment, then we strip him of another fancy, another in the long line of personal dignities he has ascribed to himself out of ignorance in times past. Speaking in the motoric tradition of Wundt, Skinner notes that he has found it necessary to attack traditional concepts which assign a spontaneous control to man's inner self: "Only in this way could I make room for the alternative explanation of action which it is the business of a science of verbal behavior to construct" (p. 460). In other words, the scientist deals in efficient-cause actions, he attempts to show what things move a man, where the source of motion "really" stems from. He provides a *more basic* and therefore more accurate picture of man. As this is generally interpreted (e.g., by Spence and others; see Chapter V), it means the scientist does not search for merely "any kind" of functional relationship between variables, since many of these laws are merely "R-R" in nature, but he seeks the ultimate *external source* of behavior, or the well known S-R law, which is "basically" in control of behavior. At this point he has a more fundamental and therefore scientific item of knowledge.

And now the S-R bind takes hold quite definitely. Man is defined as an "in-between" agent of efficient causes, all of which string out from cause to effect and back again. As Skinner notes: "Men will never become originating centers of control, because their behavior will itself be controlled, but their role as mediators may be extended without limit. . . . 'Personal freedom' and 'responsibility' will make way for other bywords which, as is the nature of bywords, will probably prove satisfying enough" (p. 460). One of the best phrasings of this S-R image of man is given by Wolpe. Taken together with Skinner's description of his personal behavior (see Chapter II, pp. 21–22) and of man's purpose by Weiss in his "raindrop analogy" (see Chapter V, p. 125), it gives us a pretty clear picture of what has happened to man in the name of scientific investigation:

> Between a stimulus and the responses that follow it there must be an unbroken network of causally related events, potentially observable by an outside beholder, no matter whether or not some of the neural

events have correlates in the consciousness of the subject. Any contents of the subject's consciousness would be *in parallel and not in series* with their neural correlates, and would in essence constitute the unique reaction of a specially placed observer (the subject) to these neural events. Thus, an image of which I am not conscious now will appear in my imagination if appropriate stimuli activate certain of my neurones. It can have no independent existence apart from the stimulation of these neurones. Within my nervous system, a *potentiality* which includes the evocation of this image may be said to exist, but *only in the same sense as it may be said that my nervous system harbors the potentiality of a knee jerk given the stimulus of a patellar tap.* If the relationship of images to the nervous system is so conceived, all talk of "mind structure" becomes nonsensical (Wolpe, 1958, p. 16).

One needs the "outside observer" because the nature of the "unbroken network of causally related events" is that of an efficient cause, it is the actual something, the force, the energy, the act-react or antecedent-consequent sequence of events, which a theorist may use in explaining the nature of some phenomenon. This outside observer is, of course, the extraspectionist, and his hope is that he can explain all the variance in man's behavior, that he can capture all the essentials of man's natural responsiveness, through use of only one or possibly two of the Aristotelian causes — efficient and material. With each successful prediction by experimental validation the extraspectionist feels he has established the validity of this image of man. But he has not. As with the basic forces or motions, the Machian criticism still holds. Causality and mechanism are not identical. Mechanism rests on the assumption of an underlying substrate in reality, a substrate identifiable by only one kind of cause (efficient), and simply because the experimental method is geared to efficient-cause (Wundt's motoric) explanation, the prediction of events within it *fails* to establish the validity of the mechanistic world view.

In stressing the theoretical "line of development" above (p. 215), what we were doing was asking that other causes — such as the traditionally conceived final causes — be scientifically accepted in the conceptualization of man, an animate creature in whom motives are apparent. If man thinks, then he somehow guides his own fate, he is *not only* a mediator of stimuli from some more basic external world, even though one might demonstrate how he gets knowledge from the environment. But if a theorist takes the individual man seriously, and ascribes to him a guiding intellect, then that theorist must still show us what the practical effects of man's thoughts are. He must still validate the comments he ultimately makes about a man thinking or growing as a person. He must reason from the theory of man to an experimental test of what he has concluded, and at that point attempt the extraspective test. When he does so he will be making use of efficient-cause constructs — the IV and DV of experimental design — but this translation from final-cause theory to efficient-cause validation does not mean he has abandoned the theory which views man as something more than a mediator of natural laws flowing in from the environment.

The ironic feature of this is that it is in psychology — the science of man — that a rejection of man's intellect is most adamantly clung to. The underpinnings of this attitude are in the outmoded view of naive realism which is still a major force in American academic psychology. Thanks to their emphasis on experimentation, psychologists such as Skinner actually believe they are "discovering" man's mechanistic nature empirically. What is more, thanks to their sense of conviction that intellectual forces are responses and not stimulating innovators, many of them refuse to argue or to "philosophize" about the nature of their investigation because this is beyond their role as scientists. This would be to introspect, to rely on non-empirical or non-objective evidence. Yet physics could free itself of Newtonian notions only after men like Mach dared to introspect, to look into their presuppositions and biases of intellect (which they believed themselves to possess as an innovative and *stimulative* aspect of their natures), and consequently changed the older ways of thought. As Cassirer remarks about the great period of revolution in theoretical physics: "From the middle of the nineteenth century onward the demand for reflective criticism in the natural sciences was urged with ever mounting emphasis" (1950, p. 82). Psychology has yet to make its great efforts at reflective criticism, at least in part because of its metaphysical assumption that scientists do not think or argue philosophically, they merely "do" experiments.

Functional vs. Compelling Causes in the Behavior of Man

In addition to the Aristotelian breakdown of causes into material, efficient, formal and final, it is also possible to think of causal sequences as either *functional,* that is, adequate to the behavior being manifested, or as literally *compelling* the behavior sequence to take place (these terms are based on Bertrand Russell's analysis, 1960, p. 181). One gets the distinct impression from Wolpe's view that man's neuron system contains a series of interlocking potential causes which are compelled to appear, once stimulated, much the way the leg must jerk when one's knee is tapped by a physician's instrument. This view of causation naturally leads to what we termed in Chapter V a "hard determinism" in human behavior. What is more, both the hard determinism and the compelling interpretation of cause seem to be suggested by the need to rely *only* upon efficient causation as an explanatory principle. That is, if one takes the view that an object under observation (say, a man) can in some way alter the course of its own events (thinking, in man), or purposively strive toward some goal of its own choosing, then one would be hard pressed to stay within the confines of a hard determinism or a compelling-cause explanation.

What clinicians and other personality theorists most often seek to do, over against what their fellow psychologists are doing in their laboratories, is to move from complete reliance on efficient-cause explanation to partial reliance on final causes. Alfred Adler reflects this desire in the following: "The fact that anxiety, for instance, affects the sympathetic and para-sympathetic nerves does not reveal the cause of an anxiety. The origin of anxiety is in the psychic and not in the somatic realm. . . . What appears to us most important is such a fact as this, for instance; that a child will make use of anxiety in order to arrive at its goal of superiority — of *control* over the mother" (1964, p. 29). The child seeks to control the mother, and then modifies its behavior accordingly; anxiety is one of these modifications, all calculated to achieve the desired end. An extraspectively-oriented theorist like Spence (1958), on the other hand, who is trying to rely exclusively on efficient causation to explain behavior, postulates no "goal" toward which the organism is striving. For Spence, anxiety is a physically-based emotional response which stimulates a drive in the organism, pushing it on to behave from out of the past, so to speak. The organism is now in a drive state, due to the physiologically-based anxiety, and it therefore "behaves" in direct relation to the strength of this drive. It does not choose to generate anxiety as one of the intermediate behaviors along the path to successful attainment of a goal, as Adler would have it.

When we begin introducing such concepts as self-directed goals or growth principles into our data, we move into a realm of personality description which most rigorous — i.e., natural-science-oriented — psychologists decry as mystical, amorphous, and outdated theorizing. It is an interesting sidelight that, if one upholds a hard determinism in physical science today, he might well be accused of foisting a religious prejudice onto nature — i.e., seeing a Creator's hand in the design of nature.

Bridgman notes that Einstein was of such a persuasion in that he: "could not bring himself to accept the idea that chance plays a fundamental role in the scheme of things, and who passionately exclaimed, *'Der Herr Gott wurfelt nicht'* ('The Lord God does not throw dice') (1958, p. 51). Yet, in psychology today, *if one questions the legitimacy* of 100 per cent determinism, he too is suspected of promoting a religious preference, the inability to reject free will, the tendermindedness of seeing man as somehow deciding his own fate. This paradoxical state of affairs stems from the rejection by all so-called toughminded (natural-science-inclined) theorists of final-cause explanations: in the case of the physicist, as regards God's hand in nature; in the case of the psychologist, as regards man's control over his own behavior. This reflects a long and hallowed tradition in the natural sciences.

The reference to Einstein underscores an important feature of the Aristotelian presentation of causation, and that is: Aristotle was attempting to show that a theorist who explains a given phenomenon can use *all four* types of causes in demonstrating that he has knowledge of it. And, although Newton did strive to limit his theoretical explanations to material and efficient causes, this does *not* mean that he rejected teleology (final causes) altogether. He, like most of the physicists of his time, and like Einstein after him, accepted the belief that a Supreme Being created the universe. His God had the properties which subsume formal and final causation. God is therefore an integral part of Newton's theory (informally appended) when he observes: "It is allowed by all that the Supreme God exists necessarily; and by the same necessity he exists *always* and *everywhere*. Whence also he is all similar, all eye, all ear, all brain, all arm, all power to perceive, to understand, and to act; but in a manner not at all human, in a manner not at all corporeal, in a manner utterly unknown to us" (Burtt, 1955, p. 259). Though it rests on procedural evidence, this belief in a God provides the underpinnings for Newton's world view and gives him the sense of confidence he has in a completely regular and causally linked universe. Indeed, as Burtt points out, when Newton theorized on the movement of bodies, he meant that these bodies were moving not only in (efficient-cause) absolute space, but literally *in God* (p. 259); and God's purpose is unknown to mortal man.

One of the major sources of distaste with the image of man reflected in Wolpe's sketch is the wooden quality, the lifeless, marionette-like behavior suggested in the hard determinism of compelling causes. This view of man is useful for certain of Wolpe's therapeutic purposes, but its mechanistic phrasing is not useful for other purposes which attract personality theorists. This has led to a great fear of mechanism among personality theorists; but actually, as we shall now attempt to show, mechanism is really no threat to final-cause explanation or teleology. The extreme reaction to mechanism is unwarranted. Bertrand Russell (1957, 1960) has shown that the cause-effect relationship is a time-bound sequence which permits us to say only what factors are related to what other factors over time. He speaks in the tempo of modern science when he notes that it is more correct to state that sequences of A to B (or S to R) reflect "functional relations" rather than causes and effects (1957, p. 201). If our minds were not so prone to reason historically, thanks to the time lapse between A and B, and the fact that we have no memory for future events, we might just as well conclude that B "causes" A. Hence, to outline a sequence of S to R in psychology is *not* to state assuredly that this or that S literally causes this or that R in any necessary or compelling manner. As Russell notes: "Causes . . . do not *compel* their effects, any more than effects *compel* their causes. There is a mutual relation so that either can be inferred from the other" (1960, p. 181).

Immanuel Kant was one of the first to point out that to assume a universe of compelling-cause determinism is to project more rationalism on the universe than it probably deserves. Newton made this assumption because of his underlying belief in a God, and this is why physicists who today hold to a hard determinism are suspected of deifying nature. But the important point is that *efficient-cause description does not demand hard determinism.* To believe that an antecedent cause and a consequent effect are compellingly related is *not* germane to the concept of efficient cause. One can see antecedents and consequents as tied to one another by a functional linking. When certain antecedents lead to certain consequents (entirely predictable within a given range of probability) we can speak of a "causal law" if we realize that this merely signifies a functional relationship between two classes of events which holds within limits and under certain circumstances. The further assertion of a compelling relationship is not dictated by empirical findings (indeed, the customary variance in our research findings argues against the thesis of compulsion). Thus, mechanism as an underlying substrate to all behaviors can be found to hold, *and* self-direction on the part of individual men who behave can also be found to hold. Both causes of behavior can be true: "The question whether, or how far, our actual world is teleological cannot, therefore, be settled by proving that it is mechanical, and the desire that it should be teleological is no ground for wishing it to be not mechanical" (Russell, 1957, p. 195).

Strangely enough, although teleology implies that an object can move in a self-determining fashion, suggesting alternative action and a non-compelling form of causation, it is also true to say that teleology and compelling causes are highly compatible at a point in the sequence of events. The object which moves under its own direction to seek a goal (the physical bodies moving within God, for Newton, or the child seeking to exert control over his mother, for Adler) *once this direction or goal has been settled on,* moves inexorably, or can be thought to move so. Thus, alternatives are open to the object conceived teleologically, but after this object decides on a course, it can move (very mechanically) in the pursuit of this now compelling goal. *Compulsion in causation is actually a teleological and not a mechanistic concept.* Russell recognized this when he noted that the reason theorists are prone to think of causes as compelling is that they analogize incorrectly from cause to volition (the act of willing) (1960, p. 180). Since volition is based upon a final-cause explanation (willing one alternative rather than another), in our terms this suggests that the hard determinist has permitted a teleology to sneak inside the limits of his efficient cause. Essentially he must presume that the S comes to know its proper R and to "will" the evocation of the latter, and no other R, in *every* instance, once a link has been established. A position of this sort was once defended in the history of thought, but we can hardly believe the S-R theorist consciously intends to do this.

A personality theorist can therefore accept the essentials of S-R theory as the functional-cause substrate in *all* behavior, and then add his more teleological explanations as they are called for to make sense of his data, particularly when these data are being conceptualized from the introspective perspective. He does not have to reduce these more teleological constructs to the functional-cause substrate, except by way of his line of development in doing an experiment to meet the demands of validation. He can thus preserve the integrity of his introspective perspective. The fact is, man needs and wants instruction from the introspective perspective, for that is the end at which he lives, and the one which affirms again and again that he is more than something compelled, an empty organism with nothing working for him except a reinforcement history outside his control. The importance of introspective theory is reflected in Russell's summary evaluation of the problem of volition (final causes) vs. mechanistic determinism (compelled efficient causes): "even if volitions are mechanically determined, that is no reason for denying freedom in the sense revealed by introspection, or for supposing that mechanical events are not determined by volitions" (1957, p. 201).

Possibly we can illustrate this issue through a simplified example. Suppose we are interested in describing the behavior of individuals who must select either of two staircases to ascend to a balcony above. We might find that when there is no one blocking the way from above, 90 per cent of the individuals observed facing this decision will select the right-hand stairway. Now, is this "causal law" a compelling or a functional law of behavior? It would be difficult to think of it as a compelling law, for, after all, any one subject *could* ascend by the left-hand stairway. In fact, if we made our law public we might find that a certain proportion of our subjects, asked to face this decision again, chose to avoid the right-hand stairway, quite by design. They might do this because they think of themselves as individualists ("for the sake of" their individuality) or as somehow different from other people, or they might do it simply for the sheer devil of it. If enough individuals decide to switch stairways, our "law" may no longer hold. In many life situations man feels he can always say "no" or in fact do the opposite of what he ordinarily does. Not in all life situations can he do this, but in some he believes he can, and this is one of them.

What would the "natural science" psychological theorist have to say about this law of ours? He would probably call it an R-R law, and state that we had simply overlooked that at some point in the past we could locate the *real* cause or causes which would explain how a person now chooses either the right-hand or the left-hand stairway. For example, the subject was reared in a right-handed culture; his parents taught him to use his right hand and not his left; his parents or various other environmental influencers taught him to think of himself (mediating responses) as an "individualist," and now, knowing what most people do, he does the opposite, and so on. If we could go back in time, down the interlocking chain of Ss and Rs, we could eventually identify the real S or Ss compelling the eventual R now observed in the subject's behavior. This would be an S-R law and it would meet the demands of natural science's reliance on efficient-cause explanation and an objectively identifiable influence in the environment. This is how the S-R theorist reasons, to preserve his concept of compelling causation. Yet, what has he in fact done? He has added to our picture of the individual certain functional relations which enrich our meaningful understanding of the latter's behavior, and then *arbitrarily* decided when to call a halt, when to name the so-called S or Ss compelling the behavior. As Russell has taught us, Ss are just as easily inferred from Rs as vice versa, and the S-R theorist has decided to play the game according to *his theory* of behavior. Beginning with the R, he reasons backward to a convenient functional relation which he can supposedly identify as an observer, and then terms *this* functional tie "the cause" of the behavior sequence, "the S-R law."

Why stop with instructions from parents, why not take their genealogy back another generation or two, until possibly we could cite the "true" S as having occurred when a left-handed grandfather decided to play third base rather than first base when he himself was a boy, and naturally had to modify his throwing arm if he were to succeed in baseball? Why not trace a family trait of individualism back to the religious upheaval the subject's forefathers might have struggled through to achieve complete freedom of worship? Then too, both baseball and religious values are learned responses to earlier stimuli, so why stop with either of these points in retrospective time? What makes any given S *the* S of importance? It is not *only* a matter of what can be observed, since each of the above is equally observable. Obviously, there is an arbitrary point at which any given theorist must stop to assert his S-R law.

One can easily agree with everything the S-R theorist objectively points to in the origins of behavior, assuming that he points to functional ties which are relevant to the behavior we are interested in. One can even help him in his quest for what are nothing more than functional relations between constructs, helping us to enrich our meaningful knowledge of behavior. *Of course* there are identifiable functional relations between environment and human behavior. An individual learns his goals or develops his intellect from his environment in an historical time sequence. One does not have to take a position as either for or against something so obvious as efficient causes in human behavior. *All behavior has an efficient cause,* and some behaviors may be easily interpreted and almost limited to such a causal analysis (certain routine or reflexive types of activity). But this does not mean we must reduce man's planful intellect to *nothing but* this form of explanation. Why not, if it works? Because though it may work within the "error limits" of predictive probability (see Chapter VI) under the restricted applications of our less life-like experiments, it fails to work in the sense of providing knowledge about ourselves as we behave in our everyday, real world. It fails to instruct us in what we know ourselves to be, as generations of men have expressed themselves in consonance with us through the history books and the pages of literature, in a meaningful way. Even where it works in the everyday world — as in actuarial prediction — it fails to instruct, it fails to answer questions such as "why" men drink or smoke to excess, even though the odds have been reported to them about the potentially harmful outcome of such activities. Men in real life ask these "whys," and someone with an interest in their behavior should be permitted to answer them, even if this answer demands a final-cause explanation from the introspective perspective.

Nowhere is this need better illustrated than in the conclusion arrived at by Immergluck (1964). This hard determinist, who fails to distinguish between functional and compelling causation, comes to the conclusion that man will always need to have an introspective sense of conviction that he is free, even when he knows better: "I propose that even in the event that such encompassing determinism should ever become unambiguously and universally accepted, we will (must?) still persist to behave *as if* inner freedom were a fact, if not for those around us, then at least for ourselves" (p. 280).* Man's sense of freedom is presented as analogous to various other perceptual distortions, but the conviction of this belief is not to be denied, and it is therefore to be frankly accepted as an "illusion" (p. 279). Immergluck would presumably instruct man as follows: "You are really not free, if by that you mean you can actually determine your own behavior; but, please go on acting as if you were free, since that is natural for you and since you will probably insist upon it in any case; this belief is an interesting aspect of your nature, kind of like the fact that you can see water on a hot road ahead when there really is none."

There are two problems with this instruction: (1) it fails to satisfy the man facing a wretched decision to know that he basically has no hand in the matter after all; (2) it is based upon a debatable interpretation of causation, one which has traditionally *not* been used to explain acts of volition. Like the patellar knee jerk of Wolpe's example, perceptual illusions persist *regardless* of our knowledge about their causes. They are tied to the automatic (compelling) reflexes of our body, and well conceptualized as efficient causes. But human goals are tied to ethical and/or aesthetic *values,* fundamentally arbitrary, although com-

---

* Here we have the fascinating paradox of a human being proposing to other human beings a principle of belief "for the sake of which" we are to behave, even though his formal position denies that human beings have such behavioral prerogatives.

pelling enough once decided upon. Such goals are not best conceptu-alized in efficient-cause terms, and have not been so conceived in the history of philosophy. They are like final causes, and if we force them into a compelling, efficient-cause form, we rob them of their meaningful essence. When it comes to ethics, knowing that one is really not free to choose among the alternatives open to him destroys or at least greatly detracts from his initiative to act. Knowing that a water puddle ahead on the road is only illusory has no direct bearing on the outcome of this dis-torted perception, which will take place in any case. Knowing that which of two roads he is to take in the fork ahead will not really be decided by the individual *does* bear on the direction he chooses. If a man really believes he lacks responsibility to choose, he may or may not take the "correct" road ahead, even when he knows which alternative is so labeled.

Values and Knowing vs. Unknowing Hedonism

An efficient cause may be thought of as the "fabric of movement," as the effective motion which brings about action (either functionally or compellingly), or as the historic past to which all things in the present are tied. But, if we assume that a *direction* in action, or a *course* in history, is *also* taking place, then the concept of efficient causation is not adequate to the theoretical task. A direction or a course of action demands that we add the idea of evaluation, it calls for a self-reflexive intelligence which can look back on itself and alter or adapt, based on certain presumptions about the worth of its movement. In other words, it calls for a knowing activity, in which values are at play. And values cannot be described in efficient-cause terms. Efficient-cause analysis can permit us to say that values are transmitted or "learned" in the past, true enough. But to show what we mean when we speak of values we must phrase our discussion in terms of future events, a fact that Bacon properly grasped in assigning the final cause to ethics and aesthetics — areas which clearly deal with values or preferences. Although learned in the past, values *as* values gain their meaning for what they have to say about the "henceforth."

If two individuals disagree over some point of value, such as how they "ought" to behave, what can we say about their predicament? Surely they have both *learned* their respective value systems in the past. They can each readily understand this, and might even agree that had they experienced reverse life histories they would now each hold to the other's value structure. But *this* agreement does not help to resolve their *other* disagreement. They would still have the value question to resolve, for values cannot be explained away this easily; values herald the future course of events and are only captured accurately in a final-cause concept. They do not draw man into the future, like some natural force of suction, nor are they always necessarily right or good or ethical (though a teleological position might make them appear to be so foreordained). As we shall see in Chapter IX, there is always room for an alternative set of values, because arbitrariness is never quite done away with in human decisions. What given datum is right or good or ethical depends upon the frame of reference within which it is to be judged. But here again values enter the picture (our "criterion problem" of Chapter VI). It would be nice to be free of the nagging necessity of values, which condition our theoretical biases, but it seems that final causes are not so easily dismissed.

In psychology, values have been most often subsumed under a hedonistic "reinforcement principle" of one sort or another, implying that animals or humans behave according to whatever furthers their sense of pleasure. But how are we to conceive of this pleasure? Is it a knowing pleasure, as conditioned by the projections of a goal in the future, or an unknowing pleasure in the ever-present behavioral activity? Psychology has made of behavior an unknowing act of stamping S to R through pleasurable aftermaths, called reinforcements. The S-R concept, since it is an efficient-cause concept, promotes a kind of blind, unknowing hedonism within which the organism is shaped into patterns of responding quite independent of any intellect (which would call for a final-cause term). Drive concepts are usually introduced at this point to explain why a satisfying state of affairs comes about; it does so whenever there is a drive-reduction, all purely mechanical and independent of the individual's awareness. The black box is at all times blind to its own chain of behavioral events.

How different it is when we propose a knowing hedonism, an extension of pleasure to a final-cause interpretation. People may seek satisfactions, not only in the mechanical on-going processes, but also in the longer-term eventuality of a "future event." In fact, the longer-term hedonism may come into conflict with the current processes of hedonistic pleasures. Many of the classical theories of ethical "self-realization" make the presumption that a man seeking to self-realize can never — even in theory — reach the exalted state for which he strives. The pleasure, the satisfaction, is gained in simply trying continuously to better oneself, to make oneself over into the person he "ought" to be (depending upon the given value system, of course). So long as this functional pleasure of striving for the future is maintained, the individual may surely be said to be under the motivation of a final cause. Why is this the case? Because it can often be shown that he *foregoes* all manner of efficient-cause hedonistic gratification to work toward the final-cause hedonistic gratification. Thus, though not all men behave this way, we do have the comrade-in-arms or the martyr who forego life itself for what they take to be a greater good in the future.

To explain such behavior exclusively on the basis of an efficient-cause analysis of a reinforcement history robs it not only of its ethical import, but of its very meaning as an item of behavior in man's repertoire. However, along with their inability to distinguish between various types of behavioral control (see Chapter VI), psychologists often find it difficult to admit a difference of this sort in their hedonistic positions. Just as controls are controls, pleasures are pleasures, so why split hairs? They fail to recognize that they have hamstrung themselves by the theoretical devices they have selected to analyze and describe human behavior. Rather than change the devices it is much easier for them to change the meanings of "personal sacrifice" or "the dignity of man."

Some Teleologies, Hidden and Otherwise

The recognition that Newton used an informally phrased final cause in his world view by employing a concept of God alerts us to the fact that other theorists must substitute various technical devices in order to deal with the issues ordinarily handled through final-cause explanation. In fact, one might well ponder whether it is possible to completely exclude teleology from the description of some phenomenon, particularly when that phenomenon is animate. That is, teleological factors may simply "go underground" or be taken for granted, like the S-R teleology referred to above (p. 231), where an S always knows its correct R. Aristotle's theoretical insight that four causes are to be used in explaining an event may be inescapable. It is fascinating to see how various personality theorists make use of teleological explanations in their views. As a brief exercise, let us examine the teleologies of Freud, Rogers, and Skinner as representatives of the psycho-analytical, neo-gestalt, and S-R traditions, respectively.

Freud is by far the most complex of these theorists in the use of a teleology. We have already shown in Chapter V that Freud was a soft determinist (p. 128), and in Chapter VII we saw him ascribe a "will" to his patients (p. 193). Even so, probably in response to the promptings of his physicalistic education and the criticisms of men like Fliess (see Chapter VII), Freud seems especially ambivalent over the use of a concept of goal-directed behavior. One sees him vacillating between an attempt to explain behavior in terms of efficient-cause instinctual energies, and final-cause intentions, cathected objects, and so on. Freud rejected any possibility of using deifying final causes in the explanation of the universe, of course, referring to the "Obscure, unfeeling and unloving powers [which] determine men's fate" (1964a, p. 167). But he also had great faith in man's intellect, and his view of science was that it is merely an extension of this intellectual creativity: "Our best hope for the future is that intellect — the scientific spirit, reason — may in process of time establish a dictatorship in the mental life of man" (p. 171). There are two varieties of science, one for the physical and one for the mental sphere: "Strictly speaking there are only two sciences: psychology, pure and applied, and natural science" (p. 179).

Since his special brand of science involved a retrospective, observational form of study rather than experimentation, it is probably not surprising that Freud's formal statement of teleology was tied to his theory of instincts, which are "given" from birth. An instinct is an inborn urge which aims at restoring all matter and mental activity (the latter stimulating overt behavior) to a previously existing condition: *"an instinct is an urge inherent in organic life to restore an earlier state of things . . ."* (Freud, 1955, p. 36). This "conservative tendency" is noted even in the sexual instincts or, as Freud came to subsume them, in Eros, where sex reproduces "primitive states of the organism" (e.g., by procreation a primitive child ensues) (p. 44); but it is most clearly evident in the death instinct (later called Thanatos by his students). That is, if you apply this reasoning to the phenomenon of death it is possible to conclude that: " *'the aim of all life is death'* and, *looking backwards, that 'inanimate things existed before living ones' "* (p. 38). Death brings about this earlier inanimate state. Thus far, if we have a teleology in the goals of instincts, it is one derived out of the past, and needing re-establishing in the future (which Freud tied to the phenomena of repetition-compulsion, the need to symbolize past concerns, the need to "work through" past conflicts, and so on).

Freud's thought did not rest with only this retrospective view of instinct. Ego-instincts most easily typify this conservative tendency, but the instincts of the sexual sphere (identified classically as the id instincts or Eros) had a more final-cause cast to them. The future goal of the sexual instinct from birth is to seek eventual union with other cells (in reproduction), and in this way to preserve life by "living on" within the cells of the offspring: "One cell helps to preserve the life of another, and the community of cells can survive even if individual cells have to die" (p. 50). This is a physical teleology, but it is interesting to note that Freud equates his line of reasoning with the philosophy of Schopenhauer, and essentially analogizes between the will to live and Eros: "For him [i.e., Schopenhauer] death is the 'true result and to that extent the purpose of life,' while the sexual instinct is the embodiment of the will to live" (p. 50). This "will to live" is about as close as Freud gets to a growth principle. As is well known, in his later years Freud was outspokenly pessimistic regarding the nature of the universe or the advance of man. Though he believed firmly in the advantages to be gained from the exercise of intellect, he did not feel that nature was in any way bound to reflect a happy development. Organic evolution can involve both higher development or involution and retrogression. When it comes to man, there is no fundamental "instinct to perfection" reflected in his nature: "What appears in a minority of human individuals as an untiring impulsion towards further perfection can easily be understood as a result of the instinctual repression upon which is based all that is most precious in human civilization" (p. 42).

The reason man "advances" is because certain instinctual sexual needs remain always unsatisfied, or partially unsatisfied, and this presses man forward to seek gratification of the repressed libidinal forces. Here we see Freud attempting to explain behavior in efficient-cause terms, but he does not succeed too well because an instinct has self-expressive (stimulus-producing) qualities. Freud's sexual instincts come to know their ends and cathect objects which would provide them satisfaction. Man has goals, but these goals are brought to bear from out of an unconscious realm of mind, from a source no one can control directly, and which ultimately depends upon instincts which know and seek certain goals (such as sexual union of a boy with his mother). Just how far any given man might "advance" would depend upon the interplay of sexual gratification and repression, and how he worked out this "vacillating rhythm" (p. 41). Only by a study of the given case history could one retrospectively determine why in one case a man sublimated properly and achieved certain heights, while another man developed a neurotic phobia (p. 42). Advances are our assessments of the ways certain men work through their repressed sexual instincts.

Of course, a theorist does not have to defend "advancement of mankind" in order to use a final cause, a purpose, a principle "for the sake of which" man might behave. Whether some goals in life advance man or lead him to retrogress is indeed an independent problem, calling for evaluation according to other principles or purposes (i.e., those of the assessor). Nor does a final cause have to be conceptualized as operating within consciousness. It appears to us that each of Freud's personality constructs — id, ego, and super-ego — had certain intentions "for the sake of which" it maneuvered and they clashed. So we do not discount Freud's use of a final cause in the description of man simply because he spoke derisively of certain forms of advancement. In subsequent chapters we shall argue that Freud's libido theory is a pseudo-physical subterfuge for more psychological (intelligent, striving) explanations of man's behavior (see Chapter X), and that Freud is the father of modern personality theory precisely because he was the first physician to make illness intelligent (see Chapter XII).

When we turn to Carl Rogers, we have none of the ambivalence over the use of final causes in the description of man that we witness in Freud. For Rogers, man is capable of consciously directing his own fate, as long as he has not become so bound up with neurotic defenses that he loses this freedom to act. All men can express willful decisions in the conscious sphere, but the neurotic "finds that he *cannot* behave in the fashion that he chooses. He is determined by the factors in the existential situation, but these factors include his defensiveness, his denial or distortion of some of the relevant data" (Rogers, 1961, p. 193). One might describe neurotic man in compelling, efficient-cause terms, for he has lost that spontaneity which final causation allows. He has lost his freedom and has given himself over to situational determination completely: he is a passive experiencer and not an active, willful stimulator of life and behavior. "The fully functioning person, on the other hand, not only experiences, but utilizes, the most absolute freedom when he spontaneously, freely, and voluntarily chooses and wills that which is also absolutely determined" (p. 193). For Rogers, science is itself an exercise of choice by the behavior of certain men; he asks that we come to view all men this way and to rid psychology of the mechanism from which it now suffers in the study of man:

> If the line of reasoning I have been presenting is valid, then it opens new doors to us. If we frankly face the fact that science takes off from a subjectively chosen set of values, then we are free to select the values we wish to pursue. . . . Suppose we start with a set of ends, values,

purposes, quite different from the type of goals we have been considering. Suppose we do this quite openly, setting them forth as a possible value choice to be accepted or rejected. . . . We might then value: Man as a process of becoming; as a process of achieving worth and dignity through the development of his potentialities; The individual human being as a self-actualizing process, moving on to more challenging and enriching experiences; The process by which the individual creatively adapts to an ever new and changing world; The process by which knowledge transcends itself, as for example the theory of relativity transcended Newtonian physics, itself to be transcended in some future day by a new perception (pp. 395–396).

Not since the days of William McDougall — who, when speaking once to a group of young psychology students touchingly ended his talk with "If then you must be behaviorists, I beg that you will be purposive behaviorists" (1923, p. 288) — has anyone argued more eloquently and with more feeling than Rogers that psychology need not limit itself to efficient-cause explanation. We have come full circle in psychology — from McDougall vs. Watson to Rogers vs. Skinner. The same points are being made, and no resolution is in sight. Doubtless, psychology will continue its schizoid pattern, because as long as it is possible to control and predict his behavior extraspectively with some success, there will be a continuing reluctance to assign self-direction to the man under observation.

Skinner has a very interesting position on the matter of teleology, one which is more complex and subtle than Rogers', but which is not quite as roundabout as Freud's. Unlike Freud, who sees stimulation to behavior as emanating from man's mind (with emphasis on the unconscious), and who therefore thinks of intellect and science as ultimately synonymous, Skinner has man mediating rather than initiating the advance of science. Man merely thinks it is he who creates scientific hypotheses; actually his "mind" is a series of responses which come to be attached to stimuli from the environment. Yet somehow, according to Skinner, there is progress in science, presumably based upon the fact that material rewards (positive reinforcements) are greater in life as time goes on during a scientific age:

The history of science is the history of the growth of man's place in nature. Men have extended their capacities to react to nature discriminatively by inventing microscopes, telescopes, and thousands of amplifiers, indicators, and tests. They have extended their power to alter and control the physical world with machines and instruments of many sorts. A large part of this achievement has been verbal. The discoveries and achievements of individual men have been preserved and improved and transmitted to others. The growth of science is positively accelerated, and we have reached a breathless rate of advance (1957, p. 459).

Skinner is indeed a visionary and here bears the message with ringing teleological overtones. He is a child of his time, and participates fully in the view of "progress" from which all natural scientists draw strength to continue their studies (Becker and Barnes, 1952, Ch. XIII). Off in the future, men will attain the power to control one another's behavior and continue to multiply the happy outcomes of the march of science (Skinner, 1957, p. 460). This is a very strong teleological theme in the behaviorist camp: that one works for the future, that it is unfair to criticize what is being done now as having no relevance for human nature because science goes where its "truths" lead, that "practical" studies of the R-R variety are premature and really fail to explain events, whereas the future S-R research will do so, and so on. It is significant that Freud's final assessment of *his* science ended on a highly pessimistic note. In one of his last papers, "Analysis Terminable and Interminable," Freud (1964b) essentially concludes that psycho-analysis cannot result in permanent cures, even for analysts themselves, who need periodic re-analyses. Psycho-analysis comes out more as a way of life than an advancing science with great prospects, and the only true termination of the analysis is brought about by death.

Summing up our review, it would probably be true to say that Freud falls between Rogers and Skinner on the question of just how free man is to act. Man has goals, but these are not always consciously striven for, nor can all of them be consciously decided upon. Rogers would feel that the latter was possible. Skinner would feel that the theoretical possibility of self-direction in man is based upon the naïveté of the theorist. Concerning the natural evolution of a positive trend in science, Freud is clearly the least teleological of the three men. And, though it may seem rather strange to typify him this way, Skinner is clearly the *most* teleological. Rogers at least recognizes a certain arbitrariness in the preliminaries of science, on which man can decide and in this way have something to say about the course of this thing called "science." Rogers is suspicious of the complete fervor with which some men jump into the "breathless rate of advance" (see Chapter VII). He would prefer to take a deep breath and look things over before plunging ahead, because science might just as well descend as ascend over the course of time (1961, pp. 384–401). Skinner, on the other hand, is confident that science will continue to prove itself and that better days are coming in the future, if only man can rid himself of some of the peculiar and disproven "responses" (values) he now holds about his nature.

Vehicular vs. Discriminal Theoretical Constructs

The generally accepted definition of psychology as the science which controls and predicts *behavior* is often an awesome burden for the personality theorist to bear. If he is completely honest about it, he must surely recognize that he is rarely interested in "behavior," a label which is too indefinite and has the connotation of "response," thanks to years of easy interchange between the terms "S-R" and "behaviorism." Everything man "does," in the sense of talking, walking, and so on, can be called an aspect of his behavior. Are we interested in how men physically speak, in what they speak about, or the influences through which their speech content comes to reflect one topic rather than another? Although providing a broad umbrella for all psychologists to nestle under, it is apparent that behavior as such is not necessarily a psychological problem. One can study behavior in the natural science tradition as a chemist, physiologist, or anatomist. Watson's great hope was that, through application of efficient causes and compelling causes he could circumscribe all of man's behavior. If this were possible, then personality theory as such would be a mere extension of behavior theory. But is it? This is the question we must now consider.

What distinguishes a personality theorist from a general behavior theorist? It would appear that a distinction can be made by discussing the goals theorists seek in formulating their theories and in gathering their data. On the one hand, we have psychologists who seek to conceptualize their data in what might be called *vehicular* theoretical constructs. Theoretical propositions making use of vehicular constructs are those which tie together regularities in behavior sequences (laws) *regardless of the particular content* of the behavior sequence under study. These propositions and constructs would presumably obtain at a high level of abstraction and would subsume lower-level constructs of a more specific and hence restricted range of convenience. Many so-called basic learning theory constructs and physiological constructs are such "vehicles" for a variety of lower-level discriminators. On the other hand, some psychologists take an interest in *certain* behavior sequences rather than others, or *particular aspects* of a given behavior sequence, and thereby phrase their data in what might be called *discriminal* theoretical propositions and constructs. These constructs have a more restricted range of convenience, but they are still very useful and instructive because they make distinctions, refine our understanding, and point in directions which further investigation can take. It would seem most plausible to think of "natural science" behavior theorists as prone to the vehicular description of behavior (drive-reduction, reinforcement, extinction, stimulus generalization), whereas personality theorists are more prone to the discriminal description of behavior. Personality theorists seek to capture certain "styles" of behavior (e.g., typologies, traits), the relationship between only certain aspects of behavior (e.g., toilet training and later character structure), or the very unique and atypical in behavior (e.g., creativity, abnormal behavior).

In doing this, personality theorists must ultimately make value judgments regarding the nature of psychological health and sickness, or creativity and non-creativity. It is necessary to have a value reference in order to make the most simple discriminating assessment, like that between the "aggressive" and the "passive" personality. As we shall see in the remaining chapters of Part Two, it is in this sense that *all* personality theorists are *ethical* thinkers. Their act of judging people as to type *forces* this role upon them.

There is no hard and fast rule distinguishing one level of theory from the other, since any given theorist can and does make use of both types of constructs. Sigmund Freud had energy concepts (vehicular) as well as other, unique concepts, such as "fixation" (discriminal). Although it is not possible to explain vehicular construct data in discriminal construct terms (since the former is more abstract than the latter), the reverse is quite possible. Sometimes it happens that a psychologist uses vehicular constructs to explain behavior first conceptualized in discriminal construct terms. Difficulties then may arise, due to a change in the meaning originally intended, or to his naive conclusion that the original construct had somehow been supplanted and even surpassed. For example, when the neo-Freudian clinician asserts that his psychotherapy client is "transferring" feelings held earlier toward loved ones onto him as therapist, the neo-behaviorist may translate this to mean that the neurotic client is unable to differentiate between an earlier stimulus pattern (father) and a later stimulus pattern (therapist); i.e., that stimulus generalization has taken place.

This is a legitimate theoretical gambit, and for all practical purposes just as true as the original assertion. But the point is, an arbitrary translation has taken place which changes nothing and may even confuse. There is no greater theoretical justification for using a stimulus generalization explanation in this case than in the one explaining why this same neurotic individual fails to distinguish between "this" love partner (currently being seen) and an "earlier" love partner (formerly seen, who coldly rejected the neurotic). Here are two different behaviors explained by use of the same vehicular construct, yet the original meanings of "transference" and "maladjusted in romance situations" must remain, if we are to make any sense of our data. The concept of stimulus generalization is a vehicular construct which can be applied whenever and wherever the given theorist chooses to use it. The concept of "transference" cannot be so applied without considerable additional commentary. If we wish to represent Freud's thought adequately, we should not speak about the neurotic transferring feelings from an earlier sex partner to a later sex partner, though something akin to this might be said to have taken place. The concept of transference has a specific role in Freud's theory (i.e., it is a discriminal construct).

This is a common practice in psychology, translating concepts first proposed as discriminal constructs into vehicular constructs. As we noted in Chapter VII, it received great impetus in the post-World War II days, thanks to the work of Dollard and Miller (1950), who set out to bring the consulting room and research laboratory into line by translating Freudian psychology into S-R terms. Although they did not state this as a conscious motive, their activity most assuredly conformed to the Wundtian idea of providing a more basic, hence "better" description of Freudian personality theory by reducing it to the more fundamental (actually, more abstract) vehicular constructs which supposedly underlay it.

Even though Dollard and Miller seem to have had an appreciation of the role Freudian theory played in generating important personality constructs, once they had successfully "explained" repression as a failure on the part of the individual to label (cue-produced response) certain aspects of his environment (1950, p. 201), it seemed to many psychologists that this was a more basic and truer statement of fact than Freud's original formulation. Putting it in vehicular terms seemed to capture the essentials of the repression construct. "Not labeling" things covers many behaviors, but it was almost natural to think that — in time — psychologists would have "discovered" repression independent of Freud through reliance on vehicular constructs of this sort. Freud was an early, imprecise pioneer who did not really have the essentials of repression clearly defined. This seems to be the attitude which resulted, even though something was again lost in the learning theory translation, because on the Freudian view repression is *not* a passive act of failing to label items in the environment. Repression is an act of commission not of omission. Freud saw man as having an unconscious intellect which worked actively to bring about repression. It was not that labeling was missed, but that an unacceptable labeling had taken place in the unconscious mind. The S-R theorist has the original idea of repressive behavior (the discriminal construct meaning) well in mind — thanks to Freud — and in a sense misleads himself into thinking that his vehicular construct satisfactorily covers all of this meaning. The Freudian "map" is retained, so to speak, but the locations and signposts on it are altogether different. Who needs Freud? Who needs all the fanciful theoretical trimmings when the basic behaviors are before our eyes? Behavior is behavior, and in time all of the vaguely phrased Freudian constructs will surely receive a more precise, scientific definition.

Another frequent result of replacing a discriminal construct with a more abstract vehicular construct is that varied theoretical concepts melt into one another, and rather than clarifying or simplifying, we can confuse our audience. This phenomenon is evident in the writings of Ford and Urban (1963), who set out to present the psychotherapies of various theorists through what they call a "monistic view of human behavior"; for them, behavior includes "the antecedents to overt behavior, that is, 'personality organization,' as well as the motor and glandular events which most people label behavior" (p. 4). Beginning with this view of behavior, the analytical and client-centered theories discussed are subsumed under an R-R designation (pp. 150, 313, 441), and many of the discriminal constructs used by the classical personality theorists come out as vehicular "mediating responses." Thus, the Freudian ego is a "class of responses" (p. 189), character is a "large constellation of behavior including many different kinds of responses" (p. 190), and thought is also a "response class" (p. 196). Even so, having subsumed all manner of lower-order discriminal constructs under the rubric "response," Ford and Urban have the self-assurance to go on and criticize Rogers for supposedly doing something comparable in his theory of psychotherapy. They remark of Rogers' "theoretical propositions" that: "the exclusive attention paid . . . to very high-order concepts has led to a corresponding omission of propositions that deal with the interrelationships between classes of events at lower levels of abstraction, and most critical of all, at the level of observable events themselves" (p. 441).

Actually, Ford and Urban's use of the high-order concept "response" makes communication about the referent "a class of responses" far more vague and unclear than anything Rogers has ever said. If we have a theory which tells us to seek responses, how can we know where to begin making our observations? Which "responses" should we look for — the class of, the large constellation, or the class? How do we begin? On the strict S-R view as applied to personality there *is no way* to begin. In order to begin to think about a specific behavior, a specific set of responses, we need to invoke some "theory of behavior" other than the S-R theory. In short, *we cannot be monistic*. We must recognize that a lower-order discriminal construct is needed to vary the *meanings* of our term "response." Something like ego or character as *more than* simply responses is needed before we can carry on a theoretical line of reasoning. Rogers has surely found this something, and carried his line of development to several empirical demonstrations of his theory's usefulness. His style of thought is distinctive, and by subsuming his "unconditional positive regard" under the vehicular rubric "mediating response," we not only violate his intent in using it (rob it of meaning), we distort the image of man on which it is based. In following their so-called monistic course on the question of behavior, Ford and Urban even refer to Rank's *will* concept as consisting of "subjectively observable responses" (1963, p. 374). Surely this is a callous distortion of a final-cause view, to make it somehow consistent with a misguided notion of monism in behavior description. This interpretation does not accurately capture what Rank meant by "will," even though it may preserve the sanctity of S-R theory and its efficient-cause limitation.

When a theorist goes to vehicular construct explanations of personality like this, there is often a concomitant adoption or presumption of an informal discriminal construct. The Freudian or the Rankian meaning is maintained on an informal, analogical basis. The vehicular construct, resting as it often does upon an efficient-cause explanation, is then pointed to as handling all the meaningful variance in the theory being presented. But in fact, if one looks more closely, he will note other sources of discriminal construct explanation. Thus, for example, a large part of the Skinnerian theory of behavior is continually left unnamed. Every Skinnerian must at some point become a sociologist or social psychologist. This is because his theory of behavior must seek an extra-individual, environmental explanation of why certain people "choose" to play tenpins while others prefer more "cultivated" leisure time pursuits. One could be 100 per cent Skinnerian and then go on to seek in socio-historical trends the source of variability in people. Skinner meshes well with Hobbesian "group mind" discriminal constructs (Allport, 1954), because it is not the individual but the environmental group which determines behavior. Of course, the question why one environment differs from another is usually left open, because one immerses his theory in what is in fact taking place at the present moment. As we have already seen above, the S-R theorist is free to say when an S is *the* S of importance to any R-R behavior now being independently observed.

Finally, the distinction between vehicular and discriminal constructs emphasizes that learning theories have no formal basis in fact as theories of personality. Learning theories are about empty organisms, devoid of specific contents, but bearing the shell of all behaviors at once. We must guard against confusing this shell with man's "real" nature. As long as we are aware of vehicular vs. discriminal tactics in the generation of constructs we should not fall into error. The essential point is that one can and should study behavior through both types of constructs. It is not true that a behavior sequence is any more fundamentally or thoroughly explained when it is conceptualized in vehicular than in discriminal construct terms. Both types of constructs are equally valid, equally legitimate, equally scientific attempts to conceptualize behavioral data. Each is to be taken and understood at its own level of abstraction, in the context of meaning for which it was intended. Anything less does violence to the knowledge being conveyed.

Summary

Chapter VIII took up the question of how man's behavior, especially that aspect of it we term "personality," is to be conceptualized. The debate among early psychologists concerning the proper method of studying man — whether by introspection or experimentation — was interpreted as really a debate over the proper image of man to be incorporated in the science of psychology. What is the proper way to think about and to describe man? That was the essential point at issue shortly after the turn of the century.

Introspection was reviewed next, as an alternative to the more commonly accepted scientific method. A comparative analysis was made of the introspective efforts of Bakan and Jung; we then appreciated more clearly that what is desirable about introspection is its theoretical perspective, not its means of verification. Introspection as method is unacceptable, due to its exclusive reliance on procedural evidence; but as the source of theoretical hypotheses from "man's perspective" (the data under study) it has no equal. The value of literature in the study of the human condition is that literary artists supply us with introspective meanings gleaned from their experience. Freud obtained such meanings directly from the introspective efforts of his clients, but he also turned to and greatly appreciated literary insights. Psychotherapy, like fiction in literature, is one of the ways man has of speaking for himself in his own conceptualization.

The real difficulty for a personality theorist comes when he tries to transfer an introspectively derived hypothesis into extraspective terms, so that a validational test can be carried out. The concept of "line of development" was introduced to underscore this theory-test sequence. If a theory is written from the extraspective perspective, its line of development can be shorter than if the theory is written from an introspective perspective. It is advocated that we permit the line of development to be extended in psychology. One cannot both "control all variables" in a study and at the same time hope to investigate highly interesting, yet poorly understood notions about man's personality. Rather than asking them to settle for a lesser goal — the performing of only tight, simple, and consequently safe research designs — it is argued that cross-validation of "looser" designs be demanded of those psychological scientists who are more attracted to the aesthetics of theory than to the aesthetics of method.

Another aspect of this is the extent of compatibility between theory and method.

In psychology, a distinction between the methodological construct of IV-DV and the theoretical construct of S-R is often obscured due to their compatibility. It is natural for theories to be framed in terms of compatible verification methods. Modern experimental science, founded as it was in the natural sciences, is highly compatible with an extraspective formulation. The introspective theorist must extend a line of development in order to validate, which seems to the extraspectionist to violate parsimony. The greatest danger of this compatibility between extraspective views of man and extraspective methods of validating hypotheses about man is that many psychologists naively believe they factually "discover," by methodological experimentation, man's nature to be that of a passive responder to stimuli outside his awareness and self-control. IV-DV findings are taken immediately as direct proof of the S-R theory, due to the identity of these two constructs. Then, as with the Newtonian physics of old, mechanistic methodology becomes a mechanistic metaphysics, and the fallacy of "affirming the consequent" is continually capitalized on to buttress an *arbitrary* view of man in the smug complacency that "facts speak for themselves."

The matter of compatibility between a theory and its method led naturally into a discussion of how one's view of *causation* in the explanation of phenomena largely determines the view of man he eventually settles for. The extraspectionist, working in the tradition of Helmholtz and Wundt, hopes to explain man's behavior exclusively on the basis of efficient-cause explanation. In this way, he seeks to continue in the "natural science" tradition of Bacon and Newton. He can thereby postulate man as an empty organism between efficient cause and effect and no more, for to impute a mind to man is to open the door for final-cause explanations.

The question was then raised as to whether it is possible and/or desirable to have *both* an efficient-cause and a final-cause explanation of man's behavior working side by side in the same theory of behavior. Would this not violate parsimony, and would not the matter of hard determinism suffice in place of some extraneous final-cause explanation? It was concluded that since efficient causes need not be thought of as compelling — but rather as functional — man can indeed be seen in both efficient-cause and final-cause terms at the same time. The hand that throws a rock can be explained by efficient-cause, but the target selected for that rock still demands a final-cause explanation. The rock itself is adequately explained by efficient causes, but is the man who aimed its flight most accurately captured in this way? Goals, once decided upon, are 100 per cent "determined." Efficient-cause description as such does not call for a hard determinism, something the physicists now recognize and accept completely. Teleology is the root source for hard determinism positions.

Chapter VIII next discussed the issue of values, and stressed that the value concept must be considered in terms of the future, not of the past. A difference was demonstrated between unknowing or blind hedonism (based on efficient cause) and knowing or intelligent hedonism (based on final cause). Teleologies, both hidden and obvious were then pointed to, and even the Skinnerian theoretical position was shown to have

·definite teleological underpinnings. Finally, a distinction was made between vehicular and discriminal theoretical constructs. Vehicular constructs are those which tie together regularities in behavior sequences (laws) regardless of the particular content of the behavior sequence under study. Discriminal theoretical constructs have a more restricted range of convenience, since they are aimed at capturing the flavor of distinct "styles" of behavior. It is argued that both types of constructs are equally scientific attempts to conceptualize behavioral data.

References

Adler, A. *Problems of neurosis* (edited by Philippe Mairet). New York: Harper & Row, 1964.

Allport, G. W. The historical background of modern social psychology. In Vol. I of G. Lindzey (Ed.), *Handbook of social psychology.* Reading, Mass.: Addison-Wesley, 1954. Pp. 3–56.

Allport, G. W. *Personality and social encounter.* Boston: Beacon Press, 1960.

Ansbacher, H. L. The significance of the socio-economic status of the patients of Freud and of Adler. *American Journal of Psychotherapy,* 1959, *13,* 376–382.

Bakan, D. A reconsideration of the problem of introspection. *Psychological Bulletin,* 1954, *51,* 105–118.

Becker, H., and Barnes, H. E. (Eds.) *Social thought from lore to science.* Washington, D.C.: Harren Press, 1952. 2 vols.

Boodin, J. E. Truth and agreement. *Psychological Review,* 1909, *16,* 55–66.

Boring, E. G. Mind and mechanism. *American Journal of Psychology,* 1946, *59,* 173–192.

Boring, E. G. *A history of experimental psychology,* 2nd ed. New York: Appleton-Century-Crofts, 1950.

Boring, E. G. A history of introspection. *Psychological Bulletin,* 1953, *50,* 169–189.

Bridgman, P. W. Determinism in modern science. In S. Hook (Ed.), *Determinism and freedom in the age of modern science.* New York: New York University Press, 1958. Pp. 43–63.

Burtt, E. A. *The metaphysical foundations of modern physical science,* rev. ed. Garden City, N.Y.: Doubleday & Co., 1955. Quotations used by permission of Humanities Press, New York.

Cassirer, E. *The problem of knowledge.* New Haven: Yale University Press, 1950.

Dollard, J., and Miller, N. E. *Personality and psychotherapy: An analysis in terms of learning, thinking, and culture.* New York: McGraw-Hill, 1950.

Ford, D. H., and Urban, H. B. *Systems of psychotherapy.* New York: Wiley, 1963.

Freud, S. *The origins of psycho-analysis, letters to Wilhelm Fliess, drafts and notes: 1887–1902.* New York: Basic Books, 1954.

Freud, S. *Beyond the pleasure principle* (1920). In Vol. XVIII of J. Strachey (Ed.), *The standard edition of the complete psychological works of Sigmund Freud.* London: The Hogarth Press, 1955. Pp. 1–64.

Freud, S. On beginning the treatment (1913). In Vol. XII of J. Strachey (Ed.), *The standard edition of the complete psychological works of Sigmund Freud.* London: The Hogarth Press, 1958. Pp. 121–144.

Freud, S. Delusions and dreams in Jensen's *Gradiva* (1906). In Vol. IX of J. Strachey (Ed.), *The standard edition of the complete psychological works of Sigmund Freud.* London: The Hogarth Press, 1959. Pp. 7–95.

Freud, S. *New introductory lectures on psycho-analysis* (1932). In Vol. XXII of J. Strachey (Ed.), *The standard edition of the complete psychological works of Sigmund Freud.* London: The Hogarth Press, 1964. Pp. 3–182. Also in Vol. 54 of R. M. Hutchins (Ed.), *Great books of the western world.* Chicago: Encyclopedia Britannica, 1952. Pp. 807–884. (1964a)

Freud, S. Analysis terminable and interminable (1937). In Vol. XXIII of J. Strachey (Ed.), *The standard edition of the complete psychological works of Sigmund Freud.* London: The Hogarth Press, 1964. Pp. 209–253. (1964b)

Fullerton, G. S. The world as mechanism. *Psychological Review,* 1902, *9,* 1–26.

Hofstadter, R. *Anti-intellectualism in American life.* New York: Knopf, 1963.

Hyman, S. E. *The tangled bank.* New York: Atheneum, 1962.

Immergluck, L. Determinism-freedom in contemporary psychology: An ancient problem revisited. *American Psychologist,* 1964, *19,* 270–281.

James, W. *The principles of psychology.* Vol. 53 of R. M. Hutchins (Ed.), *Great books of the western world.* Chicago: Encyclopedia Britannica, 1952. Originally published — New York: Holt, 1890.

Jung, C. G. *Memories, dreams, reflections.* Copyright 1963. New York: Pantheon Books, A Division of Random House, Inc., and London: William Collins Sons, Ltd.

Kantor, J. R. *The scientific evolution of psychology.* Vol. 1. Chicago: Principia, 1963.

Ladd, G. T. On certain hindrances to the progress of psychology in America. *Psychological Review,* 1899, *6,* 121–133.

McDougall, R. Mind as middle term. *Psychological Review,* 1912, *19,* 386–403.

McDougall, W. Purposive or mechanical psychology? *Psychological Review,* 1923, *30,* 273–288.

Munsterberg, H. Psychological atomism. *Psychological Review,* 1900, *7,* 1–17.

Osgood, C. E. *An alternative to war or surrender.* Urbana, Ill.: University of Illinois Press, 1962.

Rank, O. *Will therapy, and truth and reality.* New York: Knopf, 1945.

Rogers, C. R. *On becoming a person.* Boston: Houghton Mifflin Co., 1961.

Russell, B. *Mysticism and logic.* Garden City, N.Y.: Doubleday Anchor, 1957.

Russell, B. *Our knowledge of the external world.* New York: New American Library, 1960.

Sanford, E. C. Psychology and physics. *Psychological Review,* 1903, *10,* 105–119.

Skinner, B. F. *Walden two.* New York: Macmillan, 1948.

Skinner, B. F. *Verbal behavior.* New York: Appleton-Century-Crofts, 1957.

Spence, K. W. *Behavior theory and conditioning.* New Haven: Yale University Press, 1956.

Spence, K. W. A theory of emotionally based drive (D) and its relation to performance in simple learning situations. *American Psychologist,* 1958, *13,* 131–141.

Titchener, E. B. Psychology: science or technology? *Popular Science Monthly,* 1914, *84,* 39–51.

Watson, J. B. Psychology as the behaviorist views it. *Psychological Review,* 1913, *20,* 158–177.

Weiss, A. P. The mind and the man within. *Psychological Review,* 1919, *26,* 327–334.

Wolpe, J. *Psychotherapy by reciprocal inhibition.* Stanford, Calif.: Stanford University Press, 1958.

Dialectical vs. Demonstrative Reasoning in the History of Western Thought

If man is inaccurately conceptualized as an empty organism, if he is something more than a responder to past stimuli, then it follows that we should be able to point to some principle of analysis or heuristic device that shows how he differs from inanimate objects such as rocks in flight or electric machines which "think." The burden of proof is on us, and in the present chapter we hope to lay the groundwork for a distinction between animate and inanimate by tracing two styles of reasoning through the history of Western thought. Reasoning refers to the flow of thought. To reason is to draw inferences, to extend a line of inquiry, to come to some conclusion, which is then taken as either a further inference (hypothesis) to be developed intellectually or tested in experience, or as an "absolute truth" in its own right. Down through the centuries in the Western world there has been what amounts to a continuing debate over the relative merits of two types of reasoning which we will call *dialectical* and *demonstrative* (following Aristotle's terminology in the latter case).

In tracing the course of this debate through certain selected adversaries over the history of thought, we hope to provide background for a major thesis which will be greatly elaborated in Chapters X and XI. This thesis has it that what is peculiarly human is dialectical, including man's thought processes (mind) and "human" behavior in general. That is, as a form of metaconstruct (style of construing), dialectical terminology presents us with the *most accurate* picture of the fundamental human condition. Extending this, it will be argued that whereas Karl Marx knowingly deflected the dialectic into his theory of social science and from thence into economics, political science, and sociology (a well known fact), *Sigmund Freud and his followers unknowingly deflected*

255

the dialectic as metaconstruct into psychology and psychiatry (a less well known or unappreciated fact).

This chapter will first take up the meanings of dialectic in the history of Western philosophical thought, and then consider briefly the implications of this review for certain theoretical and methodological issues drawn from Part One.

Meanings of Dialectic in the History of Western Philosophical Thought

The history of dialectical vs. demonstrative reasoning is as old as the history of thought; one cannot say with any clear justification that one form of reasoning arose in man's thought before the other. It seems highly likely that both must be taken as givens within thought, and that which one is emphasized as superior at any given time over the centuries must be seen in the context of just what purpose a proponent had in mind when he argued for one or the other of these types of reasoning. This is the lesson of history: the fact that during various periods either one of these patterns was held up as superior, or more elegant, more accurate, less mystical, less critical, depending upon what case the proponent was trying to make. Our story begins with ancient Greece, where dialectic has the upper hand in the philosophies of Socrates and Plato, but before we leave that age, Aristotle has come along to frame the problem clearly for the first time, to assign names to the alternative kinds of reasoning open to man, and to set going an historical debate which has never been resolved and still plagues the contemporary mind, albeit in a somewhat different guise.

Greek Philosophy

Socrates (469 B.C.–399 B.C.) · Although he did not invent the practice, since he seems to have learned much about it from Zeno and Parmenides (Russell, 1959, p. 53), Socrates must certainly be given credit as the first great dialectician. As a young man, Socrates was apparently associated with the Greek Sophists, but he himself was never a Sophist and he later condemned their use of the dialectic for mere rhetorical advantage because it fell short of the goal of "knowledge." Sophists were "practical-minded" individuals who took pay to teach Grecians in the workings of law, philosophy, and the arts of rhetoric so that, for example, the educated businessman of the times could gain advantages over his competitors. They occasionally assisted the populace in pleading cases before the law, and so Sophists have been referred to as the forerunners of modern lawyers — though their often specious reasonings and appeals to hasty conclusion have lent a pejorative connotation to their name down through history. To this day "sophistry" denotes deception, and even the more acceptable noun, "sophistication," denotes ingenuineness and artificiality.

Plato has informed us most on the possible origins of the Sophistic movement in early Greece. It was his belief that this group could be traced to the view of Heraclitus (sixth-fifth century B.C.) that all things are in a state of flux, so change becomes the essence of existence (Cassirer, 1944, p. 47). One of the most influential and important Sophists was Protagoras (fifth century B.C.), who excites our interest because of a statement attributed to him by Plato. There are no works of Protagoras in existence, but apparently he held to the view that "concerning every subject opposite statements are possible." This belief was highly consistent with the view held by Pythagoras (died about 497 B.C.), the first man to call himself a philosopher (a "lover of wisdom"), who held that all "things are compounded of opposite qualities" and consequently nothing in existence "is simple and unmixed" (Untersteiner, 1954, pp. 19–26). Thus, notions of opposition, change, and complexity were in the air when Socrates came upon the philosophical scene.

Socrates never recorded a system of philosophy, and indeed, he never admitted that he had any knowledge to impart. Rather, he used a procedure of questioning others to bring out items of knowledge which he felt were carried by all men within their intellects, and which could be located if one had the proper method. Sophists might have used a comparable questioning method to win advantage in argument, or to persuade others of their preconceived notions or vested interests, but the genuine philosopher sought only the "truth," whatever it might be (and it was identified with the "good"). To understand this view better, we must appreciate that in the Grecian world view every man was seen as the descendant of a "Golden Age" of gods and hero figures, who naturally knew more and passed on to the lesser, human intellects of Athenian times more than the latter would have realized, had they ever made the intellectual effort. Thus, Plato (who put Socrates' thoughts to paper in the famous dialogues) has Socrates say: "and the ancients, who were our betters and nearer the gods than we are, handed down the tradition, that whatever things are said to be are composed of one and many, and have the finite and infinite implanted in them . . ." (1952, p. 612).

Knowledge is a unit, having a singleness about it, but also a diversity, and with the proper use of intellect, with the proper technique of examination, new insights can be gained, because that is the nature of the universe of things; all propositions, beliefs, or views that presently exist carry within them the seeds of new knowledge.

The remarkable implication of this view is that knowledge could be gained through discourse. Two men could talk and learn. It was not necessary for one to teach the other. It is in this sense that Socrates could proclaim ironically that he lacked knowledge himself. And his technique of instructing the young men of Athens, an association which eventually brought about or was used as an excuse for his execution, embodied this principle of interpersonal discourse. He taught (and learned) by posing a series of questions which were suggested in the discourse, checking a student's line of reasoning by taking the opposite position and, to the great consternation of many, refusing to take a dogmatic stand himself on any issue. Problems are not finally answered in the dialogues, but new levels of understanding do issue from them. His method occasionally perplexed and even irritated students, as it did Theaetetus, who once complained of feeling dizzy with all the gyrations, but Socrates could only reply that this feeling was the beginning of philosophy. The aim was, of course, to get the student to think for himself, to be self-critical, exact, and tenacious in his reasoning. Plato continued this style of instruction in his Academy, and it has come to be embodied in the classical conception of education as aiming not for the mere accretion of facts, but for the development of critical faculties in the student.

Socrates spent his life in the streets and gathering places of Athens, carrying on his talks with all manner of people. Though we will continue with his views in our consideration of his student, Plato, we want to stress at this point that the first great dialectician's philosophical life epitomized, in a way, one of the most characteristic features of dialectic: its discursive character. The dialectic of Socrates is oppositional because alternate positions are put forth by two contestants in vocal discourse, though one may do more prompting than the other. It is an interpersonal act of finding knowledge in intellects which at heart are one, reflected in each of many men. Dialectic furthers reasoning dynamically, through an interpersonal exchange.

Plato (427 B.C.–347 B.C.) · Although he continued the discursive methods of his teacher, Plato greatly raised the status of dialectic by turning it inward and essentially equating it with the power of reason.

This was consistent with Socrates' view, of course, but the major difference is in Plato's emphasis and great elaboration of the dialectic as pure reason — without emotion — seeking a perception of the absolute good. One could now think of it as taking place interpersonally, in discourse, or within the confines of one intellect, one brain, climbing the ladder of abstraction to ever greater heights for a glimpse of the higher truths before one descends again to empirical observation. Indeed, it was at the heights of abstraction that philosophic truths were to be found (which meant scientific truths as well), *not* at the levels of empirical observation. His position is made clear in the following:

> And when I speak of the other division of the intelligible, you will understand me to speak of that other sort of knowledge which reason herself attains by the power of dialectic, using the hypotheses not as first principles, but only as hypotheses — that is to say, as steps and points of departure into a world which is above hypotheses, in order that she may soar beyond them to the first principle of the whole; and clinging to this and then to that which depends on this, by successive steps she descends again without the aid of any sensible object, from ideas, through ideas, and in ideas she ends (1952, p. 387).

This is the classical "idealistic" position in philosophy. As Kant was later to observe, Plato used the term "idea" in such a way that it did not refer to the senses. Hypotheses were drawn from the senses and embodied in ideas, but one did not have to stay with sensible attachments in experience as he built upon such underpinnings and ascended the ideational levels we now call the ladder of abstraction (see Chapter II). This view was based upon the Socratic theory of ideas, which held that there were really two spheres of intelligible experience: the sphere of things as we sense them in everyday observation (which Plato termed "becoming"); and the sphere of unchanging absolutes or universals embodied in ideas (termed "being"). Only in the latter sphere could the unblemished truth be found, for ideas are the prototypes or archetypes of things as we find them in experience. The world of being was basic to the world of becoming, and it encompassed "first principles" not apparent in experience. The idea of "form" (*eidos*) is an archetype in the intellect, a *universal* truth (first principle) in which any given object in sensory experience must "participate" if it is to exist. To come to this universal requires not only skill and ability, but the exercise of a certain style of reasoning: "dialectic alone, goes directly to the first principle and is the only science which does away with hypotheses in order to make her ground secure" (p. 397).

But how is one to accomplish this feat of reasoning? Not unlike the pattern of dynamic interchange used by Socrates, the answer is simply to know when and where to differentiate from among the total (the one) various contradictory parts (the many). It is through *opposition of contradictories* that dialectical reasoning must move ever upward, toward the universal. It is a "divide and conquer" sequence, but only if the thinker can successfully bring together the differentiated members of the total into a further unity (*synopsis*). The following quote captures the flavor of dialectic as a dynamic analysis of whole to part, part to part, and part to whole, all based upon the principle of successive division into opposites:

> Then, surely, he who can divide rightly is able to see clearly one form pervading a scattered multitude, and many different forms contained under one higher form; and again, one form knit together into a single whole and pervading many such wholes, and many forms, existing only in separation and isolation. This is the knowledge of classes which determines where they can have communion with one another and where not (p. 571).

We can see in this concept of class (a type of idea) the origins of what Aristotle called "formal cause." Plato believed that "every individual thing has its own determinate idea which is always one and the same" (pp. 490–491). If this is so, then the realization of an archetypal idea (drawn from the world of being) in actuality as an item of experience (from the world of becoming) would mean that the former had served a determining role in the realization of the latter, as the blueprint served in the construction of the stereo system (see Chapter V, p. 120). Of course, Aristotle was critical of Plato's formulation. He claimed that Plato had merely substituted "idea" for the concept "number" used by the Pythagorean philosophers of southern Italy, whom Plato had visited following the death of Socrates. In explaining the nature of existence, Aristotle claimed, the Pythagoreans said that "things" merely imitated numbers, whereas Plato said they imitated ideas. Though this may well be true, it does not obviate the fact that Plato's view was very likely a precursor of Aristotle's formal causation (Russell, 1959, pp. 82–83). Plato did not view mathematics very favorably, as we shall see below. He placed geometry as an intellectual activity somewhere "between opinion and reason" (p. 387). Thus, if Plato borrowed from Pythagorean doctrine, it was more on the side of idealism than mathematical calculation, a mental facility which he felt did not come up to dialectical reasoning.

Although some interpreters of Plato believe that the theory of ideas was strictly Socratic in tone, and that Plato in his later years rejected it (Russell, 1959, p. 62), it seems clear that this second great dialectician placed much stock in the possibility of attaining knowledge through an exercise of sheer intellect. The dialectic now has an intrapersonal as well as interpersonal emphasis. Man can pull himself up by his own bootstraps, entirely within a cognitive sphere. Observations "out there" are really secondary to the inner world of thought. Plato considered experiments relating the lengths of strings to their musical tones playful games rather than serious scientific work, and his astronomy aimed not at collecting data for the verification of propositions about the physical universe, but at using such observations to throw light on the static and unchanging world of ideas (Jaspers, 1962, p. 167). Fortunately, there was a certain modicum of this idealistic attitude in Galileo's outlook at the dawn of modern science, when he considered mathematical reasoning superior to empirical experimentation. This is the heritage of Plato, the heritage of idealism, with its implicit criticisms and suspicions of a physical world too easily accepted by the naked senses.

Aristotle (384 B.C.–322 B.C.) • It remained for Aristotle to oppose his teacher and to move the locus of suspicion from the senses to the intellect; in other words, he sounded the first note for realism, although he was not a naive realist and has been termed a moderate idealist (Stace, 1955, p. 73). With Aristotle, we get a clear and highly complete examination of all those factors at play in the acceptance or rejection of propositions — he called them premises — about our experience. A premise is a sentence which affirms or denies one thing or another, such as "All men are mortal." Aristotle believed that everyone must at some point reason syllogistically, utilizing the well known sequence of major premise, minor premise, and then a conclusion drawn from an evaluation of the two; but he felt it was possible to make a distinction between the ways individuals came to their premises. This was important, because one of the most vital aspects of truth involved beginning a line of syllogistic reasoning from absolutely true major premises. After all, if one began a line of reasoning with falsehood, he could only end with falsehood. He therefore proposed the distinction which we have accepted in our review of reasoning as follows:

> Now reasoning is an argument in which, certain things being laid down, something other than these necessarily comes about through them. (a) It is a "demonstration", when the premises from which the reasoning starts are true and primary, or are such that our knowledge

of them has originally come through premisses which are primary and true: (b) reasoning, on the other hand, is "dialectical", if it reasons from opinions that are generally accepted (1952, p. 143).

By "generally accepted opinions," Aristotle was referring to the fact that Socrates had sought knowledge in discourse with some one man, let us say, who, for all we can tell, held a communal bias or opinion rather than truth (leading to "contentious" reasoning). It was inevitable that opinions would sneak into the discourse because of the very style of dialectic. Thus, whereas demonstrative premises stated one and only one of two contradictories — "X is the case (and by implication Y is not)" — dialectical premises, said Aristotle, always depend upon the adversary's choice between the two contradictories — "Which do you take to be the case, X or Y? You say X? Fine, let us proceed"; but just as likely "You say Y? Fine, let us proceed." Thus, in dialectical arguments, rhetoric (the art of persuasion) always plays a part, because the direction the argument takes is arbitrary. The dialectician is not dealing with any given reality, but only with those faculties of mind which deal with dispute, such as opinions, attitudes, and related biases: "Dialectic is merely critical where philosophy claims to know, and sophistic is what appears to be philosophy but is not" (p. 523). Thus, Aristotle hints that dialecticians can at times succumb to the same errors of reasoning they accuse the Sophists of committing. This was the price they had to pay, actually, for over-valuing the power of intellect. To turn away from the world of sensory experience into the world of thought can lead to a sense of conviction which is unwarranted and itself quite at odds with the traditions of dialectic:

Lack of experience diminishes our power of taking a comprehensive view of the admitted facts. Hence those who dwell in intimate association with nature and its phenomena grow more and more able to formulate, as the foundations of their theories, principles such as to admit of a wide and coherent development: while those whom devotion to abstract discussions has rendered unobservant of the facts are too ready to dogmatize on the basis of a few observations (p. 411).

This is Aristotle's naturalism, so much revered in psychology over the years. He was a biologist, and made many early studies of organisms through careful observation — for this is the essential point of his criticism. Man cannot find truths about reality solely through an exercise of pure reason. He must come to grasp new truth based upon sense perceptions of the past; he cannot use the inductive method unless he bases this induction on "particulars" gleaned from experience by the senses and then begins his ascent up the ladder of abstraction. Plato and Socrates revered the idea and believed that somewhere in the mind ideas take flight from the senses, but Aristotle argues that this was flatly incorrect. By turning his attention so meticulously to the nature of abstraction, Aristotle was in one sense the first semanticist. He made a clear distinction between names and things, for example, and his naturalistic bent argued that science must pin its hopes on adequate observation of the latter. By manipulating names and not things, the skillful dialectician could win arguments and show proofs which had no bearing on the reality of sense perception. If he deliberately sets out to do this, to contort and twist facts to suit his needs, a man behaves as the Sophists did. Aristotle said that what made a man a Sophist was not his use of dialectic or rhetoric, but his moral purpose in engaging in dispute. To this extent he agreed with Socrates and Plato. One way to avoid sophistry was to go to causal analysis (see Chapter V), for if one can point to the indisputable "causes" of phenomena, he cannot avoid the demonstrative line of reasoning at some point in the discourse.

Aristotle's emphasis on observation flowed directly from his view that the premises of demonstrative arguments must be "primary and true." This act of publicly doing something which can be participated in by others provided a groundwork for the various sciences and permitted them to "have communion with one another" (p. 39). If we observe something, and catalogue our findings, at that point we *have* particulars, on the basis of which we can reason inductively and demonstratively; we have not found the knowledge in our minds, we have gleaned it by the use of our senses, so that we begin with something primary and true.

Aristotle was not so naive as to assume that all knowledge was demonstrable, and he recognized that some truths had to be assumed as "basic truths" in the early stages of demonstrative reasoning. Such things as the meaning of unity, triangularity, or straightness, had to be granted as "axioms" at the outset in demonstrative reasoning. It was up to the science of philosophy to examine these basic truths, because: "it does not belong to the geometer to inquire what is contrariety or completeness or unity or being or the same or the other, but only to presuppose these concepts and reason from this starting point" (p. 524). Aristotle was a pluralist in his view of the family of sciences, and he felt that sciences such as philosophy, which would examine basic facts — even using dialectic as a vehicle for critical study — would naturally be working in a very important realm, involving an even higher type of wisdom than that demanded of the physicist.

Working together, all sciences seek to determine first principles (universals) in basic facts, combining both observation and a complete explication of the causes of phenomena. Indeed, science itself is an activity which must be understood in the same way. In answer to the question of what sort of science man must have, Aristotle observes: "this must be a science that investigates the first principles and causes; for the good, i.e. the end, is one of the causes" (p. 500). Thus Aristotle recognizes that science is teleological as an activity, and that its very nature is tied to a pursuit of what Socrates had called the good — i.e., the pursuit of truth wherever it takes us.

The impact of Aristotle on the history of dialectic was to accentuate a further characteristic we now ascribe to it; i.e., its use as a tool for the examination of assumptions, biases, and critical evaluations of all types. Although he relegated dialectic to a secondary role in the pursuit of knowledge, he did nothing to destroy the reputation of dialectic as one of the activities all philosophers must occasionally engage in — however guardedly — when they come to certain impasses in their sensory experience. Aristotle did not take such an extremely empiricistic position as to denigrate the intellect, and St. Thomas Aquinas later placed him midway between Plato, as an extremist on the side of intellect, and Democritus, as an extremist on the side of sensation (Fremantle, 1954, p. 150). But the heritage of Aristotle is observation through sensory experience. Down through history we have had this genuinely dialectical opposition between the types of thinkers William James probably referred to when he made the tenderminded-toughminded distinction in psychology. We have had those who saw in intellect a source of knowledge unattainable either exclusively or primarily through the senses, as opposed to those of a more skeptical turn of mind who see the source of knowledge as only or primarily in the sensory intake.

Medieval Philosophy

The medieval period is usually taken as that span of time between the fall of Rome to the barbarians in the fifth century and the fall of Constantinople to the Turks in the fifteenth century (Fremantle, 1954, p. x). The Western philosophers of note in this period were churchmen. Aristotle was eclipsed at the outset, with his work not being assimilated into this period's stream of thought until about the middle of the twelfth century, when translations from the Arabic were first introduced to Europe and then were followed by translations directly from the Greek. Thus Plato's influence was the first to be felt. We shall not attempt to cover this period in great detail, but will confine our comments to three philosophers, one who wrote before the Aristotelian renaissance, and two who wrote afterwards.

St. Augustine (354–430) • The first truly great medieval philosopher, it is generally conceded, was St. Augustine, who was greatly influenced by the neo-Platonists, Plotinus (205?–270) and Porphyry (233–304) (Fremantle, 1954, p. 19). There are two important developments that took place in the history of dialectic which we can trace to the influence of Augustine. First, he subtly altered or at least laid the groundwork so that his successors could alter the *intent* of dialectical argument as perceived by Socrates and Plato. No doubt this is precisely what Aristotle had cautioned against in his attack on dialectic, but with the advent of Augustine we find dialectic serving primarily a "defensive" rather than an attacking or "critical" function in reason. This development came about through Augustine's view of the nature of meaning as originating with a single, all-powerful God. Augustine argued, in the Platonic tradition, that meanings are often unclear, ensnarled with misconceptions, and at times so confused that mortal man might, for example, reason from incorrect assumptions (propositions) to valid conclusions, or vice versa. This is so because *man does not create,* he merely observes valid logical reasoning, the meanings and development of which have been created by God: "And yet the validity of logical sequences is not a thing devised by men, but is observed and noted by them that they may be able to learn and teach it; for it exists eternally in the reason of things, and has its origin with God" (Augustine, 1952, p. 652).

Man does not create the science of mathematics (numbers), for these relations exist *as laws* in the reality of life which has been created by God. This Augustinian view that what Plato had called ideas (sphere of being) had a literal existence (in the sphere of becoming) — not a prototypical but a literal existence — came to be called "realism" during the medieval period. Although we have called Plato an idealist, if one gauges his role in history correctly, it is true to say that he also influenced the development of realism. Later in medieval times the "nominalists" entered the picture to oppose the realists. Basing their argument on Aristotle, the nominalists claimed that the *universal* Pythagorean-Platonic notions of number or idea were merely *names* used by philosophers in argument, but that such universals had no existence in reality.

It is important to note that Plato's philosophy did have the two realms of being and becoming, and that he really could not be termed a realist in the sense used during medieval times, which held that being and becoming were identical, if not "one." The early churchmen succeeded in propounding a realism by equating their conception of a Supreme Being with Plato's sphere of being. They could then take the scriptural texts as examples of the revelation of truths propounded by the one God, the creator of all knowledge. Thus, rather than an act of free creativity with no predetermined intention, as in the Socratic-Platonic concept of dialectic, the medieval dialectic becomes a tool in the search for meanings hidden within the revealed truths. It is in this sense that Augustine speaks glowingly of both rhetoric and dialectic (themselves created by God) as "of the greatest assistance in the discovery of . . . meaning" (p. 654).

But whose meaning is this? Arbitrariness is lost in the convictions of faith, which was a precondition for the kind of philosophizing Augustine did. The meanings of Augustine are of God's intent, and are properly contained in the scriptures. Due to his emphasis on the theological, what he ultimately suggested was that all of man's efforts should be turned quite by design to a greater understanding of the truths revealed in holy works. It is therefore not surprising that his philosophy points continually to this goal. Natural science, history, even the mechanical arts, are considered important primarily because they can serve as exegetical aids. This was not the Grecian approach to knowledge, for it *begins* with a focus on certain elements of (scriptural) knowledge, whereas Socrates, Plato, and even Aristotle did not think of the dialectic as having a vested interest. This would have been to them a form of sophistry, an argument indulged in for practical aims, to promote a given point of view. Augustine defined sophistry as taking advantage of an opponent through a play on words, or reasoning from incorrect inferences, but he saw nothing dangerous in the use of dialectical reasoning for the further elaboration of God's meanings.

It probably never occurred to St. Augustine, so strong was his faith, that a maverick dialectic in reason could innocently tear down the city which God had built. Faith can strangle free dialectic. Thus it was that succeeding churchmen sought to prove the existence of God and/or to support other theological matters through intellectual argument. It was not always made clear, but such arguments were of course dialectical, and for a period of several centuries the demonstrative point of view was not referred to as such. By the eleventh century the typical theological problem was handled as follows: "a question would be posed (for example, whether God is the highest good), the arguments for and against stated, and a balance struck" (Leff, 1958, p. 93).

The second important development in dialectic which has been pointed to in the thought of Augustine is his use of it as a metaconstruct. That is, at least some admirers of Augustine have seen dialectical reasoning in the Doctrine of the Holy Trinity; Jaspers has opined: "The rise and influence of Trinitarian speculation are partly explained by the fact that it discloses the threefold step — dialectic — in all things, in the soul, in every reality" (1962, pp. 196–197). He goes on to show how Augustine used a triadic breakdown in many different spheres of his theology. This interpretation teaches us another role which dialectic can play. To be a dialectician in the Greek tradition was, after all, to divide, to break up experience into parts and then bring these parts back into a new unity (the many into one). Dialectical reasoning has this feature of thesis, antithesis, and synthesis. Jaspers is claiming that Augustine, in addition to reasoning dialectically, or speaking dialectically with contemporaries, used the triadic concept as a sort of model (metaconstruct) in ordering his observations of experience and cogitations about experience. We want to keep this in mind as one of the possible applications of dialectic, and indeed, a very important application in the history of thought. Like the Platonic ideas or universals themselves, dialectic may be conceived of as a "form" to be applied to the conceptualization of items of knowledge.

St. Thomas Aquinas (1225–1274) • The Aristotelian tradition, tempered somewhat by the already ascendant Platonic tradition, was given its greatest expression by St. Thomas Aquinas. The familiar dichotomy of our study is reflected in his comment: "an imperfect mode of knowledge disposes towards a more perfect, as opinion, the result of dialectical syllogisms, disposes towards science, which results from demonstrative syllogisms" (1952, p. 765). Dialectic was a means for dealing with the less well perfected knowledge, in the hope of raising it to the levels of science. Aristotle's view of the dialectic as contentless was also adopted by Aquinas: "in speculative matters . . . there is one science of dialectics, which inquires about all matters; but demonstrative sciences, which pronounce judgment, differ according to their different objects" (p. 40). It was this speculative aspect of dialectic which Aquinas made important again — as a tool in theological matters. He was trying to solve certain problems in light of the Aristotelian renaissance, and developed what one could call a Platonic dualism on the nature of knowledge so that both the senses *and* the intellect (theological argument) could be given their due. Aquinas proposed that a clear and firm distinction be made, not between two spheres of reality, as Socrates had essentially done, but between two *sources* of knowledge: the intellect and sensory experience. Each has valid truths to yield and a proper role to play in knowledge. By underscoring this distinction in the sources of knowledge, Aquinas placed greater emphasis on the derivation and statement of axioms as a preliminary to syllogistic reasoning than Aristotle had done.

What this amounted to was that dialectic was rescued from the indefinite position in which Aristotle had left it, and essentially elevated to a more prominent position. Aquinas believed sensory experience was essential to knowledge, and accepted the view that revelation was one such empirical source. By placing emphasis on the role of sensation in gaining knowledge, Aquinas helped put a stop to the more extended flights of fancy in which dialecticians had been indulging before his time (Leff, 1958, p. 91). However, his empiricism was not of the toughest-minded variety, for he also conceded that in developing certain more speculative items of knowledge, it was necessary to resort to reason and to dialectic. As is well known, Aquinas' proofs of God's existence were based in large measure upon classical Aristotelian causal analysis. It is probably correct to say that Aquinas combined Aristotelian and Platonic themes in the way which was implicitly suggested, though never formally developed, by Aristotle's polemic. Aristotle never intended to put the death blow to dialectic, and Aquinas' salvaging of it saved him from the radical empiricism which eventually came to grip the Newtonians.

William of Ockham (1300?–1349?) · The trend to an extreme empiricism was given an important impetus by one of the last of the church philosophers of the medieval period, William of Ockham. He does not compare in stature to Augustine or Aquinas in the history of philosophy, but we want to refer to him as a forerunner of Bacon, and a philosopher who was a nominalist and in the more rigorous traditions of Aristotelian empiricism. Ockham placed the greatest possible emphasis on the sense organs by claiming they were the root of *all* knowledge. The so-called Ockham's razor was aimed at eliminating the free play of intellect: "entities are not to be multiplied without necessity." This principle has been traced back to Aristotle's name vs. thing argument, as well as to various statements he made in support of sensory experience as the basis of knowledge (Fremantle, 1954, p. 202). In opposition to Aquinas, Ockham took the position that a proof of God through reasoning was impossible, and that only revelation — as a type of empirical, sensory experience — could establish His existence. To postulate universals, first principles, or arguments on the basis of reason, such as the causal arguments which even Aristotle would have accepted, was for Ockham the introduction of unnecessary entities. Ockham extended Aristotle's tougher side, and developed a semanticist-like position which held that logic is merely a verbal instrument, and that metaphysical arguments are nothing more than manipulations of words. Dialectic and the power of intellect suffered a much greater setback from Ockham's position than they had ever received at the hands of Aristotle. Anyone who now dared to reason speculatively seemed to be practicing sophistry.

British Empiricism

Although he was one of the founders of mathematical science, as we have noted above, Plato did not believe that the essential nature of things could be grasped through its application. In fact, he viewed mathematical reasoning as inferior because it could never hope to offer us a glimpse of the sphere of being, which he took to be the province of dialectic. Although mathematicians might vaguely apprehend being, as when they grasp geometrical principles, Plato felt that more generally: "they only dream about being, but never can they behold the waking reality so long as they leave the hypotheses which they use unexamined, and are unable to give an account of them" (1952, p. 397). What attracted Plato to the Pythagorean doctrine of numbers was an interest in numbers not as a substitute for the contents of mind in reasoning, but rather as one example of his fundamental belief in ideas as universals. Mathematicians have stumbled onto certain universals and thus get a glimmering of being, but since they do not go to the source of their concepts, they are inferior to dialecticians. Mathematicians may reason, Plato is saying, but they do not reason dialectically.

This insight amounts to a remarkably accurate prediction, for, as we shall now document, it was indeed the rise of mathematics following medieval times that led to an eclipse of dialectic in the seventeenth and eighteenth centuries, and which even today keeps it submerged (though not inoperative) in man's thought. Dialectic surely had begun to decline when Descartes, a philosopher whom the Greeks would have considered a great dialectician, and who was also a mathematician, so missed the point that he called dialectic valueless and relegated it to the arts of rhetoric. Descartes, whose famous question on personal existence and the dialectical argument that followed, to rival St. Anselm's ontological proof of God, could say in the seventeenth century: "Dialecticians are unable to devise any syllogism which has a true conclusion, unless they have first secured the material out of which to construct it, i.e., unless they have already ascertained the very truth which is deduced in that syllogism" (1952, p. 17). This position is flatly in opposition to the Socratic-Platonic belief that dialectic helped man discover certain truths in the mind which he might not otherwise have come to. Though he did not personally have this intention, surely a view like Descartes's could be interpreted as an attack on the powers of mind.

But it was not the philosophy of Descartes as such which presented a threat to the exercise of intellect in the practice of dialectical reasoning. What did present this threat in history, causing dialectic to be dropped completely as a topic of reasonable concern, was the philosophical tradition which has come to be known as British Empiricism. This tradition is strongly entrenched in the twentieth century, and, as we have already seen (Part One), has played an almost solitary role in the formation of American academic psychology. At this point we will review three of its early advocates to see how dialectical and demonstrative reasoning fared in its evolution.

Sir Francis Bacon (1561–1626) · We have already had considerable experience with the ideas of Sir Francis Bacon as an important figure in the evolution of modern science (see Chapters V and VIII). He is the one of our three Britishers who was not greatly taken by mathematics (probably because of its mentalistic aspects), and who is to be remembered more for his great emphasis on experimental or empirical evidence than for his stress on the manipulation of numbers. During his time the term "scholasticism" was used to describe those churchmen and other scholars who used philosophical argument (dialectical reasoning) to settle the questions of universals, existence, and so on. Bacon attacked the scholastics for being obfuscators rather than clarifiers of knowledge. Like Aristotle, he recognized that scientists cannot be continually bickering over every little assumption they make in going about their business of gathering data, or posing "silly" questions unamenable to observation, such as the classic derisive example: "how many angels can dance on the head of a pin?" Though he directed his attack at the scholastics, the implication was, of course, that dialectic would impede rather than facilitate the advance of science. In arguing this way, Bacon went further than Aristotle had by detracting from the value of creative intellect, as follows:

> Our method of discovering the sciences is such as to leave little to the acuteness and strength of wit, and indeed rather to level wit and intellect. For as in the drawing of a straight line, or accurate circle by the hand, much depends on its steadiness and practice, but if a ruler or compass be employed there is little occasion for either; so it is with our method (1952, p. 113).

When it comes to scientific method, therefore, intellect plays little or no role. In his "idols of the theatre, or of theories" (p. 113), Bacon was making the classical sophistic point of deciding beforehand to press a given theory or bias onto the facts of experience, rather than following the empirically scientific procedure of doing the opposite. Indeed, not even Aristotle's vaunted position as an empiricist was to be respected, for: "he had already decided, without having properly consulted experience as the basis of his decisions and axioms, and after having so decided, he drags experiment along as a captive constrained to accommodate herself to his decisions; so that he is even more to be blamed than his modern followers (of the scholastic school) who have deserted her altogether" (p. 114). Bacon severely criticized Aristotle for not taking up the problem of how the major premise of a syllogism is arrived at. This was a valid point, but in his attack Bacon neglected to consider one of the *two* possibilities for coming to a syllogistic major premise which Aristotle had proposed. He neglected to consider dialectical reasoning.

Aristotle did not assert that dialecticians fail to reason syllogistically, once they have come to their major premises. He merely said that they come to their major premises in a way different from the demonstrative reasoner. The latter affirmed one and only one premise, which presumably was "true." In Baconian terms, the empirical scientist using demonstrative reasoning can define empirically, can point to, can measure what he plans to begin with as a major premise in his syllogistic reasoning to follow (what we call today operationism). Dialecticians, on the other hand, said Aristotle, come to their major premises *arbitrarily,* and as a result, they can often take the flights of fancy which Bacon saw in the ruminations of scholasticism — they can depart from sensory experience (facts) out of an undisciplined intellect. At the same time, Aristotle believed there was a role for dialectic in the examination of certain questions unsuited to demonstration, a point which Kant later explicated.

Bacon's criticism of Aristotle is all on the side of demonstrative reasoning, and his only real point is that major premises must come from experience. And not just any old experience, as in casual observation, but in controlled, experimental experience. Meanings come from experience, not from God or ancestral progenitors, and they get into the mind in *only* this way. Anyone who argues otherwise is in error and not a scientist. Sometimes even an empirical scientist gets too hasty in making generalizations (deductions) from too few observations (on which we base inductions), and lets his fancy run so that he goes beyond the facts (empiric error). For Bacon, the source of meanings was in hard reality and intellect was really a secondary instrument in creating knowledge. He crystallized and firmly established the *realistic interpretation of meaning* (see Chapter II), upon which Newton was later to build. As we have seen (see Chapter VIII), Bacon also began the attack on Aristotelian causation which others in the British empiricist tradition, such as Hume, were to continue.

Thomas Hobbes (1599–1679) · Our second proponent of the British empiricist tradition, Thomas Hobbes, was a contemporary of Bacon, although he was no great admirer of Bacon as a philosopher. In his middle years, Hobbes was very much taken by the beauty of Euclidean geometry, and in working out his own philosophical stand, came to envision man's reasoning processes as analogous to mathematical manipulations. Reasoning, for Hobbes, was: "nothing but reckoning (that is, adding and subtracting) of the consequences of general names agreed upon for the marking and signifying of our thoughts; I say *marking* them, when we reckon by ourselves; and *signifying,* when we demonstrate or approve our reckonings to other men" (1952, p. 58). Notice that in making this distinction between marks and significates, discussion between men is taken as one demonstrating something to another. Thinking may go on within the skull of one of two discussants, but when a man speaks up, it is to "communicate." The Socratic dialectic, of course, did not have communication as its major goal. The Greek dialectic promotes or creates — in one sense "discovers" — new meanings within old meanings. This is the source of the *idealistic interpretation of meaning* (see Chapter II).

As an empiricist-realist who sees man getting every bit of meaning (information) from the senses, from the "outside," Hobbes downgrades the importance of intellect as Bacon does. Nothing is added from the inside, except possibly an ordering of the "signs" one gets from the environment. Thus, if a man fails to reason properly and comes up with a question having no generally understood signification, he has not committed an error of reasoning, he has merely voiced an absurdity. Error results when a man attempts to reason without the aid of words, as when he tries to speculate on what preceded some item in his sensory range, or to predict an as yet unfulfilled outcome of events. In this case, looking backward or to the future in time, he might err because he lacks the proper signs to determine empirically what did in fact happen or what might happen. He lacks the primary and true propositions.

But if this same man reasons in words of general signification, and then comes up with some kind of false inference, he is not making an error of reason, he is stating an absurdity. Reason is something which we must acquire, through study and hard work. Man is not born with it, nor does he acquire it just by aging. Hobbes even claims that philosophers are not immune to the "privilege of absurdity," and attributes this to the fact that they do not begin their ratiocinations from the clear definitions or explications of names which they use in argument. Consequently, unlike the geometer, who does do this, they arrive at absurdities: "And therefore if a man should talk to me of a *round quadrangle;* or *accidents of bread in cheese;* or *immaterial substances;* or of a *free subject; a free will;* or any *free* but free from being hindered by opposition; I should not say he were in error, but that his words were without meaning; that is to say, absurd" (p. 59).

Socrates, too, realized that words can get a reasoner into difficulty, but he believed that dialecticians help to clarify meanings-in-words. He once argued that the dialectician teaches a legislator to use the names of things correctly, and thereby helps direct him to truth just as the ship's pilot directs the shipwright in construction (Plato, 1952, pp. 88–89). But Socrates was not the realist Hobbes was. For the empiricist, words are copies of reality, hence meaningful or not meaningful insofar as they mirror this reality. If a word in cognition has meaning for Hobbes, then it is either a reality-bound, generally understood term, or it is nonsense. Therefore, if a reasoning man puts forth a proposition of the sort already pointed to by Hobbes, it is *always* his fault and never reality's. He may have reified some personal idiom (mark); he may have used metaphors or analogies in reasoning, which are inadmissible to those reckonings which seek truth; or, he may have used names which signify nothing but which have been learned by rote in a scholastic university (Hobbes, 1952, p. 59). This is another development in the semanticist position, dividing mind from reality and laying the blame on the intellect (on the cognitive map) and never on reality, for how can what is "real" be wrong? Reality is credited with a rationality and reasonableness which man merely copies in his cogitations (realistic interpretation of meaning).

But through it all, in rejecting speculative thought, Hobbes makes his case confidently on the assumption that the demonstrative is the *only* form of reasoning of which man is capable. Since his time the concept of "reason" itself has taken on much more the meaning of an orderly, appropriate, clearly sequential process. Hobbes was also an early contributor to the "common sense" notion, and can be cited as one of the initiators of that anti-intellectual strain in modern science we noted in Chapter VIII. He jolts us with the image of hoary old philosophers, filled with nothing but absurd shreds of distorted terminology learned and taught by rote but signifying nothing. To reason, for Hobbes, is to be rational and to use the common language of educated men correctly. It calls for terms demonstrably clear to all, and then a syllogistic sequence in which some message already contained in the major premise (culled from primary and true experience and therefore not born in mind) is drawn out by the minor premise and then the conclusion accurately stated and communicated to a listener. To divide, to produce many from one, to seek the opposite or the contrast or the analogy for a name or proposition *is not to reason,* if by reason we mean a way of finding truth. Truth, like reality, is implacable.

John Locke (1632–1704) · Our final representative of British empiricism, John Locke, is usually given credit as the most influential of its early progenitors, and he is surely the most direct in line of descent to twentieth-century behavioristic psychology. He is noted for the doctrine of ideas he propounded, and it is interesting to compare his thinking with that of Plato. The fundamental difference between British empiricism and the more continental views in psychology could not be epitomized better than in this comparison. For Plato, ideas were not imprintings on the mind from reality, but rather the very essence of things only dimly perceived in the environment. In the world of thought one can use reason to break up sensory input and visual memory into pieces of pure gold, the nature of which is very different from the impure slag heap of unrefined reality now separated and tossed aside. Man's reason is a wonderful and vital aspect of his experience because: "immaterial things, which are the noblest and greatest, are shown only in thought and idea, and in no other way . . ." (Plato, 1952, p. 595). Dialectical reasoning permits analysis, subdivision, and opposition, and the breaking away of slag, so that the refined product comes to stand alone as "idea."

Locke, on the other hand, sees ideas as mental copies of a given reality. Like Hobbes, he believes the contents of mind can only be that which comes in from the outside, and that nothing can be added or subtracted from the meanings so garnered by the mind *qua* mind. Each meaning is embodied in an idea, which starts out either accurately representing reality, or inaccurately doing so (Hobbesian notion of definition). Each "simple idea" is a unit of information unto itself, and *cannot be further subdivided.* The mind never creates knowledge, it merely responds passively to sensory input, though it can combine the indivisible simple ideas somehow into more complex ones, similar to the Hobbesian mathematical combinations. Unlike Platonic ideas, which were "universal totalities" acting as prototypes for reality but in themselves the *end state* of reason, Locke's ideas are "atomistic building blocks" which combine *in the beginnings* of thought, indivisible and uncreatable: "it is not in the power of the most exalted wit, or enlarged understanding, by any quickness or variety of thought, to *invent* or *frame* one new simple idea in the mind . . . nor can any force of the understanding *destroy* those that are there" (Locke, 1952, p. 128).

The main argument Locke wages is against a conception of "innate ideas," by which he seems to mean the neo-Platonic scholastic attempt to find truths in the mind which are unattainable in reality. In his famous essay on human understanding, Locke (1952) sets out to demolish universals by considering two of them: "What is, is," and "It is impossible for the same thing to be and not to be." In Grecian times, such propositions might surely have emerged in dialectical discourse. Locke claims that these propositions have been termed universally valid, and therefore presumes they must be thought of as "innate." Actually, this is not quite what universals meant, and it is an inaccurate assessment of the Platonic tradition. Plato's ideas were not inborn ideas about the truth "out there" — the reality to which they referred — so much as they were the truth "in here," to which the existential reality conformed imperfectly. By assuming that Platonists down through history had been saying that mind has inborn ideas of reality, Locke begins his argument against a straw man. The churchmen had approximated what he claimed, but their view was that God's ideas, and His plan for reality, existed independent of man's reason. Man could learn of God's plan through an exercise of his reason, but this was not a matter of just sitting down and permitting innate ideas to spring forth. As a realist, and a monist, Locke could not fully appreciate the dualism of Plato or of the scholastics.

In any case, Locke goes on to argue that such universals as have been cited are in fact not universal because there are large segments of humanity who have never voiced them — certain primitive groups, idiots, children, and so on. Yet all men should do so if they are truly innate. If something is "in" the mind, then it is in the mind. Using an argument similar to the one used by Descartes, Locke asks how reason could possibly help to bring out universal truths if these truths are in the mind in the first place. Referring to those who argue for universals he observes: "But how can these men think the use of reason necessary to discover principles that are supposed innate, when reason (if we may believe them) is nothing else but the faculty of deducing unknown truths from principles or propositions that are already known?" (p. 97). This is of course a definition of demonstrative and *not* dialectical reasoning. Locke's imaginary opponent in his famous essay is presumably both arguing in the Platonic philosophical tradition *and* accepting as his sole definition of reasoning the Aristotelian view of demonstration. It goes without saying that straw men often have peculiar views. At this time in history, therefore, we find both Descartes, who supported intellectual argument as a form of proof, and Locke, who continued the Hobbesian detraction from the powers of intellect, holding to the conviction that the only way man can operate mentally is by demonstrative reasoning. Dialectic had been successfully submerged.

Locke also continued in the semantic tradition by observing that some of these pseudo-problems of the dialectician, such as universals, were due to misuse of language. This was how Hobbes rejected at least some of the more famous dialectical problems. But Locke added another point to explain how oppositional or speculative conflicts might arise in the mind. He developed this in his discussion of probability, a very important adjunct to his theory of ideas. If simple ideas come in from the environment, and if they can be mathematically combined into more complex ideas, then whatever proposition results, whatever conclusion a reasoner comes to which then guides his course of behavior must depend upon the frequency of this or that idea-complex in his mind, considered in relation to the sum total of all ideas available. Thus, Locke concluded, the evidence nurtured by probability of the atomistic and indivisible contents is what determines the course of action that an individual will take: "Probability . . . carries so much evidence with it, that it naturally determines the judgment, and leaves us as little liberty to believe or disbelieve, as a demonstration does, whether we will know, or be ignorant" (p. 369).

Judgment is a kind of mathematical calculation of frequency probabilities (see Chapter VI); the mind is not an active but a passive process; it cannot create, but it can weigh one empirically derived probability against another. Locke then goes on and essentially accounts for those conjectures, waverings, oppositions, and doubts which Socrates would have considered fruits of the dialectical process by noting that experience often contradicts, so that ideas conflict, information from the senses which stimulate the production of ideas is frequently inadequate or at times equally important, and so on. This is where dialectic presumably might be placed in the Lockean philosophy:

> That as the arguments and proofs *pro* and *con*, upon due examination, nicely weighing every particular circumstance, shall to any one appear, upon the whole matter, in a greater or less degree to preponderate on either side; so they are fitted to produce in the mind such different entertainments, as we call *belief, conjecture, guess, doubt, wavering, distrust, disbelief*, etc. (p. 369).

The Nineteenth Century

Not since the time of the Greeks had there been such an important period in the history of dialectic. It is during the nineteenth century that we again see a recognition of the role of dialectic in human reason; a major philosophy is built around it which greatly elevates and doubtless over-estimates its role in history, and, through it all, there is a continuing sense of distrust by many for this form of reasoning. Men who considered themselves scientists were especially distrustful of what they took to be sophistry in the use of dialectic; Sigmund Freud was one of these. Even near the close of the century, when idealistic themes were gaining ascendance in the new physics, dialectic carried the negative connotation of mysticism, vested interest, and a rejection of the canons of science. But dialectic was to live on and become assimilated as a metaconstruct in the growing social sciences, as well as to help shape covertly a new conception of man in the emergence of psychiatry. Despite his attitude, Freud played a significant role in this transformation. Though we do not use the old terms "demonstration" and "dialectic," our twentieth-century debate over the proper conceptualization of man is in large measure a rephrasing of this historical bifurcation. We will omit consideration of Freud for now, in order to give his views a thorough treatment in Chapter X. Three leading theoreticians of the nineteenth century will be taken up in this chapter to show how dialectic was faring in the Continental tradition while its eclipse in the British tradition was continuing.

Immanuel Kant (1724–1804) · Although he had published his monumental work on reason in 1781, Kant's thought was so influential in the nineteenth century that he can well be considered a philosopher of this period. His mature philosophical work was stimulated in part by the skeptical analysis of David Hume (1711–1776), one of the British empiricists, and we would do well to begin a consideration of Kant by briefly pointing to Hume's argument concerning the nature of cause. Interestingly enough, he was referring to the efficient cause in his analysis, since by now Sir Francis Bacon and others had pretty well made the efficient cause synonymous with all causation, in science. Hume's argument was aimed at all those who relied upon causal analyses to support "rational" proofs, such as the attempt to prove God's existence by showing the need in nature for a "first cause" (creation). Basing his argument on the assumption that knowledge can come to man only through the senses, Hume showed that there is nothing in empirical reality to account for the "fact" of causation. One does not "see" causes, but merely attributes them to events due to a habit of mind he has acquired. To use Hume's famous example, the observer notes that when event A — e.g., a billiard ball — is conjoined or bumps into event B — a second billiard ball — the latter event seems to move *in response to* the former. Yet this is an inductive leap, based upon one's past experience with A and B events, and *not* a knowable or observable feature; we can never know with certainty that the B event will continue to move as our habit of mind expects it to. In any given instance it might not. Thus, all talk of causes as grounds for rational argument is really so much uncertain habit being projected onto events in an attempt to build a view of reality which is congenial but which transcends the facts and is therefore invalid.

Hume's analysis really comes down to the fact that inductive reasoning (from the particular A and B events to the general construct "cause") can never be as convincing as deductive reasoning (in which one begins with a general principle and comes down to the particular case in point; see Chapter V). Induction demands leaps or inferences which somehow transcend the facts, which go beyond the sensory input from the external world. It is this transcendent quality of intellect to which Kant directs his attention in trying to answer Hume. By his own estimation, Kant performed a "Copernican revolution" in turning the tables on Hume. Rather than explaining mental conceptions in terms of sensory experience, as the empiricists had, Kant explained sensory experience in terms of mental conceptions, or *categories,* as he called them. In taking this position Kant presents an interesting admixture of Platonic idealism (mental categories, coming before experience is possible) and Aristotelian caution as regards the power of intellect to know truth (the rejection of dialectic as a method of discovering truth). His treatment of dialectic is clearly Aristotelian, but much of his philosophy is very Platonic in spirit. He therefore took the middle way and neither went to the extremes of the empiricists, nor brooked the rational proofs of the scholastics. He filled in that part of Aristotelian philosophy which made it possible for dialectic to play a role in man's thought, but his comments were all calculated to restrain its use and to weaken further its role in the natural sciences.

For Kant, thinking was the act of referring so-called sensory intuitions to objects in reality. Knowledge possessed by the intellect came either from sensory experience (through the objects in reality) — called *a posteriori* knowledge — or was "given" in the structure of intellect and known to reason as *a priori* knowledge. As sensory experience is brought into the intellect, we make use of our understanding to unify such items of eventual knowledge (once they have been properly organized and worked on by reason). The understanding deals with sensory reality; but reason, which is a higher-order activity of mind, does not have any direct bearing on reality. The aim of reason is to put the contents of the understanding in rational order. As Kant says: "Reason . . . never applies directly to experience, or to any sensuous object; its object is . . . to the manifold cognition of which it gives a unity *a priori* by means of conceptions — a unity which may be called rational unity, and which is of a nature very different from that of the unity produced by the understanding" (1952, p. 110).

Now the intellect can put forth two types of propositions embodying judgments about reality (truths): "Either the predicate B belongs to the subject A, as something which is contained (though covertly) in the conception A; or the predicate B lies completely out of the conception A, although it stands in connection with it. In the first instance, I term the judgement *analytical,* in the second *synthetical*" (p. 16). The proposition "All bodies are extended," which could of course be the major premise of a syllogism, is cited as analytical because the meaning of "extended" (B) is included in the conceptual meaning of "body"

(A). (This is one kind of proposition which Aristotle referred to as "true and primary" when he discussed demonstrative reasoning, and it is so by definition. Others which are true and primary must be synthetically or operationally shown to be true and primary empirically, by pointing demonstratively to "that" over there.) Kant's second example, "All bodies are heavy," is cited as an example of a synthetic judgment, because the meaning of "heaviness" (B) is not a definitional aspect of "body" (A). If this proposition is true and primary, it is so only from having been found to be so empirically.

At this point Kant leaves the empiricist position by contending that "pure reason" contains *a priori* synthetic propositions. The British empiricists, believing as they did that all meaning comes from the environment, would have equated synthetic with *a posteriori,* and analytic with *a priori* items of knowledge. Kant, however, now invokes his categories of mind to state that there are certain givens in reason which provide intellect with the beginnings of rationality. For sensory experience to be assembled in a meaningful way, for the understanding to mediate *a posteriori* knowledge, certain categories in the mind must operate at the outset. The mind's eye looks out onto reality through an eyeglass, so to speak, which provides it with the structure and harmony needed for rationality. It never sees reality, if by that we mean the palpable material substance underlying the form of things; it never knows "things in themselves" (noumena), but deals only with sensory representations (phenomena) mediated by the understanding.

Causality was one such *a priori* synthetic proposition (we come to know the categories by way of propositions). The category of causality is within the very fabric of intellect; it helps us to order experience and, like the categories of substance and reality, it makes thinking possible. No amount of analysis will give us the thought that A causes B, because B is not included in the concept of A. This is a synthetic proposition with which we begin thought, and we subsequently see it verified in experience. The same goes for mathematical propositions such as "five plus two equals seven." Causation is not an empirically derived habit, but the very heart of an active intellect, seeking to assemble sensory data. Sensation may be passive, but thought is not. The Kantian view sees mind as an *active* agent which brings something to experience, not as a *passive* recipient of indivisible units from the environment, as the Lockean view had it.

Kant therefore agrees with Hume that we can never experience causation as a real event, or know for certain that it operates, but this is only because it is not of the sphere of palpable reality. It, like the concept of reality, comes at the beginning of thought, making it possible. The twelve Kantian categories also include such things as unity, plurality, and totality (Russell, 1959, p. 241); they are not important for our purposes, and the main point to grasp is that it would be impossible to experience anything external to the mind were it not for these organizing categories of reason, which permit us to create as well as to take in and learn. Indeed, we must take in before we can learn or know the truth; we must have an accurate grasp of reality before we can put speculation to work. Kant took a very un-Platonic stand when he observed: "It is a humiliating consideration for human reason that it is incompetent to discover truth by means of pure speculation" (1952, p. 233). He was not, after all, a thoroughgoing idealist, even if he did bristle somewhat at the naive realism of the British school. Though he made mind an active agent in the propounding of knowledge, he did not think it could discover truths *about* reality *apart* from reality. Mind can enrich the meanings of sensory information through categorical analysis and study; but it cannot transcend sensory experience without running grave risks of concocting error.

This brings us to Kant's interpretation of "idea" and his view of the role of dialectic. Ideas were those aspects of reason which went beyond sensory intuition: "A conception formed from notions, which transcends the possibility of experience, is an *idea,* or a conception of reason" (1952, p. 115). Whereas Plato had viewed ideas as the end stage of dialectical reasoning and as prototypes of things in experience, Kant viewed ideas as free of experience and as prototypes for nothing in particular. Indeed, they could be completely beyond experience. Ideas hover about in abstract mental space, so to speak, and capitalizing on sensory knowledge as ordered by the categories of reason give either an accurate or an inaccurate account of the world of reality. Ideas do not *have* to bind themselves to sensation by way of intuition. They can transcend experience and take flight in free speculative thought. This is doubtless identical to the Platonic conception, except that Kant was quick to add that such free thought is often highly spurious. Such flights of fancy must not be considered truths, for they are not capable of demonstration. Because Kant felt that thinking should properly remain reality-bound, like Aristotle before him, he kept his theory of meaning close to reality. Just because some principle is logically possible, that does not make it either true or primary; hence to speculate about possibilities, such as a life after death, is to engage in dialectic.

Reason, if it is to arrive at truth, cannot be taken up with such dialectical opinions; it must rely upon true and primary propositions, well founded in experience. Thus, Kant argues, demonstrative reasoning is to be preferred as organon (as a method for discovering truths).

Whenever anyone uses the free play of intellect as organon he is immediately involved in dialectic, because: "speculative reason is, in the sphere of transcendentalism, dialectical *in its own nature*" (p. 229). Kant used the term *transcendental logic* to refer to the form of logic we use in examining the nature of our understanding, or the means by which we come to know the categories of pure reason. We manipulate ideas in this work of transcendental logic, and doing it correctly by limiting our analysis to the study of our minds Kant referred to as *transcendental analytic*. However, when we use transcendental logic not merely to examine the structure of our intellect but to establish the so-called validity of universal truths in reality — on the order of the proofs for the existence of God — we get lost in a logic of illusion; this illusory logic Kant referred to as *transcendental dialectic*. It is illusory because in the free play of intellect, which has a dialectical nature, it is always possible to contend *either* side of a given proposition with equal justification — since there is no possible way of demonstrating which position is true.

Kant discussed many such "antinomies" (i.e., conflicts in the laws of pure reason), such as the belief that the world is finite, or its opposite, that the world is infinite. The power of such illusory questions over the mind is great, so that even when we know better we may raise such questions as if they were genuine issues, but they are not. Although such illusions are inescapable, it is our duty to follow them through and help demolish them, to help show that they are simply questions without objective meaning since they do not refer to the objective (in our terms, "real") world. The only time Kant considered it acceptable practice to engage in dialectical argument was when one is under dialectical attack. Then, it is "fair game" to use dialectical defenses, since your argument is always at least as good as your opponent's.

We see, therefore, that although he was critical of it Kant did at least acknowledge that man's reason is to a certain degree dialectical. Man is not *only* a demonstrative reasoner, though it would be good if he could stay within the limits of this form of mental cogitation, because that would keep man tied to reality and presumably, therefore, more rational. Thought gone astray is set loose by dialectic. The importance of dialectic in Kantian philosophy is further underscored by Bertrand

Russell, who notes that the table of categories proposed by Kant was made up of triads, where the third one listed in each grouping is a combination of the first and second, which are opposites: "Thus *unity* is in a sense the opposite of *plurality,* whereas a *totality* contains a manifold of units, and this unites the two first notions" [italics added] (Russell, 1959, p. 245). The "one and the many" comes back into the history of thought, disguised now as a conceptual scheme for the functioning of mind. Although still under fire, dialectic was back in the picture on the Continent.

Georg Wilhelm Friedrich Hegel (1770–1831) • With the possible exception of Plato, Georg W. F. Hegel did more to elevate the dialectic as method and as metaconstruct in the history of thought than any other philosopher. His name is taken as virtually synonymous with dialectic by many in the twentieth century. Hegelian philosophy has been said to have either directly or indirectly influenced every major movement in thought over the past two centuries, both in the sense of its role in the communistic movement, and as a target for those who reacted to his systematization and complex form of idealistic monism. Hegel is the last of the great systematic thinkers who strove to give a complete picture of the universe in their philosophies. Up to his time, all those philosophers who took an idealistic position — either fully and gladly, like Socrates or Plato, or somewhat reluctantly and critically, like Aristotle or Kant — had at least tempered their idealism with a dualistic conception of the universe (Stace, 1955, p. 76). Plato and Aristotle spoke of "matter," which underlay the form of things, and Kant had believed that "things in themselves" existed, even if we could not know them as such. Hegel pointed to the contradictions in such views, which posit formless substances that cannot be known by the senses. He proposed a monistic idealism: there is only one substance, and that is mind. It was not a subjective, chimerical world, however, because the mind which made itself manifest in experience was that of a Divine Spirit, coming to self-consciousness by stages in history. The world as perceived was not "our" subjective mind played out to suit our whims, but the entirely objective mind of a Supreme Being. Hegel's philosophy has been termed by some a "pantheism" or "theodicy" and an "evolutionary idealism" (Hook, 1962, p. 54).

Hegelian philosophy begins with this great stress on reason, logic, and the workings of mind; history is not the unfolding of cause-event sequences, but more like the activity of intellect, as when the mind moves in logic from premises to the reaching of a conclusion (Stace,

1955, p. 22). If Hume had charged that inductive knowledge is never as certain as deductive, in Hegel we see a bold effort to answer this skepticism by attempting to derive a complete system entirely through deduction. Hegel begins his analysis by accepting the Kantian categories. Kant has correctly noted that all knowledge is conceptual, beginning with certain categories which, if drawn out in detail, will help us to explain the nature of the universe. Extending the thinking of Kant, Hegel notes that since the categories did not come from experience, it follows that we cannot hope to find their justification outside the intellectual sphere. Philosophy begins with intellect, with the exercise of reason. Reasoning is a *process* or movement of Kantian-like categories. Aristotle had postulated a "hierarchy of forms" in existence, from the lower levels of inorganic matter, on up through animate forms and thence to man, the highest "form" on earth. Hegel took this hierarchy notion and added to it the idea that each lower-order concept in the interlocking lattice is somehow "deducible" from a higher-order concept. Indeed, lower-order concepts are "within" the higher-order concepts, so that a relationship exists throughout the entire ladder of abstraction.

Plato believed his universals (ideas in being) to be a more noble and accurate representation of concepts than actual empirical examples. The idea of a horse is more beautiful than any given horse; purity or whiteness is far more noble as a universal idea than any pure or white "thing" in existence can be. A universal makes reference to nothing in particular, it is just the essential concept epitomized by and "riding above" the mundane world of everyday reality. But Plato had no way of explaining why horses or pure things or white things existed simply because there was an idea of them at some highly abstract level of mind. For Plato, higher ideas do not contain the lower ideas, thus one cannot extract the latter from the former. Kant had his universal categories of mind, but he never tried to tie them all together deductively. This is what Hegel set out to do. In time, he increased the list of categories to several dozen, tried to deduce them logically from one another, and finally, tried to show how they all form a large complex, a single unity which is self-determined and sufficient unto itself (the one and the many); in short, how it is all contained in the one intellect of God.

This was a very large task, and it called for (1) a point at which to begin, and (2) a method by which to proceed. Hegel's starting point had to be at some highly abstract level — at the level of universals — for if a category is highly abstract, then it follows that lower-order categories can be deduced from it. The higher we climb the ladder of abstraction, the more concepts we subsume (see Chapter II). He concluded that an excellent starting point would be with the category of *being,* for all objects in our experience have this in common — each of them "is." As an idealist, Hegel held that things as we know them are merely congeries of universals: an ice cube is white, an ice cube is cold, and so on. Whiteness and coldness are universals; to be is to know, and knowing about some object is dependent upon such universals. When we strip an object of universals, all that is left is its "is-ness," its being, which is also a universal. This is how Hegel found his first category, from which he could begin to deduce others. Now he needed a method.

Hegel's method was one of logic, since reason is the very essence of his world view. When he speaks of logic, however, Hegel departs from the Aristotelian conception. Had he accepted the view that all men reason syllogistically once they decide upon their major premise, Hegel would have argued that there *is* a formal way in which man can come to the major premise *dialectically.* There is a certain method for coming to the correct "opposite." Aristotle felt this always depended upon the choice of an adversary in conversation, was therefore arbitrary, and consequently resulted in poor science. In this sense Hegelian logic begins *before* the Aristotelian variety. As we have seen, Aristotle was greatly attracted to the extraction of truth once the major premise had been asserted. The demonstrative reasoner begins with primary and true propositions because he defines them as immutably so (to his satisfaction, thus dogmatically) or because he claims to have acquired a true insight from experience (as an operationist would claim to work today). As dialectician, Hegel is interested in how the demonstrative reasoner comes to his proposition in the first instance. He questions whether too much concern with the extraction of the supposed truth already asserted in the major premise has not beclouded the falsity of the major premise as phrased. This is nothing more than the old Platonic argument against the mathematician. But finally, and more basically, Hegel rejects the view that man reasons *only* in a demonstrative manner; rather, he views this as a mechanical parody on true intellect, for in the Hegelian world view, as in the Platonic: "the essential movement of thought is dialectic" (Hegel, 1952, p. 53).

Having perched himself at least halfway up the ladder of abstraction with his beginning (universal) category of "being," how can Hegel begin deducing lower-level categories? He does this by a brilliant variation on the original Socratic "divide and conquer" dialectical process. He finds within the first category its opposite, and thus creates two poles of meaning from the one; and from these two he "deduces" a third, which gives the total effect of a triad. Whereas the Lockean presumably begins at the low levels, with indivisible units of meaning (simple ideas) picked up from empirical reality, and climbs the ladder of abstraction from the lowest rung by induction, making his Humean-like inductive leaps on the basis of habit, the Olympian Hegelian descends deductively from above with his certainty well in hand. The Hegelian fashions a tripod of solid meaning on which to base his analysis, and such triads can go to make up other triads (really, deduced to be a part of another triad), so he too can ascend as well as descend the ladder of abstraction. But unlike the hapless Lockean, the Hegelian manages to pull himself up by a "magical" method of continuing deduction, by the extraction of contradictions and their resolution in a completely new alternative.

Indeed, it is true that Hegel performed something of a "Copernican revolution" on the confident assertions of Aristotle. This happened as follows: Aristotle had evolved certain "primary and true" propositions with which the demonstrative reasoner begins his case; presumably, such propositions were unquestionably self-evident. One such proposition, which we saw Locke using above (p. 275) in his argument against innate ideas, was the well known "law of contradiction." Aristotle phrased this proposition as follows: "we have now posited that it is impossible for anything at the same time to be and not to be, and by this means have shown that this is the most indisputable of all principles" (1952, p. 525). As if to show that demonstrative reasoning is indeed smug in its overconfidence about what is or is not indisputable, Hegel begins his deductive analysis by proving that something can both be and not be at the same time.

The argument runs as follows: If we take an object which has being, as well as the other universals giving it its quality, and begin to strip from it each of these universals in turn, we are left in time with only its "is-ness" or its being. If we take from a rock its irregular spherical form, its hardness, its heaviness, we are left with a void of "being." At this point the rock merely "is," and it has no other attribute. But this void is precisely what we mean by "nothing." Therefore, being and nothing are identical. But this is certainly a contradiction of sorts, one quite different from Aristotle's. In his rephrasing of contradiction, Hegel asserts that it is possible for something to both be and not be when it is in the process of "becoming." *Being* contains within it the seeds of its opposite, *nothing,* and through this contradiction, we can deduce a new category: becoming. Becoming resolves the contradiction, and completes what has been termed the "first triad" of Hegelian logic (Stace, 1955, p. 90).

Since reasoning is a process, a flow from one category to another, pushed on by a compulsion of the Divine Spirit to come to know itself, it is to be expected that becoming will also contain its own contradiction, and that it will touch off a new triadic interrelationship of the type from which it was born. The three aspects of Hegelian dialectic forming such triads are often referred to as the thesis (being), antithesis (nothingness), and synthesis (becoming). Thus, synthesis always suggests its antithesis and acts as a new thesis. In Hegelian philosophy (except for so-called "late Hegel," when his politics entered in, bringing the dialectic to a halt), nothing is self-evident, nothing stands apart from everything else as an unrelated item of knowledge, and change is the very essence of experience, because there is an "unchanging Absolute" which makes itself known in change. This is a very fluid, organismic conception of knowledge. As Hook has observed: "In effect, if not in intent, what Hegel did was to dissolve all things into their relations, construe these relations as logical categories and present the interrelationships of the logical categories as a process" (1962, p. 54). Sometimes these relations and the triads seem rather far-fetched, as in the one which brings together art, religion, and philosophy; it is also true that Hegel was not above stretching the concept of triad by proposing *four* terms rather than three (Stace, 1955, p. 97). But the important thing for our purposes is to see how the dialectic was applied in Hegelian philosophy.

Having now put together a method of analysis, Hegel effected a further revolution by applying it to history, to make his case of a Divine Spirit coming to self-consciousness. History is not only the unfolding of a divine intellect; it becomes a huge stage, on which the dialectical drama is played out, as one civilization passes into another by the fact that it contains within itself the seeds of its own contradiction, hence destruction. He ranged far over the field of civilization, and at one point observed that, whereas Western man has tended to emphasize the distinctions between things, thus developing a precise mind with mathematical clarity, Eastern man emphasized the identity of things, and is said to be more vague and mystical. Either pattern of thought is one-sided and not representative of the unity of things, if it remains unchecked by the other. Man must find a synthesis of the two if he is to fulfill his potential.

The movement of history is dialectically logical. Here is Hegel's evaluation of the ancient Egyptian spirit (nature): "If . . . we combine what has been said here of the peculiarities of the Egyptian spirit in all its aspects, its pervading principle is found to be, that the two elements of reality — spirit sunk in nature, and the impulse to liberate it — are here held together inharmoniously as contending elements" (1952, p. 257). In time, these inharmonious elements contributed to the decline of the Persian world, and brought about the new Greek spirit, in which democratic freedom and free individuality were realized (p. 258). There is a dynamic conflict at play in history, which brings about change, movement, and ultimately progress as the Divine Spirit comes to self-consciousness. Hegel thus makes use of dialectic as a metaconstruct, as a vital model of how to capture most accurately the essentials of history, art, religion, and philosophy. The dialectic is now at the very core of existence; it has been liberated from the single mind and made into a world principle second to none. This was one of the most complete world views ever expounded. The dialectic awaited only Karl Marx for a more down-to-earth, practical application.

Karl Marx (1818–1883) · Although he was forced to do his major writing in England due to political ostracism, Karl Marx was a thinker deeply entrenched in the Continental tradition, one who never completely escaped from the German idealism he claimed to have rejected. For Marx, the dialectic continues to be a world principle, a law of nature manifested in historical change; but it is conceived as a play of opposites within the economic and materially palpable means of production which each society in turn manifests. Ideas do not create institutions, make class distinctions, evolve governments, or discover gods within the fabric of mind. As the empiricists contended, ideas are the *result* and not the cause of material reality. Social institutions, which nurture our political attitudes, philosophies, and religions, not to mention all the petty foibles of class consciousness (pride, covetousness, and so on), are merely the superstructure of society which has been built upon the soil of its own peculiar brand of material production. The entire purpose of this superstructure is to retain the status quo, the material advantage of some and the subjugation or expropriation of others. In the England of his time, Marx observed the worker, the proletarian, getting a meager return for the amount of actual production he contributed to the material gains of society; while the capitalist, the bourgeois, who like a "leech" did not himself work to produce wealth, reaped greater and greater rewards.

Borrowing the Hegelian dialectic, Marx saw in this unfair distribution of wealth or material reward for work a "class struggle," the formation of a triad. One class (bourgeois) which had been the synthesis of a bygone era was now facing its contradiction in a new class on which it must prey (the proletarian); consequently, what would most certainly issue from this "tension of opposites" was a revolution (a negation) and the establishment of a classless society (communism). Just as Hegel had terminated the advance of dialectic in the "ideal" Prussian monarchy, Marx was prepared to declare its termination in the "ideal" classless society. Conflict (dialectical opposition) would no longer be necessary, for in this final "negation of a negation," the bourgeoisie would disappear from the face of the earth, and peace with plenty for all who produced would be achieved.

In his youth Marx was an advocate of Hegelianism, and he always made it perfectly clear where his dialectic came from: "I . . . openly avowed myself the pupil of that mighty thinker [Hegel]" (1952, p. 11). He did this even after Hegelian philosophy had come under serious attack. Marx believed that Hegel's dialectic was a mystical form because the old court philosopher was motivated to glorify the existing state of things; whether knowingly or not, Hegel with his Divine Spirit defended an anachronistic era. Yet that in itself did not detract from the fact that Hegel was the genius who first saw dialectic at work in history, permitting a comprehensive examination of events which combined every conceivable aspect of societies as they evolved (the one and the many). The trouble was, Hegel had the dialectic topsy-turvy. He had mind creating material, whereas it should be just the other way around: "With him it is standing on its head. It must be turned right side up again if you would discover the rational kernel within the mystical shell" (p. 11).

Marx therefore set the Hegelian dialectic upright and conducted his analysis of history through what is called "dialectical materialism." When it came under attack as mystical or as "Hegelian sophistry," Marx observed that such reactionary comments were actually due to the fact that the dialectic was "a scandal and an abomination to bourgeoisdom and its doctrinaire professors because it includes in its comprehension an affirmative recognition of the existing state of things, at the same time, also, the recognition of the negation of that state, of its inevitable breaking up . . . and is in its essence critical and revolutionary" (p.

11). The attacking, critical nature of dialectic had now become a tool to be used in class warfare, even against the hoary philosophers who had used it to advantage over the centuries, and was thus shaking the very foundations of society, just as it had done since the collapse of Persia and the birth of Greece.

Though he did not live to see it, and though its actual emergence was very different from what he had predicted, Marxian communism was to become an actuality in the twentieth century, and the dialectic was to continue providing it with an active, dynamic rationale. Communists believe that their system *must* negate capitalism, for that is the nature of the evolving, material reality. There is a compulsion about material things in the same way that there was a compulsion for Hegel's Divine Spirit to know itself. Communism would be realized, for the dialectic is a universal reality. Following Marx's death, his friend and ally Friedrich Engels (1820–1895) said: "Dialectic . . . is nothing more than the science of universal laws of motion and evolution in nature, human society and thought" (Hook, 1962, p. 75).

The Twentieth Century

Although science was given a great boost by the revival of Platonic philosophy at the beginning of the seventeenth century, it was the idealism suggested (mind could manipulate matter by mathematics) rather than the dialectic method of discovering truths which provided the impetus. At the beginning of the twentieth century, the nature of truth was a topic of concern, and there was much talk in philosophical circles of the relative merits of two theories: the correspondence vs. the coherence theory of truth (Adler, 1927, p. 18). The correspondence theory is based on empiricism and holds that truth is what fits the facts, whereas the coherence theory places its emphasis on the understanding as it asks: does the item of information under consideration cohere with the entire nexus of extant knowledge? From our review of dialectic thus far it is obvious that the latter question is a dialectical one, and that the former definition is more the attitude of empirical (demonstrative) science.

Thanks to the developing roles of empiricism in Britain and pragmatism in America, the correspondence theory won ascendance in scientific circles, and with it a decline in the use of "dialectic" as such was effected. The emphasis was now all on the side of demonstration. The truth became that which "worked" in actuality, which permitted a prediction in the material world, or which could be pointed to operationally. Even on the Continent, where traditions of dialectic are strongest, the *term* was avoided because of its connotations of mysticism and anti-science. Doubtless the communistic usage also served to make dialectic a rabidly sophistic word, an act of pure phantasy done to justify the most preposterous flights of imagination in the name of vested interest. As we shall attempt to show in Chapter X, the dialectic was forced underground, and, through the fertile mentality of Freud, helped shape an image of man for the twentieth century which was to contradict the demonstrative image of science, so that the old conflict was resumed on a slightly different battleground. Battlegrounds change, but it is still the same war. We have chosen two theoreticians of the twentieth century, one a mathematician who founded an important approach to the study of communication and self-regulating systems, the other a noted scholar, philosopher, and teacher. They present a nice contrast, reflecting in their comments the classical divergences with which we have become so familiar.

Norbert Wiener (1894–1964) • Norbert Wiener has been called the "father of cybernetics." Cybernetics is derived from the Greek word meaning "steersman," and this science has to do with steering, controlling, directing, and communicating information. Communication is taken as identical to control, for "when I control the actions of another person, I communicate a message to him," and vice versa (Wiener, 1954, p. 16). Cybernetics therefore has as its purpose the development of techniques for the exercise of control over the environment. It is important to control nature, for nature does not stand still. The universe is gradually deteriorating, losing its organization and fineness of differentiation, and melting into sameness. The central concept here is "entropy," an estimate of the extent of disorganization in the universe, arrived at mathematically in the statistical theories of Bolzmann and Gibbs (p. 7). Cybernetics begins with the assumption that the universe is disintegrating at a greater or lesser degree of entropy, and that anything which "swims against" this tide can be considered "living." One of the most powerful vehicles for the perpetuation of life, for the countering of entropy, is the use of language — especially because language contents can be stored in memory. By searching his memory, a man can "adapt" in the face of changing circumstances. Men can take in data from their environment (called *input*), and then use this input information to effect changes in the outer world (called *output*). Further, thanks to their sensory receptors and memory, men can alter their performance as they go along, basing each successive act on how they had actually performed rather than on how they thought they might perform when they first started to behave (called *feedback*). Interestingly enough, machines can do all these things too. Extending this analogy, Wiener argues that machines and men are much alike:

> It is my thesis that the physical functioning of the living individual and the operation of some of the newer communication machines are precisely parallel in their analogous attempts to control entropy through feedback. Both of them have sensory receptors as one stage in their cycle of operation: that is, in both of them there exists a special apparatus for collecting information from the outer world at low energy levels, and for making it available in the operation of the individual or of the machine (p. 26).

Machines and men are therefore much alike: not in the sense that living mechanisms are merely electrical circuits, but that both organizations of behavior counter entropy, retain their integrity in the face of a type of "universal pragnanz" which exerts great effort for simplicity and sameness, the lack of distinctiveness, and ultimately a featureless chaos on the face of reality. The central nervous system of man, with its synaptic connections for the transmission or blocking of messages, is like the electrical machine with its switches; both utilize feedback to "learn" and to guide future behavior using the facts of the past. Indeed, the machine "reasons" in a logical way: "I have often said that the high-speed computing machine is primarily a logical machine, which confronts different propositions with one another and draws some of their consequences. It is possible to translate the whole of mathematics into the performance of a sequence of purely logical tasks" (p. 154). Thinking machines do "think," they reason, they apply logic. *But,* and this is very important for our survey, *they reason demonstratively.* "True and primary" principles are fed in or recorded as a result of literal performance (through feedback and a memory bank), and then, from these "different propositions," a most probable alternative is selected and recommended or acted out. Machines do not dream up "possibilities," they do not state opinions (unless by opinion we mean a certain frequency probability level), they do not create (unless we mean that they extract all the possible combinations from a mass of data handed to them), and they do not "transcend" their nature by self-exploration in the way Kant said a man could.

This is not to detract from cybernetics, of course. But we should be aware of the intellectual traditions within our sciences, and Wiener is clearly aware of them. In elaborating on his psychology, Wiener places himself accurately in the history of thought by comparing Pavlov's work with John Locke's. In discussing Pavlov's conditioned reflex, which he takes as the proper means of explaining the acquisition of knowledge from the environment, Wiener notes: "Here we have on the level of the animal reflex, something analogous to Locke's association of ideas, an association which occurs in reflex responses whose emotional content is presumably very strong" (p. 69). Subcortical associations, not between ideas but of salivary glands with sounds, for example, Wiener took to be more base emotional motivators, but man could also associate one idea to another and be motivated by higher thoughts (p. 68). The conditioning of a man or animal was one form of input, or learning, and this is analogous to what the cyberneticist terms a *change in taping* on the machine. As we learn, a synaptic pathway is opened which would otherwise have been closed, just like the switches in a machine.

The Hobbesian and Lockean tradition may also be seen in Wiener's treatment of Freudian psychology. After first reviewing the decline of hard determinism in the physical sciences, Wiener goes on to say that both modern physics and Sigmund Freud have pointed to an irrationality in nature. Presumably, 100 per cent determinism implies rationality, but the acceptance of probability for Wiener suggests an element of irrationality in the universe: "This recognition of an element of incomplete determinism [by the physicists], almost an irrationality in the world, is in a certain way parallel to Freud's admission of a deep irrational component in human conduct and thought" (p. 11). He goes on to speak about Freud as in the tradition of St. Augustine, but bases his case not on their similarities in the use of dialectical metaconstructs or reasonings, but on the fact that both would favor probability theories over certainty, both would accept irrationality over complete understanding. This is all very reminiscent of Locke's view that doubt, wavering, or bifurcation in attitude is due to a situation of equal probabilities for alternatives. There is no place for dialectic in the British tradition.

More fundamental and germane, however, is the patent insight before us that Wiener has adapted demonstrative reasoning as the *only* model for man's thought. If St. Augustine transferred dialectic into the Trinity and many other of his theological concepts, Wiener has most certainly transferred demonstration into his concept of mind. He has used demonstration as a metaconstruct. The brain is an extremely complex computing machine which reasons demonstratively. Since it is an imperfect machine it makes errors, "forgets," and lacks the impartiality of the unemotional electrical circuits. Even when memory is correct, emotion can enter in, to foul up the appropriate probabilities so that man does not always learn the facts by experience. In the twentieth century the machine has become a model for the way people ought to reason, or at least for the way they would like to reason if they were not damned to their human condition. Wiener was a great champion for the open society and the furthering of different points of view, so we do not mean to suggest in any way that he consciously furthered the dehumanization of man. We shall have more to say on this matter in Chapter XI.

Mortimer Adler (1902–   ) · No man in the twentieth century has been more in tune with the possibilities and limitations of dialectic than Mortimer Adler. His book *Dialectic* (1927) must go down as one of the greatest expositions of this subject in history, and the subsequent treatment of it in the *Syntopicon* of the *Great Books of the Western World* series (Hutchins, 1952), of which he was Editor-in-Chief, is also a significant contribution. Adler's interpretation of the dialectic is more on the side of conversation than metaconstruct; it is more like Socrates than St. Augustine, more like Aristotle than Plato, more like Kant than Hegel. He defines dialectic as "thinking in discourse" (1927, p. 28). It is an affair of words, which are themselves symbols and statements of meanings. Meanings are not always clear in discourse, so we can speak of the connotations words take on. If language were always factual, and linguistic propositions were always "true and primary," there would be no need for dialectic: "If language were entirely denotative, discourse would not have the elaborate ramifications that it has, for the elaboration of language, its store of definitions and distinctions, is largely due to the connotative properties of its verbal elements . . . [and] to solve the lack of clarity engendered by connotative aspects of language, we must resort to dialectic" (p. 85).

Adler believes that language might have originated in some demonstrative form, as when primitive man gestured or pointed to what he wished to communicate about. Dialectic came only later, when there was a sophisticating of language, fulfilling an inevitable need for clarity, since man probably began using analogies and metaphors in his attempts to communicate. Words were invented, sometimes with unclear referents. It was at this point that dialectic was needed to help make meanings clear, to further understanding. Although he is somewhat cautious in his choice of words, Adler proposes a rather interesting role for dialectic:

It may be, but is not here asserted, that the end of dialectic is understanding rather than truth, that dialectic seeks to determine the meaning of propositions or opinions in debate, rather than the relative truth of them. If this were so, the conclusion of an argument by agreement, would imply the achievement of understanding, or the ability to translate mutually from one system into another, rather than the attainment of truth. Truth in dialectic or argument may mean nothing more than such agreement or translation. In other words, arguments may lead to truth when they lead to common understanding (p. 22).

This implies that dialectic is relevant to a coherence theory of truth, just as demonstration relies on a correspondence theory.

Enlarging this theme, Adler observes that dialectical discourse does not rest on factual information. Facts cannot be discovered in discourse, and when we go to seek facts, dialectical discourse is at an end. This is because facts are dogmatic. They are simply givens, true by definition or observation. The spirit of dialectic, on the other hand, is completely undogmatic. In the Socratic tradition, Adler here recognizes that dialectical examinations go where reason takes them. But as Aristotle had noted, science cannot countenance such freedom of thought. It demands factual discipline. It is for this reason that Adler can say: "Science like theology is profoundly religious. . . . It postulates the law of contradiction, and the law of uniformity and determination. But this is dogmatic rather than dialectical postulation. It does not admit of alternatives. The ideal of science, in terms of these initial assumptions, is the achievement of an ultimately true system of knowledge" (p. 227). Adler rightly recognizes that the spirit of dialectic is never to accept a final truth, an immobile and indisputable "fact." That was the error of both Hegel and Marx, thinking that dialectic could *ever* come to rest. That is its basic divergence from the Lockean view of an indivisible unit of knowledge. The dialectic is ever moving and alive with the possibilities in things.

Adler also shows convincingly how anyone who has posed the simple question "What do you mean by that?" has invited the exercise of dialectic in common speech. This was the starting point for Socrates, and it is for anyone who seeks to actualize the various relationships implicit in the structure of language (to find the many meanings in the one universe of discourse). At the same time, as Socrates was to demonstrate so clearly in his style of life, dialectic is the heart of philosophy. Philosophy is dialectical activity in general: "Philosophy is thus concerned with truth only as a relation among propositions, as a systematic relation of propositions intrinsic in discourse. And there are no absolutely true or false propositions in the universe of philosophic discourse" (p. 225). Finally, Adler proposed that dialectical features in language might well be involved in neurotic behavior, and might thus be amenable to psycho-analysis, since the latter discipline is based upon a dialectical examination of doctor and patient, with the latter carrying on a sort of internal dialectic.

His reasoning is as follows: neurosis might be thought of as a type of language barrier between conscious and unconscious — or disso-ciated — realms of personality. Adler suggested that the impulses as-sociated with repressed materials formed a complex, and then, cut off as they were from conscious language patterns by the censor, chose to express their unsatisfied presence by use of metaphorical language, such as the dream's latent content. The individual therefore literally does not understand himself, because two systems of language are functioning without really communicating, within the partial systems of the person-ality. Neurosis is a disintegrated condition of the personality, and the cure of psycho-analysis is to instruct the patient in self-criticism by means of translation (dream analysis, and so on), thus furthering self-understanding. Once this is accomplished, the individual can again act as a unit (as a whole person) and the neurotically based symptoms dis-appear. Thus: "Psycho-analysis . . . is a dialectic of the neurotic per-sonality, a dialectic of the soul which has been split into two universes of discourse, and which must be reunited by the establishment of trans-lation between them" (p. 116).

Now this is surely a remarkable insight. Although he did not try to establish that Freud consciously or unconsciously employed dialectical reasoning, and proposed his theory of neurosis merely as one possible explanation of how it might function in a person's life and in therapy, we are nevertheless encouraged in our thesis about Freud to note that Adler had so early drawn a parallel between dialectic and psycho-analysis. Freud was indeed dialectical in outlook, not only as to his technique of interviewing, or his attempt to teach the patient a new language of internal communication, but down to his very teeth in the ruminative activity of digesting materials proffered by the client in free association. He used dialectic as metaconstruct at every turn, once he sensed its applicability to the conceptualization of his patients.

Some Implications of the Alternatives in Reasoning
for Method, Theory, and Ethics

Having completed our review through selected examples of the developing themes of dialectical vs. demonstrative reasoning, it may be instructive now to take up some of the major points discussed thus far in terms of this historically important distinction. Can we see the effects of dialectic and demonstration in the many problems and concepts already covered? We will put off until later their relevance to the specific problems of personality theory and other matters having to do with the conceptualization of man. For now we simply want to consider this chapter's contents in terms of the general topics of method, theory, and ethics.

Implications for Method

It is now obvious that in our definition of method we have tried to encompass the historical dichotomy by distinguishing between validating evidence (research method), in deference to the Aristotelian-Kantian criticism, and procedural evidence (cognitive method), in deference to the Platonic-Hegelian awareness that mind is not to be denied. What Aristotle and Kant wanted was the recognition that theory could not go unchecked by empirical test of those conclusions which seemed plausible to intellect. Plato's attitude — that reality was a lesser sphere than intellect — might have led to extreme distortions had it not been challenged by a more pragmatic test of truth. It rests on a faith in the ability of all minds to come to the same conclusions, assuming that they are healthy and of equal endowment. Modern philosophy has challenged this view in its recognition that what we say about reality is at least in some measure dependent upon the language we use, including its implicit assumptions, so that different language structures might lead to differing views of reality, or at least to the posing of different questions about reality. Some of the problems posed for dialectical analysis are problems of language syntax rather than legitimate problems in the world of experience. British empiricism has played an important part in altering the role of philosopher from that of the learned systematist to something akin to a wise philologist who helps us escape the traps of verbal predicament which our language sets for us.

On the other hand, Aristotle failed to take an interest in precisely how major premises do in fact come about. He seemed to feel that as long as man stays close to nature, this reality-boundedness is sufficient to keep him from running wild intellectually and all will fall into place. Though this may be true, it still does not face up to the matter of precisely how ideas or hypotheses are framed in the mind. Kant resolved this problem by assuming certain givens in mind which got the process of thought going. The British empiricists resolved it by simply presuming that mind copies reality with little bits of information, which then total up to big bits of information. Kant felt that only in examining the categories does dialectic play a serious role in man's intellectual life; otherwise, it is to be distrusted and kept in check (to be used mainly in self-defense during debate). The empiricists simply let dialectic drop altogether, and tried to deal with such questions as attitudes, disagreements, oppositions, and doubts on the basis of probability.

Now, in Chapter VI we saw that this attempt to deal with probability entirely through the British demonstrative approach resulted in some confusion about just how probability can work in routine clinical practice. Clinical prediction, which is based upon logical probability, is a dialectical formulation; statistical prediction, which is based upon frequency probability, is a demonstrative formulation. As with Wiener's thinking machines, the statistical predictor (a test) begins with Lockean probabilities of a "primary and true" nature (indivisible bits of information), and then mathematically derives a "best guess" based on fact. Logical probability, however, must deal with those distribution-free situations where the clinician has no factual pattern to go on. He must weigh one logical opinion against another and then make his best guess. We said in Chapter VI that to show accurately how man *does in fact reason,* we must include some form of logical probability, or the weighing of dialectical comparisons. This was something Aristotle failed to appreciate, for he was not concerned with the psychological question "how does man reason?" but rather with the question "how ought man to reason, if he wishes to be correct?" In dealing with the philosophical question he simply made the obvious psychological assumption that man reasoned *both* dialectically and demonstratively.

Continuing in the more psychological vein, note that our insight now allows us to see how man can *reason by way of analogy.* This anticipates our next section, but we should note at this juncture that the Rule of Bayes is in part an analogous use of probabilities which *have no existence.* One can analogize from related albeit different "possibilities" to the case at hand. In fact, by reasoning through opposites it is possible for man to make an "educated guess" about something which has never happened to him before at all. Although he anchors his reasoning processes in past experience, man can analogize by opposites and arrive at judgments of the probable in unique situations facing him in the present. It is this "creative potential" to transcend literal past experience as programmed by the "real" environment which we usually take to be the mark of human intelligence (see Chapter XI). We see here the glimmerings of both human creativity and idealism, as somehow related to the dialectical features of man's intellect.

We have tried to deal with Aristotle's concern about how man *does* think and how he *ought to* think by recognizing a difference between theory and method, yet acknowledging that both are fundamentally theoretical or "thinking" enterprises. They are affairs of reason. Man, if he is to make himself clear, if he is to be objective, *ought* to strive to reason demonstratively (methodologically) at times, because only in this way can he meet the Aristotelian-Kantian criticism. But this is not to deny that he *does* also reason dialectically. The problem comes in, as we have seen, when man attempts to translate constructs phrased from his perspective "as man" into a demonstrative framework, when he moves from the introspective to the more extraspective perspective in proving his point. This is complicated by the recognition that *introspection breeds dialectic*. Yet, can we ignore the discoveries of immediate reason? By dismissing introspection as method can we also dismiss dialectic? It does seem a little foolish to dismiss the lessons of history, which clearly indicate in the writings of most philosophers an introspective tussle going on within mind, the recognition of something akin to two brands of reason, one exciting but a little too dangerous, the other flat but reliable.

That dialectic is tied to introspective effort was shown clearly in Chapter VIII. When Bakan posed his question at the typewriter — probably something like "What is the nature of secrets?" — he was framing a dialectical question. Jung's dialectical discourse with his inward complexes, and the voice of the anima speaking out to him, is an even more dramatic example of this tendency for introspection to breed dialectic. Bakan's "possibilities" are the fruits of dialectic; they are the very items which Kant eyed so suspiciously as not true simply because intellect suggested they were possible. But what if they turn out to be empirically true? Then, we have that human act of creation which no thinking machine will ever generate, a dialectical creation of something new, an *alternative* to what was, an opposition to the *fact* of things. Of course to claim that our creations are true we must first demonstrate them in an objective way. We must, if you like, extend a theoretical line of development from the act of dialectical creation and procedural test to the empirical demonstration of the new "possibility" (hypothesis) generated. This creative act, we have said, is *not* primarily a methodological but a theoretical act. Scientific method calls for a public test of our possibility "out there," and is therefore best suited to demonstrative reasoning; speculation set free among plausibilities is more the sphere of dialectic. Though dialectic is involved with the cognitive method, it is surely true to say that it is most admirably suited to theoretical matters. Mortimer Adler has stated flatly that "Dialectic is a theoretical enterprise" (1927, p. 104). All of this brings us to our next focus of this chapter's contents.

Implications for Theory

We now see the origin of the ladder of abstraction which was the first topic of Chapter II. This ladder dates back to the time of the Greeks, where it was seen as an important stepping-stone to the realm of pure ideas in the Platonic philosophy. Down through history there has not been much debate over the fact of having to abstract, in the sense of leaving out details as we ascend the ladder, but much debate has focused on the lowest or "first level" of abstraction (labeling). Does it spread itself across a world of matter or things-in-themselves, or is there nothing but mind and no matter? The side one chooses here places him on one end or the other of the realism–idealism dimension. Hegel would be extremely idealistic, and Locke would be extremely realistic, while Kant would represent a moderate position on this dimension. Kant has been considered a moderate idealist (in the sense that his categories infuse reality with shape), and yet he termed himself a "critical realist." He is also a dualist, as were Plato and Aristotle, whereas Hegel and Locke were monists. Hegel made everything into mind and Locke considered everything material reality. This seems like a reasonable move, in the direction of parsimony or Ockham's razor, but monistic views generate their own special problems.

One of the problems stemming from a materialistic monism, as handed down to modern psychology from the British empiricists, has to do with their treatment of meaning. By stressing demonstration as a metaconstruct for the mind of man, meanings become extra-individual and there is no theoretical device by which it is possible to describe how a human act of creativity can take place. *British associationist* psychology is a passive hooking up of one construct meaning to another, always on the basis of some "input" information from reality (realistic interpretation of meaning). Just how the machine-like man comes upon new insights is beyond the theory. To call an innovation "creative" is probably one of those cases Hobbes spoke about — a misuse of terminology; for how can a man literally "create" anything with an intellect in which he has only the *tabula rasa* potential for storing and coding meanings from an independent natural order? The behaviorist, in describing how a man can come up with new hunches, must therefore ask for time until he knows a good deal more about the central nervous system. His theory suggests that input, feedback, and output (or antecedent, intervening, and consequent variables) will someday be empirically discovered to account for everything we now call "mind."

The dualistic theorist, on the other hand, whether he is idealistic in orientation or not, can take his lead from Adler (1927) and use the dialectic metaconstruct to state that man gets only the raw data of a rather crude language from the reality of his environment, with its metaphorical possibilities and other unclear connotations. He must then *actively* (dialectically) work over these data, and in doing so he literally creates new meanings through the power of his intellect. Freudian associationistic psychology is like this — the intellect is alive and contributory, with unconscious hidden meanings as well as the more apparent meanings of consciousness. Freud can therefore have something to say about the creative act. On his view a man can indeed come up with new possibilities, sometimes bizarre, but just as often constructive contributions to his life and times.

However it comes about, we have called this creative ability theory generation. In Chapter III we outlined several ways in which the theorist can "come up with" new ideas purely within intellect. It seems clear now that dialectical reasoning must play a significant role in such generation. It is thoroughly undogmatic and free of facts, so that it can always "take flight." Dialectic also lies at the root of theoretical integration, for it has this characteristic of bringing all the parts into a unified whole (the many into the one). Indeed, as both Hegel and Marx sensed, dialectic has a certain compulsion about it to bring everything into a totality, under one grand insight; it pushes us on to seek the "this is it" feeling of grand finality. However, once we give in to this great insight and assert it, we have both welcomed a fact and bid good-bye to dialectic, for it is by nature ever restless and moving on.

Those pockets of finality, those definitions which state boldly "this is it, and only it, a fact to be reckoned with" are in the spirit of demonstrative reasoning. Theoretical description, though it may begin as a dialectical analogue of some sort, once it has been frozen into a demonstrative construct and proven to be "fact" (taken seriously by all those who know the area of study in question), it is no longer a resident of the speculative regions which greatly attract dialectic. The same is true of theoretical delimitation. It is difficult if not impossible for dialectical reasoning to delimit one and only one factor for consideration. Dialectic sweeps to great generalities and similarities, seeming at times to take on an entropic character, only to break up just as quickly the mass of over-generalization into fine points of reason, if not pedantic, fussy points. Though it needs the steadying hand of demonstrative reasoning, dialectic can act as a check on the too-confident delimitation of what this or that construct implies, or literally means. If closeness to nature and a demonstrative turn of mind is healthy for the dialectician, it is just as healthy for the demonstrative reasoner to back off and examine dialectically precisely what he is doing from time to time. This is something Aristotle did not realize might happen — that being too reality-bound could lead to uninteresting and routine theoretical positions being evolved. We have argued in Part One that this is what seems to be happening in psychology. We favored letting out the reins a bit in psychology, permitting a longer line of development from theory generation in procedural test to definition, delimitation, and ultimate validational test.

As already suggested above, in the discussion of method, the concept of a different theoretical perspective from which constructs could be phrased is also underlaid by the dialectical vs. demonstrative reasoning distinction. Just as introspection breeds dialectical theoretical constructs, demonstration breeds extraspective theory. The extraspective theorist is in the harder traditions of the Aristotelian-Kantian criticism, and he draws his most direct line of descent from the British school and the world view of Newton. We might also suggest that the essential characteristic of William James's toughminded and tenderminded thinkers in psychology has to do with whether a given theorist is on the side of demonstration or dialectic. He who splits hairs and says "yes, but what if I really don't define anxiety the way you do?" is tendermined and just too finicky to be doing the work of science. As Aristotle and Bacon said, the natural scientist cannot be hidebound by complete clarity at every turn. He is moving too fast and can leave this mopping-up activity for the tenderminded philosophers.

The universals of ancient philosophy may now be seen to bear a close resemblance to what we have called constructs, and especially to the more abstract metaconstructs. Universals can also be thought of as clearly objective (having a general or universally recognized meaning due to the clear, public analysis of them) rather than subjective constructs. Objectivity has to do with meanings, and meanings, as we have seen in Part One, are woven into the fabric of a given group's common sense, which nurtures its procedural evidence. Thus, when the ancients spoke of universal ideas, rather than inborn ideas as Locke would have it, they were speaking of meanings which any man in their sphere of common-sense knowledge could grasp if he put his intellect to the task. Universals had objective meaning, even though one might well debate whether they had literal existence. The concept of "law" was also a late descendant of the earlier universal propositions. In medieval times, lawfulness was used more in the theoretical than the methodological sense. God's mental laws (final causes) were being made manifest in reality and therefore could not result in error. Out of this conception came the belief in hard determinism. Thus, when Wiener speaks of soft determinism as a kind of irrational element in nature, he is speaking in the tradition which saw the universe as being directed by the intellect of a Divine Spirit, either Hegelian or Christian; this Absolute Mind was rational and, as Einstein later said, "did not throw dice."

Implications for Ethics

Ethics of course refers to the way one "ought" to behave, and since ethical decisions seek to define a given way of behaving, it seems reasonable to suppose that they make use of demonstration. "This is the right way" and "that is the wrong way." Although doubtless important in much of ethical thought, demonstrative reasoning does not exhaust the possible ways of thinking about ethical matters. In fact, if it comes down to this, assertions such as the Golden Rule or Kant's Categorical Imperative are really more on the side of introspection and dialectic than extraspection and demonstration. Ethical decisions are like Hegelian philosophy; they demand a great deal of consideration *before* one comes to the major premise of an Aristotelian syllogism. The "criterion problem" of Chapter VI is a problem for experimental ethics precisely because it raises a dialectical question: "What do you mean by the greatest happiness for the greatest number? What about the individual?" When dialectical argument is used, as in medieval times or more recently by the communists, to "sell" someone's vested interest, it is used more as rhetoric and sophistry than as true dialectical inquiry. It may be very difficult for anyone to achieve a completely open, uncommitted attitude, ready for any alternative which might be suggested in discourse. But as long as the psychologist makes an honest effort to do so he is participating in a time-honored pattern of thought which is as important to the march of mankind (whether up or down the stairs of progress) as the style of reasoning we have called demonstrative. The approach one takes as a psychotherapist determines his manner of interpreting "control" (Chapter VI). The demonstrator is inclined to use control as a means of social influence, and thus to frame an ethic of manipulation. The dialectician strives to keep all alternatives open and to turn over responsibility to his client whenever possible.

It seems clear now that the reason so many psychologists cannot appreciate what someone like Rogers means when he says he strives not to control his client is that they have no accounting for dialectical reasoning in their theories. Nurtured in the traditions of British empiricism, they find all such talk preposterous. Their world view is the same as that of Wiener, who said communication is an act of control, because the communicator *always has something to communicate.* He has the bits of information copied from the environment (input) ready to be sent out (output), with possibly some slight modification based on intermediate factual inputs (feedbacks). This communicator is not seeking in dialectical fashion to help another individual, a discussant in dialectical relations with him, to make *his* — and by definition *their* — thinking clear. The spirit of the dialectic is undogmatic. To claim that a psychotherapist must set out to control the behavior of his client is to make a demonstrative claim, not a dialectical one.

Socrates did not set out to make any given point in his discourses; he merely went where they led him (if we can believe him; and even if we doubt that he could stick to this, we must at least recognize that this was his intention). Any clinician who approaches his client in the hope of helping to further the latter's self-understanding rather than to control him into some preconceived pattern of "mental health" follows the dialectical path. For him, since there are no "primary and true" items of factual knowledge to be communicated, *there is no control,* even according to Wiener's definition. Though it is difficult to achieve, an undogmatic attitude, an openness and complete honesty, *can at least be furthered* by the use of dialectical reasoning. If the therapist used it only to achieve some preselected goal which he had in mind as he entered the relationship, then we would have to consider this another case of sophistry. In this sense psychotherapists can legitimately claim to be "marginal men," transcending the usual moral code — the "norms" of behavior — when that is called for, in an attempt to find the subjective "truth" for their clients (self-understanding nurtured by the client's procedural evidence).

Summary

Chapter IX traced the history of a debate which has been reflected within the various philosophies of Western mankind down through the centuries. It has to do with a distinction between demonstrative and dialectical reasoning. To reason is to draw inferences, to extend a line of inquiry, to come to some conclusion which is then taken as either a further inference (hypothesis) to be developed intellectually, or an "absolute truth" in its own right. Dialectical reasoning has been given many different interpretations, but essentially it stresses an active role for the mind, in which meanings are generated, new relationships in language are found by opposing any term or proposition with its opposite or an alternative. As Protagoras said, "concerning every subject opposite statements are possible," so every denotative assertion implies by definition its opposite. Some of the philosophers discussed placed greatest stress on the interpersonal or discursive use of dialectic, which originated with the Greek Sophists and was made famous in the Socratic dialogues. Aristotle took this view, and stated that although all men reason syllogistically, a dialectician comes to his major premise arbitrarily, ready to take either side of an issue depending upon the position selected by his adversary in debate. Plato, St. Augustine, and Hegel modified this position, giving dialectic a more honored role in thought than as merely an arbitrary rhetorical device; in particular, they advocated its use as a critical tool of analysis, and stressed its potential for creativity. Hegel and Marx even made it into a world principle. Adler, Kant, and St. Thomas also recognized a certain role for dialectic, but they stressed the need for empirical facts in the generation of knowledge. Dialectic need not relate to a factual world.

When the theorist begins his reasoning with assumptions, or items of information that he takes (or "knows") to be primary and true from the outset, Aristotle called this a demonstrative line of reasoning. Whereas the dialectician seeks to divide into opposites and thus to find or create new meanings, new relations within the total language structure, the demonstrative reasoner aims primarily to extract the inferences which an *already defined* truth has for him. The attitude of the operationist who says that "for my purposes, operationally, we shall define X as so and so" is in line with demonstrative reasoning, for he has his meaning confidently in mind before he proceeds. It is in this sense that dialectic has a critical role to play before coming to this definition or to the major premise. The dialectician would have started by saying "what is the nature of X?" Can the same theoretician use both types of reasoning? Of course he can; assuming that we really believe man has the capacity to reason in both of these ways. Aristotle, St. Thomas, Kant, and Adler were all very clear in their recognition that dialectic was one way of reasoning which man used, even though they were more or less critical of its use as a substitute for empirical demonstration. On the other hand, the British empiricists Bacon, Hobbes, and Locke seem to have overlooked the dialectical alternative, and to have defined man as *only* a demonstrative reasoner. This view, which was reflected in the thinking of Wiener, is of great importance because it is widely held in twentieth-century psychology. It is a reflection of the "hard side" of Aristotle, a very rigid interpretation of his naturalistic bent.

Another way in which dialectic and demonstration have been employed is as metaconstructs, ways of conceptualizing or organizing the contents of observation or intellectual debate. Dialectic was said to have served as such a model for St. Augustine, and we have seen how demonstration was taken over as a model for man's brain by cybernetics and the thinking machines. After the philosophical overview of Chapter IX was completed, several topics which had been covered in earlier chapters were mentioned so that the reader might place them in proper historical context. It seemed fairly evident at this point that the matter of dialectical vs. demonstrative reasoning is one of the most important issues ever to have been considered by the philosophers. It recurred at every period in history, one way or another, and lies at the heart of most disagreements in theory which now plague psychology. This will be made plainer as we continue with our thesis that Freud deflected dialectical thought into psychiatry and thence into the twentieth-century image of man.

References

Adler, M. J. *Dialectic*. New York: Harcourt, Brace & Co., 1927. Quotations used by permission of Harcourt, Brace & World, Inc., and Routledge & Kegan Paul Ltd.

Adler, M. J. (Ed.-in-Chief) *The great ideas: A syntopicon.* Vol. 2–3 of R. M. Hutchins (Ed.), *Great books of the western world.* Chicago: Encyclopedia Britannica, 1952.

Aquinas, T. *Summa theologica* (excerpts). Vol. 20 of R. M. Hutchins (Ed.), *Great books of the western world.* Chicago: Encyclopedia Britannica, 1952.

Aristotle. In Vol. 8 of R. M. Hutchins (Ed.), *Great books of the western world.* Chicago: Encyclopedia Britannica, 1952.
On generation and corruption. Pp. 409–441.
Metaphysics. Pp. 499–626.
Prior analytics. Pp. 39–93.
Topics. Pp. 143–223.

Augustine. *On Christian doctrine.* In Vol. 18 of R. M. Hutchins (Ed.), *Great books of the western world.* Chicago: Encyclopedia Britannica, 1952. Pp. 621–698.

Bacon, F. *Novum organum.* In Vol. 30 of R. M. Hutchins (Ed.), *Great books of the western world.* Chicago: Encyclopedia Britannica, 1952. Pp. 105–195.

Cassirer, E. *An essay on man.* Garden City, N.Y.: Doubleday & Co., 1944.

Descartes, R. *Rules for the direction of mind.* In Vol. 31 of R. M. Hutchins (Ed.), *Great books of the western world.* Chicago: Encyclopedia Britannica, 1952. Pp. 1–40.

Fremantle, Anne. *The age of belief.* New York: New American Library, 1954.

Hegel, G. W. F. In Vol. 46 of R. M. Hutchins (Ed.), *Great books of the western world.* Chicago: Encyclopedia Britannica, 1952.
The philosophy of history. Pp. 153–369.
The philosophy of right. Pp. 1–150.

Hobbes, T. *Leviathan.* In Vol. 23 of R. M. Hutchins (Ed.), *Great books of the western world.* Chicago: Encyclopedia Britannica, 1952. Pp. 49–283.

Hook, S. *From Hegel to Marx.* Ann Arbor, Mich.: University of Michigan Press, 1962.

Hutchins, R. M. (Ed.) *Great books of the western world.* Chicago: Encyclopedia Britannica, 1952. 54 vols.

Jaspers, K. *The great philosophers.* New York: Harcourt, Brace & World, 1962.

Kant, I. *The critique of pure reason.* In Vol. 42 of R. M. Hutchins (Ed.), *Great books of the western world.* Chicago: Encyclopedia Britannica, 1952. Pp. 1–250.

Leff, G. A. *Medieval thought: St. Augustine to Ockham.* Chicago: Quadrangle Books, 1958.

Locke, J. *An essay concerning human understanding.* In Vol. 35 of R. M. Hutchins (Ed.), *Great books of the western world.* Chicago: Encyclopedia Britannica, 1952. Pp. 85–395.

Marx, K. *Capital.* In Vol. 50 of R. M. Hutchins (Ed.), *Great books of the western world.* Chicago: Encyclopedia Britannica, 1952. Pp. 1–393.

Plato. In Vol. 7 of R. M. Hutchins (Ed.), *Great books of the western world.* Chicago: Encyclopedia Britannica, 1952.
Cratylus. Pp. 85–114.
Parmenides. Pp. 486–511.
Philebus. Pp. 609–639.
The republic. Pp. 295–441.
Sophist. Pp. 551–579.
Statesman. Pp. 580–608.

Russell, B. *Wisdom of the west.* Garden City, N.Y.: Doubleday & Co., 1959.

Stace, W. T. *The philosophy of Hegel.* New York: Dover Publications, 1955.

Untersteiner, M. *The sophists.* New York: Philosophical Library, 1954.

Wiener, N. *The human use of human beings.* Boston: Houghton Mifflin Co., 1954.

The Role of Dialectic
in Freudian and Jungian
Psycho-analytical Theory

Introduction

Though we might argue that the personality study initiated by Freud and his students is really not science, no one can doubt that in the nineteenth century for the first time men began seeking *scientifically true* explanations of human behaviors previously left to the comments and opinions of philosophers, religious thinkers, and artists. But when science comes to the study of human behavior, not just behavior of the vehicular variety, in which individual differences are submerged, but to all the nuances of inaccurate and self-contradictory things that men do, a special brand of reasoning and conceptualization is required if we are to make sense of the inconsistency within the cold facts of observation. It was Freud's particular genius that he could look at such non-primary and non-true facts of behavior — such as the hysteric's belief that a certain body function had been lost, though it had *not* been lost — and make this belief a false fact of life, without dismissing them as idiotic, interpersonally deceitful, or psychologically meaningless.

As we saw in Chapter VII, in seeking the cause of neurosis Freud took his clients' testimony seriously, and studied the content of their verbal statements to find the life story which prompted the presenting symptom picture. And at every turn he resorted to the use of dialectic. In this chapter we shall trace this aspect of his thought in his early theory, and also speculate on the source of Freud's dialectical bias. A similar analysis will then be made of his most important student, Carl G. Jung, for the dialectical play of opposites is equally apparent in Jung's writings.

309

Sigmund Freud and the Dialectic

Freud's Dialectical Bias Generally Recognized

It is appropriate at the outset to note that Freud's inclination to dialectical reasoning has been generally recognized, though it has usually been phrased in other terms. We have seen in Chapter IX how Mortimer Adler (1927) was quick to identify the dialectical aspects of psycho-analytical therapy. Even before his observations had been made, however, Fritz Wittels, an early student of Freud who fell out of favor for a time and during the interim wrote a biography of his teacher, referred to the fact that the Freudians were easily noted by their "love for a tripartite subdivision" in making theoretical statements (1924, p. 34). Anyone who reads Freud must be greatly struck by the truth of this observation. The psyche or personality structure is first broken down into conscious, unconscious, and preconscious factors, with acceptable ideas, unacceptable ideas, and a censor that knows the difference between them acting as guardian; later, we have the id, ego, and super-ego overlaying but not greatly different from the first tripartite conception. The typical ploy is to oppose human behaviors of all sorts, including thoughts, desires, and impulses, and then to find a middle ground, compensation, compromise, substitution, alteration, or a complete reversal as an alternative outcome to what might otherwise have taken place. The defense or adjustment mechanisms are names applied to all manner of dialectical oppositions and combinations (the one into many and back again), with resultant conflicts being handled or resolved — however inadequately — by repression, sublimation, projection, reaction formation, or the like. If no resolution is possible, then a stalemate in ambivalence or a complete breakdown of behavior is the result. Freud is most certainly in the tradition of St. Augustine in using a dialectical metaconstruct.

Freud's student, biographer, and apologist, Ernest Jones, has also mentioned the dialectical bent in Freud's thinking, though Jones does not appreciate its actual nature and has proposed a dynamic, psychoanalytical explanation for this tendency, which we will take up below. Thus, while discussing one of Freud's papers, and Freud's tendency to make instinctual energies beat an alternating theoretical path (the so-called vicissitudes of the libido), Jones observes:

> A striking feature of the essay is the prominence in it of one set of contrasts, and one pair of opposites, after another. It vividly illustrates

a peculiar feature of Freud's thinking throughout his life, his constant proclivity to dualistic ideas. Any kind of pluralism was quite alien to him. Someone once said facetiously that he had never learned to count beyond the number two.*

Heinz Hartmann was to describe this "dualistic" tendency more accurately as Freud's "very characteristic kind of dialectical thinking that tends to base theories on the interaction of two opposite powers." †

Philip Rieff has also named the dialectical bias as such, and properly placed Freud in the history of thought: "in the nineteenth century science was entirely identified with the 'physical' method; 'dialectical' explanations were consigned to religion and philosophy. Freud gave a new impetus to the dialectical tradition, but psychoanalytic doctrine owes nothing to the older religious psychologies" (1959, p. 16). What Rieff here calls the "physical method" we of course recognize as the natural science emphasis on demonstrative reasoning, the need to define concepts as operationally and primarily true, from the extraspective perspective, and to rely upon efficient causation rather than reifying nature through the use of final-cause explanation.

This need to meet the demands of both the scientific community and his clients plagued the young Freud, as we might recall from Chapter VII. The Fliess correspondence may now be seen in its more accurate context — as a running debate between the two forms of reasoning, each of which suggests different theoretical directions or ways in which a phenomenon is to be delimited and described. As we shall now attempt to show, Freudian theory is a monumental attempt to tie together the demonstrative and the dialectical metaconstructs into one image of man. Freud could not completely shake his medical school education or his identity with the natural science traditions of his German instructors; but neither could he be placated with a physical description of man which amounted to a scientific fairy tale, and a bad one at that. Above all, he sought to capture the basic nature of what he took to be the human being, as he saw this introspectively in his self-analysis, and as he observed it in his clinical practice. To grasp better how Freud must have wrestled with the demands of Germanic science and the more French-like clinical-practical sense, we will now consider two converging influences on his early theorizing.

---

* From *The Life and Work of Sigmund Freud,* Volume II, Copyright 1955 by Ernest Jones, Basic Books, Inc., Publishers, New York, p. 320.
† *Ibid.,* p. 422.

*Psychic Energies: Mayer, Helmholtz, Brücke, and
the Constancy Principle*

It would seem from a reading of both Jones's biography (1953, 1955, 1957) and the commentary accompanying Strachey's translation (1955, p. xx) of Freud's early work (e.g., Breuer and Freud, 1955) that Freud's scientific attitude was very strongly rooted in the principle of constancy, or conservation of energy, a concept proposed initially by the German physicist and physician, Julius Robert Mayer (1814–1878), and later refined by the psychologist Helmholtz. Since Breuer and Freud later used this idea in their *Studies on Hysteria* (1955), and Freud never rejected its import, Jones concludes that it had "captivated" the young scholar, who probably first read of it in the published lectures (1874) of his beloved teacher Ernst Brücke:

> Organisms differ from dead material entities in action — machines — in possessing the faculty of assimilation, but they are all phenomena of the physical world; systems of atoms, moved by forces, according to the principle of the conservation of energy discovered by Robert Mayer in 1842, neglected for twenty years, and then popularized by Helmholtz. The sum of forces (motive forces and potential forces) remains constant in every isolated system. The real causes are symbolized in science by the word "force." The less we know about them, the more kinds of forces do we have to distinguish: mechanical, electrical, magnetic forces, light, heat. Progress in knowledge reduces them to two — attraction and repulsion. All this applies as well to the organism man.*

It will be recalled (see Chapter VIII) that Helmholtz presumed there was a substrate of "simple forces" which underlay all physical phenomena, and that it was the purpose of science to reduce all descriptions to this mechanistic base. Wundt then saw in this idea of force an even more basic motion, and Brücke here is saying that the forces of motion within a system, as conceptualized in atoms, although they may distribute themselves unequally, always sum to a constant total — at least as long as the system remains isolated. Breuer and Freud then adopted this notion of a constancy in the central nervous system, as follows: "The nervous system endeavors to keep constant something in its functional condition that may be described as the 'sum of excitation.' " †

---

* From *The Life and Work of Sigmund Freud*, Volume I, Copyright 1953 by Ernest Jones, Basic Books, Inc., Publishers, New York, p. 41.
† *Ibid.*, p. 386.

This says nothing of any isolated system, and has the implication of homeostasis, the desire to keep a certain level of tension, neither too much nor too little. Freud made this even clearer in a lecture he delivered in 1893, when he said: "If a person experiences a psychical impression, something in his nervous system which we will for the moment call the 'sum of excitation' is increased. Now in every individual there exists a tendency to diminish this sum of excitation once more, in order to preserve his health" (Freud, 1962, p. 36). Note that the principle has a psychological interpretation now, and would apply even to the individual's conscious awareness of a heightened state of excitation. The *Studies on Hysteria* were not nearly so colored by the constancy principle as was the ill-fated *Project* (see Chapter VII).

In the latter work we see Freud speculating freely about the possible nature of the central nervous system. The constancy principle is now termed the "principle of neuronic inertia" (Freud, 1954, pp. 356–358). Thus, neurons seek to rid themselves of quantities of energy, which allows the nerve impulse to be transmitted, but at other times they sustain or bind certain quantities within them. A "cathected" neuron is one which is filled with a certain amount of energy, and pleasure is "the sensation of discharge" when a neuron gives up its energy (p. 373). Sensations of pleasure and unpleasure accompany the rise and fall of cathexes in the neurons; to have pleasure, first one's neurons must have a certain amount of energy cathexis, so the nervous system seeks to keep a constant level within the fluctuating changes of its energy charges — not too much, not too little. The ego is a collection of impermeable neurons, in which energy is stored and memory therefore is possible. The ego retains an identity within the changing conditions of the nervous system. *Does this sound like Freud?* We know that even he did not understand himself in trying to write this kind of psychology (see Chapter VII, p. 176), no matter how much it might have pleased Brücke (then deceased) had he done so. There would have been many men to applaud an effort of this sort. But Freud knew this was all a vain and pretentious farce, at best an academic exercise. This was a vehicular psychology, and he was above all a personality theorist interested in discriminal constructs.

The drive-reduction learning theories are identical in outlook to the view represented by the conservation-of-energy principle. A theorist of this persuasion, relying upon efficient causation exclusively (see Chapter VIII), views his "drives" as (potential) energy transformations of matter — a measurable "something" which propels the organism to act when it rises but ceases this propulsion as it falls off. Hence, an unknowing, blind hedonism can be used to explain behavior in extraspective fashion. However, as we argued in Chapter VIII, Freud did not see behavior as *primarily* the result of efficient causes, and thus due to the rising or falling of energy levels alone. It was not the unidirectional flow or redistribution of energy (force) according to a constancy principle which afforded psycho-analysis its peculiar and original flavor. Rather, it was the *opposition* of two intentions (final causes held to by the ego, id, or super-ego), wishes, or ideas — one clashing with the other — which brought about human action and gave Freudian thought its uniqueness. Unfortunately, Freud could not stand completely apart from his medical background, so what actually happened was that he combined his dialectical approach with the more demonstrative tradition then in ascendance in medical circles, and continued to use an energy concept as a sort of pseudo-drive for the organism.

We say "pseudo" because the true theoretical formulation always sprang from a dialectical ploy of some sort, and it was then rephrased in energy terms. It was not merely the instinctual drive or its energy which provided the dynamics of motion, but the energy as stimulated and then opposed by another, with the resultant repression, projection, or sublimation, which gave personality its Freudian impulse. Instinctual energies were more like ideas, which could help set a *teleological line of behavior* by affixing cathexes to certain consciously or unconsciously determined goals. The psyche (which amounts to saying "a system of ideas") could also remove these charges of energy according to circumstance. Just as ideas are never lost to the unconscious mind, libidinal energy is never dissipated or used up within the psychic system. Such energy could be opposed to itself, so that the three parts of the psyche might wage an internal war, based upon opposing ideas of right and wrong. And the possible ways in which this energy can be transformed, altered, or turned away from its natural object are legion. In short, an honest appraisal can only suggest that in his desire to meet the needs of the physiological science of his day, *Freud made his energies behave dialectically.* At least he did so for the sexual energies, suggesting that polarity may not be characteristic of the nutritional instinctual energies (Nunberg and Federn, 1962, p. 86). The energy of the sexual instincts was very mobile and easily moved about in service of the mental contents or ideas of the various portions of the psyche. As is well known, the libido's versatility is limited only by Freud's genius in making it do his theoretical bidding.

Since the conservation-of-energy principle suggested a balancing of forces as well as the opposition of an attraction and a repulsion, it served as a convenient link with the more traditional science of the academic circles and an honest subterfuge for Freud and those who would align him with the more extraspective sciences. But Freud was a great dialectician, and the single effort he made to describe humans as he had been accustomed to describing lower animals in the laboratory of Brücke (the *Project*) ended, as we have seen, in nothing but failure and confusion for him. To shed light on the more accurate wellspring of Freudian thought we will now turn to some other influences on his early career as psychotherapist and theorist.

Mental Contents: Charcot, Janet, Breuer, and Antithetical Ideas

Ernest Jones would have Freudian theory traced to the principles of physiology that Freud learned in Brücke's laboratory (1953, p. 45). Others of Freud's interpreters have placed greater stress on his contacts with the French as having stimulated his theoretical ideas, especially Charcot, whom Freud greatly admired. For example, Wittels observes:

> Charcot showed that in a hysterical subject it is possible, under hypnosis, to arouse ideas — with the aid, perhaps, of some trifling physical impression, such as a tap on the skin — which lead to a paralysis of one of the limbs, a hysterical paralysis. . . . Charcot thus proved that ideas can induce bodily changes. . . . He [Freud] came to study under one who, like Freud's teachers in Vienna [Brücke], had graduated as pathological anatomist, and had therefore been well grounded in the field of natural science. This man [Charcot] maintained, and could prove, that mere ideas were able to cause disease. It is probable that Freud was not slow to realize that he was learning something which would bring him into collision with the Viennese School (1924, pp. 29, 31).

One of the most fundamental differences between dialectical and demonstrative explanations is that the dialectician can more readily stay within the realm of discourse, within the *content* of the material under consideration. That is, since he is engaged in conversation, with another or with himself, he accepts the import of the content meanings of these verbal exchanges. He does not set as his goal the attainment of an explanation other than and entirely outside these contents, in a new sphere of construct meanings removed from the import of the initial constructs. And he never completely dismisses the contents and their implications in forming an explanation of the phenomenon at hand. This permits him to deal with what Aristotle called opinions, for the truth or falsity of some content may bias the theoretician into rejecting the import of a verbal content. If a man speaks nonsense, the best thing to do is simply ignore what he says and get on with the facts of the case; this is the way a demonstrative reasoner proceeds, as we recall in the case of Hobbes (see Chapter IX). Yet, as we now know, facts are a special form of opinion, buoyed up by two kinds of evidence but subject to change. Modern science has taught us that today's facts may well crumble into tomorrow's opinions, and that it is possible to hold opinions within facts or to hold two mutually contradictory facts at different times without violating reason. The dialectician is prepared for such alternatives, but it seems like pure sophistry to those who believe there are true and primary bits of reality about which someday all can be known.

Aristotle was the first to note that dialecticians dealt with the more obvious and apparent aspects of behavior, whereas the demonstratively-inclined physicist strove to be more complex. Complexity depended upon the number of causes used in explanation by a theorist. Thus, Aristotle said:

> a physicist would define an affection of soul differently from a dialectician; the latter would define e.g. anger as the appetite for returning pain for pain, or something like that, while the former would define it as a boiling of the blood or warm substance surrounding the heart. The latter assigns the material conditions, the former the form or formulable essence; for what he states is the formulable essence of the fact, though for its actual existence there must be embodiment of it in a material such as is described by the other (1952, p. 632).

Now, as this came to be interpreted, it seemed that the physicist, by adding a new causal element to the description of anger, was adding new meanings to the nature of what we call anger. The Helmholtzian call for a reduction to basic forces rests squarely on this interpretation. Until such time as the theoretician brings his explanation down to the basic forces in anger — the boiling blood or the whipping about of atoms — he will not have captured its essential nature, nor added to the meaning of anger.

Yet, in the French school of Charcot and Bernheim, in which the straightforward mental contents such as proffered by the hypnotist to a subject were the focus of theory, it might have been shown how in opposing one idea with another an interesting alternative developed, shedding new light on the meaning of some behavioral phenomenon. If the appetite to return anger with anger were mentally opposed by another appetite, *not* to express anger, then the dialectician and his mental contents might still be able to shed light on the nature of hostility, or even on the origins of hysterical symptoms. This possibility was demonstrated most clearly to Freud in the post-hypnotic suggestion experiments performed by the French. When asked why he was opening an umbrella indoors — while he was under post-hypnotic suggestion to do so — one of Bernheim's subjects replied that he wanted to check to make certain it was not his personal umbrella (Wittels, 1924, p. 39). Here was the evolution or creation of a compromise, a self-deluding falsehood conceived to ameliorate two impulses within the mind, to obey and to appear plausible. No mere reduction to more basic forces could ever hope to capture *this* meaning. Meanings have levels of abstraction and contexts of applicability (multiordinality), and it just so happened that the kinds of meanings in which Freud as analyst was interested were not those which attracted Fliess or Brücke. When pressed to recall the real reason for opening the umbrella, in time Bernheim's subject did so. Observations such as these, made in 1899 (p. 38), could hardly fail to impress the ambitious and intellectually daring young Freud, who was then setting his own medical and theoretical course.

It is therefore not surprising that in what appears to be his very first publication of a theoretical position on hysteria, Freud made use of the concept of *antithetic ideas* (Jones, 1953, p. 240). This paper was published in 1892, the year preceding the first publication of the *Studies on Hysteria,* which appeared over a two year span in the literature, with Breuer and Freud's "Preliminary Communication" reaching print in 1893. Freud mentions the antithetic idea theory in the *Studies,* while discussing the case of Frau Emmy von N., one of his first clients. The case of Frau von N. was probably begun in 1888 or 1889 and was terminated after about one year. Interestingly, although Strachey (1955, p. xii) seems to feel that Freud used primarily post-hypnotic suggestion with Frau von N., Freud at least believed he had relied primarily on the cathartic method. This is important, because post-hypnotic suggestion ("do this — or, don't do that — upon awakening") is very much in the style of demonstrative reasoning, whereas the cathartic method, in which the client searches his own memory, to recall and talk out a situation long pushed out of his awareness, is more in the style of dialectic. The information to be used and acted upon is proffered by the client and used by one of the two participants in discourse, as he assists the other to elucidate, and so the process continues. Freud was to make this procedure entirely open, carried on within the relationship of two conscious discussants, very much in the Socratic tradition. We feel, therefore, that these early cases are extremely important in that they reflect Freud's dialectical awakenings even before his theories of repressed sexuality had been formulated. *Indeed, it is our thesis that the repression theory would not have been possible without its dialectical underpinnings.*

Freud's theory of antithetic ideas was used to explain the origin of hysterical symptoms as "conversions." Thus, in discussing how it was possible for Frau von N. to exhibit such noisy tic-like movements as the clacking of her tongue, stammering, and the calling out of names or certain exclamations like "Don't say anything!" Freud reasons as follows:

> Our hysterical patient, exhausted by worry and long hours of watching by the bedside of her sick child which had at last fallen asleep, said to herself: "Now you must be perfectly still so as not to awaken the child." This intention probably gave rise to an antithetic idea in the form of a fear that she might make a noise all the same that would wake the child from the sleep which she had so long hoped for. Similar antithetic ideas arise in us in a marked manner when we feel uncertain whether we can carry out some important intention. . . . It appears that a conflict had occurred between her intention and the antithetic idea (the counter-will) and that this gave the *tic* its discontinuous character and confined the antithetic idea to paths other than the habitual ones for innervating the muscular apparatus of speech.*

We see in this quote not only Freud's tendency to use final causation as a theoretical description (which he later masked in the libido theory), but also the clear tendency to explain how a mental conflict might be the result of dialectical opposition. The concerned mother has an *intention,* and this intention suggests its opposite spontaneously, by the very fact that it was framed. Though he never appreciated the precedent, Freud now begins to put himself in the intellectual tradition which dates

---

* From J. Breuer and S. Freud, *Studies on Hysteria.* Vol. II of J. Strachey (Ed.), *The Standard Edition of the Complete Psychological Works of Sigmund Freud,* pp. 92–93. London: The Hogarth Press, 1955. (Also in *Studies on Hysteria,* by Josef Breuer and Sigmund Freud, Basic Books, Inc., Publishers, New York, 1957.)

back to Protagoras' view: "concerning every subject opposite statements are possible." Another insight we gain here is that, if the mind suggests opposites in this spontaneous fashion, then it just might be that *unique* final causes can also be projected by way of such a dialectical opposition. Man can project something which *never was* simply because he can reason to the opposite of what "is." His Lockean inputs generate a *dimension* ranging from the "fact as gleaned from experience" to "the opposite of the fact as experienced." Reasoning further, man can now project an "ought," or hope, or wish "to shoot for," which is in part what Aristotle meant by the final cause. It is in this sense that final causes differ from efficient causes; they can be worked over and altered to meet the needs of an intellect responding actively to the strict inputs of experience.

This dialectical tactic of Freud's represents his fundamental divergence from the style of thought used by Breuer and by Pierre Janet, the famous student of Charcot who is sometimes said to have been the source of the dualistic opposition of mind that Freud adopted in his theoretical outlook. Both Janet's concept of "dissociation" and Breuer's concept of "hypnoid state" explained the dualism in the mind demonstratively. That is, they *asserted it;* the mind of the hysteric had simply set free an idea, according to which the body acted in consonance. A "fixed idea" which had been dissociated from the rest of the reality-testing apparatus of the mind took over control of the personality, said Janet, and now exerted great influence:

> There are such kinds of fixed ideas in somnambulisms and fugues; the idea of one's mother's death, the idea of visiting tropical countries, etc. There are such ideas in systematic contractures, for instance, when a patient seems to hold her feet stretched because she thinks herself on the cross. There are such ideas in visceral disturbances, and I have shown you the observation of a patient who died of hunger because she had the fixed idea of the turnips she had eaten when at school [that they were poisoned] (1920, p. 324).

Breuer's "hypnoid state" held the identical notion of a form of self-hypnosis brought on by any of a number of reasons (Breuer and Freud, 1955, pp. 215–222). In their demonstrative approach, both Janet and Breuer favored physical explanations, straightforward reasons why ideas should get split off or fixed. For example, in his discussion of how a writer's cramp might arise, Janet suggests the plausible possibility that writing is a highly complex behavior, and therefore it may be more subject to loss of function due to neurosis than other, less complex functions; or, that "physiological laws" may account for the fact that hysterical symptoms always arise during an emotional state, and presumably therefore run afoul of physical complexities in the body and mind (Janet, 1920, p. 336).

Freud cannot rest with such speculations. Why, he wants to know, does the person get emotional in the first instance; why is it *this* complex activity and not *that* complex activity which is adversely affected in the neurosis? In discussing Breuer's "hypnoid state" Freud observes: "In his view what happens in hypnoid hysteria is that an idea becomes pathogenic because it has been received during a special psychical state and has from the first remained outside the ego." * Breuer talks as if his famous client, Anna O., in the first cathartic therapy, had just been the unhappy victim of an unnatural state of affairs, and that nothing had led up to the pathogenic situation from which her symptoms stemmed. Freud claims, on the other hand, that he has never found a case of pure hypnoid hysteria, for there has always been something behind the pathogenic situation, there has been a *strangulator* of what Breuer called the "strangulated affect" of the hysteric. This was the unconscious opponent which Freud as master detective put himself to finding. And his entire approach was that of the dialectician, in theory formulation as well as in the way he carried on the discursive treatment. Freud threw his lot entirely with the theory of oppositions in the mind, which he termed "defense," rather than with the hypnoid-state view. Even before he had discovered his personal defensiveness in his self-analysis Freud found that: *"by means of my psychical work I had to overcome a psychical force in the patients which was opposed to the pathogenic ideas becoming conscious (being remembered)."* †

The censor was tenacious and did not easily give up hidden secrets. It exerted a force against the prying eye of the analyst. But what kinds of things could there be lying beneath? What sorts of ideas could provoke such an ambitious attempt at secrecy? Freud answers: "I recognized a universal characteristic of such ideas: they were all of a distressing nature, calculated to arouse the affects of shame, of self-reproach and of psychical pain, and the feeling of being harmed; they were all of a kind that one would prefer not to have experienced, that one would rather forget." ** Here is the essential difference between Freud and Janet or Breuer; by looking at the other side, the opposite

* *Ibid.*, p. 285.
† *Ibid.*, p. 268.
** *Ibid.*, p. 269.

of things as they appear, Freud could suggest a generalization to answer questions of "why," one that he took to have universal validity.

The hysteric's "not knowing" was really a case of "not wanting to know." Writer's cramp now becomes tied to the hidden motives of the writer *in every instance;* moreover, the nature of the symptom dialectically suggests its possible cause, so that we can take it as a first hypothesis clinically that the writer is rejecting writing as an activity. (The opposite of writing is *not* writing.) Is it something he fears he will write, or is it his unconscious refusal to continue in an occupation which makes him unhappy? Whatever is at the basis of the problem, we begin our dialectical analysis with those manifestations in conscious life which are the opposite counterparts of contents in the unconscious life. Nothing ever merely "happens" in the psyche, for everything has a meaning, everything has a determination for everything else, tied together in one large complex of associations (the many into one). Freud shares with Marx and Hegel the need to apply analysis to the more obvious, the more patent manifestations of things, because truth is never what it appears. Intellect must be applied to the state of things before truth will issue.

The decade spanning the 1890's, covered well in the Fliess correspondence (see Chapter VII), was a time of increasing reliance upon dialectical maneuvers for Freud. He began using the dialectic as a major metaconstruct, and thereby put together some of the most remarkable insights about man. Though Jones (1953, p. 241) apparently dismisses the antithetic idea theory as minor in Freud's early development, we note that as late as 1896 he uses the phrasing "antithetic symptom" in discussing the return of repressed ideas in the obsessional neurosis. By the close of the decade (1899) we find him confidently proposing to Fliess the most astonishing theories, based upon the dialectical maneuver, such as the following: "It turns out, for instance, that hysterical headaches are due to a fantastic parallel which equates the head with the other end of the body (hair in both places — cheeks and buttocks — lips and labiae — mouth and vagina); so that a migraine can be used to represent a forcible defloration, the illness thus again standing for a wish-fulfilment." * Symptoms are interpreted as the "coupling of opposites" (p. 279); in the symptom we see both the repressed and the repressing ideas made actual. Freud tells Fliess of

* From *The Origins of Psycho-analysis, Letters to Wilhelm Fliess, Drafts and Notes: 1887–1902,* by Sigmund Freud, Basic Books, Inc., Publishers, New York, 1954, p. 273.

the case of a woman who had developed hysterical vomiting. This symptom "meant" or symbolized both that she had been impregnated by an imaginary lover and was now ill with child (repressed wish) *and* that she would soon become emaciated from illness and therefore lose her sexual attractiveness for other lovers (repressing wish). We have here the formation of a content psychology, in which the motive power is supplied by the dialectical clash of ideas, and in which *energy notions are superfluous*. Man had been shown, at Freud's hands, to be what the artists had proposed — namely, a "clever work of fiction" and full of contradictions (p. 279).

It was while he was discussing what he took to be a sophistic trend in dialectical reasoning that Aristotle proposed his famous law of contradiction (see Chapter IX, p. 286). Yet here is Freud, at the end of the nineteenth century, arguing that *unconscious* man can have his cake and eat it too, especially in his dream life:

> The way in which dreams treat the category of contraries and contradictories is highly remarkable. It is simply disregarded. "No" seems not to exist so far as dreams are concerned. They show a particular preference for combining contraries into a unity or for representing them as one and the same thing. Dreams feel themselves at liberty, moreover, to represent any element by its wishful contrary; so that there is no way of deciding at a first glance whether any element that admits of a contrary is present in the dream-thoughts as a positive or as a negative (1953, p. 318).

Freud took great satisfaction in the fact that he had discovered a special kind of truth about man. In discussing his personality construct "id," though he does not refer specifically to Aristotle, Freud comments: "The logical laws of thought do not apply in the id, and this is true above all of the law of contradiction" (1964, p. 73). Demonstrative givens, either clearly true or clearly false as major premises, may exist in logic, Freud is saying, but man is not always this kind of animal. By so commenting on the Aristotelian law of contradiction, Freud unknowingly places himself in the traditions of *another* form of logical analysis — the dialectic. As we have seen, this brand of logical analysis has a long history, dating back to the Sophists, and as recently as the century of which he was a product the view was embodied in Hegel's belief that any thesis carried within it the seeds of its own contradiction.

In 1910, Freud published a little paper on "The antithetical meaning of primal words" (1957). It was based upon the work of the philologist Karl Abel, and it delighted Freud, for Abel had evidence to suggest that in the earliest known examples of human languages, such as the Egyptian, "there are a fair number of words with two meanings, one of which is the exact opposite of the other" (p. 156). If man had first communicated, as Mortimer Adler (see Chapter IX) had suggested, demonstratively — by pointing to things — then man had probably first reasoned, first learned to distinguish between things, by dividing them into opposites. This was Abel's thesis: "Man was not in fact able to acquire his oldest and simplest concepts except as contraries to their contraries, and only learnt by degrees to separate the two sides of an antithesis and think of one without conscious comparison with the other" (p. 158). Thus, the concept of strength doubtless first held together or subsumed the contrary ideas of "strong" and "weak." It was the relationship between opposites that man first captured in a single term. Abel was arguing that the process of construing was fashioned dialectically, and Freud happily concurred, for it met with his clinical experience. Once again, though he accepted its import as a scientific fact, Freud would never have accepted the label of dialectician. Indeed, he would have been riled by the suggestion, for he equated dialectic with sophistry, and sophistry with senseless argumentation, engaged in more for personal than scientific reasons. Personally, he avoided public debates whenever possible. His attitude is made plain in the following:

> I have never been able to convince myself of the truth of the saying that "strife is the father of all things." I think the source of it was the philosophy of the Greek sophists and that it errs, as does the latter, through the overestimation of dialectics. It seems to me, on the contrary, that scientific controversy, so-called, is on the whole quite unfruitful, apart from the fact that it is almost always conducted in a highly personal manner. Until a few years ago I could boast that I had only once been engaged in a regular scientific dispute, and that with one single investigator, Löwenfeld of Munich. The end of it was that we became friends and have remained so to this day (1952, pp. 545–546).*

These are very strange words from the mouth of a man who fought the resistances of the censor, broke with almost every one of his old friends, said of himself that he always needed an enemy to oppose as well as a close friend in whom to confide, stood against a generation

* From: *A General Introduction to Psychoanalysis* by Sigmund Freud. By permission of Liveright, Publishers, New York. Copyright © renewed 1963 by Joan Riviere. And by permission of George Allen & Unwin Ltd, Publishers, London.

of his fellow scientists on the confident belief that they were too threatened or constricted by their own sexual repressions to look objectively at the truth, and who spent the larger part of his life in dialectical exchanges with both patients and students. Only Freud "in all his contradictions," the man who could give the most banal acts an oppositional twist to set one's head spinning, could also in 1937 dismiss the dialectic with a cool sentence in a letter to R. L. Worrall concerning Marxian theory: "As to the 'dialectic' I am no clearer, even after your letter" (Jones, 1957, p. 345). Taking a page from his analytic notebook, could it be that Freud did not want to find the hidden meanings in this case? All of this brings us to the possible sources of Freud's dialectical bias.

The Sources of Freud's Dialectic

Freud was a very complex man, and to attempt an analysis of the roots of his thought is a task fraught with contingencies, blind alleys, and speculative guesses. The master sleuth is himself the most difficult to detect anything about. From what others have claimed or presumed, and from what we know of his time in history, there seem to be three possible sources of influence to which we can trace Freud's dialectical orientation: (1) his method of psycho-analysis and consequent use of the introspective theoretical perspective; (2) his Jewish identity; and (3) the philosophical climate of his time. Each of these probably contributed to the emergence of his style of thought, and we will now take them up in turn.

Method of Psycho-analysis and the Introspective Theoretical Perspective

Whereas the Frenchmen Charcot and Bernheim drew parallels between hysteria and hypnosis, and Janet could see in the hysteric's fixed ideas a phenomenon similar to post-hypnotic suggestion, Breuer and Freud introduced an entirely new aspect to psychopathology. The French were studying hysteria in a way which made the individual hysteric a mere pawn in the game of science, a kind of specimen for observation and hypnotic experimentation. But the Viennese practitioners, Breuer and Freud, found that the neurotic patient, with the aid of hypnosis, or, as Freud later adapted the procedure, with free association in a relaxed atmosphere, could search his memory and recall a pathogenic situation in his past, one in which an emotional response had been choked off or strangulated. By subsequently talking out the feelings associated with this situation, and overcoming certain resistances along the way with the help of the therapist, a removal of the symptom could often be effected. In the Breuer-Freud technique the focus of study clearly shifts from the hypnotist to the subject, from the therapist to the patient. The evolving psycho-analytical technique succeeded in *shifting the locus of theoretical perspective from the extraspective to the introspective end of the continuum.*

Unlike the French, who placed their subjects under hypnosis, got them to behave in various ways — even against their symptom pictures — and then speculated on various psychological and physical causes *for their clients,* Breuer and Freud let their clients speak for themselves. Anna O. even named her own therapy, which came upon Breuer quite by accident, as a "talking cure." The client was important to the Viennese in a way never quite appreciated by the French. Unfortunately, Breuer could not accept this introspective attitude as completely as Freud did, but his contribution to the development of psycho-analysis in this sense cannot be overlooked. As Freud's therapy came to be perfected, one did not "do" anything to the client — on the order of post-hypnotic suggestion — one merely proposed (theoretical) explanations to cover the recollections a client proffered as he searched his own unique life history.

However, we now know that discourse, whether carried on interpersonally or intrapersonally, breeds dialectic. Dialectic is, among other things, "thinking in discourse." Whether posed by the analyst or by the client, a "why" to any behavior, dream, or emotion promotes a dialectical process of examination. This is the very essence of the insight therapy introduced by Freud. We know that for centuries, whenever man turned to the examination of his basic premises, he had to forego demonstrative reasoning and seek his answers dialectically. Why should it be any different for the greatest analyst of all times? Even his own psyche was not spared as he turned the process to self-analysis. He looked inward, and analyzed his unconscious motives as best he could in much the same way that Bakan and Jung looked into theirs (see Chapter VIII). And on his own testimony we can show that he thereby generated dialectically opposite ideas. Thus, in *The Psychopathology of Everyday Life* (1901), while he introspectively analyzes one of his personal "screen memories" (an idea which overlays a deeper, more significant, or more meaningful idea) Freud tells us: "Strangely enough my next thought was not a maxim but the following sentence: 'God created man in His own image' and the same idea in reverse: 'Man created God in his'" (1960a, p. 19). Ernest Jones's explanation for Freud's dialectical propensity is traced to the *insights* which presumably issued from this introspective effort, rather than, as we would have it, from the tactics of the method itself.

Jones believed that the source of Freud's "dualistic" tendencies lay in a personality quirk, one of which Freud was well aware, and which showed itself in his many oppositional tendencies, such as his attraction to science but also to free speculation, his masculinity and femininity, his conflict over dependency and independence. As if not to presume too much, Jones develops his case slowly, eventually letting Freud speak for himself on the matter: "I cannot but recall in this connection that Freud once told Jung that were he ever to suffer from a neurosis it would be of the obsessional type. That signifies, as Freud himself taught us, a deep ambivalence between the emotions of love and hate, and much in his own self-descriptions undoubtedly accords with this" (Jones, 1955, p. 423). For Jones, then, Freudian dialectic is at heart an ambivalent attitude stemming from certain (presumably anal) personality characteristics.

Though it is properly analytical, one can hardly take this suggestion very seriously. It may be one of the reasons for Freud's dialectical approach, but it seems far more plausible to assume what is the basic suggestion of the present section — i.e., that in relating dialectically both intrapersonally and interpersonally, and being called upon to reason dialectically to propose introspective insights to his clients, Freud simply furthered and elaborated an approach which grew naturally from his method of study and therapy. If we *must* then assume that the results of his self-analysis provide a clue to his dialectical bent, we would favor the lead given us by David Bakan (and also Freud): When he looked inward, Freud had to discover there his Jewishness. If he did not personally realize the full importance of his Jewishness to the edifice of psycho-analysis, at least others have. Although drawn in large measure from the introspections of one man, psycho-analysis does not rest on the accidents of a single life, as Jones might have it, because Freud's most personal and intimate self had already "contained within it a culture" long before he introspected analytically (Bakan, 1958, p. 46). Here is our next lead to the origins of Freudian dialectic.

Freud's Jewish Background

In the minutes of the Vienna Psycho-Analytic Society, during a 1907 meeting, there is recorded an observation made by Sadger to the effect that all Jews are prone to develop obsessional neuroses, and further, that this is doubtless due to their intellectual ruminatory tendencies (Nunberg and Federn, 1962, p. 98). For thousands of years, claims Sadger, Jews have been studying, interpreting, and reinterpreting the contents of the Talmud. This is an interesting thesis, one which apparently never occurred to Jones, but in putting himself on the line as a potential obsessive, Freud was, according to Sadger at least, stating a reasonable probability for *any* individual of Jewish nationality. In their analysis of the eastern European Jewish community — the *shtetl,* a cultural heritage very much in Freud's background (he was named after a Polish king) — Zborowski and Herzog (1962) underscore Sadger's thesis by drawing out the dialectical nature of talmudic analysis. The young talmudic scholar (yeshiva boy) literally partakes in re-enactments of arguments advanced several centuries past by eminent rabbis, and comes in time to his own measured view of the issue under consideration. Knowledge is not gained passively, but demands active seeking and exchange with others; and debate, whenever called for, is entered into as part of the analytical procedure: "The popular picture of the Jew in Eastern Europe, held by Jew and Gentile alike, is true to the talmudic tradition. The picture includes the tendency to examine, analyze and reanalyze, to seek for meanings behind meanings, and for implications and secondary consequences" (Zborowski and Herzog, 1962, p. 121).

Bakan has drawn noteworthy parallels between Freud's work and his cultural heritage. For example, Freud's willingness to accept many alternative explanations of the same phenomenon, and to pile one concept on top of another until quite a complexity resulted is seen as typically Jewish. There is a Jewish proverb to the effect that "All dreams follow the mouth" or "All dreams follow their interpretation" (Bakan, 1958, p. 261). This is very much like the Hegelian view that truth issues only when reason is applied to the apparent facts of things in experience. The positivist would find truth in the immediately identifiable, the facts as defined operationally and demonstrably there before his eyes. This Jewish proverb Bakan believes is reflected in Freud's willingness to transcend Aristotle's law of contradiction. Bakan relates a vignette taken from the *Berakoth,* about the Jew who had a dream and had it interpreted by twenty-four different dream interpreters. Each gave a different interpretation of the dream, yet all were fulfilled. Presumably, had he gone to a twenty-fifth interpreter the list of fulfilled alternatives would have increased by one. In like fashion, argues Bakan, Freud was never bothered by inconsistencies:

> In usual scientific thought, one pits one explanation against another in logical counterposition. Freud, however, with his doctrine of over-determination and overinterpretation of dreams, made such counter-position inappropriate for dream interpretation. In his view, different and contradictory interpretations could be maintained simultaneously, and hence the doctrine that "dreams follow their interpretations" could never be violated (p. 262).

Though Bakan here phrases his argument in terms of religious writings, the extent of this "alternative explanation" tendency in the eastern European Jewish culture was great. Nothing was simple or straightforward in the world of the shtetl:

> It is proverbial in Eastern Europe that a Jew will avoid answering a question by a simple yes or no [which of course is the demonstrative way]. According to his tradition it is the business of the thinker to recognize incompatibilities or opposites, in the realm of spirit and in the practical world — realms which themselves are inseparable [the many in the one]. . . . Countless anecdotes, told by and about the Jews of Eastern Europe, are based on the ingrained assumption that in any situation "there are always two possibilities." If the worst one comes to pass, there are still two possibilities; and if the more evil of those eventuates, there are two possibilities in that — and so on, *ad infinitum*. One never forgets that "every stick has two ends" (Zborowski and Herzog, 1962, p. 123).

This seems a more plausible explanation of Freud's dualism than the one offered by Jones; nothing could better sum up the dialectic, with all its complexities and possibilities born of introspective intellectual effort. Zborowski and Herzog note that the Poles, who were apparently more straightforward in thought, used to say, when they developed a sense of frustration over some difficult task: "This is as difficult as getting a Jew to tell you the way" (p. 121). The saying is based on the un-happy fact that whenever the Polish gentile who was traveling asked a Jew for direction, he was likely to receive a lengthy discourse on how *not to* proceed. The dialectic, emerging from the minute examinations of the Talmud, must truly have permeated the Jewish character in order for a humorous manifestation such as this to have developed.

Freud was much taken with jokes spun around the Jewish character; and, as Rieff has noted, the essence of Jewish humor is that it is based in large measure on dialectical shifts, oppositions, changes of pace (Rieff, 1959, p. 80). Although he rejected all religious ties, Freud's identity with the Jew was great (Jones, 1955, p. 398). He once referred to himself as a "Jewish father" of the psycho-analytical movement (Freud, 1960b, p. 302). Another time he suggested that he was not unlike a talmudic scholar in his work, wresting every last bit of meaning from his text or from some utterance (Jones, 1955, p. 398). But perhaps the clearest indication of the importance of his Jewishness was given by Freud on the occasion of his seventieth birthday, when he spoke to the B'nai B'rith Lodge in Vienna, to which he had proudly belonged for twenty-nine years. In this remarkable statement, Freud not only sums up his feelings about being a Jew, but almost identifies his people as an opposing counterforce, a human antithesis, to the broader majority, the thesis of humanity. It was this character, he says, which helped him over the lonely years of non-recognition:

That you are Jews could only be welcome to me, for I was myself a Jew, and it has always appeared to me not only undignified, but outright foolish to deny it. What tied me to Jewry was — I have to admit it — not the faith, not even the national pride, for I was always an unbeliever, have been brought up without religion, but not without respect for the so-called "ethical" demands of human civilization. Whenever I have experienced feelings of national exaltation, I have tried to suppress them as disastrous and unfair, frightened by the warning example of those nations among which we Jews live. But there remained enough to make the attraction of Judaism and the Jews irresistible, many dark emotional powers all the stronger the less they could be expressed in words, as well as the clear consciousness of an inner identity, the familiarity of the same psychological structure. And before long there followed the realization that it was only to my Jewish nature that I owed the two qualities which have become indispensable to me throughout my difficult life. Because I was a Jew I found myself free of many prejudices which restrict others in the use of the intellect: as a Jew I was prepared to be in the opposition and to renounce agreement with the "compact majority." *

* From *The Letters of Sigmund Freud,* Selected and Edited by Ernst L. Freud, Basic Books, Inc., Publishers, New York, 1960, pp. 366–367.

One can see in this remarkable statement how it was possible for Freud to accept the Jungian hypothesis of a "collective unconscious." He never really dismissed this possibility, and surely, Jung's view that "man is men" must be seen in Freud's readiness to identify his own historic roots. It therefore seems not too presumptuous to suggest that, if it is true that Jewish culture is heavily saturated with dialectical reasoning, at least a partial explanation for Freud's dialectical bias stems from his national origin. Whether from his sense of identity with a discriminated-against minority, or from the patterns of thought in this minority, it may well have been easier for Freud to ask the whys at the proper time, to be less disturbed by inconsistency in a client's answers, and to keep an open mind, thanks to the sociocultural heritage he carried within him as one of the Jewish people.

Continental Philosophy

The third possible explanation of Freud's dialectical orientation is involved with the more formal philosophical currents of thought in the Europe of his time. It is of interest to note that Freud made some highly contradictory statements regarding philosophy over his lifetime. He was obviously attracted to it at certain points, yet believed it was somehow beneath the scientist to cultivate this interest — attitudes which we believe reflect his educational preparation and his fear of being dismissed as someone who plays with ideas or phantasies rather than facts. Thus, in 1895, writing to Fliess during the difficult years of isolation, the younger Freud could argue confidently for theoretical speculation: "We cannot do without men with the courage to think new things before they can prove them." * At this point in his life philosophy seems to have been an acceptable complement to his active and highly creative intellect, a worthwhile endeavor not to be denied. On the first day of January, 1896, he writes to Fliess: "I see that you are using the circuitous route of medicine to attain your first ideal, the physiological understanding of man, while I secretly nurse the hope of arriving by the same route at my own original objective, philosophy. For that was my original ambition, before I knew what I was intended to do in the world." †

* From *The Origins of Psycho-analysis, Letters to Wilhelm Fliess, Drafts and Notes: 1887–1902*, by Sigmund Freud, Basic Books, Inc., Publishers, New York, 1954, p. 137.
† *Ibid.*, p. 141.

We know that as a student Freud had translated one volume of John Stuart Mill's work, containing a section on Plato; we also know that he had some knowledge of Kant (Nunberg and Federn, 1962, p. 320) and Hegel (Freud, 1952, p. 822). In his later years Freud did some reading of Nietzsche and Schopenhauer. But there are very few references to philosophy as such in his writings, including the correspondence. He makes many more literary than philosophical allusions, and he had a particular fondness for Goethe, a fact we shall want to keep in mind because it parallels an attraction that Jung felt toward the great German poet. By 1906 Freud had acquired a group of students and together they founded the Vienna Psycho-Analytical Society. In the Society's minutes of that year there is a very interesting notation. During a discussion of the possible influence of philosophical thought on the psycho-analytical movement, Freud appears to have become if not annoyed at least slightly threatened by the prospect that his edifice might be explained away as just another intellectual wrinkle in the fabric of philosophical history, for after stating that he had not yet read any Nietzsche, Freud affirmed that he had renounced the study of philosophy because its abstract nature was highly unpleasant to him (Nunberg and Federn, 1962, p. 359).

He seemed to renounce philosophy whenever he felt he was under attack, whenever the old charge of "thought-reader" (see Chapter VII) might be leveled. For example, in 1927, writing to a Mr. Achelis, and defending himself against the charge that he had made a blanket statement regarding the nature of dreams, Freud once again ascends his scientific high horse: "I believe that one day metaphysics will be condemned as a nuisance, as an abuse of thinking. . . . However this may be, it is certainly simpler to find one's way in 'this world' of facts than in the 'other world' of philosophy." * Freud's need to identify himself with scientific rigor is also reflected in the following: "Even when I have moved away from observation I have carefully avoided any contact with philosophy proper. This avoidance has been greatly facilitated by constitutional incapacity." † However, as Jones points out (p. 335), in his closing years Freud once again spoke of his love for philosophy, by which he seems to have meant the desire to answer those ineffable questions stimulated by problems from another sphere of man's nature.

* From *The Letters of Sigmund Freud,* Selected and Edited by Ernst L. Freud, Basic Books, Inc., Publishers, New York, 1960, p. 375.
† From *The Life and Work of Sigmund Freud,* Volume III, Copyright 1957 by Ernest Jones, Basic Books, Inc., Publishers, New York, p. 335.

If we attempt to ferret out the actual formal themes at play, we find Freud's philosophical background to be highly complex and his theory buoyed up by positions which are intermixed and almost confused. As a physician, Freud seems to have been deeply indoctrinated with the realism of Helmholtz and Brücke, even though, Jones notes, his psychiatry instructor Meynert was a philosophical idealist (1953, p. 376). The science taught by Brücke was Newtonian, aimed at capturing the basic structures and forces in a real world, extraspectively and with precision. Freud carried this ideal with him throughout life, and, not having kept in touch with the new physics emerging at that very time in Vienna — thanks to the work of Ernst Mach — never gained an appreciation of what it all meant. Despite his great reverence for science, Freud was no more informed about its changing face than he was about the formal schools of philosophical thought which were making themselves felt on the Continent (Rieff, 1959, p. 26). As was noted in Chapter VIII, Mach was advocating a phenomenological physics, in opposition to the realistic views of men like Helmholtz and Wundt. Mach argued that there was no need for science to make any assumptions concerning the ultimate nature of reality. Scientific statements did not refer to a reality, but to the sense impressions on which they were based. Freud was so irritated with Mach's (neo-Kantian) position that he apparently avoided the social philosopher Josef Popper-Lynkeus, a man he admired, because the latter had Mach as a friend. He did not want to bestir the waters in his relations with Popper-Lynkeus, who could somehow cultivate a social life with the "intellectual nihilist" Ernst Mach (p. 26).

Freud thus succeeded somehow in placing himself within the demonstrative traditions of science, and fooling many, including Jones, into thinking that there was no essential difference between his outlook and the outlook of all physical scientists. Of course, there were enough parallels between his attitude and the Newtonian tradition to make this seem plausible. Like Aristotle, he believed one could gather scientifically true statements about reality by carefully looking *at* reality, and checking one's thought against the facts before one's eyes. His method of investigation — as we saw in Chapter VII — he considered analogous to microscopic rather than experimental investigation. He once said that he could *not* experiment in the analytical hour, along the lines of physics or physiology, but that even so his working hypotheses were always the direct result of many observations made upon his clients: "Later on, whenever I had the opportunity of recognizing an hypothesis of this kind to be erroneous, it was always replaced — and I hope improved — by another idea which occurred to me (based on the former as well as new experiences) and to which I then submitted the material." * This stress on observation, the careful selection of hypotheses from client behavior, was seen by Freud as serious scientific business. He was not toying with a mere idea world of sensory impressions, as Mach would have it. There was a *right* and a *wrong* interpretation of behavioral affairs, there was a *reality in mind* which could be circumscribed by the analyst's practiced eye. Having stipulated the real state of affairs, as we have seen, Freud went on in the traditions of Helmholtz, Wundt, and Brücke to translate his completely psychological theory into what we take to be superfluous concepts of energies running hither and yon within the psyche.

But though he made a valiant attempt to stay within the fold of Brücke's Newtonian science, Freud again and again suffered opposition and ridicule from certain members of the broader scientific community. He was a dialectician speaking as stepbrother to the demonstrative group, which lacked an appreciation of the dialectic. Freud saw in their rejection of his views only that opposition bred by their revulsion to his sexual theories; but, there was a fundamental difference in outlook here which submerged even the sexual theory — a deep gulf between dialectic and demonstration which could not be bridged. Not even Freud, the great weaver of opposites into one, could bring together this monumental contradiction. The more extraspective, realistically-inclined scientists, who see science as primarily a methodological matter, not only do not work the way he worked, they do not even *think* about data the way he thought. Yet it is precisely Freud's loyalty to the realistic interpretation of science which makes him so difficult to understand as a methodologist. He, like Einstein, is a transitional figure in the history of science, appearing on the scene at precisely the time when the older science was moving into the new; and, like Einstein, Freud found himself committed in principle to the older ways. He never fully appreciated the strongly idealistic component in his analytical thought. If this component came from a formal philosophical school, how did it happen to intrude itself on Freud's developing outlook? That is the question we now turn to.

In the minutes of one of the Vienna meetings, it is recorded that Alfred Adler — who was more drawn to philosophy than Freud — tried

* From *The Letters of Sigmund Freud,* Selected and Edited by Ernst L. Freud, Basic Books, Inc., Publishers, New York, 1960, p. 396.

to establish a direct line of descent from Schopenhauer through Marx and *Mach* to the psycho-analytical movement (Nunberg and Federn, 1962, p. 358). He added, and Federn supported him in this view, that Nietzsche was probably a progenitor of the psycho-analytical way of thought. It is at this point that Freud notes that philosophy as an abstract endeavor (presumably not based on observation) is unpleasant to him, and that he has never read Nietzsche (p. 359). Nevertheless, it is significant that at least some of his students had realized that psycho-analysis was forming within a certain philosophical tradition — one which embraced even Ernst Mach. And the tradition they had singled out was the Platonic, *idealistic* one.

A common attribute of all philosophers, down through history, who have argued on the side of Plato is their desire to challenge basic assumptions, attack presuppositions, and question the very nature of the realities so easily accepted by their more demonstratively-inclined contemporaries. Thus, as with Socrates and Plato, Nietzsche's strength lay not so much in putting together a systematic, interdependent philosophical system — since it was precisely this overconfident tying together he was opposing — but in critically and dialectically challenging those primary and true Aristotelian "givens" which others had accepted without adequate examination (Kaufmann, 1956, p. 66). Only Hegel was able to be both dialectical and highly systematic, taking as his rationale the force of historical truth to say what developed and why. All the other great proponents of dialectical activity fell short of such systematization. Dialecticians are the great analysts, the questioners, the examiners of thought. Freud was no exception to this rule, though his questioning and challenging occurred directly in the patient-therapist relationship, where he was always ready to cast doubt on the easy explanation or the apparent reality of some behavior. It may be, as his students were implying, that the Zeitgeist which moved Schopenhauer, Hegel, Marx, Nietzsche, and, of all oddities, Mach, also moved Sigmund Freud.

But then Freud was also influenced in his contacts with the French, and it is very interesting to note that another early student, Fritz Wittels, actually traced his teacher's idealistic bent (the explanation of hysterical disorders completely on the basis of ideas) to the time spent with Charcot. The philosophical underpinnings of Charcot's psychogenic view of hysteria is attributed by Wittels to a revival of idealism in the France of that period:

At the Sorbonne, the philosopher Paul Janet (not to be confused with Pierre Janet, the neurologist, one of Charcot's pupils) was then engaged in an attempt to counteract the predominance of materialism in philosophy. There was a similar idealistic trend in contemporary Germany, the classic land of idealist philosophy. Perhaps it was in the wards of the Salpêtrière that this swing of the philosophical pendulum first showed its influence in the medical domain. Charcot taught that hysteria is psychically engendered; that the disease is not due to any tissue changes, but arises from purely spiritual causes, which are not recognizable under the microscope. This conception of "psychogenic" disease seemed incomprehensible to the doctors who regarded themselves as modern at that date (1924, p. 28).

Wittels goes on to argue that Freud's emancipation from the materialism of his medical school training was due to the French idealism with which he came into contact. He shows how others of Brücke's students, like Sigmund Exner, continued in the extraspective vein, explaining the nature of mind entirely on the basis of materialistic efficient causes (p. 30).

Was Freud an idealist or a realist? It appears that he consciously espoused a realistic position on the nature of science, but at least two of his more sophisticated students see in his mature outlook a primarily idealistic bent. There is an interesting parallel here with the theory of Marx, who began his intellectual development in the camp opposite to Freud's early conviction. Marx was a confirmed idealist as a young man, and supported Hegelian philosophy as initially conceived. Then, when he adapted Hegelian philosophy to the class struggle he moved to a staunchly realistic bias. The Marxian dialectic is a "dialectical materialism," a law of nature in real things and guiding real things somewhat analogous to the notion of efficient causation in material nature (antecedents preceding consequents). Yet, as with Freud, it is not difficult to see as much idealism as realism in Marx. In fact, Freud actually noted this complexity in outlook himself:

> There are assertions contained in Marx's theory which have struck me as strange: such as that the development of forms of society is a process of natural history, or that the changes in social stratification arise from one another in the manner of a dialectical process. I am far from sure that I understand these assertions aright; nor do they sound to me "materialistic" but, rather, like a precipitate of the obscure Hegelian philosophy in whose school Marx graduated (1964, p. 177).

One could paraphrase this and say that there is much in Freud which does not sound realistic, no matter how much he would have preferred it to be so. Dialectic is at heart a "free spirit" in the realm of cognition, and therefore to tie it down to reality is to take something away from it — that arbitrariness which Aristotle recognized as the wellspring of opinion but also of creativity. Thus, what binds Freud, Hegel, and Marx together is neither realism nor idealism so much as it is their common use of dialectic as the dynamic principle which moved events. Hegel had man changing in personality according to the working through of contradictions in the evolving flux of the Absolute Spirit, coming dialectically to consciousness in history. It has even been suggested that he thought of his own individuality as nothing more nor less than a kind of verbal vehicle for the expression of the Absolute. Man did not shape history in Hegel's view; history, or the Spirit in it, shaped man. Marx took this same position, and saw the roots of man's personality in the class struggle. There was a typically bourgeois way of behaving, a proletarian way of behaving, and so on. To psychologize about the individual man was foreign to the Hegelian-Marxian line of thought. Freud, on the other hand, though attracted to the origins of society and the movements of culture, placed his emphasis on the individual man. A single man — say, Moses — could exert tremendous influence on the course of history. In the Platonic tradition, whereas Hegel and Marx stressed the many over the one, the class over the individual, Freud singled out for special consideration the one from the many, the individual person who was worthy of consideration in his own right. But all three men gave their theories a dynamic flavor by stressing the play of opposites, the clash of contradictions.

Whether Freud received this influence directly from the Germans, or indirectly from the French, there is sufficient evidence drawn from the intellectual climate of his time that Freud may have had a formal philosophical influence bringing him round to his dialectical bias, in addition to the other two sources already reviewed. This brings us to the end of our consideration of Freud. We will now look at his most important student, Carl G. Jung, who probably did as much to advance dialectical thought in the twentieth century as Freud.

Carl Gustav Jung and the Dialectic

Jung, more openly and consciously than Freud, propounded a theory of human psychology and a method of psychotherapy based upon the dialectic. At the height of his career, he observed: "I see in all that happens the play of opposites" (Jung, 1961, p. 337). This is the key to the understanding of Jungian psychology, where nothing stands alone, and every aspect of human behavior has an offsetting, opposite tendency which is either acknowledged and experienced by the individual, or slips down into that unconscious realm of mind where it can later make itself known in dreams or possibly even in abnormal conditions (certain complexes). Man grows as a person to the extent that he can balance the contents of consciousness against those of his unconscious, to the extent that he can avoid that one-sidedness more typical of the mass man, the neurotic, and the psychotic. A perfect life synthesizes all aspects of behavior and acknowledges the promptings of the unconscious. Thanks to his skillful use of dialectic, Jung could turn the obvious and the apparent to look at the underside of things (shadow), so that he recognizes, for example, that good calls for evil, and that religion is the need in man to balance the spiritual against the daily need to stress the flesh (1963, p. 335). Man is an interconnected whole, within which contradictions are to be expected. Speaking of himself in later years, Jung muses: "I had to obey an inner law which was imposed on me and left me no freedom of choice. Of course I did not always obey it. How can anyone live without inconsistency?" (p. 357).

In this self-observation we see the Platonic tradition, in that: (1) inconsistencies are to be expected in the conscious world of material experience (recall that the realm of becoming is an imperfect copy of the realm of being); (2) certain remnants of a "past" are within man, potentially or actually influencing his present behavior. The realm of being comes before and manifests itself in the realm of becoming, if conditions are made right. Like Hegel and Marx, and unlike Freud, Jung emphasizes that man is more the product of his collective identity than he is a product of the accidents of his unique life history. The individual man has a "subjective" identity in his earthly past, but he also has an "objective" identity in the group of men from which he evolved biologically and psychologically: "Ideas spring from something greater than the personal human being. Man does not make his ideas; we could say that man's ideas make him" (Jung, 1961, p. 333). The one-in-the-many is de-emphasized in the Jungian dialectic: "we are not the personal creators of our truths, but only their exponents." * This theme of man being propelled by forces from out of his past group identity is made explicit in Jung's concept of the archetype, a decidedly Platonic-Kantian

---

* From *The Collected Works of C. G. Jung,* Vol. 16, *The Practice of Psychotherapy,* Bollingen Series XX.16. New York: Pantheon Books, and London: Routledge & Kegan Paul Ltd, 1954, p. 69.

notion which stresses the dialectical "possibilities" of things based upon *a priori* "givens" possessed by man at birth. Archetypes are not factual and literal ideas, but rather "*a priori* categories of possible functioning," * which may or may not be made manifest in any given life history, just as Socratic wisdom might or might not have been "discovered" had not two men set out to dialectically exchange ideas, and thereby actualize the potentials in things. Archetypes may or may not appear in a given life history (though they are likely to), but the individual can surely prompt their occurrence by developing one-sided, by overlooking the opposite qualities of his manifest behavior.

As with others of Freud's students, Jung was far more learned in Western philosophy than his teacher. He actually discussed the dialectical nature of his psychotherapy in terms not unlike those used by Mortimer Adler:

> If I wish to treat another individual psychologically at all, I must for better or worse give up all pretensions to superior knowledge, all authority and desire to influence. I must perforce adopt a dialectical procedure consisting in a comparison of our mutual findings. But this becomes possible only if I give the other person a chance to play his hand to the full, unhampered by my assumptions. In this way his system is geared to mine and acts upon it; my reaction is the only thing with which I as an individual can legitimately confront my patient. . . . In other words, the therapist is no longer the agent of treatment but a fellow participant in a process of individual development.†

As with the Socratic method, the activator of the psychotherapeutic process must become a part of it, he must not set out with dogmatic "basic and true" principles which he then plans to communicate or to effect in his client. Indeed, it is a good idea to refrain from setting clear-cut goals in therapy because this detracts from the possibility of a mutual influence between doctor and patient. The doctor who sets out to control his client in some one fashion and no other is himself behaving one-sidedly and not giving full appreciation to the forces of psychic heredity: "As far as possible I let pure experience decide the therapeutic aims. This may perhaps seem strange, because it is commonly supposed that the therapist has an aim. But in psychotherapy it seems to me positively advisable for the doctor not to have too fixed an aim. He can hardly know better than the nature and will to live of the

* *Ibid.*, p. 34.
† *Ibid.*, pp. 5, 8.

patient. . . . You can exert no influence if you are not susceptible to influence." * This was a theme which Jung and Rank were to develop, and which — thanks in part to Rank — Rogers was to pick up and make into a major viewpoint (see Chapters VI and VII).

Jung's ability to bear up under contradiction and inconsistency is in the best traditions of the dialectic. Even when he discussed the nature of psychological science, like Plato and Nietzsche before him, he questioned the too easy acceptance of material reality as reflected in consciousness. Like the Jew with the dream in the *Berakoth,* Jung was not upset by the multiplicity of things, nor did he mind having several contradictions nestled side by side within psychological theory. Indeed, he invited them:

> Our psychological experience is still too recent and too limited in scope to permit of general theories. The investigator needs a lot more facts which would throw light on the nature of the psyche before he can begin to think of universally valid propositions. For the present we must observe the rule that a psychological proposition can only lay claim to significance if the obverse of its meaning can also be accepted as true.†

To the demonstrative reasoner, who begins from major premises taken as *true* — and not "not true" at the same time — this must surely represent a call for pure sophistry. Jung is a twentieth-century dialectician, there can be no doubt about it.

The Sources of Jung's Dialectic

The question arises whether Jung was prompted to take over the dialectical bias of his teacher, or whether he quite independently had come to some leanings in this direction. Since we consider Freud to be the main source of dialectical thinking in modern psychiatry and psychology, there is no need to devote excessive space to a consideration of Jung's intellectual background. However, Jung has at various times acknowledged his dialectical or oppositional bias, and we have several interesting comments by him on this specific point. He was not quite so ready to disown all philosophical ties as Freud was, although Jung too was eager to point out that he was an empirical scientist and not an "armchair philosopher." Jung has also drawn some interesting parallels

* *Ibid.,* pp. 41, 71.
† *Ibid.,* p. 115.

between literary products and the dialectic, which we will want to keep in view for a discussion in Chapter XI on the image of man. There seem to be three main sources of dialectic in Jung's background, each of which he has commented on at one time or another. They are introspection, literature, and philosophy.

Introspection

As we have already seen in Chapter VIII, Jung was quite open in revealing the nature and contents of his personal introspective efforts. We know that he strongly advocated and personally practiced inward living, or introspective investigation. This in itself can bring about dialectical oppositions or divisions. Though he was speaking in another vein, Jung did bring introspection and such bifurcation into one idea when he said of himself: "Like anyone who is capable of some introspection, I had early taken it for granted that the split in my personality was my own purely personal affair and responsibility" (1963, p. 234). He would not have believed that his inward ruminations *brought about* this split, of course, but we know that such an outcome is quite likely. Those who look inward, either personally or within the psychic structure of another, are quickest to find diversity and even contradiction. We are all more complex than we seem on the surface when we take the time to contemplate our unique natures and ask "why do I do this or that?" Dialectical self-examination breeds diversity and hence complexity. Jung may well have come to the dialectic as method and as metaconstruct through his use of introspective examination. Interestingly, he saw a parallel between his own condition and that of Goethe's epic hero: "Faust, to be sure, had made the problem somewhat easier for me by confessing, 'Two souls, alas, are housed within my breast.'" (p. 234). This brings us to our tie between Jungian psychology and literature.

Literature

Jung was greatly drawn to Goethe, not the least of reasons being that his grandfather was rumored to be an illegitimate son of the great poet and scientist (Jung, 1963, p. 234). In fact, he goes so far as to date the point in life when he was first made aware of the principle of opposition by having read Goethe. It happened, according to his testimony, even before his commitment to the Freudian movement:

In my youth (around 1890) I was unconsciously caught up by this spirit of the age, and had no methods at hand for extricating myself from it. *Faust* struck a chord in me and pierced me through in a way that I could not but regard as personal. Most of all, it awakened in me the problem of opposites, of good and evil, of mind and matter, of light and darkness. Faust, the inept, purblind philosopher, encounters the dark side of his being, his sinister shadow, Mephistopheles, who in spite of his negating disposition represents the true spirit of life as against the arid scholar who hovers on the brink of suicide (p. 235).

Mephistopheles, the "Spirit of Contradiction" (Goethe, 1952, p. 98), the "Part of that Power which would the Evil ever do, and ever does the Good" (p. 33) is for Jung the embodiment of a dialectical opposition.

It is generally recognized that *Faust* draws its action from the dialectical conflict between opposed historic forces (Spender, 1958, p. xvii). Goethe held to the view that "All things weave themselves into a whole" (p. viii), and he extended this Platonic view into his scientific endeavors, so that it can be said of him that he "was the last of the universal scientific minds, still able to encompass the whole of nature" (Magnus, 1949, p. 38). Unfortunately, this logic did not always hold and some of his scientific work was probably hindered by this need for a final unity. But in ever so many ways he is within the Platonic line of descent, and, if it is true that Jung's developing mind was greatly impressed by insights from *Faust,* then this would be the proper tradition for our thesis. Speaking of traditions, what if Jung were asked directly to comment on our thesis that dialectical reasoning had played a major role in the evolution of psycho-analytical thinking? What might he say to it? This brings us to the final possible source of influence on Jung.

Philosophy: A Letter from Jung

Before Jung's death, the writer was fortunate enough to communicate with him and to put the question to him in a general way, as to the possible influence of the dialectic on his thought. At that time some clear parallels between certain features of Hegelian philosophy and Jungian thought were of interest, so the inquiry sent to Jung focused in particular on the possible impact of Hegel on the Continent during Jung's student days. Naturally, there was no reason to expect a great thinker such as Jung to know for certain the sources of his theoretical proclivities, but it did seem plausible to expect at least some kind of estimate. It would help our thesis, for example, if Jung spoke more kindly of the idealistic philosophers than of the realistic. If he asserted that John Locke attracted him, or that he found Plato confusing, then one could certainly not accept the thesis too readily or without serious doubts. In any case, here is the reply, a letter dated April 27, 1959:*

Dear Mr. Rychlak:

The philosophical influence, that has prevailed in my education, dates from Plato, Kant, Schopenhauer, Ed. v. Hartmann and Nietzsche. These names at least characterize my main studies in Philosophy. Aristotle's point of view had never a particular appeal to me; nor Hegel, who in my very incompetent opinion, is not even a proper philosopher, but a misfired psychologist. His impossible language, which he shares with his bloodbrother Heidegger, denotes the fact, that his philosophy is a highly rationalized and lavishly decorated confession of his unconscious. Owing to the fact, that I use the term "dialectic procedure" or something to this extent, exposes me to the misunderstanding, that I am envisaging an intellectual proceeding, which is not the case, but in truth a practical method of dealing with the very concrete propositions, the unconscious is presenting us with. This is a very important chapter of psychotherapy, since neurosis consists in a dissociation of personality. One is always confronted with an opposite or a vis-à-vis, you have to reckon with; a fact, which is only unknown to people, who know of nothing else, but the contents of their consciousness. Moreover the science of all moving as well as living bodies is based upon the concept of energy. Energy itself is a tension between opposites. Our Psychology is no exception from the principle, that embraces about the whole of natural science.

In the intellectual world, in which I grew up, Hegelian thought played no role at all; on the contrary, it was Kant and his epistemology on the one side, and on the other straight materialism, which I never shared, knowing too much about its ridiculous mythology. Hegel's dialectics, I can safely say, had no influence at all, as far as I know myself. The German term "Auseinandersetzung" was used by me in its colloquial sense. Being an empiricist and not a philosophical thinker the terms I chose, have their real source in experience; thus when I speak of "Auseinandersetzung," it could be just as well the discussion between Mr. A and his wife. Another common misunderstanding is, that I derive my idea of "archetypes" from Philo or Dionysius Areopagita, or St. Augustin. It is solely based upon empirical data, vis. upon the astonishing fact, that products of the un-

---

* This letter is reprinted by permission of Dr. C. G. Jung's heirs.

conscious in modern individuals can almost literally coincide with symbols occurring in all peoples and all times, beyond the possibility of tradition or migration, for which I have given numerous proofs.

I have never studied Hegel properly, that means his original works. There is no possibility to conclude to a direct dependence, but, as I said above, Hegel confesses main trends of the so-called unconscious and can be called "un psychologue rate." There is, of course, a remarkable coincidence between certain tenets of Hegelian philosophy and my finds concerning the collective unconscious.

Hoping that I have answered your question satisfactorily, I remain

yours faithfully

C. G. Jung (Signed)

Although he rejects any direct tie to Hegel by naming Plato, Kant, Schopenhauer, Ed. v. Hartmann, and Nietzsche, Jung has accurately placed himself in the dialectical tradition (see Chapter IX). His disinterest in Aristotle is significant, and the reference to the "ridiculous mythology" of materialism furthers his tie to idealism and the dialectic. The letter is very interesting in rejecting Hegel as a direct influence, yet admitting to certain coincidences between Jungian psychology and Hegelian philosophy. Jung has, in fact, many similarities to Hegel in his tendency to stress the collective history of peoples, the play of supra-individual forces on a given life, the importance of a balanced existence, and an identical interpretation of the dialectic. The writer has found analogies and similes used by both writers in making critical points for their respective views, which of course prompted him to make the suggestion eventually rejected by Jung.

That Jung could refer to Hegel as a "misfired psychologist" evidences the compatibility he sensed in their views. Man is men on both positions, and can be properly understood only through an examination of historical (including mythological) background facts. History has a content which may be used to explain current behavior discriminatively. That is to say, history is not a vehicular device; when one deals with the history of a given life as Freud generally did, or with the history of a people having common roots, as Jung was more likely to do, he is still dealing with discriminal constructs. He is attempting to explain the uniqueness of a present line of behavior, or the facts of *this* rather than *that* state of affairs. In our terms, *history is discriminal in its concepts*. Jung feels that Hegel projected his unconscious promptings onto mankind, but be that as it may, there is surely a great similarity in their outlooks and one finds it difficult to give up at least a global, "Zeitgeist" type of relation between them.

The final point of importance in our consideration of the Jungian dialectic is his attempt to tie this concept to a universal energy notion. We have already seen how Freud made his energy concept behave dialectically in the psyche. Energy concepts are essentially vehicular constructs, in that they are invoked to explain *all* behaviors, and rarely do they clarify our grasp of the unique, at least in human affairs. Jung, like Freud, seems to have felt it necessary to provide his content psychology with a vehicular underpinning of energy expenditure. He said, both in the letter above and in many other contexts, that all energies known to man begin with tensions brought about by opposites, as in the positive and negative charges of electrical energy. Here is a good example of the way Jung develops this idea in commenting on ego-formation:

> Just as all energy proceeds from opposition, so the psyche too possesses its inner polarity, this being the indispensable prerequisite for its aliveness, as Heraclitus realized long ago. Both theoretically and practically, polarity is inherent in all living things. Set against this overpowering force is the fragile unity of the ego, which has come into being in the course of millennia only with the aid of countless protective measures. That an ego was possible at all appears to spring from the fact that all opposites seek to achieve a state of balance. This happens in the exchange of energy which results from the collision of hot and cold, high and low, and so on (1963, p. 346).

This idea of a dialectic in nature is very similar to some of the views taken by Marxian theorists. Although Marx never used the term, many of his students referred to a *Natur-Dialektik* at play in not only the discriminal *history* of peoples, but in the vehicular *material reality* as such (Hook, 1962, p. 75). There have even been attempts to explain Einstein's theory and all of physics on the basis of a physical dialectic, which presumably brings about the opposition of atomic structures and thus all energy (Wilson, 1940, pp. 191–192). The problem with these views is that not *all* the opposites in nature are truly dialectical. When a moving object meets an immovable obstacle, that is not an opposition in the sense of dialectical bifurcation based upon the nature of the moving object. Dialectically speaking, the moving object would carry within its essence the seeds of its own opposition; or it would be directed to a *certain* obstacle. Although it leads to an arbitrary positing of contraries in many instances, the dialectic is after all a directional concept. It tells us where to look. Seek the opposite of what is given. The opposite of moving is immovable. But, the opposite of a moving sexual force is different from the opposite of a moving hostile force. In brief, the dialectic furthers *discriminative* theorizing. Since it can be posed at any time and at any level, it leads to refinements in *thought;* it is at the root of idealism and strains against realistic certainty and self-assurance.

Jung denies that in using his principle of opposition he is dealing with an intellectual process. He claims to have observed, as have all scientists, this *literal* opposition in nature. Despite this move to scientific integrity, when he goes on to use as examples of opposition the "collision of hot and cold, high and low," he reveals the weaknesses of his claim. The scientist may be able to prove beyond doubt what things are "hotter than" or "higher than" others, in observation. He may even show, for example, when cold air meets hot air a thunderstorm results from the collision of such "opposites." But does he ever prove that cold air carries within it hot air, and that in this way an opposition of forces is generated? Is not the intellectual *concept* of hotness merely implicit as a verbal opposite of coldness *by definition* in thought? It sccms obvious that it is the latter sense in which the dialectic can be said to be at play in nature. The dialectic is our term for man's ability to reason in a certain way about experience. Opposites which suggest themselves in thought do not have to *be* at all, they may merely remain possibilities. Historically, this tendency to assume that everything in reality had to have its opposite in reality was used by dialecticians to prove very dubious points. For example, if one wanted to prove that an opponent were dishonest, then he might begin an oppositional definition of honesty. After honesty had been drawn out in elevated and exalted form, it was a simple trick to look at one's opponent with a jaundiced eye and imply what everyone could see — that he was *not* that honest. Hence, he must surely be dishonest. This is an old trick, first used by the Sophists, and there is now a maxim to the effect that proving the opposite of a point does not make one's original case.

Dialectic is a *verbal,* an *intellectual* procedure; Freud seems to have appreciated this fact better than Jung, in stressing the oppositional origins of speech. If we tie the dialectic down to nature as some kind of vehicular principle, we take away that arbitrariness which is its essence. Even if we were to show its practical effects through methodological validation, this would not make it any more "real" than it is now. Those who would view the dialectic as a law of natural energy generation in reality, for example, are either overly anxious to stay within the bounds of conventional vehicular science, or are letting their realistic bent get the better of them. Possibly Jung was more tainted by materialism than he realized, but we prefer to think he was simply trying to be properly empirical and scientific in making his claim that even natural forces begin in oppositions. The dialectic is more properly aligned with the idealistic tradition, and, as anyone who reads the great dialecticians knows, one man's opposition is sometimes another man's absurdity. If we make the dialectic an observable, concrete, hence "primary and true" principle of nature, the next step is to begin predicting its course, and naming the oppositions about to come up. When that happens — and it will not — we will have succeeded in killing off the dialectic. For this will be demonstration, pure and simple: arbitrariness will be error, creativity will be change, and oppositions will be merely related rather than contradictory.

The Dialectic in Twentieth-Century Social Science

Except for an occasional reference to the Marxian materialistic variety, the dialectic as such is rarely mentioned in modern times. Dialectic is equated with and dismissed as sophistry, or as a quaint but outmoded method of instruction, or as some form of armchair nonsense about the flow of nature. It is not taken seriously, at least in the sense of the nineteenth-century view of dialectic as an important aspect of logic and creative thought. Hidden or partially camouflaged within the theories of Marx and Freud, however, the dialectic does receive a more balanced and genuine hearing in the twentieth century. For this is a century of class rebellion. It is a time of the emancipation of woman, the revolution of workers against the economic tyranny of the moneyed classes, the impatient demands of racial minorities and industrially backward countries, each rebelling against a world in which they are ignored like some devalued or despised contradiction to the broader order of things. A theory such as Marx's, which makes use of dialectical analysis, is well suited to the conceptualization of the times even though in its essentials it violates the facts. Indeed, what is most true about Marxian theory, and most often borrowed, is not the economic theory — which would make predictions other than those which are now coming to be — but rather the certainty of class conflict in the movement of mankind.

The twentieth century is also a time of growing interest in the workings of man as a human being, caught within the dynamic flow of his personal life's events. Though the more doctrinaire phrasings of psychoanalysis may be giving way to other formulations, the dialectical style of thought which is its heritage has not spent itself and doubtless never will. One can be quite certain that when a client in psychotherapy opens his first contact by stressing that he is greatly in love with his wife, one of the *first* hypotheses this is likely to generate in the therapist will continue to be something like: "this man may well hate his wife, now let us see if this is so, and why he may do so." The love-hate contrast provides a *dimension of meaning* along which to array client behavior, and the therapist can then help the client to see that he is vacillating between extremes on the dimension, or that he has expressed one end of it while unconsciously feeling (believing) the other is true. As he combines this dimension with others proffered by the client, in time he frames an image of the client which may be more in line with what the client actually feels, and on the basis of such comments and the client's use of procedural evidence, a therapeutic outcome may be effected.

Like the Socratic discussions of centuries past, the therapist is working with his client to discover those truths which at the outset neither knows. Rather than the heritage of a Golden Age locked in each man's intellect, we now have the repressed meanings of one man's life under dialectical investigation by two men, or the archetypal heritage of a bygone era now manifesting itself but being grasped by only one man — the therapist — though it shows itself in the psyche of the other. But the search is the same. To aid him in the discovery of insights regarding his client, a therapist must, as we have noted, often rely upon inverse probability judgments (see Chapters VI and IX): "What is the probability that a man would say that he loved his wife at the outset of a therapy contact when not asked, and mean it, against the probability that if he really loved his wife, and so on." Here we have the often cited "clinical method" beginning to unfold in dialectical comparison, and the conceptualization of the patient's behavior which ensues is also likely to be entirely dialectical — that is, if the clinician operates within the psycho-analytical tradition.

Freudian psychology is a "man in the middle" view; there are three identities within one psyche, each with its own particular goal (final cause) in the living reality facing the individual. The man in the middle, the ego, must somehow keep his loosely knit group together, and in any given behavior seek to satisfy all concerned. Like the little tramp in the Charlie Chaplin motion pictures, the ego can at times be perfectly proper and considerate; but beware, for at any moment he may pull the chair out from under the fat lady, or worse, because he also has darker needs to satisfy. This interplay between the demands of the id and the super-ego is in all essentials identical to the Hegelian-Marxian theoretical analysis of the interplay between various civilizations and then between class levels within a given civilization. The motive power is always a dialectical clash, and the budding opposition always emerges somehow within the framework of a given construct — a human being or social group, as the case may be. What gives Freudian theory its most significant quality is the way Freud opposed *value* structures. He spoke about libido as though energies somehow move the organism called man. But energies have no more to do with values than the stomach and its digestive juices have. It is the direction taken, the intent, and the consequent (value) conflict of the "man in the middle" which gives Freud lasting significance as a personality theorist. How "ought" we to behave? That insight is the goal which his method and theory seek to provide.

This dialectical approach is properly seen as within the Continental line of descent. A psychotherapy within the tradition of British empiricism would of course not call for a mutual search for meaning between two people. The Continental tradition has also been seen in the twentieth century within the gestalt and the existentialist movements. Often American therapists, such as Rogers, have tied Rankian-psycho-analytical views to gestalt-existentialist views, a union which is particularly easy to effect because of their common Platonic heritage. Rogers finds his clash much more in the interpersonal pressures of parent-against-child, or in the need of certain individuals to influence or "control" others. Rather than accepting one another and appreciating each individual's ability to decide for himself and to grow under the weight of his own potential, Rogers finds myriads of what Marx would have termed "expropriators" — individuals who selfishly feed on the behavior of others. We have the mother who must live her son's life, and hence assures his collapse as a spontaneous individual being. We have the self-assured scientist with a comparable gleam in his eye, out to save the world from spontaneous — hence uncontrolled — nature. Showing through the Rogerian criticism is a gnawing dialectical question: "why this way, and not that; why not leave it up to the individual?" Control is not *only* a vehicular concept. The dialectician takes an interest in the refined discriminants; he wants to know what kinds of controls these are which one person wants to effect in another.

And so it goes. The dialecticians, having been greatly submerged in the natural sciences, where reality is much less arbitrary, now emerge doubly important in the social science of our time. It is probably no accident that the twentieth century witnessed the emergence of the social sciences. As the nineteenth century found the role of the philosopher shifting from that of the Hegel-like speculative and all-encompassing systematist, to that of one who assists the scientist in making his ideas more logically clear and consistent, much of the commentary on man made by the earlier philosophers was now being made by various other specialties. This group of social evaluators and critics has emerged in the twentieth century as what we call social scientists, and, although the orientations among them vary considerably, we can count within this group theorists from anthropology, economics, psychiatry, psychology, and sociology. Speculation has moved to the latter sciences from its earlier home exclusively within philosophy, and speculation is nurtured by dialectic. More important, the nature of the data is well suited to dialectical theoretical constructions. That is, for centuries men had been trying to verify their belief methodologically through dialectical argumentation. When talk gave way to empirical validation there was no room for dialectic in *method*. Yet, what better way to capture man *theoretically* as known in the philosophies of history than to think of him as a dialectical being? What better theoretical construct can one have than a dialectical construct? Is this not what makes man different from a raindrop or a calculating machine, that he can reason in a peculiarly "human" way? He has been doing so for centuries, if we can believe history. Why not capture him in this way theoretically?

This will be our next point. Not only do we claim that dialectic has been deflected into the twentieth-century social and psychological sciences; we now argue that this is how it *ought* to be. If we, as scientists, hope to capture the essentials of our data, then we cannot overlook any aspect of behavior which seems to fit the facts. If our datum is man, then all those behaviors which have relevance to that "image" we call man must be given their proper weight in the theoretical description of him. This is not a question to be dismissed in the name of parsimony, it is not a matter of how far we can get *without* assuming that he has the ability to reason dialectically. It is purely and simply a challenge to capture him accurately, based upon how we know him to be, in ourselves. What do we mean by a man, or a human being, as opposed to just any other form of organic, natural life? That is the next point to consider. Can we show that those unique characteristics ascribed to man, or bemoaned when left out of a description of man, have a dialectical quality about them? If we can, then our thesis is greatly strengthened. This will be our task in Chapter XI, where we will study the contrasting uses of demonstrative and dialectical metaconstructs in the description of man.

Summary

Chapter X was devoted to a development of our thesis that Freud and his students deflected dialectical reasoning and dialectical meta-constructs into the study of the individual, while Marx and his followers were doing the same thing in the study of group behavior. Psycho-analysis and various derivatives of Marxian socioeconomic theory have been the modern havens for dialectic. After citing several examples of Freud's penchant for the dialectical twist, and showing how Freud relied on a dialectical explanation even before he made use of energy notions, we made some speculations on the possible sources of his bias. It was suggested that psycho-analysis as an introspective procedure may en-courage dialectical usages, because introspective examination begins with the sorts of questions dialectic is based upon. Freud's Jewishness was also credited with playing a role in his dialectical leanings. Finally, cer-tain Continental idealistic philosophical trends, particularly stemming from the French, were introduced as possible sources of influence on Freud. One of Freud's most important students, and a great dialectician in his own right, Carl G. Jung was also looked at in Chapter X. We saw some direct evidence for our thesis in the form of a letter from Jung, which seemed to place him clearly within the idealistic dialectical tra-dition. Jung also may well have been influenced by his introspective efforts, but a clear tie to literature in his outlook provided us with a unique influence, hinted at in Freud's ideological background but not quite so apparent. Finally, in Chapter X, the role of dialectic in twen-tieth-century social science was underscored, and the position was taken that it is right and proper for theorists to make use of dialectical con-structs in conceptualizing man.

References

Adler, M. J. *Dialectic.* New York: Harcourt, Brace & Co., 1927.

Aristotle. *On the soul.* In Vol. 8 of R. M. Hutchins (Ed.), *Great books of the western world.* Chicago: Encyclopedia Britannica, 1952. Pp. 631–668.

Bakan, D. *Sigmund Freud and the Jewish mystical tradition.* New York: D. Van Nostrand, 1958.

Breuer, J., and Freud, S. *Studies on hysteria.* Vol. II of J. Strachey (Ed.), *The standard edition of the complete psychological works of Sigmund Freud.* London: The Hogarth Press, 1955. Also, J. Breuer and S. Freud, *Studies on Hysteria.* New York: Basic Books, 1957.

Freud, S. *A general introduction to psychoanalysis.* In Vol. 54 of R. M. Hutchins (Ed.), *Great books of the western world.* Chicago: Encyclopedia Britannica, 1952. Pp. 449–638. Also published — New York: Liveright, and London: George Allen and Unwin, 1963.

Freud, S. *The interpretation of dreams* (Parts I and II). Vols. IV and V of J. Strachey (Ed.), *The standard edition of the complete psychological works of Sigmund Freud.* London: The Hogarth Press, 1953.

Freud, S. *The origins of psycho-analysis, letters to Wilhelm Fliess, drafts and notes: 1887–1902.* New York: Basic Books, 1954.

Freud, S. The antithetical meaning of primal words (1910). In Vol. XI of J. Strachey (Ed.), *The standard edition of the complete psychological works of Sigmund Freud.* London: The Hogarth Press, 1957. Pp. 153–161.

Freud, S. *The psychopathology of everyday life* (1901). Vol. VI of J. Strachey (Ed.), *The standard edition of the complete psychological works of Sigmund Freud.* London: The Hogarth Press, 1960a.

Freud, S. *The letters of Sigmund Freud* (edited by E. L. Freud). New York: Basic Books, 1960b.

Freud, S. On the psychical mechanism of hysterical phenomena; a lecture (1893). In Vol. III of J. Strachey (Ed.), *The standard edition of the complete psychological works of Sigmund Freud.* London: The Hogarth Press, 1962. Pp. 25–39.

Freud, S. *New introductory lectures on psycho-analysis* (1932). Vol. XXII of J. Strachey (Ed.), *The standard edition of the complete psychological works of Sigmund Freud.* London: The Hogarth Press, 1964. Pp. 3–182. Also in Vol. 54 of R. M. Hutchins (Ed.), *Great books of the western world.* Chicago: Encyclopedia Britannica, 1952. Pp. 807–884.

Goethe, J. W. *Faust.* Vol. 47 of R. M. Hutchins (Ed.), *Great books of the western world.* Chicago: Encyclopedia Britannica, 1952.

Hook, S. *From Hegel to Marx.* Ann Arbor, Mich.: University of Michigan Press, 1962.

Janet, P. *The major symptoms of hysteria,* 2nd ed. New York: Macmillan, 1920.

Jones, E. *The life and work of Sigmund Freud.* New York: Basic Books.
  Vol. 1. *The formative years and the great discoveries,* 1953.
  Vol. 2. *Years of maturity,* 1955.
  Vol. 3. *The last phase,* 1957.

Jung. C. G. *The practice of psychotherapy.* Vol. 16 of H. Read, M. Fordham, and G. Adler (Eds.), *The collected works of C. G. Jung.* Bollingen Series XX.16. New York: Pantheon Books, 1954.

Jung, C. G. *Freud and psychoanalysis.* Vol. 4 of H. Read, M. Fordham, and G. Adler (Eds.), *The collected works of C. G. Jung.* Bollingen Series XX.4. New York: Pantheon Books, 1961.

Jung, C. G. *Memories, dreams, reflections.* Copyright 1963. New York: Pantheon Books, A Division of Random House, Inc., and London: William Collins Sons, Ltd.

Kaufmann, W. *Nietzsche.* New York: Meridian Books, 1956.

Magnus, R. *Goethe as a scientist.* New York: H. Schuman, 1949.

Nunberg, H., and Federn, E. (Eds.) *Minutes of the Vienna psychoanalytic society: 1906–1908.* Vol. I. New York: International Universities Press, 1962.

Rieff, P. *Freud: The mind of the moralist.* New York: Viking Press, 1959.

Spender, S. (Ed.) *Great writings of Goethe.* New York: New American Library, 1958.

Strachey, J. (Ed.) Editor's introduction. In Vol. II of *The standard edition of the complete psychological works of Sigmund Freud.* London: The Hogarth Press, 1955.

Wilson, E. *To the Finland station: A study in the writing and acting of history.* Garden City, N.Y.: Doubleday Anchor, 1940.

Wittels, F. *Sigmund Freud: His personality, his teaching, and his school.* New York: Dodd, Mead, 1924.

Zborowski, M., and Herzog, Elizabeth. *Life is with people.* New York: Schocken Books, 1962.

The Play of Metaconstructs
in Personality Theory and
the Images of Man

XI

An image is a fancy, born of imagination, and then taken ever so subtly as the presumed nature of some phenomenon. The introspectionists are influenced by their personal cogitation and self-study. They understand themselves as they discover themselves to be while looking inward. And the extraspectionists are also influenced by the needs of what they call science, with its demands of validation. If only one could "control and predict" introspectively in the same way that he can extraspectively. But he cannot; hence, unless we are prepared to accept a uniting notion such as the "line of development" from theory to methodological test, an unyielding line is drawn between the images fostered by our respective theoretical perspectives.

It is our thesis that the single most important issue in the history of thought concerning *man's nature* is the problem of whether dialectic is to be used in framing his image, or whether a demonstrative metaconstruct will suffice in describing him. As we have seen, down through history there have been repeated disputes over this question of how best to *think about* the data of the senses. Earlier, the point at issue was not how to think about *man* as a datum, but rather how should man *himself* think in solving problems about data based upon his perception of things, and his use of reason. The early philosophers were in agreement that they were beings who reasoned *both* dialectically and demonstratively. In forging the methods of science to place restrictions on this free intellect, these men gradually elevated the role of demonstration to a prominent position. Since dialectic has been so successfully eclipsed, the question for the twentieth century is: Do we need this concept at all, or is it so fraught with error and devious sophistry that it will lead to scientific decline?

353

One may not need a dialectical metaconstruct in the theory of natural science. But what of a science of man? We are still speaking of data, but now these data are "human," whatever we mean by that. It was not until the advent of social science that such a question might legitimately have arisen. What the poet and dramatist had been trying for centuries past to capture was now made the content of a science. Can the image of man gleaned through the arts meet with the image scientifically "discovered" in the laboratory, and if not, why not? As we shall see, the question of dialectical conceptualization meshes with our argument of Chapter VIII, that final causation distinguishes human from natural science theory. Dialectic shall become our heuristic aid in describing how truly original final causes arise in man's personality.

Our initial purpose in the present chapter is to isolate a few of those aspects of man's nature which we ordinarily consider "human," and to show how they most often lend themselves to a dialectical phrasing. We will then identify and name several other metaconstructs which have been generated in the historical exchanges between those who favored dialectic and those who did not. An attempt will be made to subsume many of the important terms in modern personality theory under these metaconstructs and thereby bring greater coherence to a field which now appears more disjointed than it actually is.

Dialectical vs. Demonstrative Metaconstructs

History, Religion, Language, and Man

We have not yet attempted to answer the question of why or how the dialectical vs. demonstrative distinction might have arisen in man's thought, and what it specifically implied for his self-conceptualization. There is no agreement on origins, as we can see in contrasting Mortimer Adler's view that man's thought processes probably began in a form of denotative pointing with Freud's advocacy of the theory that primitive language combined opposites in single terms from the outset. In the latter case, even the pointing would suggest two meanings. There are those who would argue that our ancient bifurcation stemmed from man's religious inclinations, the tendency he had to divide reality into a world of spirit and a world of matter (e.g., Baker, 1961, p. 111). Here again, it is virtually impossible to say from where this tendency stems; but if we can accept the testimony of a modern man, we would do well to listen to Julian Huxley. In his fascinating introspective book, *Religion*

Without Revelation, Huxley tells how a developing sense of "power" came into contact with his being:

> I had no picture of this power, no belief that it was personal. On the other hand, I felt about it that it somehow worked by contraries and was concerned not to let poor mortals have too good a time — that same feeling which finds it unlucky to say that a child is pretty, which mistrusts too much happiness, and especially mistrusts the mention of it, the arousing of which in ourselves makes us oppose an argument for the mere reason that the other man has put it forward. If, for instance, I was extremely anxious to have a fine afternoon, I would not like to confess it openly, even in thought, but would feel that if I said, or ostentatiously thought, the opposite, I might get what I wanted. This idea of going by contraries is widespread among all races and almost all classes; and yet, if I may trust my own recollections, it was in my own case a quite spontaneous rationalization, whose logical implications (of a malicious personal power in control of events) were, however, not followed out: most likely it arises with equal inevitableness elsewhere and equally remains in one of the mind's watertight compartments (1957, pp. 68–69).

If we begin from such personally derived, introspective sensing of a "power within," we might conclude that man's theories of dualism, "luck," religious guilt, and so on, were generated from a dialectical, oppositional tendency he came up against within his own psyche. We must at least acknowledge that demonstration and realism, and dialectic and idealism are very compatible notions. Dialectical generation of the possibility in things calls for a certain disdain for the hard facts of reality, and an attempt to transcend the status quo of empirical data to grasp something beyond the apparent. Man seems always to have made this attempt to work over reality intellectually and alter its import, or merely to express ideas for the sheer joy of doing so, no matter how unrealistic they might be. Susanne K. Langer has seen in this self-expressive facility the basic difference between man and beast (1948, p. 46).

As Freud recognized, the matter of language and communication seems very much involved in the dialectical process. Cassirer makes a distinction between signs and symbols in language expression which has implications for the role of language in dialectical vs. demonstrative reasoning (1944, pp. 80–84). Signs are attached to certain elements of experience and come to stand for these elements in thought and communication; but symbols have meaning even though they may not relate to anything existing in reality except themselves. Symbols express or create meaning in and of themselves, whereas signs merely reflect the meaning in other things — i.e., their referents. The numeral "7" has a sign function when it is proxy for the idea of seven days in the week, but it becomes a symbol when it helps us to conceptualize "luck," or the social situation we call "a lucky break." As Langer observes, "Symbols are not proxy for their objects, but are *vehicles for the conception of objects*" (1948, p. 61). To believe that the data of the senses are somehow reducible to signs, and this alone, or that signs are primary and symbolic activity is a generalization done after the fact of sign learning, would of course suggest a demonstrative position. This is what Hobbes and Locke believed. A dialectical conception, on the other hand, would suggest that things are not always what they seem, and from the very beginning of meaningful understanding, something else — something opposite to or alternative to the given sign — is suggested. As with Huxley's self-examination, happiness suggests sadness, beauty implies ugliness, mortality leads to immortality. It is at this point that idealism and symbolism meet, and we are reminded of the many-and-the-one thesis of the early Greeks.

In fact, one could argue that Greek philosophy, which has been typified as having struggled with the basic theme of how to account for change within permanence (Baker, 1961, p. 3), epitomizes the dialectical vs. demonstrative distinction. Demonstrative reasoning settles on *permanent* facts so that a methodological test of some hypothesis can be made. Dialectic is better suited to the conceptualization of *change*. As we have seen, the Platonic view solved the riddle of permanence in change by postulating a world of unchanging absolutes and another of altering reality. The dialectical method permitted a thinker to move from one world to the other by an exercise of intellect. In trying to bring his more fanciful colleagues back to earth, Aristotle then called for some ground rules in demonstration and thereby framed our historical bifurcation. But, there is every indication that this dichotomy in human thought is as old as man's history, and very likely as unresolvable as it is ancient.

Ernst Cassirer has underscored the great lucidity with which Blaise Pascal (1623–1662) put his finger on this recurring historical dichotomy. As mathematician and philosopher Pascal recognized better than most the implications of demonstration vs. dialectic for the image of man. He spoke of the "geometrical spirit" vs. the "acute or subtle spirit" (Cassirer, 1944, p. 27). The geometrical spirit of man, said Pascal, reasons from axioms and draws inferences, the truth of which can be demonstrated by universal logical rules, such as the Aristotelian law of contradiction. However, there are some things which cannot be treated in this way, and the mind of man is one of the most outstanding examples. This "subtle spirit" cannot be framed in geometrical mathematics, said Pascal, because man is full of contradictions and he must be described as we find him. Man has no primary and true "nature" which can be pointed to as an axiomatic substrate for demonstration. Man is a strange admixture of being and non-being. He is tossed hither and yon between the dialectical poles of existence, and must be understood in this context (p. 28). Cassirer then goes on to show how man's nature is not a substance, not a material essence to be credited to heredity, but rather a functional manifestation of his work, his religion, his art; in brief, his "nature" is his cultural symbols as revealed in his history. Man is men, as Jung has attested (see Chapters VIII and X). But there is a dilemma in all this, for as history proceeds dialectically and men seek to express what they sense in themselves, alternative views are continually suggested, and in time they become points of conflict that can divide mankind: "Thus what was intended to secure the harmony of culture becomes the source of the deepest discords and dissensions. This is the great antinomy, the dialectic of the religious life. The same dialectic appears in human speech. Without speech there would be no community of men. Yet there is no more serious obstacle to such community than the diversity of speech" (p. 167).

When one generates the possibilities in things, the possible ways of thinking about a Supreme Being once this idea has been suggested, the possible ways of enunciating and delivering meaningful ideas in self-expression, it is doubtless inevitable that different men will develop different possibilities, which in time may become vested interests. The dialectic is father to strife. This is why in science we resort to demonstration as a stabilizing measure. But how can we capture and communicate the *fact* of a multiplicity in man's nature as reflected in his history better than by thinking of it in dialectical terms? And how much do we lose in accuracy if we disregard this sequence of dynamic events? These are the points at issue, and we would argue that a personality theorist cannot let the descriptive concept of dialectic slip from his grasp and hope to do justice to the object of his study.

Art and Man

It is often said, in referring to some applied aspect of psychology, such as clinical work, that the clinician is an artist in addition to or rather than being a scientist. Art is so firmly opposed to science in the minds of many psychologists that they believe no one could perform both activities without injuring one or the other. Being called an artist in academic psychological circles is like being called a little soft in the head. What is the fundamental distinction between artist and scientist? Presumably, it is the belief that scientists are more objective, swayed less by their emotions, and more prone to define their terms clearly, so that generalizations can be drawn from their statements. The artist is moved by impulse, he is entirely subjective and not interested in learning how he achieves his effects. All of this has a certain ring of truth; but, the fundamental difference stems from reliance in each realm of knowledge on either primarily demonstrative or primarily dialectical metaconstructs and reasoning processes. The toughminded psychologists, who speak from a demonstrative viewpoint, sense the dialectical maneuverings of their clinical colleagues, who are continually questioning assumptions, avoiding taking a stand, and decrying natural science, yet refusing to stipulate a better alternative. And dialectic, as we shall soon see, is quite accurately tied to artistic expression.

The gestalt psychologists made a criticism of academic psychology not unlike the clinician's lament, as when Kurt Koffka observed: "The denunciation of the intellect which has assumed such tremendous proportions in some parts of our world with such far-reaching consequences, seems to me the outcome of the wrong scientific attitude . . ." (1935, pp. 8–9). The problem stemmed, said Koffka, from the rising trend to rabid empiricism, which chose to ignore many aspects of man's existence; it was his hope in time to alter the nature of science to help "re-create that original unity which it had to destroy in order to develop" (p. 9). As is well known, by stressing the dynamic organization of things, the one-in-many features of the whole as more than the sum of its parts, gestalt psychology furthered a Platonic theme in modern psychology. The typical maneuver of the gestaltist was to devise an experiment which could not be explained through the simple, efficient-cause theories of the behaviorist. Thus, it was Koffka and other gestaltists who argued for a reintroduction of final-cause terms such as "will" and "level of aspiration" into psychology. Of course, unlike some dialectically-inclined theoreticians, the gestaltists strived to retain an extraspective perspective, so that *will* became actions in the *field* controlled by forces emanating from an individual *ego* in the field (pp. 417–421).

Other neo-Platonists, such as the existentialists, who are also in the Continental gestalt-phenomenological tradition, seek to make their theoretical statements from the introspective perspective. It is the uniqueness of the individual as the "one" having "many" interlacing dynamic elements that they try to capture (Boss, 1963). Now, as we have noted in Chapter VIII, this has been one of the major motives in literature, to capture experiences for the reader. Even "art for art's sake" is properly understood as an expression of experience by a man, from his perspective and to suit his personal conceptualization. When disparate items of experience are united, we can say that something has been created, and, if the beholder can now put himself in the proper perspective, he too might appreciate the expression (meaning) embodied in the art object — though it is not essential that anyone do so. If the work lends itself to many interpretations and many emotive experiences, then we are not disturbed by such multiplicity, for art is not discredited by holding to inconsistencies. Art, like man, has no substantial essence beyond its history; as a cultural artifact, it is best conceptualized and understood in dialectical terms.

It is not difficult to find support for this view if we turn to those who have written on the nature of art. Typically, one finds that artistic expression, to be accurately grasped, demands a "tension of opposites" phrasing. In his four-volume work, *The Social History of Art,* Hauser uses this device in discussing architecture (1951, I, p. 242), the drama (III, p. 85), the novel (IV, p. 28), poetry (IV, p. 168), and painting (IV, p. 168). Each art form is seen to lend itself to a dialectical analysis. Music has been said to be a highly versatile art form because it permits the simultaneous expression of opposite tones and emotionally expressive melodies (Langer, 1948, p. 48). In discussing the historical development of literature, Shipley states his thesis in clearly dialectical terms: life is a conflict, a battle, and: "The plot of a novel or play grows out of this conflict. But beneath the story, and in every work of art, the artist takes his stand. The literary 'schools,' romanticism, realism, and the rest, represent the different bivouacs in the unending struggle" (1949, p. 11). How reminiscent this is of the analyses of Hegel, Marx, and Cassirer; how consistent it is with the views of Freud and Jung! What moves the artist is what moves all men, namely the conflict engendered by opposing convictions, opposing "natures," located either within or between persons.

It has been said that the genius of Shakespeare was that he, for the first time in history, expressed to the public, and to the most pedestrian among us, the conflict which springs from the realization that pure, unadulterated *ideas* of truth, fidelity, and so on, cannot be realized in everyday life without their being wracked with compromise and defiled with petty realities. Shakespeare's heroes are caught up in this problem of how what one thinks about reality is often a far cry from what is realized in reality. Hellenistic and medieval dramatists portrayed no such conflict in their heroes. The two worlds of Plato had always been kept quite distinct, as in Greek drama, in which divine beings with man-like characteristics interceded to help a hero, or in medieval drama, in which the saint-like hero rejected the contradictions of reality and took flight into a spiritual life.

Shakespeare was able to capture the more true-to-life circumstance which faces every man at some point, and thus to portray for the first time a truly "human" man. As Hauser observes: "Shakespeare's . . . character-drawing is naturalistic, the differentiated psychology of his figures and the human lifelikeness of his heroes, who are a bundle of contradictions and full of weaknesses" (1951, II, p. 168). To achieve this descriptive feat, Shakespeare continually resorted to the use of dialectical phrasings (p. 171). Whether we think of Hamlet's tortured self-examination — "To be or not to be" — or Iago's treacherous self-observation — "I am not what I am" — the respective conflict in moral decision and the deceitfulness of apparent reality is best captured as a dialectical matter. For centuries, Shakespeare's insight into the human condition has been unquestioned. Can this be due simply to the fact that he demonstratively pointed to the right and not the wrong variables in man's nature, or did he touch on something more basic in the union of contradictories we call life?

Of course, we should not conclude from all this that artists have never utilized a demonstrative metaconstruct in their conceptualization of man. Though dialectical phrasings are far more frequent, Balzac and Zola may be compared in this sense. Balzac was well received by Marx and Engels because of his sensitivity to the class struggle. Balzac wrote of the clash between classes, each with its own vested interest. The poor man gets sent to prison for some minor infraction, while the rich man who ruins many people through unethical business practices is merely fined, being protected by laws written to favor the rich. Balzac did not feel, as Marx did, that the lower classes were any more noble or on the wave of a future tide than the upper classes. Each class, and hence each person, had his own vested interest, though it was possible to be caught between them, as in one sense Balzac himself was. He identified with the upper classes even as he presented the nature of the class struggle objectively and with great sensitivity, and this made him a favorite of the originators of communistic theory. Zola, on the other hand, though he shared the communist's faith in the advance of science, did not characterize man or the society in which he lived in dialectical terms. Zola was greatly taken by the demonstrative methods of science, and he believed that art should be servant to science, that it should show how man's behavior is shaped by natural laws in the environment. Zola even spoke of the novel as "simply the application of the experimental method to literature" (Hauser, 1951, IV, p. 87). Man was a mechanism shaped by natural forces which could be identified quite certainly through the exercise of scientific methods.

The rise of the science-fiction novel in the twentieth century also parallels a rise in the demonstrative conceptualization of man's intellect. The citizens of Walden Two (Skinner, 1948) are not like the characters portrayed by Shakespeare. They are not rent with conflict, for that would suggest abnormality and the book is about a utopia. Utopias have always been presented as isolated islands of happiness amid oceans of varying miseries (Becker and Barnes, 1952, Ch. VIII). They are specially designed closed societies in which only *certain* alternatives are to be entertained, lest the balance of the group be upset; in short, they are under some *one* person's social control (see Chapter VI). The citizen of such a utopia is made happy from somewhere outside his head. How does he know he's happy? What does happiness mean for him? How does he recognize unhappiness? Skinner has had difficulty convincing his readers that happiness could be achieved in his utopia, but he has had no difficulty keeping his citizens convinced, for they are demonstrative creatures.

Balzac's genius lay in his recognition that all individuals identify themselves invariably with some group or class and seek advantage, which, as Cassirer has observed, generates conflict. Hence, a truly *classless* utopia is just so much nonsense based upon a myth of the "downtrodden." Such suffering masses must indeed be satisfied, must be clothed and fed, but this does not insure the dissolution of class distinctions. Diversity, competition, and the clash of vested interest is not so easily extinguished, for it is generated by the very nature of human intellect. Changes take place in the structure of advantage, but that is all. In this sense, Balzac, like Freud, is a more consistent and indomitable dialectician than even Hegel or Marx. Balzac, Freud, and Shakespeare were more pessimistic about what advances men could make, precisely because they could not see the clash of dialectic coming to a halt either in man's psyche or in his social structure.

Creative vs. Computer Intellect

The fact that a dialectical manner of reasoning is possible in man but not in a "thinking machine" lies at the heart of the fear that modern science is making men into machines. We have already touched upon this in our discussion of Wiener's adoption of demonstrative reasoning as the only model for man's thought processes (see Chapter IX). The point is, thinking machines — at least up to now — have been made to reason according to a binary system in which the law of contradiction has been applied exclusively (Adler, 1961, p. 31). Propositions fed into the machine are either true or false, and in no case is something both true *and* false. As Wiener indicated, thinking machines reason syllogistically; but we must realize that their major premises are not arbitrarily decided upon, therefore the thinking machine cannot carry on two lines of argument at the same time, or arrive at contradictory conclusions after an act of reasoning — as man can and frequently does. Thinking machines have "true and primary" *bits* (short for "binary digits") of information stored away in their memories, and it is their inability to subdivide and rearrange these Lockean bits which gives their reasoning a wooden, uninspired, literally "mechanical" quality. By processing vast amounts of data very quickly they can make proper comparisons and come to the "correct" conclusions. Indeed, if the data on which they base their conclusions have been entered properly, a machine *cannot* make a mistake — itself a clearly human prerogative, the other side of making a creative contribution.

It is the man who runs the machine, who puts the properly determined primary and true data into it, that initiates the reasoning process and must reason dialectically. The machine begins its line of reasoning with the major premise already decided upon. It may be that science will someday construct a machine which will choose its own major premises. The machine might then begin by examining the contrasting side of any issue presented to it in proposition form, such as the opposite of truth, falsehood; or the opposite of falsehood, which may not quite be truth as originally conceived. This is the strange thing about dialectical reasoning. What is opposed to thesis (antithesis) must literally be created by the reasoner, and should he oppose a second antithesis to the first, he does not always arrive back at the original thesis. At this point meanings may be altered sufficiently to justify speaking of a creative line of thought, because now the initial stimulus from the environment no longer exists, and a spontaneously arrived at derivative is being developed. Rather than the binary division "A vs. B" fed into the machine, we would now have "non-A vs. non-B," or "non-non-A vs. B" programmed into the machine by itself. The machine would be doing what in a human we would call "following through" on the implications of an exciting, interesting, or playful line of thought.

Such a machine would surely be a maverick. It would not always solve the problems put to it. In fact, it would begin by suggesting alternative problems to the ones posed by the operator. It would rattle the association network of a body of knowledge and begin some real "noise in the network." It would arrive not at errorless conclusions but at hunches and hypotheses and, in those cases where two lines of reasoning on the same issue resulted in equally plausible outcomes, it would present its proud owner with an *opinion* on which of the two alternatives it preferred, based on other grounds. Along with its opinions and hunches such a machine would soon begin making mistakes. In short, it would behave humanly. One can only guess at how much interest a machine like this would generate in science. It would be an oddity, but hardly a thing calculated to excite the toughminded scientist, who would doubtless sum it up as an inferior organism — just like the man who made it.

The real irony in all of this is that so many psychologists are pleased to accept the machine as paradigm for man, even though they also admit we have no "scientific" way of accounting for the creative act. Simply recognizing that man does reason dialectically may not provide such an explanation in research terms, but we would argue that this recognition does call for a re-examination of the ways we seek to describe and think about his behavior as an organism. What has been dropped in scientific reasoning — oriented as it is to the methodological side of knowledge — is precisely what we mean to capture when we use terms such as "invention," "self-expression," or "creativity." The dialectical potential of man's intellect provides him with the option of accepting things as they stand or varying the facts in some way to suit his fancy. He proceeds by forming dimensions, X to non-X, and through repetitions of this procedure rearranges circumstances in such a way as to create new combinations by detecting parallels in disparate events (analogizing). Note that we said *he* does this; he creates, by articulating the potentials in so-called *input* information, and his *output* is just as likely to be a bird of another color. This is what Plato was really saying, that man's intellect is active and ever alive to the possibility of things. The computer intellect is not alive, and cannot transcend the possibility of its input information. Computers do not act, they do not express, they respond and follow through. They are Lockean beings, with minds which truly begin as *tabula rasa* and give back only the information which goes into them at some point, albeit in refined ways.

This is what the neo-Platonist takes to be innate, the potential to create ideas; what is innate is the dialectical potential and not ideas *per se*. Neo-Lockeans frequently misconstrue the issue, as Locke himself did, claiming that the content of ideas is being referred to in using a term such as "creativity." They ask, "Where do these created ideas come from; are you born with them; does a god put them in your head?" Naturally, the ideas as expressed must be phrased in "idea forms" or in words, and everyone knows that we learn words from our environment, our culture. But the *act of creating* ideas as an exercise of intellect does not have to be thought of as coming from the environment; it can be thought of as the equipment all humans have potentially at their disposal in behavior. The neo-Lockean might more properly ask, "Where does this creative ability come from?" and when he has done that he can ask himself, "Where does the memory of the *tabula rasa* come from?" for the two queries are parallel. If memory intellect stores ideas gleaned from the environment as mental contents, then creative intellect can deal with this same group of ideas. Specific ideas, we are saying, are quite irrelevant to the point at issue. Man is either potentially capable of *creating stimuli* within his mind's eye, or he is nothing but a *responder* to environmental inputs. The neo-Platonists believe the former, based upon a dialectical rationale; and the neo-Lockeans believe the latter, holding as they do that reasoning means only demonstrative reasoning.

The point of how ideas are expressed in language brings us back to this very important topic. It is probably a further clarification of the truth that man has no essence other than a historical one to say that man's history is literally born of signs and symbols, verbal collages delineating his experience in abstract terms. When a man speaks, does he *express* an idea he has generated dialectically, or is he letting flow a charge of nervous energy to excite certain muscular or glandular responses acting as surrogate to the idea (which is really not "his" if by that we mean created by him)? In Cassirer's terms, is man merely a sign-responding animal, or is he also a symbol-expressing animal? The image of man one takes on this point will largely determine how he explains the origins of speech. Brown has summed up this issue in a nutshell:

> One type of theorist conceives pre-linguistic man to have been a higher anthropoid motivated by biological needs and alterable through conditioning and instrumental learning. For this theorist the problem of speech origin is the problem of explaining the accidental development of speech habits and of demonstrating the survival value of such habits. Another sort of theorist imagines pre-linguistic man to have had the impulse to symbolize and communicate. For this theorist the problem of speech origin is the problem of explaining how men found suitable representational symbols to function as surrogates for concepts (1958, p. 135).

This is all very true, and we know full well which image is most presumed in American academic psychology. But those who favor the latter image ordinarily wish to do more than merely explain how man found suitable representational symbols to function as surrogates for concepts. This would be mere sign learning and not symbolic expression. If one believes that man has an active intellect, and a need to infuse his existence with meaning (to create stimuli), then language is a tremendous vehicle for the *creation* of — rather than simply a means of recording — knowledge. Symbols are not limited to the response side of a cause-effect chain; they are essentially *stimuli.* The creative man — be he artist, political thinker, religious figure, or scientist — *does* something to the environment through an act of symbolic expression and creation. With his new ideas and behaviors of all sorts he can move mountains, or misfire completely, in error. In its impractical, often stupid manifestations, human creativity is literally human nature made manifest. As Langer has observed, "If a savage in his ignorance of physics tries to make a mountain open its cavern by dancing round it, we must admit with shame that no rat in a psychologist's maze would try such patently ineffectual methods of opening a door" (1948, p. 42).

A most interesting truism about language expression is that as each concept, each image which a sign or symbol mentally generates, is stipulated, its opposite is also suggested immediately or potentially. Language terms are always pregnant with more meaning than their strict denotation signifies. Symbolic rites in particular are fraught with such oppositional tendencies, very reminiscent of Huxley's introspection, and it is no coincidence that some students of language feel that man's language originated in religious or magical rituals. During times of famine, primitive man dances for a good hunt; or in times of drought, he carves a totem to the gods for rain. Gradually, the carvings or paintings used in conjunction with the ritual become the basis for written communication. The symbolic manifestation of opposites can also be found in happier times, as when groups re-enact and relive old wars or tragedies in their history. In this case it is not the permanent return of a former state which is desired, but the sense of commitment and communal identity which was born of past trials which is being sought and re-affirmed. By reliving the difficult past in symbolic recollection we can reassert our identity, "lest we forget," in the more easy present.

Man, says Langer, is the only animal that has the *"need of symbolization"* (1948, p. 45). Man must transcend mere sign language if he is to further his human nature. His language, Sapir says, serves him as a heuristic device in thought (Langer, p. 113). If he thus symbolizes to understand, and in so doing grasps both the thesis and antithesis of concepts, we have here a marvelous potential for creativity; for this creative act does not depend only upon the realities of his environment. He has seen the heads of men and the bodies of lions, but the god to whom he now bows with a man's head and a lion's body has never before walked this earth as stimulus. No thinking machine now in operation would cross its wires in quite this symbolic way. If nature has decreed that man's intellect originates in *tabula rasa* fashion, then she has also allowed that intellect certain *carte blanche* privileges in the matter of altering the impressions etched upon it by experience.

Emotional vs. Intellectual Factors in Human Behavior

The recognition that man can create alternatives to what is given by way of a dialectical maneuver leads us into the next area which is usually brought up in discussions of human nature. Man, unlike machines, must deal with emotional forces in his being; and, unlike lower animals, he need not always give in to them — at least not in any apparent or overt sense. Man is an emotive animal, and if modern science were to take this characteristic away from him by insisting on its machine model, then this would be no better than (and actually the other side of) conceiving him in base, animalistic terms. Neither conception accurately captures the human condition.

Everyone knows that an emotion is, among other things, a physical reaction of some sort, that it hinges in large measure upon body chemistry, and that it influences behavior in certain ways. Psychologists have ordinarily thought of emotional factors as providing the energizing power for behavior, adequate if not too strong, but highly disruptive if it exceeds certain bounds. An emotional animal is unpredictable, and emotional factors can disrupt cortical activity (Hebb, 1949, p. 148). The man who is subject to emotional forces is also unpredictable, or at least unreliable, even to himself. He says things and does things quite in opposition to his typical nature. He alibies, rationalizes, projects, does everything possible at conscious and unconscious levels to distort the truth. The man of intellect, on the other hand, the cool, rational being who has a grip on himself, is far more logical. He does not distort facts to suit his personal emotional needs; he does not lack the self-control to look reality in the face and speak the known truth. Such a man can be counted upon to make as little error as humanly possible in whatever task he may face. He is predictable.

Without questioning the essential truths contained within these characterizations, we must frankly recognize that they are stereotypes based upon a reification of the dialectical vs. demonstrative distinction. Emotional man is dialectical man become Sophist. He is committed to a given position and uses all the wiles of his creative intellect to make his case, or to carry on his belief in the face of contradictory facts. It is not that he loses intellect in becoming emotional, but that he foregoes the stabilizing influence of demonstrative reasoning. As William James said, "Even in soliloquizing with ourselves, we construe our feelings intellectually" (1958, p. 330). Emotional man still reasons, but in a way which commits him so completely to what he "wants" to believe (a type of final cause) that he begins to overlook other relevant data. This is exactly what Aristotle inveighed against in first making the distinction in the ways we reason. Hauser has accurately captured this point in noting that the Romantic in history, though he is often concerned with introspective oppositions, behaves more sophistically than dialectically (1951, III, p. 181). Romanticism, full of emotional zeal, is prone to overlook the possibility of alternatives (objectivity) because of its great commitment. Emotional man is man so desirous of making a predetermined case (according to a belief "for the sake of which" he lives) that he would choke on reality before acknowledging the truth of things. Of course, there are all levels of emotional behavior, but the general pattern is the same and easily recognized.

Now, the other side of this is that an emotional man who also happens to be correct can carry on zealously in the face of much opposition to make a contribution he might otherwise have given up on. One is not either-or in these matters, and it is probably most correct to state that man in every situation in which he finds himself is drawing upon his emotions for strength, or striving to ignore their frightening import or their biasing nature, but in any case he is best described in dialectical terms. Langer (1964) has made the interesting case for emotions serving as heuristic devices, analogous to the role of language discussed above. Emotions provide meanings by cultivating a form of rapport among peoples which is preliminary to communication, and therefore language is dependent to a certain exent on an emotional community of human beings. The very idea of self-expression has an emotive connotation, and it has always been our belief that art capitalizes on this common bond among peoples. Art transcends cultural bias and captures the eternal human condition, as Cassirer here makes plain:

> What we feel in art is not a simple or single emotional quality. It is the dynamic process of life itself — the continuous oscillation between opposite poles, between joy and grief, hope and fear, exultation and despair. To give aesthetic form to our passions is to transform them into a free and active state. In the work of the artist the power of passion itself has been made a formative power (1944, p. 190).

Probably in no other activity is the law of contradiction proven so false as in emotional behavior. As we shall stress in Chapter XII, as a "human" being, man is simply not that logical. Anyone who has felt strongly about something knows full well that many "emotions" may be sensed from moment to moment or even at the same time. Man swallowed up by love for woman feels lust and tenderness, jealousy and hostility, toward her, all in one fleeting instant as she strolls by on the arm of another man. The cool, dispassionate observer of a scientific experiment, if he long remains so dispassionate, may begin feeling more boredom and hostility than serene self-control, or some combination of them all. The diversity produced by introspection is very often a result of "emotional" self-exploration. The client in psychotherapy, for example, looks inward to find his "true self" and discovers there a number of individuals, a number of feelings all somehow intertwining about things which are often quite contradictory. "How can I both love and hate my mother so?" he asks, and it required a Freudian dialectic to make sense of such talk, for the client was not in error, his cortical circuits were not jumbled, he was speaking the emotive truth.

The tendency to speak out with precisely "what we feel," come what may, is valued in certain circles of psychology as "spontaneity," another feature of behavior often cited as peculiarly human. The human being has a spontaneous nature which, if developed properly, leads to a happy life and a true sense of self-realization. It is when people must hide behind Jungian masks in life and run away from their honest feelings that psychological maladjustment is likely to result. This is the essential message of the Rogerian school of thought, for example, in which a client in therapy is continually encouraged to examine *his* feelings, and come to the truth of *his* emotional attitude toward various aspects of his existence (Rogers, 1951). As we saw in Chapter VII, the Rogerian client *feels* rather than *thinks* his way through problems, for thinking is unfortunately taken by Rogers to be a kind of demonstrative labeling of things in either-or terms. He does not appreciate the role of dialectical *thinking* in the emotional self-searching which his clients engage in.

If we contemplate the description of emotional behavior for a moment, it soon becomes apparent that one cannot quite capture the essence of emotion without at some point sketching the social situation which prompts it. We use symbolic metaphors and stereotypes, such as "rejected lover," "carefree as a child," or "blue-Monday blues," and each of us has in mind a ready, almost artistic representation or stylization of what this particular social situation might be for us. Rather than telling how we literally feel, all we need say is that we are waiting for the birth of our first child — or our first son after several daughters — in order for another individual to understand our mood. He may not have it precisely accurate, but this is still the most succinct way we have of communicating our emotion. In fact, were we to discuss it with him, to dialectically examine how we feel in our situation, he might well help us to recognize a few nuances of feeling that we did not know we had before he came on the scene. With any luck, and a little Socratic examination, in time we can settle on a pretty fair conceptualization of how we feel. But note that in large measure this feeling-meaning is *social* rather than *physiological*.

In Chapter X we noted how the emotions of humor were communicated in the Jewish jokes through a dialectical ploy, a fact which we suggested is the reason Freud was so taken with them. We can now build on this and see how it is possible for much or all of humor to be construed in dialectical terms. There is no settled, primary and true course of events to the humorist, who delights us with his ability to do the unexpected. The unlikely or even preposterous circumstances which jokes or other humorous situations thrive on is well captured in such terms. The sudden burst of laughter in a tense situation is most easily brought on by the unexpected and hence incongruous nature of the situation. Although one need not over-generalize on the matter, it is surely a defensible first proposition to say that humor is in large part a dialectical affair.

Natural Laws vs. Social Laws in Man's Behavior

The natural science view has man responding to environmental stimulations of one sort or another on a lawful basis. It holds that these laws can be pointed to if conditions are right, and that man's behavior can be understood in terms of them, just as the behavior of any natural phenomenon can be so understood. Yet, even as we follow this prescription in the laboratory we find some interesting things taking place. Subjects from different sociocultural backgrounds respond quite differently to the same experimental procedures. This is often dismissed as due to lack of sample control, and all manner of precautions are taken to rule out such "individual differences" (discriminal constructs) in search of the "natural" laws (vehicular constructs) at play in human behavior. If he is lucky enough to have a problem suitable to animal study, the psychologist can rule out such social class or ethnic differences altogether. The question is, has he in so doing ruled out that which is human as well?

If one peruses the many psychological texts now available, he observes the striking fact that more and more of our theoretical rationales hinge upon social-psychological, economic, and cultural explanations. Think of the import of social class difference alone, on attitude studies, child-rearing practices, intelligence, achievement striving, and mental illness, to name only a few of the areas greatly indebted to socioeconomic theory. The realization is growing in psychology that it may be possible to describe man in natural science terms, yet be forced to acknowledge enough of these "non-natural" variables, such as social class, to make the picture an impossible one without a greater emphasis being placed on the latter than the former. A heart beats, and all animals can be equated in natural science terms with regard to their hearts; but the human heart and no other quickens its pace in response to the aesthetic qualities of a beautiful painting, or at a physical examination, even when it should know better, "because the doctor is going to help and not hurt."

There is the attitude held in psychology that physical laws are un-bending and never arbitrary, but that socioeconomic laws are really not immutable, could have gone another way, and therefore are not to be considered as basically scientific as the natural (physical) behaviors of man. The study of individual differences is a secondary quest, to be undertaken after the "real" controllers of the action have been fully isolated and named. Let us assume for the moment something we know is not the case: that natural lawfulness means 100 per cent determinism and that in time all of man's behavior can be completely controlled on the basis of certain naturalistic measurements. Even if this were the case, we would still face the problem of how — after all — to have him be-have. If we admit that men who are now under naturalistic influences behave differently, then we must also admit that in time we must choose from among these alternatives the one or two behaviors that we are going to allow men to emit. In other words, we are going to have to make a decision, and sadly or happily — depending on one's attitude about the dialectic — the truth is that *all decisions are at some point at least par-tially arbitrary.* One cannot escape the dialectical necessity of at some point deciding on the major premise, "All men are . . . ," and this inevitably involves us in the "criterion problem" discussed in Chapter VI. Even if it were possible to stipulate all the primary and true natural factors in man's behavior, this decision would still have to be made.

Such decisions, as we have seen, are likely to be the contingencies of class bias or other sociocultural influences, including the exaltation of scientific methods. This is one of the few clear advances the modern intellect has attained over earlier intellects, such as the Grecian; i.e., appreciation of the role of social factors in thought. It took time and the rise of natural science for man to turn to a consideration of his own nature and thus to beget a social science. He is now thinking through the implications of this study in which he is both observer and observed. This science must somehow combine the past with the future, man's history with his new directions and aspirations. Skinner has said that as science advances "it strips men of fancied achievements," as when Copernicus and Darwin altered man's role in the universe by making him just another animal on a minor planet (1957, p. 458). Yet the newer physical science, which accepts the inevitability of a certain arbitrariness in its methods, has placed man back on center stage in recognizing that he is in some measure the creator of the universe he studies. Science, like art and like man himself, is a cultural product and cannot be properly understood unless placed in historical perspective.

In his study of the universe man may take away from himself, but it is difficult to see how the product of his own intellect as embodied in his history can really do anything but add to his long list of achievements, fancied and otherwise.

When we turn to those theorists who have attempted to describe man's social behavior, it is clear that a dialectical metaconstruct has very often been at play in their thought (Becker and Barnes, 1952). Collective identities as an organism (the many in the one), the opposition of class interests, the wars which arise from national consciousness and competition between countries, all such factors are best captured in dialectical terms. Social history, like emotion, is not an either-or proposition, and the contradictions it holds are legion. The advance of society through stages has often been used in sociological theory, and Hegel helped establish here a dynamic, usually three-step tradition in which one stage is destroyed or dissolved by the increasing capabilities of the next. We do not need to review the Marxian world view, and no one would seriously question the immense impact this dialectical theory has had in the twentieth century.

Turning to social psychology, we see there also the frequent use of dialectical notions. A tension of opposition is usually postulated as facing the individual, and he must in some way decide between alternatives, make peace with his class or his group, and in the process either resolve the tension or risk expulsion, mental illness, or isolation. To live socially the human being must make certain contracts, he must bargain with his group and come to a settlement. Thus Parsons and Shils (1951) develop the idea of social dilemmas, Bales (1949) uses the term "strain," and Merton (1949) has used a concept called "dysfunction," with similar dialectical implications. Limiting his analysis to the modern big-business enterprise, Argyris (1964) has discussed the conflicts which result when the individual's needs and the organization's needs must both be met; and Levinson *et al.* (1962) have attempted to show that a lack of proper balance in the bureaucratic structure can lead to mental illness for the individual. The rubric "balance theory" has been used to describe a certain tradition of social-psychological theory typified by the work of Heider (1958).

But the most important development in balance theory has been the "cognitive dissonance" hypothesis of Festinger (1957). Considering the above trend, it is not surprising that Festinger as a social psychologist formulated this hypothesis about how individuals solve their problems. The theory is in every respect a modern manifestation of dialectic. Festinger's central notion is that an individual experiences cognitive dissonance whenever he must entertain the likelihood of two contradictory statements, behaviors, or attitudes facing him in life. Two such "elements" of experience are dissonant if, considering these two alone, *"the obverse of one element would follow from the other"* (p. 13). Some examples of dissonant relations would be contemplating or actually voting for a Republican candidate when one thinks of himself as a Democrat, eating chicken with the fingers in violation of proper etiquette, or standing in the rain without getting wet (p. 14). All manner of Aristotelian logical inconsistencies illustrate cognitive dissonance. Now, when such obverse elements of cognitive dissonance arise, the individual is supposedly motivated to reduce the inconsistency, and Festinger's broader view has many ingenious speculations as to which way this decision will go. The trouble is, whichever way it goes is often still consistent with cognitive dissonance theory, and therefore Festinger's view has come under attacks not unlike those made upon Freud. This is as it should be, of course, for both Festinger and Freud rely on dialectic. Though he does not use the phrase "tension of opposites," Festinger is clearly attempting to show how man can live within contradictions by altering reality to suit his needs.

The Human Image

If we now put all these features together, man's historical-religious identity, his active and creative intellect, his need to express the emotional significance of life in art and other symbolic forms, and his overriding social reliance on others for language, ideas, competition, and companionship in the face of existence, we fairly well summarize what most people mean by the phrase "human being." To the personality theorist, who takes great interest in these features, this is not an idle phrase. His interest is in *these* features primarily, he wishes to adapt his method of study to capture *these* data essentials, and if for any reason this proves unacceptable to the needs of the broader scientific community, in psychology or elsewhere, a very special "tension of opposites" is likely to arise. If one closely examines this opposition, he can see rather clearly and definitely the ancient problem of demonstration vs. dialectic, for human nature as viewed by the personality theorist is dialectical, in addition to being demonstrative; but science as evolved by men is founded on an anti-dialectical philosophy. Great ingenuity and understanding on both sides will be needed in bargaining for a contract in this realm of discordant and dissonant scholarly behavior.

Other Major Metaconstructs at Play in Personality Theories

We now come to several other metaconstructs which have played an important role in the fashioning of modern personality theories and images of man. The list of five or six is not to be considered exhaustive, since these are merely heuristic measures taken so that we can understand better the ramifications of various issues which arise when men begin commenting on the natures (in the sense that we know that term) of other men. The important point to remember is that the metaconstructs now to be discussed all emerged in some way from the historical dialogue of Chapter IX. Although we shall see here other threads in the image of man, the fabric itself is spun from the fundamental issue of dialectical vs. demonstrative reasoning. Take, for example, those metaconstructs which will be traced back to the causal types proposed by Aristotle. We must remind ourselves that Aristotle developed his four causes in order to elucidate the differences between the demonstrative and the dialectical reasoner. The remaining metaconstructs will also be seen to carry a strong flavor of the points which have typically been made by dialecticians since before the time of Plato.

Antecedent-Consequent, Efficient Cause, Behavior, Law, and Drive

The "antecedent-consequent" metaconstruct, to which we have already referred at various points in the book, stems directly from the Aristotelian conception of an efficient cause. The terms themselves are actually taken from logic, in which we speak about the antecedent and consequent of a hypothetical or implicative proposition of the variety: "If, then." We have already mentioned this relationship in Chapter V. But if one thinks about how *verbal* hypotheses are phrased, it is easy to see how this was gradually extended to data — as if they themselves consisted of two independent but joined elements, a cause (antecedent) and an effect (consequent).

We have referred to this theory of little pieces of fluctuating variables, all somehow regularly being attached one to another, as the "mechanistic" world view. Hence, it seems extremely natural to the experimentalist to frame his thinking by saying, "Now what are the antecedents here and what are the consequents of these factors in the behavior of that man or animal I am observing?" The antecedent is the efficient cause, the immediately preceding "push" which gets things done. Reasoning of this sort is so pervasive in psychology that we have termed it the "S-R bind" (see Chapter III). Man is now a complex combination of consequents, all tied in some way to the antecedents of a genetic or reinforcement history. The social history *created* by other men, as discussed earlier in this chapter, with all its artifacts and multiplicity of viewpoints, is considered — analogous to the Darwinian view of natural selection — as just so many chance variations which proved viable (that is, led to a "reinforcement") for some reason and hence were retained.

Two important concepts are related to, if not actually developed from, the antecedent-consequent metaconstruct. The first is the idea of "scientific law." When the natural sciences rejected final and formal causes in favor of material and efficient causes, the belief in regularities to be identified by scientific observation went very nicely with the concept of a lawfulness in nature, which is itself a time-bound succession of antecedent and consequent events—or can be so conceived. As we may recall from Chapter V, the mechanical, cause-effect world view of Laplace was based on a faith in 100 per cent determinism, which is another way of saying 100 per cent lawfulness. Without the notion of cause-to-effect, which is the synonym for this metaconstruct, there would be no need to think of lawful regularities. As we have seen thus far in our consideration of determinism, lawfulness is so much a part of our thinking that it almost seems a contradiction in terms to think of both lawfulness and anything less than a hard determinism. Yet, there is no real contradiction here because any regularity in events — whether subject to arbitrary sources of influence or not — might be captured in some lawful way by an observer, and thus improve his chances of predicting above the chance level, as long as there is a pattern in the arbitrary choices made. The issue is not whether the observational data are completely determined, but whether such arbitrary actions as are taking place may be patterned and therefore predicted with some degree of success.

The second concept widely used in psychology which stems from our reliance upon an antecedent-consequent metaconstruct is the notion of a "drive" which impels the organism's behavior. Psychology borrowed this concept from the natural sciences, which use the theoretical maneuver of explaining how things move by showing how energies are transformed (conservation of energy) and in the process bring about some cause-effect sequence of events (see Chapters VIII and X). What moves the organism? Why, some form of drive or a physical something embodying energy expenditure, much like the energy exchanges of inanimate particles which find their way about in the universe. The concept of rein-

376 · A Philosophy of Science for Personality Theory

forcement now completes the picture, for, coming as it supposedly does later in the antecedent-consequent sequence, it serves as the strengthening agent (literally "reinforcer") of the bond between the two elements. And, some say, its power to unite comes from drive reduction, which is analogous to the energy exchanges taking place according to the law of energy conservation. After a great deal of debate over how many or which drives must be reduced to effect a reinforcement, many psychologists have now given up this argument. It is not uncommon today to hear it said that whatever strengthens this bond is a reinforcer, as long as it can be shown empirically that a strengthening has taken place (an empirical law of effect).

The tie between drives and the antecedent-consequent metaconstruct, and the important relation of the latter to the conceptualization of "behavior," is nowhere better exemplified than in the post-World War II tendency of psychologists to substitute other kinds of drives for the physically based drives used before the war. Earlier, it was some physically based substrate, such as the ingestion of food at the time of or shortly after responding which supposedly united the S-R bond. All higher-order motivations were to be reduced to some such Helmholtzian-Wundtian, lower-level energy exchange. More recently, the range of the drive construct has been extended, so that it has become possible to think of its energy as being expended and reinforcements ensuing from the activities of behaving, seeing, and doing themselves, such as exploring one's environment out of curiosity. The bonding now takes place *not* as a form of reinforcement secondary to the more basic physico-chemical energy exchange, but as a direct result of behavioral activity as such.

Koch has commented on this anachronistic theoretical perseveration among psychologists as follows: "One can only wince at the current tendency to talk about such things as 'curiosity drives,' 'exploratory drives,' 'sensory drives,' 'perceptual drives,' etc. as if the 'activities' which are held to 'satisfy' each of these 'drives' (if indeed they are distinct) were just so much undifferentiated neutral pap that came by the yard" (1961, p. 633). Though many call for its discontinuance, it is difficult to see how the drive concept can be dropped or even weakened until such time as the other Aristotelian causes are seen to move organisms. Efficient-cause elements, the antecedents and consequents, must after all be hooked up in some fashion so that behavior comes about in its patterned, lawful way. What other way is there to explain this regularity besides postulating a drive or energy to bring about a cause-effect sequence? Since there is no self-direction issuing from the organism under observation, how else can we think of its behavior but as "due to" one of several drives being reduced, satisfied, or dissipated? This is a problem born of the behavioristic tactic which stretches the natural science view to cover man.

Prototypes, Formal Causes, Hierarchies, and Symbols

Our next metaconstruct, "prototype," which dates from early Greek thought, was embodied in the Platonic concept of a world of being, became the historically important issue of universals in thought, and was included among the Aristotelian causes as a way of explaining something by showing the formal properties it shared with other things. Is the phenomenon before one's eyes a reflection of the more general class of things like it, which ties together its essentials? If so, then we are using a formal cause in explaining what we know about this phenomenon and all others like it by elucidating their common properties. We are framing a prototype or general case in order to understand the particular better. Some such motive is surely involved with the process of abstraction itself — a need to conceptualize common properties in order to bring together constructs and thereby manipulate diverse "things" through a smaller number of descriptive concepts. Indeed, the heuristic device we are now using, framing metaconstructs in personality theory, is just such a procedure. This is a preliminary step in meeting the demands of objectivity.

As we leave out details in order to classify, we must inevitably begin thinking and communicating at different levels of discourse. Thus, prototypical usages presume some form of *hierarchy*, since something is believed to have come before, as in the knowledge Plato believed man possessed from the Golden past, however imperfectly; or, in abstracting the essential details of objects observed we must eventually postulate a ladder of abstraction from lower to higher which explains the relationship among the various abstractions. Hence, a hierarchical concept is immediately suggested when one thinks of the formal properties of particulars, each of which belongs to a certain class of now more abstract, universal forms.

In addition to its general importance to all theorizing as an abstract enterprise, the prototype metaconstruct has had many other very important applications in personality study. Freud's use of the antecedent-consequent metaconstruct was almost always combined uniquely with a prototype interpretation. Everything which has happened earlier (antecedent) to a person comes someday to color his present pattern of behavior (consequent) in a way reminiscent of this earlier event (prototype). Thus, a grown man's personality takes on oral or anal characteristics, depending upon just when certain things happened to him as a child, determining his level of partial fixation in a prototype period of some sort. The dream symbol is an excellent example of prototype application, for it presumably recreates, re-enacts or expresses some preoccupation or problem in a stylized way. The symbol is analogous to the item or area of concern, so that all erect structures in the dream are taken as phallic symbols, for example. Universal symbolism presumes some form of prototype classification. Freud used prototype explanations almost routinely, so that sucking mother's milk is the prototype for introjection, birth anxiety is the prototype for all later anxieties, and the prototype for the Oedipal conflict is man's original attempt to form a society in the primal horde, including the killing off of the patriarch.

Probably the most widely recognized prototype concept in psychology is Jung's "archetype," which is virtually identical to the concept used by Plato, as Jung was apparently often reminded (see his letter, pp. 342–343). Jung had this to say of dreams, phantasies, visions, legends, myths, religions, fairy tales, and even manic ideas:

> Over the whole of this psychic realm there reign certain motifs, certain typical figures which we can follow far back into history, and even into prehistory, and which may therefore legitimately be described as "archetypes." They seem to me to be built into the very structure of man's unconscious, for in no other way can I explain why it is that they occur universally and in identical form, whether the redeemer-figure be a fish, a hare, a lamb, a snake, or a human being (1954, p. 124).

Thus, as a neo-Platonist Jung tells us: "a child is not born *tabula rasa,* as one assumes. The child is born as a high complexity, with existing determinants that never waver through the whole life and that give the child his character" (Evans, 1964, p. 34).

How might these archetypal ideas come to influence us as we study their meaning? Are they programmed ideas, stamped on our intellects by nature to direct us in a demonstrative fashion? *Not at all.* The point of a formal examination is that one must look at all sides in order to grasp the essential universal. A "redeemer-figure" demands some awareness on our part of what redemption means and why anyone should have need for the redeemer. Archetypes are meaningful and significant, Jung is saying, because through an examination of their manifestation in dreams and myths we come to understand better some of the most vital aspects of life. We come to this understanding through *our* introspective efforts, and this is not an either-or matter, evolving new meanings from older meanings. Take, for example, Jung's testimony on how he came to grasp what was for him the most true conception of God through introspective analysis. By contemplating the archetype which embodies the supreme-being figure, Jung says, he finally realized that God had his darker sides: "God is not human, I thought; that is His greatness, that nothing human impinges on Him. He is kind and terrible — both at once — and is therefore a great peril from which everyone naturally tries to save himself" (1963, p. 55). Neither Gods nor men can be accurately captured through a one-sided primary and true statement that "All . . . are. . . ." A force for good implies a force for evil. Archetypes are the means, therefore, by which we can come to understand "essences," the formal qualities of things. This is the Jungian view and it is entirely Platonic.

In his literary work, *Anatomy of Criticism* (1957), Northrop Frye grasps this Jungian insight and makes use of it in the formal analysis of literature, or what he calls "archetypal criticism." In the following quote Frye beautifully shows how archetypal images can exert a dialectical influence on the reader of poetry:

> The conception of a garden develops the conception "weed," and building a sheepfold makes the wolf a greater enemy. Poetry in its social or archetypal aspect, therefore, not only tries to illustrate the fulfilment of desire, but to define the obstacles to it. Ritual is not only a recurrent act, but an act expressive of a dialectic of desire and repugnance: desire for fertility or victory, repugnance to drought or to enemies. We have rituals of social integration, and we have rituals of expulsion, execution, and punishment. In dream there is a parallel dialectic, as there is both the wish-fulfilment dream and the anxiety or nightmare dream of repugnance (p. 106).

There are, of course, many other instances of prototype theorizing which might be mentioned. Alfred Adler's birth order views rely on this metaconstruct, as when the baby of the family continues this personality pattern as an adult (Ansbacher and Ansbacher, 1956). Sheldon's constitutional psychology, which sees behavior and personality as prearranged by nature's somatotyping, is also heavily indebted to the prototype metaconstruct (Sheldon, Stevens, and Tucker, 1940). R. B. Cattell's belief that a universal index of central and all-pervasive factors, much like the natural scientist's chart of basic elements, can be determined through factor analysis rests ultimately on a prototype use of theory (1950). George Kelly's "personal constructs," which people acquire and adapt to meet the upcoming and unexpected in life, are essentially tentative prototypes used to order and to predict the turn of events (1955). And finally, we contend that Gordon Allport's use of "functional autonomy" draws from a prototype rationale (1937). Allport's aim in proposing this construct was to go beyond antecedent-consequent drive-reduction theory and assert that some behaviors might function in their own right, so to speak. Though a man may have begun going to sea in order to catch fish to eat (reinforcers), in time the sea-going man may acquire a love for the sea quite independent of this food-getting motive. His earlier behavior of sailing about in ships and possibly even of fishing becomes a prototype for the later activity, which he might now be doing for the simple joy of the activity itself. The earlier drive reduction may have fixed a stylistic pattern, but the present activity is now functionally independent of these drives and is not best understood as an extension of them.

Stereotypes vs. Theorotypes • There is a special case of the prototype metaconstruct which, although it is extremely important in personality theorizing, rarely gets the emphasis it deserves. Usually the influence which emanates from this form of prototype maneuver is very subtle and informal, so that it is likely to be overlooked. We refer to the unnamed influence of stereotypes. In 1922, Walter Lippmann called attention to the use of stereotypes in his book, *Public Opinion* (1946). Analogizing from the printer's page layout, which is often blocked out using routine stories or advertisements, so that it has a certain prearranged form even before the major story of the day is slipped in, Lippmann observed that people carry about in their mind's eye various stereotypes which frame their attitudes toward public issues, or toward other people. Following this observation, psychologists spent considerable time studying the ways stereotypes influence attitudes and vice versa. These studies, particularly the "authoritarian personality" researches following World War II (Adorno, Frenkel-Brunswik, Levinson, and Sanford, 1950), usually presented evidence that stereotyping was somehow tied to rigidity, maladjustment, and even psychosis, so that in general there is a negative connotation associated with the term. Stereotypes include such things as "the stupid and shiftless Negro," "the scheming and predatory Jew," "the literal-minded and authoritarian Catholic," and so on. Yet the fact is, and Lippmann was quite sensitive to the truth of this, all men must process their impressions through what Kelly (1955) would call "personal constructs," hence each must inevitably resort to stereotyping of one sort or another to order his intellect. This Kantian insight is the natural outcome of our abstracting processes. Personality theorists have often relied on stereotypes to convey their impressions and to make their thinking clear.

Take, for example, Hermann Rorschach's personality characterization of subjects who report inkblot responses which are uninspired and routine, but rigidly precise and accurate (the D response). These individuals, Rorschach said, are not unlike "certain 'schoolmaster' and bureaucratic types, where daily exercise supports and emphasizes the attitude. Here the precision of self-control and the pride in consistency gives rise to ideas of superiority, overcompensating the feelings of insufficiency in the individual" (1942, p. 58). Anyone who has had to deal with a testy bureaucratic clerk, or a smug third-grade teacher can immediately understand what Rorschach is trying to communicate here. Of course, the testy and the smug individuals may be greatly outnumbered by the many helpful clerks and unassuming teachers we have known. But we are dealing here with a prototype use of an abstraction which tries to capture a certain interpersonal relation; and a stereotype serves quite well in this case as a *symbol* of the meaning we are trying to communicate. Freud's concept of the censor also seems to have been patterned on the stereotyped image of the rigid border guard, who held back (repressed) certain items from crossing the border and leaving his region. That Freud had a fairly common stereotype in mind is clear in his statement that a "Russian censorship" takes place in mental disorder; it is for this reason that the psychotic's language seems so meaningless, because words are blocked at the border of consciousness and therefore we do not hear the full story in communicating with them (1954, p. 240).

Of course, it would be possible to think of *all* attempts to classify personality into formal unities as stereotypes, so that Freud's "oral" and "anal" types, or Fromm's "marketing personality" (Fromm, 1941), Sheldon's "somatotypes" (Sheldon *et al.*, 1940), and indeed the "authoritarian personality" itself (Adorno *et al.*, 1950), might all come under this rubric. Considering the pejorative connotation the term has acquired, we do not think it would be wise to do this. At the same time, it seems important to capture the obvious truth that personality theorists order their perceptions of others in helpful if stylized ways. We therefore propose that the term *theorotype* be used to capture this more sophisticated application of a formal-cause notion. Theorotypes are presumably applied with more discretion than stereotypes, and only after a proper observation and weighing of all facts. They would be more flexible, more readily given up, and in the final analysis taken not as reified entities but as heuristic devices. They issue from the perceiver's intellect, *not* from the "true" characteristics of the person observed. In the Cassirer sense, they symbolize our intended meaning rather than label some palpable reality. Theorotypes may be used like stereotypes, but they would then lose their great usefulness and become labels rather than symbols. What we hope to do in personality study is add to and refine our symbols rather than continue drearily hanging the same old labels on people.

Growth, Advancement, Development, and Final Causes

The next important metaconstruct is "growth," which follows from what Aristotle termed a final-cause explanation. If we think of an organism as orienting its behavior in terms of goals, rather than being driven blindly by drives, then we leave open the possibility that the organism can select one goal rather than another. Psychologists who rely exclusively on efficient causation must trace this selection of alternatives to some form of positive reinforcement determining the decision, no matter how subtle and far-removed its influence may be. If a man chooses to give up his life in an act of bravery, the efficient-cause analysis must trace this act back to a "positive" reinforcement working usually in a "secondary" way. Sometimes there is a bit of undeclared dialectic tossed in, like the man who would rather avoid the negative reinforcement of being labeled a coward. Better to die with the positive reinforcement of knowing one is a hero than to live in the recognition that one is a coward. But what if a man is in no danger of being called a coward, yet still does something we might term an act of bravery, such as standing up for an unpopular view in the face of group pressure and social ostracism? In this case too, the efficient cause must be traced back, stepwise down the preceding antecedents, until we can say that the man who behaves this way learned to do this because of some positive reinforcement in the past. As we noted in Chapter VIII, the S-R conceptualization handles all cases through this maneuver, for if a man acted with cowardice and conformed to the group pressure, we could easily find some positive reinforcement in the *present* (such as avoiding loneliness) or learned in the past (such as a parent who taught that everyone must compromise sometime) to explain this behavior.

Those who are willing to describe man in final- as well as formal- and efficient-cause terms can see in an act of bravery the ethical intent of "how one ought to behave." This is a goal in the future, not yet realized, or a principle "for the sake of which" present behavior *may be* self-directed (learned in the past, to be sure, but adhered to or not); it says nothing about what *is*. The brave man is motivated not only out of past experience, but also out of future goals (principles), and through his mental evaluation of the "right, good, and proper" way to behave; quite by style of living he chooses *certain* goals rather than others to shoot for. All such goals have been learned, gleaned from past experience (to do what is right, as mother taught, or to sometimes compromise, also as mother taught). One behaves "bravely" because that is the way one should or ought, hence *must* behave, out of one's personally decided upon sense of duty. In Chapter VI we observed that this ethical view was based upon an intrinsic rather than an instrumental interpretation of value. Reinforcement interpretations are based upon the instrumental view.

Yet positive reinforcements really do not help us explain why one man acts bravely and another cowardly, since both individuals presumably seek a "positive" state of affairs. We must always invoke other theoretical terms and propositions which clarify the nature of *what* this positiveness is; and there lies the rub, for its meaning changes dramatically from one instance to another. Once it is merely food gratification, another time it is the status drive to be satisfied, yet another time, the gratification of sweet revenge, and so on. All this amounts to is beginning with a proto-type presumption that "whatever" we can locate in the history of the organism that relates in some plausible way to the present behavior must be the positive reinforcer. Thus a lower-level (discriminal) theory of some sort must be brought in to explain those remarkable twists of in-strumentally motivated behavior in which people seem quite willing to face unequivocally negative reinforcements.

It is proper to begin a consideration of the growth metaconstruct with what is actually an ethical discussion, for as we recall from our discussions of values in Chapters V and VIII, historically, final causes and ethical issues have been considered together. If one begins with a goal concept, then it seems only the greatest common sense to ask, "Is it a worthwhile goal?" Those who have an ethical bent are naturally attracted to the growth metaconstruct; for example, it is no accident that Carl Rogers has the following "growth principle" as one of the tenets of his theory of personality and behavior: *"The organism has one basic tendency and striving — to actualize, maintain, and enhance the experienc-*

ing organism" (1951, p. 487). The behaving organism seeks to actualize its potentials or, in more dialectical terms, to realize the possibility of things — to achieve the "ought" and improve its existence. This belief in a growing, expanding, directional tendency is not limited to individual organisms, of course. We have seen in Chapter VIII how Skinner reflects the final-cause theory that all modern scientists hold to, which is contrary in spirit to the Grecian view that man had descended from a golden past. Today we accept without question the view that man is progressing through science, which is believed pointed toward a golden future.

The growth metaconstruct has an affinity for the hierarchical arrangement of abstracts or behaviors, just as the prototype metaconstruct was seen to have. Plato's realm of being was a hierarchy of mental steps or stages, each leading to the ultimate goal of "truth"; the philosopher was admonished to seek this goal, to grasp the prototype by degrees as he developed his powers of dialectical reasoning. All subsequent theories of advance, progress, or growth have used a similar type of hierarchical arrangement of things — as in the "stages" of mankind's evolution to higher forms, the "ladder" of success, and so on. Of course, there are those who make use of a hierarchical concept without implying any direction to the organization of behavior, without suggesting the *necessary* concomitant of growth. At least, they try to do this. Take, for example, Dollard and Miller's use of "hierarchy of response," which is a ranking of responses from the one least likely to be made by an organism to the one most likely to occur when the proper stimulus is presented (1950, p. 36). According to their strict view, we are all born with a limited innate hierarchy of this type and, through learning, acquire several "resultant" hierarchies over the years, any of which — when it is frozen momentarily in place — may be considered an "initial" hierarchy. This is what might be termed a demonstrative application of the hierarchy concept; as it stands there is no suggestion that the most probable response is necessarily any better or higher or more "self-realized" than the lower. Such an evaluation would presumably go beyond the bounds of the scientific theory Dollard and Miller espouse.

The trouble is — and it is no fault of their own — these psychologists cannot avoid the "growth" implication of their hierarchies. In trying honestly to capture the human social animal, Dollard and Miller must admit that an "age grading" (p. 171) takes place, so that giggling in church, for example, at one level may be tolerated as childish, while at another it is quite inappropriate and possibly even an indication of severe maladjustment. But if this hierarchy is not arrayed by circumstance in each individual's life, then there is an overriding directional influence suggested. Someone, some force, some influence has inveighed against or shown the way, so that man can scratch where he pleases in private, but must bear up under certain annoyances when in the company of others. Unless one makes the assumption that such patterned hierarchies grow by chance occurrences in a world of nothing but efficient causes, then he *must* consider the likelihood of a final cause lurking somewhere in his theoretical position. Simply assigning the weight of explanation to the social environment by saying that man "learned" this or that does not answer the question. The social environment or culture implies by definition man's influence on himself, for man is men and vice versa; man's nature is his history. Animals scratch where and when they please, and there are no "chance" hierarchies of an ethical or aesthetic variety emerging in their behavior. There are no data of this sort *in* physical nature, which makes it easily conceptualized in efficient-cause terms. But there *are* such features in man's behavior, and for this reason we cannot continue talking as if there were no need for final-cause analyses in human behavior.

The reference to age grading reminds us that much of psychology is dependent upon some such growth notion, for we see the adult as a product of various stages of development, as having moved through infancy and childhood to "adulthood." These stages imply more than mere physical growth, as a tree might grow. We mean here quite literally a type of advance, a movement toward maturity, and at every point along the way there are numerous value judgments of the "ought" variety suggested, which every mother who follows the latest fad in child-rearing practices surely knows. Turning to some specific personality theories, we might note that Freud, Sullivan (1953), and to a lesser extent Jung, all make some use of developmental stages. Freudian psychology has at times been typified as very much biased in the direction of a "Victorian" maturity. Spontaneity and childlike innocence are taken by many in the Freudian tradition as something akin to fixations. Adler's "level of aspiration" concept is of course clearly in the growth tradition, for it suggests that man by his very nature has a tendency to improve on past performance (Ansbacher and Ansbacher, 1956). Horney's "real self" is based upon a growth principle, suggesting as it does that honest and sincere advance can be made in the personality if the individual can avoid the crippling effects of neurotic striving for superiority (1950). Rank's concept of "will" is a similar growth notion, at least when used in the sense of one's "positive" will to seek his true identity and to express his personal potential (1945).

In the more clearly gestalt tradition, Rogers (1951), Kelly (1955), and especially Maslow (1954) have all phrased their comments on man in terms of his potential for self-direction and growth. Man, on this view, is basically capable of making his own decisions and has the ability to make changes for the better if certain preconditions are laid down for this development. Abraham H. Maslow in particular has painted the picture of man as motivated by certain layers of needs, in hierarchical fashion. The order of these needs from most to least potent is as follows: physiological needs, such as hunger, are most basic; then come the needs for safety, belongingness, love, esteem, self-actualization, knowledge, and finally, beauty. Man will develop, and will ascend this hierarchy of needs, given the proper physical and social environment, even though he often falls short of reaching the apex. But one cannot look at the basest of needs and speak for *all* mankind from such a restricted view.

Maslow uses "growth" in a conventionally positive sense and, in fact, whenever we use terms such as "final causes," or other growth concepts which imply a striving for the "better" or "hoped for" ends of life, a tacit assumption is made that these ends are always the *conventionally good* ones. This need not be the case, of course. Final causes, and with them the ends which they nurture, are themselves framed by a *set of values*. To say that a man strives for some goal, projects an aspiration, or is working to achieve something he personally desires, is not to say that everyone who examined his motivation would agree on the goodness of this end. Murray and Kluckhohn (1953) recognized this when they altered the meaning of Freud's ego-ideal by taking it out of the super-ego sphere (conventional morality of the larger culture) and making it an ego image which portrays the person "at his future best," realizing all of his ambitions (p. 40). Murray and Kluckhohn then go on to note that "Ego ideals run all the way from the Master Criminal to the Serene Sage" (p. 40). In other words, to know what a personal advance *means* to the individual, we must have some knowledge of his value system. Some young men actually do strive to become anti-social heroes, to make the "most wanted criminal" list, or the like. Adler was also cognizant of this tendency for certain (often unconscious) drives of individuals for superiority to be entirely immoral in terms of the broader morality of the group (Ansbacher and Ansbacher, 1956).

If more psychologists were aware of this fact there might be less reluctance to admit that we do indeed utilize final-cause concepts in psychology. Two major misunderstandings arise whenever one begins speaking of "final causes" in theorizing, and both stem from the fact that ethical thinkers and theologians have made such extensive use of this construct. First of all, it is assumed that a final cause *must* be tied to a deity concept, a supreme intelligence which has in mind what man ought to be doing with his life. At the very least, it is assumed that a final cause *must* relate to some "goody-goody" intention which man is said to seek on the basis of conventional morality. The more rigorous scientific theorist winces at such indirect theological attempts to theorize about man, and, we would argue, with good reason. The second misunderstanding that arises is due to a technical confusion over what is meant by a final cause, brought on by the wedding of efficient and final causes. Due to theological arguments in times past, a confusion has arisen between final causes (God's intentions), and the end state of a succession of immutably determined efficient causes, each attached to its successor.

Thus, looking backward in time, we might argue, with St. Thomas Aquinas and others, that "every 'effect' has an efficient cause." If there are efficient causes stretching back in time, then it follows that at some point, some *thing* gave the first cause, or more properly, the first *impetus* to the fabric of movement we have called efficient causation. This Prime Mover, theologians have argued, must have been God. Now, regardless what one thinks of this argument — based on *efficient* causation — the point is that something akin to it has been used as a projection into the future, and it is this latter confounding of a final (directional) cause with an efficient cause which has led to our current misunderstanding of the nature of final causes.

Many psychologists have it in mind that a final cause is the "last efficient cause," somewhere in the future, directing or pulling us down a predetermined road of efficient cause-to-effect. This attitude originated in the treatment Aristotle afforded the question, essentially, "how do we know a *truly* final cause?" In answering this question, he was forced to bring in the matter of values. Recognizing first of all that natural events continually change over time, Aristotle observes: "For if a thing undergoes a continuous change and there is a stage which is last, this stage is the end or 'that for the sake of which' " (1952, p. 270). How does one assess what is last? Aristotle goes on to note that: "not every stage that is last claims to be an end, but only that which is best" (p. 270). This is the root source of teleologies, as being tied to the "best" progress of matter. What this amounts to is that, since we must judge an end state (when is a product truly "finished"?), we must also judge the *value* of that product. We must exercise intelligence. Plato would have seen the "end" as the realm of being. As we noted in Chapters V and VIII, a final-cause usage automatically imputes *intelligence* (evaluation, judgment) to some aspect of the data being described, or to its presumed creator.

Now, the way theologians were later to develop this view, the Prime Mover was a "best" or "good" influence at the outset of time; and, off in the future, the *intentions* of this Prime Mover had it in mind where matter (including man) was to go for its own good, a "best" end state. As we noted in Chapter VIII, the inexorable direction that was therefore assumed in the world of physical matter is due to *this* form of "deity teleology." Newton's hard determinism was just another way of expressing his theological convictions (see Chapter VIII, p. 229). A final cause or an end state toward which a deity is casting the fabric of movement (efficient cause-to-effect) for its own good would most surely be *in effect* a kind of "last efficient cause." It would be the last act in man's history, and presumably, since God knows what is "best," it would be a "good" act. This is what most psychologists think of when one speaks of final cause or teleology.

However, one is *not* committed to this interpretation if he chooses to apply final causes to the individual man. In this sense, we would have a "human teleology" rather than a deity teleology. We would argue that a man *does* have an active, evaluative mentality which permits him to judge an end for the sake of a set of values. *Our* values may not jibe with *his* values, but as long as he can aspire to his "end," he is most assuredly being directed by a final cause "out of the future." But this future is not inexorable. In judging what is "best" man has had to begin with certain major premises which framed the beginnings of his judgment process. We might think of these as *meanings* asserted in the very act of conceptualization (see Chapters II and III), and usually referred to as "assumptions."

In time, these assumptions might well change, altering any given man's value system and concomitantly altering the course of *his* unique fabric of movement (the efficient causes occurring in his behavior). This is what we mean by a self-reflexive intellect in the human being. There is absolutely no reason we cannot make use of the Aristotelian final cause in this manner, even though Aristotle did not address himself to the question "how do psychological factors influence man's selection of his major premises?" Freud taught us something of this, and we now must carry on and make our theories clearer regarding man's (in this sense) final-cause intellect. The historical tie of final causation to ethical, aesthetic, and theological theories makes it extremely difficult to get a fair hearing in the natural and social sciences. It is, of course, only the minimum courtesy to hear out those who choose to use final-cause constructs, for they may not be nearly so religiously "lily white" or moralistic *in their intentions* as was originally supposed.

Purity and the Questioning of Premises or Constructs

We may recall at this point that the dialectician has typically been a questioner, a doubter, a critic of those premises taken by the demonstrative reasoner as true and primary items of knowledge. Dialecticians have often raised more questions than they can answer. Out of this tradition has grown a certain doubt as to the validity of conceptualization *per se,* so that there has been, since at least the nineteenth century, a tendency among certain critics of science and philosophical positions to claim that to label an item of knowledge, by that very act, chokes off some of the true nature of the item in question. To abstract is to leave out details (see Chapter II), and, though this leads to objective generalization, it also calls for a certain disregard for what another person might take to be "important details." These meaningful details are often considered more important than the resulting generalization, more "true to life" than what can be said from the refined abstraction of conceptualization. Also, when we generalize — extend our verbal constructs — from one phenomenon to another, we run the risk of distorting the newer phenomenon by forcing it into the constructs of the older. Labels are sometimes reified to make spontaneous observations act as we want to see them act; a simple case of this is the functioning of stereotypes. All such criticisms as these are the result of what we might term the "purity" metaconstruct, which is a long-standing reaction to the fixing of abstractions in formulating bodies of knowledge.

Although the purity metaconstruct is essentially a dialectical criticism, born probably in Plato's call for the application of intellect to sensation before truth could be arrived at, this does not mean that dialecticians themselves have not been accused of falling into the trap of believing their own arbitrarily formed premises to be primary and true. Thus, Hegel wrote his *Logic* in reaction to the supposedly false type of abstraction which Aristotle used in his logic. Rather than merely "concocting" his logic, said Hegel, he would prove it an historical truth that there was an Absolute's reasoning manifesting itself dialectically over the ages. Historical truth was for him a kind of "operational definition." Yet Kierkegaard attacked Hegel for merely substituting one grand abstraction of "Absolute" for the equally arbitrary but more numerous abstractions proposed by Aristotle. Hegel was essentially accused of falling in love with his own cogitations and therefore believing that they were true for all men and all times. And Hegel was obviously sensitive to this criticism, as the following defense of his dialectical method clearly indicates:

> this dialectic is not an activity of subjective thinking applied to some matter externally, but is rather the matter's very soul putting forth its branches and fruit organically. . . . To consider a thing rationally means not to bring reason to bear on the object from the outside and so to tamper with it, but to find that the object is rational on its own account; here it is mind in its freedom, the culmination of self-conscious reason, which gives itself actuality and engenders itself as an existing world. The sole task of philosophic science is to bring into consciousness this proper work of the reason of the thing itself (1952, pp. 19–20).

The phrase, "to bring reason to bear on the object from the outside and so to tamper with it" is a fair definition of the purity criticism, and this is precisely what Kierkegaard accused Hegel of doing, phrasing it succinctly in the well-known passage from his journals: "If he [Hegel] had written his whole *Logic* and in the Preface had disclosed the fact that it was merely a thought-experiment (in which, however, at many points he had shirked something), he would have been the greatest thinker that has ever lived. Now he is comic" (Lowrie, 1961, p. 95). Kierkegaard accepted the validity of the dialectic, but spoke of it as a purely subjective, "qualitative dialectic" which each man uses in searching his own psyche to find the unpredictable, unique meanings of his personal introspective world (Aiken, 1956, p. 227). We see here the natural affinity the dialectic has for multiplicity, or, in other terms, for *subjectivity* in viewpoint. Through introspective, dialectical self-examination, we can find ourselves as no man can know us, completely subjectively and completely "free" of those designations which other people or institutions are only too willing to place on us. This is what Kierkegaard had in mind, and it is the kind of freedom which is basic in those who reject the utopian life of Skinner's *Walden Two* (1948). It is not political but *conceptual* freedom they seek; freedom from being "what you say I am, if what you say does not meet my self-examination."

This tendency to reject the conceptualizations of others has taken some extreme forms, and has often been phrased in terms such as "intellect" vs. "emotion." The cold, unfeeling language of the intellect is opposed to the warm, genuine language of the emotions. Mystics, many artists, and certain philosophers have framed views of this sort. For example, the philosophy of Henri Bergson regards all abstract conceptualizations as a distortion or falsification of reality, and turns instead to a reliance upon inarticulate feelings and intuition for guidance (Langer, 1964, p. 62). The "purity" metaconstruct has appeared in various guises within psychology. When William James observed "in every concrete individual, there is a uniqueness that defies all formulation" he was reflecting its influence (1911, p. 109). Jung phrased it another way: "What we are to our inward vision, and what man appears to be *sub specie aeternitatis,* can only be expressed by way of myth. Myth is more individual and expresses life more precisely than does science. Science works with concepts of averages which are far too general to do justice to the subjective variety of an individual life" (1963, p. 3).

One of the most important proponents of the purity metaconstruct in psychology has been Carl Rogers, whose entire view has been greatly influenced by it (see Chapter VII). For Rogers, man is potentially capable of growing if he is left unmolested by others' needs to press him into a preconceived pattern. As he says, "I find that when clients are free to be any way they wish, they tend to resent and to question the tendency of the organization, the college or the culture to mould them to any given form" (1961, p. 169). What happens, says Rogers, is that when we press others into our preconceived notions we lose that spontaneity of interpersonal relations so essential to the growth of both ourselves and others to whom we relate — and they may similarly be pressing us into their preconceived molds. Hence, we begin to lose interpersonal contact as "persons" and begin treating one another as "objects," for that is all a label of this sort is, the preliminary step to a routine handling. We do not come to know the "real person" when we begin by labeling; we are maneuvering for advantage and the desire to get things over with. In therapy this is crucial, for: "The more the therapist perceives the client as a person rather than as an object, the more the client will come to perceive himself as a person rather than an object" (p. 207). Both Jung and Rank had made similar points, by reacting to the highly doctrinaire theories of personality with which Freud had infused his psychotherapy; Rank would have agreed entirely with Jung, who once said that the therapist "should remember that the patient is there to be treated and not to verify a theory" (1954, p. 115). Finally, Rogers is of the view that the only learning which can significantly influence one's behavior is the learning he has discovered himself, through his own efforts. He takes here the typical dialectical position that each person must find his own way, though another may help by making circumstances appropriate for self-study. But ultimately, knowledge is subjective, in the sense that it is personal. Rogers has even drawn parallels between his position and Kierkegaard's on this matter of personal knowledge (Rogers, 1961, p. 276).

Views of this general type, including those of Kierkegaard, are frequently lumped under the rubric "existentialist," and the philosophy of existentialism is in large measure a reactionary criticism, voiced against the self-satisfied certainty of modern demonstrative science. Take, for example, the following account of (existentialist) daseinsanalysis by Boss:

> It is fortunate that Daseinsanalytic thinking does not require us to accept a ready-made conceptual framework and to learn it by heart. On the contrary, analysis of *Dasein* [translated "being there," or luminating the nature of the human being] urges all those who deal with human beings to start seeing and thinking from the beginning, so that they can remain with what they immediately perceive and do not get lost in "scientific" abstractions, derivations, explanations, and calculations estranged from the immediate reality of the given phenomena. It is of paramount importance to realize from the start that *the fundamental difference which separates the natural sciences from the Daseinsanalytic or existential science of man is to be found right here* (1963, pp. 29–30).

This criticism goes beyond the point we have made — i.e., that psychological scientists are prone to confuse methodological with theoretical constructs, hence to cast man in needlessly mechanistic terms. Boss is extending this to say that scientists literally blind themselves to the potentials of data by getting so caught up in their own preconceived abstractions that they overlook the most elemental of notions. As he observes: "Daseinsanalysis starts with the observation of facts so simple that many contemporary philosophers and psychologists, accustomed to complicated speculations, have a hard time grasping them" (p. 31). This is the dialectician's historic distrust of settled-upon abstractions. By pressing for such a close tie to only the "observable facts" psychology has invited a reaction of this sort, the rejection and subtle ridicule of science itself as a rote labeling process flying in the face of introspectively simple and humanistically true but extraspectively undefinable facts of existence.

As noted in Chapter VIII, the very act of putting an introspective theoretical construct into operational terms robs it of much impact and meaning, for we lose that sense of immediacy and self-expressiveness that we get when we speak about our private lives. Empirical, scientific accounts never carry the ring of conviction and genuineness that a good novel, biography, or historical diary seems to offer. Once we leave the particular, the "true" account which was really lived, and ascend the ladder of abstraction to the general, we feel cheated and wish that we could both comment on everything and yet also carry this sense of the "actually experienced" in our constructs. Objective knowledge is always a purée rather than a meaty stew. Gordon Allport's extensive treatment of the idiographic vs. the nomothetic study of personality deals with this very problem, and is a special case of the purity metaconstruct. These terms were taken from Windelband, who declared the judgments of natural science are nomothetic, those of history idiographic. The former give us general facts with no literal content implied, and the latter give us particular facts which have been literally alive (Cassirer, 1944, p. 235).

The challenge here, according to Allport (1940, 1962), is to build a psychology in which we have not only nomothetic laws based upon the frequency-probability approach (see Chapter VI), but also laws which can predict the course of life for an individual. As Jung says, when you have an "average man," you have a nobody, for the average is a statistical fiction. Allport's thinking is highly sophisticated on this matter, for he recognizes that one cannot reject the demands of science for objectivity, which is ultimately at stake in the purity criticism. The solution he recommends combines the purity and the prototype metaconstructs, for he essentially is asking that we modify our methods to admit new formal causes. This is made clear in a paper (1962) in which he changes terminology from "idiographic" to *morphogenesis,* the study of patterns in living. Biologists must deal with nomothetic common facts, such as the obvious similarity in chemical structure of enzymes, protein molecules, and so on, for all living organisms, whether they study the antelope or the human being. Yet, the structure (pattern, form) of man differs from that of the antelope, and morphogenic studies try to find out how this takes place. In like fashion, Allport argues, we must devise new morphogenic ways of discovering styles of living which capture the whole man as we know him, rather than as dissected into the common but unreal substrate. He advocates the use of "liberal" research methods, such as matching methods and rating scales, or asking subjects what *they* think is at play in their lives (1962). In our terms, he would advocate a lengthening of the theoretical line of development. All those who would like to see a change in the study of man within psychology must applaud his efforts.

However, we doubt that one aspect of the basic issue from which his critique takes flight can be solved through a change in scientific techniques. When Allport requires that the "morphogenic interpretations we make should be testable, communicable, and have a high measure of predictive power" (1962, p. 410), he flirts with the counter-effects of the purity construct, which must forever rear its shaking head at such stable items of nomothetic or morphogenic knowledge. Just as soon as he *or his subject* is fortunate enough to coin a new, reliable, predictable morphogenic construct — let us say, "materialistic" — Allport will have to meet the challenge of the subject to whom the term is to be applied, who will doubtless introspectively say, following a wonderful demonstration of this construct's validity: "Yes, we predicted that someday I'd 'marry for money not love,' but that *still* doesn't mean I'm quite *that* involved in materialistic values, because look at my love of community service," and so on. If one assumes that this subject is in fact materialistic and is now denying it, if one accepts a demonstratively settled label, then of course we have here merely a defensive individual. But what if he really is not "all *that* materialistic," as the label suggests? To the dialectician this would be no inconsistency, to be both materialistic and not materialistic. He does not believe that humans will lose this ability to create alternatives by making, if nothing else, today's wishes tomorrow's facts. To the call for new formal-cause constructs, the idiographic or morphogenic answers well, but its overtones of the reaction to labeling that we call the purity criticism will never be satisfactorily answered, for this is a dialectical issue. When we dare to introspect, we are all variations on a theme, even those themes we ourselves compose to express our peculiarly idiographic temperaments.

Organismic, Balance, Well-Roundedness, and
the One in Many

The consideration of a morphogenic unity in nature and human behavior provides a natural transition to our next metaconstruct, which shares its origin with the same Platonic world view that prompted the purity criticism. The "organismic" metaconstruct can be traced to the belief held by the early Greek dialecticians that knowledge was never a thing of bits and pieces but existed as a totality — the one in the many — and could never be properly grasped by proceeding from "givens" to "givens." Data of the senses must be submitted to an overall evaluation before the truth of reality can be isolated, for intellect brings to bear on one given all the potential and possible (dialectical) alternatives generated by other propositions which, though they began as unquestioned givens, were subsequently revised in light of (dialectical) analysis. Knowledge is "one ball of wax," so to speak, and must be interrelated to be properly grasped. This long-standing belief has shown its influence through history in theories of art, principles of pedagogy, and various philosophical propositions. Its importance in psychology has already been pointed to in the work of gestalt psychology, where the very notion of gestalt configuration implies that one must look for a whole which is more than the sum of the parts.

There have been many attempts to apply gestalt principles directly to personality. Not only Koffka (1935) and Lewin (1935) but Goldstein (1939), Rogers (1951), and Murphy (1947) have formulated personality theories in which the individual personality is portrayed as a total configuration of interlacing portions all potentially influencing one another at any given moment. Often there is an analogy drawn between the gestalt concepts of figure (personality) and ground (environment), with the admonition not only that the individual is a self-sustaining total, but that the environment in which he lives is also an organized whole which cannot be dissected without being distorted (note here the purity implications). Sullivan's (1953) concept of personality as a system of interlacing dynamisms (roughly, "habits") within a field of interpersonal relations also reflects this organismic influence. By viewing the individual as an interdependent organism within the social group, theorists of a gestalt persuasion have been reviving the "one and the many" thesis of Socrates and Plato. Note that it is a thesis that works better as criticism than as a program for direct action. If the personality is so complex, how in the world can we study it? If every time we nail down our constructs at this end some gestaltist reminds us that things over on the other end of our controlled gaze are running wild, how frustrated we feel! Gestalt psychology, phenomenology, and existentialism all have this common dialectical tradition of reactionary criticism.

Another way the organismic metaconstruct has been used is as an evaluative judgment made of the "kind" of personality or adjustment the individual has achieved. Indeed, the very notion of a total unity, well put together, is what we ordinarily mean by "adjustment," and therefore the organismic metaconstruct has been quite important in the area of mental health evaluation as well as in ethics — if these two can really be separated (see Chapter XII). Along with the growth metaconstruct this has been used by many students of the "normal" personality as a kind of guideline for evaluating the adequacy of a person's style of life. Take, for example, Freud's tripartite conception of personality (id, ego, and super-ego), each component of which had to be balanced against the others as an organismic totality for proper functioning to take place. But Freud was not greatly attracted to this phenomenological or gestalt way of thinking. Two of his important students were, however, and we can see that Jung and Rank made of their views a kind of grand evaluation of the individual in terms of how well rounded his personality was in light of all the possibilities that were open to him.

As we have already suggested in Chapter X, Jung's entire outlook involved an attempt to balance consciousness against unconsciousness; only then would the "self" emerge as a unity symbolized in the "mandala" archetype (1963, p. 195). His thesis that "man is men," and his great stress upon the collective aspects of the unconscious are also manifestations of the organismic viewpoint. Rank's concept of "will," in addition to having a final-cause tone, captures the organismic idea, in that what the individual seeks in coming to psychotherapy is a unified self-conception; and it is the will which eventually guides and organizes his reintegration. In giving his instructions for free association, Rank paraphrases the Freudian instruction in a way which clearly reflects the organismic metaconstruct. He tells the client: "Say whatever you wish, for it is all one what you say" (1945, pp. 16–17).

There have been similar evaluative uses of the organismic metaconstruct in the gestalt tradition. Thus, Lecky (1945) hypothesized that individuals seek not pleasure but a sense of unity in self-identity, which he termed "self-consistency." The extent to which an individual has achieved self-consistency is a rough yardstick for assessing his adjustment level. It was from Rank and Lecky that Rogers then borrowed (1951) in putting together his own view of personality; the idea of seeking self-expression and unity doubtless went well with Rogers' ethical concern for the proper form of interpersonal relations among humans (see Chapter VII).

Finally, there are those who have stressed an organismic theory at the society level, suggesting that man can find balance, harmony, and good personal adjustment only within a certain type of social context. In his later years Adler relied increasingly on a belief in "social interest" (Ansbacher and Ansbacher, 1956) to explain how mental health may be brought about in an individual. Only the man who cultivates the innate propensity for warm human relations can, in the long run, achieve full personal development as a human being. Fromm (1941) has something of this same idea in his "productive orientation"; i.e., that which characterizes the individual who truly loves and accepts in himself a reflection of the "one out of many" — as a "human," who must live among humans and find meaning in life. The productive form of living can best be multiplied through group measures, through a revision of the social structure within which we live (Fromm, 1955). We must first alter the "one" pattern of living before we can alter the effects for the "many."

Actually, this organismic unity is also at the heart of the Skinnerian world of *Walden Two* (1948), except that in this case there is no suggestion of spontaneous growth within the individual as a result of group changes. Walden Two, unlike Fromm's Sane Society, is simply an efficient way of manipulating the behavior of large numbers of people. The collective as such has no emergent quality about it. It is not something better than a mere agglutination of independent items. Fromm and Adler have more of the Platonic image of man in the conception of unity, believing that all men of healthy disposition are potentially capable of *knowing* what is the good way to behave. Skinner's image of man has him often ignorant of but responsive to the lawful regularities which shape his destiny; it is not important that man should know of these things in any event. The clearest way to see this is to note that both Adler and Fromm ask the many (the large number of individuals in a social group) to begin making those changes which will alter the one (the society). They admonish each of us saying, "You are a human being, and you ought to. . . ." Skinner does not so entreat; he manipulates the one (the laws controlling social behavior) in order to influence the many (the controlled citizens of his society).

Alienation, Conflict, and the Many in One

Personality theorists have also found use for what we might term an "alienation" metaconstruct, which is of course the reverse of the organismic metaconstruct. Recall that dialecticians have argued that at times knowledge appears to have certain inconsistencies or contradictions within the sum total of interlacing parts. Hegel made this internal strife of evolving classes the very core of his historical theory. A portion or several portions of the "one" become opposed to other portions within the unity. When this occurs, reasons the dialectician, tension and conflict result, leading usually to change (Hegel) or to new arrangements within, hence a new understanding of the total (Plato). These contradictions are not particles which had been agglutinated previously and now simply are disassembling. The idea "alienation" frames is that of an internal inconsistency, an opposition of "natures" so that it is never simply any kind of dissolution but strictly and narrowly a tension of opposites. Of course, the opposites may or may not be diametrically different; one never knows until they have been subjected to careful dialectical analysis. But at least for the present, one can see in the bifurcation that takes place two or more subparts which have direct implications for one another, which grate on the meanings of one another, which call for a change in one or the other.

As might be expected, virtually every one of the theorists who stress the organismic metaconstruct also uses an "alienation" notion. Ordinarily this is not simply a question of claiming that the organism goes out of balance. Freud's tripartite breakdown of the personality has a certain flavor of alienation, suggesting as it does the cross-purposes at which the id and super-ego work. Freud derives his "dynamic" coloring from this maneuver. But the alienation metaconstruct is not given the great emphasis in Freudian theory that the more phenomenological Jung was to give it. For Jung, if adequate balance was not maintained, in time a truly alienated aspect of the personality — the "shadow" — would be formed and make its appearance in the conscious sphere *outside the control of consciousness.* By ignoring promptings from the unconscious to balance behavior, one can create a personal Frankenstein monster. He begins to act differently, does not know himself anymore, and feels torn by conflicting emotions. Freud would explain these same manifestations as being under the direction of unconscious motives and potentially identifiable as having originated in early experience. Jung believes the roots of many such complexes emerge from the past group identities of the collective unconscious, and that when alienation takes place it is not always a matter of what one has *lived;* it could be a matter of what one has *failed* to live, at least consciously. There is a way to avoid this split in personality before the contents going into the complex become powerful enough to function on their own within consciousness. Jung tells us that: "The essential thing is to differentiate oneself from these unconscious contents by personifying them, and at the same time to bring them into relationship with consciousness" (1963, p. 187). One resolves the alienation by seeking an intrapersonal synthesis before serious trouble arises, a time-worn dialectical outcome in a modern therapeutic role.

The gestalt group also has made use of alienation to describe personality conflicts. Goldstein speaks of "unnatural figures" in the organism's adjustment, which is somewhat analogous to the forcing of a puzzle part into a context where it does not really fit (1939). The person is not what he seems, he is not functionally and interdependently "whole." Rogers has a similar idea in his concept of "distorted symbolization," which occurs when an individual takes on values or beliefs he does not truly feel congruent with, but complies with because of the feelings of others (1951). Lewin, who sees personality even more in spatial terms than Rogers, captures this idea in his concept of a "lack of communication" between regions of the "life space" (1935). This ability which the mind seems to have — to operate within inconsistency by not tying together or communicating inconsistencies within its total grasp of things — is what Huxley meant by "watertight compartments" in the statement quoted at the beginning of this chapter (p. 355). It is the recognition that alien thoughts, desires, and the like, must at times be blocked off from the rest of the personality structure, or conflicts endangering the totality will result. It is a way of maintaining stability in the unity of parts, and is the same device utopians use when they place their societies in remote areas in order to filter out undesirable "outside" influences. As Festinger has demonstrated, man fortunately has the dialectical capability of resolving such cognitive dissonances even when the watertight compartment springs a leak.

Some theorists have looked at the other side of alienation, at the reticence which a family totality may have in permitting contradictions to arise in its members. The overprotective mother, whatever her reasons for behaving this way, is fighting giving up control of what she takes to be an extension of herself, or of her family unit. The child, too, fears separation and the challenge of having to stand apart from or possibly even against the will of his parents. We usually credit Rank with developing this theme most thoroughly in psychology. In his view, people either attain this separate identity within a new relationship or they are swallowed up in maladjustment. As Rank says, "the problem of the neurosis itself is a separation problem and as such a blocking of the human life principle, the conscious ability to endure release and separation, first from the biological power represented by parents, and finally from the lived out parts of the self which this power represents, and which obstruct the development of the individual personality" (1945, p. 73). Each of us must at times bear up under an alienation in order to bring about a change for the better.

Finally, the alienation theme has been used in trying to capture man's plight as a social animal. Adler's man, who fails to evolve social interest (Ansbacher and Ansbacher, 1956), or Karen Horney's predatory neurotic, who moves against or away from people out of a compulsive need to become a Godlike figure (1950), are drawn in these terms. The basic tenet of existentialism is that man has become alienated from his fellow man, has lost touch with him, and now merely uses him or is used with no sense of personal commitment or involvement. Erich Fromm's major thesis in *Escape From Freedom* (1941) is that modern man, thanks to the changing social structure and the increasing scientific knowledge he possesses, no longer feels a part of the natural order, nor subservient to his God and to those who represent Him in society. Man is free to decide his own fate, yet rather than reveling in this freedom, he cowers at his alienation from the stable, structured world of yesteryear. Rather than shape his own destiny, he escapes from the freedom his growing intellect makes possible by fleeing to mass movements, passing popularities, the "state," and other ingenuine or unproductive character orientations. As with Rank's overprotected child, who cannot forego the will of the mother, modern man finds it impossible to stand on his own two feet. He cannot bear up under his alienation from the natural order; he is a higher animal but lives out a lower purpose.

Organismic-Alienation Cycle

There is a special case combining the organismic and alienation metaconstructs into a kind of repetitive cycle which is worth singling out for consideration. This is a favorite maneuver of developmental psychologists or personality theorists who are greatly committed to a phenomenological approach. The idea is that there is some phenomenon occurring in behavior or development as a mass initially, but then, in order to develop or change in some systematic way, the organism must go through a phase of slight disorganization before finally recombining into a new and well-organized unity. Coghill (1929) used this notion to capture the developing behavioral changes which accompanied the maturing central nervous system of the salamander, and Gesell and his associates (1940) also relied on it to explain such things as the developing motor coordination of young children. Babies learn to make gross movements, out of which differentiated movements arise, awkward at first, then more coordinated, reaching a new or more mature level, only to have differentiations and awkwardness come about once again, and so on. In this way, by combining growth with an organismic-alienation cycle we can present a flowing theory of change. Drawing his theory from the work of Coghill, and adapting some of the Rankian terminology, Frederick Allen formulated a theory of child behavior and therapeutic cure based very much on the organismic-alienation cycle (1942). Children must learn to identify themselves as independent of their parents, and, Allen reasoned, psychotherapists must act as vehicles for this self-discovery in play therapy. They must serve as counterpoints against which this self-definition can occur, filling in as surrogates for parents who have had little success in furthering the psychological growth of their offspring. Murphy has also made extensive use of the organismic-alienation cycle, explaining in these terms not only the structure and development of personality, but perceptual development as well (1947).

A Plethora of Metaconstructs?

We could of course continue our analysis of major themes or metaconstructs in psychology. We might, for example, coin a special "predisposition" metaconstruct based upon the material cause for theories which rely on genetic transmission — the stuff of life that determines the nature of being, and so on. However, it was not our intention to present an exhaustive review of all the common themes that might be isolated. Rather our purpose has been to show that virtually all of those points which first arose from the fundamental bifurcation of demonstration vs. dialectic are somehow active now in modern theories of man. The points which dialecticians were making centuries ago are still with us, doing their jobs of keeping man's image somehow different, subjective, and even mysterious. Yesterday's "universal" or "inherited idea" is today's "creative intellect." The human being remains human to the extent that he can retain those factors which dialecticians have attributed to him, argued for, muddied the waters about, and generally advocated as a result of their introspective efforts. The twentieth century now has its dialectician making his case as a personality theorist. But what a problem he has — being forced to "put up or shut up" on the basis of a methodological rationale which admits of no dialectic. If he therefore must at times resort to sophistry, perhaps we can forgive him and recognize in this very maneuver the truth of his introspective efforts — that there is something terribly undemonstrative about his behavior if we give him a completely free and open stage on which to act.

Summary

In Chapter XI we attempted to show how the effects of dialectic vs. demonstration have been felt in modern personality theories. In particular, we proposed and documented the thesis that what we mean by the nature of man as a human being is very often best phrased in dialectical terms. Thus, history, art, symbolic expression and creativity, emotional display, and social forces, all were shown to be best described in dialectical terms. The "human image" is not to be discovered in the present or even in the future. It grows out of our past, and it has been reflected in many different forms over the centuries. One could not start afresh in the present and discover anything beyond what the ages have already taught us, for man's nature evolves out of past behaviors, about which he has had something to say. He has brought a kind of ability to the hard facts of life, so that he could interpret these facts, assess their import, judge their worth, and, if they did not suit his purpose, change them to meet his aspirations for what "could be" in the future. This future is now man's past, and as his heritage, it is thus not to be denied. Modern man has failed to divest himself of ancient dialectical issues, and in showing how they now are manifested, we have acquired a new appreciation for the "kind" of being who first proposed them. He was surely not an either-or animal then, and we can hardly believe that he will ever become one, save on the drawing boards of the more ambitious human engineers.

In the latter half of Chapter XI several metaconstructs were suggested and their role in modern psychology was underscored. The "antecedent-consequent" metaconstruct, based upon efficient causation, is extremely important to S-R theory. Freud's antecedents were usually given the additional meaning of "prototype" or formal cause in setting a style from out of the past to color a man's behavior in the present. The "growth" metaconstruct follows from a final-cause explanation, and is seen in many theories such as Maslow's, which take a more positive view of man. The "purity" metaconstruct is based upon the dialectician's tendency to question basic assumptions, and may be seen operating in the Rogerian dislike of forcing terms upon human beings, presumably changing persons into "objects." The "organismic" and "alienation" metaconstructs flow from the "one and the many" thesis of the ancient Greek dialecticians. Whether seen as important to the individual, as in Jungian psychology, or to the group, as in Frommian psychology, the idea of having unity out of diversity, of having an organismic totality rather than an alienation among subparts, has proved to be a very important theme in modern personality theory.

References

Adler, I. *Thinking machines.* New York: New American Library, 1961.

Adorno, T. W., Frenkel-Brunswik, Else, Levinson, D. J., and Sanford, R. N. *The authoritarian personality.* New York: Harper, 1950.

Aiken, H. D. *The age of ideology.* New York: New American Library, 1956.

Allen, F. *Psychotherapy with children.* New York: W. W. Norton, 1942.

Allport, G. W. *Personality: A psychological interpretation.* New York: Holt, 1937.

Allport, G. W. The psychologist's frame of reference. *Psychological Bulletin,* 1940, *37,* 1–28.

Allport, G. W. The general and the unique in psychological science. *Journal of Personality,* 1962, *30,* 405–422.

Ansbacher, H. L., and Ansbacher, Rowena R. (Eds.) *The individual psychology of Alfred Adler.* New York: Basic Books, 1956.

Argyris, C. *Integrating the individual and the organization.* New York: Wiley, 1964.

Aristotle. *Physics.* In Vol. 8 of R. M. Hutchins (Ed.), *Great books of the western world.* Chicago: Encyclopedia Britannica, 1952. Pp. 257–355.

Baker, H. *The image of man.* New York: Harper & Row, 1961.

Bales, R. F. *Interaction process analysis.* Reading, Mass.: Addison-Wesley Press, 1949.

Becker, H., and Barnes, H. E. (Eds.) *Social thought from lore to science.* Washington, D.C.: Harren Press, 1952. 2 vols.

Boss, M. *Psychoanalysis and daseinsanalysis.* New York: Basic Books, 1963.

Brown, R. *Words and things.* New York: Free Press of Glencoe, 1958.

Cassirer, E. *An essay on man.* Garden City, N.Y.: Doubleday & Co., 1944.

Cattell, R. B. *Personality: A systematic, theoretical, and factual study.* New York: McGraw-Hill, 1950.

Coghill, G. E. *Anatomy and the problem of behavior.* Cambridge: Cambridge University Press, 1929.

Dollard, J., and Miller, N. E. *Personality and psychotherapy: An analysis in terms of learning, thinking, and culture.* New York: McGraw-Hill, 1950.

Evans, R. I. *Conversations with Carl Jung.* New York: D. Van Nostrand, 1964.

Festinger, L. *A theory of cognitive dissonance.* Evanston, Ill.: Row, Peterson, 1957.

Freud, S. *The origins of psycho-analysis, letters to Wilhelm Fliess, drafts and notes: 1887–1902.* New York: Basic Books, 1954.

Fromm, E. *Escape from freedom.* New York: Farrar and Rinehart, 1941.

Fromm, E. *The sane society.* New York: Rinehart, 1955.

Frye, N. *Anatomy of criticism.* Princeton, N.J.: Princeton University Press, 1957.

Gesell, A. *The first five years of life.* New York: Harper, 1940.

Goldstein, K. *The organism.* New York: American Book Co., 1939.

Hauser, A. *The social history of art.* New York: Vintage Books, 1951.
Vol. 1. *Prehistoric, ancient-Oriental, Greece and Rome, middle ages.*
Vol. 2. *Renaissance, mannerism, baroque.*
Vol. 3. *Rococo, classicism, romanticism.*
Vol. 4. *Naturalism, impressionism, the film age.*

Hebb, D. O. *The organization of behavior.* New York: Wiley, 1949.

Hegel, G. W. F. *The philosophy of right.* In Vol. 46 of R. M. Hutchins (Ed.), *Great books of the western world.* Chicago: Encyclopedia Britannica, 1952. Pp. 1–150.

Heider, F. *The psychology of interpersonal relations.* New York: Wiley, 1958.

Horney, Karen. *Neurosis and human growth.* New York: W. W. Norton, 1950.

Huxley, J. *Religion without revelation,* rev. ed. New York: Harper & Row, 1957.

James, W. *Memories and studies.* New York: Longmans, Green, 1911.

James, W. *The varieties of religious experience.* New York: New American Library, 1958.

Jung, C. G. *The practice of psychotherapy.* Vol. 16 of H. Read, M. Fordham, and G. Adler (Eds.), *The collected works of C. G. Jung.* Bollingen Series XX.16. New York: Pantheon Books, and London: Routledge & Kegan Paul, 1954.

Jung, C. G. *Memories, dreams, reflections.* Copyright 1963. New York: Pantheon Books, A Division of Random House, Inc., and London: William Collins Sons, Ltd.

Kelly, G. A. *The psychology of personal constructs.* Vol. 1. *A theory of personality.* New York: W. W. Norton, 1955.

Koch, S. Psychological science versus the science-humanism antinomy; intimations of a significant science of man. *American Psychologist,* 1961, *16,* 629–639.

Koffka, K. *Principles of gestalt psychology.* New York: Harcourt, Brace & Co., 1935.

Langer, Susanne K. *Philosophy in a new key.* New York: Penguin Books, 1948.

Langer, Susanne K. *Philosophical sketches.* New York: New American Library, 1964.

Lecky, P. *Self-consistency: A theory of personality.* New York: Island Press, 1945.

Levinson, H., et al. *Men, management and mental health.* Cambridge, Mass.: Harvard University Press, 1962.

Lewin, K. *A dynamic theory of personality.* New York: McGraw-Hill, 1935.

Lippmann, W. *Public opinion.* New York: Penguin Books, 1946.

Lowrie, W. *A short life of Kierkegaard.* Garden City, N.Y.: Doubleday & Co., 1961.

Maslow, A. H. *Motivation and personality.* New York: Harper, 1954.

Merton, R. K. *Social theory and social structure.* Glencoe, Ill.: Free Press, 1949.

Murphy, G. *Personality: A biosocial approach to origins and structure.* New York: Harper, 1947.

Murray, H. A., and Kluckhohn, C. Outline of a conception of personality. In C. Kluckhohn, H. A. Murray, and D. Schneider (Eds.), *Personality in nature, society, and culture,* 2nd ed. New York: Knopf, 1953.

Parsons, T., and Shils, E. A. (Eds.) *Toward a general theory of action.* Cambridge, Mass.: Harvard University Press, 1951.

Rank, O. *Will therapy, and truth and reality.* New York: Knopf, 1945.

Rogers, C. R. *Client-centered therapy.* Boston: Houghton Mifflin Co., 1951.

Rogers, C. R. *On becoming a person.* Boston: Houghton Mifflin Co., 1961.

Rorschach, H. *Psychodiagnostics.* New York: Grune & Stratton, 1942.

Sheldon, W. H., Stevens, S. S., and Tucker, W. B. *The varieties of human physique: An introduction to constitutional psychology.* New York: Harper & Bros., 1940.

Shipley, J. T. *Trends in literature.* New York: Philosophical Library, 1949.

Skinner, B. F. *Walden two.* New York: Macmillan, 1948.

Skinner, B. F. *Verbal behavior.* New York: Appleton-Century-Crofts, 1957.

Sullivan, H. S. *The interpersonal theory of psychiatry.* New York: W. W. Norton, 1953.

Career and Professional Problems of Psychology as a Science of Man

Introduction: Issues Which Divide

One of the avowed intentions of the present volume was to provide a frame of reference within which the long-standing problems of not only the science but the profession of psychology might be interpreted and better understood. In the years immediately following World War II, when non-academic professionalism in psychology was clearly going to be a major aspect of its future, much internal dissatisfaction was voiced from the academic circles as to precisely what the role of a psychologist was to be. Professional rivalries from external regions, such as those with psychiatry and social work, were soon to follow. Many young career psychologists who left the academic circles to take up positions in the field found their jobs unrewarding, unclear as to responsibility, subservient to the needs of medicine, spilling over into the bordering regions of social work, public relations, religion, and so on. Professional self-identity was a thing difficult to come by. Many professional psychologists, prepared in university circles for one kind of major activity, later found themselves unprepared to conceptualize and deal adequately with the tasks called for in non-academic settings.

Aside from some very important financial and political reasons for their professional rivalry and jealousy, it is our contention that divisions within the psychological community stem from different and opposing uses of the theoretical and methodological constructs we have been considering throughout this volume. There is a fundamental conflict over the proper treatment of data, which is closely tied to a resulting difference in the image of man held by psychologists of different professional persuasions. In particular, there are five basic issues which divide the psychological community, and each of these has been given

407

considerable treatment in Part Two: (1) the motives to psychotherapeutic contact; (2) introspective vs. extraspective theoretical perspectives; (3) differentiating theory and method; (4) the employment of dialectical vs. demonstrative reasoning and metaconstructs; and (5) efficient- and material-cause vs. final- and formal-cause analyses of behavior. These issues are not given in any particular order, but they are numbered here to set them off clearly and give them proper stress. They shall provide a general framework for the discussion which follows.

There are other issues, of course, a few of which will be mentioned below, but in the main it is felt that these five points of conflict throw greatest light on the problems of psychology. The tactic of Chapter XII, therefore, is to show how these "issues which divide" have been at play in psychology and its relations with other professions. We shall begin with a consideration of clinical psychology as our model profession, follow it through its conflict with academia and its role among the healing professions, and then close with a discussion of some adjustment problems made to order by the demands of service work in an applied situation.

Clinical Psychology and its Contradictions

Psychology has gleaned hypotheses from, and has served several professional contexts, such as industrial, military, or school; but probably no other profession has been the focus of debate for matters such as science vs. technology, basic vs. applied science, or art vs. science, as much as clinical psychology. We have therefore selected clinical psychology as merely one of the many professional extensions which could be singled out to bring into relief those topics generated by the debate referred to in the introduction. But our discussion will have relevance for all non-laboratory professional activities in that broad field of knowledge we know as "applied" psychology.

The Profession of Clinical Psychology

The phrase "clinical psychology" was first used by Lightner Witmer, who is generally conceded to be the founder of the first psychological clinic at the University of Pennsylvania in 1895 (Watson, 1953). Witmer also founded and edited a journal entitled *The Psychological Clinic*. His orientation, and the orientation of many of the early clinicians was demonstrative rather than dialectical or "dynamic." Freud's more dynamic psychology came into clinical psychology by way of psychiatry, as reflected in the work of William Healy, who founded the first child guidance clinic in Chicago in 1909. Whereas Witmer was interested in the study of physical-sensory defects in exceptional children — demonstratively "given" disorders in the material- and efficient-cause reality of body tissues — William Healy adapted Breuer and Freud's term "abreaction" to explain how delinquents often steal in order to reduce tension which has been generated by family strife (Healy, 1917, p. 31). The latter is a dialectical explanation. As Robert Watson has accurately noted, "Although a pioneer, Witmer turned his back on almost all that was to predominate in the later days of clinical psychology and became of historical significance only. Healy is still a contemporary" (1953, p. 329).

It was not until World War II, when psychologists and psychiatrists were brought together into teams with social workers, that the profession of clinical psychology as we now think of it began to crystallize. The job facing each of these specialties was one of assessing the intellectual abilities, the psychological health, and the potential fighting capabilities of American soldiers. In order to serve in his team role, the clinician embraced projective tests and accepted the Freudian dynamic approach all the more, which in many cases was the language of his psychiatric teammate. But there was another language flourishing in psychiatry, with a firm grip upon the medical intellect of its practitioners, and that was of course the "physical" thesis as to the origin of mental illness. This conflict over how one should think about the emotionally disturbed individual has persisted, and plagues the relations of the psychiatric team to this very day, as we shall see below. The team arrangement worked fairly well for clinical psychology, but following the war, when the clinician had to return to the academic setting and begin instructing the new Ph.D.'s that were following in his wake, the clinical psychologist began a process of painful soul-searching in an effort to define his legitimate role in the *science* of psychology. Was he, after all, a scientist or a technologist; a scholar or a practitioner?

Academic psychology up until this post-war era had faced many challenges to what it took to be its proper method of scientific investigation. After the initial clash with introspectionism (see Chapter II), which ended in success for extraspectionism, there were the gestaltists and their phenomenological method to deal with. Next, the ambitions of the group testers and the great visionaries of applied psychology in the 1920's and 1930's had to be put down lest they unravel the carefully spun conception of what proper psychological study amounted to. Each time, the image of psychology as an objective, basic science, with its greatest potential realized only in the laboratory, had been retained untarnished — at least within academic circles. Now to have to swallow hordes of prospective "soothsayers" and "healers" armed with inkblots, subjective case histories, and dog-eared copies of Freud was an unhappy prospect to the academician. It is not surprising, therefore, that an atmosphere of potential conflict was ready and waiting for the clinical psychologist who came home from the ravages of one war to wage another war on the ravages of mental disorder. An admirable goal, but was it a scientific goal?

Clinical psychology, as a profession of major importance in the American Psychological Association, is therefore primarily a post-World War II phenomenon. To get a better picture of the growing pains involved in the process of clinical self-definition immediately after the war, let us take a close look at the themes which developed over roughly the first decade following World War II. Interestingly enough, the exchange of views will remind us of the Freud-Fliess correspondence of Chapter VII. Most of the points made by the emerging profession had been made earlier in the century by psychologists with humanistic leanings who were other than clinicians. More fundamentally, we see in the exchange a modern rephrasing of our historically important bifurcation between those committed to a demonstrative metaconstruct and those committed to a dialectical metaconstruct in the conceptualization of their data — in this case, the behavior of man. History has its well known way, and the history of psychology is no exception to the repetitive rule. We shall study these very important post-war years from the pages of the *American Psychologist,* the professional organ of the American Psychological Association, first published in 1946.

A Modern Rephrasing of the Historical Bifurcation

At the very outset of that decade, Krech (1946) heralded the "spectre of fission" haunting academic psychology — i.e., the split between experimental and professional psychology. With the war hostilities ended and social needs painfully evident, Krech argued for the study of human beings rather than lower animals, suggesting that the method might prove more difficult but that with ingenuity and effort it could be perfected. He proposed that a distinction be drawn between "pure" experimental and "applied" pure experimental psychology. The former type of psychologist experiments only to shed light on systematic scientific concepts. The latter psychologist experiments to help answer specific questions, whether or not those questions bear on a systematic point of view. Yet both researchers would be "pure" in their experimentation. Crannell (1947) answered Krech with the argument that certain basic laws and principles can better be studied in rats than in men, reaffirming the notion that such a procedure teaches one the *basic* tools of science.

The issue was joined then, making it appear to be merely a question of method in the accrual of knowledge. Academia wanted laboratory experimentation with conditions of extensive control enforced, a goal which was unattainable if experimentation were continually being tailored to some social necessity. Unfortunately, the role of theory in the conceptualization of man was not discussed as such. Since it seemed to be primarily a matter of methodological verification, those who were prone to demonstrative reasoning pressed a strong argument. Clinicians did not attempt to defend their activity as the seeking of personality constructs which would never be attainable in the laboratory context — at least, not at first. The first move was to draw a parallel between clinical and laboratory work. Thorne expressed this view initially: "Although the primary emphasis is on the individual case, the basic methods of clinical science involve the same techniques of description, classification, and explanation as are standard in experimental laboratory science" (1947, p. 160). This seemed to suffice for a time, since over the next few years the issues were not prominently discussed. Graduate education and the Veterans Administration training programs were of major concern, culminating in the Boulder Conference on training of clinical psychologists in late 1949.

The following year, Guthrie (1950) discussed the role of clinical psychology in the context of systematic psychology. Using a rather heavily-drawn analogy between clinical psychology and medicine, Guthrie placed both of these "practices" outside the realm of science. The reason for this decision was that neither discipline is interested in explaining what it deals with — disease or behavior, as the case may be — except insofar as such explanation facilitates a cure or, presumably, a change in behavior. Science, on the other hand, is concerned with explanation *per se:* "Science aims at generalization and theory. Practitioners aim at cures" (Guthrie, 1950, p. 99). Psychologists need adequate theoretical models, and the psycho-analytical models do not serve for science because they are prescientific. For Guthrie, a scientific model would be one like *cybernetics*. Summing up, he suggests that the practice of psychology be left to physicians and social workers, whose training better fits them to the job in the first place, and that psychology take its place as one of the basic sciences.

This is an historically important paper. It reflects all the points we noted in the introduction to this chapter. Guthrie here assumes the role for psychology that Fliess played for Freud. Both presumed that clinicians and clients had as their major motive to psychotherapy the curing of some affliction. Guthrie dislikes Freudian (dialectical) models and asks for a Wienerian (demonstrative) model. He attacks the clinician — where up to now the clinician had been strongest — as theoretician for man, as someone who phrased theory introspectively with the use of "mental" (final-cause) constructs. He encourages the ever growing tendency, noted in Chapter VII, to let personality theory — in the sense of theory about human behavior — emanate from the laboratory rather than the clinic. The traditional role of personality theorist is here preempted in the name of science.

It would seem, then, that Krech's prediction was taking form, assuming that Guthrie's attitude reflected the position of a fair segment of academicians. The argument now sounds as if it were an argument over theory, but the underlying strength is still gained from the side of method. Science is a *basic* theoretical activity, which means it is carried out in laboratories with great methodological control over theoretical variables. Non-laboratory study is "applied," hence unscientific by definition. We saw that this belief in unscientific, applied studies first arose in physical science (see Chapter V) as a form of social-class bias. This pejorative connotation was also contained unintentionally in the famous definition of applied psychology by Bingham (1923) as "psychology in the service of ends other than its own." Applied psychologists must surely sell their souls to effect a cure or a desired change in human behavior, and science be damned. In any case, as might have been expected, psychologists with applied interests answered this attitude of Guthrie's by stating that there were no basic differences between applied and pure research, or between the clinician and the systematist (Gabriel, 1950; Newman, 1950).

It was Rosenzweig (1950) who then brought the issue down to one of the proper study of *personality* in psychology (Rosenzweig, 1951; Super, 1951). Rosenzweig's general contention was that, as he interpreted several APA committees studying the problems of clinical psychology, the overwhelming emphasis in the training of clinicians was being placed on professional competence. He feared that in the profession's desire to respond to a social need, and to define minimal standards of professional competence, clinicians might well overlook the fact that as of that time, no one could state precisely *what* a clinician should be. Such principles must be based upon firm experimental evidence. He asked that a committee dealing with the coordination of professional and scientific functions of the clinician be formed, lest psychology face the likelihood that it is "destined to become a science foreign to personality — as used to be the case — and a profession foreign to science — as should never be the case" (Rosenzweig, 1950, p. 680).

In a series of exchanges which followed, many opinions were voiced and attitudes crystallized; the upshot of it all was that the clinician refused to accept the inevitability of a schism and was now definitely committed to being a scientist *as well as* a practitioner. "Fusion" replaced "fission," and no doubt there were lamentations on both sides. Although phrased in terms of professional practice, what this *meant* was that now psychology must attempt to merge two lines of thought, two forms of metaconstruct, into one orientation. Few other sciences in the history of thought had to wrestle with quite this problem. Hunt (1951) continued in the same vein as Thorne and, accepting the affinity of clinical psychology and medicine, took the position that the physician is a scientist using well-tested techniques: "Too often we concentrate upon the physician and his bedside manner but overlook the scientific basis of his method" (Hunt, 1951, p. 686). He further underscored the empirical basis of clinical intuition and buttressed his case by citing probability theory from Reichenbach. Thus, Hunt strengthened the clinician's methodological arguments by helping to initiate the trend to philosophy of science as a rationale for clinical psychology.

The personality theory side of the question was then brought to the fore again by Bach (1952) when he asked: "Who are the discoverers of psychological knowledge?" He pointed out that well known practitioners — such as Freud, Rorschach, and Rogers — have stimulated tremendous amounts of significant research. Bach's argument advanced Rosenzweig's precaution, to suggest that a major responsibility and privilege of the clinician is to formulate hypotheses from personal contact with people, and then to submit these hypotheses to experimental test. Moreover, the two aspects so delineated were to be viewed as parts of the same *scientific* process. Rogers clarified the elements of this argument when he noted that psychologists doing psychotherapy "will develop their hunches, their theories, their concepts, their research projects, not only from knowledge of animals and laboratory subjects, but from intimate contact with the psychological dynamics of individual human beings in a process of change" (1953, p. 50). Although it is not stated in our terms, we see here quite clearly the call for theory phrased from an introspective rather than merely from the extraspective perspective. Clinicians would become, then, the "applied" pure psychologists Krech spoke of, but they would never participate in ends other than their own.

From this point onward we see attempts on the part of clinicians to bring together — not merely to integrate — the roles of practitioner and scientist, to somehow bridge the gaps caused by differences on our five central issues. Not all clinicians took this tack. For example, Ruth Tolman quoted from a personal communication from the clinician E. L. Kelly, who wrote:

> Clinical psychologists must become more and more schizophrenic. When functioning as clinicians, they must behave as intuitively and artistically as do psychiatrists, who as Eysenck points out do not have a satisfactory science to apply as yet. When functioning as scientists . . . they should accept the canons of science and act like scientists. This is not to say that one role is more important or better than another, but they should not be mixed *at the same time* (Tolman, 1953, p. 723).

Here is one man's solution to the problem of being both spontaneously artistic (dialectical in relating to the client) and scientifically rigid (demonstrative in proving hypotheses). If they followed this, clinicians would play dual roles, according to the situation. Presumably the situations would ultimately influence one another, but the important factor Kelly seems to be stressing is that ground rules in one activity should not dominate or restrict clinicians carrying through in the other activity. Although it is a feasible program of action, as formulated it seems to have confused some individuals who had difficulty shifting roles. The simple truth is, laboratory skills taught in graduate programs generate theoretical formulations based upon the demonstrative metaconstruct, whereas clinical skills demand a certain flair for the dialectical or dynamic conceptualization. It is therefore not surprising that one student of the period complained about dual roles for experimentally and clinically inclined psychologists (Solomon, 1955). He emphasized, as others did (Kahn, 1955), that the real difference lay in the opposing *interests* of individual psychologists, interests which *could not be successfully integrated* by the same person. This reminds us of Yerkes' admission (see Chapter VII) that he had never wanted to be a psychologist, in the sense of studying people introspectively. We interpret this to mean that some psychologists sense the very deep cleavage between those who proceed from demonstrative positions and those who proceed from dialectical positions in the study of man. Can we ever bridge this cleavage? Rogers thinks we can, and he next picked up the trend of thought he had helped to initiate. His contention was that a clinician can function as *both* scientist and clinical therapist in the *same* situation:

> I can abstract myself from the experience and look upon it [i.e., therapy] as an observer, making myself and/or others the objects of that observation. . . . To avoid deceiving myself as observer, to gain a more accurate picture of the order which exists, I make use of all the canons of science. . . . A deeper understanding of therapy . . . may come from living it, or from observing it in accordance with the rules of science, or from the communication within the self between the two types of experience (1955, p. 278).

Note what Rogers is saying here. He believes that one can profit from considering himself, as clinician, extraspectively. Indeed, one can do researches on oneself to help prove certain beliefs he holds about the therapeutic process. At the same time, the effective therapist must never lose that introspective sensitivity, that openness to his client's subjective beliefs and opinions. We view this paper as the most important answer to Guthrie's criticism. Rogers here makes it plain that method *influences* theory, in that theories and method strive for compatibility as we know from Chapter VIII. A science which pays attention only to its methods will soon find its theories taking on the coloring of those methods. What is needed is a balance between demonstratively-oriented science — as traditionally presented in the physical sciences — and a more dialectically-oriented science, one which appreciates the need to use constructs which "fit" the data object from "its" perspective. After all, it was not until the advent of social science that a science was called upon to *instruct* as well as to study its data. Even early medicine, with its physical hypotheses, did not claim that physicians had to instruct their patients in the nature of the diseases for which the latter were being treated. Psychology, Krech and Rosenzweig and Rogers are saying, *does* have this responsibility, this social obligation.

The problem really lay in the definition of science, with its great stress on method. If only the clinician could broaden the scope of "science" somehow, his laboratory counterpart might come to accept him as the scientist he felt himself to be. This has become the general approach to clinical psychology — i.e., to bring together in some way activities in the clinic with activities in the laboratory. The latter half of the twentieth century is likely to see a continuing trend in this direction. Facing the austere definition of science proffered by the academicians who have chosen to write on this topic since the beginning of this century, psychologists with an applied interest responded by going to the writings of their peers in the physical sciences to see what they were saying. How adequately was the current trend in the physical sciences being translated into the science of psychology? At the close of the decade we have been studying, we see the initiation of a series of papers addressed to the question "what is science?" (Bakan, 1956; Crannell, 1956; Skinner, 1956; Strupp, Castore, Lake, Merrill, and Bellak, 1956; Berenda, 1957; Rychlak, 1959).

When he turned to the history of science, or to the writings of eminent physical scientists, the clinician was pleasantly surprised to find that he was *more in step* with the science of the times than he would have supposed from the writings in most psychology texts. As we thoroughly demonstrated in Part One, the Newtonian world view which had been brought into psychology during the first half of this century was not the *only* one then ascendant in physical science. In fact, it had been undergoing steady decline in physical science during this half-century while it was growing in stature within psychology. Attempts to change the nature of scientific investigation, to broaden its base in accordance with the needs of a new science continue to be made in psychology by clinicians and psychologists with comparable interests. But this has been a slow and difficult process, because the cultural lag is great and the needs of academia are not always those of the field. Despite the myriad sources of evidence cited in Part One, despite the efforts of many liberally-inclined physical scientists, and despite the direct exhortation of Oppenheimer (1956) to psychologists to update their thinking, in the midst of the second post-war decade Koch could make this relatively modest evaluation of the prevailing psychological Zeitgeist: "the philosophy of science still talked in psychological literature is approximately 20 years out of date" (1961, p. 631).

Professional Fission and the Future of a
Useful Science of Man

As we have seen, events over the first decade succeeding the world conflict were to prove Krech a remarkable prognosticator. Psychology did indeed generate internal fission, and the resulting stress has never quite been dissipated. Some would claim that it continues to increase with the passing years. Surely there is little to indicate that things are improving significantly. It is one thesis of this book that such improvement will be forthcoming only when both sides clearly understand the issues which divide them, and when a conception of science has been worked out that is more compatible with "applied" psychologies than the definition which has held sway over the first two-thirds of the twentieth century.

Over this period, it was fashionable to use as an opprobrious allusion the image of an "armchair" psychologist. Such an individual, presumably, rather than leaving the comforts of a cool spot in the parlor to seek validation in the hotter world of events, preferred to spin theoretical nonsense to support his favorite subjective biases. More recently, there has been another image taking shape, which, like the earlier stereotype, has a certain amount of odious truth about it. This is the image of the "gadget" psychologist — too busy collecting data to think, to deliberate, to question the usefulness of his research activity. Whereas the armchair theorist put the world together to suit his cogitations, the gadget theoretician now puts the world together to suit his apparatus. He multiplies his gadgets just as readily as his counterpart multiplies his homespun notions. Neither seems prepared to appreciate the orientation of the other. They do not understand each other, and fail to grasp that one errs on the side of dialectic while the other errs on the side of demonstration. The gadgeteer says "All men are completely predictable scientifically" because his apparatus captures them remarkably well in contrived situations, and the armchair thinker serenely assures himself that "Man is too complex ever to be grasped fully by science" because he looks inward to find there new, inexplicable possibilities of things not yet or never to be validated.

It is not a question of which psychologist is right. We must grasp the fundamental truth that psychology cannot prosper unless a dialectic helps in the generation of hypotheses, and that objectivity is unattainable short of a demonstrative freezing of major premises which can then lead us to empirical tests of our theoretical position, our style of thought about the data, our now more sophisticated and testable biases. Complete reliance on either metaconstruct in the conceptualization of human data can only lead to emptiness of description and the decline of our science. Psychology will either slip into an inconsequential role as a minor technology — at best a stopgap science, waiting for some physical science to take the lead in explaining human nature — or be completely swallowed up as a modern art form of some sort, related to literature and drama. For the lover of truth, for those who want to come up to the standards of validation yet study the "person" they know themselves to be, either form of decline would surely be a senseless waste of the potential we know psychology has as a unique science.

Some people, of course, will never have an actively scientific interest — such as those who enter the laboratory following attainment of a doctor's degree as a stepping-stone to administrative or instructional academic careers, or those who seek to be directors of clinics designed for meeting community needs. Doubtless all sciences have this problem — if that is the way to phrase it — of having men among their numbers who really do not care to advance or who simply cannot advance knowledge in an independent and devoted manner. Other individuals will simply be unable to think about data in both dialectical and demonstrative fashions, especially since there are so many related issues, as we have noted in the introduction to this chapter. We shall doubtless have a range of commitment to these combined metaconstructs among psychological scientists. Some men will never forego their convictions of a unique nature, not amenable to scientific study; others will find dialectic sheer madness. But we speak here of the advisability of a middle ground purely in the ideal sense. It would be helpful if all psychologists were to appreciate the influence of our contrasting metaconstructs on their science. At the very least, an appreciation of this sort may bring together factions which are simply unable at the present time to find a common talking ground.

One of the clearest indications we have that there is a tremendous practical need for the insights of psychology can be found in this very fear of psychology's contamination by "applied" considerations. Academia's hysteria is an accurate reflection of the fact that psychology is open to the fervid clawings of people seeking help — in industry, mental hospitals, schools, government agencies, and so on. It is also probably true that in this applied context psychologists as well as other scientists will be prone to give in to the pursuit of material wealth *per se,* foregoing a more disinterested pursuit of knowledge. But surely the way to help them return to their identities as responsible, dedicated scientists is by improving their scientific status and increasing their self-respect, rather than by damning them as second-class citizens, as "applied," hence good for nothing to science. We must realistically face up to the instructional demands of the culture which press upon them, or yield our place on the rostrum. We must find an orientation which admits them to a place of dignity and honor among the family of sciences. Once they comment upon man in his social environment, *all* psychologists become "applied," and essentially take the role of personality theorists. One cannot refer to man in his everyday world without doing the job of a personality theorist. Whether one makes man an automaton or a dynamically-driven complexity of conscious and unconscious minds, as this picture is drawn out in the "real world" beyond the gadgets a personality theory takes form. Let us hope the gadgets mirror the real situation accurately, including life as seen from the perspective of the man who walks about in this world and who seeks self-knowledge. Let us hope that even the armchair theoretician will stroll about and come back with suggestions for his friend in the laboratory, or better yet, construct a few gadgets of his own. As we psychologists mingle with the data, capturing them as persons in our theories about personality, there is another aspect of man's existence we come up against. That is, as we have seen (see Chapters VI, VII, and VIII), personality comments have a kind of value or ethical intonation when they are pronounced about individuals in relation to other individuals. If "all (or even most) men behave thus," but Mr. X does not behave so, regardless how scientifically hygienic we prefer the implied conclusion to be, the fact is, Mr. X is "different" from all or most of his fellow men. In human relations, this inevitably leads to an ethical judgment being pressed. We may just as well face it, ethics and personality commentary are fundamentally related. This is doubtless the reason all the truly great personality theorists are also profound social critics; they have "oughts" in mind, either stipulated or implied in their assessments of man.

Abnormal Behavior and the Healing Professions

The Psychiatric Team and Member Motives

In addition to the internal conflict over the nature of psychology as science, the clinician has had to deal with professional problems stemming from his early participation on the psychiatric team. There are, once again, many political and economic motives reflected here, particularly with psychiatry — issues which are beyond the scope of the present inquiry. But there are also fundamental problems of a theoretical nature which face the team when its members set out to assume their community responsibilities. In Chapter VII we reviewed three motives to the psychotherapeutic contact, and probably in no other meeting of minds does the confusion over how to approach clients make itself plainer than in the activities of the psychiatric team. It would simplify our exposition if we could make the blanket assertion that all psychiatrists, since they are basically physicians, take the curative approach, all social workers the ethical, and all psychologists the scholarly tack in dealing with clients. This meets a certain stereotype of the professional groups, and for any one team arrangement this is not an unlikely lineup of motives. But often there are individual variations in the pattern within a profession, as we know from the fact that within any one professional identity all three motives operate.

The writer has been present at many team presentations or case staffings, when the confusion in motives has been made painfully clear by interprofessional tensions. Often the matter goes as follows: the psychiatrist, trained as a physician and dedicated to the curative role, views mental illness as analogous to physical illness. He takes it as his major premise that the patient has come for treatment, with self-knowledge or ethical promptings being merely secondary aspects reflecting anxious self-concern or some such. Ethical considerations are presumed to fall only in the classical doctor-patient relationship. If he is a toughminded practitioner in the old-school tradition, he may question a patient being presented before the team in rather straightforward terms, much as he would conduct an examination of an ulcer patient, in a manner which offends the professional sensibilities of the social worker (or psychologist), who sees in this "cold" approach precisely that rejection and unfeeling lack of concern which has brought the patient to the hospital in the first instance. Stressing the relationships between people, the "sharing" of one's experience with others on a common level, the social worker thinks of mental illness as stemming from (ethical) problems in interpersonal contact. The psychiatrist's feelings about this fall somewhere between embarrassed tolerance of an overly emotional colleague and frank irritation at the implied criticism of his time-tested medical approach. He is seeking a diagnosis which can lead to an identification of the (usually presumed) physical disturbance at the heart of the illness, and thence to a cure. He deals with his client's mental ailment demonstratively, as he would a kidney ailment, and is naturally at a loss to understand the social worker's great concern — if, indeed, he grasps it at all. Fortunately for him, he is usually at the top of the team pecking order, and is therefore spared the side glances being thrown the psychologist's way.

The psychologist, for his part, is more likely to be in sympathy with the social worker, since he is not so committed to the physical hypothesis. Having been trained in interviewing and in accepting the client on his own terms, the psychologist is less demonstrative in therapeutic approach. At the same time, he does feel some need to frame the mental health issue in demonstrative research terms. He thinks that the very first thing we should be doing is conducting extensive research to see what are the possible causes of mental illness. These causes often transcend merely physical matters, touch upon the socioeconomic condition of a *client* (the term he prefers to use), and are very likely to end up as "basic" personality studies having no direct bearing on healing or curing at all. Indeed, the psychologist might even want to study the utility of a psychiatric team arrangement, which may not be the most effective way to deal with emotionally disturbed individuals. But how to test all these points empirically is the concern of the psychologist on the team, and he might well think of clients as subjects for research rather than as patients in therapy.

The social worker dislikes this fanatical need of the psychologist to reduce everything to numbers, and, in the best traditions of the purity metaconstruct, often takes the position that this turning of patients into "guinea pigs" is just as bad as turning them into childlike pawns in the medical game. The psychiatrist is probably less likely to attack the psychologist's scientific inclinations. In fact, he would prefer to see psychologists move exclusively into assessment and research (which really are closely related), because there is a direct professional confrontation here over the matter of who should be doing private psychotherapy. The psychiatrist argues that since he is a physician, and since mental illness is an illness, he, as major healer, should assume the role of therapist. Both psychology and social work now question the "illness" label, and also the wisdom of assuming that only physicians can heal whatever it is we call mental illness. Some psychiatrists have been giving them substantial help in this area, but the professional patterns of acceptable behavior remain poorly ironed out.

So much for our stereotyped account. It goes almost without saying that this is a highly erroneous description of what many psychiatric teams have become, and that reversals in the motives to psychotherapy occur among team members even though the resultant confusions and tensions remain. But there *is* a definite truth in the fact that motives to the meeting of an applied goal such as treating mental illness differ, and that as a result professional strife is generated due to a lack of understanding. The moral seems to be that each individual entering a healing profession should begin by making it as clear in his mind as he can how he personally rank-orders our three motives. If he then attempts to assess the motives of other colleagues as he comes to know them, he may be able to make sense of the points on which they diverge from his view. One can tolerate opposition to one's view if all presumptions are made clear and are shown to be more than the subjective idiosyncrasies of one or two individuals. One's biases may continue to prejudice his feelings about such a member of the team, but it will then be clear that this is due to one's *own* basic (major) premises. The problem arises in part from personal presumptions, although these may also be widely held in the profession.

This is not unlike the conflict within psychology, of course, where we have argued that understanding of one another's position can lead to greater tolerance on all sides. The real danger seems to be that one viewpoint may begin to hinder or restrict the other, as when the laboratory scientist belittles the applied scientist, or when the ethically motivated therapist attacks the personal character of the curatively motivated. One cannot hope to prevent such prejudice from forming altogether, but it surely is intolerable to raise it to a professional status, where the prejudice might actually be translated into an overt act of discrimination. The healing professions, as well as the schools of thought within psychology, benefit from diversity and a vigorous pursuit of alternative hypotheses. Professional concerns sometimes militate against this process, and it is therefore a form of ethic in itself to seek to understand oneself quite clearly, not only personally, but professionally, as one of a group which is united to serve society in a patterned mode of endeavor.

Theories of Disease, Personality, and the Changing Conception of Mental Illness

A continual source of difficulty for both psychology and psychiatry is the disparity they find between their more conventional scientific viewpoints and the demands of their clients for insight and understanding. Like Freud, the psychiatrist with a dynamic orientation finds it difficult to rely entirely on physical theories in his daily practice; his psychological counterpart often balks at the opportunity to apply S-R theories to human beings who come seeking help for personal problems. The inapplicability of both the physical and S-R views stems from our introductory issues, especially the one relating to final causes. We can make this point clearer by looking more closely at the changing view of mental or emotional illness.

Primitive peoples viewed their psychotics as being possessed by a spirit (usually evil), so that in one sense the "intentions" of this other-worldly spirit might be thought of as an early "final-cause" theory of mental illness. But it was Hippocrates (460–377? B.C.) who introduced the first generally accepted medical model of human behavior, sub-suming both normal temperamental patterns and disordered or "sick" behavior. He postulated the operation of four humors at work in the body. There were black and yellow bile, blood, and phlegm, and these combined in various ways to produce certain physical and emotional ill-nesses (MacKinnon, 1944, p. 15). The humor was essentially an effi-cient cause of both certain temperamental tendencies and the propensities for certain types of mental illness. The fact that certain humors — blood and phlegm — were observable and could be pointed to, lent this view a certain material-cause plausibility as well. This physical model of a palpable substance (material cause) affecting the individual from within his body (efficient cause) was to become the predominant style of theorizing in the medical sciences. The third of our Aristotelian causes — formal — can be seen in the physician's quest for a particular pattern of symptoms, or a syndrome of clues to the nature of the dis-turbance. Therapy became a question not of understanding the inten-tions of the physicians' data — which would imply a final cause — but rather of merely identifying the operation of a blindly operating sub-stance which had been doing its worst, and then applying counter-measures. The physician — never the disease — had intentions. The patient's intentions, such as they were, had nothing directly to do with the illness from which he suffered.

If we think about it, then, we realize that Hippocrates' theory of temperament or personality and his theory of illness overlapped. More-over, since the theory was primarily aimed at explaining physical and emotional illness, we can see that it made no allowance for intelligent design in the behavior of its data. As with all such physical theories, the typical Hippocratic medical theory was designed extraspectively, and its style of conceptualization is demonstrative. It seeks a vehicular gen-eralization of causes which effect *all* data similarly, in every instance and at all times. The symptoms of smallpox are demonstratively given clues to a universally valid condition. This is comparable to the physical theories of the universe, where intelligence need not be attributed to the movement of stars.

Now, although there had always been a recognition in medicine of the influence that mind seemed to have on matter, it is true to state that up until the latter portion of the nineteeth century a broadly useful personality theory failed to emerge precisely because there was no attempt to assign *mentality* to the disease process. As late as the 1830's we find the historically eminent physician Marshall Hall explaining neuroses in terms of "reflex irritability," an inherited propensity — which means an efficient cause — that could be located in the cerebrum, spinal column, or ganglionic system (Stainbrook, 1953). Kraepelin was to follow and put together our modern theory of diagnosis entirely in this vein of physically based diseases which run their course entirely outside of final-cause intellect. Karl Menninger refers to Kraepelin's system, with its constructs limited to efficient, formal, and material causes, as follows:

> Kraepelin lived in the golden age of "causal" diagnosis. The "cause" of typhoid fever had just been identified, and that scourge was being eliminated. The "cause" of syphilis had been discovered and effective treatment soon followed. The "cause" of diphtheria had been identified and that dreadful affliction stayed. . . . Kraepelin admitted that he could not *find* the "causes" for the mental disease syndromes which he defined, but he was convinced that the conditions which he had identified *had* causes which would some day and in some way be found; then the disease could be eliminated (Menninger *et al.*, 1963, pp. 46–47).

Though Menninger here uses the blanket term "cause," it is clear he means to say "all those causes except the final." Final causes are goals; hence they have not "happened," they need not "exist" and cannot be discovered without taking the patient's intellect into consideration. They are the possibilities of the dialectician, the hopes and foolish dreams of a man who can rise above what is, or what was, to seek something that is unattainable even in the future. There was no opportunity to speak this way about a human being, sick or healthy, because the theories being proffered by physicians (as well as other physical scientists) did not permit the use of a final cause. What is more, physically based theories phrased from the extraspective perspective were proving highly useful in the treatment of sick and disordered people. Such theories have their disadvantages, of course, but at least they had improved the lot of the mentally ill person by changing his designation from "witch" or "werewolf" to "sick human being." Modern personality theory had to wait on the cyclical evolution from an incorrect intentions theory (evil spirits directed the mentally ill) to an only partially correct physical theory (the effects of humors or other disordered physical conditions blindly led to mental illness) to a more correct intentions theory.

A completely useful personality theory could only have arisen because someone like Freud *unknowingly* added to the other theoretical devices a final-cause explanation, of unconscious minds with distinct goals in view. Our stomachs work outside conscious awareness, and it is not necessary to ascribe a "goal" of digestion to the stomach. We therefore do not think of our internal organs as possessing intellect. But though he spoke in terms of instinctual promptings (see Chapters VI and VIII), Freud's "unconscious" was an *intelligent* sphere of activity, one which did indeed have "in mind" certain things to be accomplished. Thus, a final-cause explanation had been wrung upon the scientific community. It was now possible to formulate personality theories people could use, for, from within what they took to be their personal intellects, they could see the plausibility of Freudian explanations. People live within a world of intentions and aspirations — beliefs, attitudes, hopes "for the sake of which" they behave — and therefore they need some way of thinking about that world in precisely these terms. Because of this final-cause tactic in explanation, as we have seen, there is a continuing resistance within the scientific community to personality theory. The resistance is not always phrased in our terms, but we can now see the real problem without great difficulty.

Freud used a model of illness in which the personality structure sought a certain adjustment level, with the ego as the "man in the middle" seeking a balance of forces between the unacceptable intentions of the id and the socially more appropriate intentions of the super-ego. If some form of stalemate was possible, then, considering all things, we could speak of mental health. If for any of a number of reasons the personality structure deteriorated, then neurosis or psychosis was the result. This made illness an assessment of the adequacy of personality functioning. It was not illness which acquired a final cause, not disease which gained a mentality, but rather the man, or the "personality," about whom a judgment of mental normality was being made. If the manifestation of illness had a meaning suggesting intelligent design, as in the immobility of writer's cramp to the man who can no longer stand job pressures, it was not the hand or the fingers which acquired intellect, but the "man within." For the first time in medical history, there was now a clear distinction drawn between an intelligent process of human behavior in disease, and the purely mechanical action of the disease process itself. One could even forego interest in the disease process and study the various types of adjustments which non-sick people achieved. Freud thus initiated the *modern era* of personality study, a study which though it began with mentally sick people was soon extended to all people.

The other side of the coin here is that now normal persons could be said to be mentally sick, from time to time, or for all time, even though they might not be under treatment. That is, evaluations of their continuing adjustment could be made and what was once disease theory could be used to explain their current "personality" behavior. In the mid-twentieth century we began seeing theorists use psychotic labels to describe individuals in what we would ordinarily have called a personality sense. The view now was that due to early influences on their developing personalities, some individuals learned to behave schizophrenic-like, for example, when they reached maturity; this is like saying they learned to be dominant or passive. When disturbed they might have to be hospitalized for a time, when less disturbed they might carry on as usual, but in each circumstance they can be identified as schizophrenic. Their projective tests, for example, would show the underlying stamp of schizophrenia. This position is reflected in the work of Beck (1954), and many clinicians now take such a view. We are back to the earlier mixing of illness and personality, but in a new way. This is a dangerous reversal of the Freudian view, because of the difficulties one finds in evaluation, the necessary core of such a theory of "illness-to-personality."

That is, in the modern world with its mass communications, against which standard a psychotic can check his thinking and even share less commonly held views with others, it is not quite so easy to get off into that world of phantasy which Cameron called a "pseudocommunity" (1963, p. 486). Modern man, even modern psychotic man, is more sophisticated, less likely to deviate from the reasonable and become bizarre, as suggested by the fact that we see fewer cases of anatomically impossible glove and stocking anesthesias among hysterics today. Thus, differentiating between a sick mind and a mind that embraces what we consider sick beliefs (two different matters) gets to be a ticklish affair. Evaluations depend upon values, and values are not clearly enunciated in the data before us.

As a result, we have the increased danger of calling "sick" someone who holds to the extreme views of some minority group, to a legitimate but restricted body of procedural evidence. The community which supports this individual's belief is no longer a pseudocommunity. Yet, because he holds to the minority view and is assessed accordingly, he might well be considered abnormal on personality grounds because he manifests a value system at variance with the broader convictions of the culture at large. This highlights the fact that procedures of medical diagnosis, like the procedures of any science, do not merely depend on the discovery of clues nestled within a reality of facts. They are often arbitrary constructions, biased by the values of a given point of view. By using mental illness terminology as one uses personality constructs, it is very easy to point to "signs" of mental illness in each person. Drawing an analogy with physical illness, this would be like saying that everyone is physically sick all the time, mildly so when fatigued from work or play, more so when suffering from a cold. This has a certain plausibility and saying it would not cause too much concern. But in mental illness, with its suggestion of irrationality and implied negative assessment of how well the individual is managing his personal affairs, this would stretch the meaning of the illness construct beyond all constructive bounds.

Coming back to our main point, over the past several decades one can definitely see a development *away* from the heavy reliance upon efficient-cause explanation in clinical psychiatry and psychology, and toward descriptions which can embrace final-cause explanations. Values are tied to final causes, goals which men find worthwhile and which guide their present behavior from out of the future in intelligent fashion. Menninger has agreed with this analysis, since he threw support to Mac-Leod (1957), who argued for the extension of scientific explanation to final causes (Menninger *et al.*, 1963, p. 113). Menninger rejects the use of what he terms "name-calling" in modern psychiatry, and he defines illness in typical (dialectical) Freudian fashion as "an extremity to which the organism is pushed and must await release by overbalancing pressures in the other direction" (p. 282). His grasp of the fact that mental illness is somehow involved in final causes is also reflected in the following:

> Medical science traditionally has never been much concerned with motivation, while religion and philosophy — and later psychology — have long had a proprietary attitude toward it. The right, the wrong, the reason, the need, the wish, the fear, the intention, the stimulus, the inhibition — all these things existed, of course. They were known to doctors as to everyone else. But who could bring order and structure to the whims of the human heart? (p. 108).

Who indeed? The liberal sprinkling of final-cause terms here reminds us that an eighteenth- or nineteenth-century scientist felt he surely could not. Bacon relegated final-cause explanation to philosophy, and especially to ethics. Well, if mental illness touches upon final causes, then it should not surprise us to find that some modern theorists may see parallels between ethics, morals, or religion *and* mental illness. And they have.

Ethico-Religious Interpretations of Abnormal Behavior

We see more clearly now that the dilemma of the clinician is somehow to grasp his client's presumably self-directed, intelligent behavior, while refraining from theorizing about it in final-cause terms — that is, if he wishes to remain a scientist in the traditional sense. As the American philosopher C. S. Peirce once observed: "Teleological considerations, that is to say ideals, must be left to religion; science can allow itself to be swayed only by efficient causes . . ." (1958, p. 353). Yet, how does one listen to a disturbed fellow human being, caught up in the turmoil of mental conflict — which so often means frustrated ambitions, self-accusations of having fallen short of an ideal, or guilt-ridden commentaries on his personal situation in life — without finding at least some form of final-cause explanation? To be honest, we have to admit that one cannot; nor have personality theorists since Freud's innovation been able to avoid this in their explanations.

Alfred Adler made it perfectly clear in his theory of personality that he viewed men as behaving in terms of life goals. Though he did not phrase his theory in religious terms, one would surely have to say that he took a more stringent, moral tone in analyzing and treating his cases than Freud. For example, he showed how it was possible to use one's guilt to gain advantage: "This is often seen in the case of a child, who tells a lie and gets a complex about it, by which arrangement he can play a rôle of distinguished uselessness. Everyone will be struck by his honesty if he worries so much about having told a fib" (1964, p. 25). The boy's intention here was to avoid taking genuine responsibility in life. Adler also initiated a kind of game analogy in personality theory, speaking about "moves in the game" of psychotherapy (p. 25) and the fact that schizophrenics are people who have been completely "checkmated" in life (p. 13). The underlying theory here is that there are certain rules of the game of life to be followed, but that certain individuals avoid facing up to them, or construct their own rules of procedure as they go along — their own "ethic" of how things ought to be played out. Adler was a genius in identifying these highly subjective ethical systems.

We might ask ourselves at this point, how does a person come to project an "ought"? If ideals transcend the existential reality of the here-and-now, and project something to be attained — or, as in self-actualization, never really to be attained but to be striven for in the future — how do they come about in the first instance? Does experience teach us our oughts by a programmed "this is good, that is bad" form of instruction administered by significant others in our formative years? If a child has been reared in a home lacking in interpersonal love and devotion, does he acquire the ideal or value "people ought to love one another and show it" from those few times when his parents may have briefly shown him affection, or can he merely sense and hence project an ought of this sort as being "right and good" out of his misery, out of his continuing *lack* of affection? Either source of learning would be a past event, a stimulus from the past environment applied to the present, but surely there is a difference. In one case he learns the ethic from being loved occasionally, in the other from *not* being loved at all. A dialectician would appreciate the latter explanation, whereas demonstrative theorists would be more likely to seek the former, since they hope to begin with those experiences which have actually taken place (the presumed "primary and true" events of the past which can be pointed to extraspectively). The dialectician takes it as his maxim that one grasps *both* love and hate in truly understanding *either* of these experiences as they take place in his past life (see Chapter XI). One need not experience hate directly to understand what it means, though of course, having a hateful experience doubtless brings home certain features of hate not before anticipated. The potential is always there for the human being to project something in the future which has never occurred in his past. He is a stimulus-creating animal, not only a responding mechanism.

Indeed, when an individual is caught up in personal turmoil, when frustration and failures in life are greatest, the time is most ripe for an act of personal commitment, for an involvement in "oughts." Goals are stimulated at the darkest hours, and if they are not, the individual is lost, for he has given up on life. Viktor E. Frankl witnessed this basic truth as a prisoner of war. His moving account of the mistreatment of Jews in Nazi prison camps showed how the prisoner who had given up his faith in the future soon deteriorated both physically and psychologically. To have value, life must extend into the future, for values are not only in our past. As Frankl notes, "Values . . . do not drive a man; they do not *push* him, but rather *pull* him" (1963, p. 157). It is for this reason that Frankl rejects homeostatic balance (constancy principle) as a fruitful model for mental health. He favors the view that man needs "not a tensionless state but rather the striving and struggling for some goal worthy of him. . . . What man needs is not homeostasis but what I call 'noödynamics,' i.e., the spiritual dynamics in a polar field of tension where one pole is represented by a meaning to be fulfilled and the other pole by the man who must fulfill it" (p. 166). A dialectical inner tension of moving toward some greater goal is the way many theoreticians have discussed the origin of religious living. When this tension of opposites is great, and when the goal is suddenly crystallized, said William James, a dramatic conversion to some faith is often the result (1958, pp. 184–185).

The direct paralleling of religious turmoil with mental illness was actually begun in the 1930's by Anton Boisen, a Protestant minister who had himself visited "The Wilderness of the Lost" (1962, Ch. I). In his remarkable book, *The Explorations of the Inner World,* Boisen effectively argued against the physical theories of mental illness, and concluded that psychotics were individuals with disorganized inner worlds, which they strive to put straight much the way the prisoner of war already referred to does. They seek the oughts and try to catch sight of a goal toward which we might all better move. They sometimes acquire a messianic zeal precisely because they do have some measures in mind to help set the world straight. Those who pass through psychoses successfully, says Boisen, emerge triumphant, better for the experience, and frequently capable of helping others make similar journeys. He discusses many religious founders, including Jesus, in these terms, and strives not to lower the value of religion as something psychotic but to raise the value of psychosis as something akin to religion. God, for Boisen, though presumably also an intelligence which has actually influenced his life (see esp. p. 115), is described in organismic terms: ". . . the idea of God is the symbol of the collective at its best" (p. 178). Boisen believes that the problem of mental illness has to do with man's philosophy of life, especially with man's sense of failure and estrangement from others (the collective).

Boisen was the first to stress that the problems of sin and salvation are to a large extent identical to those of mental illness and its cure. This is not to say that every sinner was mentally ill, or vice versa, but: "For the most part . . . what we know as mental illness represents either the crucial or the terminal stage of inner conflicts which arise within those who are trying to serve two masters, those who recognize and accept an ultimate loyalty but have not been able to give up desires and tendencies which belong to an earlier stage of development" (p. 209).

Religion, therefore, has to do with the organization of personal and social experience into a collective, to which we pay homage in the God concept. Presumably the more generally accepted definition of religion as an "attitude of devotion to something greater than the self" might then be applied here. The religious man devoutly sets himself a course of action, because he has answered the final-cause query: "Who am I? What is my place in the universe? What am I intended to do or be?" (p. 138). Unlike the inner adjustment of Freudian man, this man would find his highest level of adjustment in the collective. It remained for O. Hobart Mowrer to give this argument a sophisticated theoretical phrasing. Apparently Mowrer, a psychologist, arrived at much of his thinking quite independent of Boisen's writings. And we can see glimmerings of Mowrer's finished view in some of his early experimental researches (e.g., Mowrer, 1948).

It is Mowrer's contention that Freud has led us down the garden path in our thinking about mental illness, as regards who is to be held accountable in its genesis (Mowrer, 1961). In one sense Mowrer picked up the trend of thinking begun by Adler, but in quite different terms. Freud was the first person to oppose the idea of a clash between the collective, as represented by the super-ego with its systems of oughts, and the animalistic nature of the individual, represented by the libidinal and hostile promptings of the id. As his theory was completely worked out, Mowrer observes, the fault for mental illness seemed to be primarily if not entirely on the side of the collective. It is the demands of the group made manifest in repressive measures such as lawfulness and moral tenets, imposed on group members to facilitate collective solidarity, that ultimately lie at the root of mental illness, in the Freudian view. The neurotic is someone who has been damned with a too-rigid super-ego, and who therefore is caught up in unrealistic guilt feelings and diverted natural impulses making their presence known in his symptoms. Mowrer takes the other side of this dialectical opposition, and stresses the fact that neurotics are not suffering from pseudo-guilt but from true guilt. The neurotic or psychotic individual has failed to put himself in a genuine and truthful relationship with the collective, has failed to digest the moral tenets and teachings of his sociocultural heritage; consequently he suffers a hell-on-earth in mental illness.

Anything which furthers this descent into mental illness Mowrer takes to be a *sin:* "Irresponsibility, wrongdoing, immorality, sin: what do the terms matter if we can thus understand more accurately the nature of psychopathology and gain greater practical control over its ramified forms and manifestations" (p. 48). Because of his paralleling of religion and mental illness, Mowrer has come under criticism in psychology, much of it by people who do not read him carefully. For example, a common argument against his position is that he argues for the status quo. This is no more true than to say that Adler argued for the status quo in his concept of social interest, or that Fromm does so in his concept of productive love. Mowrer just happens to believe that moral or religious tenets are not to be discounted simply because they lack scientific origins. If these are thought of as time-tested oughts, arbitrarily arrived at but proven to be challenges equal to man's worth, then can we afford to dismiss them so easily? Furthermore, there are many types of religious leaders, and some of them have been decidedly revolutionary in approach, as Jesus was. Religions deal with values, and simply because a value is old does not mean it cannot be revolutionary. Some would feel that, in today's highly competitive and materialistic world, the older values of brotherly love and disdain for wealth as such, which Jesus advocated, are still decidedly revolutionary in their message, since they contradict the prevailing value structure.

Another criticism of Mowrer has to do with the therapy he advocates; in it a neurotic is expected to admit his deviousness and be moved to rectify the situation, to confess his guilt in the presence of those against whom he has "sinned." This seems to stimulate visions of hairshirts and burnings at the stake in the minds of some clinicians, when actually, of course, the practical outcomes of many psychotherapy series are precisely of this sort. Jung spoke about it as the neurotic throwing off the "mask" he wears in relations with others, and Rogers' discussion of "congruence" is very much on this order, where guilt becomes just that — guilt — with sincere promptings to repent not taken lightly but encouraged and accepted for what they are. Any single therapist might indeed abuse the Mowrerian approach and revile his client, but it is hardly fair to hold the point of view responsible, any more than it would be Freud's fault if an unscrupulous psycho-analyst related sexually to his client in the name of "therapeutic release of the client's pent-up libido."

A final criticism often heard of Mowrer is that he needlessly brings in religious terminology, when he could limit his commenary to terms such as ethical tenets or group mores. He does this by design, of course, because he feels that psychology is doing very poorly in the mental health field, and he sees no reason why we must ask religious people to change their introspectively meaningful terms to suit us. In fact he takes ministers to task for giving up their potential usefulness as psychotherapists. Mowrer feels they are too readily accepting the notion that only someone called a psychotherapist, with his so-called specialized training, can help a human being suffering through a neurotic or psychotic problem. Mowrer definitely advocates that ministers can and should provide such psychotherapy, in light of their religious heritage, which, as one aspect of the collective wisdom of mankind, surely gives them as much right to cure sick souls as the psycho-analysts, who only recently came on the scene (p. 171).

The important point for our consideration is to recognize that all of these attempts to unite religion or ethics and mental illness put their emphasis on the final cause. *Mental illness is seen as a disorder not of efficient but of final causation.* Something has gone wrong with the life plan, and consequently the individual is out of kilter. He has made up his own rules or justifications, in a selfish fashion, or he is completely at sea as to what to do, disorganized, estranged, and alone. He retreats into a world of his own, but finds no lasting peace of mind. Can a physical therapy treat such an illness? Only if the final-cause disruption is itself contingent upon an efficient-cause physical disruption. But there hangs the tale. The physical thesis has been with us for centuries, seemingly unable to provide a meaningful picture of things. Frankl, Boisen, and Mowrer ask that we consider the possibility that final-cause disruptions are to be cured only through application of that area of knowledge with the greatest experience in such study — religion and/or the related ethical philosophies of man.

The psychiatrist Thomas S. Szasz has made this point another way in his book, *The Myth of Mental Illness* (1961). He does not draw a parallel with religion, but, like Adler before him, he goes to game theory as a heuristic device and asserts that the mentally ill are those individuals who have problems in living due to the kinds of games they and their environmental associates play (p. 255). Szasz does not seem to be directly influenced by Adler, but rather more by the mathematical models group which was spawned in the growing mathematical idealism of modern physics (see Chapter V). It has become acceptable to refer to mathematical models as games, and there has been considerable cross-breeding of mathematics with actual games, such as chess. The various chess moves have been programmed into computers and thus it is said that machines have been taught to play games by the rules, to make moves giving the greatest mathematical probability of success, and so on. Szasz, however, acknowledges a certain affinity with the thinking of

Adler, and the following quote might just as well have been taken from the founder of Individual Psychology: "it seems worth pointing out that in many of these games ('mental illnesses'), the chief aim of the player ('patient') is to control his opponent ('significant object') and/or to prove his superiority and omnipotence" (p. 288).

It is surely clear that whether one refers to the rules of the game, social interest, ethico-religious mandates, or the Ten Commandments, he is speaking not only about what is, but about what ought to be. And, if difficulties in personal adjustment arise because these prescriptions, beckoning values, sought-for aspirations are not clear, or are unmentioned or despoiled in some way — i.e., if these problems are the *causes* rather than the *effects* of mental illness — then psychology would indeed do well to turn part of its attention to those classical areas of human concern we know as ethics and religion. At least, some of our number should be given the opportunity to make this plausible investigation, and to evolve theories of mental illness and its cure in light of their preferred terminologies. One can always translate terms if that is what really disturbs him. We could not validate ethical systems in this study (see Chapter VI), but we would be seeking a relationship between future projections and their hypothesized effects on the intelligent human being functioning in the present. The influence of ethical systems, with specific beliefs varying across criteria selected to assess them, could then become a matter of demonstrative investigation within a particular point of view. We might well reach this level of study in psychology, if only the line of development from theory to test were extended in the name of a science of thinking, intelligent mankind.

Adjustment Problems of the Clinician as Applied Psychologist

Once the clinician has left the university and set foot in the world of "practical affairs," he must face many problems brought about by this very circumstance. Bingham's definition (see above, p. 412) takes on a ring of truth, because the clinician is not always certain at this point precisely what are his "ends" as a theoretician or as a scientist in this clamoring world of "data" which seek to gain advantage or help through his services. He has to operate within the conflicting motives to psychotherapy. Attracted to the profession by an "interest in people," which translates into a scholarly curiosity about their natures, he now finds that such study may simply take up valuable time during the consulting hours of a working day. Time means money, and the clinician is a businessman, so the next development in his thinking is to raise the question, "what is the most efficient method of clearing up client symptoms?" It is only a short step then to the realization that, after all, insight is really unnecessary to the effecting of a cure. His motive thus shifts ever so subtly to the curative, and in time, lest he find adequate satisfaction in curing others or in expanding his business, he begins to suffer from a certain lack of personal fulfillment. Then too, he may not be certain precisely why he administers his clinical tests to clients, and he frequently questions the worth of clinical reports to other professions. Sometimes he finds that he can best help his data (people) by being illogical and sophistic. Add to these points the constant demands of his academic friends that he seek to validate his dialectically-phrased case interpretations, and it is obvious that the professional lot of a clinician is not without its drawbacks.

Even so, we do not agree that a solution can be found in simply defining all applied psychologists as outside the realm of basic science. As we saw in Chapter V, science is merely a tool designed to help make our thinking clear as we formulate theories and hunches about our world. The world of practical affairs *is* our world just as clearly as the world of natural affairs is. Man's social behavior, though it may depart in absolute respects from the behavior of a raindrop or a monkey, is not therefore less worthy of scientific study. One does not let the method dictate what are proper data; one adjusts the method to suit the data. Data are constructs, and we as social scientists must work to provide proper data language for a science which has meaning to other aspects of our data. Certain of our constructs talk back to us, a disconcerting experience at times, but this should not dissuade us in our efforts to be correct, to put forth theories which are meaningful and valid. We cannot leave the field and, in ignorance of human affairs, hope to construct a worthwhile theory of man's personality. Let us now turn to a few problem areas of the clinician in the field, and examine them in light of our "issues which divide."

Test Prediction and the Intent of Clinical Instruments

In his book on *Theory and Research in Projective Techniques* (1963), Murstein contrasts the needs of a practicing clinician with those of a researcher on the matter of test usage as follows:

> The practicing clinician . . . is more directly concerned with the immediate availability of valid test procedures which can be used with

the client or patient he is seeing now. He is very much concerned with the ability of the tests he may employ to predict the personality status of a given individual. With regard to the research findings, therefore, the fact that a new method of analyzing the TAT correlates .40 with a diagnostic criterion may leave him cold if the error in *individual* prediction remains high. The researcher, contrariwise, may be delighted that his new method of analysis apparently contributes valid variance to the prediction of the criterion even if the practical utility of such a method is not currently realizable (p. 361).

Though there is a certain amount of truth in this observation, we might pause to consider precisely what is the "practical utility" a clinician seeks in administering his objective or projective tests. Why does the clinician administer the Rorschach or TAT to his client? Is it his hope to predict client behavior someday at the 1.00 level? Is that what he is striving for as a practical goal? We frankly doubt that this is his primary goal. Since he must validate his theories of personality in time, the clinician may say and somehow even believe that he wants to predict in the sense of validation (theory of knowledge), with increasing accuracy. But the problem is, one can predict client behavior with great accuracy yet *fail* to have a theoretical grasp — literally, a genuine understanding — of what he is predicting about. If the diagnostic criterion to which the TAT is predicting fails to instruct the clinician as regards his client's dynamics, no manner of correlational value will excite him to take an interest in it. As we noted in Chapter VI, the actuary does not have to know why a man drinks to predict accurately that he is a bad bet for automobile insurance. Similarly, the clinician does not have to understand the personal idiosyncrasies of his client to make some rather remarkable predictions, such as the length of time he will stay in the hospital, his potential diagnosis, or the kinds of phrases the staff is likely to use in describing him. He can let an objective test such as the MMPI work for him in this regard. But can he "get a feel for the person" who took the test, can he spontaneously generate a new label or alter the meaning of an old one to fit his particular client through the use of such a testing procedure?

This is the reason many clinicians, who view it as their task to "understand" their individual clients, find the empirical study of projective tests, or the use of objectively constructed tests such as the MMPI hollow and devoid of meaning. They seek to use tests such as the Rorschach or TAT not only or even primarily for *methodological prediction,* but to *describe theoretically* what they take to be a person emerging spontaneously before them. They seek a language of description and not merely a fixed actuarial prediction of the sort we hope for in methodologically validating some hypothesis formed after we have done our theorizing and made use of our "data language." They are interested in the theoretical style of conceptualizing, the examination by dialectical analysis of what makes the client "tick." To the client, questions such as "why do I drink?" or "why did I land in the hospital?" or "why am I so miserable?" are of the utmost practical utility. Many clinicians try to stylize and systematize a way of thinking discriminally about client problems in their clinical instruments. This *style* of thought must fit *all* clients, though its particulars in the description of individuals may vary for different clients. Freudian thought was accepted not because it had 100 per cent predictability, but because it provided a language of theoretical description equal to the task, whereas the physical languages did not.

Questions such as "what kind of an automobile risk is this man?" or "what diagnosis would this patient carry if he went into hospital X?" or "how long will this patient remain in hospital X?" are not of practical utility to the client so much as to the personnel who must sell him insurance, or treat his mental illness. As we have seen, not all clinicians feel they "treat" others so much as they help others to learn about themselves; they are consequently less attracted to this brand of practical utility. If they remain unenthused about some new scheme for scoring the TAT, it is usually due not to the .40 correlation this scheme achieves, but to the fact that it fails to help them conceptualize their client's situation. Schemes which *do* help will be embraced even if the predictive correlations remain at .00, as experience over the years surely should have taught us by now. The Rorschach has failed to be highly predictive over the years, and it has consequently fallen from favor as a topic for research investigation. Yet, it is the most frequently used instrument in actual practice because of its great utility as a language of description. Even those who support the Rorschach's standardization have rejected the predictive validity of more objective tests, such as the MMPI, because of their presumed inability to capture "all" of the personality. A typical attitude of this sort is expressed in the following:

> Such well-known paper-and-pencil approaches to the study of personality as the Minnesota Multiphasic Personality Inventory, the Edwards Personal Preference Schedule, and Cattell's Junior Personality Quiz provide a convenient, though severely limited, approach to the validation of other methods of personality assessment. Unfortunately they all have the common characteristic of dealing only with the sub-

ject's superficial response to items the content of which is often transparent. Although ingenious methods have been developed to disguise this content and force the subject to make choices which can then be scaled and treated psychometrically, the fundamental, superficial nature of such tests still persists. In fairness to the self-inventory approach, it should be pointed out that scales from these tests usually have fairly high reliability and often correlate with socially observable behavior to a higher degree than any projective technique. Such correlations, however, can frequently be traced directly to the fact that the individual has a conscious self-concept that dominates his test responses and is not unrelated to his social behavior as judged by others (Holtzman, Thorpe, Swartz, and Herron, 1961, pp. 179–180).

The tougher-minded researcher must surely look on the last line of this quote as a bit of word magic, since it calmly writes off any and all correlations between tests tapping the conscious self-image and independent measures of overt behavior. Validity is simply dismissed here in favor of a theory about unconscious behavior, a theory which the clinician finds essential to his practice and which is thus far more important than mere prediction of something called conscious self-images at no matter how high a correlation level. As we noted in Part One, theories are rarely if ever rejected because of something so limiting as validating evidence; theories are dislodged only by better theories — with evidence coming in after the fact as an arguing point if it happens to be in the theorist's favor.

A point which relates to this matter of usefulness of theory is the fact that so many of our test subjects find the items on objective tests arbitrary and inapplicable to them. Objective test items are actually written like final givens, like the premises of a demonstrative line of reasoning. One feels ensnared, as if he were being described in the syllogism which began demonstratively "All men are evil. This is a man. Hence. . . ." Can we question this major premise? Not if the demonstrative reasoner has defined his "evil" construct operationally and sticks to his guns. In the same way, test subjects feel that test items are immutable givens, stipulations which cannot be altered even though they feel strongly that this or that item "really does not apply to me." The actuarial clinician does not split hairs about MMPI items. They are dropped into the IBM hopper like so many black and white balls in an urn (see Chapter VI) and predictions result with little emphasis given to an analysis of the item content as such. When the items *are* looked at and interpreted individually, it is not for the sake of prediction but for the sake of theory. Berg (1957) has shown us how to predict when the item content is virtually or apparently non-existent for the test taker.

But subjects do not realize that we can be indifferent to what they say about themselves from item to item. They relate such item content to themselves, and find through such dialectical examination and introspective effort that the items really misfire with regard to their personalities. At least, many of them seem to do this. Consequently, they feel misunderstood and arbitrarily forced into pigeonholes against their wills. To a certain extent, this purity criticism is well taken, but such charges naturally irritate the actuarial clinician, who simply wants cooperation in making predictions. He is on the side of method, while the client is on the side of theory, at this point. He is the demonstrative reasoner, the client the dialectician. Because of their disguised purpose, the traditional projective tests avoid this problem. The test taker has no way of evaluating the Rorschach or TAT content, and thus rarely feels so definitely that he is being arbitrarily labeled.

Coming back to the clinician who seeks understanding as well as prediction, we find that he now often uses his objective tests much the way he formerly used his projective instruments. The sophisticated clinician can analyze an MMPI profile of scores very much as he had formerly analyzed the contents and scores of a Rorschach protocol. He has worked out a new language of description, one which can be greatly extended beyond the narrow limits of the test's original nine or ten scales. He manipulates the theorotypes embodied in the subscales — schizophrenia, hysteria, and so on — in such a way as to come up with new combinations of personality descriptions and hypotheses unique to the individual. He capitalizes on our overlapping of illness theory and personality theory. This client has a spot of hysteria and a dash of psychopathy, and that one combines depression and a certain paranoia.

By enlarging upon such syndrome pictures as models for behavior, the clinician can manufacture all manner of commentary in the best tradition of the dynamic projective testers. He makes a mockery of Holtzman's criticism and becomes just as "deep" in his analysis as the Rorschach test user. In addition, he combines certain of the profiles and establishes empirically that newly emerging valid constructs can be demonstrated in research (Cronbach and Meehl, 1955). Thus vindicated, he can go on cooking up his own special brew of unique, individualistic interpretations for each new client he meets. Whereas before he had pondered over the intricacies of a unique Rorschach or TAT protocol, now he ponders over the jumbled deck of theorotypes before him in the MMPI profile. He does this because he *must* have a theoretical language of description which permits variation, which departs from the "All men are this way all the time" phrasing of a demonstrative test, and comes down to "This man is different in certain ways from all or most others I have seen, in the following ways" dialectical phrasing.

The Clinical Report and Professional Problems

A word should be said about the clinical report, which must often be written by the clinical psychologist for other team members — the psychiatrist in particular — or for professional groups, such as court authorities, who seek to evaluate the mental status of an individual client. The problem here, of course, issues from the myriad theories each professional identity holds to in conceptualizing its realm of activity. Take, for example, the psychiatrist. When he asks the clinician to evaluate his patient, there is an unmentioned and debatable assumption made that the clinician's theory of illness is congruent with the psychiatrist's. Often this is the case, but just as often it is not, as our discussions of the motives to psychotherapy have already taught us. Many psychiatrists think of a clinician's role as analogous to that of a laboratory technician's. If one is seeking a diagnosis of a physical malady, then send the patient off to the laboratory and have some tests run. Similarly, if an emotional disturbance exists, send the patient off to the psychologist and see what might turn up.

What does turn up when the psychologist is given a free rein in conceptualizing his case is often superfluous and unusable. Whereas laboratory reports fit nicely into the psychiatrist's theory of illness, psychological reports often do not. The psychiatrist wonders where the psychologist gets all the fanciful insights into the case, and cannot help noting the similarity of some psychological reports to dime store novels. Often the clinical psychologist, in making his recommendations for psychotherapy, strongly urges that important figures in the client's life be seen, such as his teachers, relatives, or religious counselor. The physician is reluctant to take quite this broad a sweep in viewing his responsibility to treat patients. Indeed, he senses correctly that the psychologist would really prefer to work on a team arrangement with *these other* individuals than with his more conventional team peers. In a team of this sort the physician would have less clear authority to call the shots, and the psychologist would be a decided threat. If he wishes to interview or to visit the relatives in many cases, the psychologist challenges the professional identity of the social worker, who asks, "Why should this fall within the realm of the psychologist at this late date?" We have already noted (p. 420) how intrusions on one another's "areas" of professional practice are an ever-present problem in the field situation. Such intrusions result because of the basic assumptions made by each professional specialty; even psychologists, in their continuing battle for a share in psychotherapy, to the psychiatrist's displeasure, rail at the social worker who is more and more drawn into therapeutic contact with disturbed individuals.

Not all psychologists are given such leeway in writing their reports. Sometimes the psychiatrist, as he makes his referral, stresses that he wants a "brief picture" — about two paragraphs — which will help him to make a diagnosis, and no more. He might like a few lines on the "dynamics" of the case, but he has many patients to take up each day at the case staffings, and he is simply unable to devote any more time to the extensive accounts which the clinical psychologist feels the need to write. The psychiatrist has noted in the past that these more fanciful excursions into dynamics usually result in long-winded exchanges among team members — including himself — but they are more for the theoretical "play" of the staff (scholarly motive) than for the benefit of the patient (curative motive). Or, a psychiatrist may desire a brief report from the clinician because he has some technical question to answer, such as "what is the IQ score?" or "is this an organic or a functional disorder?" His referral question is quite specific, and he sees no reason why it should not be treated in the same way the blood serologist treats a query about white-to-red blood count.

Now, from the psychologist's point of view, asking him a simple-minded question of this sort — one which is often based upon a debatable physical thesis as to the origins of abnormality and behavior in general — is a definite affront. He not only feels "caught" within the theoretical orientation of a politically strong majority, but he recognizes that this majority is "putting him down" in posing questions of this sort for him to answer. If this is the only role he is to play, then there is surely little room on the psychiatric team for him and his extra-medical theories of abnormal behavior. He therefore turns whenever he can to research or, more frequently, to administrative interests. He falls back on routine objective tests and what he considers to be a more humdrum report, but he justifies this by stressing that this is what the psychiatrist wishes him to do. He may just as well get lost in his researches and the daily problems of looking after his subordinates, if he is fortunate enough to pull together a staff. Frequently there is a psychological trainee (or "intern") about to answer the psychiatrist's technical question, so the issue is usually resolved through delegation.

Finally, of course, we should note the frequently made criticism that it really does not matter *what* is written in a report, because the nature of the psychiatric treatment is always the same. At least, the amount of variation in treatment due to findings described in the psychological report is negligible. Every patient is put through roughly the same procedure — of rest, pills, the various physical therapies, such as electro-convulsive shock — and even in the case of two-person psychotherapy, the psychological report is not germane. Freud would have scoffed at needing a psychological report based upon tests to teach him about his patient. Many modern therapists take the same view, noting that one must wait for the client to discover himself in any case, and that a biasing psychological report might do more harm than good to the therapeutic relationship. One cannot catalogue the client's disorders demonstratively, he must wait for the client to discover himself introspectively as he daily relates to his therapist.

Naturally, in some of the more dynamically oriented institutions, the psychological report is given more weight and even considerable respectability. We are surely being unfair in our characterization for many clinics and hospitals. Based on Menninger's analysis of mental illness (above, p. 427), one would like to believe that his view of the ideal clinical set-up is of this more liberal variety, where clinical psychologists might be given the chance to write up and then follow through on a program of therapy consistent with their theories. But note the reluctance he reflects in the following, in which he is speaking about the role a clinical psychologist might personally play in following through on his therapeutic recommendations to the psychiatric team: "The psychologist will assist in the continuing observation of psychological change and reactions, checking the course of the illness. He may also personally assist the patient to make corrections in his perceptions, associations, attitudes, and behavior; in short, he may undertake, vis-à-vis, some form of re-education or psychotherapy with the patient" (Menninger *et al.*, 1963, p. 335).

This rather uncertain acceptance of the psychologist as psychotherapist (re-educator) is actually a definite step forward, and it bodes well for the profession of clinical psychology. Yet, feeling as he does that the question of mental illness is still open, the clinical psychologist is not placated by what he takes to be such "little favors" from psychiatry. He would like to have far more to say and do than merely "some form" of re-education or psychotherapy, but he recognizes that he surely will have great difficulty in succeeding, because his role on the team is designed to meet the needs of another profession's theory about what should be done with the mentally ill. Though he continues to press his case, he looks around nervously for other avenues in which to develop a more independent self-image.

The Uses and Abuses of Insight

Slowly but surely the clinical psychologist has captured a certain right to see clients in psychotherapy. But this has brought on additional adjustment problems stemming from the resulting disagreements over whether or not the use of insight in psychotherapy is necessary. This problem is not unlike the one already discussed concerning tests which can predict adequately in the actuarial sense, but not provide a satisfactory theoretical understanding of the test subject. As we saw in the case of Wolpe (see Chapter VII), cures can be brought about without providing the client with an explanation of how his illness may have arisen in the first place. As the therapist Phillips has expressed it in speaking about the need for dealing with so-called depth questions which a client might raise — such as "why did I start drinking in the first place?" — what the therapist must do is

> to show that *they are the wrong questions to ask*. It is not a matter of *Why*, thus implying a genetic or historical answer-seeking process. The proper questions, it is contended, have to do with "How" and "What," meaning "How does the patient act to produce his troubles?" and "What situations and attitudes give rise to the behavior and symptoms in question?" (1956, pp. 36–37).

One might well ask, "proper for whom — the client or the therapist?" Insight is just one of the names we use for a man's thirst for knowledge, and the client does not find such "Why" questions beyond reasonable consideration. This is how man makes sense of his existence, and he hopes to be so understood by his therapist. If he has to bargain with his doctor and ignore this question as a cooperative patient should, as long as his drinking can be stopped by a therapist who finds such questions irrelevant to the cure, he will doubtless do so — at least in the presence of this very helpful doctor. Later, in talking over his problems with friends, of course, all sorts of speculative theories as to why he began drinking will doubtless be generated.

It is relatively easy to become disenchanted with insight therapy if one does not find great satisfaction in ferreting out the intricacies of personality functioning and theorizing about them. As a therapist, one soon learns that theoretical explanations of client behavior are legion, and that, thanks to the functioning of the client's procedural evidence, contradictory explanations can lead to comparable therapeutic outcomes. It sometimes becomes a tedious game of drowsy wits, trying to cook-up consistent pictures from the statements, dreams, and free associations of a none too interesting client. The hushed excitement, the glamour of Freud's initial insights is played out. One finds himself repeating "dynamics" across clients, and wondering whether this is generalized lawfulness of behavior, or a general projection of one's pet hunches. Even Phillips must cast all client behavior in a neo-Adlerian frame of reference to make sense of it (p. 39). It is difficult to repress this compulsion to understand others, or oneself, even if the truth resulting from this activity is often arbitrary and tentative. The immediate experiencing of procedural evidence in the clinical situation is sobering for the clinician, who up until that time may not have recognized its importance in his more academic theoretical and research pursuits.

Another source of conflict for the clinician who uses insight, if he is at all sensitive to the implications of his method of interpretation, has to do with the violation of logic entailed in many insights. As we noted in Chapter X, Freud took pride in the fact that his method could encompass the illogical maneuvers of his patients. Therapy clients proffer "good reasons" in place of the "real reasons" motivating their behavior. Emotional man is highly illogical and sophistic. Thus, when the clinician discredits what his client contends on the grounds that he has a hidden reason, an unconscious reason, a devious reason for arguing one way when the truth lies in another, he effectively employs an *ad hominem* argument to counter a client's sophistry. He takes up not the content of the client's assertion but rather the presumed unconscious and unrelated reason for making it. The client says, "I fight with my boss because he is an evil man, as the following example of his nature will surely convince you. . . ." and the clinician says at the appropriate point in therapy, "You are finding reasons to dislike your boss because he represents your father, whom you hate. . . ." A counter of this sort would not be permitted in logical debate, no matter how many instances of father rejection and hostility could be cited from the remarks of the discussant who made the initial assertion about his boss. The boss's behavior would have to be evaluated in its own right. But that is of no matter to the clinician. Ordinary people are surely not logicians, hence we are justified in "using fire to fight fire," in meeting clients' deviousness with illogical counter-arguments.

Trouble arises for us when we leave the consulting room, however, for we tend to continue such illogical analyses in our dealings with professional peers. This tendency to use *ad hominems* often colors the clinician's style of debate when he meets the criticisms of the broader scientific community. We know that Freud gained a certain reassurance and strength of purpose in the belief that hostile physicians were rejecting his views not on the merits of their criticisms but simply because they could not face up to their own sexual promptings. This type of argument is frequently leveled at the experimentalist by the clinician. If the experimentalist asks for controls in research, the clinician counters with some veiled interpretation of the former's toilet training, or worse (see, for example, Chapter III, p. 50). Even if there is truth in such charges, which might be quite useful to the experimentalist as a client in therapy — where he would want to study his motives on a personal, introspective basis — there is surely no call for them in an objective debate over questions of scientific fact. One must transcend such subjectivities and make his case at the level of the community in scientific exchange. If clinicians fail to appreciate this distinction between subjective therapy debate and objective research debate, then they surely will fail as scientists. Moreover, by justifying their stand through the use of *ad hominem* arguments, they open the door to such counter-arguments from their opponents, for they are no longer "the doctor" in the situation and hence are not to be considered any more expert at this sort of thing than their opponents. Although some clinicians would still prefer to thrive on the vagaries of such subjective entanglements and bits of gossip, they surely are not to be emulated, for then they encourage the regression of a scientific discipline into sophistry.

An interesting variation on the Freudian *ad hominem* has emerged in the years since World War II, nurtured by the growing influence of existentialism, with its stress on openness and commitment in interpersonal relations. In this case, the psychologist seeks to disarm his therapy client with his desire to create an open relationship in the therapy hour. Instead of taking the "you hate your boss because you hate your father" tack, this form of therapeutic *ad hominem* would run: "you are not really open and honest, but are merely clothing your true feelings in words, in barriers to direct communication and experience, hence you are avoiding a true relationship." Having discredited the client's intellectualized, or reticent approach to self-understanding, the therapist can then get him to make all manner of new self-evaluations. He argues: "strip yourself of your pretenses and be free; discover the 'real you' by voicing how you *truly* feel." The purity metaconstruct is quite apparent in all of this, and the theory which underlies this interpersonal ploy doubtless has considerable merit. We do hide behind Jungian masks, and we do avoid expressing our "true" feelings in many instances. An experience of this sort in psychotherapy can be helpful.

However, when used as a ploy in debate or in social relations outside the therapy room, it is quite inappropriate. The usual course of this *ad hominem* is as follows: The clinician becomes embroiled in a point of disagreement. He is very open and frank about his own personality inclinations, and invites his opponent to do the same. He essentially challenges his opponent to admit to presumed biases motivated by personality defenses — such as admitting that he feels a personal hostility toward the psychologist, who is "sensing" this interpersonal tension as they talk. If the opponent denies that he is feeling any undue hostility or tension, except in the sense that he is aggressively pressing his point in the debate, the psychologist then makes his *ad hominem* carry the day by either stating or implying: "you are not as completely open and honest as I am. You are unaware of what *really* is prompting you. I am not *defensive,* but you are. It therefore follows that your argument is leveled merely to sustain these irrelevant defensive pretenses. My argument is *genuine,* hence it is *true.*" This can be a particularly vicious *ad hominem* in social relations, because it puts the complete weight of involvement on the opponent. The disarming openness of the clinician and his assumption that what is said "genuinely" must therefore be true are quite convincing ploys. If one looks closer, however, the "purity" implied in stripping oneself of "intellectualized" words is not so pure. It smells of sophistry.

Dialecticians into Demonstrators and Back Again

If we had to single out the major source of conflict for the clinician, it would be the fact that his situation demands that he move from a dialectical to a demonstrative orientation in thinking about his data. The clinician who feels he must work with and appreciate the significance of a client's verbalizations is inevitably put into a dialectical framework. He is at the nerve center of theoretical speculation, so to speak, in that his client is always prepared to shape a slightly different account of his personal life history. Theoretical subjectivity is another way of saying that each client has this option, of accepting, rejecting, or altering constructs to suit his special case, to meet with his personal procedural evidence. The intent of the purity metaconstruct is to assert this prerogative for each of us. Mere words, abstracted from the behavior of others, cannot capture in any genuine way the exact situation which confronts each of us in his "one and only" life. The clinician (at least the more traditional variety) is prepared to let us take this approach; he comes to expect and to encourage expression of the dialectical peculiarities of each client. However, when the clinician takes leave of his client, he faces another responsibility, that of scientifically proving the theories which have been generated in their contact.

He must do at this point precisely what we have not wanted him to do with us. The clinician must abstract a subtle generality, an objective terminology, from contacts within a series of subjective variances. As Jung has noted, it would be impossible to have any science if each client were literally a personality theory unto himself. Though he has come to accept the utility and legitimacy of thinking in dialectical terms, we now ask the clinician to frame an experiment in fixed, demonstrative terms. After he has permitted the client to come to his own major premises dialectically and to distort the terminology as it is proffered in the therapy hour, we now want the clinician himself to describe what he does in operational, primary and true terms. It is very difficult to make this switch, just as it is difficult for the psychologist (and he too may be a clinician such as Wolpe) who is accustomed to thinking primarily in demonstrative fashion to begin theorizing dialectically. One prefers to stay with what has been meeting his purposes in the past.

This is why it is so difficult to get certain clinicians to appreciate the need for an occasional demonstrative attack on their theories. To do research, one has to settle on a major premise or two, on an hypothesis that he considers worth testing. Too often, the dialectically-inclined theorist sees so many alternatives, so many contingencies, that he cannot take any single hypothesis seriously. Research studies are indeed rather restricted commentaries, filled with concern about controls of all that seems spontaneous and interesting. Even when he does get involved in research and finally obtains proof for his hypothesis, the clinician may find that there are alternative hypotheses which can explain the results just as easily, a fact he knew from the outset. So, it all seems a little wasteful of time to him, time he might well have spent in other pursuits — which means that the other motives in his work may begin to gnaw at him. There are countless clinicians who fail to see the importance of research to their work, and who shrug it off as merely another tool in the game of professional advancement, or academic chess.

It is probably too much to expect that the demonstrative and dialectical styles of theorizing and testing hunches can be highly perfected in the same individual. All men make use of both forms of reasoning to various degrees, but they seem to gravitate to one or the other, as our review of history over the centuries has clearly shown (see Chapter IX). But the point is that we must appreciate how peculiarly susceptible the clinical situation is to conflicts in this sphere. The contrasting needs of an applied and a so-called basic psychology were never more apparent. Having now pinpointed as well as we can the *major* source of our professional fission, we might at least get it under moderate control. We might recognize that it is possible to err in both directions, and that though one need not find a middle way combining both, he ought to acknowledge at least that the direction he takes, down one or the other of our two paths, will surely color his journey and determine its endpoint. Let us hope that at least some of us walk both paths, for that is how true understanding is most likely to ensue — through personal experience and travel in many lands.

Summary

Chapter XII dealt with the many problems which arise when psychology is practiced in an applied setting. It was suggested at the outset that five "issues which divide" were at the heart of most professional and career misunderstandings in psychology and related professions. These included the motives to psychotherapy, the need for an introspective as well as an extraspective perspective in theory formulation, the different demands of theory and method, the employment of dialectical vs. demonstrative reasoning and metaconstructs, and the use of efficient- and material-cause vs. formal- and final-cause explanations. Clinical psychology was then selected as a model form of applied psychology, and its history traced rather carefully over the decade following World War II. The "issues which divide" were seen in this unfolding picture.

Some consideration was given to problems of the psychiatric team, where the motives to psychotherapy generate professional strife. The point was made that modern personality theory could emerge only after a distinction had been made between physical illness theory and a theory of intelligent human behavior, moved by the attraction of final causes. This led into a general discussion of the nature of mental illness, and it was made clear that in all the emerging views of mental illness which depart from the physical model of illness, the shift is toward a final cause explanation. A dialectical metaconstruct permits us to see how man generates final causes. Mental illness is increasingly seen as a disorder of final rather than efficient causation.

In the final sections of Chapter XII some thought was given to the problems faced by the clinician in the field, who must move out of the more demonstratively oriented academic world into the more dialectically oriented world of individual clients. It was noted that clinicians do not always administer tests to predict to some criterion with great efficiency, and that at times they forego prediction — a methodological matter — in favor of understanding — a theoretical matter. Writing clinical reports was considered a highly disillusioning experience. Insight was seen to be often based upon illogical arguments, and the danger of extending this practice to scientific discourse was underscored. Finally, the fact that the clinical situation is peculiarly susceptible to the confrontation of dialectical and demonstrative strategies in theoretical and methodological matters was reaffirmed as a major source of difficulty.

References

Adler, A. *Problems of neurosis* (edited by Philippe Mairet). New York: Harper & Row, 1964.

Bach, G. R. Who are the discoverers of psychological knowledge? *American Psychologist,* 1952, 7, 131–132.

Bakan, D. Clinical psychology and logic. *American Psychologist,* 1956, *11,* 655–662.

Beck, S. J. *The six schizophrenias.* New York: American Orthopsychiatric Association, 1954.

Berenda, C. W. Is clinical psychology a science? *American Psychologist,* 1957, *12,* 725–729.

Berg, I. A. Deviant responses and deviant people: The formulation of the deviation hypothesis. *Journal of Counseling Psychology,* 1957, *4,* 154–161.

Bingham, W. V. On the possibility of an applied psychology. *Psychological Review,* 1923, *30,* 289–305.

Boisen, A. T. *The exploration of the inner world.* New York: Harper & Bros., 1962.

Cameron, N. *Personality development and psychopathology.* Boston: Houghton Mifflin Co., 1963.

Crannell, C. W. Are rat psychologists responsible for fission? *American Psychologist,* 1947, *2,* 22–23.

Crannell, C. W. Fission resolved? *American Psychologist,* 1956, *11,* 636–638.

Cronbach, L. J., and Meehl, P. E. Construct validity in psychological tests. *Psychological Bulletin,* 1955, *52,* 281–302.

Frankl, V. E. *Man's search for meaning: An introduction to logotherapy.* New York: Washington Square Press, 1963.

Gabriel, E. A clinician answers Guthrie. *American Psychologist,* 1950, *5,* 495.

Guthrie, E. R. The status of systematic psychology. *American Psychologist,* 1950, *5,* 97–101.

Healy, W. *Mental conflicts and misconduct.* Boston: Little, Brown, 1917.

Holtzman, W. H., Thorpe, J. S., Swartz, J. D., and Herron, E. W. *Inkblot perception and personality.* Austin, Texas: University of Texas Press, 1961.

Hunt, W. A. Clinical psychology: Science or superstition. *American Psychologist,* 1951, *6,* 683–687.

James, W. *The varieties of religious experience.* New York: New American Library, 1958.

Kahn, T. C. Clinically and statistically oriented psychologists split our profession. *American Psychologist,* 1955, *10,* 171–172.

Koch, S. Psychological science versus the science-humanism antinomy; intimations of a significant science of man. *American Psychologist,* 1961, *16,* 629–639.

Krech, D. A note on fission. *American Psychologist,* 1946, *1,* 402–404.

MacKinnon, D. W. The structure of personality. In Vol. I of J. McV. Hunt (Ed.), *Personality and the behavior disorders.* New York: Ronald Press, 1944. Pp. 3–48.

MacLeod, R. B. Teleology and theory of human behavior. *Science,* 1957, *125,* 477–480.

Menninger, K., Mayman, M., and Pruyser, P. *The vital balance.* New York: Viking Press, 1963.

Mowrer, O. H. Learning theory and the neurotic paradox. *American Journal of Orthopsychiatry,* 1948, *18,* 571–610.

Mowrer, O. H. *The crisis in psychiatry and religion.* New York: D. Van Nostrand, 1961.

Murstein, B. I. *Theory and research in projective techniques.* New York: Wiley, 1963.

Newman, S. H. Should psychological theory and practice be divided? *American Psychologist,* 1950, *5,* 495–496.

Oppenheimer, R. Analogy in science. *American Psychologist,* 1956, *11,* 127–135.

Peirce, C. S. *Values in a universe of chance* (edited by P. P. Wiener). Garden City, N.Y.: Doubleday Anchor, 1958.

Phillips, E. L. *Psychotherapy: A modern theory and practice.* Englewood Cliffs, N.J.: Prentice-Hall, 1956.

Rogers, C. R. The interest in the practice of psychotherapy. *American Psychologist,* 1953, *8,* 48–50.

Rogers, C. R. Persons or science? A philosophical question. *American Psychologist,* 1955, *10,* 267–278.

Rosenzweig, S. Imbalance in clinical psychology. *American Psychologist,* 1950, *5,* 678–680.

Rosenzweig, S. (Ed.) Balance in clinical psychology: A symposium in correspondence. *American Psychologist,* 1951, *6,* 208–212.

Rychlak, J. F. Clinical psychology and the nature of evidence. *American Psychologist,* 1959, *14,* 642–648.

Skinner, B. F. A case history in scientific method. *American Psychologist,* 1956, *11,* 221–233.

Solomon, L. N. The paradox of the experimental clinician. *American Psychologist,* 1955, *10,* 170–171.

Stainbrook, E. Some historical determinants of contemporary diagnostic and etiological thinking in psychology. In P. H. Hoch and J. Zubin (Eds.), *Current problems in psychiatric diagnosis.* New York: Grune & Stratton, 1953.

Strupp, H. H., Castore, G. F., Lake, R. A., Merrill, R. M., and Bellak, L. Comments on Rogers' "Persons or science?" *American Psychologist,* 1956, *11,* 153–157.

Super, D. E. Reply to Rosenzweig. *American Psychologist,* 1951, *6,* 128.

Szasz, T. S. *The myth of mental illness.* New York: Hoeber-Harper, 1961.

Thorne, F. C. The clinical method in science. *American Psychologist,* 1947, *2,* 159–166.

Tolman, Ruth S. Virtue rewarded and vice punished. *American Psychologist,* 1953, *8,* 721–733.

Watson, R. I. A brief history of clinical psychology. *Psychological Bulletin,* 1953, *50,* 321–346.

An Orientation for
the Future

Introduction

Having completed our review of the many issues at play in a philosophy of science for personality theory, it now behooves us to tighten the threads of development and formalize the position into an orientation for the future. Since it is the style of thought and not specific points of argument which must stand as a legitimate alternative in the future, the important thing seems to be to articulate the goal at which we have now arrived. In this closing chapter we shall therefore organize the viewpoint around succinct points, present a table and a final overview, and also take some cognizance of the most frequent objections engendered by this view.

The Personality Student's Frame of Reference

The general approach taken in this volume was to ask the questions: How do certain men think — or theorize — about other men? What are their major assumptions, and what factors seem to be logically determining these assumptions? We have tried to avoid the tactic of looking to underlying subjective motives, the personality-determined promptings which might well play a part in any given instance, because such approaches rely upon *ad hominems*. We believe an illogical argument is acceptable within the four walls of the consulting room, but it is beneath the role of the scientist to attempt such personality analyses of one's opponent on a point of theoretical dispute. Since there are legitimate arguments to be made, drawn from the history of science, why settle for such an inconclusive and irritating rejoinder? Students of personality should be especially careful to avoid this tactic; they are the most susceptible to its use due to their area of interest. Freud's lasting mistake was that he could not avoid it.

A truism we have come to in our review of theory is that the days of hoping to find a single, all-encompassing theory — about anything — are surely past. This plausible assumption of yesteryear was based upon an inaccurate interpretation of the nature of meaning. In the future, the student of personality must come to know *all* theorists equally well. He cannot pick sides without first examining the premises within which he is to evaluate the selection of theories before him. Rather than asking questions like "who is right, Freud, Jung, or Sullivan?" or "which theory is most scientific, Rogers' or Wolpe's?" he must ask: "what meanings were these men seeking? What was their *purpose* in theorizing?" If purposes differ, then grounds for evaluation differ.

Though there is nothing wrong with holding to *one* position, hoping to further its terminological development, experience suggests that what any single theorist has to offer of worth is a given vantage point rather than a completely viable terminology. Even the "single truth" approach benefits from a complete understanding of alternative interpretations. As dialecticians we might now grasp the fact that one of the best ways to know our own meaningful position is to study carefully that view which is most in opposition to it. Understanding is furthered by bringing to bear on human behavior the contrasting images of man implied in diverse theories. This is like playing the same melody with different instruments simultaneously; each one adds something to the total production — including a modicum of cacophony. Now, having argued for such a diversity in outlook, does this mean we must abandon hope of ever achieving a single language of discourse, a consistent frame of reference within which to consider and debate the merits of our views on man? No, we think it is still possible to have a unifying organization at another level.

The proper ground for a unifying outlook is several steps up the ladder of abstraction. Rather than taking a stand with one personality theorist, the more sophisticated student will seek his unifying outlook in the basic issues which come into *all* such lower-level points of view. Where does the theorist stand on the use of causation in the formulation of his constructs? This will ultimately affect his use of determinism and dictate whether or not he will make room for intelligent self-direction in the description of his data. What are his predilections as to the nature of meaning — on the side of realism or idealism? This will tell us where he will begin his descriptive task of capturing data, which then must dictate what kinds of things he will consider it interesting to theorize about. In a tactic of this sort, we ask the right type of question. We begin tying *this* theorist to *that* intellectual tradition, no matter how he might wriggle to free himself and shout in the name of purity that he will be his own man. As a cultural product, man's knowledge is the knowledge of men. The more we study our supposedly unique natures and decry our unique problems — and *also* read history — the more we see that there have been men like us, saying the same sorts of "unique" things for centuries, only in different contexts.

This is not to say that there is nothing new under the sun. It is simply to recognize that at the highest levels of abstraction there are unifying issues from which we are unable to free ourselves, and which therefore come into play in all manner of lower-level formulations. The Greeks called them universals and Kant later called them the categories of reason. We have selected a handful of such basic parameters within which to study the problems of psychology as a science of man. We now argue that personality theorists in particular must come to know more about these abstract parameters, so that they can have a comprehensive frame of reference within which to study *all* men — as now conceptualized or as yet to be conceptualized in tomorrow's theories.

Theoretical Terms and Intellectual Traditions

In Chapter I we promised the reader that he would find at the end of his philosophical journey a conceptualization which might tie things into one grand, overriding issue. The dialectical vs. demonstrative bifurcation provides us with precisely this opportunity. We take it to be one of the most abstract of higher-level metaconstructs, a dimension of contrast so towering in its significance that it penetrates the upper regions of man's understanding. It cannot in itself be subsumed by a higher-order theory resolving the contradiction that is its fundamental nature, though we might value one side or the other and in this way subsume the bifurcation under our theory of value. We have groped upward and now, accepting the wisdom of Plato, Aristotle, and Kant, we stand before the two traditions of thought merely to accept them as unresolvable "givens." However, within the descending rays of their influence on lower-order conceptions we can see a pattern of light

Topics of This Book That Lend Themselves to the Historical Bifurcation

Dialectical Tradition	vs.	Demonstrative Tradition
Idealism		Realism
Subjective		Objective
Introspection		Extraspection
Informal (hidden) theories		Formal (explicit) theories
Theory stressed		Method stressed
Cognitive method (procedural evidence)		Research method (validating evidence)
R-R laws (researching)		S-R laws (experimenting)
Hypothetical constructs		Intervening variables
Dualistic or pluralistic		Monistic
Intrinsic value (reasoned)		Instrumental value (rewarded)
Ethics of freedom		Ethics of control
Logical probability		Statistical probability
Soft determinism		Hard determinism
Final causes accepted (mind)		Efficient causes stressed (body)
Functional causation		Compelling causation
Knowing hedonism		Unknowing hedonism
Teleology "within" man		Teleology "within" science
Discriminal constructs		Vehicular constructs
Long line of development		Short line of development
Coherence theory of truth		Correspondence theory of truth
Behavior is active-stimulating		Behavior is passive-responding
Becoming, process, dynamic, conflict		Being, regular, fixed, routine
Contradictions accepted		Law of contradiction accepted
Self-reflexive intelligence		Input vs. output intelligence
Create		Communicate
Purity or spontaneity		Clarity or definability
Connotation		Denotation
Humanistic science (anthropomorphic)		Naturalistic science (mechanistic)
Idiographic		Nomothetic
Symbols		Signs
Tenderminded		Toughminded
Cognitive		Behavioristic
Clinicians		Experimentalists
Applied		Basic
Nurture		Nature
Armchair thinkers		Gadgeteers
Dreamers		Reifiers
Sophistic		Rigorous
Sentimental		Sagacious
"Philosophers" or "artists"		"Scientists" or "engineers"

taking shape. Thus, virtually *every* major issue of our volume can be seen to fall between the contrasting ends of our grand dimension. The accompanying table abstracts the major issues discussed, and the reader can assess the legitimacy of our claim by perusing its contents.

Two points must be quickly added: (1) It goes without saying that we have oversimplified here to make a point, and that all manner of finer distinctions could be made among these contrasting issues. We have not arrayed this table to say that all these issues are "one." We simply wish to use our historical bifurcation as a heuristic device, and to note at this point that within these two lines of descent one can array a remarkable number of lower-order dimensions of conflict. (2) A theorist does not have to accept *all* the tenets of one side or the other. He can be realistic in outlook, for example, yet accept functional causation and the legitimacy of introspective theorizing. We merely say that the (frequency) probability is that more of one side of the table will tend to hang together, and that crossings-over should be less the rule than the exception for any given theorist.

The question of how properly to mix the dialectical with the demonstrative strategies of theorizing must be the single most important one for psychology to answer. In thus mixing the two ends of our dimension, what sort of activity would we be involved in? To what does this dimension specifically and meaningfully refer? What are the "relations" brought under the rubric "dialectical vs. demonstrative traditions"? Why, these are none other than the *two ends of the dimension of meaning itself,* now so abstract and all-encompassing that we can truly speak of it as *knowledge.* This historical bifurcation speaks out to proclaim that meanings, facts, ideas, hunches, and so on, vacillate between the poles of doubt and certainty, denotative clarity and connotative implication, creative error and creative accuracy, and so on. These are different ways of expressing the same thing — i.e., that knowledge grows as meanings change and as evidence is brought to bear. Our dimension is unresolvable because in its essentials it describes what *must take place* for meaning to advance. Its import is that it charges each of us with the responsibility of not overlooking his left hand while he turns the knobs of science with his right. A complete explication of our data cannot be found *only* in one end of this dimension of meaning. We must avoid thinking in terms of only one side, and cross over whenever and wherever it is possible to do so. The more crossings the better, for such journeys to the other side will serve to educate us and raise our level of meaningful understanding.

Since we have now summarized the book's content within this single dimension of dialectical opposition, it may appear that we deviously sought to elevate the contribution of dialectic, that we saw it as something more basic, hence "better" than demonstration. Though one can see the truth of Kant's assertion that pure reason is dialectical in its essentials, we must also see the merit of Kant's claim that *subjective* reasonings are also generated by this dialectic. When we seek to make personality statements about people "in general," we must extend our construct meanings beyond the individual and seek objectivity. Hence, though dialectic may be basic to man's free use of reason, it is a demonstrative tactic which brings him the ultimate fruit of that creative intellect. Only in this way can he acquire a lasting body of knowledge. Those who would stay exclusively on the side of dialectic must end their theoretical days in sophistry. We want open systems in psychology, opened by dialectic to be sure, but also brought to points of reference for experimentation in demonstrative fashion. They may then be opened once again by a dialectical tactic, and so forth.

Some Philosophical Implications

We shall now enumerate certain implications of the philosophy of science we have been advocating throughout the book. We have chosen as specific points only those conclusions and assumptions which seem most germane to the view. Each point will be followed by a brief commentary.

1. *A final, all-encompassing theory is impossible, because at the higher levels of abstraction all theoretical formulations rest upon arbitrary premises.*

By arbitrary we do not mean capricious or unreasoned, but rather that the premises on which arguments ultimately hinge *could* have gone another way. If pure reason is dialectical in its essence, then this acknowledges that the reasoner can take *either* side of a position. Indeed, the reasoner can take *both* positions and follow through on the logical implications of two mutually contradictory points of view. We feel that this peculiarly human ability greatly enriches meaningful understanding.

At the higher levels of abstraction, one man's assumption (thesis) is — by the very fact that he expressed it — another man's challenge to meaning (antithesis). In taking such diametrically opposed positions — for any of a number of reasons — theorists do not necessarily lose their ability to communicate objectively, hence to understand one another. We can fully understand the premises on which our opponent's position is based, yet *disagree* with that position. Some people seem to have the naive view that man will someday clear out all the "noise" in his communication channels, and then, when everyone is getting the message being sent "loud and clear," a state of complete agreement will be possible. We reject this view, and assert that it is the nature of human intellect to fashion a variant point of view — if for no other reason than just for the "devil" of it. How then do we select a theoretical point of view?

2. *At the highest level of abstraction, choices in point of view rest upon what can only be called a value preference.*

There are countless reasons why a position is challenged by its opposite or an alternative position (alternatives begin in the pole of opposition). Some of these reasons include personal factors of a subjective nature (the *ad hominems*), but most of them have been handed down objectively in the historical evolution of what man takes to be knowledge. They frame his biases and condition his use of procedural evidence so thoroughly that when all other arguments seem to fail in defense of his view, he must rest with a final assessment of worth: "I hold to this view because it makes better sense, and therefore meets my purposes."

3. *The worth or value of any theory is ascertainable only in terms of the purpose it is to serve.*

To ask how good a theory is, or to cite ground rules for theory, is only to presume certain valued higher-order assumptions from the outset. Take, for example, the often cited rule of thumb in psychology that "theories must generate testable hypotheses." Although admirable from demonstrative assumptions, this limiting canon has been shown to have stifled a creative urge among psychologists. If one hoped to further creativity in potential theorists, this would surely be a "bad" admonition. Hence, the only way to evaluate the worth of various theories is to make clear precisely what higher-order value judgments we are invoking while making the assessment. We must make explicit our theory of value. Recognizing this, we might now say that a "good" theory is one which serves its purpose.

One of the aims of the present volume has been to force psychologists to consider their value preferences in setting out to do their jobs. If it can be admitted that contrasting systems of values ultimately result in contrasting interests and definitions of the work to be done, and that *this has nothing to do with empirical validation,* then possibly a certain bemused tolerance for one another's inability to resolve the stand-off will be engendered. This calls for a return to philosophical examination and, even more importantly, for a recognition of something Aristotle named a "final" cause.

4. Values are the final causes which define the purposes of our theories.

We must not overlook the fact that in expressing his views on causation, Aristotle was presenting a *theory of knowledge.* This view was subsequently altered over the ages, and today the concept of "cause" is virtually synonymous with what he called "efficient cause." But the meanings imputed by Aristotle in his constructs are still with us, regardless what we call them. We think it honest to recognize this fact and to put ourselves in proper historical alignment. It should now be clear that whatever Aristotle meant by "final" cause in his theory of causation is what we as scientific theorists base our judgments of value on. The final cause in this case is the meaningful premise *for the sake of which* other premises are selected, believed in, and defended. As influences from higher levels, final causes frame our lower-level theories. At the higher levels they *are* our values. They represent what we "stand for" when all argument fails. Not all men have the courage to take such a clear-cut stand, of course. But when they do stand — and we cannot say why they do so without resorting to irrelevancies or to discussions about the historical roots of their views — we have reached the abstract region of value judgments. There is nothing further to do in this arid plain but pitch our tents and honor our opponents — for they have as much right to a campsite as we do.

5. Theorizing is thought in the process of evolving meaning out of existence.

We accept the view that theorizing and thought are one and the same process, the attempt to forge and extend meaningful relations within the poles of our historical bifurcation. One cannot accomplish this as a scientist unless he occasionally freezes the process and objectifies his constructs. It is demonstration which furthers such denotative meaning by way of method. Whether we begin from the plausibly given (procedurally tested), "primary and true" premises of cognition, or the objectively prescribed (validated), "operationally defined" premises of experimentation, a demonstrative tactic is called for. Then, as clues for the future, the connotative meanings of theoretical terms invite dialectical analogies and metaphorical creation of new hypotheses. In this case, we theoretically generate new meanings from old, and error along with insight, until such time as we can return again to a demonstrative tactic.

6. *Psychology suffers from a lack of idealism in theoretical outlook.*

By stressing the contribution of an active, dynamic intellect to meaning, we have placed ourselves on the side of idealism. We do this quite by design, because it is our considered (valued) opinion (major premise) that psychology suffers from an overstuffing of undigested realism. It is about time for a change in diet. We feel at this juncture that if one were to select a title for the point of view being espoused, it would be something like "objective idealism." This is in the spirit of crossing-over from one side of the table (see above) to the other and it merely suggests that we can be objective yet not feel constrained to keep our theoretical models in line with some other science's models simply because it arrived on the scene first, with an equally arbitrary realistic thesis on the nature of meaning.

We are essentially neo-Kantian in outlook, and Kant referred to his position as "critical realism" (as opposed to naive realism). Ordinarily, this title would do nicely, but we feel it is important at this point to stress the term *idealism,* because of psychology's historical tendency to accept realism without question. So long as we keep objectivity as well as idealism in our value system we do not have to fear losing our identity as scientists. Indeed, this brings us to our next point.

7. *The scientist is a theorist who moves to validate propositions drawn from his thought at least some of the time.*

This is the most liberal definition of science that we can propose, short of throwing out validation as a method — an alternative we simply cannot accept. We cling to this theory and method of aquiring knowledge not because of any hallowed identification with the other sciences, but simply because we are unable to think of a more legitimate procedure for resolving disputes, refining our thought, or curbing our speculative zeal. However temporary a scientific insight may be, it *is* at least "there" to be had by all, stripped of pomposity and authority. Those who swim in deeper waters have their role in life as mystics and seers. But science demands that at certain points within our theoretical plunge we come up for air and thus "show ourselves" to others. There is no way we can avoid this responsibility.

8. *Knowledge is a cultural product, transmitted in a supra-individual sense.*

It is a reasonable first hypothesis that sociocultural factors such as group identities help determine the values men express. Knowledge is cultivated and furthered by group identities of many sorts. As human beings, we seem to need a meaningful identity, and it is in this identification process that values are delimited and then nurtured. The "tough-minded scientist" identification has certain built-in role prescriptions which condition the way we choose values in "science" contexts. There are those who feel that they can somehow flee this inevitable identification with a position (the purity criticism), but we can see no evidence that identification is ever truly avoided. Individualists look remarkably alike at certain levels of abstraction.

Science itself is such a cultural product. The demonstrative socio-cultural tradition on which science rests is most valued in the Western world, where it has been greatly enhanced by material progress. Eastern (Oriental) man, on the other hand, seems to have placed greater value on the dialectical tradition of self-investigation, contemplation, and the acceptance of contradictions as a natural course of events. It is no accident that he puts to himself the dialectical question: "What is the sound of one hand clapping?" This is pure nonsense in the Hobbesian-Lockean world of demonstrative reasoning.

Some Reactions to This Philosophy of Science

Following the style of enumeration and brief commentary, we will now review the most frequently cited objections to the philosophy of science espoused in this volume. Doubtless there are many other, even more germane criticisms to be made. But these seem to be the most spontaneous reactions and therefore deserve our most direct consideration at this point.

1. From toughminded critics: "Since it is admitted that the S-R and related theoretical views are legitimate, why this 'straw man' attack? Why dictate what we should be doing as scientists?"

Due to the consistent bias of this book, it may seem that we have argued that everyone should think the way we think. This is a false conclusion, of course. The view expressed is that we should have a common body of terminology at the higher levels of abstraction so that we might better classify one another and come to understand our particular strengths and weaknesses. The amusing irony of this criticism is that we view the present volume as a plea for freedom, not a dictation of what everyone should do. Sometimes this criticism is phrased: "Why do you throw up the sister sciences of physics, chemistry, and others, in talking about the nature of science? Does psychology *have* to be like other sciences?"

The reason for taking this approach is that we found from reviews of the literature of the 1920's and especially the 1930's that when psychology was ironing out its current image as a "natural science," our foremost theorists relied heavily upon the sister sciences (especially physics, à la Bridgman) in making their case. At least, they argued from their interpretation of what was supposedly taking place in the other sciences. It therefore seemed reasonable to argue on the other side of the issue through other modern developments in the physical sciences. *Of course,* we need not pattern psychology on the physical sciences completely. Indeed, if final causation is accepted in psychology as a useful theoretical maneuver, then we will be a truly "different" science.

The "straw man" charge is arrived at in two slightly different ways, but both have the same reference point. Some claim that they in no way intend to comment on the so-called "image of man" in doing their learning experiments, and that they frankly resent being forced into the mold we have selected for them. Others say that by drawing examples primarily from the Skinnerian camp we have overgeneralized and misconstrued the more sophisticated S-R approaches of modern times, which are not as rigid, mechanical, and naively realistic as we make them out to be. From our view, those who say they make no comment about man's nature are simply refusing to look at the *implications* of what they are claiming about the learning processes they are supposedly studying without becoming involved in personality issues. The charges that we have overdone our Skinnerian attack seem to overlook the fact that we have cited at least a half-dozen theorists who have in some way reflected the S-R image of man in their writings. Putting our two "straw man" counters together, we now observe that the main reason Skinner is such a useful theorist to use as an example is that he had the courage to follow through on the implications of his point of view. He construes man *in terms of* his conception of science very clearly. The allegedly more sophisticated S-R theorist is less likely to be caught up in an extreme example simply because he lacks the Skinnerian boldness to follow the lines of development outward from his theoretical vantage point. In any case, it will be left to the reader to decide how unfair and inaccurate our presentation has been.

2. *From tenderminded critics: "Since this view has not provided an alternative to the method now in scientific vogue, there is no hope of*

truly liberalizing psychology. One can never break the S-R bind or hope to capture human nature in the IV-DV methodology."

A criticism of this sort is really an expression of exasperation with the way we have been interpreting scientific methods. It must ultimately arrive at the conclusion that either (a) an alternative *scientific* methodology is in the offing, or (b) psychology need not necessarily be a science. "What is so precious in science that we must bow down to it as to a golden calf?" is the attitude expressed by some who make this criticism. Since it is our conviction that psychology ought to remain within science, and that thus far no adequate alternative to validation has been offered as a scientific method, we cannot accept this criticism. People who make it sometimes write a lot, and they have some interesting subjective things to say. But they do not advance science.

What we need is not a new method but more daring use of the present research strategy of control and prediction. We need the original design, the speculative venture, and this will come about only if we are not afraid to begin with loosened controls — this stimulates creativity — and rash predictions. We need professional journals which will give as much time to evaluation of the theory being tested as they now give to the method of verification. Good ideas remain good ideas whether the theorist has been lucky enough to think of a research design to prove them or not; as long as he has tried to validate, he should be given the chance to be read as a scientist, regardless of his statistical findings in the actual study. There are two ways to be afraid of error: the toughminded way, in which the solution is to design studies which cannot go wrong; and, the tenderminded way, which disparages all attempts to control and predict as mechanical and unlifelike. What makes a true scientist is his utter devotion to his job in the expectation that he will be wrong most of the time — if not now, then surely at some future time. This means, however, that he will have something generally valid to say for all of us (objectively) *some* of the time.

3. *"You have made truth into a higher-level form of opinion. You have disparaged intellect rather than raising it in idealism as you imply."*

This is a Platonic criticism. It seems a disparagement of intellect to claim that man is unable to arrive at a final point of "truth," which is to say, a final agreement at the highest levels of thought. This criticism rests on a predicated theory of truth as some form of higher-level universal which all men might arrive at, given the proper circumstances and information. We have an alternate theory of truth, one which says that some truths are simply the recognition that a single position of "the truth" is impossible, and that an arbitrariness shall always intrude itself at the higher levels.

We would prefer to use the term "truth" at the lower levels of abstraction, where truths are indeed communal opinions, held on the basis of evidence. This is the reason we felt it necessary to distinguish so definitely between theory and method. But at the higher levels of abstraction the concept of truth is so dependent upon one's definitions and premises that it seems better merely to speak of "positions" held and to avoid the construct of truth. Experience over centuries of philosophical analysis should have taught us by now that we do not find truth in the upper philosophical regions. Truth seems to be a lower-order construct, a discriminal and not a vehicular notion, so to speak.

Note that we have avoided a solipsism in outlook by stressing the need for both theory and method in our interpretation of knowledge. Truth may be one kind of opinion, but it is belief nurtured by evidence, and an *objective* truth escapes the pitfalls of *subjective* truths or opinions. Solipsistic views, which are in the idealistic line of descent, as we are, embrace a subjective interpretation of meaning. Validation in experimental method would, therefore, be considered a form of communal self-delusion. This is not the view we take of communal opinions or truths. We recognize the role of intellect in the conceptualization of data, but this we have said is primarily a theoretical matter. It is incumbent upon the theorist now to submit his theory to communal test. Intellect is thus raised on the side of theory, but tempered on the side of method.

4. "There is a circularity in asserting that values are the determiners of theories, yet also act as higher-level theories themselves."

This criticism is well taken, but inevitably those systems which attempt to explain their own status must make it. By noting that values influence lower-level theories, yet also act as theories themselves in the upper regions, we merely recognize the multiordinality of the term "theory." We do not imply an identity here in the types of theory at the two levels. When we are unable to point to a higher-level construct which might resolve some point of contradiction — as in the historical bifurcation, above — we are left with two traditions within which to begin phrasing our major premises. We have a special case of the Heisenberg principle. Depending upon the premises (parameters) selected, the theories written at lower levels will be determined accordingly. Since the parameters are in fact arbitrary, there seems no way to describe this theoretical predilection except to observe that such preferences are conditioned by a "theory of value." In this case, the higher-level abstraction resolving our difficulty is the theory "this is better, more reasonable, meets my purposes *better,* than that." We rise above the historical dilemma only by making it a value judgment, which is another way of saying that a theory of value operates as a standard for the exercise of procedural evidence.

5. *"How can anyone who calls himself a scientist accept teleology? Can you not revise your position on science without having to become an advocate of final causes?"*

This criticism seems to be based upon a problem of terminology. Ordinarily when one uses terms such as "final cause" or "teleology," he seems to begin mixing science and values somehow in the *sphere of method.* Arguments in theology and aesthetics, for example, might be phrased "What would a perfect God do . . . ?" or "What has the artist intended . . . ?" The logical development then carries on, and, based upon the exercise of procedural evidence, the case rests with such a cognitive proof. Arguments of this sort, which are termed "arguments from definition," encourage us by plausibility to accept a major premise, and then, using the flow of reason, lead us to an inescapable conclusion. Accepting the major premise — which itself may and often does include a final-cause assumption — one is drawn necessarily to the end implied at the outset.

But we have not argued for teleological *proofs.* We have not suggested that final causes be used in method. The scientific method is to retain its efficient-cause nature. Final causes are to be *theoretical* devices, brought to bear in method by way of a line of development. A student once put the question: "When a rat goes toward a food box, and runs faster if more food is in the food box, does the rat have this as a goal, or as a final cause?" One finds the answer here not in methodological factors, but rather in asking himself what purpose the *scientist* has in mind as he formulates his *theory.* Does he assume that rats *have* final causes or that they *do not have* final causes, as they have eyeteeth, or some such? If the purpose is to discover what rats really have, then the question makes sense, and we can let the scientist wrestle with the problem of measurement. But so-called rat psychologists do not all have this purpose of discovering "things" in the minds of lower animals. Their purpose is primarily to show a regularity of behavior, as conditioned by environmental manipulations of one sort or another. Since rats do not ask to be informed about their behavior, and since thus far they have not begun expressing aspirations in their behavior, we might be foolish to introduce additional causal constructs into our theory about their behavior. No such purpose is called for in *our* theoretical behavior, whether or not the rat has any purpose in his behavior. We could not possibly hope to educate one another.

But when a man is in the maze, and expresses goals as a rule and believes that he really has them, and when that man looks to us for instruction, how foolish is it to begin a theoretical formulation with final causes included? We can study him in rat terms if we like — "extraspectively" as we have called it — but we can *also* study him in human terms, which, as we have argued, demands the "meaning for the sake of which behavior takes place" theoretical development. If a man can find meanings in the past, thanks to his memory capacity, then he can also find meaning in the future, thanks to his grasp of time perspective. There is nothing mysterious or spiritual about this. This is what happens. How can anyone hope to be a scientist and ignore what is happening?

6. *"No one can seriously accept an idealistic position. It is sophistry pure and simple to say that you study mere chimeras in the mind's eye, and that your models need have no referent in the world of reality."*

It seems a desperate theoretical trick to some when we argue on the side of idealism. All one can do here is to reiterate that in light of modern advances in physical science an idealistic position is far easier to live with than a realistic position. Further, we take the idealistic stand for a definite purpose. It is our feeling that the kinds of data personality theorists hope to capture have been cut off from them by psychology's extreme reliance on realism. We want now to temporize. If tomorrow we were to find that personality theorists are neglecting validation in the name of idealism, we would argue on the realistic side of the issue, for the Aristotelian-Kantian criticism is well taken. If it is any consolation, we might note that an idealistic theorist can believe things "exist" even when he is not thinking of them. His wife and children are "really there" while he is at the office. In the same way, the realist does not ask for an operational definition when his children express their love for their father. The point the idealist makes is that whatever "is there" (things in themselves) derives its meaning in the act of conceptualization, *not* from the fact of existence alone. Whether something exists independent of this conceptualization *in no way affects such meaningful ties of experience made by the theorist.* We take our place with Kant on this matter, and, for the present at least, ask the realists to show how it profits us to believe *also* that our models exist independent of our intellect. It is validation we must encourage, not a belief in just another "realistic" nether land or spirit world.

7. *"This view makes the same type of error you accuse the S-R theorists of making. You have made a metaphysic of a theory in speaking about man's nature, rather than making a metaphysic of a method."*

This may well be, but one must realize, in making this criticism, that a metaphysic *is* on the side of what we have been calling "theory." The universals of the ancients, for example, which might be thought of as truly metaphysical assumptions, were rooted in thought (i.e., theory). We have already asserted that such universals are for us the value-laden assumptions on which we base our reasoning and procedural evaluations. Such theories as we arrive at must then be shown to have objective validity by the demonstrative tactic of doing an experiment. Hence, we do not see this as the same error the S-R theorists fall into, because we do not claim to be scientifically *discovering* that man is the way our (efficient-cause) methods make him out to be. We merely claim that our methodological verification is consistent with our theoretical line of reasoning. Indeed, if another theory were invoked in opposition to ours, it might well explain the methodological sequence of events just as consistently as we have done. Methodological factors are not the only grounds for believing in theories.

8. *"In merely aligning the two so-called traditions of thought, a genuine solution has not been effected. You have straddled the issue rather than pointed to a clear-cut 'new way.'"*

This brings us back to the half-solutions promised the reader in Chapter I. Occasionally a tenderminded reader will accuse us of being too timid to press the point that dialectical traditions have to be considered superior to the demonstrative, because our table (p. 456, above) is predicated on such an opposition. Getting a winner or a "punch line" at the tail end of a presentation does seem more satisfying, but we cannot accept the logic being used for this particular problem in meaning. This criticism is founded on the belief that a theorist must always either take a stand or be forced to straddle issues. We think that in certain cases, for certain purposes, this belief is sound. But in others it is necessary to accept as one's position a mutual interplay, a crossing-over at different points along the dimension of abstraction and in different contexts of meaning. Though we have tried to take a strong stand on issues throughout the book, and have spoken in terms of presenting a legitimate alternative to the S-R world view, we feel that this is the time to move about and spend time on both sides of the question. This is not straddling an issue but enriching our understanding.

9. *"This view is too philosophical, and psychology as science has to be especially careful not to get too philosophical."*

We have tried throughout to show that scientists are more, not less, interested in philosophy than they were a century ago. They do not seek answers in philosophy as a method alone, but primarily use philosophical examination to sharpen their thought about their assumptions, and to keep themselves in trim for changing circumstances. Some psychologists feel that as long as their assumptions seem to be working in the laboratory methods, there is no need to examine them. This would be perfectly acceptable, if it were not for the fact discussed under point one of this section — that our methods seem ever to color our theories and vice versa. Methods are based upon theories of knowledge, and lest we be led astray by an unexamined major premise and set of values operating from above, we had better look to our science as an offspring of philosophy. Finally, we would like to think that we have been psychologizing about philosophy rather than philosophizing about psychology. We have learned that the problems of philosophy are the problems of man, and, as personality students, we hope to study man in all his endeavors. Philosophers are no less men than psychologists; and psychologists are no less men than the human laboratory subjects they put through their methodological procedures.

A Final Overview of Our Image of Man

It has not been our purpose to write a "personality theory." However, as we have continually argued, one cannot talk about methods of studying man without proffering what might be termed an "image of man." In order to leave no doubt on the matter, and at the risk of some repetition in this closing chapter, we might now finish the volume with a final overview of how man looks from our perspective. The writer has had some trying experiences in attempting to discuss the nature of man with psychologists who view this matter only in terms of demonstrative computer analogues. One is flooded with talk of input loads and information, gathered from the environment helter-skelter (this is where they usually say a so-called dialectic may fit in — as garbled information), or in more ordered fashion, and then sorted according to various scanning procedures. When you ask if a machine-analogue man will also generate opposites for every item or at least some of the input items, there is usually a kind of amused reaction, followed by mumblings, and then the conversation deteriorates in short order into a polite jocularity, if not worse. One senses that he has been scanned and cast into the sophistic slot.

We would say that man's cycle of awareness, reasoning, meaning formulation, and so on, takes place as follows:

1. Man meets experience with meaningful conceptions or basic premises, and fashions it at least as much as experience fashions him.

Depending upon the theory one wishes to invoke at this point, the meaningful conceptions may be such things as self-concepts, phenomenal fields, life lines, personal constructs, the stereotypes of an authoritarian bigot, the theorotypes of a practicing psychotherapist, the rules for experimental controls used by a laboratory scientist, and so on. Such Kantian-like assumptions, made by a reasoning intellect, cannot be thrown off, for they attire man with rationality — and that is man's peculiar nature, that he has the potential to *understand* his predicament either correctly or incorrectly.

2. Man's experiencing of his environment, which frames his understanding, is at heart a search for meaning.

Man not only begins his experience with a framework of understanding in delimiting that experience, he also seeks to extend this grasp in the creation of new meanings. Meaning is a relational term and it signifies that man can extend these relations, tie one signification into another, and thus enlarge his scope. He has the ability to create stimuli for further meaning, *not only* the ability to respond to the etchings of the environment on his intellect.

3. Man stores information obtained from the past in memory, but he also creates meanings for the future by reasoning for the sake of older meanings.

This is our final-cause argument. Man's meaningful ties are not limited to material in the past, for he has a self-reflexive intelligence which can turn in on itself. We subscribe to the view that man, at some time in his life, *can* think self-reflexively, *can* evaluate what has happened to him or to other men, and from this self-examination project an entirely unique, creative goal. We might also at this point introduce the hypothesis of an unconscious intellect, and observe that such goal formulations need not operate only in awareness. Mentality does not *have* to be thought of as a single unity of consistent intentions. There is no reason cross purposes might not arise within one individual.

4. The mental mechanism for a creative human act which is not an accident begins in dialectical opposition, which generates at some point an alternative not now realized and possibly unrealizable. Man's creative intellect can result in subjective error, so a demonstrative tactic is called for to establish objective truths.

Final causes would be unparsimonious hence superfluous theoretical constructs if man were *only* a demonstrative being. That is, we would then be limited to seeing goals or principles "for the sake of which" men behave as limited to the Lockean "inputs" of yesterday. But *if* man can also reason dialectically, *then* he can "come up with" causes of behavior which have no necessary replicative tie to yesterday. The human mind considers what "is" and the opposites implied (the "what is not"), and then from among the dimensions thus generated, selects and projects an "ought." This "ought" might be something like "good gang members never squeal on a pal" or "only those concepts which can be operationally defined have meaning for our purposes." Once asserted, the "ought" suggested can act as a guide not only for *this* intellect but for the intellects of others as well. To check on the plausibilities of single intellects, which might influence through the weight of procedural argument alone, man fashioned science. He brought demonstrative tactics in as counter-weight, for he learned in time that creativity does not mean empirical truth.

The difficulty with accepting the final-cause construct lies in the fact that experiential contents from which final causes may be framed are always learned in the past. Hence, "if learned in the past, then efficiently caused in the past." This is the logic suggested, and as far as it goes, it is correct. There can be no argument with the fact that current behavior has flowed (efficient cause) out of the past. Men influence one another, they "program" one another, in demonstrative fashion. Idiographically and very specifically, as men we are where we are because we came this way — and no other way.

But could we have gone *another way?* If so, how might this have been accomplished? Those who argue that man could *not* have gone another way can restrict their theories to an efficient-cause tactic. In cataloguing what *did* happen they assume that this is all that could have happened. Those who say that another path might have been selected — if, for example, some individual in a position of power or influence had reasoned in another fashion, and so on — would look for a final cause at some point. They would say we are products of a past, but that this has been in some measure an intelligently decided, self-reflexive past which projected designs for any of a number of reasons. Many of these designs have proven stupid and erroneous, but in their very stupidity they reflect man's unique intelligence. Nature's "errors" of the natural-catastrophe variety seem highly rational and completely sane by comparison.

5. Once an "ought" is projected, it takes on the characteristics of a value.

Once man arrives at even an erroneous "ought," he often gains a sense of conviction which nothing can shake. His course is set and he is no longer open to the possibilities which transcend his particular frame of reference. He is a valuing animal and he has made his judgment. These judgments are sometimes made informally and subtly, even unconsciously. Or, having been influenced by someone else who made this judgment, man now simply clings to his value out of an identity with a particular group. That is, social pressures, the weight of a community of common sense, serve to determine his plausibilities, and he is now subject to the "values of the group." He is programmed, good and proper.

Fortunately, every now and then, one among the programmed majority rises up as a voice in the emptiness of opposition and dialectically creates a minority of dissent. New adherents quickly follow, and they see in the alternative a value system equally or possibly even more viable than the older system. Modern man's plight seems to be that he now fully recognizes the inevitability of this process, and that he must live within arbitrary points of reference for all time. His valued beliefs claim certainty and finality, hence this is a frightening conclusion to draw. It seems in flat contradiction to man's valuing intellect. But draw it he must.

6. Since men do not all reason creatively all of the time, remarkable consistencies in their behavior permit us to predict their behavior by use of statistical probability.

We wish to make it perfectly clear here that men are not to be thought of as proceeding creatively in *every* life situation. Most men, most of the time, proceed routinely and without any need to challenge their "inputs." There is no need here to deny the obvious fact that consistency in behavior is the rule. Solutions to problems, after all, are difficult to come by. Once settled upon, there is a great attraction to simply staying with them if they continue to do their jobs well. Also, the majority of behavioral conventions are simply not worth challenging or modifying. Historical evidence is available which suggests, however, that the most viable civilizations have been those in which conflicting views have been generated, and where the populace has been able to bear up somehow within inconsistency and rise above it to new solutions, which of course are arrived at by intellects working their way through the so-called hard facts of reality.

7. *Emotional man is dialectical man reasoning sophistically.*

Hemmed in by the import of his valued beliefs, a comforting situation which has nurtured his meanings in the past, the man faced with an unacceptable alternative in the present now argues in favor of his belief with all the cunning at his disposal. He strives to cling to the meanings he wants to believe rather than accepting others. If this takes place within a single man, as in the Freudian man-in-the-middle theory, we speak about internal or unconscious conflicts. If this conflict shows itself interpersonally, we might then observe two men much committed to their points of view. Each is described by the other as a sophist, since presumably neither seeks a disinterested truth but rather aims to defend his vested interest. In the tradition of Aristotle, we do not see this form of sophistry as a really *bad* variety, since it is genuine and not insincere. Any man with a sense of commitment must seem sophistic to another man who does not see the cogency of the former's case. Thus, only if a man *intends* to lead us astray in false conclusions should he be considered sophistic in the pejorative sense. Otherwise, we must recognize that this stubborn advocate of a point of view might "really be saying something." He could be an innovator.

8. *Man can make the possibilities he dreams of into a reality by living them.*

Thanks to his self-awareness, man can cling to his position long enough to occasionally "make it so" in his life style. The man of conviction, the moralist, the revolutionary, the zealot, shows us the way simply because he is so committed to the final-cause value he champions that he proves its validity in his own case. Moreover, he makes it clear that we too can live out his value system in our lives. He gives us a goal to shoot for. Indeed, this is the way our modern conceptions of science were worked out — as much by example as through practical result. This is also the reason there will always be something other than scientific knowledge moving man on to new insights, new positions, new frontiers to conquer. We would be naive in the extreme to assume that validation is the only test of knowledge that has worth or import in the story of mankind.

Such things as the internal consistency of arguments, the plausibility of assumptions based upon sociocultural identities, the proofs of introspective feeling-tones, the weight of logic in arguments from definition, all shall continue to exert a major influence upon man. These enter into science, but the scientist does not rest his case with them. It was not the purpose of this volume to make an exhaustive review of such "other than scientific" means of proof. We simply lumped all these variants together into the category of procedural evidence. There are many reasons which prompt men to base their meaningful self-definitions on one or another of these non-scientific or incompletely scientific theories of knowledge. But the point we would like to make in closing is that, in acting thus, each man will surely reflect a self-image of the sort we now hold the mirror of analysis up to for instructive intentions.

REFERENCES

Adams, D. K. Note on method. *Psychological Review*, 1937, *44*, 212–218.

Adler, A. *Problems of neurosis* (edited by Philippe Mairet). New York: Harper & Row, 1964.

Adler, I. *Thinking machines*. New York: New American Library, 1961.

Adler, M. J. *Dialectic*. New York: Harcourt, Brace & Co., 1927.

Adler, M. J. (Ed.-in-Chief) *The great ideas: A syntopicon*. Vol. 2–3 of R. M. Hutchins (Ed.), *Great books of the western world*. Chicago: Encyclopedia Britannica, 1952.

Adorno, T. W., Frenkel-Brunswik, Else, Levinson, D. J., and Sanford, R. N. *The authoritarian personality*. New York: Harper, 1950.

Aiken, H. D. *The age of ideology*. New York: New American Library, 1956.

Allen, F. *Psychotherapy with children*. New York: W. W. Norton, 1942.

Allport, G. W. *Personality: A psychological interpretation*. New York: Holt, 1937.

Allport, G. W. The psychologist's frame of reference. *Psychological Bulletin*, 1940, *37*, 1–28.

Allport, G. W. Personalistic psychology as a science; a reply. *Psychological Review*, 1946, *53*, 132–135.

Allport, G. W. The historical background of modern social psychology. In Vol. I of G. Lindzey (Ed.), *Handbook of social psychology*. Reading, Mass.: Addison-Wesley, 1954. Pp. 3–56.

Allport, G. W. *Personality and social encounter*. Boston: Beacon Press, 1960.

Allport, G. W. The general and the unique in psychological science. *Journal of Personality*, 1962, *30*, 405–422.

Ansbacher, H. L. The significance of the socio-economic status of the patients of Freud and of Adler. *American Journal of Psychotherapy*, 1959, *13*, 376–382.

Ansbacher, H. L., and Ansbacher, Rowena R. (Eds.) *The individual psychology of Alfred Adler*. New York: Basic Books, 1956.

Aquinas, T. *Summa theologica* (excerpts). Vol. 20 of R. M. Hutchins (Ed.), *Great books of the western world*. Chicago: Encyclopedia Britannica, 1952.

Argyris, C. *Integrating the individual and the organization*. New York: Wiley, 1964.

Aristotle. In Vol. 8 of R. M. Hutchins (Ed.), *Great books of the western world*. Chicago: Encyclopedia Britannica, 1952. Quotations by permission of Encyclopedia Britannica and Oxford University Press.

On generation and corruption. Pp. 409–441.

Metaphysics. Pp. 499–626.

Physics. Pp. 257–355.

Posterior analytics. Pp. 95–137.

Prior analytics. Pp. 39–93.

On the soul. Pp. 631–668.

Topics. Pp. 143–223.

Augustine. *On Christian doctrine.* In Vol. 18 of R. M. Hutchins (Ed.), *Great books of the western world.* Chicago: Encyclopedia Britannica, 1952. Pp. 621–698.

Ayer, A. J. *Language, truth and logic.* New York: Dover Publications, 1946.

Bach, G. R. Who are the discoverers of psychological knowledge? *American Psychologist,* 1952, *7,* 131–132.

Bacon, F. In Vol. 30 of R. M. Hutchins (Ed.), *Great books of the western world.* Chicago: Encyclopedia Britannica, 1952.

Advancement of learning. Pp. 1–101.

Novum organum. Pp. 105–195.

Bakan, D. Learning and the scientific enterprise. *Psychological Review,* 1953, *60,* 45–49.

Bakan, D. Learning and the principle of inverse probability. *Psychological Review,* 1953, *60,* 360–370.

Bakan, D. A reconsideration of the problem of introspection. *Psychological Bulletin,* 1954, *51,* 105–118.

Bakan, D. Clinical psychology and logic. *American Psychologist,* 1956, *11,* 655–662.

Bakan, D. *Sigmund Freud and the Jewish mystical tradition.* New York: D. Van Nostrand, 1958.

Baker, H. *The image of man.* New York: Harper & Row, 1961.

Bales, R. F. *Interaction process analysis.* Reading, Mass.: Addison-Wesley, 1949.

Barrett, W. Determinism and novelty. In S. Hook (Ed.), *Determinism and freedom in the age of modern science.* New York: New York University Press, 1958. Pp. 30–39.

Beck, S. J. *The six schizophrenias.* New York: American Orthopsychiatric Association, 1954.

Becker, H., and Barnes, H. E. (Eds.) *Social thought from lore to science.* Washington, D.C.: Harren Press, 1952. 2 vols.

Berenda, C. W. Is clinical psychology a science? *American Psychologist,* 1957, *12,* 725–729.

Berg, I. A. Deviant responses and deviant people: The formulation of the deviation hypothesis. *Journal of Counseling Psychology,* 1957, *4,* 154–161.

Bergmann, G., and Spence, K. Operationism and theory in psychology. *Psychological Review,* 1941, *48,* 1–14.

Bingham, W. V. On the possibility of an applied psychology. *Psychological Review,* 1923, *30,* 289–305.

Black, M. Making something happen. In S. Hook (Ed.), *Determinism and freedom in the age of modern science.* New York: New York University Press, 1958. Pp. 15–30.

Boisen, A. T. *The exploration of the inner world.* New York: Harper & Bros., 1962.

Boodin, J. E. Truth and agreement. *Psychological Review,* 1909, *16,* 55–66.

Boring, E. G. Temporal perception and operationism. *American Journal of Psychology,* 1936, *48,* 519–522.

Boring, E. G. Mind and mechanism. *American Journal of Psychology,* 1946, *59,* 173–192.

Boring, E. G. *A history of experimental psychology,* 2nd ed. New York: Appleton-Century-Crofts, 1950.

Boring, E. G. A history of introspection. *Psychological Bulletin,* 1953, *50,* 169–189.

Boss, M. *Psychoanalysis and daseinsanalysis.* New York: Basic Books, 1963.

Breuer, J., and Freud, S. *Studies on hysteria.* Vol. II of J. Strachey (Ed.), *The standard edition of the complete psychological works of Sigmund Freud.* London: The Hogarth Press, 1955. Also, J. Breuer and S. Freud, *Studies on hysteria.* New York: Basic Books, 1957.

Bridgman, P. W. *The logic of modern physics.* New York: Macmillan, 1927.

Bridgman, P. W. Determinism in modern science. In S. Hook (Ed.), *Determinism and freedom in the age of modern science.* New York: New York University Press, 1958. Pp. 43–63.

Bridgman, P. W. *The way things are.* Cambridge, Mass.: Harvard University Press, 1959.

Bronowski, J. *The common sense of science.* Cambridge, Mass.: Harvard University Press, 1958.

Brown, J. F. *Psychology and the social order.* New York: McGraw-Hill, 1936.

Brown, R. *Words and things.* New York: Free Press of Glencoe, 1958.

Burtt, E. A. *The metaphysical foundations of modern physical science,* rev. ed. Garden City, N.Y.: Doubleday & Co., 1955.

Calverton, V. F. The rise of objective psychology. *Psychological Review,* 1924, *31,* 418–426.

Cameron, N. *Personality development and psychopathology.* Boston: Houghton Mifflin Co., 1963.

Carnap, R. *Logical foundations of probability.* Chicago: University of Chicago Press, 1950.

Cassirer, E. *An essay on man.* Garden City, N.Y.: Doubleday & Co., 1944.

Cassirer, E. *The problem of knowledge.* New Haven: Yale University Press, 1950.

Cattell, R. B. *Personality: A systematic, theoretical, and factual study.* New York: McGraw-Hill, 1950.

Coghill, G. E. *Anatomy and the problem of behavior.* Cambridge: Cambridge University Press, 1929.

Conant, J. B. *Modern science and modern man.* Garden City, N.Y.: Doubleday Anchor, 1952. (Originally published, New York: Columbia University Press, 1949.)

Crannell, C. W. Are rat psychologists responsible for fission? *American Psychologist,* 1947, *2,* 22–23.

Crannell, C. W. Fission resolved? *American Psychologist,* 1956, *11,* 636–638.

Cronbach, L. J., and Meehl, P. E. Construct validity in psychological tests. *Psychological Bulletin,* 1955, *52,* 281–302.

Cronbach, L. J. The two disciplines of scientific psychology. *American Psychologist,* 1957, *12,* 671–684.

Cureton, E. E. Validity, reliability, and baloney. *Educational and Psychological Measurement,* 1950, *10,* 94–96.

Dallenbach, K. M. The place of theory in science. *Psychological Review,* 1953, *60,* 33–39.

De Morgan, A. *An essay on probabilities.* London: Longmans, 1838.

Descartes, R. *Rules for the direction of mind.* In Vol. 31 of R. M. Hutchins (Ed.), *Great books of the western world.* Chicago: Encyclopedia Britannica, 1952. Pp. 1–40.

Dewey, J. *Democracy and education.* New York: Macmillan, 1916.

Dollard, J., and Miller, N. E. *Personality and psychotherapy: An analysis in terms of learning, thinking, and culture.* New York: McGraw-Hill, 1950.

Eddington, A. *The nature of the physical world.* New York: Macmillan, 1929. (Also available in paperback — Ann Arbor, Mich.: University of Michigan Press, 1958.)

Eddington, A. *The philosophy of physical science.* Ann Arbor, Mich.: University of Michigan Press, 1958.

Einstein, A. *Essays in science.* New York: Philosophical Library, 1934.

Ellenberger, H. F. A clinical introduction to psychiatric phenomenology and existential analysis. In R. May, E. Angel, and H. F. Ellenberger (Eds.), *Existence: A new dimension in psychiatry and psychology.* New York: Basic Books, 1958. Pp. 92–124.

Evans, R. I. *Conversations with Carl Jung.* New York: D. Van Nostrand, 1964.

Feigl, H. The scientific outlook: Naturalism and humanism. In H. Feigl and May Brodbeck (Eds.), *Readings in the philosophy of science.* New York: Appleton-Century-Crofts, 1953. Pp. 8–18.

Fernberger, S. W. Behavior versus introspective psychology. *Psychological Review,* 1922, *29,* 409–413.

Festinger, L. *A theory of cognitive dissonance.* Evanston, Ill.: Row, Peterson, 1957.

Ford, D. H., and Urban, H. B. *Systems of psychotherapy.* New York: Wiley, 1963.

Frank, P. *Philosophy of science.* Englewood Cliffs, N.J.: Prentice-Hall, 1957.

Frankl, V. E. *Man's search for meaning: An introduction to logotherapy.* New York: Washington Square Press, 1963.

Fremantle, Anne. *The age of belief.* New York: New American Library, 1954.

Freud, S. *A general introduction to psychoanalysis.* In Vol. 54 of R. M. Hutchins (Ed.), *Great books of the western world.* Chicago: Encyclopedia Britannica, 1952. Pp. 449–638. (Also published — New York: Liveright, and London: George Allen & Unwin, 1963.)

Freud, S. *The interpretation of dreams* (Parts I and II). Vol. IV and V of J. Strachey (Ed.), *The standard edition of the complete psychological works of Sigmund Freud.* London: The Hogarth Press, 1953.

Freud, S. *The origins of psycho-analysis, letters to Wilhelm Fliess, drafts and notes: 1887–1902.* New York: Basic Books, 1954.

Freud, S. "A child is being beaten"; A contribution to the study of the origin of sexual perversions (1919). In Vol. XVII of J. Strachey (Ed.), *The standard edition of the complete psychological works of Sigmund Freud.* London: The Hogarth Press, 1955. Pp. 175–204.

Freud, S. *Beyond the pleasure principle* (1920). In Vol. XVIII of J. Strachey (Ed.), *The standard edition of the complete psychological works of Sigmund Freud.* London: The Hogarth Press, 1955. Pp. 1–64.

Freud, S. The future prospects of psycho-analytic therapy (1910). In Vol. XI of J. Strachey (Ed.), *The standard edition of the complete psychological works of Sigmund Freud.* London: The Hogarth Press, 1957. Pp. 139–151. Also in Vol. II of *The collected papers of Sigmund Freud.* New York: Basic Books, 1959.

Freud, S. The antithetical meaning of primal words (1910). In Vol. XI of J. Strachey (Ed.), *The standard edition of the complete psychological works of Sigmund Freud.* London: The Hogarth Press, 1957. Pp. 153–161.

Freud, S. On beginning the treatment (1913). In Vol. XII of J. Strachey (Ed.), *The standard edition of the complete psychological works of Sigmund Freud.* London: The Hogarth Press, 1958. Pp. 121–144.

Freud, S. Delusions and dreams in Jensen's *Gradiva* (1906). In Vol. IX of J. Strachey (Ed.), *The standard edition of the complete psychological works of Sigmund Freud.* London: The Hogarth Press, 1959. Pp. 7–95.

Freud, S. *The psychopathology of everyday life* (1901). Vol. VI of J. Strachey (Ed.), *The standard edition of the complete psychological works of Sigmund Freud.* London: The Hogarth Press, 1960.

Freud, S. *The letters of Sigmund Freud* (edited by E. L. Freud). New York: Basic Books, 1960.

Freud, S. On the psychical mechanism of hysterical phenomena: a lecture (1893). In Vol. III of J. Strachey (Ed.), *The standard edition of the complete psychological works of Sigmund Freud.* London: The Hogarth Press, 1962. Pp. 25–39.

Freud, S. *Jokes and their relation to the unconscious* (1905). Vol. VIII of J. Strachey (Ed.), *The standard edition of the complete psychological works of Sigmund Freud.* London: The Hogarth Press, 1962.

Freud, S. *Introductory lectures on psycho-analysis.* Part III: *General theory of the neuroses* (1915–1917). Vol. XVI of J. Strachey (Ed.), *The standard edition of the complete psychological works of Sigmund Freud.* London: The Hogarth Press, 1963.

Freud, S. *New introductory lectures on psycho-analysis* (1932). In Vol. XXII of J. Strachey (Ed.), *The standard edition of the complete psychological works of Sigmund Freud.* London: The Hogarth Press, 1964. Pp. 3–182. Also in Vol. 54 of R. M. Hutchins (Ed.), *Great books of the western world.* Chicago: Encyclopedia Britannica, 1952. Pp. 807–884.

Freud, S. *Moses and monotheism* (1934–1938). In Vol. XXIII of J. Strachey (Ed.), *The standard edition of the complete psychological works of Sigmund Freud.* London: The Hogarth Press, 1964. Pp. 1–137.

Freud, S. Analysis terminable and interminable (1937). In Vol. XXIII of J. Strachey (Ed.), *The standard edition of the complete psychological works of Sigmund Freud.* London: The Hogarth Press, 1964. Pp. 209–253.

Fromm, E. *Escape from freedom.* New York: Farrar and Rinehart, 1941.

Fromm, E. *The sane society.* New York: Rinehart, 1955.

Frye, N. *Anatomy of criticism.* Princeton, N.J.: Princeton University Press, 1957.

Fullerton, G. S. The world as mechanism. *Psychological Review,* 1902, 9, 1–26.

Gabriel, E. A clinician answers Guthrie. *American Psychologist,* 1950, 5, 495.

Gesell, A. *The first five years of life.* New York: Harper, 1940.

Goethe, J. W. *Faust.* Vol. 47 of R. M. Hutchins (Ed.), *Great books of the western world.* Chicago: Encyclopedia Britannica, 1952.

Goldstein, K. *The organism.* New York: American Book Co., 1939.

Grunbaum, A. Causality and the science of human behavior. *American Scientist,* 1952, 40, 665–676.

Guthrie, E. R. The status of systematic psychology. *American Psychologist,* 1950, 5, 97–101.

Hall, C. S., and Lindzey, G. *Theories of personality.* New York: Wiley, 1957.

Hauser, A. *The social history of art.* New York: Vintage Books, 1951.
   Vol. 1. *Prehistoric, ancient-Oriental, Greece and Rome, middle ages.*
   Vol. 2. *Renaissance, mannerism, baroque.*
   Vol. 3. *Rococo, classicism, romanticism.*
   Vol. 4. *Naturalism, impressionism, the film age.*

Healy, W. *Mental conflicts and misconduct.* Boston: Little, Brown, 1917.

Hebb, D. O. *The organization of behavior.* New York: Wiley, 1949.

Hegel, G. W. F. In Vol. 46 of R. M. Hutchins (Ed.), *Great books of the western world.* Chicago: Encyclopedia Britannica, 1952.
   The philosophy of history. Pp. 153–369.
   The philosophy of right. Pp. 1–150.

Heider, F. *The psychology of interpersonal relations.* New York: Wiley, 1958.

Hobbes, T. *Leviathan.* In Vol. 23 of R. M. Hutchins (Ed.), *Great books of the western world.* Chicago: Encyclopedia Britannica, 1952. Pp. 49–283.

Hofstadter, R. *Anti-intellectualism in American life.* New York: Knopf, 1963.

Holt, R. R. Clinical and statistical prediction: A reformulation and some new data. *Journal of Abnormal and Social Psychology,* 1958, *56,* 1–12.

Holtzman, W. H., Thorpe, J. S., Swartz, J. D., and Herron, E. W. *Inkblot perception and personality.* Austin, Texas: University of Texas Press, 1961.

Hook, S. (Ed.) *Psychoanalysis, scientific method, and philosophy.* New York: New York University Press, 1959.

Hook, S. *From Hegel to Marx.* Ann Arbor, Mich.: University of Michigan Press, 1962.

Horney, Karen. *Neurosis and human growth.* New York: W. W. Norton, 1950.

Hull, C. L. Mind, mechanism, and adaptive behavior. *Psychological Review,* 1937, *44,* 1–32.

Hull, C. L. *Principles of behavior.* New York: Appleton-Century-Crofts, 1943.

Hull, C. L. The problem of intervening variables in molar behavior theory. *Psychological Review,* 1943, *50,* 273–291.

Hunt, W. A. Clinical psychology: Science or superstition. *American Psychologist,* 1951, *6,* 683–687.

Hutchins, R. M. (Ed.) *Great books of the western world.* Chicago: Encyclopedia Britannica, 1952. 54 vols.

Huxley, J. *Religion without revelation,* rev. ed. New York: Harper & Row, 1957.

Hyman, S. E. *The tangled bank.* New York: Atheneum, 1962.

Immergluck, L. Determinism-freedom in contemporary psychology: An ancient problem revisited. *American Psychologist,* 1964, *19,* 270–281.

James, W. *Memories and studies.* New York: Longmans, Green, 1911.

James, W. *The principles of psychology.* New York: Holt, 1890. Also in Vol. 53 of R. M. Hutchins (Ed.), *Great books of the western world.* Chicago: Encyclopedia Britannica, 1952.

James, W. *The varieties of religious experience.* New York: New American Library, 1958.

Janet, P. *The major symptoms of hysteria,* 2nd ed. New York: Macmillan, 1920.

Jaspers, K. *The great philosophers.* New York: Harcourt, Brace & World, 1962.

Johnson, W. *People in quandaries.* New York: Harper & Bros., 1946.

Jones, E. *The life and work of Sigmund Freud.* New York: Basic Books.

Vol. 1. *The formative years and the great discoveries,* 1953.

Vol. 2. *Years of maturity,* 1955.

Vol. 3. *The last phase,* 1957.

Jourard, S. I-thou relationship versus manipulation in counseling and psychotherapy. *Journal of Individual Psychology,* 1959, *15,* 174–179.

Jung, C. G. *The practice of psychotherapy.* Vol. 16 of H. Read, M. Fordham, and G. Adler (Eds.), *The collected works of C. G. Jung.* Bollingen Series XX.16. New York: Pantheon Books, and London: Routledge & Kegan Paul, 1954.

Jung, C. G. *Freud and psychoanalysis.* Vol. 4 of H. Read, M. Fordham, and G. Adler (Eds.), *The collected works of C. G. Jung.* Bollingen Series XX.4. New York: Pantheon Books, 1961.

Jung, C. G. *Memories, dreams, reflections.* New York: Pantheon Books, and London: William Collins Sons, Ltd, 1963.

Kahn, T. C. Clinically and statistically oriented psychologists split our profession. *American Psychologist,* 1955, *10,* 171–172.

Kant, I. *The critique of pure reason.* In Vol. 42 of R. M. Hutchins (Ed.), *Great books of the western world.* Chicago: Encyclopedia Britannica, 1952. Pp. 1–250.

Kantor, J. R. *The logic of modern science.* Chicago: Principia Press, 1953.

Kantor, J. R. *The scientific evolution of psychology.* Vol. 1. Chicago: Principia Press, 1963.

Kaufmann, W. *Nietzsche.* New York: Meridian Books, 1956.

Kelly, G. A. *The psychology of personal constructs.* Vol. 1. *A theory of personality.* New York: W. W. Norton, 1955.

Kelly, G. A. Personal construct theory and the psychotherapeutic interview. Unpublished manuscript, 1963.

Koch, S. Psychological science versus the science-humanism antinomy; intimations of a significant science of man. *American Psychologist,* 1961, *16,* 629–639.

Koffka, K. *Principles of gestalt psychology.* New York: Harcourt, Brace & Co., 1935.

Korzybski, A. *Science and sanity: An introduction to non-Aristotelian systems and general semantics,* 2nd ed. Lancaster, Pa.: Science Press, 1941.

Koyré, A. Influences of philosophic trends on the formulation of scientific theories. In P. G. Frank (Ed.), *The validation of scientific theories.* Boston: Beacon Press, 1956. Pp. 192–206.

Krasner, L. Behavior control and social responsibility. *American Psychologist,* 1962, *17,* 199–204.

Krasner, L. The therapist as a social reinforcement machine. In H. H. Strupp and L. Luborsky (Eds.), *Research in psychotherapy.* Vol. II. Washington, D.C.: American Psychological Association, 1962. Pp. 61–94.

Krech, D. A note on fission. *American Psychologist,* 1946, *1,* 402–404.

Kuo, Z. Y. The fundamental error of the concept of purpose and the trial and error fallacy. *Psychological Review,* 1928, *35,* 414–433.

Ladd, G. T. On certain hindrances to the progress of psychology in America. *Psychological Review,* 1899, *6,* 121–133.

Langer, Susanne K. *Philosophy in a new key.* New York: Penguin Books, 1948.

Langer, Susanne K. *Philosophical sketches.* New York: New American Library, 1964.

Lecky, P. *Self-consistency: A theory of personality.* New York: Island Press, 1945.

Leff, G. A. *Medieval thought: St. Augustine to Ockham.* Chicago: Quadrangle Books, 1958.

Levinson, H., *et al. Men, management and mental health.* Cambridge, Mass.: Harvard University Press, 1962.

Levy, L. H. *Psychological interpretation*. New York: Holt, Rinehart & Winston, 1963.

Lewin, K. *A dynamic theory of personality*. New York: McGraw-Hill, 1935.

Lippmann, W. *Public opinion*. New York: Penguin Books, 1946.

Locke, J. *An essay concerning human understanding*. In Vol. 35 of R. M. Hutchins (Ed.), *Great books of the western world*. Chicago: Encyclopedia Britannica, 1952. Pp. 85–395.

Lowrie, W. *A short life of Kierkegaard*. Garden City, N.Y.: Doubleday & Co., 1961.

MacCorquodale, K., and Meehl, P. E. On a distinction between hypothetical constructs and intervening variables. *Psychological Review*, 1948, *55*, 95–107.

MacKinnon, D. W. The structure of personality. In Vol. I of J. McV. Hunt (Ed.), *Personality and the behavior disorders*. New York: Ronald Press, 1944. Pp. 3–48.

MacLeod, R. B. Teleology and theory of human behavior. *Science*, 1957, *125*, 477–480.

Magnus, R. *Goethe as a scientist*. New York: H. Schuman, 1949.

Marx, K. *Capital*. In Vol. 50 of R. M. Hutchins (Ed.), *Great books of the western world*. Chicago: Encyclopedia Britannica, 1952. Pp. 1–393.

Maslow, A. H. *Motivation and personality*. New York: Harper, 1954.

McDougall, R. Mind as middle term. *Psychological Review*, 1912, *19*, 386–403.

McDougall, W. Purposive or mechanical psychology? *Psychological Review*, 1923, *30*, 273–288.

Meehl, P. E. *Clinical versus statistical prediction*. Minneapolis: University of Minnesota Press, 1954.

Meehl, P. E. When shall we use our heads instead of the formula? *Journal of Counseling Psychology*, 1957, *4*, 268–273.

Meehl, P. E. Schizotaxia, schizotypy, schizophrenia. *American Psychologist*, 1962, *17*, 827–838.

Menninger, K., Mayman, M., and Pruyser, P. *The vital balance*. New York: Viking Press, 1963.

Merton, R. K. *Social theory and social structure*. Glencoe, Ill.: Free Press, 1949.

Mowrer, O. H. Learning theory and the neurotic paradox. *American Journal of Orthopsychiatry*, 1948, *18*, 571–610.

Mowrer, O. H. *The crisis in psychiatry and religion*. New York: D. Van Nostrand, 1961.

Munitz, M. K. The relativity of determinism. In S. Hook (Ed.), *Determinism and freedom in the age of modern science.* New York: New York University Press, 1958. Pp. 63–69.

Munsterberg, H. Psychological atomism. *Psychological Review,* 1900, 7, 1–17.

Murphy, G. *Personality: A biosocial approach to origins and structure.* New York: Harper, 1947.

Murphy, G. Trends in the study of extrasensory perception. *American Psychologist,* 1958, 13, 69–76.

Murray, H. A., and Kluckhohn, C. Outline of a conception of personality. In C. Kluckhohn, H. A. Murray, and D. Schneider (Eds.), *Personality in nature, society, and culture,* 2nd ed. New York: Knopf, 1953.

Murstein, B. I. *Theory and research in projective techniques.* New York: Wiley, 1963.

Nagel, E. Principles of the theory of probability. *International Encyclopedia of the Unified Sciences.* Vol. 1, No. 6. Chicago: University of Chicago Press, 1947.

Nagel, E., and Newman, J. R. *Gödel's proof.* New York: New York University Press, 1958.

Newman, S. H. Should psychological theory and practice be divided? *American Psychologist,* 1950, 5, 495–496.

Nunberg, H., and Federn, E. (Eds.) *Minutes of the Vienna psychoanalytic society: 1906–1908.* Vol. 1. New York: International Universities Press, 1962.

Oppenheimer, R. Analogy in science. *American Psychologist,* 1956, 11, 127–135.

Osgood, C. E. *An alternative to war or surrender.* Urbana, Ill.: University of Illinois Press, 1962.

Palter, R. Philosophic principles and scientific theory. *Philosophy of Science,* 1956, 23, 111–135.

Parsons, T., and Shils, E. A. (Eds.) *Toward a general theory of action.* Cambridge, Mass.: Harvard University Press, 1951.

Peirce, C. S. *Values in a universe of chance* (edited by P. P. Wiener). Garden City, N.Y.: Doubleday Anchor, 1958.

Phillips, E. L. *Psychotherapy: A modern theory and practice.* Englewood Cliffs, N.J.: Prentice-Hall, 1956.

Plato. In Vol. 7 of R. M. Hutchins (Ed.), *Great books of the western world.* Chicago: Encyclopedia Britannica, 1952. Quotations by permission of Encyclopedia Britannica and Oxford University Press.

Cratylus. Pp. 85–114.

Parmenides. Pp. 486–511.

Philebus. Pp. 609–639.

The Republic. Pp. 295–441.

Sophist. Pp. 551–579.

Statesman. Pp. 580–608.

Prior, M. E. Bacon's man of science. In P. P. Wiener and A. Noland (Eds.), *Roots of scientific thought.* New York: Basic Books, 1957. Pp. 382–389.

Rank, O. *Will therapy, and truth and reality.* New York: Knopf, 1945.

Reichenbach, H. *Experience and prediction.* Chicago: University of Chicago Press, 1938.

Rieff, P. *Freud: The mind of the moralist.* New York: Viking Press, 1959.

Rogers, C. R. *The clinical treatment of the problem child.* Boston: Houghton Mifflin Co., 1939.

Rogers, C. R. *Counseling and psychotherapy.* Boston: Houghton Mifflin Co., 1942.

Rogers, C. R. *Client-centered therapy.* Boston: Houghton Mifflin Co., 1951.

Rogers, C. R. The interest in the practice of psychotherapy. *American Psychologist,* 1953, *8,* 48–50.

Rogers, C. R. Persons or science? A philosophical question. *American Psychologist,* 1955, *10,* 267–278.

Rogers, C. R. *On becoming a person.* Boston: Houghton Mifflin Co., 1961.

Rogers, C. R. Learning to be free. In S. M. Farber and R. H. L. Wilson (Eds.), *Control of the mind.* Vol. 2. *Conflict and creativity.* New York: McGraw-Hill, 1963. Pp. 268–288.

Rogers, C. R., and Skinner, B. F. Some issues concerning the control of human behavior: A symposium. *Science,* 1956, *124,* 1057–1066.

Rorschach, H. *Psychodiagnostics.* New York: Grune & Stratton, 1942.

Rosenthal, D. Changes in some moral values following psychotherapy. *Journal of Consulting Psychology,* 1955, *19,* 431–436.

Rosenzweig, S. Imbalance in clinical psychology. *American Psychologist,* 1950, *5,* 678–680.

Rosenzweig, S. (Ed.) Balance in clinical psychology: A symposium in correspondence. *American Psychologist,* 1951, *6,* 208–212.

Rotter, J. B. *Social learning and clinical psychology.* Englewood Cliffs, N.J.: Prentice-Hall, 1954.

Rubinstein, E. A., and Parloff, M. B. (Eds.) *Research in psychotherapy.* Vol. I. Washington, D.C.: American Psychological Association, 1959.

Russell, B. *Mysticism and logic.* Garden City, N.Y.: Doubleday Anchor, 1957.

Russell, B. *Wisdom of the west.* Garden City, N.Y.: Doubleday, 1959.

Russell, B. *Our knowledge of the external world.* New York: New American Library, 1960.

Rychlak, J. F. Clinical psychology and the nature of evidence. *American Psychologist,* 1959, *14,* 642–648.

Sanford, E. C. Psychology and physics. *Psychological Review,* 1903, *10,* 105–119.

Schrödinger, E. *Science theory and man.* New York: Dover Publications, 1957.

Shaw, F. J. Clinical psychology and behavior theory. *Journal of Abnormal and Social Psychology,* 1950, *45,* 388–391.

Sheldon, W. H., Stevens, S. S., and Tucker, W. B. *The varieties of human physique: An introduction to constitutional psychology.* New York: Harper & Bros., 1940.

Shipley, J. T. *Trends in literature.* New York: Philosophical Library, 1949.

Sidgwick, H. *Outlines of the history of ethics.* Boston: Beacon Press, 1960.

Skinner, B. F. *The behavior of organisms: An experimental analysis.* New York: Appleton-Century, 1938.

Skinner, B. F. *Walden two.* New York: Macmillan, 1948.

Skinner, B. F. Are theories of learning necessary? *Psychological Review,* 1950, *57,* 193–216.

Skinner, B. F. The control of human behavior. *Annals of the New York Academy of Science,* 1955, *17,* 547–551.

Skinner, B. F. A case history in scientific method. *American Psychologist,* 1956, *11,* 221–233.

Skinner, B. F. *Verbal behavior.* New York: Appleton-Century-Crofts, 1957.

Solomon, L. N. The paradox of the experimental clinician. *American Psychologist,* 1955, *10,* 170–171.

Spence, K. W. The nature of theory construction in contemporary psychology. *Psychological Review,* 1944, *51,* 47–68.

Spence, K. W. The postulates and methods of "behaviorism." *Psychological Review*, 1948, *55*, 67–78.

Spence, K. W. Theoretical interpretations of learning. In C. P. Stone (Ed.), *Comparative psychology*, 3rd ed. Englewood Cliffs, N.J.: Prentice-Hall, 1951. Pp. 239–291.

Spence, K. W. *Behavior theory and conditioning*. New Haven: Yale University Press, 1956.

Spence, K. W. A theory of emotionally based drive (D) and its relation to performance in simple learning situations. *American Psychologist*, 1958, *13*, 131–141.

Spender, S. (Ed.) *Great writings of Goethe*. New York: New American Library, 1958.

Stace, W. T. *The philosophy of Hegel*. New York: Dover, 1955.

Stafford, J. W. Fact, law, and theory in psychology. *Journal of General Psychology*, 1954, *51*, 61–67.

Stainbrook, E. Some historical determinants of contemporary diagnostic and etiological thinking in psychology. In P. H. Hoch and J. Zubin (Eds.), *Current problems in psychiatric diagnosis*. New York: Grune & Stratton, 1953.

Stevens, S. S. The operational definition of psychological concepts. *Psychological Review*, 1935, *42*, 517–527.

Stone, G. R. Prediction in clinical psychology and behavior theory. *Psychological Review*, 1952, *59*, 95–97.

Strachey, J. (Ed.) Editor's introduction. In Vol. II of *The standard edition of the complete psychological works of Sigmund Freud*. London: The Hogarth Press, 1955.

Strupp, H. H. The outcome problem in psychotherapy revisited. *Psychotherapy*, 1963, *1*, 1–13.

Strupp, H. H., Castore, G. F., Lake, R. A., Merrill, R. M., and Bellak, L. Comments on Rogers' "Persons or science?" *American Psychologist*, 1956, *11*, 153–157.

Sullivan, H. S. *The interpersonal theory of psychiatry*. New York: W. W. Norton, 1953.

Super, D. E. Reply to Rosenzweig. *American Psychologist*, 1951, *6*, 128.

Szasz, T. S. *The myth of mental illness*. New York: Hoeber-Harper, 1961.

Titchener, E. B. Psychology: science or technology? *Popular Science Monthly*, 1914, *84*, 39–51.

Thorne, F. C. The clinical method in science. *American Psychologist*, 1947, *2*, 159–166.

Tolman, E. C. The determiners of behavior at a choice point. *Psychological Review,* 1938, *45,* 1–41.

Tolman, E. C. Freedom and the cognitive need. *American Psychologist,* 1954, *9,* 536–538.

Tolman, Ruth S. Virtue rewarded and vice punished. *American Psychologist,* 1953, *8,* 721–733.

Untersteiner, M. *The sophists.* New York: Philosophical Library, 1954.

Voltaire, F. M. A. *Candide.* New York: J. J. Little & Ives, 1930.

Waters, R. H., and Pennington, L. A. Operationism in psychology. *Psychological Review,* 1938, *45,* 414–423.

Watson, J. B. Psychology as the behaviorist views it. *Psychological Review,* 1913, *20,* 158–177.

Watson, J. B. An attempted formulation of the scope of behavior psychology. *Psychological Review,* 1917, *24,* 329–352.

Watson, R. I. A brief history of clinical psychology. *Psychological Bulletin,* 1953, *50,* 321–346.

Watson, R. I. *The great psychologists.* Philadelphia: J. B. Lippincott, 1963.

Webster's *Third new international dictionary of the English language unabridged.* Springfield, Mass.: G. & C. Merriam Co., 1961.

Weiss, A. P. The mind and the man within. *Psychological Review,* 1919, *26,* 327–334.

Wiener, N. *The human use of human beings.* Boston: Houghton Mifflin Co., 1954.

Wiener, P. P., and Noland, A. (Eds.) *Roots of scientific thought.* New York: Basic Books, 1957.

Wilson, E. *To the Finland station: A study in the writing and acting of history.* Garden City, N.Y.: Doubleday Anchor, 1940.

Winter, J. E. The postulates of psychology. *Psychological Review,* 1936, *43,* 130–148.

Wittels, F. *Sigmund Freud: His personality, his teaching, and his school.* New York: Dodd, Mead, 1924.

Wolpe, J. *Psychotherapy by reciprocal inhibition.* Stanford, Calif.: Stanford University Press, 1958.

Yerkes, R. M. Concerning the anthropocentrism of psychology. *Psychological Review,* 1933, *40,* 209–212.

Zborowski, M., and Herzog, Elizabeth. *Life is with people.* New York: Schocken Books, 1962.

Zilsel, E. The origins of Gilbert's scientific method. In P. P. Wiener and A. Noland (Eds.), *Roots of scientific thought.* New York: Basic Books, 1957. Pp. 219–250.

NAME INDEX

SUBJECT INDEX